CONTENTS

CONTRIBUTORS

ANNA ALEXANDROVA is an Assistant Professor in philosophy at the University of Missouri St Louis. She specializes in philosophy of social sciences. Her recent papers deal with the nature and use of formal models in economics ("Making Models Count" forthcoming in *Philosophy of Science*) and with the measurement of well-being and happiness in psychological sciences ("Subjective Well-Being and Kahneman's 'Objective Happiness'" *Journal of Happiness Studies* 2005). She is particularly interested in the use of social scientific knowledge for policy.

ERIK ANGNER is Assistant Professor of Philosophy and Economics at the University of Alabama at Birmingham. He hold separate PhDs in History and Philosophy of Science and in Economics from the University of Pittsburgh, and is the author of *Hayek and Natural Law* (Routledge, 2007). He is currently writing (with George Loewenstein) a book titled *Foundations of Behavioral Economics*.

CRISTINA BICCHIERI is the Carol and Michael Lowenstein Professor of Philosophy and Legal Studies at the University of Pennsylvania, where she is also a member of the psychology graduate group. Her research interests lie at the intersection between philosophy, game theory, and psychology. Her primary research focus is on judgment and decision making with special interest in decisions about fairness, trust, and cooperation, and how expectations affect behavior. Her most recent book is *The Grammar of Society: the Nature and Dynamics of Social Norms* (Cambridge University Press, 2006).

KEN BINMORE, CBE FBA PhD BSc, is a mathematician turned economist and philosopher. He has held chairs at LSE, the University of Michigan and University College London. A wide range of applied work includes the design of major telecom auctions in many countries across the world. As a consequence of the £23.4 billion raised by the telecom auction he organized in the UK, he was described by *Newsweek* magazine as the "ruthless, poker-playing economist who destroyed the telecom industry." He nowadays devotes his time to applying game theory to the problem of the evolution of morality. His recent books include *Natural Justice* (Oxford University Pess), *Does Game Theory Work?* (MIT Press), and *A Very Short Introduction to Game Theory* (Oxford). He is currently a Visiting Professor of Economics at the University of Bristol and a Visiting Professor of Philosophy at LSE.

NANCY CARTWRIGHT is Professor of Philosophy at the London School of Economics and at the University of California at San Diego, and from 2006–2009, Director of the Centre for Philosophy of Natural and Social Science at LSE. She has written extensively in the philosophy of physics but since going to LSE has been concentrating in the philosophy of the social and economic sciences, especially on question of modelling and causality. She is a Fellow of the British Academy and the American Philosophical Society, a former MacArthur Fellow, and a member of the American Academy of Arts and Sciences and the German Academy of Natural Science.

SIR PARTHA DASGUPTA FBA FRS is the Frank Ramsey Professor of Economics at the University of Cambridge and Fellow of St John's College, Cambridge. His work has ranged over welfare economics, intergenerational ethics, environmental and resource economics, the pure theory of games, and the economics of science and technology. His most recent book is *Economics: A Very Short Introduction* (Oxford, 2007). He is a Member of the Pontifical Academy of Social Sciences and a Foreign Member of the US National Academy of Sciences, the American Academy of Arts and Sciences, and the American Philosophical Society.

JOHN B. DAVIS is Professor of History and Philosophy of Economics at University of Amsterdam and Professor of Economics at Marquette University. He is author of *Keynes's Philosophical Development* (Cambridge, 1994), *The Theory of the Individual in Economics* (Routledge, 2003), co-editor with Wade Hands and Uskali Mäki of *The Handbook of Economic Methodology* (Elgar, 1998), former editor of the *Review of Social Economy*, and currently co-editor of the *Journal of Economic Methodology*. He is writing a book on identity and the individual in recent approaches in economics.

KEITH DOWDING is Professor and Head of the Program in Political Science in the Research School of Social Sciences at the Australian National University, Canberra. He has published widely in social and political philosophy, political science, public administration and urban politics recently with a jindyworobak slant. His recent research interests include the measurement of freedom and rights, satisfaction with public services and the career paths of senior politicians.

STAN DU PLESSIS is a macroeconomist at the University of Stellenbosch in South Africa where he is a Professor in the Department of Economics. He is also the vice president of the Economic Society of South Africa and treasurer and secretary of the African Econometric Society. He teaches macroeconomics, monetary economics and advanced econometrics, mainly to graduate students. His academic publications have focused on monetary policy and the business cycles but he has also written on fiscal policy, economic growth, the exchange rate, institutional economics, and law and economics.

GARY FIELDS is Professor of Labor Economics and Economic Development at Cornell University. His research is on labor markets and income mobility in developing countries. He serves as a consultant to the World Bank, Asian Development Bank, and United Nations as well as private sector companies. Fields holds BA, MA, and PhD degrees in economics from the University of Michigan.

FRANCESCO GUALA is Associate Professor of philosophy at the University of Exeter (UK). He is the author of *The Methodology of Experimental Economics* (Cambridge, 2005), *Filosofia dell'economia* (Bologna, 2006), and of several articles in philosophy and social science journals. In 2002 he has won both the International Network of Economic Method Prize and the History of Economic Analysis Award. His current research concerns the application of empirical methods to the study of social ontology.

DANIEL HAUSMAN is the Herbert A. Simon Professor of Philosophy at the University of Wisconsin–Madison. He is a founding editor of the journal *Economics and Philosophy of Economics* and author of *Causal Asymmetries*, *The Philosophy of Economics: An Anthology*, and (jointly with Michael McPherson) *Economic Analysis, Moral Philosophy, and Public Policy*. He is current working on issues in health measurement and a book on preferences.

KEVIN D. HOOVER is Professor of Economics and Philosophy at Duke University. He is the author of *Causality in Macroeconomics, The Methodology of Empirical Macroeconomics* and many articles on macroeconomics, monetary economics, history of economic thought, economic methodology, and philosophy. His current interests include causality and the philosophical foundations of econometrics.

PAUL HUMPHREYS is Professor of Philosophy at the University of Virginia. His current research interests include computational science, emergence, and heterodox economics. Recent publications include *Extending Ourselves: Computational Science, Empiricism and Scientific Method* (Oxford, 2004); and *Emergence: Contemporary Readings in Science and Philosophy*, co-edited with Mark Bedau (MIT Press, 2008).

HAROLD KINCAID is Professor and Chair in the Department of Philosophy at the University of Alabama at Birmingham. He is the author of *Philosophical Foundations of the Social Sciences* (Cambridge, 1996) and *Individualism and the Unity of Science* (Rowman and Littlefield, 1997) and with John Dupré and Alison Wylie, *Value Free Science: Ideals and Illusions* (Oxford, 2007). He has published numerous articles and book chapters in the philosophy of social science and philosophy of economics.

USKALI MÄKI is Academy Professor at the Academy of Finland and former Professor at Erasmus Institute for Philosophy and Economics. He is Chair of the International Network for Economic Method and a former editor of the *Journal of Economic Methodology*. He is editor of *The Handbook of the Philosophy of Economics* (Elsevier). Much of his current work is on models, realism, and interdisciplinarity.

PHILIP MIROWSKI is Carl Koch Chair of Economics and the History and Philosophy of Science, and Fellow of the Reilly Center, University of Notre Dame. He is author of *Machine Dreams* (2002), *The Effortless Economy of Science?* (2004), *More Heat than Light* (1989), and the forthcoming *ScienceMart™: the new economics of science*. Outside of work on the commercialization of science, he has edited with Wade Hands on a history of the theory of demand theory in the twentieth century entitled *Agreement on Demand* (2006), and with Dieter Plehwe, *The Making of the Neoliberal Thought Collective* (2008).

ROBERT NORTHCOTT is Assistant Professor in the Department of Philosophy at the University of Missouri-St Louis. He works on causation and on methods of apportioning causal responsibility, with particular reference to the special sciences. Recent publications include: "Causal efficacy and the analysis of variance" in *Biology and Philosophy* (2006, 253–276), "Causation and contrast classes" forthcoming in *Philosophical Studies* (published online May 2007), and "Weighted explanations in history" forthcoming in *Philosophy of the Social Sciences.*

ALEX ROSENBERG (Ph.D. 1971, Johns Hopkins) joined the Duke faculty in 2000. Previously he was professor of philosophy at Dalhousie, University, Syracuse University and University of California, Riverside. Rosenberg is the author of 11 books, including *Microeconomic Laws: A Philosophical Analysis* (University of Pittsburgh Press, 1976), *Philosophy of Social Science* (Clarendon Press, Oxford, and Westview Press, Third Edition, 2007), *Economics: Mathematical Politics or Science of Diminishing Returns?* (University of Chicago Press, 1992), and *Darwinism in Philosophy, Social Science and Policy* (Cambridge, 2000), and most recently, *The Philosophy of Biology: A Contemporary Introduction* (with Daniel McShea, Routledge, 2007)

DON ROSS is Professor of Philosophy and Professor of Economics at the University of Alabama at Birmingham and Professor of Economics at the University of Cape Town, South Africa. His recent books include *Economic Theory And Cognitive Science: Microexplanation* (MIT Press), *Every Thing Must Go: Metaphysics Naturalized* (with J. Ladyman; Oxford) and *Midbrain Mutiny: The Picoeconomics And Neuroeconomics Of Disordered Gambling* (with C. Sharp, R. Vuchinich and D. Spurrett). His research interests include game-theoretic modeling of socialization, the neuroeconomics of addiction, technical relationships among theories from different sciences, and infrastructure and industrial policy in Africa.

JACK VROMEN is Professor of Philosophy and the Academic Director of *EIPE* (Erasmus Institute for Philosophy and Economics) at Erasmus University Rotterdam. Recent publications are "Routines, Genes and Program-Based Behavior" (*Journal of Evolutionary Economics*, 2006) and "Neuroeconomics as a Natural Extension of Bioeconomics: The Shifting Scope of Standard Economic Theory" (*Journal of Bioeconomics*, 2007). His research focuses on philosophical aspects of the relation between economics and evolution.

JIM WOODWARD is the J.O and Juliette Koepfli Professor of the Humanities at the California Institute of Technology. He is the author of *Making Things Happen: A Theory of Causal Explanation* (Oxford, 2003). He works primarily in philosophy of science but also has an interest in empirical approaches to ethics and political philosophy.

THE OXFORD HANDBOOK OF

PHILOSOPHY
OF ECONOMICS

CHAPTER 1

INTRODUCTION:
THE NEW
PHILOSOPHY OF
ECONOMICS

DON ROSS AND HAROLD KINCAID

THIS volume—its selection of topics, authors, and approaches—reflects a specific vision of what philosophy of economics should be. In this chapter, we outline and defend that vision. Past philosophy of economics was guided in large part by assumptions derived from both philosophy of science and economics that have been displaced by more recent developments in both fields. It is these developments that motivate the orientation of this book.

Our focus is on economic science, as opposed to the somewhat broader field taken by the philosophy of economics in general. In drawing this distinction we follow Lionel Robbins, whose *Essay on the Nature and Significance of Economic Science* had its seventy-fifth anniversary of publication celebrated last year (2007). Robbins carefully distinguished economic science, by which he meant the systematic search for objective economic relationships, from the many purely practical aims to which economic reasoning is put. The manager of a warehouse deciding how much floor space to devote to aisles, thus trading off between storage capacity and ease of access, is engaged in economics but not, Robbins would say, in economic *science*. Similarly, the ruler who decides that every family should have a free weekly chicken in their pot hands over to economic technicians the problem of selecting a means of funding the redistribution. Everyday, practical economics is arguably more important than economic science, and certainly far more wide-spread. It is also less shrouded in philosophical confusion—populist obtuseness about trade and other matters being dire *confusion* but not *philosophical* confusion—and so is best left in the hands of outstanding commentators such as Kay (2005) and Harford (2005). The topics taken up in this book are more arcane then theirs, and harder to get unambiguously right.

OLD AND NEW PHILOSOPHY OF SCIENCE

Philosophy of economics through the 1980s had an intimate relationship both to developments in economics itself and to the predominant approaches in philosophy of science, though with some lag in responding to developments in both areas. The technical innovations that dominated economics from the 1950s to the 1970s combined with some general philosophy of science assumptions in the 1950s to produce a philosophy of economics with a distinct character. Understanding that history is important for seeing how and why the philosophy of economics is undergoing a major change in character.

Recent historical and sociological studies of science have deepened our understanding of the extent to which "official" paradigms—that is, graduate textbook presentations—of scientific disciplines can hide much heterogeneity in actual practice and interpretation among researchers. This was true of the economics of the 1950s and 1960s, where practical empirical and policy work went on in parallel with the development of advanced mathematical theory. However, technically extending the neoclassical paradigm certainly garnered the greatest prestige in the profession. In the hands of theorists such as Samuelson, Arrow, Debreu, and McKenzie, microeconomics was preoccupied with theorem proving, much of it clearly motivated by ambitions to achieve maximum generality. Formalization was thus a paramount consideration. Consistent marginalist models of consumer and producer behavior were developed. This work culminated in the Arrow-Debreu-McKenzie model, which showed that, under certain assumptions about consumers and producers, such as convexity of demand and constant returns to scale, an equilibrium exists in that there is a set of prices such that aggregate supply will equal aggregate demand for every commodity in the economy. The First Theorem of Welfare Economics showed that every general equilibrium is Pareto efficient, and the Second Theorem establishes that every general equilibrium can be brought about by some set of prices. Though these achievements occurred before the 1970s, they furnished the image of economics on which leading philosophers of economics were still mainly focused in the 1980s and 1990s; see, for example, Hausman (1992) and Rosenberg (1993), which were arguably the most influential publications in philosophy of economics during those decades.

Parallel influences from philosophy of science that informed thinking about economics in the 1970s and 1980s generally involved a core set of assumptions that do not fall under any standard label. Those assumptions included the following:

1. Theories are the central content of science. A mature science ideally produces one clearly identifiable theory that explains all the phenomena in its domain. In practice, a science may produce different theories for different subdomains, but the overarching scientific goal is to unify those theories by subsuming them under one encompassing account.
2. Theories are composed of universal laws relating and ascribing properties to natural kinds and are best understood when they are described as formalized systems. Philosophy of science can aid in producing such formalizations by the application of formal logic.
3. The fundamental concepts of science should have clear definitions in terms of necessary and sufficient conditions. General philosophy of science is in large part about clarifying general scientific concepts, especially *explanation* and *confirmation*. The goal is to produce a set of necessary and sufficient conditions for application of these concepts. These definitions are largely tested against linguistic intuitions about what we would and would not count as cases of explanation and confirmation.
4. Explanation and confirmation have a logic—they conform to universal general principles that apply to all domains and do not rest on contingent empirical knowledge. A central goal of philosophy of science is to describe the logic of science. Explanation involves, in some sense still to be clarified, deductions from laws of the phenomena to be explained. Whether a science is well supported by evidence can be determined by asking whether the theory bears the right logical relationship to the data cited in support of it.
5. Holism: Theories are wholes that are evaluated as units against the evidence. Evidence always bears on theories as totalities, not on single hypotheses considered one at a time. This thesis was a common meeting ground of the descendents of logical empiricism, such as W.V. Quine and philosophers usually perceived as the leaders of logical empiricism's overthrow, Thomas Kuhn and Imre Lakatos. Lakatos's specific incorporation of holism through his conception of the units of scientific testing as entire research programs, which include abstract 'hard-core' assumptions buffered from direct confrontation with observation and experiment, seemed to many philosophers to fit economics especially closely.
6. The criteria for explanation and confirmation allow us to demarcate properly scientific theories from pseudoscientific accounts, which tend to sacrifice due attention to confirmation in favor of apparent explanation, and in so doing fail to be genuinely explanatory.

7. It is a serious open question to what extent any of the social sciences are real sciences. This question is best explored by comparing their logical structures with those characteristic of physics and, to a lesser extent, chemistry, geology, and biology.

These were some of the key ideas in the philosophy of science in the 1960s and 1970s that shaped how philosophy of economics was done. Of course, not all tenets were equally influential in every application nor were they always explicitly advocated. However, a significant subset of them were implicit in most philosophical accounts of economics.

We may note an important feature that general equilibrium theory and the kind of philosophy of science just described have in common: both emphasize highly general, abstract, unifying structures that are independent of and prior to specific empirical research projects. Neoclassical general equilibrium theory was precisely the kind of scientific product that philosophy of science saw as its target, for reasons internal to its own dynamic that had emerged from the logical positivism and logical empiricism of the earlier twentieth century. Understanding economics meant understanding the status of general equilibrium theory. That understanding would come from identifying the fundamental commitments of the theory and clarifying their cognitive status. What were the theoretical laws? Did they have the proper logical form of laws? What were their truth conditions? What was their connection to observation, especially given the simplifying assumptions that seemed essential to all theory in the neoclassical vein?

As we noted, the two most influential philosophers of economics of the last three decades of the previous century, Alex Rosenberg and Daniel Hausman, were centrally concerned with these questions. Rosenberg's (1976, 1992) main preoccupation was the question of whether the laws of microeconomics have the right form to be laws, while Hausman (1981, 1992) primarily investigated the truth conditions for ceteris paribus generalizations and sought to identify the fundamental general assumptions of contemporary neoclassical economics. Economic methodologists took similar approaches in assessing current theory. For Blaug (1980) the key question was the alleged need for falsifiablity of the neoclassical paradigm and the extent to which stringent tests as defined by Popper were present in economics. His judgment was largely negative. Cauldwell (1982) shared the emphasis on assessing neoclassical theory and on the importance and possibility of determining its scientific status by means of general criteria drawn from the philosophy of science. Others asked similar questions through the lenses of Lakatos (Hands 1993) or Kuhn. Is neoclassical theory a progressive or degenerating research program? What were the paradigm shifts in the history of economic thought? Is the abstract character of general equilibrium theory defensible on grounds that every research program includes a sheltered hard core that does not make definite empirical predictions on its own, or is its protective belt so resistant to efforts at falsification as to render the approach pseudoscientific, as Blaug has repeatedly alleged? To repeat, not all these authors affirmed all seven of the assumptions listed earlier, and they did not uniformly interpret the ones they did affirm. Yet they shared a commitment to using general philosophy of science criteria to assess the epistemic status of neoclassical theory as the fundamental preoccupation of philosophy of economics.

Useful work was done using the seven tenets, and we do not deny that there is some truth in each of them, provided that enough (relatively massive) qualifications and escape clauses are added. However, as philosophers and philosophically inclined economists began turning their attention to economics, philosophy of science was moving beyond the tenets toward a more subtle understanding of science. All the tenets are, to a significant extent, misleading as descriptions of actual scientific practice. Let us consider them again one at a time, now with an eye for their problems.

1. Theories as central: "The" theory in a given discipline is typically not a single determinate set of propositions. What we find instead are common elements that are given different interpretations according to context. For example, genes play a central role in biological explanation, but what exactly a gene is taken to be varies considerably depending on the biological phenomena being explained (Moss 2004). Often we find *no* one uniform theory in a research domain, but rather a variety of models that overlap in various way but that are not fully intertranslatable. Cartwright (1980) gives us the example of models of quantum damping, in which physicists maintain a toolkit of six different mathematical theories. Because these aren't strictly compatible with one another, a traditional perspective in the philosophy of science would predict that physicists should be trying to eliminate all but one. However, because each theory is better than the others for governing some contexts of experimental design and interpretation, but all are reasonable in light of physicists' consensual informal conception of the basic cause of the phenomenon, they enjoy their embarrassment of riches as a practical boon. There is much more to science than theories: experimental setup and instrument calibration skills, modeling ingenuity to facilitate statistical testing, mathematical insight, experimental and data analysis paradigms and traditions, social norms and social organization, and much else—and these other elements are important to understanding the content of theories.

2. Theories, laws, and formalization: Laws in *some* sense play a crucial role in scientific theories. Absent any trace of what philosophers call modal structure, it is impossible to see how scientists can be said to rationally learn from induction (Ladyman & Ross 2007, Chapter 2). However, some of our best science does not emphasize laws in the philosopher's sense as elegant, context-free, universal generalizations, but instead provides accounts of temporally and spatially restricted context-sensitive causal processes as its end product. Molecular biology is a prime example in this regard, with its emphasis on the causal mechanisms behind cell

functioning that form a complex patchwork of relations that cannot be aggregated into an elegant framework. Expression in a clear language, quantitative where possible, is crucial to good science, but the ideal of a full deductive system of axioms and theorems is often unattainable, and not, as far as one can see, actually sought by many scientific subcommunities that are nevertheless thriving.

3. Conceptual analysis: Some important scientific concepts are not definable in terms of necessary and sufficient conditions but are instead much closer to the protypes that, according to cognitive science, form the basis for our everyday concepts of kinds of entities and processes. The concept of the gene is again a good example. There is no definition of gene in terms of its essential characteristics that covers every important scientific use of the concept. Cartwright (2007) has argued recently that the same holds even for so general and philosophical an idea as *cause*: there are different senses of *cause* with different relevant formalizations and evidence conditions. Equally important, the traditional philosophical project of testing definitions against what we find it appropriate to say is of doubtful significance. Who is the relevant reference group? The intuitive judgments of philosophers, whose grasp of science is often out of date and who are frequently captured by highly specific metaphysical presuppositions, do not and should not govern scientific usage at all (Ladyman & Ross 2007, Chapter 1). Questions about the usage of scientists is certainly more relevant, but this also may not be the best guide to the content of scientific results; when scientists pronounce on the limitations of concepts, they, in effect, step outside their professional roles and don philosophical mantles. The most important aspect of science's relationship to everyday *or* philosophical conceptual order is its relentless opportunism in pursuit of new observations and new ways of modeling data, which leads it to resist all attempts to restrict it within comfortable and familiar metaphysical or epistemological boundaries.

4. The logic of confirmation and explanation: Confirmation and explanation are complex practices that do not admit of a uniform, purely logical analysis. Explanations often have a contextual component set by the background knowledge of the field in question that determines the question to be answered and the kind of answer that is appropriate (van Fraassen 1981). Sometimes, that context may invoke laws, but often it does not, at least not in any explicit way. Confirmation likewise depends strongly on domain-specific background knowledge in ways that make a purely logical and quantitatively specifiable assessment of the degree to which specified evidence supports an hypothesis unlikely. Such general things as can be said about confirmation are sufficiently abstract that they are unhelpful on their own. The statements, "A hypothesis is well supported if all sources of error have been ruled out" or "A hypothesis is

well supported by the evidence if it is more consistent with the evidence than any other existing hypothesis" are hard to argue with. Yet to make any use of these standards in practice requires fleshing out how error is ruled out in the specific instance or what consistency with the evidence comes to in that case. Other all-purpose criteria such as "X is confirmed if and only if X predicts novel evidence" or "X is confirmed if and only if X is the only hypothesis that has not been falsified" are subject to well-known counter examples and difficulties of interpretation.

5. Holism: It is a fallacy to infer from the fact that every hypothesis is tested in conjunction with background theory that evidence only bears on theories as wholes (Glymour 1980). By embedding hypotheses in differing background theoretical and experimental setups, it is possible to attribute blame and credit to individual hypotheses. Indeed, this is how the overwhelming majority of scientists view the overwhelming majority of their own research results. Judged on the basis of considerations that scientists typically introduce into actual debates about what to regard as accepted results, the relationships between theories, applications, and tests propogated by Quine and Lakatos look like philosophers' fantasies. In particular, they make science seem like unusually empirically pedantic philosophy. It is no such thing.

6. Science and pseudoscience: Several of the insights about science already discussed suggest that judging theories to be scientific or pseudoscientific is a misplaced enterprise. Scientific theories and their evidence form complexes of claims that involve diverse relations of dependence and independence and, as a result, are not subject to uniform or generic assessment. Any general criteria of scientific adequacy that might be used to distinguish science from pseudoscience are either too abstract on their own to decide what is scientific or is not, or they are contentious (Kitcher 1983). This is not to deny that astrology, creation "science," and explicitly racialist sociobiology are clearly quackery or disguised ideology; it is merely to point out that these judgments must be supported case by case, based on specific empirical knowledge.

7. Scientific social science: The foregoing discussion of science and pseudoscience should make it obvious that questions about the "genuine" scientific status of all, or some particular, social science are sensible only if (1) they are posed as questions about specific bodies of social research, and (2) they are approached as concrete inquiries into the evidential and explanatory success of that body of work. Assessing scientific standing is continuous with the practice of science itself.

From the perspective of this more nuanced philosophy of science, traditional philosophy of economics was often engaged in unfruitful projects. Adherence to the seven tenets has encouraged engagement in discussions conducted at levels of abstraction too elevated and remote from empirical research to contribute to understanding the practice or content of economics. Economic methodology, following McCloskey (1985) has more than one form: *M*ethodology is abstract philosophical commentary on science, whereas *m*ethodology informs the day-to-day concerns of practicing economists and is taught, for example, in econometrics courses. Contra McCloskey, it is not reasonable to think of this as a simple dichotomy rather than a continuum. For example, is one teaching *M*ethodology or *m*ethodology if one explores the difference between so-called Granger causation in Markov process models of financial systems and more general relationships of asymmetric influence transmission between variables that a philosopher would be more likely to regard as "real" causation? Notice that an economist might be interested in this issue for reasons that have nothing to do with philosophical curiosity; consulting clients are often looking for levers they can pull that will have predictible effects, something that merely Granger-causal relations don't, in general, deliver. However, we agree with McCloskey that much philosophy of economics has been conducted toward the extreme *M*ethodology end of the spectrum and, as a result, is of little consequence for economics. Asking whether neoclassical economics meets Popperian falsificationist standards or whether its statements have the right logical form to be laws is unlikely to be of much relevance because these questions presuppose the simplistic picture of science that we reject. Philosophical commentary, to be useful, must engage much more closely at the other end of the spectrum where *m*ethodology influences the practice of economics.

Philosophy of economics also needs to change in order to give appropriate weight to major innovations that have transformed practice in economics since the midcentury heyday of general equilibrium theory that has been the prime focus of most recently past philosophy of economics. To these innovations, and to the bases of their significance, we now turn.

OLD AND NEW ECONOMICS

As noted earlier, from the 1950s through the 1970s scientific economists were preoccupied with highly abstract models. These included not only general equilibrium models, taken as foundational for microeconomics. Though philosophers at the time largely ignored macroeconomics, the period was dominated first by technical debates between Keynesians and monetarists over the character of the Phillips curve, and later (then on into the 1980s) by the rise of rational expectations modeling. Since the 1980s, however, there has been a dramatic expansion of the range of modeling activities and forms of model testing. This expansion can mostly be attributed to four developments. In order of importance as we see them, they are: (1) the development of massive computing power, facilitating the testing of highly specified causal

models against ever larger data sets; (2) the rise of game theory, which made economists' outputs useful to more agents than just government planners, and provided
a rigorous theoretical framework for relaxing unrealistic informational symmetries;
(3) the increasing integration of economic research with work from other disciplines;
and (4) the increasing turn among economists to empirical experimentation.

We will briefly discuss each of these exciting developments. However, we want
to make it clear that we do not think of these developments as paradigm shifts in
the Kuhnian sense. We are indeed suspicious of the value of that hoary idea to any
science, at least to any science once it establishes a track record of techniques for
modeling relatively clean empirical data. The view that whole disciplines undergo
revolutions—that is, transformations in their fundamental ontologies—crucially
rests on the assumptions about holism and the putative logic of confirmation in
philosophy of science we questioned earlier. It is far from clear that scientists make
implicit metaphysical reference to so-called natural kinds, as many philosophers
imagine. In general, we doubt that there is typically a precise fact of the matter
about what terms used in scientific theories refer to; we deny that philosophers
have sound motivation for supposing that such reference is intended given that
most scientists find the suggestion strange; and we think the main epistemic
import of science is missed if too much attention is paid to the semantic formulation of theories. Ladyman and Ross (2007) argue that sciences appear far more
progressive than Kuhnians imagine if one attends, not to statements of theories,
but to mathematical structures that guide the design of experiments and tests of
observations. Like physics, economics has *accumulated* and *refined* mathematical
structures for use in modeling, rather than *replaced* earlier structures with novel
ones. Computable general equilibrium models differ in their detailed structure
and in their purpose from the general equilibrium models of the 1950s and
1960—they are about detailed empirical investigation rather than proving uniqueness and stability. However, they are in their abstract structures clearly related to
and successors of those models from the 1950s and 1960s.

(1) Number Crunching

As Paul Humphreys (2004 and this volume) argues, it is probable that the sciences
will turn out never to have experienced a technological development more significant in the long run than the staggering expansion in computational capacity
that has followed the innovation of microprocessing, and which is still far from
complete.

Critics of economics have long scoffed at economists' defense of heroically
simplified models on mere grounds of tractability. (See, for one of many examples,
Addleson 1997.) Such critics have not generally had in mind, one hopes, that economists ought to use *intractable* models instead. Rather, the intended view (unusually
explicit in Addleson) has been that economists should give up on attempting quantitative representation in favor of qualitative and empirically richer understanding.

What formerly made richer quantitative models intractible was not economists' inability to write them down or imagine what operations it would take to solve them. What generated most intractability was the physical incapacity of teams of human brains to compute solutions to models with as many variables as we can often see should appear in ideal pictures of real systems of interest. Beginning slowly in the 1940s, but multiplying on an annual basis since the late 1980s, this capacity constraint is now triumphantly shattered. Ever-greater complexity is worth modeling because ever-more complex models can be solved.

What is relevant here is not literally the limiting case of the representation of complex reality, a single supermodel (so to speak) literally isomorphic to the world itself. Such a model would be epistemically pointless. Understanding *consists in* generalization, which is a species of simplification. On the other hand, there is no doubt that, for most of its history, computational restrictions forced economists to make do with the frustrating method of asking what circumstances would be like if they were based upon interaction of far fewer variables than clearly made real differences to parametric outcomes. This formerly nonoptional method puts a huge premium on the economist's power of imagination—a factor that critics of "toy" modeling seldom credit—and is indeed the source of a good deal of the intellectual thrill that economists appreciate. Every economist, for example, at some point in her or his early training saw in a rush the stunning implications of extending Adam Smith's trivial model of the pin factory to the whole interlocked network of global production. The lucky economist's whole career is a series of such leaps of imagination.

It is, thus, to be feared that economics might become more boring, as computers take over where insight was once necessary. However, where accuracy is concerned, there is no serious room for doubt that real computation is vastly superior to intuition. It might be objected that—at least for the moment, while we wait upon the fuller flowering of artificial intelligence—computers in economics can only do what we already understand clearly enough to program them to do. Here, however, supply of a problem and resulting demand for solutions have worked their usual effects; the explosion of computational capacity has been closely followed by a boom in invention of new econometric techniques. As Kincaid's and Du Plessis's papers in this volume remind us, at the moving frontier, critics are naturally alert to the imperfections of these techniques, and restlessness for improvement in them will be a permanent state of affairs. However, only the ignorant could deny that our ability to model increasingly rich causal hypotheses grows steadily, along with our capacity to subject these models to ever wider ranges of tests, with complementary strengths and weaknesses, against ever larger sets of data. This is reflected in the proportion of cousework a typical doctoral student in economics now must devote to learning analysis packages compared to her predecessor of a decade ago. This quiet revolution in the curriculum is tangible evidence that economists *are* becoming more like dentists in the way Keynes (1930) hoped they would. Perhaps this is sad for economists but a breakthrough for economics—and for its consumers.

The importance of the computational boom at the philosophical level is straightforward. It simultaneously reduces reliance on high abstractions, and permits greater weight to be given to empirical testing of hypotheses—especially causal hypotheses—by means of regression analyses on independent variables in models that aim at completeness. Prestige in the discipline, we believe, is beginning to accrue to highly fruitful achievements in model specification in just the way it has for decades been associated with elegant uniqueness proofs. Continuing worries of Popperians such as Blaug (2002) that economics is unmoored from confrontation with recalcitrant nature are increasingly anachronistic.

(2) Game Theory

The rise of game theory as the single most important branch of mathematics in microeconomics unfolded glacially, beginning in 1944 but not emerging into the central precincts of the discipline until the 1980s. Notwithstanding the fact that game-theoretic reasoning is now second nature to every economist under 50, its significance is often underappreciated. Economists still frequently express the opinion, for example, that game theory has obviously been useful in industrial organization and auction theory, but it has otherwise not fulfilled its promise. It is clear enough what people who say such things are getting at. Game theory has not been very productive of sweeping theoretical generalizations. Game-theoretic models of phenomena tend to have shallow reach and to need rewriting from scratch, whenever data force even minor adjustments to specifications of players' utility functions or strategy sets. In consequence of both this very real limitation and of the multiplicity of Nash equilibria in most games of interest, game-theoretic models usually fare poorly at quantitative prediction except when applied to designed mechanisms. The equilibrium refinement program (Kreps 1990), which was launched in the hope of providing relief from the embarrassing richness of equilibria, quickly degenerated into a formalized philosophical argument about what we ought to mean by the honorific "rational."

The problem with this familiar way of trying to minimize the importance of game theory is that it interprets the sources of value and potential influence of formal technology too narrowly. In general, anyone who becomes excited about a new kind of mathematics because they think they'll at last be able to deductively *nail* a range of empirical magnitudes is on the road to disappointment. (Philosophers are invited to reflect on their experience with formal logic at the beginning of the previous century.) The misleading example of Newton notwithstanding, that is not mainly how mathematics transforms science. It does so, instead, by providing scientists with fruitful new ways of organizing and representing phenomena. By this criterion, game theory has had a more transformative impact on economics than any other set of tools since differential calculus in the 1870s. We pointed out in the first section that much science is not about abstract theories but about providing detailed causal mechanisms according to context of application. That is what current game theory seeks to do.

Game theory has radically expanded econonomists' sense of how much of the social and commercial world it is possible for them to rigorously model. The example of industrial organization (IO) theory is illuminating in this regard. Before game theory, economists could formally handle monopolistic and perfectly competititive markets. This made their work interesting to government planners concerned with efficiency limits for the purpose of identifying targets, but it left economic modeling and advice far less relevant to business people, the majority of whom live in ologopolistic environments, often characterized by increasing returns to scale. Game theory took over IO because it is tailor-made for oligopoly and wholly unreliant on the decreasing returns assumption. Its resulting relevance to the real domain of commerce persists despite the limitations of the game theorist's ability to make reliable quantitative predictions (except about designed mechanisms); used with due care and understanding, game theoretic models of oligopolistic industries are devices of unsurpassed power for identifying the parameters on which strategists must focus, and for further specifying those to which major regime shifts are most sensitive (Ghemawat 1998, Sutton 1998). In turn, the basic property of game theory that permits the rigorous modeling of oligopolistic scenarios is its ability to capture asymmetries among agents. These include asymmetries in utility functions and strategy sets, but, most importantly by far, they include asymmetric information.

In a quite deep sense, game theory is *based on* information. The fundamental solution concept of game theory, Nash equilibrium (NE), can be defined in terms of it: a vector of strategies is a NE if (1) each player has information about the strategic choices of the other players, and (2) the strategy of each player is the best for herself, given her information about the strategies of the other players. What is important about information here, in philosophical terms, is that there is no such thing as *false* information (Dretske 1981); yet NE analysis carries no commitment to players having *full* information. In NE, each player does the best they can relative to what they're in a position to know. This is distinct from bounded rationality, in which agents fail to compute consequences of what they *are* in a position to know.

It is difficult to exaggerate the importance to contemporary economics of asymmetric information models, based on the game-theoretic analysis of signaling and screening, for which Akerloff, Spence, and Stiglitz shared the Nobel Prize. It is the basis for contemporary understanding of incomplete contracting, which is in turn criterial for the economic understanding of law, regulations, and the importance of institutions. It underscores the many specific, path-dependent explanations of failures of convergent development in political economy. (See Kincaid's and Fields's chapters in this volume.) It accounts for instabilities in markets even when traders take due care to protect themselves from their own tendencies to asymmetrically evaluate risks of gains and losses or underweight small probabilities. Most importantly, attention to informational asymmetries encourages economists to attend to distinguishing parameters of relatively specific situations instead of turning to the most general model that represents a phenomenon at a high level of abstraction. Again, this doesn't imply a flight from generalization, but rather a means to achievement of generalizations that deliver more fruitful, often qualitative, predictions.

This perspective suggests a better conceptualization of the venerable distinction between 'institutional' and 'neoclassical' economics than is typical of older treatments in the philosophy of economics and methodology literatures. The overwhelming majority of economic models are intended as accounts of short-run phenomena. Following Binmore (1998), something relatively precise can be meant by 'short run': this denotes a range of time scales in which games are played among agents whose utility functions are stable and whose preferences can thus be treated as exogenous. This is the familiar domain of neoclassical economics. Now suppose we think of institutions as the sources of determination of game structures, including not only strategy sets and distributions or flows of information, but also of preferences. Then we can think of the medium run as denoting the range of timescales in which, due to the influence of an institutional framework treated as constant, agents seek new sources of information and their preferences adapt in consequence. Game theory, now applied according to the principles of 'behavioral game theory' (Camerer 2003), remains the necessary modeling technology on this timescale. Since behavioral game theory models the influence of institutions (including social norms) on the dynamics of preferences, it implements the research program traditionally associated with institutionalism (as standardly constrasted with the neoclassical research program; see, e.g., Bowles et al. 2005, Chapter 2). Because preferences are allowed to move in the medium run, if we follow tradition by identifying agents with utility functions then the agents playing medium-run games cannot be numerically the same agents as feature in the short-range games the medium-range games determine, even if the same biological entities instantiate the agents at both timescales (Ross 2005, 2006). The idea here is that nothing forces us to identify the agent in some market transaction with the whole career of a biological person; the agent need last only as long as the episode being modeled, especially if 'agency' is understood as a modeling device rather than the name of a natural kind. Finally, following principles pioneered by Young (1998) but now in wide use, we can deploy evolutionary game theory (Weibull 1995) to model the long run, in which even the variables used to define institutions are controlled endogenously. At this timescale the players of games are strategies themselves, which transcend their biological embodiments who come and go with each generation.

In this framework the principles of game-theoretic reasoning and representation provide new methods for modeling economic processes at every level of abstraction and aggregation. Where once economics could model only the input-output properties of entire markets, treating both production and consumption functions as black boxes, thanks to the flexibility of game theoretic representation we can, at least in principle, model almost any social process in terms of responses to changes in relative scarcities and/or availability of information. The old tension between neoclassical and institutional economics is dissolved in recognition of the fact that modeling is scale-relative. Without the resources provided by game theory that allow us to implement this insight in real working models, this could at best have been a vague philosophical suggestion.

Game theory provides a powerful new basis for enriching the interactions between economists and workers in other disciplines. To this we now turn.

(3) Interdisciplinarity

Economists have a long history of defending their separateness from other branches of science. This gave rise to a main preoccupation for past philosophy of economics, encapsulated in our citation of Hausman's (1992) *The Inexact and Separate Science of Economics* as an exemplary consolidation of the previous generation's perspective. The tradition Hausman represents is a venerable one among philosophers of science who engaged with economics; his title alludes to John Stuart Mill.

When Hausman, and also Rosenberg (1992), focus on the separateness of economics, the main neighboring discipline that interests them is psychology. Several narratives of the campaign by economists to distance their activity from psychology have been written, from diverse and often incompatible perspectives. All tend to agree in emphasizing a tradition of "de-psychologizing" the concept of utility, which began with Pareto (1909 / 1971), was given rhetorical clarity and prominence by Robbins (1935), and was completed by the banishment from economics of mentalistic concepts (belief, desire, agency itself) in Samuelson's (1947) methodology based on revealed preference theory. A currently popular interpretation of this tradition (Bruni & Sugden 2007, Angner and Loewenstein forthcoming) depicts it as basically a long *mistake,* in which preference for a certain form of theory driven by physics envy (Mirowski 1989) later joined forces with primitive and ill-digested behaviorism to cause a divorce that did far more damage to economics than to psychology. Fortunately, according to this widespread view, the new behavioral economics (e.g., Camerer & Loewenstein 2004) represents a return to courtship, with remarriage clearly around the corner.

Alternative narratives of the historical relationship between economics and psychology are possible. Ross (2005, forthcoming) argues that economists after the 1930s seemed committed to an account of individual decision making that competes with—and ultimately loses the competition with—accounts emanating from psychology only because of the rhetorical commitment of many famous economists to methodological individualism. However, Ross argues, methodological individualism has done little if any work in driving important economic hypotheses; its motivation has been primarily ideological, and secondarily philosophical, rather than scientific. The strongest apparent counterexample to this suggestion is the microfoundations movement in macroeconomics that arose in the 1970s. However, the representative agent approach to modeling that forms the core of microfoundations makes no pretense to providing a plausible account of actual individuals; it is simply a device for bringing the technical rigor of microeconomics to bear in macroeconomics. If macroeconomics had clearer mathematical foundations than microeconomics, instead of the other way around, economists would doubtless have been busy seeking "macrofoundations," with just as little philosophical significance. Ross's revisionary account reads the history of economics as the history of models of opportunity-cost minimization by production-consumption systems, almost all of which, in the actual applications of economic theory that have been empirically important, have been identified with social aggregates. If economics is the science of opportunity-cost minimization, then behavioral economics might most accurately be conceived as a branch of psychology, specifically, the psychology of valuation and reward learning.

Neither side in this argument can or should want to deny that the level of interaction between economists and psychologists has been steadily increasing over the past two decades. It is readily accepted in contemporary economic literature, as it once was not, that findings from psychology may motivate the modeling of agents with utility functions that are exotic by comparison with simple maximization of expected financial returns or, alternatively, hedonic utility. Daniel Kahneman was awarded the Nobel Prize in Economics in 2006 for his lifetime of work that used ingenious psychological experiments to establish the theoretical and empirical value of Prospect Theory (which then spawned a family of variants) as an alternative to Expected Utility Theory (EUT) in providing a basis for representing choice and valuation functions. Neither EUT nor any of its rivals has proven *generally* superior as empirical accounts of the human computation of behavioral choice (Camerer & Harless 1994; Hey & Orme 1994; Ross 2005, 174–176; Binmore 2007, 21–22). Rather, psychology and economics share with other sciences, as Cartwright (1989 and elsewhere) has stressed, availability of a handy multiplicity of reduced form modeling equations for opportunistic exploitation of data in a range of recurrently constructed experimental paradigms. Guala (2005) shows how experimenters have used these as tools for gathering a "library of phenomena," rather than the basis (at least, so far) for an overarching theory of the behavioral response to scarcity and risk. We should expect this library to be of direct relevance to both the psychology of valuation and a more abstract theory of opportunity-cost minimization (where the latter incorporates constraints on the availability of, and asymmetries in, information).

That one can distinguish economics and psychology by reference to different primary objectives does not entail that, with respect to any given exercise in experimental design, prediction, or explanation, we ought to be able to draw an unambiguous line of disciplinary demarcation. We pointed out earlier that it is often a mistake to identify scientific areas with their abstract theories, and it equally can be a mistake to see differences in abstract theories as defining the different sciences. The boundaries of *three* disciplines—economics, psychology and computational neuroscience—blur in the thriving new enterprise of neuroeconomics (Montague

& Berns 2002; Glimcher 2003; Montague *et al* 2006; Politser 2008). The essential motivation for this mélange is the development of several technologies that permit controlled observation of correlates of live functional processing in the brains of humans (and other animals), including brain areas associated with valuation and reward. Interpretations of the role and place of economics in this enterprise, and of the possible significance of the resulting discoveries to microeconomic theory and methodology, are multifarious and in too early a state of ferment to be profitably grouped into classes in a general review like the present one. For preliminary articulations of perspectives in the gathering debate see Camerer *et al* 2005; Caplin & Dean 2007; Ross et al. 2008, Chapter 8; Gul & Pesendorfer 2008; and Ross's chapter in this volume).

Our earler emphasis on economics as a science frequently preoccupied with aggregate phenomena should remind us that pschology is only one neighboring science whose borderland with economics has come under extensive review. Indeed, the frontier over which sorties have been fought for longest is that between economics and sociology. In classical political economy the border was scarcely demarcated at all. It later hardened under the idea that the two disciplines rested on rival accounts of fundamental human motivation, with economists emphasizing individualistic aviriciousness and sociologists emphasizing drives for social status. The emerging reconciliation between institutional and neoclassical approaches to modeling, as discussed earlier, now allows us to see this implausibly totalistic pair of commitments in terms far more charitable to both sides; we can say that sociologists concentrated mainly on phenomena best captured by medium-run models, with endogenous institutional and group-normative variables, whereas economists modeled short-run phenomena in which preferences remained fixed. This potential compatibility was obscured for decades by the fact that economists embraced formal and quantitative models long before sociologists did, combined with the fact that, before the rise of game theory, economics lacked technology for linking these models to accounts of the medium or long runs. However, we can see in the work of Goffman (1959), and other sociologists influenced by him, anticipation of game-theoretic insights in everyday descriptive prose. Since then, sociology (at least in North America) has experienced a massive infusion of what economists regard as rigor. On the other side of the fuzzy border, we find theorists of social norms modeling them as objective functions optimized by agents who are generated, at the medium-run scale, by processes of socialization (Bicchieri et al. 1996; Mantzavinos 2004; Bicchieri 2005; Woodward's chapter in this volume). If it becomes widely recognized in economics, as we think it should, that methodological individualism is an ideological or philosophical prejudice rather than a scientifically justified principle, then an eventual fusion of economics and sociology seems to us more likely than the much-prophecied merger of economics and psychology.

Game theory plays an equally important, though not exclusive, role in another thriving interdisciplinary bridge into and out of economics, that with biology. The game-theoretic route was opened by Maynard Smith's (1982) depiction of Darwinian selection as the play of multiple long-run games among strategies embodied in genetic dispositions of individual organisms. The maximand in these games is fitness rather than utility, with each generation of genetically similar organisms representing a tournament among some of the possible moves. A rich formal literature quickly developed that establishes bidirectional mappings between Maynard Smith's dynamical equilibrium concept, the Evolutionary Stable Strategy, and Nash equilibrium (Weibull 1995). This work has contributed to economics in two important ways. First, it provides a canonical and rigorous framework for modeling evolutionary competition among firms and other strategies for the organization of production, which had been introduced into economics by Hayek and brought into the mainstream by pioneering work of Nelson and Winter (1982). This is precisely the technical bridge between medium-run modeling of institutional change and short-run modeling of prices and quantities to which we have continually referred in the present section. Second, establishment of formal relationships between dynamic and static solution concepts in game theory has been the basis for a formal theory of the learning of equilibrium play that allows intuitively dubious Nash equilibria to be selected against by forces less arbitrary than philosophically motivated and computationally demanding refinements of rationality (Samuelson 1998).

Economic and game theoretic reasoning inform parts of biology more basic than abstract evolutionary modeling. The field of behavioral ecology, which models animals and plants as interactively adapting to (and sometimes partly constructing) their environments so as to maximize expected fitness, is directly informed by game theory (Krebs & Davies 1997; Dugatkin & Reeve 2000). Economists are apt to doubt that this activity has much to do with them. However, an intriguing new literature has begun to emerge that models some behavior of nonhuman animals in terms of participation in competitive markets (Noë et al. 2001). The key to this is partner choice, which many game-theoretic models in behavioral ecology assume away without biological motivation. For example, small, reef-dwelling fish visited by larger fish who come to have parasites eaten out of their mouths extract payment by devouring some of their client fish's scales. The cleaners have been found to practice systematic, and optimal, price discrimination against clients who have fewer service options because their ecology requires them to stay close to a single reef (Bshary & Noë 2003). These markets appear to stabilize at competitive (Bertrand) equilibrium. Instances of this kind should interest all economists, because they vividly illustrate selection of efficient outcomes under circumstances where there is no temptation to think that the agents consciously deliberate.

This need not be mysterious. One possible mechanism suggested by a great deal of evidence in the animal-learning literature is that implementation of simple matching algorithms allows animals to maximize reward rates (Gallistel 1990). This will tend to produce behavior corresponding to utility maximization in environments where there is no significant opportunity for investment. Where animals are faced with investment choices, such as in parenting, the theorist may need to consult the long run and search for genetic dispositions learned over the evolutionary lineage of the animal in question. Then people, who regularly encounter ecologically non-natural investment choices, emerge as the especially interesting case. Perhaps people adapt to environments with non-natural investment opportunities only by relying on institutions, such as financial markets, that quickly punish them (by rising capital charges) whenever they use biologically natural melioration under circumstances in which utility-maximization would have delivered higher expected returns.

When their attention is turned in this way to human cultural adaptation, as mediated through institutional change, economists naturally become involved in explanatory projects shared with anthropologists. Recent work that has attracted considerable attention in the literature exploits anthropologists' understanding of the ways in which alternative organizations of production in different societies are stabilized by specific social norms that adapt people's incentives efficiently. The best-known application of this body of knowledge is Henrich et al.'s (2004) interdisciplinary project to determine how members of different small-scale societies expect one another to play in ultimatum games. Other notable recent applications of economic logic to long-run cultural evolution are provided by Seabright (2004) and Clark (2007), who each study, in very different ways, the cultural adaptations that make capitalism possible. In the case of Clark's analysis, this controversially involves an aspect of genetic adaptation, thus simultaneously integrating economic, anthropological, and biological analysis.

We conclude this section by considering a related group of disciplines with which economics has always been in close contact: the broadly philosophical cluster composed of political philosophy, public choice political science, and normative decision theory. What is recently novel in this area is not the existence of interdisciplinary relations *per se* but their nature.

Formal welfare analysis and its close cousin in philosophy, applied utilitarianism, both petered out in the decades after the war due to doubts about quantitative interpersonal comparisons. While economists spent several years first showing that perfectly competitive markets achieve welfare optima at general equilibrium, then expended further effort discovering that this fact has far less policy significance than imagined (Lipsey & Lancaster 1956), philosophers interested in the normative domain busied themselves with conceptual analysis of moral language. (In our view, the economists' voyage into a cul-de-sac was illuminating and important, whereas the philosophers' trip down *their* blind alley was merely a disciplinary embarrassment.) Substantive normative theory was reborn in philosophy thanks to Rawls (1971). At first, Rawls's approach might have been thought to provide limited scope for interanimation with economics, due to his explicit rejection of utilitarianism in favor of broadly Kantian foundations. (As a caveat, it must be noted that Amartya Sen and a few other economists sympathized with Rawls in this respect, and have been strongly influenced by him.) However, a surprisingly strong bridge to Rawlsian justice has recently been built up by Binmore (1994, 1998, 2005), who in turn relies crucially on Harsanyi's (1955, 1977) resuscitation of formal utilitarianism. The key here, yet again, is game theory. It furnished Harsanyi with the tool for breaking out of the dead end in welfare economics that had been arrived at by the combination of skepticism about interpersonal comparisons, the Lipsey-Lancaster theorem, and Arrow's impossibility theorem. Binmore then uses Nash bargaining theory to show how people with plausible Darwinian psychologies, which emphatically do not include Rawls's transcendent Kantian moral commitments, can nevertheless arrive at Rawlsian justice rather than the maximization of net collective utility. On Binmore's analysis, norms of justice are institutions in the strict sense discussed earlier, that is, endogenous long-run variables in evolutionary games that constrain bargaining equilibria in shorter-run models.

We have not included first-order discussions of justice and distribution in this *Handbook*. We could at best have covered these topics inadequately, a poor compromise in light of the many excellent sources to which readers can be referred instead. In any case, these issues do not mainly fall within the purview of the philosophy of science, or, therefore, that of philosophy of *economic* science. They are topics for political philosophy informed by economic analysis. However, we *have* included some second-order work on the nature of the economic analysis that political philosophers receive as consumers. Methodological questions about this activity *are* questions for economic scientists and philosophers of science.

Just at the point in time when Rawls was reviving substantive political philosophy and Harsanyi was breathing life back into welfare economics, a rude shock was experienced by the main community of applied welfare economists, the development theorists. Their orthodoxy, derived from Solow's (1957) exogenous growth model, led them to expect that the economies of the rich and poor countries should converge due to faster growth in markets where relative capital shortages would generate higher average returns. However, beginning in the mid-1970s two of the world's three less developed continents, Africa and South America, went into comparative decline. At first, this was partly masked by the co-occurrence of a long recession in the rich world. However, by the end of the 1980s it had become clear that if the Solow model's prediction was correct, this must be only in a significantly longer run than previously thought. South America returned to decent growth in the 1990s. However, up until the resurgence of commodity prices in 2005, most of sub-Saharan Africa endured three full decades of economic shrinkage. To insist on faith in long run convergence in that context would simply be a way of seeking to excuse evident irrelevance to real policy choice.

Most economists of course did not do this. As reviewed in Kincaid's chapter in this volume, the Solow growth model has been largely supplanted by so-called endogenous growth models, according to which poverty traps are a recurrent possibility due to mutual co-dependence of financial, physical, and human capital accumulation. Most theorists believe that Africa has been mired in such a trap.

This *Handbook* is of course not the venue for exploration of the contest between exogenous and endogenous growth models. However, the rise of the new growth theory has had important consequences for methodological issues in policy-led economic science.

Where belief in the Solow model encouraged relative passivity (with some infusion of financial capital from outside poor economies called for if one wanted to speed up growth processes that would occur naturally anyway), the endogenous growth perspective implies a need for activism to pull countries out of poverty traps. However, the search for *effective* bases for activism has been deeply frustrating. It cannot be said that economists, in their role as positive scientists, have identified any clear recipes for bringing about sustainable upward inflection points in national growth curves of poor countries (Easterly 2001).

It is a standard dogma among philosophers of science, of all theoretical persuasions, that scientists do not discard prevailing models until replacements are available. This is for the pragmatic reason that, in the absence of a model, no one knows what to do that would qualify as knowledge development. We agree that the history of science largely bears out this belief. However, matters are importantly different where policy choices, especially policy choices relevant to the health and even survival of millions of people, are concerned. Persisting with application of a model in which theorists have lost confidence, merely because a consensus alternative is not yet on the scene, is politically and perhaps also morally unacceptable. At the very same time, the perceived need for better policy-relevant science grows more urgent. Development economics is in a state of high crisis, and, *therefore*, there is more development economics being conducted than ever before.

It would be a peculiar philosopher of economics who did not find this situation extremely interesting. It is too soon for us, or anyone, to be able to say how the passage through the current crisis will ultimately transform economics. However, we will be so bold as to speculate a bit. We think the urgent quest for effective growth policies will greatly accelerate current trends, repeatedly indicated earlier in this chapter, toward a preference for models of local scope, emphasizing historically and institutionally contingent asymmetries of information, over putatively general, ahistorical, nonsituational models such as the Solow growth model or—to cite another example for the sake of generality—the Heckscher-Ohlin theory of international trade. Heckscher-Ohlin models are increasingly giving way to so-called gravity models in which the underlying theoretical assumption is extremely banal—that contingent historical and geographical relationship variables between countries determine their comparative levels of trade—and all of the economist's acquired skill, knowledge, and ingenuity go into constructing specific models of this relationship that are sufficiently complete, and sufficiently carefully constructed with respect to partitioning of independent variables, to allow for convincing econometric estimation and testing.

Very often, the small-scale models coming to dominate economics are game theoretic. Indeed, game theory may be the key basis for understanding the record of failure in development policy in Africa. Public choice models, the major contributions of political scientists to a particularly close interdisciplinary partnership with economics, often predict rent-seeking activities of individuals and institutions that reflect deep learning and will thus tend to be highly resilient and persistent in the face of attempts at altruistically or disinteresedly motivated reform. Public choice models have come in for a good deal of harsh criticism (see, e.g., Shapiro 2005). This has mainly focused on the features they allegedly share with neoclassical microeconomic models: overgenerality, insensitivity to historical and institutional contingencies, commitment to methodological individualism, and reliance on a version of *Homo economicus* whose motives are unreasonably consistent and self-centred. In our opinion, the public choice literature has indeed (with important exceptions) been more deserving of these charges than the mainstream tradition in microeconomics. However, it is possible to enrich the first generation of public choice models by drawing on the resources of multiscale game theory as outlined in earlier sections.

A movement in this direction is evident in the development literature (Platteau 2000). We predict that the key scientific contribution to more successful antipoverty policy over the coming years will lie in the area of mechanism design. This requires, first, that one achieve focus on an appropriate scale, at which modeling simplifies phenomena sufficiently for *important* variables to stand out as salient, but not so drastically that causal pathways connecting *control* variables—potential policy levers—with dependent variables targeted for reform disappear inside black boxes. Then, one searches for a game-theoretic model that identifies a set of institutional structures, which some authority could plausibly put in place by manipulation of the levers identified in step one, that would incentivize individuals and groups to act as if they valued the public interest in economic growth rather than to impede it through rent-seeking.

Though activity of this kind is engaged in for the sake of policy, and policy is ultimately driven by normative commitments, the commitments in question tend to be relatively banal and noncontroversial by comparison with the epochal "markets or governments?" ideological battles that political philosophers have often identified as undercurrents in economics. (Dasgupta's chapter in this *Handbook* provides rich and eloquent detail on this theme.) The hard questions in the new policy economics, as it operates closer to the ground and relies on game theory and the econometric applications made possible by vast number crunching resources, are methodological and scientific far more than they are normative. Readers of Fields's chapter will gain a good sense of the extent to which leading methodological debates in economics now tend to take pragmatism for granted, and to focus on how we can derive the maximum quantity of *useful* information from the lavish streams of data now available to us. It is for this reason that, in a volume that confines its focus to economic *science* rather than to every kind of debate in which economists engage, we have included chapters on the pragmatic foundations of welfare and development economics, while leaving arguments between Kantian and utilitarian normative-foundational frameworks for continued treatment in other sources.

Its richer set of tools having opened new veins of activity, economics as a discipline has been growing steadily in confidence. This has made economists impatient with methodological arguments—there are so many more pressing things to get on with. At the same time, confidence encourages them to engage opportunistically with contributions from other disciplines, rather than devote energy to patroling their own boundaries. We do not think that economics is blending into psychology or any other discipline (though it might swallow sociology). However, it is certainly being importantly changed in its scientific character, and for the better, by interacting with the neighbors.

(4) Experimentation

Some commentators, including some economists, give the impression that controlled experimental testing of economic hypotheses is a recent and novel phenomenon. It is not. As early as 1931, L.L. Thurstone attempted to experimentally derive subjects' utility functions from their choice behavior in his laboratory. The experimental work for which Vernon Smith shared the Nobel Prize with Kahneman goes back to the 1960s. What certainly *is* true is that economists are doing far more experimental work than at any past time and, more importantly, that this research has recently begun to be taught in leading economics graduate programs. Increasing numbers of graduate students are even encouraged to learn laboratory methods. Experimental economics is shedding its status as a fringe practice.

Because the very essence of an experiment as a contribution to knowledge is replicability, experimentation gains positive value from methodological dogma to a greater extent than other kinds of scientific activity. Experimental economics has accordingly stabilized around several distinctive norms. Guala (2005, 232–233) identifies four methodological "precepts." These are rules which, if broken, will preclude publication of an experiment in an economics journal unless the economist in question has a specific, scientifically based, and scientifically persuasive, explicit justification. Guala's precepts are:

1. *Nonsatiation:* choose a medium of reward such that of two otherwise equivalent alternatives, subjects will always choose the one yielding more of the reward medium.
2. *Saliency:* the reward must be increasing in the good and decreasing in the bad outcomes of the experiment.
3. *Dominance:* the rewards dominate any subjective costs associated with participation in the experiment.
4. *Privacy:* each subject in an experiment receives information only about her own incentives.

We have some doubts about whether privacy merits being regarded as a genuine precept. Though it is indeed more often observed than not, we suggest that this is mainly because it is often necessary to try to maintain dominance. Dominance is often very difficult to achieve, or to be confident one has achieved, as Ken Binmore in particular has repeatedly pointed out. This is just one aspect of a general, partly philosophical, question to which experimental economists should, in our view, devote substantial attention: What circumstances are necessary and sufficient for belief that an experiment is *externally valid,* that is, that it successfully models in the laboratory the structural parameters and (parametric and nonparametric) incentives relevant to whatever class of ecological circumstances the experimenter is ultimately interested in predicting and explaining?

As Cartwright (1989) has emphasized, this general issue arises for all laboratory experimentation in science, but different sciences have varying means available for dealing with it. Experimental economists are particularly limited by ethical proscriptions against confronting subjects with coercive incentives or allowing them to exit experiments poorer in monetary wealth than they entered. Guala fails to include one clear precept of experimental economics, namely, nondeception, which further challenges designers' ingenuity in contriving to achieve external (and internal) validity. Economists are conditioned by their training to perceive experimenter credibility with subjects as a commons good. That is, any single team of experimenters could gain a degree of design freedom by being willing to deceive subjects about real payoffs. Deception is not ethically proscribed by institional review boards and research ethics committees, since psychologists engage in it as a matter of course. However, if many economic experimenters regularly deceived subjects, word might be expected to get around in subject pools that economists' subject briefings cannot be trusted. In an economic experiment, confidence that subjects operate in accordance with the incentives ascribed to them, as reinforced by the experimental design, is crucial to the point of the enterprise. Thus the community of experimental economists faces a many-person Prisoner's Dilemma unless outside authorities act to change the game. The outside authorities in question are journal editors, who coordinate on a rule according to which they will not publish reports of experiments in which subjects are deceived. Economists determined to deceive subjects can seek to publish their results in psychology journals, and then take their chances with their tenure and promotion committees. However, one cannot ask one's graduate students to take chances with the acceptability of their thesis chapters. The nondeception precept has been extended to neuroeconomics, following a 2004 vote by the founding membership of the Society for Neuroeconomics.

To avoid problems of external validity, economists are increasingly conducting field experiments in which subjects' incentives are known to be those operative in the wild because the subjects are not taken out of the wild in the first place. Duflo (2006) provides a review and extended discussion of two representative examples. As she indicates, field experiments have lately become especially emphasized in development economics. This reflects the fact, as discussed in the previous section, that development models are becoming increasingly local and situational. Assumptions about information, costs, and incentives built into such models, not being typically defensible merely by appeal to generic ideas about rationality, require explicit empirical testing. A common design involves finding two similar local populations—for example, two villages—one of which is designated a treatment group and receives a policy initiative intended to change incentives or information, while the other control group does not receive the initiative. Underlying the experiment must be a causal model in which administered variables appear on the left-hand side of the model equation and some independent policy objective (e.g., an increase in per capita household consumption expenditure, or the proportion of women's days occupied by fetching fuel and water, etc.) appears on the right-hand side. Following a prestipulated observation period, the model is tested econometrically to determine how well it accounts for variance in outcomes between the villages. We think it is accurate to say that this methodology is quickly coming to be accepted as the gold standard in development economics. Note that the only restrictions on independent variables arise from testing constraints, not from an a priori model of economic agents or of markets.

We have placed experimentation at the bottom of our list of main sources of recent change in economics. This is in part because we dispute the stereotype common among philosophers that economists have been, at least until recently, uninterested in testing their models against reality. According to our reading of the history, they were always willing enough, but labored under severe limitations. The most important of these was shortage of computational power needed to test models that were not drastically simplified. The second, interacting directly with the first, was the fact that introducing interactivity into models through use of game theory usually blows up complexity. The *best* strategy when a scientist cannot rigorously test finely fitted models is to retreat to models of wide scope that rely on maximally general theoretical principles. A justification that economists for years *could have* given for extreme idealization, regardless of whether they perceived the need for such justification, was that they had no other effective choice in many domains of interest.

Consequently, the mainstream core of economics for several decades looked just like what a science, according to the received view in mid-twentieth-century philosophy of science, was supposed to look like. We believe that the received view is and always was largely mistaken. Therefore, it mistook a virtue economists made of necessity for a deep methodological commitment based on philosophical presuppositions. Later, when received opinion in philosophy of science came increasingly into question, economics as philosophers had *mis*understood it fell under suspicion as well.

We suggest that a more accurate narrative is as follows. Economists have generally been sceptical about the importance of grand methodological and philosophical principles. The rhetoric of the discipline resonates, throughout its whole history, with an ideal of close empirical testing of hypothesized relationships. This is reflected in, among other things, economists' perennial resistance to the kinds of highly abstract constructs that dominate psychology. (A reader who doubts what we're saying here is advised to consult the first few chapters of Samuelson's *Foundations*. If any document has a claim to being the high church expression of mainstream postwar philosophy of economics among economists, this is it.) Modern classics in the philosophy of economics, Hausman (1992) and Rosenberg (1993), missed this underlying spirit in the discipline because they were written at the end of a long period of frustration with the available tools. A decade-and-a-half later, an extraordinary new set of instruments delivered from the work-shops of computer science and mathematics have profoundly altered capabilities. Sensibilities, which always adjust with a lag, are duly following. It is no surprise that it is time to re-cast the philosophy of economics.

ORGANIZATION OF THE *HANDBOOK*

A standard but tedious practice in introductions to collections is to briefly describe the contents of each chapter. We suppose this is intended to serve two purposes. First, it might demonstrate that the collection in question has a *raison d'être* expressed in its ordering and development of topics. Second, it can guide a con-sumer who is trying to decide which chapters to actually read.

We will eschew this approach. We believe we have now adequately explained why we have edited this new *Handbook,* and included in it the material that we have. We also hope that readers will be able to gather which chapters interest them by looking at the titles and the names of the authors. The one traditional introduc-tory function we do think still needs to be performed is to briefly state the book's principles of organization. This is for the benefit of the particularly devoted student of the philosophy of economics who plans to read the *Handbook* right through, and would like a bit of orientation first.

We referred at several points in the Introduction to classic statements of the conception of philosophy of economics that, according to us, are now being dis-placed, thanks to changes in disciplinary practice. The clearest and most influen-tial expressions of this conception, in our view, are due to Daniel Hausman and Alex Rosenberg. A third equally influential contributor of their generation, at least in Europe, has been Uskali Mäki. We therefore deemed it appropriate to open the *Handbook* by asking Hausman, Rosenberg, and Mäki to restate their general ori-entations and motivations. We explicitly requested them to write partly from auto-biographical standpoints, since the point of this exercise is increased clarity about recent intellectual history. The first part of the *Handbook* is comprised mainly of these three chapters. It is rounded off and balanced with a chapter from Philip

Mirowski, who has been the most provocative, but also widely read and highly influential, critical historian of the grand neoclassical self-conception. Taken together, Part I of the *Handbook* showcases the image of economics against which a majority of philosophers of science have increasingly reacted. It thus describes a platform relative to which the rest of the book's contents amount to a complex response.

Part II surveys the impact on microeconomics of the new technologies, methods and interdisciplinary relationships described in this Introduction. The topics covered are the evolution of the concept of personal utility in game theory, social preferences, the nature of the individual as incorporated in economics, the relationship between behavioral economics and neuroeconomics, issues in the design of economic experiments, methodological questions from mechanism design, and evolutionary economics.

Part III turns to issues in the study of aggregate phenomena. The topics taken up are the impact of cheap computational power on modeling, the current status of microfoundations for macroeconomics, methods for trying to isolate reliable policy levers from macroeconomic data, the turn from general to situational explanations and policy studies of growth, and the similar turn in studies of labor markets.

Part IV concerns the relationship between current controversies in economic science and welfare. Topics considered are the nature and measurability of welfare, the justification and methodology of interpersonal utility comparison, recent proposals to revive broadly Benthamite (that is, psychologistic) conceptions of well being for use in economics, and the relationship between facts and values in development economics.

It will be obvious from a cursory inspection of these topics that this *Handbook* covers significantly different ground from previous volumes that aimed at presenting the state of the art in philosophy of economics. Our aim in this Introduction has been to explain why this is so, and to identify underlying general changes in both philosophy of science and economics that explain the more specific aspects of novelty.

We conclude by summarizing the general message. Economists are far less preoccupied with abstract, grand, unified theories than they once were. Therefore, philosophers of economics should be less interested in this, too. Led by Nancy Cartwright and others, this was a conclusion many philosophers of science had arrived at independently. But this has led many to criticize economics because they did not quickly pick up on changes taking place in economics graduate curricula or circulating working papers. The new, situational, and pragmatic economics beautifully exemplifies the themes that philosophers of sciences had recently gathered from other disciplines.

However, in saying that economists are less devoted to grand, unified *theories*, we do not at all deny that there are unifying *themes* in contemporary economics. We agree with Gintis (2007) that use of game theory, with its associated focus on informational asymmetries, underlies not only what is most distinctively novel across most of economics, but extends the discipline's integration in the larger suite of behavioral sciences. Unlike Gintis, we do not interpret game theory as itself a behavioral theory; it is a part of mathematics, making no empirical claims. To this extent, our stance harkens back to aspects of positivism and even Kantianism, so we are not dismissive of the relevance of philosophy. The key is for philosophers to keep their ears as close as possible to the ground—in this case, the ground being the economics seminar rooms around the world in which the graduate students gather. We hope this *Handbook* aids that purpose.

REFERENCES

Addleson, M. (1997). *Equilibrium Versus Understanding.* London: Routledge.

Angner, E. & Loewenstein, G. (forthcoming). "Behavioral Economics." In U. Mäki, Ed., *Handbook of the Philosophy of Science Volume 13: Economics.* London: Elsevier.

Binmore, K. (1994). *Game Theory and the Social Contract, Volume 1: Playing Fair.* Cambridge, MA: MIT Press.

Binmore, K. (1998). *Game Theory and the Social Contract, Volume 2: Just Playing.* Cambridge, MA: MIT Press.

Binmore, K. (2005). *Natural Justice.* Oxford: Oxford University Press.

Binmore, K. (2007). *Does Game Theory Work? The Bargaining Challenge.* Cambridge, MA: MIT Press.

Blaug, M. (1980). *The Methodology of Economics.* Cambridge, England: Cambridge University Press.

Blaug, M. (2002). "Ugly Currents in Modern Economics." In U. Mäki, ed., *Fact and Fiction in Economics,* 35–36. Cambridge, England: Cambridge University Press.

Bicchieri, C., Jeffrey, R. & Skyrms, B., eds. (1996). *The Dynamics of Norms.* Cambridge, England: Cambridge University Press.

Bicchieri, C. (2005). *The Grammar of Society.* Cambridge, England: Cambridge University Press.

Bowles, S., Edwards, R. & Roosevelt, F. (2005). *Understanding Capitalism.* 3rd edition. Oxford: Oxford University Press.

Bruni, L. & Sugden, R. (2007). "The Road Not Taken: How Psychology Was Removed from Economics and How It Might Be Brought Back." *The Economic Journal* 117: 146–173.

Bshary, R. & Noë, R. (2003). "Biological Markets: The Ubiquitous Influence of Partner Choice on the Dynamics of Cleaner Fish—Client Reef Fish Interactions." In P. Hammerstein, Ed., *Genetic and Cultural Evolution of Cooperation,* 167–184. Cambridge, MA: MIT Press.

Caldwell, B. (1982). *Beyond Positivism.* London: George Allen and Unwin.

Camerer, C. & Harless, D. (1994). "The Predictive Utility of Generalized Expected Utility Theories." *Econometrica* 62: 1251–1290.

Camerer, C. (2003). *Behavioral Game Theory.* Princeton: Russell Sage / Princeton University Press.

Camerer, C. & Loewenstein, G. (2004). "Behavioral Economics: Past, Present, and Future." In C. Camerer, G. Loewenstein & M. Rabin, Eds., *Advances in Behavioral Economics*, 3–51. Princeton: Princeton University Press.

Camerer, C., Loewenstein, G. & Prelec, D. (2005). "Neuroeconomics: How Neuroscience Can Inform Economics." *Journal of Economic Literature* 43: 9–64.

Caplin, A. & Dean, M. (2007). "The Neuroeconomic Theory of Learning." *American Economic Review* 97: 148–152.

Cartwright, N. (1980). "The Reality of Causes in a World of Instrumental Laws." In P. Asquith & R. Giere, Eds., *PSA 1980, Volume 2*, 38–48. East Lansing, MI: Philosophy of Science Association.

Cartwright, N. (1989). *Nature's Capacities and their Measurement*. Oxford: Oxford University Press.

Cartwright, N. (2007). *Hunting Causes and Using Them*. Cambridge, England: Cambridge University Press.

Clark, G. (2007). *A Farewell to Alms*. Princeton: Princeton University Press.

Dretske, F. (1981). *Knowledge and the Flow of Information*. Cambridge, MA: MIT Press.

Duflo, E. (2006). "Field Experiments in Development Economics." In R. Blundell, W. Newey, & T. Persson, Eds., *Advances in Economics and Econometrics Volume II*, 322–348. Cambridge, England: Cambridge University Press.

Dugatkin, L. & Reeve, H. (2000). *Game Theory and Animal Behavior*. Oxford: Oxford University Press.

Easterly, W. (2001). *The Elusive Quest for Growth*. Cambridge, MA: MIT Press.

Gallestel, C.R. (1990). *The Organization of Learning*. Cambridge, MA: MIT Press.

Ghemawat, P. (1998). *Games Businesses Play*. Cambridge, MA: MIT Press.

Gintis, H. (2007). "A Framework for the Unification of the Behavioral Sciences." *Behavioral and Brain Sciences* 30: 1–16.

Glimcher, P. (2003). *Decisions, Uncertainty and the Brain*. Cambridge, MA: MIT Press.

Glymour, C. 1980. *Theory and Evidence*. Princeton: Princeton University Press.

Goffman, E. (1959). *The Presentation of Self in Everyday Life*. New York: Anchor.

Guala, F. (2005). *The Methodology of Experimental Economics*. Cambridge: Cambridge University Press.

Gul, F. & Pesendorfer, W. (2008). "The Case for Mindless Economics." In A. Caplin & A. Schotter, Eds., *The Handbook of Economic Methodologies, Volume 1*. Oxford: Oxford University Press.

Hands, W. (1993). *Testing, Rationality, and Progress*. Lanham, MD: Rowman and Littlefield.

Harford, T. (2005). *The Undercover Economist*. Oxford: Oxford University Press.

Harsanyi, J. (1955). "Cardinal Welfare, Individualistic Ethics, and the Interpersonal Comparison of Utility." *Journal of Political Economy* 63: 309–321.

Harsanyi, J. (1977). *Rational Behavior and Bargaining Equilibrium in Games and Social Situations*. Cambridge: Cambridge University Press.

Hausman, D. (1981). *Capital, Profits, and Prices*. New York: Columbia University Press.

Hausman, D. (1992). *The Inexact and Separate Science of Economics*. Cambridge, England: Cambridge University Press.

Henrich, J., Boyd, R., Bowles, S., Camerer, C., Fehr, E. & Gintis, H. (2004). *Foundations of Human Sociality*. Oxford: Oxford University Press.

Hey, J. & Orme, C. (1994). "Investigating Generalizations of Expected Utility Theory Using Experimental Data." *Econometrica* 62: 1291–1326.

Humphreys, P. (2004). *Extending Ourselves*. Oxford: Oxford University Press.

Kay, J. (2005). *Culture and Prosperity*. London: Collins.

Kitcher, P. (2003). *The Advancement of Science*. Oxford: Oxford University Press.

Keynes, J.M. (1930 [1963]). "Economic Possibilities for Our Grandchildren." Reprinted in Keynes, J.M., *Essays in Persuasion*, 358–373. New York: Norton.

Krebs, J. & Davies, N. (1997). *Behavioral Ecology: An Evolutionary Approach*. 2nd ed. London: Wiley-Blackwell.

Kreps, D. (1990). *Game Theory and Economic Modelling*. Oxford: Oxford University Press.

Ladyman, J. & Ross, D. (2007). *Every Thing Must Go: Metaphysics Naturalized*. Oxford: Oxford University Press.

Lipsey, R. & Lancaster, G. (1956). "The General Theory of Second Best." *Review of Economic Studies* 24: 11–32.

Mantzavinos, C. (2004). *Individuals, Institutions and Markets*. Cambridge: Cambridge University Press.

Maynard Smith, J. (1982). *Evolution and the Theory of Games*. Cambridge: Cambridge University Press.

McCloskey, D. (1985). *The Rhetoric of Economics*. Madison: University of Wisconsin Press.

Mirowski, P. (1989). *More Heat Than Light*. New York: Cambridge University Press.

Montague, P.R. & Berns, G. (2002). "Neural Economics and the Biological Substrates of Valuation." *Neuron* 36: 265–284.

Montague, P.R., King-Cassas, B. & Cohen, J. (2006). "Imaging Valuation Models in Human Choice." *Annual Review of Neuroscience* 29: 417–448.

Moss, L. (2004). *What Genes Can't Do*. Cambridge: MIT Press.

Nelson, R. & Winter, S. (1982). *An Evolutionary Theory of Economic Change*. Cambridge, MA: Harvard University Press.

Noë, R., van Hoof, J. & Hammerstein, P., Eds. (2001). *Economics in Nature*. Cambridge, England: Cambridge University Press.

Pareto, V. (1909 / 1971). *Manual of Political Economy*. New York: Augustus Kelley.

Platteau, J. (2000). *Institutions, Social Norms and Economic Development*. London: Routledge.

Politser, P. (2008). *Neuroeconomics: A Guide to the New Science of Making Choices*. Oxford: Oxford University Press.

Rawls, J. (1971). *A Theory of Justice*. Cambridge, MA: Harvard University Press.

Robbins, L. (1935). *An Essay on the Nature and Significance of Economic Science*. 2nd ed. London: Macmillan.

Rosenberg, A. 1976. *Microeconomic Laws*. Pittsburgh: University of Pittsburgh Press.

Rosenberg, A. (1992). *Economics: Mathematical Politics or Science of Diminishing Returns?* Chicago: University of Chicago Press.

Ross, D. (2005). *Economic Theory and Cognitive Science: Microexplanation*. Cambridge, MA: MIT Press.

Ross, D. (2006). "The Economic and Evolutionary Basis of Selves." *Journal of Cognitive Systems Research* 7: 246–258.

Ross, D., Sharp, C., Vuccinich, R. and Spurrett, D. *Midbrain Mutiny: The Picoeconomics and Neuroeconomics of Disordered Gambling*. Cambridge, MA: MIT Press.

Ross, D. (forthcoming). "The Economic Agent: Not Human, but Important." In U. Mäki, Ed., *Handbook of the Philosophy of Science Volume 13: Economics*. London: Elsevier.

Samuelson, P. (1947). *Foundations of Economic Analysis*. Cambridge, MA: Harvard University Press.

Samuelson, L. (1998). *Evolutionary Games and Equilibrium Selection*. Cambridge, MA: MIT Press.

Seabright, P. (2004). *The Company of Strangers*. Princeton: Princeton University Press.

Shapiro, I. (2005). *The Flight from Reality in the Human Sciences*. Princeton: Princeton University Press.

Solow, R. (1957). "Technical Change and the Aggregate Production Function." *The Review of Economics and Statistics* 39: 312–320.

Sutton, J. (1998). *Technology and Market Structure*. Cambridge, MA: MIT Press.

Thurstone, L. (1931). "The Indifference Function." *Journal of Social Psychology* 2: 139–167.

van Fraassen, B. (1981). *The Scientific Image*. Oxford: Oxford University Press.

Weibull, J. (1995). *Evolutionary Game Theory*. Cambridge, MA: MIT Press.

Young, H.P. (1998). *Individual Strategy and Social Structure*. Princeton: Princeton University Press.

PART I

RECEIVED VIEWS
IN PHILOSOPHY
OF ECONOMICS

CHAPTER 2

....

LAWS, CAUSATION, AND ECONOMIC METHODOLOGY

....

DANIEL M. HAUSMAN

As someone who has been working on philosophy of economics for more than a generation, I was asked by the editors of this *Handbook* to summarize my view of the subject. Since I have already done that elsewhere,[1] I shall focus in this essay on the relations between my work on methodology, developments in philosophy of science, and the contributions of other methodologists.

This chapter consists of five sections. Section 1 explains how my work derives from philosophy of science, as the subject was understood in the 1970s. It is autobiographical, not because I think my biography is of great interest, but because my story may help readers to understand the outpouring of writing on economic methodology beginning in the 1970s, of which my work was just one small part. Section 2 sketches a view of philosophical methodology that articulates the roles that reflection, analysis and study of economics ought to play. Section 3 summarizes the views on economic methodology that are developed in my principal contributions. Section 4 relates that work to the contributions of other writers on economic methodology, particularly Uskali Mäki and Alexander Rosenberg.[2] Section 5 discusses new directions in which my work on methodology is moving in response to developments in both economic methodology and philosophy of science.

1. THAT SEVENTIES SHOW

I was a graduate student at Columbia from 1973–1978. I had planned on studying social and political philosophy, but I was particularly influenced by courses taught by Isaac Levi, Sidney Morgenbesser, and Howard Stein, which provided me with a solid background in philosophy of science. These courses were largely devoted to the questions asked by the logical empiricists concerning laws and explanation, confirmation, and the meaning of theoretical terms, along with the logical empiricist's careful but often unsuccessful answers. Pragmatist concerns with the goals of science and the relations between science and practical endeavors were prominent, too, and all my teachers were well informed about the details of particular scientific disciplines. They were all engaged with the burgeoning efforts to link philosophy of science to more detailed historical and sociological studies of scientific practice, which followed in the wake of Kuhn's and Lakatos' work.

Although I had not studied much economics, I had political reasons to be intensely interested in questions of political economy; and for that reason, I sat in on a series of lectures on the so-called Cambridge Controversy in the theory of capital and interest, which John Eatwell gave during the Fall of 1976. Since the history he recounted matched neither the idealized views of scientific rationality and change sketched by the logical empiricists nor the supposedly more sociologically detailed accounts offered by Kuhn or Lakatos, I decided to write a dissertation in philosophy of science focusing on the Cambridge Controversy, general equilibrium theory and Sraffa's *Production of Commodities by Means of Commodities* (1960), which ultimately became my first book, *Capital, Profits and Prices*.

The kind of project I was undertaking was typical of a good deal of work in philosophy of science at that time: study some compact area of science and use what one observes to test and improve some relevant thesis in the philosophy of science. Of course, things are more complicated than this, since naive empiricism is no better as a method in philosophy of science than as a method in science; but the vision of philosophy of science as itself a sort of social science directed toward questions of normative epistemology was a common and, I think, fruitful one. And I even had a model in Rosenberg's *Microeconomic Laws: A Philosophical Analysis*, which came out just as I was starting work on my dissertation.[3] *Capital, Profits and Prices* was more influenced by developments in philosophy of science in the 1970s and more engaged with the details of economics than was *Microeconomic Laws* (which makes no references to the work of Kuhn or Lakatos), but there are nevertheless many similarities in the way that Rosenberg and I conceived our tasks and in the philosophical training and perspective that we brought to our reflections on economic methodology. Although we were philosophical innovators in our attention to economic theory and practice, we were at this time fundamentally old fashioned in our philosophical reference point.

In particular, we thought of laws as fundamental to science because of their role in explanation (which we took to conform roughly to the deductive-nomological model) as well as in prediction. We thought of scientific testing as testing of lawlike statements and confirmation (like refutation) to be concerned with lawlike statements. We had been taught that causation was a matter of lawlike regularity with temporal priority of the cause to the effect. We conceived of theories as sets of lawlike statements. So-called theoretical terms were problematic, because it was unclear how statements concerning such terms could be meaningful and hence eligible to be laws. We took the central philosophical questions concerning science to revolve around the analysis, confirmation, and application of laws.

Both Rosenberg and I accordingly zeroed in on questions about laws in economics. Such questions were not only the central questions concerning any science, but they seemed particularly pressing with respect to economics, whose central "laws" are platitudes which, if construed as universal generalizations, are obviously false. Having isolated essentially the same fundamental questions, Rosenberg and I then followed different paths in addressing them, and I'll leave Rosenberg's story for Rosenberg to tell. In my own case, I was very puzzled when I realized how homely and mangy were the fundamental generalizations of economics. Although I was tempted to declare that the emperor wore no clothes and that economics was just ideological claptrap dressed up as science, I'd come to have too much respect for both the character and intellect of the great economists, both past and contemporary, to make any such simple condemnation. (And I would certainly never have been able to get a simple-minded condemnation past either Isaac Levi or Sidney Morgenbesser, both of whom were far too knowledgeable about economics.) Of course, economists might make specific blunders. Indeed, given both the sensitivity of the subject matter and the human fallibility of the investigators, there are bound to be many failures within economics. But it didn't seem likely that the whole discipline was without cognitive merit.

So if the apparent difficulties with economic laws did not justify condemning the whole discipline, I needed either to show how economics could be a significant cognitive endeavor even though it possesses few if any laws or to show how the generalizations of economics could count as laws despite their apparent defects. It seemed to me (mistakenly, in retrospect) that these two alternatives might not be very different. Consider, for example, a false quantitative generalization whose implications always lie within some relatively narrow margin of error around the true value. How much difference is there between, on the one hand, defending the cognitive merits of such a generalization while denying (on the grounds of its falsity) that it is a law and, on the other hand, weakening the criteria so as to count such generalizations as laws? Rather than challenging received views in philosophy of science and denying the centrality of laws to science, I explored the possibility that the basic generalizations of economics might be regarded as in some sense approximate laws.

This choice led immediately to a research agenda: To say that economics relies on approximate laws raises a raft of questions. What could it *mean* to say that some statement is an approximate law? To say that a claim is approximate seems to imply that it is false, and how can a false statement explain anything? Is there some sense of approximation in which approximate claims might be regarded as true? How can approximate claims be tested? How can they be refuted or confirmed? Can one hold a realist view of a theory whose fundamental "laws" are merely approximate? How important is exactness? To what extent should approximation be tolerated?

These are general philosophical questions, and satisfactory answers either have to conform to accepted philosophical analyses of concepts such as confirmation, explanation, realism, meaning and so forth, or they call for revisions in the philosophical understanding of such concepts. So my research agenda for philosophy of economics inevitably posed fundamental philosophical questions. My philosophical training supplied initial answers to the fundamental questions, but it also supplied me with considerable skepticism about those answers and a general suspicion that when abstract philosophical reasoning apparently condemns what scientists do, the fault is more likely to lie with the philosophizing than with the scientific practice. This pragmatist presumption reinforced the historical and sociological mantra of the time and led me to tackle the questions about whether economics contains approximate laws by looking carefully at what economists say and do. But such looking is hardly just a matter of opening one's eyes and reading some books and articles or going along to some classes and seminars. The looking was heavily constrained by the questions I was asking and especially by the presumption that laws are central to science.

In looking both at what capital theorists did and also at what economists said when they reflected on their practice, I was fortunate to find a remarkable methodological predecessor, John Stuart Mill (1836, 1843). Although Mill's economics is not the same as contemporary economics and his philosophy of science not the same as logical empiricism, his problem resembled mine, and I was able to modify his account of inexact laws and inexact science to show how economic generalizations could be of value despite their apparent inaccuracy. Moreover, in studying his works carefully and in reading contemporary economics (not contemporary economic methodology) with Mill's views in mind, I developed a model of the global structure of economic theorizing that is fundamentally at odds with accounts drawn from Kuhn and Lakatos.

2. METAMETHODOLOGY: WHAT HAVE WE METHODOLOGISTS BEEN UP TO?

I see economic methodology as a normative enterprise. It attempts to answer questions such as what the goals of theorizing *ought* to be, how economists *ought* to explain, or what economists *ought* to regard as evidence and how evidence *ought* to influence their assessments of hypotheses, models, and theories. Although these are normative questions, they are not moral questions. The "ought's" here are matters of rationality, and they are conditional. For example, in asking whether economists ought to take introspection as a source of evidence, the methodologist is asking whether economists are more likely to achieve the cognitive, epistemic, and practical goals aims of economics if they take introspection as evidence.

The answer to a normative question such as, "Should economists make use of introspection?" thus depends on the answer to two other questions: "What are the consequences of economists making use of introspection (as compared to the alternatives)?" and "What are the objectives of economics?" Logic and conceptual analysis can help answer the first question. No empirical investigation is needed to know that accepting contradictions is not a good way to avoid error or that, in the long run, if one repeatedly applies Bayesian updating, the influence of prior probabilities washes out. The consequences of practices are also open to historical, sociological, psychological, and computational investigation. The answer to the second question, concerning the objectives of economics is partly up to economists, though they are heavily constrained both by the social demands made of economics and by what economists and others think is feasible. Questions about what economics can achieve are again partly philosophical, since conceptual and logical impossibilities are also empirical impossibilities, but they, too, are in large part empirical. So there is a role for both empirical investigation and logic and conceptual analysis in economic methodology.

The empirical approach to the philosophy of science, which has informed my work, places particular emphasis on empirical investigations of the consequences of alternative methodological practices and of what kinds of results economists are capable of achieving. Economic methodology is thus in large part itself a peculiar kind of social science whose empirical investigations are designed to help answer normative methodological questions. Understanding methodology this way may seem paradoxical. If the task is to apply scientific methodology to learn what scientific methodology is, it would appear that one needs to know the results of the investigation before one can undertake the investigation. So the investigation is either pointless or impossible. If the goal is to use history of science to learn what science is, it would appear that one needs to know what science is in order to know what to study. To study laws, theories, models, explanations, or data in economics, one has to know what count as laws, theories, models, explanations, or data.

These complications show that one cannot begin with a blank slate. To study economic methodology empirically, one needs to take for granted distinctions between science and nonscience, between economics and other inquiries, between justified and unjustified uses of evidence, between acceptable and unacceptable inference patterns, between laws and nonlaws, between reasonable and unreasonable constraints on theory and model construction, and so forth. One has to start out assuming that one already knows a good deal about the world and about how to acquire knowledge. Without that knowledge, the methodologist could not inquire into the nature of knowledge and the means of its acquisition— but then the methodologist would lack not only the means to carry out such an investigation but also an object to investigate. The real danger to which the circularity points arises when inquiry into economic methodology or philosophy of science in general is structured so that its presuppositions cannot be questioned. If studying economic methodology cannot lead one to revise the methodological presuppositions with which one began, then there is not much point to the investigation.

In practice, this problem has not been pressing in economic methodology, because the methodology that is manifested in the practice of economics is not in accord with the methodology that has guided the empirical-philosophical study of that practice. If the philosophy of science that the methodologist unavoidably brings to the study of methodology were solidly supported, then the methodologist could react to the discrepancy between economic practice and philosophical precept by criticizing economic practice. Some of the work of Mark Blaug (1980) and Terence Hutchison (1977) is like this. Convinced of the correctness of Karl Popper's falsificationist philosophy of science, they criticize economists for failing to behave as Popper specifies. Although Rosenberg is not a follower of Popper, he, too, has maintained that economics fails as an empirical science, because it fails to meet the standards laid down by philosophy of science (1992).

As I have already mentioned, my training and experience have made me more ambivalent about conflicts between economic practice and the findings of philosophy of science. Though those who study economic methodology cannot start from scratch, they also cannot take their philosophical presuppositions as authoritative dicta. When practice fails to match principles argued for by philosophers of science, the methodologist's task is to find the best explanation for the discrepancy. Sometimes practice will be faulty. Like everybody else, economists make mistakes; and with such enormous material interests at stake, ideological factors are bound to intrude. But what passes for philosophical wisdom may be mistaken, too, especially since philosophy of science has been so heavily influenced by the study of physics, which is just one of many sciences and in many ways atypical.

I expect that philosophy of economics will show that the state and development of economics manifest imperfect rationality. The standard of rationality comes, as it must, from philosophy of science. Methodologists should seek the most compelling explanation for what they observe, whether those explanations wind up vindicating or condemning economics. But methodologists should not be quick to condemn, and they should be suspicious of accounts that attribute to economists egregious and persistent errors.

3. ECONOMICS AS AN INEXACT
AND SEPARATE SCIENCE

This section presents, in bare-bones outline, my view of the methodological fundamentals of microeconomic and general equilibrium theorizing. This view is already present in *Capital Profits and Prices,* but it expressed better a decade later in *The Inexact and Separate Science of Economics.* As explained below in section 5, my views have since evolved in a different direction.

I characterize the fundamental theory of microeconomics and general equilibrium theory as a set of inexact laws such as "People prefer more commodities to fewer" or "Firms attempt to maximize profits." What makes these laws inexact is that they contain *ceteris paribus* clauses. Those clauses, in context, denote predicates which, if explicitly incorporated into the antecedents of the laws, would result in exact rather than inexact laws. Inexact laws are, in effect, exact laws inexactly specified. Inexact lawlike statements are true or false, and they express laws only if they are true. Economists are justified in believing that a statement such as "*Ceteris paribus,* people prefer more commodities to fewer" is an inexact law only if it satisfies a list of justification conditions. I characterize four of these conditions: lawlikeness, reliability, refinability, and excusability.

Economic theories and models do not consist only of laws (and indeed chapter 5 of *The Inexact and Separate Science of Economics* equates models with predicates or definitions of predicates rather than sets of assertions). Models and theories also characterize details of the circumstances to which they are applied, and those characterizations are often highly simplified or exaggerated. So problems about the apparent falsity of statements within economics extend beyond questions about the fundamental explanatory principles. My tactics for dealing with simplifications are analogous to those employed for dealing with inexact generalizations. I ask when theories can provide knowledge despite containing simplifications and turn to issues about approximation and robustness.

Among the basic principles of economics is the implicit claim that people are rational, at least to the extent that their preferences are transitive and their choices reflect their preferences. This is a remarkable fact, which raises questions about the relations between economics on the one hand and action theory and the theory of rationality on the other. This fact bears on questions of theory appraisal and revision, and especially on the character of explanations in economics, which cite the reasons for choices as well as arguably the causes. Because of both its concern with rationality and the importance of its subject matter to human interests, economics is inevitably intertwined with ethical questions concerning welfare, freedom, equality, and justice.[4]

Although my work in the philosophy of economics has been mostly a rerun of that seventies show—a mixture of logical empiricism, pragmatism, and the first days of the historical and sociological turn in the philosophy of science—issues within economics have carried it beyond the limits of the philosophy of science with which it began. In particular, both the detailed peculiarities of the economic theories I studied most carefully and the details of methodological reflections by economists from Mill to Herbert Simon (especially Simon 1953 and Simon & Rescher 1966) led me to take a very different view of causation than the logical empiricists had. Only by taking causal claims seriously as involving a good deal more than mere regularity could I come to terms with Sraffa's *Production of Commodities by Means of Commodities* (1960) or with the difficulties of incorporating accounts of capital and interest into the framework of general equilibrium theory, as revealed, for example, in Christopher Bliss' *Capital Theory and the Distribution of Income* (1975). Some of the most important questions concerning theories of capital and interest turned on questions of causal priority, which could not in turn be cashed out in terms of time order.

Coupled with difficulties in the account of inexact laws, this work on causation and its role within economics gradually undermined the logical empiricist premises of my philosophy of economics and set the stage for a fundamental revision, emphasizing causes rather than laws, which is sketched below in Section 5.

4. Mäki, Rosenberg, and Others

The differences between the contributions Mäki, Rosenberg, and I have made more often reflect differences between our characters or the questions we have asked, than disagreements about the answers to common questions. Mäki's and Rosenberg's work accordingly often complements mine, and for that reason, only some of the distinctions between our approaches imply criticisms of one another.

Unlike Rosenberg and me, Mäki's interest in economic methodology grew out of a serious interest in economics. These origins, coupled with Mäki's intellectual character—his patience, his taxonomic approach, and his insistence on deferring judgments until they can be made fairly and comprehensively—have led Mäki to defend economics from many of its methodological critics. Instead of criticizing economists for failing to live up to some set of methodological rules, he has sought to characterize the methodological commitments that are implicit in the practice of economics. Although, as explained earlier, I have been hesitant to criticize economists, Mäki has been even more hesitant.

Describing Mäki's approach this way makes it sound as if he would walk hand-in-hand with Deirdre McCloskey, who apparently denies that any intellectual standards apply, which are not already manifested in the work of economists (1985, 1994). But unlike McCloskey, Mäki does not reject methodology or the epistemological and particularly ontological inquiries that ground methodology, and he certainly does not believe that what economists do cannot be criticized on philosophical grounds.

As Mäki explains, the broader intellectual concerns that have grounded his work on economic methodology are ontological and socioeconomic rather than epistemological. Although he has not ignored questions concerning confirmation and disconfirmation, his focus has been on questions of realism, unification, and the social shaping of economic theorizing. My own concerns are quite different. Epistemological and semantic questions are for me fundamental, and when I have broached ontological questions (especially concerning causation or laws) or broadly sociological questions concerning the disciplinary structure of economic theorizing, it has been in the service of determining whether we have good reason to investigate, employ and believe the claims that economists make. So, for example, when addressing questions concerning unification, my concerns have been tied to questions about whether more unified theories are better supported by the evidence. The ontological questions about unification that interest Mäki are good ones, but they are not my questions, except insofar as they help us to grasp the cognitive status of economics.

Unlike Mäki I've had little professional interest in work on the sociology of economics or science in general, except to criticize unfounded and often absurd leaps from sociology to sweeping claims about epistemology or ontology, such as the claim that causal interactions between scientists and the phenomena they investigate have no influence on the conclusions scientists draw (Hands 2004). Mäki is no more sympathetic toward absurd claims such as this one than I am—though he is, characteristically, more patient with them (2002). Apart from specific details, our differences with respect to the sociology of economics are mainly differences in our interests and intellectual personalities.

With respect to realism, Mäki and I have disagreed sharply in print (Hausman 1998b, 2000; Mäki 2000), and because the issues bear on central features of our approaches to economic methodology, I want to return to them briefly. On my reading of the literature in philosophy of science, scientific realists and antirealists disagree about the meaning, truth, and evidence for claims about unobservables postulated by scientific theories, while the controversy between realism and instrumentalism concerns the goals of science (Morgenbesser 1969). Because most economic theories do not postulate unobservables, beyond those to which daily life already commits us, whether scientific realists or antirealists are right is largely irrelevant to most methodological questions concerning economics. Questions about unobservables have nothing to do with what one should say about what economists call "unrealistic assumptions." Disagreements among economists about the goals of science are of some importance, but the controversy between realism and instrumentalism is largely orthogonal to the issues that divide realists and antirealists.

Even though Mäki agrees that economic theories typically do not postulate new unobservables—that (in his terminology) economic theories deal in "commonsensibles"—he reports that questions about scientific realism have always been at the core of his work on economic methodology. Starting with a familiarity with exactly the same philosophical literature and agreeing about the limited role of unobservables (apart from "commonsensibles"), we nevertheless reach what appear to be diametrically opposed conclusions about the relevance of scientific realism to economic methodology. How can this be?

There are two answers. First Mäki and I are disagreeing about what questions to ask and about how to describe inquiries governed by the questions at issue. In a series of papers, Mäki has asked the question, "What realist theses are consistent with the claims made by prominent economists?" (for example, Mäki 1990, 1992, 1998, 2004), and he has taken this question to define a realist research program in economic methodology. I don't think that this is an interesting philosophical question to ask (though it may be an interesting historical question), because everybody who supposes that his or her words have meaning and that there is any way of getting things right or wrong counts as a realist of one sort or other. It is misleading to speak of a realist research program here, because one would get exactly the same results, though negatively characterized, by asking "What antirealist theses are consistent with the claims made by economist X?"

The second factor that explains our disagreement grounds the first. Mäki writes that his "obsession to render as much of economics as possible [as] being in line with general realist canons is motivated by the idea that this will create—or help unearth—common ground for focused debate and help resist some of the unjustified and misdirected criticisms." Consider one of Mäki's cases. Milton Friedman (1953) argues that economic theories should be assessed by their predictions concerning market phenomena and that the realism of their assumptions is irrelevant to their assessment. Like many others, I interpret Friedman's position as instrumentalist, on the grounds that Friedman takes the goals of economics to be exclusively predictive. (Unlike early commentators such as Ernest Nagel [1962], I do, however, point out that Friedman's views differ from the sort of instrumentalism defended earlier in the twentieth century by pragmatists and positivists.) In my view, Friedman's thesis is neither antirealist nor realist. Since there are essentially no unobservables, the issues that divide realists and antirealists concerning unobservables do not arise. Mäki argues that one can instead read Friedman as a realist, since Friedman does not deny that unrealistic assumptions are true or false and because he talks about capturing "essential" features of the economy (Mäki 1992). How is this identification of Friedman's kind of realism supposed to "create—or help unearth—common ground for focused debate" or help to defuse unjustified or misdirected criticism?

Mäki maintains that " 'Realism' is a label which helps us carry out focused and philosophically informed discussions on *the* major issue in economic methodology: how do economic theories and models relate to economic reality?" (Mäki 2000, 110 [Mäki's italics]). I, too, am eager to assist in carrying out "philosophically informed discussions" on "how do economic theories and models relate to economic reality." Though much of the task is empirical, there's a great deal of philosophical work to do. Before economic theories and models can be confronted with evidence, one needs to address semantic questions about what they mean, ontological questions about their referents, pragmatic questions about their aims and strategies, and a variety of epistemological questions about the ways in which theories and models can be appraised. In my view, discussions about realism are only a small part of the philosophical task with respect to economics, in which unobservables other than commonsensibles are rare and unimportant. Mäki, in contrast sees issues about realism as crucial.

The main reason why we disagree is, I think, that Mäki reads a philosophical question such as, "How could a model of markets like Robert Aumann's (1966), which involves a continuum of traders, tell us anything about real economies?" as a question about whether markets with a continuum of traders are real, and he takes that question as a question about realism. Mäki writes that "an early insight took [him] away from a naive condemnation of unrealistic assumptions.... Falsehood in assumptions will not be sufficient for an antirealist instrumentalism about economic theory" (this volume). This quotation suggests that he identifies the question of whether claims with false assumptions may be empirically valuable with the question of whether such claims can be given a realist reading, while I would separate the two questions.

Rather than a disagreement about what philosophical tasks need to be undertaken in order to make possible an appraisal of economic theories and models or a disagreement about how to carry out these tasks or how to prioritize them, Mäki and I mainly disagree about whether to label these tasks as inquiries concerning realism. This disagreement is not insignificant, but the bottom line is that the differences in the way Mäki and I classify the task of interpreting economic theories and models and ask how they can bear on economic reality does not prevent our drawing very much the same conclusions—though in different terminology.

Like Mäki, Rosenberg has been concerned with questions about ontology, but his questions concern what *kinds* of entities and processes economics is concerned with, not whether these entities and processes are *real*. Although Rosenberg has been deeply involved with questions of appraisal and especially with the predictive weakness of economics, his diagnoses of the apparent empirical inadequacies of economics rests on ambitious ontological and metaphysical theses rather than on distinctive accounts of testing or theory appraisal.

In developing his diagnoses of the apparent inadequacies of economics, Rosenberg has also been willing (unlike Mäki and me) to offer sweeping global characterizations and assessments of economics. Although Rosenberg has often insisted that his diagnoses were not meant to be condemnations, it is hard to read his views of a decade ago any other way. In *Economics: Mathematical Politics or Science of Diminishing Returns?* (1992) Rosenberg maintains that economics is not an empirical science and could not possibly become one without jettisoning its fundamental principles.

One sees here, among other differences, a dramatic contrast in philosophical temperament. Although Mäki and I ask questions that are as bold and general as the ones that Rosenberg asks, and we would like to offer such striking and far-reaching answers, we are much more cautious. Neither of us would ever assert, as Rosenberg (1992) has, that economics is either applied mathematics or normative political philosophy. It might seem that we would obviously be right not to make such a claim, since, as Rosenberg would now agree, it is not true. But philosophy of economics would lose a great deal if no one were willing to stick his or her neck out and enunciate such provocative theses.

Rosenberg's current views are friendlier to the empirical claims of economics, though no less sweeping. In his view, the principal methodological peculiarities of economics can all be explained once we recognize that the subject matter of economics concerns the interactions among members of a single self-conscious and intelligent species in one spatiotemporal location. Given such a subject matter, it follows that economics (like biology) is a historical science. Its generalizations are not genuine laws, and they can be expected to break down. Natural selection (by which Rosenberg includes more than the effects on gene frequencies of differential reproductive success) governs economic institutions, processes, and outcomes; and the human capacities that enable this wider range of selection mechanisms ensure that equilibria and the regularities that characterize them will be short-lived.

Although I would quibble with many details, this picture is much more powerful and plausible than its predecessor. Moreover, it has useful implications for controversial questions concerning economic methodology. Consider, for example, the sacred dogma of many contemporary macroeconomists, that all macroeconomic generalizations must derive from the choices of a rational representative agent. One doesn't need Rosenberg's vision of economics to question the rationale behind this dogma (Kirman 1992; Hoover 1995 and this volume), but if one accepts Rosenberg's views of the basic principles of economics as generalizations about individual characteristics that currently have a selective advantage, then there is little reason to insist on microfoundations for macroeconomic generalizations, let alone the pseudo microfoundations provided by representative agent models. Qualms about whether macroeconomic generalizations are more than accidental correlations and whether they can ground policy conclusions are better addressed by looking at selection mechanisms rather than at hypothetical rational choices.

To say a bit more about the implications of Rosenberg's current views, some specificity will help. Consider the fundamental principles of consumer choice theory:

(1) Consumers' choices are rational (that is, their preferences are complete and transitive and their choices track their preferences).

(2) The preferences of consumers depend exclusively on their own consumption bundles, with larger bundles preferred to smaller.

(3) Consumer preferences show diminishing marginal rates of substitution—roughly that consumers are willing to pay less for additional units of commodities when they have more of them than when they have few of them.

It is obvious that these generalizations are rough and not always true. Yet a great deal of human behavior is consistent with them and can be perspicuously described by them. They are exactly the sort of generalizations one would expect to find if Rosenberg's view of economics as a historical science is correct.

Moreover, Rosenberg's view predicts that this state of affairs is irremediable. Though it might be possible to find other generalizations that were superior in one or more regards, it is impossible to find genuine laws. So, Rosenberg's view apparently implies that my efforts to characterize the fundamental generalizations of economics as inexact laws were fundamentally misconceived. Because of their reference to spatiotemporal particulars, the generalizations of economics cannot be laws at all.

As striking as this conclusion may be from the perspective of logical empiricism, it does not, tell us very much. Claims in biology concerning, for example, the ways in which DNA sequences code for various proteins are not laws either, but they differ in at least the following six ways from generalizations such as "People prefer more commodities to fewer":

1. They are more precise.
2. Within certain well-specified domains they are almost exceptionless.
3. They constitute new knowledge, not platitudes.
4. Their scope is broad.
5. They are unchanging for long periods of time.
6. They are less sensitive to context and environment.

If economists were to uncover generalizations like those discovered daily in contemporary molecular genetics, they would think that they had died and gone to heaven. The differences between generalizations in economics and certain areas of biology are at least as important as any similarities they may have in virtue of both biology and economics being historical sciences.

Rosenberg's view has some resources for addressing these differences, since natural selection operates differently in economics than in molecular biology. But the interpretative tasks and epistemological questions with which my work has grappled remain. It is an exaggeration to maintain, as Rosenberg does, that "Almost everything mysterious and problematical to the empiricist philosopher of science about economics is resolved once we understand economics as a biological science" (this volume).

5. NEW DIRECTIONS

In reflecting on the work that Rosenberg, Mäki, and I have done over the past generation, one should be struck by the complexities of the philosophical questions implicit in the problems of economic methodology. Economics is an enormous, diverse, and intellectually compelling discipline, whose empirical credentials are suspect. Despite its diversity, it is dominated by specific commitments concerning explanatory principles, mathematical techniques, and the interpretation of data. It bears strongly on people's interests, and its intellectual integrity is thereby constantly threatened. Its models are abstract and unrealistic, full of claims that if taken literally are false. Its central explanatory principles are generalizations concerning individual belief, evaluation and choice.

To characterize and assess this enterprise with the tools of logical empiricist philosophy of science or of the scientific realists Mäki mentions is like characterizing and assessing impressionism without the use of color terms. As Rosenberg points out—though he does not put things this way—many of the central concepts of logical empiricism fail to mark the significant distinctions one wants to draw. Since there are no laws and could not be any laws, the distinction between laws and nonlaws does not help one to draw distinctions among economic theories. Methodologists need a metaphysics, a pragmatics, a semantics, and an epistemology that permit them to draw enlightening and justifiable distinctions among intellectual enterprises that flunk the logical empiricist tests.

Largely as a result of studying James Woodward's work (2000, 2003), I've gradually become convinced that the philosophy of economics needs to be built around the concept of causation rather than the concept of law. It is more enlightening to interpret the generalizations economists make as causal claims than as inexact laws. Regardless of whether generalizations concerning demand deserve to be called laws, recent increases in the nominal price of gasoline have caused people to drive less, and they have hurt sales of SUVs. Economists have true and important things to say about the causal consequences of shocks, market structures, tax policies, and so forth. The most natural way to characterize and assess this work relies on theories of causation and causal explanation.

To say merely that economists explain why SUV sales have slumped by citing a cause of the slumping sales is, however, closer to a restatement of the problem than to a solution. What does it mean to say that economists have identified causes? How can one judge whether this claim is true? Does explanation require only that one cite a cause? According to the most widely accepted theories of causation (including Hume's account), x's cause y's only if there is some law relating x's to y's or relating x's to the probability of y's. If one accepts one of these theories of causation (as, I think, Rosenberg does—see Beauchamp and Rosenberg 1981), then it seems that one is right back to the problems concerning laws. The proposal to cast away the apparatus of laws makes sense only if at the same time one casts away accounts of causation in terms of laws.

There are accounts of causation that do not rely in this way on the notion of a law. I personally defend one such account in my *Causal Asymmetries* (1998a). These accounts are, however, speculative and controversial, and it is undesirable to base a defense of economics on such shaky reeds. This is one of the reasons why previously I've tried to stay on a more conventional path. Given the unsatisfactory destination to which that path leads, perhaps it is time to throw caution to the winds and see where another path leads.

Explanations answer *why* questions, and, as philosophers such as Achinstein (1983), Miller (1987), and Van Fraassen (1980) argue, one can learn a good deal about explanation by thinking about the questions that explanations answer. Here are some of the things one learns:

1. When people ask, "Why did the explanandum phenomenon f happen?" they want to know what caused f. One can explain events by citing their causes, but not by citing their effects. For example, the height of a flagpole explains the length of its shadow and not *vice versa,* because the shadow's length causally depends on the flagpole's height.

2. Citing some cause of f will not explain f if the cause that is cited is already well know or if the cause does not discriminate between f and the contrasting outcomes that are implicit in the question. Although causally relevant to falling SUV sales, the principles of thermodynamics do not explain why people are buying fewer SUVs this year.

3. An explanation should provide some account of *how* the cause gives rise to the explanandum, unless the way in which the cause operates is already well known. Although not formalized, economists have a convincing story to tell about how price changes influence individual choices, and how individual choices influence market outcomes.

4. Explanations are better if they are *deeper.* There are at least two dimensions of depth. First, if an explanation can account for many contrasts or contrasts within a larger range, then it is deeper. Second, if the mechanism linking cause and effect is robust—if it would not break down readily and would still function as background conditions vary—then the explanatory account one has given is more satisfactory. It may be true that deficit spending in the 1960s caused an increase in real economic growth, but if that causal relationship broke down in the different economic circumstances of the 1970s, then the explanation of economic growth in the 1960s is superficial.

Why are *why* questions requests for information about how deep and discriminating causes lead to the phenomena to be explained? What drives the human practice of asking explanatory questions? Rosenberg's perspective helps with the answer: People are not passive knowers. They *act.* They seek, among other things, to survive and reproduce, and accordingly they seek knowledge to help them control their environment. People would like to know how to bring about consequences they desire or prevent outcomes they wish to avoid, and only causal knowledge gives them that power. Human interest in the answer to why questions extends, of course, far beyond the realm in which interventions are possible, but this is, I suggest, a generalization of this practical interest.

Knowing that x causes y, unlike knowing merely that x and y are correlated, provides one with a recipe for manipulating y via x. For example, the connection between the rate of unemployment and the rate of inflation captured in the Phillip's curve could not be used to control the rate of unemployment, because one did not know what the specifically causal relations were. Because people's concern is to control events of particular *kinds*, they want not just information about causes but information that bears on the events being of *this* kind as opposed to *that*. Knowledge of where to intervene (if possible) and what the results of intervention would be is severely limited if one did not understand *how* the cause gives rise to the effect. Thus one wants more than merely knowledge of what some of the causes are. Because intervention with respect to a superficial cause could be efficacious in furthering one's ends only in a very limited domain, explanations that cite deep causes are more satisfactory than explanations that cite superficial ones.

By developing theories of causation and causal explanation, one seeks to distinguish what has explanatory value from what does not, while conceding that no laws are to be had. What matters to the explanation of slumping SUV sales is not whether demand for complements always decreases when prices rise but whether *on this occasion* the higher gas prices caused demand for SUVs to decline. The concern with laws is a residue left over from an untenable Humean theory of causation. The issue is whether economists are right about the causes, not whether their principles are laws.

Can the question about causes be divorced from questions about laws? One can read Hume as attempting to replace the notion of a necessary connection with the notion of what he calls "constant conjunction"—to explicate necessity as universality. But he failed, and so have his successors. Claims can be universal without expressing laws. Even if, as seems likely, the universe does not contain a solid sphere of gold weighing 10,000 kg, the generalization that there is no such gold sphere is not a law. Even though not sufficient for lawfulness, universality is still widely felt to be *necessary*. One might offer the following intuitive argument in support of this necessary condition for something to be a law: If the connection between F and G and other antecedents is lawful, then the relationship should either be universal, or claims about the conditional probability distribution should be universally true. Irregularity shows that the relation is not lawful.

This intuitive argument is fallacious. Consider the following point, which derives from Jerry Fodor (1991). Suppose that F and G are macroscopic properties whose instantiations are realized by the instantiations of micro properties, upon which the macro properties supervene. Suppose that, in virtue of instantiating the micro properties, there are laws relating each realization of F to a realization of G, and some of these laws are not deterministic. If the marginal probability distribution of instantiations of the micro properties that realize F is in the relevant sense accidental, then the nonaccidental connection between F and G (in virtue of the lawful connections between their realizations) is consistent with there being no deterministic or probabilistic law relating F and G. Alternatively, suppose that some of the microproperties upon which F and G supervene stand in lawful relations and some do not. In this way, too, there could be causal relations between instantiations of F and instantiations of G even though there is no law—either deterministic or probabilistic—relating F and G. It is plausible that both these sorts of irregularity obtain in economics.

Although Fodor's account undermines the claim that causal relations between instantiations of F and G imply laws *relating F, G, and other predicates,* it does not question the more general intuition that causal connections presuppose some sort of law. So Fodor cuts some slack for nonuniversal macro causal generalizations without apparently challenging the view that token causal claims imply laws.

Having in this way satisfied metaphysical scruples about the impossibility of causation without laws, one can study causal explanations of economic phenomena without worrying about whether there are economic laws. For practical purposes, one can specify subdomains in which counterexamples to the relevant causal generalizations are rare, and in those subdomains the generalizations serve the purposes of explanation and prediction as well as universal laws would. One could instead incorporate domain restrictions into the antecedent of economic generalizations, and in that way attempt to make them universal, but doing so merely pays lip service to the demand for universality. Nobody regards claims about the domains in which people tend to be more or less selfish as part of any economic laws, and it is better that they don't. Woodward rightly insists that the messy business of specifying when one can and cannot rely on the generalizations of special sciences ought to be kept out of the generalizations themselves (2000, 228–235).

It is too much to demand even restricted universality. The explanatory credentials of a causal generalization, such as the so-called law of demand, do not require that one be able to specify a domain in which this generalization holds without exception. It is enough if one can specify a domain in which exceptions are rare and usually explicable in terms of known varieties of "disturbing causes." Given Fodor's point about supervenience, there is no reason to expect that there will be significant domains in which generalizations stated in the macro vocabulary will hold universally.

Causal explanation does still require rough restricted universality or its probabilistic analogue. Without rough restricted universality or its probabilistic analogue, a purported explanation cannot be known to have identified causes, and it thus does not respond to the ultimately practical interests that underlie *why* questions. If no generalization linked any known property of an event x to a property of an event y, there would be no way to test the claim that x causes y. Furthermore, to know what would happen if one were to intervene to change the value of x, an explanation needs to invoke some generalization relating the value of x to the value or probable values of variables that depend on x. The generalizations can be probabilistic, restricted, and rough, but without at least this much uniformity, one fails to explain.

So an explicitly causal account of explanation leads one back to a nomological necessary condition on explanations. But it does not lead one back to the one I gave in my account of inexact laws, and it does not justify worrying about whether the generalizations that economists rely on count as laws. Inexact generalizations have explanatory power if they provide the information that people seek when they ask *why* questions. They do that if they identify deep discriminating causes and the mechanisms by which those causes give rise to the phenomena to be explained. The inexact generalizations that describe the operation of those causes can succeed in conveying this information only if they possess at least a restricted rough universality. Within a domain including not only the actual circumstances but also the circumstances envisioned in possible interventions and in the contrast class, their consequents or the probabilities of their consequents must hold nearly invariably. (And the wider the domain of possible interventions for which the generalizations continue to hold, the deeper and more satisfactory the explanation.) Although the causal model of explanation leads in this way to a complex nomological necessary condition on scientific explanations, there is no argument here for resuscitating the deductive-nomological model of explanation or the insistence that science requires laws. The nomological necessary condition is only a fragmentary implication of the causal model. The vague nomological necessary condition lacks the content of the causal model and cannot supplant it.

To fill in and defend this sketch requires a great deal more work. Like Mäki and Rosenberg and so many others studying economic methodology, I've got lots more to do. Economic methodology is a large field, with room in it for our three research programs and so much more!

NOTES

1. *The Inexact and Separate Science of Economics* (1992) is the most comprehensive statement of my views on economic methodology. These views are also summarized in the entries I wrote for the Routledge *Encyclopedia of Philosophy* (Craig 1998) and the *Stanford Internet Encyclopedia of Philosophy* (http://plato.stanford.edu/).

2. I focus on them, because the editors of this *Handbook* have asked them to summarize their views in this volume. Several of the other contributors to this *Handbook* could just as well have been invited to present overviews, and authors who are not represented in this volume who have made lasting contributions to the resurgence of economic methodology include Roger Backhouse, Mark Blaug, Bruce Caldwell, Terence Hutchison, Tony Lawson, and Deirdre McCloskey.

3. Indeed, my first publication was a review of Rosenberg's book, and it was through correspondence related to that review that Rosenberg and I got acquainted. As it happens, my first contact with Mäki came via his review of *Capital, Profits and Prices*. The review was in Finnish, and I couldn't read it, but in correspondence and conversation, we found a great deal of common ground. Mäki also came to economics with training in 1970s philosophy of science. Obviously there were important differences between Helsinki, Johns Hopkins, and Columbia, and Rosenberg's Ph.D. was several years earlier than Mäki's and mine. But there are many similarities among our philosophical backgrounds.

4. In clarifying how the relations between economics and ethics influence the methodology of economics, I wound up writing a great deal about the relations between economics and ethics, mainly in collaboration with Michael McPherson, who co-founded with me the journal *Economics and Philosophy*. Our main work is *Economic Analysis and Moral Philosophy* (1996), an expanded version of which appeared under the title, *Economic Analysis, Moral Philosophy and Public Policy* (2006).

REFERENCES

Achinstein, P. (1983). *The Nature of Explanation*. Oxford: Oxford University Press.

Aumann, R. (1966). "Existence of Competitive Equilibria in Markets with a Continuum of Traders." *Econometrica* 34: 1–17.

Beauchamp, T. & Rosenberg, A. 1981. *Hume and the Problem of Causation*. Oxford: Oxford University Press.

Blaug, M. (1980). *The Methodology of Economics: Or How Economists Explain*. Cambridge, England: Cambridge University Press.

Bliss, C. (1975). *Capital Theory and the Distribution of Income*. Amsterdam: North Holland.

Craig, E., Ed. (1998). *Routledge Encyclopedia of Philosophy*. London: Routledge.

Fodor, J. (1991). "You Can Fool Some of the People All of the Time, Everything Else Being Equal; Hedged Laws and Psychological Explanations." *Mind* 100: 19–34.

Friedman, M. (1953). "The Methodology of Positive Economics." In *Essays in Positive Economics*, 3–43. Chicago: University of Chicago Press.

Hands, W. (2004). "Constructivism: The Social Construction of Scientific Knowledge." In J. Davis, A. Marciano, & J. Runde, Eds. *The Elgar Companion to Economic and Philosophy*, 197–212. Northampton, MA: Edward Elgar.

Hausman, D. (1981). *Capital, Profits and Prices: An Essay in the Philosophy of Economics*. New York: Columbia University Press.

Hausman, D. (1992). *The Inexact and Separate Science of Economics*. Cambridge, England: Cambridge University Press.

Hausman, D. (1998a). *Causal Asymmetries*. New York: Cambridge University Press.

Hausman, D. (1998b). "Problems with Realism in Economics," *Economics and Philosophy* 14: 185–213.

Hausman, D. (2000). "Realist Philosophy and Methodology of Economics: What Is It?" *Journal of Economic Methodology* 7: 127–133.

Hausman, D & McPherson, M. (1996). *Economic Analysis and Moral Philosophy*. Cambridge University Press. 2nd. ed. retitled *Economic Analysis, Moral Philosophy, and Public Policy*. Cambridge, England: Cambridge University Press, 2006.

Hoover, K. (1995). "Is Macroeconomics for Real?" *The Monist* 78: 235–257.

Hutchison, T. (1977). *Knowledge and Ignorance in Economics*. Chicago: University of Chicago Press.

Kirman, A. (1992). "Whom or What Does the Representative Agent Represent?" *Journal of Economic Perspectives* 6: 117–136.

Mäki, U. (1990). "Mengerian Economics in Realist Perspective." *History of Political Economy, Annual Supplement*. 22: 289–310.

Mäki, U. (1992). "Friedman and Realism." *Research in the History of Economic Thought and Methodology* 10: 171–195.

Mäki, U. (1998). "Is Coase a Realist?" *Philosophy of the Social Sciences* 28: 5–31.

Mäki, U. (2000). "Reclaiming Relevant Realism." *Journal of Economic Methodology* 7: 109–125.

Mäki, U. (2002). *Fact and Fiction in Economics: Models, Realism and Social Construction*. Cambridge, England: Cambridge University Press.

Mäki, U. (2004). "Realism and the Nature of Theory: A Lesson from J.H. Von Thünen for Economists and Geographers." *Environment and Planning A* 36: 1719–1736.

McCloskey, D. (1985). *The Rhetoric of Economics*. Madison: University of Wisconsin Press.

McCloskey, D. (1994). *Knowledge and Persuasion in Economics*. Cambridge, England: Cambridge University Press.

Mill, J. S. (1836). "On the Definition of Political Economy and the Method of Investigation Proper to It." Reprinted in *Collected Works of John Stuart Mill*, vol. 4. Toronto: University of Toronto Press, 1967.

Mill, J. S. (1843). *A System of Logic*. Reprinted London: Longman, Green & Co., 1949.

Miller, R. (1987). *Fact and Method*. Princeton: Princeton University Press.

Morgenbesser, S. (1969). "The Realist-Instrumentalist Controversy." In S. Morgenbesser, P. Suppes & M. White, eds. *Philosophy, Science, and Method*, 106–122. New York: Harcourt, Brace & World.

Nagel, E. (1963). "Assumptions in Economic Theory." *American Economic Review Papers and Proceedings* 53: 211–219.

Rosenberg, A. (1976). *Microeconomic Laws: A Philosophical Analysis*. Pittsburgh: University of Pittsburgh Press.

Rosenberg, A. (1992). *Economics—Mathematical Politics or Science of Diminishing Returns?* Chicago: University of Chicago Press.

Simon, H. (1953). "Causal Ordering and Identifiability." In W. Hood & T. Koopmans, Eds. *Studies in Econometric Method*, 49–74. New York: John Wiley & Sons.

Simon, H. & Rescher, N. (1966). "Cause and Counterfactual." *Philosophy of Science* 33: 323–340.

Sraffa, P. (1960). *Production of Commodities by Means of Commodities*. Cambridge, England: Cambridge University Press.

Van Fraassen, B. (1980). *The Scientific Image*. Oxford: Oxford University Press.

Woodward, J. (2000). "Explanation and Invariance in the Special Sciences." *British Journal for the Philosophy of Science* 51: 197–254.

Woodward, J. (2003). *Making Things Happen: A Theory of Causal Explanation*. Oxford: Oxford University Press.

CHAPTER 3

IF ECONOMICS IS A SCIENCE, WHAT KIND OF A SCIENCE IS IT?

ALEX ROSENBERG

ECONOMICS strikes most people, including most well-informed people, as a science, or at least more of one than the other social sciences. Among some, perhaps, what led them to treat it as one was the wish that economic decisions could be reduced to matters a science would make easy. For reasons Kuhn (1962) catalogued in *The Structure of Scientific Revolutions,* economics it is only natural to view it that way.

To begin with, economics has a paradigm, as plainly exhibited by the uniformity of its textbooks. It is a commonplace that unlike every other social and behavioral science, the introductory texts in economics are all pretty much the same. By and large you could permute the problems at the ends of chapters among the five largest selling textbooks in the field and still test students' understanding of the chapters they had actually read.

Second, the language of the discipline is highly mathematized. It's obvious that one cannot really understand microeconomics, even as it was presented by Quirk and Saposnik (1968) forty years ago or by R.D.G. Allen (1938) sixty years ago, without differential calculus. Since then, a good deal more mathematics has become indispensable, whether it be fixed point theorems in topology for general equilibrium, or set theory for social choice, or probability for econometrics, or simultaneous estimation techniques for computational general equilibrium, and so forth.

Third, the discipline has identifiable proprietary laws, albeit inexact ones, and a set of proprietary kinds, which the discipline's "discipline" requires be applied to the solution of puzzles. And it rewards most generously those who find new puzzles to which to apply the laws and concepts. This progressive expansion of the domain of economics is often decried by some social scientists as economic imperialism. But economic imperialism is carried on by noneconomists as well as by guild members in good standing, and is on the one hand a reflection of the belief, widespread beyond economics, that it is a science or more of one than other "preparadigm disciplines" among the social and behavioral sciences, and on the other hand an expression of the confidence of economists that they are on the paradigmatic highroad, and have been since perhaps as far back as Adam Smith, but certainly since Walras and Marshall.

If we were less sophisticated, we might even add as a reason economics is viewed so widely and firmly as a science that it has its own Nobel Prize. Of course we know that it doesn't. But let us not underestimate the symbolic value of the Sveriges Riksbank Prize in Economic Sciences in Memory of Alfred Nobel both within and beyond the profession.

It was all but the last of these features that led me in the late 1960s to turn my attention to economics and its philosophy of science. There were at that time two approaches to answering the question about whether economics is or could be a science. One *appeared* to be motivated by and answered in accordance with standards drawn from Logical Positivism, postpositivism, and economists under the influence of Popper. *Appeared to be* bears emphasis. Although there were attempts by economists such as Papandreou (1958) to clothe economics in the mantle of hypothetico-deductivism and "partial interpretation," and economists such as Lipsey (1963) expressed a commitment to falsificationist methodology, in reality none of these figures honored empiricist demands on empirical content. A second answer to the question about whether economics could be an empirical science derived from a pervasive view of social science influenced by the later work of Ludwig Wittgenstein, and animated by what Donald Davidson called a tide of little red books, all emanating from Britain, of which the most notorious was Peter Winch's *The Idea of a Social Science* (2007), or as we were wont to parody it, "the very idea of a social science." It would be nice to say that these books are now *thankfully* forgotten. But in fact, they are only forgotten. Many a philosopher would gladly bring them back as interlocutors in the philosophy of social science. For, unlike much of what goes by the name of philosophy of social science these days, emanating as it does from France and the sociology of science, highlights from the tide of little red books are paragons of intelligibility and cogent argument.

The threat that these books and the general influence of Wittgenstein posed for social science was the notion that the study of human action could not be empirical; instead it had to be somehow or other *a priori*. It could not be causal, rather it had to be conceptual, or linguistic. Both human action and the study of human action were, on this view, games, but not the strategic interactions that nowadays interest us and others, but "language games" in which learning the rules was both necessary and sufficient for full understanding.

This was the state of play at the frontiers of debate in the philosophy of social science before philosophers took much of an interest in economics. Not Popper's strictures, not Logical Empiricism's demands for testability, still less historicism à la Dilthey, but the cultural anthropologist's problem of understanding and assessing the rationality of another culture, dominated the agenda of the subdiscipline. Quine had already written *Word and Object* (1961) some years before, but the message had not apparently reached Oxford.

The first book-length treatment of the cognitive status of economics, *Microeconomic Laws* (Rosenberg 1976) was in written large part to test the picture of social science advanced by the tide of little red books, and its associated Wittgensteinian philosophy of mind. By this time Logical Positivism's account of theory was already in eclipse. In turning attention to the subject, philosophers could, of course, find those few documents, from Robbins (1932), Hutchison (1938), Machlup (1955, and Keynes *père* (1917) that constituted the philosophy of economics before we philosophers got hold of it. And then there was Milton Friedman's "Methodology," which, had it not existed, would have had to be invented, because it has single-handedly justified our existence from that day it was published in 1953 to this! By and large, the work of these economists could not provide much of a basis to underwrite the possibility of an economic science. So, in order to refute the Wittgensteinians, in *Microeconomic Laws* I had to elaborate an account of the discipline and its credentials to constitute an empirical, explanatory science of the causes and effects of economic events and processes. There was, I held, no philosophical obstacle to the discovery of economic laws, some reason to think that rational choice theory constituted a first approximation to such laws, and, in its implications for firms, consumers, and markets, a scientific theory of economic phenomena.

The trouble with my argument that economics satisfied formal, semantic, and syntactic requirements on a science is that it didn't really go far enough to underwrite the conclusion that it is one. As Imre Lakatos long ago pointed out, scientific research programs have to be empirically progressive. Economists like Weintraub (1985) were eager to show that, though their discipline did not satisfy empiricist or pragmatist strictures on adequacy, it did pass muster on Lakatosian ones. It was empirically progressive. This claim was of course controversial. Influential economists like Leontief (1982) rejected it out of hand. Moreover, few of the problems philosophers ever raised about the difficulty of making Lakatos' demand precise were ever solved, and, again, Quinean strictures explain why this is so (cf. Rosenberg 1986). So arguments like Weintraub's never got much traction among philosophers. Nevertheless, I came to realize that for a discipline to be a science, it was not enough that it looked like one; it had to show long-term net improvements in predictive power. I emphasize the qualifications *net* and *long term*. The first qualification, *net*, recognizes the possibility (overemphasized by Kuhn) that there can be losses as well as gains in scientific change. The second qualification, *long term*, reflects the fact that predictive improvement cannot be expected on a schedule, or to be expected at evenly spaced intervals, or even at all for significant periods of time. Nothing so much reflects this feature more than evolutionary biology. Predictive improvement comes in at least two varieties: (1) improvements in the range of phenomena predicted, for example the extension of Newtonian mechanics from predictions of planetary motion to aerodynamics; and (2) improvements in precision of prediction, prediction to more decimal places: for example improvements in predictions of the precession of the perihelion of mercury affected by the special theory of relativity.

Soon after I had completed my defense of the conceptual possibility of economics as an empirical science, David Braybrooke impressed on me first of all that economics did very poorly on even the most generous version of a demand that scientific disciplines satisfy demands for predictive improvement. I explored some of these relatively undemanding criteria in papers like "Is generic prediction enough?" (Rosenberg 1989). In this paper and others I acknowledged that whether a theory is experiencing predictive improvement is often a controversial matter, and, by and large, it is the specialists in a scientific discipline who are the authorities about whether a discipline is showing such progress. In economics, however, the question of predictive improvement turned out to be controversial. It was easy to line up distinguished economists on one side of the question. As already noted, Vassily Leontief, for example, long insisted on economics' predictive weakness. It was not easy to find economists who argued for the predictive strength of economics, but easy to identify those who rejected the demand for it: Diedre McCloskey (1985) and Roy Weintraub (1985).

Having despaired of economic theory's prospects for predictive improvement, I began to ask two related questions: First: Why does economic theory face these limitations? Second: What does the enterprise of economics aim at, what are its criteria of adequacy, if not predictive improvement? My answers to the second question (all the way from "If economics is not a science, what is it?" (Rosenberg 1983) to *Economics—Mathematical Politics or Science of Diminishing Returns* (Rosenberg 1992) have never satisfied me or any one else for that matter. My answer to the first question, of what prevents economics from moving beyond generic prediction at most, initially focused on the limitations it shared with psychology because of their shared reliance on intentional states. Since such states are impossible to individuate accurately, we cannot establish exactly what individual economic agents' preferences and expectations are, and so we are deprived of the very sort of information about the causes of individual economic behavior (choice) that we require in order to improve the theory. I still think this is part of the story, but not as large a part as I used to think.

The period from 1970 onward has seen the development of an entire subdiscipline of philosophy of economics, with its own journals, several score of monographs, a text book or two, anthologies of influential papers, a learned society, and some very distinguished contributors, including most insightful and influential of all, Daniel Hausman (1981, 1991), Marc Blaug (1980) and C. Wade Hands (2001). But after about fifteen years of work in the subdiscipline, what became apparent to me was that the economists were not going to take much notice of the work done in the philosophy of economics. There have been and are highly visible economists who have dipped into the field, people like Amartya Sen (1982) and Hal Varian (Gibbard & Varian 1978). But by and large, economists who were not openly hostile to the philosophy of economics, like Diedre McCloskey, were more than satisfied that the last word on the subject that any economist needed to take heed of were penned by Milton Friedman in 1953. For that reason, after the mid 1980s I moved away from the philosophy of economics to work in the philosophy of biology, a subdiscipline in which the cognate scientists have shown more sympathy, interest, and willingness to be influenced by philosophers.

This bit of autobiography would be of interest only to my obituary writer, except for the fact that my absorption in biology finally led me to solve my problems about economics. It was by studying the aims and limits of biological science that I realized what the scope and limits of economics really are. Almost everything mysterious and problematical to the empiricist philosopher of science about economics is resolved once we understand economics as a biological science. Such an understanding pretty much leaves economics as it has been—indeed it vindicates the present shape of economics' proprietary theory far more responsibly than a purblind instrumentalism. What is more, it solves both of my problems: it explains what the reasonable limitations should be on any predictive demands about economics, and it explains why economics should not be expected to look like those sciences in which there are laws, exact or inexact, that we mistakenly wanted economics to look like.

First I will sketch the conclusion, then I will provide the argument: Economics, like all the social sciences, is a historical science. It constitutes a set of factual claims about historical trends of greater or lesser generality on this planet. Because of its spatiotemporally restricted character, and more important, because of the reflexive character of economic interactions, economics comports no laws, exact or inexact. Those generalizations of economics we mistake for its inexact empirical laws describe fairly common and enduring but nevertheless local trends, which are the result of the operation of exact laws (but not economic ones) on local initial conditions. Economics does also develop and employ a significant number of mathematical models, sets of necessary truths, which are to greater or lesser extents, applicable or inapplicable to actual processes. Because of the reflexive character of economic processes, along with the persistence of exogenous shocks, none of these models can be expected to have permanent applicability even to their intended domains. As such there are severe limits to economic theory's predictive powers; in particular there are limits to our ability to establish values for its parameters and coefficients that hold constant long enough to make any predictions. These are not reasons to cease seeking predictively powerful results in economics, but they are reasons to think that such results will not be easy to achieve or very enduring when achieved. And all this follows from two considerations: first economics is a biological science, and second, all the features just attributed to economics are inescapable features of all biological sciences.

I won't spend much time arguing that economics is a biological science; all the social sciences are biological sciences. They are sciences devoted to the study of the causes and effects of the behavior of members of a particular species, *Homo sapiens*. That species exists only on the Earth and not elsewhere. Anyone tempted to define economics in Lionel Robbins' terms, as the general science of the efficient employment of scarce resources, without essential reference to human (and perhaps a limited number of other species on this planet), is, in effect, committed to treating economics as the abstract and purely mathematical enterprise of pure linear (and nonlinear) programming.

More important and more interesting are the nature and scope of biological sciences. Biology is an *almost* completely historical science. That is, its subject matter is almost exclusively what has happened to biological systems on this planet over the last 3.5 billion years of its almost 5 billion year history. From molecular biology to paleobiology, and including all the compartments of the subject in between, the explanatory problems of biology involve explaining either particular events (e.g., the Cretaceous extinction, the effectiveness of antiretrovirals for HIV-A) or historical patterns of longer or shorter scale (the 1:1 male:female ratio among sexually reproducing species, the persistence of the sickle-cell trait in malarial regions). By contrast, a nonhistorical science—chemistry or physics—is one whose kind terms, laws, and theories do not make essential reference to particular places or times in the history of the universe.

Now, in biology there is only one set of exact laws. And the reason is that the one undoubted biological law or set of laws makes impossible the existence of any other laws, exact or inexact, or at least any laws about particular species. The exceptionless law is the principle or principles of natural selection, which describe the way in which adaptations come about in a purely mechanistic world bereft of causally efficacious purposes, goals, or ends; a world in which random, or better, blind variation in fitness differences occur; and a world in which there is natural selection, or better, environmental filtration, which results in persistent increases in fitness or adaptation in the solution of a lineage's, or group's, or organism's local "design problems." The mechanism of natural selection provides the only mechanism possible for the appearance of purposiveness in a world without final causes. As apparent purposiveness is evident throughout the biological realm, and especially in human affairs, the law or laws that Darwin discovered operate throughout these realms.

It is of the greatest importance to see that the mechanism of natural selection is the only game in town when it comes to the production of adaptive traits, behaviors, institutions, and so forth. Besides its phylogenetic operation in creating adapted lineages, it operates developmentally and ontogenetically at many levels.

Daniel Dennett (1995) has given handy names to the most important of these onto-genetic processes of natural selection that produce apparently purposive behavior: To begin with, natural selection creates Darwinian creatures—ones with geneti-cally adapted traits. Long afterward, Skinnerian creatures emerge, organisms whose external behaviors are subject to selection by environmental reinforcers. More recently there are what Dennett calls Popperian creatures, echoing Sir Karl's suggestion that cognition is a process in which randomly generated hypotheses are allowed to die in our stead. In the Popperian creature, the environment that does the selecting obtains inside the head. It carries a lot of information about the outer environment, and filters hypotheses in ways that in effect preselect them for outer environmental appropriateness. It's easy to see how advantageous it is to be a Popperian creature. Dennett's latest stage are Popperian creatures whose inner environment contains information about the features of the outer environment created by themselves or other Popperian creatures. (He calls them Gregorian creatures after the psychologist Richard Gregory.) This stage will include us, other tool users like Chimps and organisms with theories of mind, second order inten-tionality, and languages of thought. Dennett calls these layers produced by natural selection, within which natural selection operates, a "tower of generate and test." It is crucial to see that, other than by magic, there is no way to produce the appear-ance of purpose at any level except by generate and test, vary and filter, i.e., natural selection.

Natural selection operating on genes, within environments that don't change over long periods, produces patterns that look to biologists like laws, or at least first approximations to them: lions are green/brown color blind, the widow bird mimics the finch call, the robin's egg is blue. These patterns aren't laws—they have exceptions, and even if they didn't, there are at least two other reasons they would not be laws. First they mention spatiotemporal individuals, particular species. But this is in the nature of a symptom of their nonlaw-like status. The second rea-son reveals a fundamental obstacle to biological laws, one that even more strongly obstructs the possibility of laws in the human sciences.

Nature sets design problems that lineages of organisms must solve. And in most cases the environment remains mercifully stable for long enough that many species can find relatively long-lasting (satisficing) solutions to these problems through the mechanisms of blind variation and natural selection. These solutions are sometimes so good and the environment is so stable that they will become almost universal in the species and last for hundreds of millions of years. It's tempting to mistake the description of such long-term solutions for laws.

But one species' (or population's or even individual's) solution to a design prob-lem is almost always another species' (or population's or individual's) new design problem. Thus, in the high grass of the African veldt, the zebra's stripes solve the problem of camouflage presented by predatory but color-blind lions. However, in the long run, the zebra's solution puts pressure on lions to acquire green/brown discrimination. And if lions acquire such discrimination, a new design problem will have been set to the zebra, a problem its lineage will solve or that will lead to its extinction. This "arms race" as evolutionary biologists have called it, recalling strategic nuclear rivalries, occurs wherever species constitute one another's (competitive) environments. Once evolution has proceeded even a little way, arms races are the rule, not the exception. Indeed, the earliest arms races began at the level of competing polynucleotide sequences; many genes have been in an arms race with one another for geological epochs, including many genes in us.

The ubiquity of arms races means that the patterns that are often mistaken for permanent laws can always and will almost always come to an end. The biological possibility of arms races saps the counterfactual force of any apparent generalization about any particular species. "The robin's egg is blue" turns out to be the description of a pattern or trend—a local equilibrium—lasting perhaps a few million years, but which will succumb to the strategy of some parasitizing cuckoo with a mutant blue egg shell sometime in the future, unless robins go extinct first. Arms races among Skinnerian and Popperian creatures will proceed at paces many orders of magnitude faster than among mere Darwinian or Skinnerian creatures.

In the human sphere the moves and counter-moves characteristic of strategic interaction alternate so rapidly that few trends last long enough even to tempt the social scientist into thinking they are laws. Indeed, the few trends persistent enough to tempt social scientists into thinking of them as laws will almost always turn out to be solutions to design problems in competitions with infrahuman species, or solutions to (parametric) design problems set by nature and not by other species. An example of the first is the organization of humans into egalitarian groups of reciprocally altruistic hunter-gatherers until they hunted mega fauna to near extinction. An example of the second is reflected in the patterns of xenophobia and incest avoidance, which make for genetically optimal inbreeding. It is difficult to give examples of such widespread economic trends that are mistaken for laws, since even so low-level a generalization as Gresham's law turns out to be a necessary truth once fully stated.

If there is only one law or set of laws in biology, then it must be the case that the explanations biology and the human sciences offer (certainly all their functional explanations) are all historical explanation sketches, in which the connection between explanandum and explanans is implicitly secured by repeated applications of the principle of natural selection. It is easy to show how the principle of natural selection operates as an implicit law when we explain various biological phenomena. It is harder to do so in the case of social and, in particular, economic phenomena. To do so requires that we bear in mind: (1) that blind variation/environmental filtration is a mechanism that can operate at many levels, and makes arms races always possible and usually likely; (2) that the mechanism of natural selection does not require that traits on which it operates be genetically encoded, or even copied one from another with much accuracy at all; and (3), most important of all, that natural selection is the only causal mechanism that can give rise to the appearance of purposive design in nature or human neural processing, and to the reality of functionally adaptive states, processes, or structures among humans.

So, once any economic institution, practice, stratagem, or other innovation comes into existence, through a process of selection for some particular effect on some range of variations, the inevitable result will be the encouragement of some other institution, practice, or stratagem, to take advantage of the initial innovation. The result will be at least to change the working of, and, more usually, to reduce the success of the earlier innovation. This effect will in turn stimulate a new round of selection on variations that have effects selected for in the economic environment created by the initial arms race, and so on. This account of why anything like laws as we recognize them in physical science are impossible in economics and the other social sciences requires some comment. First of all, though the conclusion will be much the same as that argued for by those who focus on the *reflexive* character of social science and social processes, the source of the reflexivity is quite different, more pervasive, and much better established in evolutionary considerations. Second, the argument is quite different from the suggestion that unpredictable, unknown, or chaotic exogenous shocks undermine general patterns. Here the undermining is completely endogenous. This is important since the *ceteris paribus* clauses of many generalizations in economics may be held cogently to insulate them from exogenous disconfirmation. Third, because of the fact that arms-race undermining is endogenous, multifarious, and always possible, the generalizations that arms races—actual and possible—threaten lack counterfactual force, and so cannot be laws, inexact or otherwise.

Students of Austrian economics may see in this argument a commitment to dynamic processes and a rejection of conventional economic, and especially equilibrium, analysis to which they will be sympathetic. Too much should not be made of this similarity. First of all, the grounds on which I argue that economic processes reflect the succession of design problems and solutions, which simply pose new design problems and elicit new solutions, is far more general and well grounded than anything Austrian economics usually appeals to. Second, in this analysis, there will be scope for the sort of economic analysis familiar from neoclassical theory, just as there is scope for such analysis in evolutionary biology. The account of economics as a biological science leaves its actual character both largely untouched and endorsed as scientifically responsible after all, in spite of its predictive weakness.

In terrestrial biology, states of affairs under the control of natural selection approach and remain in the vicinity of equilibria frequently, and sometimes for very long, indeed sometimes geologically long, time periods. These periods of course come to an end, owing to exogenous nonbiological, or much more usually endogenous arms-race undermining. However, until this happens, they sufficiently closely approximate or satisfy relatively well-understood mathematical models that these models are important components of the explanation of why these states of affairs approximate the equilibria derivable in the models. One of the nicest examples of the role of such necessarily true mathematical models in biology is the Fisher 1:1 sex-ratio model. This model provides a deductive derivation of the 50:50 investment in males and females at equilibrium in a sexually reproducing population, from a set of axioms that includes, in particular, the principle of natural selection. The model has no more (and no less) empirical content than the proof of a theorem in geometry, and there are well-known biological systems—female and male skewed species—in which it is not realized (because of its being undermined in an arms race). For this reason, it is no law, inexact or otherwise, that "sexually reproducing species invest equal resources in each sex." Nevertheless, because of the close-enough satisfaction of its assumptions in most extant species during this geological epoch, the model has considerable explanatory value, and the generalization that approximates it was widely, though mistakenly, viewed as a law, indeed, one that reflected the wisdom of the creator in providing a mate for every male, *ceteris paribus*.

The parallel between Fisher's sex-ratio model and the model of a competitive equilibrium should not have escaped notice. Consider how we explain why price changes in a real economy almost never destabilize markets. We claim that they approximate to provably stable general equilibrium models of market exchange. This is a model that derives the existence of a general equilibrium from assumptions so stringent that no market could come very close to realizing them: the weak axiom of revealed preference among an infinite number of omniscient agents, infinite divisibility, no returns to scale in production, and a complete market for every commodity at every instant in the future. But, each of the axioms is alleged to be closely enough satisfied by whatever real market's stability properties are being explained that the model's deductively derived conclusion can be said to be closely enough satisfied as well. The same story can be told about any other piece of pure economic theory.

It used to be fashionable to deny that biology had much explanatory power. It is still correct that the combination of evolutionary theory and the most complete statement of initial conditions we can come up with has little long-term predictive content, since there are so many different ways in which most biological systems can solve the design problems they face. And the same state of affairs explains the predictive weakness of economics and the rest of social science. Most human interactions are strategic and so provide occasions for the selection of new strategies that upset temporary equilibria early and often. Since genetically encoded design solutions vary much less and vary much more slowly than neurologically encoded design solutions, an evolutionary equilibrium model will be closely approximated among biological lineages for appreciable periods, certainly for long enough periods that biologists will be able to state the model and even to estimate the degree of fit to the world. The applicability of an equilibrium model or any model is much more short-lived among humans, as the success of any one or more strategies quickly elicits new strategies which trump them. For this reason, those employing equilibrium models must usually be satisfied with at most generic predictions. Success in predicting the details of particular events will be rare in the human sciences.

I am hardly the first to claim the relevance of evolutionary theory to economics. Even before Nelson and Winter attempted explicitly to approach the theory of the firm from this perspective, more conventional economists were doing so. As far back as fifty years ago, economic theorists sought the protection of the theory of natural selection at a time when it lacked testability and had little predictive content. Both Alchian (1949) and Friedman (1953) appealed to natural selection to vindicate economic theory on the grounds that individuals and firms who did not act in accordance with its strictures would sooner or later become extinct. Alas, among economists, Gary Becker (1962) revealed that natural selection was too good a cover for the theory. It could be shown to produce the theory's conclusions about excess demand even when combined with the denial of its axioms about rational choice. Even worse for the strategy of hiding behind a predictively weak theory in natural science, developments in biology began rapidly to add predictive content and considerable testability to the theory of natural selection in the years after 1953.

The role evolutionary theory plays for my view of economics is quite different from its largely rhetorical invocation to protect the methodological status quo so dear to Chicago school economics. What evolutionary theory has done for me is to change my old question, "If economics is not a science, what is it?" into the question, "If economics is a science, what kind of a science is it?" And it has provided me with an answer to that question: It's a biological science. This answer to the question was, however, not very helpful to me until I had managed to figure out for myself what a biological science is, and how it differs from a physical science, in particular how it differs in its theories and laws, generalizations and models, and most of all, in the historical and terrestrial character of its intended domain. Only when it became evident to me that biology is a historical/terrestrial science, in which Dobzhansky's dictum is literally true—that nothing makes sense in it except in the light of evolution—did I begin to understand the character of economic theory.

There are, of course, some substantive and methodological implications about how economics should proceed if it really is a biological science. Happily, over the last twenty-five years or so, and long before I came to the conclusion that it is a biological science, economics started acting like one. There seem to be at least three sea changes in the discipline over the last thirty years that have made economics a much more scientifically interesting enterprise than it was when I first began thinking about the subject. To begin with, game theory provided economics with tools to explore strategic interactions, and, thus, eventually to treat the impact of increasing returns to scale on the creation of many other kinds of asymmetries. And when harnessed together with a Darwinian replicator dynamics, game theory began to be able to explain as adaptive a great deal of economic and near-economic behavior that rational choice theory had to stigmatize as irrational or employ ad hoc devices with which to reconcile itself.

A second sea change among economists was the sudden willingness to take into account the findings and theories of cognitive and social psychologists, not to mention neuroscience, about both preferences and expectations, the two causal variables in economic choice. The new-found willingness to even consider relevant psychology was of course signaled when the Nobel Prize for economic science was awarded to Daniel Kahnemann for his work with Amos Tverski. To this trend must be added the field of experimental economics, to which few economists paid any attention in 1970, for which of course that same Nobel Prize was awarded to Vernon Smith as to Daniel Kahnemann. Experimental economics has of course made explicit common cause with evolutionary biology in the work of Erst Fehr. In doing so it has transformed what James Buchanan called 'Constitutional economics' and what others call the economics of institutions. Developments in both game theory and experimental economics have enabled it suddenly to become as relevant to institutional design as evolutionary biology has become to ecology. Consider the design of bandwidth auctions just for starters. These trends reveal economists now acting with the opportunism that characterizes science. Behavioral economists, especially in finance, have been working hard over the last decade or more, against strong resistance, most of it emanating from Chicago, to employ these findings and models to undermine cornerstones of theoretical complacency in economics like the efficient markets hypothesis and the limitless power of arbitrage to enforce the law of one price. In this and in other areas, they have especially benefited from systematic research in psychology about uncertainty and risk.

Third, nothing has been more breathtaking in economics over the last three decades than the freedom that strategic interaction models gave economic theory to waive the assumption of perfect and symmetrical information. Ever since Akerlof (1970), economists have been developing models that allow for asymmetries of information, and so stand a chance of enhanced applicability and at least generic prediction to a wider range of real-world cases than economic models that began with complete information.

Add, to all these, ever-increasing computational power that econometrics shares with computational genomics, and suddenly there is the prospect of turning mere existence proofs into results of computational general equilibrium.

REFERENCES

Aklerlof, G. (1970). "The Market for 'Lemons': Quality Uncertainty and the Market Mechanism." *Quarterly Journal of Economics* 84(3): 488–500.

Alchain, A. (1949). "Uncertainty, Evolution, and Economic Theory." *Journal of Political Economy* 57: 211–221.

Allen, R. (1938). *Mathematical Analysis for Economists*. New York: St. Martin's Press.

Becker, G. (1962). "Irrational Behavior and Economic Theory." *Journal of Political Economy* 70: 188–196.

Blaug, M. (1980). *The Methodology of Economics*. Cambridge: Cambridge University Press

Dennett, D. (1995). *Darwin's Dangerous Idea*. New York: Norton.

Freidman, M. (1953). *Essays in Positive Economics*. Chicago: University of Chicago Press.

Gibbard, A. & Varian, H. (1978). "Economic Models." *Journal of Philosophy* 75: 664–677.

Hands, W. (2001). *Reflections without Rules*. Cambridge, England: Cambridge University Press.

Hausman, D. (1981). *Capital, Prices and Profits*. New York: Columbia University Press.

Hausman, D. (1991). *The Separate and Inexact Science of Economics*. Cambridge: Cambridge University Press.

Keynes, J.N. (1917). *The Scope and Methods of Political Economy*. London: .A.M., Kelly.

Kuhn, T. (1962). *Structure of Scientific Revolutions*. Chicago: University of Chicago Press.

Leontief, V. (1982). "Academic Economics." *Science* 9 July, p xii.

Lipsey, R. (1963). *Introduction to Positive Economics*. London: Weidenfield and Nicholson.

Machlup, F. (1955). "The Problem of Verification in Economics," *Southern Economic Journal*, 22: 1–21.

McCloskey, D. (1985). *The Rhetoric of Economics*. Madison: The University of Wisconsin Press.

Papandreou, A. (1958). *Economics as a Science*. Philadelphia: Lippencott.

Quine, W.V. O. (1961). *Word and Object*. Cambridge, MA: MIT Press.

Quirk, J. & Saposnik, R. (1968). *Introduction to General Equilibrium and Welfare Economics*. New York: McGraw Hill.

Rabin, M. (1998). "Psychology and Economics." *Journal of Economic Literature* 36: 11–46.

Robbins, L. (1932). *An Essay on the Nature and Significance of Economic Science*. London: St. Martin's Press.

Rosenberg, A. (1976). *Microeconomic Laws*. Pittsburgh: University of Pittsburgh Press.

Rosenberg, A. (1986). "Lakatosian Consolations for Economists.." *Economics and Philosophy* 14: 127–139.

Rosenberg, A. (1989). "Are Generic Predictions Enough?" In B. Hamminga, ed., *Philosophy and Economics II*. Dordrecht, The Netherlands: Reidel.

Rosenberg, A. (1992). *Economics—Mathematical Politics or Science of Diminishing Returns*. Chicago: University of Chicago Press.

Sen, A. (1982). *Choice, Welfare and Measurement*. Cambridge: Cambridge University Press.

Weintraub, R. (1985). *General Equilibrium Analysis*. Cambridge: Cambridge University Press.

Winch, P. (2007). The Idea of a Social Science and Its Relation to Philosophy. London: Routledge.

CHAPTER 4

REALISTIC REALISM ABOUT UNREALISTIC MODELS

USKALI MÄKI

My philosophical intuitions are those of a scientific realist. In addition to being *realist* in its philosophical outlook, my philosophy of economics also aspires to be *realistic* in the sense of being descriptively adequate, or at least normatively non-utopian, about economics as a scientific discipline. The special challenge my philosophy of economics must meet is to provide a scientific realist account that is realistic of a discipline that deals with a complex subject matter and operates with highly unrealistic models. *Unrealisticness in* economic models must not constitute an obstacle to *realism about* those models.

What follows is a selective and somewhat abstract summary of my thinking about economics, outlined from two perspectives: first historical and autobiographical, then systematic and comparative. The first angle helps understand motives and trajectories of ideas against their backgrounds in intellectual history. My story turns out to have both unique and generalizable aspects. The second approach outlines some of the key concepts and arguments as well as their interrelations in my philosophy of economics, with occasional comparisons to other views. More space will be devoted to this second perspective than to the first.

HISTORICAL

During my second undergraduate year at the University of Helsinki in 1971, I decided to become a specialist in the philosophy and methodology of economics. No such (institutionalized) *field* of inquiry existed at that time, but this was no reason not to make the decision. I studied economics and philosophy parallel to one another. I was attracted to economics by my perception of its importance and rigor, while philosophy was more a matter of intellectual passion. Having taken introductory courses in economics, I was, just like many other fellow students, deeply puzzled by utility maximization, perfect competition, and other assumptions that appeared bizarrely unrealistic about the social and mental world as we knew it. There was so much obvious falsehood in the models of the queen of the social sciences that I did not know what to make of it. Then I read Milton Friedman's 1953 essay—cited in Richard Lipsey's *Introduction to Positive Economics* (1971) that was at that time used as the major text—that argued in defense of such assumptions. The first encounter with Friedman's essay made me feel like being intellectually insulted. I viewed its message as manifesting an irresponsible academic opportunism that did nothing to ease my puzzlement. On the contrary, it made the puzzlement deeper. These two experiences at an intellectually sensitive age were sufficient to result in a lifelong commitment and devotion.

Intermediate and advanced courses in economics did nothing to alleviate the puzzlement and discomfort. It would probably have been impossible for me to continue my studies in economics had I not also been a student of philosophy. I decided I would survive my economics studies by combining the two, by looking at economics from the point of view of the philosophy of science. I hoped this would help me understand the discipline that appeared so odd to this student. I was lucky because Helsinki was at that time one of the centers of frontline postpositivistic philosophy of science. Naturally, we learnt about Popper, Kuhn, Feyerabend, Laudan, and Lakatos, but at the core of the attention was scientific realism as conveyed by two distinguished advocates, Ilkka Niiniluoto and Raimo Tuomela. I also studied the works of other scientific realists such as Wilfrid Sellars, Mario Bunge, Jack Smart, Clifford Hooker, Hilary Putnam, Richard Boyd, and others. We examined the structuralist (Sneed-Stegmüller) conception of theory structure and dynamics as well as the work by Leszek Nowak and the rest of the Poznan school on idealizations in scientific theorizing (Nowak 1980). In the latter part of the 1970s, I was also rather influenced by Roy Bhaskar's first two books (Bhaskar 1975/78, 1979) and by some works by Rom Harré (e.g. Harré 1970).

So when the 1980s dawned and the new field of the philosophy and methodology of economics started taking shape, I had a very different (post-Popperian) background than many of the visible players, such as Larry Boland, Mark Blaug, Neil DeMarchi, Bruce Caldwell, Wade Hands, and others. As I was to complain later, the field initially came to be dominated by Popperian and Lakatosian themes and conceptual tools (1990a, 2008c). I was closer to Alex Rosenberg and Dan Hausman than to those others in my philosophical training, yet there were two things that distinguished me from these two pioneers: my strong antipositivism, due to my early exposure to European and Australian versions of scientific realism, and the problems on my agenda being primarily prompted by my experiences as an economics student. It was to become a major concern of my research agenda to look at the falsehood we students discovered in economic models from the point of view of a realist conception of science.

Soon after Rosenberg's *Microeconomic Laws* (1976) was published, I got hold of a copy of it (with quite some difficulties in that ancient world without Google and Amazon). I admired its argumentative qualities, but it did not very strongly connect with my concerns since its key issues were derived from those of general philosophy of science and philosophy of social sciences rather than from within economics. Hausman's concerns in his *Capital Profit, and Prices* (1981) were closer to mine, and have been ever since—even though here, too, I feel like being closer to the concerns of the students and practitioners of economics. This has shown, among other things, in my reluctance to talk about "laws" in a manner that joins the positivist legacy and that Rosenberg and Hausman have shared in their accounts of economics. I rather talk about causes, powers, mechanisms, and dependency relations in my ontology of economics.

The constitutive questions on my agenda have had less to do with Rosenberg's "Is it a science?" and more closely linked to Hausman's "What kind of science is it?" My life-long preoccupation was to be with the more specific question that derived from the worries of an undergraduate economics student: "How does economics relate to the real world?" Virtually everything I have done somehow connects with this broad question that can be approached from a variety of angles.

From early on, I sought a connection between scientific realism and what I would later call the issue of *realisticness* in economics. In the early 1980s, I discarded Bhaskar's framework as I found it too simplistic to be of much help in understanding such a complex subject as economics (much later, Bhaskar was to be rediscovered by others in economic methodology). I moved on to developing a more nuanced discipline-sensitive scientific realism following a bottom-up approach that would be responsive to empirical and local discoveries about peculiar features of various research fields (some might call it a "grounded theory" approach at the meta level). This search was based on the conviction that such a local scientific realism must indeed be actively created given that no sufficiently rich and powerful version was available in the philosophical literature. (Mäki 1989, 1996b, 1998a, 2005a)

An early insight directed me away from a naïve condemnation of unrealistic assumptions. Economic models involve idealizations just like the most respectable physical theories do: just think of the idealizations of frictionless plane, perfectly elastic gas molecule, rigid body, planets as mass points, two-body solar system. So what's the trouble, if any, I asked. It became clear that falsehood in assumptions will not be sufficient grounds for an antirealist instrumentalism about economic theory. This insight would drive and shape my later inquiries. The key idea that gradually emerged was that false idealizations often serve an important purpose, that of theoretically isolating causally significant fragments of the complex reality. Getting to this idea was helped by studying Marshall's writings on economic method, J.H. von Thünen's model of the isolated state, and Nowak's work on idealization. The analogy with experimental method also facilitated developing the idea: experimental isolation and theoretical isolation have a similar structure. (Mäki 1992a, 1994a, 2004a, 2004b, 2005c) Among other things, these insights enabled me to overcome my early dislike of Friedman's essay and to develop a generous interpretation of it as a realist statement (Mäki 1986, 1989, 1992b, 2003, 2008a). I have been rather lonely with this interpretation, because most other commentators of Friedman have labeled him an antirealist instrumentalist.

Alan Musgrave's seminal 1981 paper inspired me to revise and elaborate his suggestions as part of a larger attempt to develop a set of principles and categories that would help identify the various functions that unrealistic assumptions serve in models (Mäki 2000a, 2004c). Indeed, it became a crucial idea in my framework that any assessment of an assumption (and more broadly of a model) must be dependent on a sound understanding of its function, and more generally on the pragmatics of research questions. These ideas have been helpful also in examining debate and change in economic theorizing: debate and change can often be redescribed in terms of (contested, requested, and suggested) isolation, de-isolation (supplementation) and re-isolation (replacement) (Mäki 2004a).

Three other perspectives have been important in my attempt to understand economic inquiry and its real world connections. One has been the ontology of isolation. Here I have emphasized causes (causal processes and mechanisms) rather than laws (while Hausman used to frame his arguments in terms of laws), and I have entertained an "essentialist" notion of the world having an objective structure, including ideas of stronger and weaker causes and connections as well as of real modalities of possibility and necessity. The idea of ontology entailing evidential constraints on theorizing naturally evolved, to supplement the focus on empirical tests by most other economic methodologists (Mäki 2001b). Case studies on Austrian and New Institutionalist Economics have been of help here. Rosenberg's suggestions about the role of folk psychology inspired the development of the generalized idea that economics deals with commonsense items such as preferences, households, prices (coined by me as "commonsensibles") by variously modifying and rearranging them. (Mäki 1990b, 1992b, 1994b, 1996b, 1998a, 2002a, 2005a)

Another perspective has been provided by the insight that economists appreciate theoretical and explanatory unification. Economic theorizing and modeling are driven and constrained by the ideal of explanatory unification and the dislike of ad hoc features in models. Economists pursue explanations that derive from a shared set of principles, or from an "ur-model" and its specific variations. A unified theoretical framework capable of accounting for a large variety of different kinds of phenomena has been established as a regulative ideal of economic inquiry. This has further ramifications for the expansion of economics to the domains of neighboring disciplines, as in the much disputed "economics imperialism." (Mäki 1990b, 2001a, 2002b, 2004a, 2009c; Mäki and Marchionni 2009)

The third perspective deals with the social conditioning or shaping of economic theorizing, including the rhetoric, sociology, and economics of economics. My friendly confrontations with Deirdre McCloskey have given me the opportunity and incentive to develop a realist account of rhetoric, one that accommodates the reality of rhetoric in scientific work while not compromising basic realist tenets (Mäki 1988, 1993a, 1995, 2000a). My work in the sociology of scientific knowledge in the context of economics (Mäki 1992c, 1993b) followed up on Bob Coats's pioneering work and may have served as a bridge from his work to that of Wade Hands (Hands 1994, 2001). Exercises in the economics of economics—examining economics itself in economic terms—have given rise to exciting issues of reflexivity (Mäki 1993b, 1999, 2005b). Economic inquiry is social activity shaped by various social conditions, but as such this should not undermine its capabilities in accessing real-world facts.

Strategic

Most of this work, and its connection to scientific realism, has been motivated and guided by *general strategic principles* like these:

1. Much of the criticism of economics is directed at wrong targets, and is based on the mistaken belief that criticism is easy—such as when inferring from unrealistic assumptions to models being incorrect. Economics is not at all flawless, but it is not easy to reliably identify its flaws (and even less easy to remedy them), almost regardless of how serious they are. Careful scrutiny is needed to locate the appropriate targets of criticism. Given that the most central set of issues deal with the relationship of economics to reality, an enriched and discipline-sensitive scientific realism offers an appropriate philosophical framework for the required scrutiny.

2. The approach is bottom-up rather than top-down. Economics is a complex subject that has many peculiar characteristics in comparison to other scientific disciplines; it is different from natural sciences and from other social sciences, although it also has similarities with both (themselves far from uniform sets of disciplines). One will not develop an adequate understanding of economics by way of imposing upon it some fancy doctrines borrowed from popular abstract philosophies of science. This easily leads to accounts that distort economics as it is actually done, or to methodological rhetoric that has little to do with actual practice (Popperian and Bhaskarian economic methodologies may have had this inclination). The alternative is to be sensitive to the complexities and

peculiarities of economics, and to develop whatever philosophical tools may be required to accommodate those features. This approach is hoped to result in a *realistic* realism about economics.

3. Many people have wondered about my obsession to render as much of economics as possible being in line with general realist intuitions. I admit the obsession. It is motivated by the hope that this will create—or help unearth—common ground for focused debate. It will help resist some of the unjustified and misdirected criticisms, while also supporting the elaboration of sound criticisms that will hit the target. Some of the misguided criticisms are based on attributing to conventional economics philosophical commitments that are not there (such as "positivism") or on adopting perspectives that ignore the obvious realist aspects of much of economic inquiry (such as radical social constructivism). The obsession also seeks to block certain evasive justifications of unrealistic economic models, in particular those that complacently declare that all models are false anyway, that they are to be judged only in terms of convenience and instrumental usefulness, so why bother taking any criticisms about their falsehood seriously! My hope is that once it is agreed that (at least many) economic models are (at least potentially) attempts to acquire truths about the real world, and that such attempts are fallible (but do not fail just because their assumptions are false), the debate will be focused on the right targets (on whether the attempts succeed or fail) and will improve in quality.

4. The role of realism in my work can also be viewed from the point of view of debates within the philosophy of science between scientific realists and antirealists. Two kinds of issue arise. First, philosophy of science has a legitimate concern with the question, How does scientific realism as a doctrine within the philosophy of science cope with a peculiar discipline such as economics? Supposing scientific realism is an adequate philosophy of chemistry and geology, does it manage to accommodate economics? My answer is: yes. Second, scientific realism has traditionally been formulated as a global doctrine about all of (good or successful) science, but it is obvious that not all of science conforms to its conventional canons. Does information about the peculiar features of economics have implications for our understanding of the contents of scientific realism in general and for the appropriate strategies of arguing about it? My answer is: yes.

5. My work has sought the attention of multiple audiences, including not just other philosophers and methodologists of economics but also practicing economists, historians of economics, philosophers of science, and other social scientists. This has been a fascinating challenge and a source of difficulties. Each discipline and research community functions in an institutional framework with distinct values and norms, agendas and standards, languages and methods, conventions and traditions, loyalties

and rivalries, rankings and authority structures. Having worked in economics and philosophy departments and having participated in many interdisciplinary encounters has helped me entertain several insider's perspectives, but obviously the success in addressing that multiplicity of audiences has been partial at most. This is a more general issue: any intrinsically interdisciplinary field faces similar challenges with their multiple audiences.

Systematic

My work involves—builds upon and contributes to—an emerging systematic portrait of economics as an intellectual endeavor and as an epistemic institution. The disciplinary portrait is a vision that integrates a range of ideas, from those about the nature of economic reality and truth about it, through those about theoretical and explanatory structure and dynamics, to those about the institutions of economic inquiry. What follows is a summary outline of the basic ideas and their relationships in their current form. Throughout, the puzzle and struggle is over whether and how theoretical economics connects with the real world. The concept of model provides an illuminating perspective to this issue. First, though, it is useful to offer a brief and simplified characterization of scientific realism as I see it.

1. Scientific Realism

My conception of generic scientific realism is rather thin and flexible. The world has an objective structure that is not created by scientists as they create their theories and models about that structure. Those theories and models are true or false by virtue of the ways of that objective structure—not by virtue of whether evidence supports them or whether we are otherwise persuaded to believe in them, for example. Finally, good science pursues theories that are true, while being prepared for the possibility of error.

In contrast to standard conceptions of scientific realism in the philosophy of science, my generic or minimal conception does *not* include claims such as these: (1) Actual science has most of its theories (at least approximately) true; (2) actual science is predictively successful; and (3) the theories of actual science refer to unobservables such as electrons. In my view, these things are empirical and local matters, they vary from case to case, from theory to theory, from field to field, from discipline to discipline. Those ingredients in standard formulations of scientific realism should perhaps be included in a realism about (the most successful) parts of physics, but not in a realism about archaeology or economics. My scientific realism is *local realism* with regard to these and other specific issues. The *global or generic realism* I endorse is the simple and minimal composite idea that, descriptively, there is a fact of the matter concerning the ways of the world and whether our theories have got those ways right, and that, normatively, it is the task of science to get them right. (Mäki 1990b, 1996b, 2001d, 2005a, 2008b)

2. Models as Representatives, or as Surrogate Systems

Economics is a modeling discipline alongside others that deal with a complex subject matter, such as biology and meteorology. Therefore, a key to understanding the practice of economic inquiry is to have a refined concept of model. This is not easy given the ambiguity of the term *model* and the multiplicity of kinds of models, and of ways of describing them (Mäki 2001c, 2005c, 2008c). I take models to be *representations* of some target (such as a real world system, a set of data, or a theory). And I take representation to have two aspects, the *representative* aspect and the *resemblance* aspect. The metaphor I have come to entertain to illustrate this idea is representative democracy: a small set of our fellow citizens are elected to serve as our representatives, and the chronic issue is whether, once elected, the goals they pursue as our representatives resemble our interests that we sought to express in the elections. Scientific models are like those representative citizens in that capacity: models resemble those citizens in interesting ways. So, in an obvious sense, representative democracy can be used as a model of theoretical modeling in science.

Scientific representation is not just a matter of some representative M possibly resembling some target R, such as a boxes-and-arrows diagram or a set of equations having a fit with some real-world structure. Representation involves an agent A (economist, scientific community) employing and using an object M as a representative of target R for some purpose P. This makes representation four placed, and there is now general agreement that this is how models as representations should be conceived. I have added two further components: an audience E, its expectations and background beliefs; and a commentary C that is used for specifying the other components and aligning them with one another (see also Mäki 2009a, 2009b).

> Agent A uses object M (the model) as a representative of target system R for purpose P, addressing audience E, prompting genuine issues of resemblance between M and R to arise; and applies commentary C to identify the above elements and to coordinate their relationships.

An important feature of this account of models as representations is that it does not require resemblance with the target to occur, it only requires *resemblance-related issues to arise (or to be capable of being raised) as genuine issues*. In order for them to be genuine issues, it is presupposed that a model has the capacity to resemble its target and that not just any arbitrary resemblances are considered. So a model is used as a representative of some target, and this potentially prompts issues of resemblance between the representative and what it is a representative of. A realist will take the stance that a successful representation does resemble its target in some desired ways—while these desired ways are relative to the relevant purposes and audiences.

The *representative aspect* of representation can be characterized in terms of *surrogate system,* in contrast to the real systems in the social world. Models are surrogate systems, and economic inquiry is *directly* concerned with the properties of such surrogate systems—rather than the properties of real systems. Much of economics consists of the investigation of the properties of model worlds ("Let's check what happens in this model"). This is an important observation, because herein lies a major source of possible complaint, based on some sort of realist intuitions: economics (or this or that of its subfields) appears to be preoccupied with a study of imaginary model worlds only, detached from the real world. This is a suspicion that must be taken seriously, but meeting the challenge is not easy. It would be intellectually irresponsible and arrogantly complacent to dismiss it as being just based on ignorance about the achievements of economics or on misunderstanding the scientific method.

Economists build models by imagining and describing and manipulating model worlds populated by perfectly rational agents, games with two players, trade with two countries and two goods, perfectly competitive firms, representative agents, closed economies, zero-transaction-cost situations. There is no doubt that through their investigations—by manipulating assumptions, performing inferences, deriving results—economists learn a great deal about the properties and behavior of such model worlds. What is not a matter of self-evidence is whether they also thereby learn about the properties and behavior of the real world. This is what prompts the issue of resemblance.

3. Models and the Issue of Resemblance

The main challenge derives from a worry about the other aspect of representation, that of resemblance. The suspicion is that viewed as representatives, as surrogate systems, (at least many prestigious) economic models do not resemble real systems in some desirable manner. And because of the lack of resemblance, and economists' lack of interest in it, economic inquiry becomes predominantly a matter of examining the properties of those imagined systems only. The accusation boils down to the thought that the study of model systems literally *substitutes for* the study of real systems.

In response to such charges, one must consider the representative and resemblance aspects of economic modeling together. If one is to please the realist intuitions of the critic, one must show how an interest in the properties of model systems not only does not rule out an interest in the properties of real systems, but also serves the satisfaction of the latter.

The key is to see the difference between direct and indirect access to one's subject matter along the following lines: Economists build (or should build) theoretical models as representatives of real systems, as surrogate systems, the properties of which are *directly* examined in order to *indirectly* acquire information about real systems. Models are built and studied because there is no epistemically reliable "direct" access available to some deep facts of economic reality. All access is necessarily indirect and mediated by simple images of complex things. However, in order for such indirect epistemic access to the real world to be possible and successful, model worlds must resemble the real world in some required ways.

In order to see the issue more clearly, we can draw a pragmatic distinction between models as surrogate systems and models as substitute systems. This is a pragmatic distinction in the sense that it is based on economists' attitudes and practices in relation to their models. *Surrogate systems* are treated as mediating vehicles in attempts to gain indirect epistemic access to the real world: surrogate systems are examined in order to acquire information about the real systems. The issue of resemblance remains a genuine shared concern. *Substitute systems*, on the other hand, are examined only for their own sake, with no further aim or wish of connecting with real world systems: the study of substitute systems substitutes for any interest in real systems. The issue of resemblance becomes neglected. (This revises the more neutral use of 'substitute system' in the terminology of some of my earlier work.)

This can be used to identify two kinds of legitimate criticism from a realist point of view. One kind of criticism attacks styles of inquiry that treat a model as a substitute system only, not even intending it as a means for gaining access to the real world. The alleged problem is that there is *no attempt*. The other kind of criticism acknowledges a model being treated as a surrogate system, but blames it for failing in accessing the social world. The alleged problem is that there is a *failed attempt*. The history of economics exhibits both kinds of criticism.

Three remarks are in order. *First*, it is not always easy to apply this distinction in practice. What appears to be a model treated as just a freely floating fictional substitute system may be defended as a surrogate system by arguing that its connections to real systems are just very indirect or that those connections will be created in a long enough run. *Second*, as a special case of the first, a model may be treated as a substitute system and as such it may serve as a test bed for developing concepts and techniques that may find useful applications in later models that will be treated as surrogate systems. The general principle is that there is no fully reliable way of identifying a model either as a surrogate system or as a substitute system in isolation from other models and its own development. *Third*, even if the distinction is primarily pragmatic, one in terms of attitudes and practices rather than in terms of the "intrinsic" properties of models, those intrinsic properties (together with the media of their description, such as mathematical equations or diagrams) often have pragmatic consequences for how the models are treated. Some models are easier to treat as surrogate systems than others, while these others may tend to invite attitudes that enable or even encourage treating them as substitute systems only (my conjecture is that using very demanding mathematical techniques for describing and manipulating a model is generally more likely—than, say, using diagrammatic methods—to discourage attention to real world systems and thereby encourage treating it as a substitute system only; but note that *more likely* definitely does not imply *necessarily* or the like).

Even if economists were ambitious and optimistic enough to treat a model as a surrogate system, there is still an objection or suspicion that naturally arises: models just do not resemble their targets, or do so only very remotely or in otherwise wrong ways. So how can models possibly help us acquire truthful information about the real world? In order to answer this question, we need to understand how the apparent gap or distance between models and the world is created, what this gap consists of, and how it is possible for this gap to help scientists gain epistemic access to the world—indeed, *what appears as a gap from one perspective may be a bridge from another.*

4. Theoretical Isolation by Idealizing Assumptions

Models characteristically are, or describe, imaginary situations. These situations are imaginary in two ways. First, they are imagined by economists. They are not observed or discovered, they are constructed by economists using their imagination. The power of imagination enables a second sense in which models are imaginary. Namely, those imagined situations are imaginary in that they do not include most of the ingredients in real situations; some ingredients are represented in very idealized form; and yet others may be added even though they do not have obvious correlates in real situations. There is no way that models can avoid being "unrealistic" in many such ways.

In describing imaginary model worlds, scientists employ idealizing assumptions that are false, if taken literally as statements about the real world. Perfect information, zero transaction costs, closed economy, ceteris paribus—these are characteristics of surrogate model worlds, not of the real world. Physical sciences employ such assumptions in abundance—just think of frictionless planes, mass points, rigid bodies. Idealizing assumptions are false, they distort the facts. But these falsehoods are *not errors*. They are not hypotheses or conjectures that are proposed with the hope that they will turn out to be true—and in case they turn out to be false, they are to be rejected and replaced by others hopefully closer to the truth. Idealizing assumptions are deliberately employed, often with full awareness of their falsehood. At any rate they are not hypotheses conjectured to be true. What is the point? How does a realist accommodate these falsehoods?

The important thing to understand is that *idealizations are strategic falsehoods.* They serve some higher purpose. This purpose is that of theoretically *isolating* some important dependency relation or causal factor or mechanism from the involvement and influence of the rest of the universe. Consider Galileo's law of freely falling bodies, Milton Friedman's (1953) favorite example. The simplest statement of the law only cites time, distance, and gravity—while implicitly or explicitly assuming that air pressure is nil, magnetic and other forces are absent, and so on. The point of these idealizing assumptions is to help isolate the impact of the earth's gravity—gravity alone, undisturbed by anything else—on the falling body (Mäki 1992b, 2003, 2008a).

This is also the point of much of economic modeling. Consider my favorite example, the very first economic model in the modern sense, J.H. von Thünen's (1826/1842/1910) model of agricultural land use in the Isolated State. It is built on highly unrealistic assumptions, such as a city without dimensions; no other towns; no rivers, no mountains and valleys; uniform fertility and climate; transportation costs a function of distance from the city alone (rather than of the availability of roads, etc.); the state closed off from the rest of the world, thus no trade; strict rationality of agents; and so on. In these imagined circumstances, a pattern of concentric rings emerges, representing zones of cultivation. But such a pattern cannot be observed in the real world, it is a feature of the model world only. And the idealizing assumptions that imply the pattern also fail to state any facts. So what's the point? The point of von Thünen's highly unrealistic simple model is to isolate one major causal factor that shapes land use patterns, namely, distance (or transportation costs), and to show how it works its impact through to the outcome in the imagined conditions. (Mäki 2004b, 2005c, 2009a)

Economists can be philosophical realists about their models even though these describe imaginary situations (von Thünen was a realist about his simplest model of the Isolated State). This is because it is possible that the mechanisms in operation in those imaginary situations are the same as or similar to those in operation in real situations. A model captures significant truth if it contains a mechanism that is also operative in real systems. This significant truth can be attained thanks to the false idealizations employed by the model. Capturing this truth does not require any de-idealization by way of relaxing those assumptions.

Unrealisticness in models is not intrinsically a bad thing. It is often a very good thing. It may even be necessary for achieving important epistemic goals. Unrealistic assumptions must be assessed in relation to their functions in modeling (such as fixing a causal background in contrastive explanations, see Marchionni 2006). Whether an assumption is duly or unduly unrealistic depends on its location in a theoretical structure and the functions it is designed or able to serve.

5. Model and Experiment

Theoretical models are structurally and functionally similar to ordinary experimental setups: both pursue isolation. The major differences lie in the methods of control used in accomplishing isolation and in the nature of the materials that are being manipulated (e.g., real people in contrast to imaginary agents). In an ordinary laboratory experiment, various causally efficacious measures are adopted to control for other things so as to neutralize their impact, while in theoretical isolation, the controls are effected by the force of assumption: those other things are assumed to be absent, constant, in normal states. In this sense, *much of theoretical modeling is a matter of thought experimentation* and the world of theoretical models is a kind of intellectual laboratory world (Mäki 1992a, 1994a, 2005c). On the other hand, *material experimentation is a species of modeling:* It is a matter of building and examining surrogate systems as representatives of real systems out in the wild. Hence my slogan, "models are experiments and experiments are models" (Mäki 2005c). In both cases, issues of resemblance arise. We have already discussed the case of theoretical models. Similar issues are involved in building and using experiments that employ causal controls, captured by the notion of external validity (see Guala 2005; cf. also Morgan 2005).

6. Isolation and Metaphor

Economists examining the rhetoric of their discipline, such as Deirdre McCloskey (1994) and Arjo Klamer (2007), emphasize that models *include* metaphors. Sometimes they suggest that models *are* metaphors. While it is easy to agree on the former idea—just think of *equilibrium, dictator game, human capital*—I would only go along with the latter if qualified as the weaker claim that models *are akin to* metaphors. The reason I think so is that I take both to be isolations. Metaphors and models are essentially similar in that both highlight limited aspects of their targets. In the case of metaphor, it highlights those aspects of the target that are believed to be similar to some limited aspects of the source. Thus, the metaphor of human capital helps isolate those aspects of education that are believed to be similar to, say, financial capital.

7. Isolation as Key to Inexactness and Separateness

Daniel Hausman (1992) has argued that, descriptively, economics is an inexact and separate science. I have argued that both of these characteristics, properly understood, are derivatives of theoretical isolation (Mäki 1996a). Hausman says inexactness lies within economic theories (in their premises or laws), but I find it more natural to say that inexactness is a feature of the implications of theories or models. I would say predictive implications are inexact in two ways: they typically have a chance of coming out true only if formulated in terms of permissive degrees of approximation; and they often fail if presented in very precise quantitative terms. As a feature of theory's implications, inexactness is a consequence of a feature of theories or models, namely, their incompleteness. Theories and models are incomplete just because they isolate small slices of the world, they capture just a small subset of the whole set of causal factors that in the real world shape the behavior of phenomena. So inexactness turns out to be a consequence of isolation.

The same can be said about separateness. As I read Hausman's notion of separateness, he mostly uses it for characterizing economics as a discipline that studies the consequences of rational greed, or, more generally, as a discipline that employs a very parsimonious set of theoretical principles having a very broad scope. Separateness turns out to be based on a radical isolation of a small set of explanatory factors that also have an extended explanatory reach. In sum, theoretical isolation is the more basic notion that underlies those of inexactness and separateness.

8. Capacities and Lies

There are many similarities between Nancy Cartwright's (1989) account of economic theory and that of mine. We both believe (that economists believe) in capacities or causal powers; agents have powers of rational deliberation, money has purchasing power, price changes have the capacity to transmit information, smart fiscal policy has the capacity to smoothen business cycles. We both believe that the conception of laws as regularities is not a recommendable idea; regularities tend to break down as circumstances change. We both believe that the world is a rather messy place, in certain respects (we might differ somewhat about those respects). I believe that the notion of capacity is not sufficient for having a sound economic ontology, but that a separate notion of mechanism is needed, and that capacities are properties of both mechanisms and their component parts: much of economic modeling amounts to attempts to describe economic mechanisms (Mäki 1992a, 1994a, 1998b, 2009a). And whereas Cartwright has thought that the theoretical models of economics lie just as the laws of physics lie (Cartwright 1983) when considered as claims about the happenings among the messy empirical phenomena, I think that if conceived as representations of capacities and mechanisms, economic models do not necessarily lie, they rather have a chance of being true. Much of the time, Cartwright seems to think that the applicability conditions of a model are given by its idealizations, including the associated ceteris paribus clauses, and that the model has a chance of being true only provided those highly restrictive conditions hold. I don't impose this requirement, but have instead defended the idea that simple and highly idealized models may be true of simple facts about the world while getting more complex facts wrong. I take this view to be part of the long tradition within economics, from Senior through J.S. Mill and J.E. Cairnes to Lionel Robbins and much of contemporary economics. (Mäki 1994a, 2004c, 2009a)

9. Ontological Convictions and Tractability Conventions

The method of isolation may be motivated by ontological conviction, the belief that models with unrealistic assumptions are needed to isolate and describe causal factors or mechanisms and their characteristic ways of operation in the real world. Economists at least implicitly distinguish between surrogate model systems and real systems—those in which disturbances are absent and those in which they are present, that is, closed and open systems. These distinctions coincide, implying that economists believe real systems are open and model systems are closed. Another way of speaking about this is in terms of simplicity and complexity. Economists build simple models because they believe the world is complex. They don't build simple models because they believe the world is simple. They build models based on theoretical isolation because they believe this is the only or the best way to get access to the deeper causes of the phenomena in complex reality. All this is fine for my scientific realism. (Here my realist portrayal of economics seems different from that of Lawson 1997.)

There is another possible motivation behind economic models and their idealizing assumptions that is a little more difficult for a realist to accommodate. Some assumptions are made to facilitate the formal treatment of a model. They increase or enable the tractability of the problems cast in terms of the model, thus they could be called *tractability assumptions* (Hindriks 2005, 2006). The primary motivation in such a case is pragmatic convenience, constrained by a given mathematical technique or framework. Often this is no problem, provided the assumptions that serve a tractability function serve as harmless formal auxiliaries rather than as distortions of an actually held deeper worldview.

Sometimes this is not the case, which gives rise to a serious issue. In such situations, pressures of tractability override important ontological considerations, and the values of formal rigor take over in shaping the focus and strategies of research. This is a worry about contemporary economics that many commentators share (e.g., Mayer 1993; Blaug 2002). A few decades ago economists lacked the mathematical tools for dealing with increasing returns and monopolistic competition in a general equilibrium framework. This violated the ontological convictions of many economists working on development issues, particularly those economists who conceived of (major parts of) the economy as being governed by positive feedback mechanisms and market imperfections. In case a conflict between ontology and tractability is resolved in favor of tractability while suppressing ontology, the obvious suspicion is that the models that ensue are (or are to be) treated as substitute systems only. Such a situation may or may not create a disturbing tension that motivates building further models that relax at least some of the relevant tractability assumptions, such as in recent developments in growth and trade theory that now employ models with increasing returns and monopolistic competition. Even though there is no full harmony established here between ontological conviction and the properties of the new surrogate systems, it seems that the process has been at least partly motivated by ontological constraints. In general, I believe *the tension between tractability conventions and ontological convictions is one of the driving forces of progress in economics.* If the tension were to be systematically resolved by privileging tractability and formal rigor while suppressing ontological convictions, economics would be on the wrong track.

10. Paraphrasing Assumptions so as to Give Them a Chance of Being True

Assumptions serving to exclude factors that are irrelevant or negligible from the point of view of the purpose of inquiry are often formulated as deliberately false idealizations. So formulated, they appear to make false claims about the absence, constancy, or zero strength of a variable. But they can often also be transformed into claims about properties such as the *negligibility* of a factor, and as such claims, they are given a chance of being true (Musgrave 1981). What first appears as a false claim about the absence of a factor F can sometimes be paraphrased as a potentially true claim about a property of F, namely, its negligibility. This property is relational in that it connects a causal fact of the matter (F has impact C on some further variable G) with a pragmatic fact about our purposes and interests (such as the required accuracy when predicting the value of G). Thus, a negligibility assumption claims that C is negligibly small given our purposes. Such a claim may be true and it may be false (Mäki 2000b, 2004c).

If we were to consider von Thünen's model of the Isolated State as a predictive model, the assumptions of no rivers and uniform fertility cannot usually be paraphrased as true negligibility assumptions; the impact of rivers and variation in fertility are not negligible for most predictive purposes. On the other hand, in two-body models of the solar system, the exclusion of interplanetary attraction can usually be interpreted as a negligibility assumption because, for most accuracy preferences, the strength of that attraction is negligibly small compared to the attraction between a planet and the Sun.

Similar issues can be raised about, say, models of two-country trade, asking whether other trade relations are negligible; or about models of closed economy, asking whether all trade relations of a given economy are negligible for some legitimate purpose. In answering such questions, one first has to fix the purposes that a model is expected to serve. This determines the upper limit of causal impact that can be neglected. Thereafter, the challenge is the empirical one of estimating the actual impact and checking whether it is below or above that limit.

In case a factor excluded by an assumption is not negligible, the options include relaxing the assumption and paraphrasing it as an *applicability assumption*. There is more on the former in Section 11 on The Needs and Roles of De-Isolation and Re-Isolation. In the latter case, what starts out as an assumption about the absence of factor F may be transformed into a claim about the applicability of the model to situations in which F indeed is absent or at least negligible in its impact, and about its inapplicability to situations in which this is not the case. A closed economy model may be claimed to be applicable to large economies in which the role of foreign trade is negligible for a given purpose of model use. Applicability is a relational property of a model, connecting the model with a domain in the world. Claims about applicability and inapplicability can be true, even though assumptions about the absence of F were false.

A realist should have no complaint about the preceding procedures of turning apparent falsehood into truth. But consider other possible uses of the art of paraphrase. A false assumption $A(F)$ about the absence of F might be paraphrased variously as true claims that make no reference to the real world, such as these: $A(F)$ serves useful pedagogical purposes; $A(F)$ helps build aesthetically pleasing models; $A(F)$ facilitates calculations about the model; $A(F)$ is a precondition for accepting a paper about the model for publication; $A(F)$ manifests a gender bias in economic inquiry. These paraphrased claims may well be true, and may reveal very interesting facts about economics. But from the point of view of model/world relations, they are true about wrong sorts of thing, so fail to please the realist in looking for a justification for apparently false models. They are about scientific practices only, not about the real world subject matter of economics (Mäki 2000b, 2004c). If those kinds of paraphrase dominate as the only available options, then the suspicion may arise that the respective models are nothing but substitute systems with little or no contact with the real world.

11. The Needs and Roles of De-Isolation and Re-Isolation

I have defended the thought that false idealizing assumptions and the highly isolative models they help build are not as such problematic for a realist. This is because, subject to some further conditions, this style of inquiry may promote the attainment of small yet significant truths about the real world. In some cases, false assumptions may be paraphrased as potentially true assumptions about negligibility and applicability. But economists often also relax some of the unrealistic assumptions, they practice de-isolation by de-idealization, adding further causal factors on top of previously isolated ones. Or they may re-isolate by re-idealization, which is a matter of removing previously included factors and replacing them with previously excluded factors. These procedures treat the original assumptions as *early-step assumptions* that give way to later-step assumptions. These practices have their reasons, too.

One may want to generate more detailed explanations or predictions of phenomena than is possible without adding further factors and complexity into one's model; de-idealization is needed. More generally, one may want to explain a different aspect of the phenomenon, which requires an adjustment in the explanatory factors by de-isolation or re-isolation (Mäki 2004a). Or one performs de-idealization for the purpose of testing and confirming a model. This is because the empirical data characteristically manifest a multiplicity of causal influences, while a theoretical model typically isolates just one or a few causal mechanisms. In order to align the two with one another, so as to ensure that the data help test what one wants to test, either the data must be adjusted (by data mining) or the model must be de-isolated, or both. Testing may also proceed by way of the theoretical maneuver of checking the robustness of certain presumed facts to various assumptions or the factors they depict. One relaxes an assumption and thereby determines whether the conjectured fact is sensitive to that assumption (see Lehtinen & Kuorikoski 2007; Kuorikoski, Lehtinen, Marchionni 2008). Another way of putting this is to say that robustness tests are ways of checking whether an assumption can be treated as a true negligibility assumption. Sometimes the discovery may be devastating, requiring a major revision in one's assumptions. For some important research questions, one is forced to relax earlier idealizations and replace them by others such as when assuming increasing returns, asymmetric information, or positive transaction costs simply because assuming otherwise will yield models that miss causally powerful factors that are far from negligible.

From another perspective, a need for de-isolation or re-isolation may arise when there is reason to believe that previous isolations violate the ontic unity in the world; they impose divisions where the world is indivisible. Just as biologists will fail in representing a system such as the human organism if they consistently exclude the brain or the heart from their theory, economists might fail in representing an economic system for certain explanatory purposes—such as for explaining the performance of a developing economy—if the isolations they employ exclude the role of institutions. Sticking to such ontologically ungrounded isolations would be tantamount to dealing with models that are nothing but fictional substitute systems.

These concepts can be used to deal with debate and progress in economics. Indeed, much of the difference, disagreement, debate, change, and progress in economics can be described in terms of rival and complementary isolations as well as requested and suggested de-isolations (whereby an assumption is relaxed so as to incorporate an additional causally relevant factor in one's model) and re-isolations (whereby the isolations of a model are revised so as to replace previously isolated factors by different ones). Such changes may contribute to progress in the sense of scope expansion (whereby new kinds of phenomena are successfully explained in terms of the same explanatory principles) or causal penetration (whereby black boxes are opened so as to reveal deeper causal mechanisms responsible for the phenomena to be explained). The debates and progressive moves in and around transaction cost economics exemplify these categories (Mäki 2004a).

12. Explanation, Mechanism, and Unification

Much of the time, economists describe their activities in terms of prediction, but there is no doubt that they also engage in explanatory practices. These practices, as *explanatory* practices, are still not very well understood, but a few things can be safely said about them. Explanatory practices typically involve theoretical modeling, and theoretical modeling is typically a matter of isolating causal mechanisms (Mäki 1992d, 1998b). Indeed, *mechanism* is one of economists' favorite words, used in a variety of contexts such as kinds of market mechanism, incentive mechanism, and transmission mechanism. Characteristically, mechanisms reside inside input-output systems, where they serve as the mediating causal chains between the input and output phenomena. A simple model is supposed to depict the bare skeleton of such a mediating economic mechanism. A mechanism in a successful surrogate system is sufficiently similar to the mechanism in the modeled real system. This is also what makes a model explanatory. By representing a mechanism inside an input-output system, economists not only convey knowledge *that* the input and the output are connected, they also conjecture *how* the input, together with the mechanism, produces the output. Answering *how* questions (How does input *I* produce output *O?*) enables economists to answer *why* questions (Why *O?*). And answering such *how* questions enables economists also to be more assured *that* there is a causal connection between *I* and *O,* thereby establishing a causal relationship where there appeared to be mere correlation or empirical regularity. Representing mechanisms may, therefore, also promote confirmation.

Much of theoretical model building in economics aims at explaining patterns of some generality—"stylized facts"—rather than singular events. It proceeds abductively, often attempting to answer the question, "What mechanism could have generated this pattern?" Such a model gives a possible (partial) explanation for the pattern by isolating a possible mechanism that could be causally responsible for, or could have significantly contributed to, the pattern. Much of economic modeling aims at *inference to a possible explanation*—rather than inference to the best explanation. A scientific realist should find such *how-possibly explanations* perfectly appropriate stages in an intellectual process towards *how-actually explanations* that describe the mechanisms and processes that actually have brought about the *explanandum* phenomenon. But if a how-possibly explanation appears to be the final destination rather than a phase on the way toward a how-actually explanation, the realist will raise questions about whether the exercise is leaning too much toward examining mere substitute systems. However, there is no denial that even a true how-possibly explanation may convey information about the modalities of the real world. Naturally, this presupposes that what the model describes is something stronger than just logical and physical possibility, namely, some sort of real social and cognitive possibility.

Much of explanatory activity in economics is driven by the ideal of *unification:* the urge to explain much by little, to explain many kinds of phenomena in terms of the same parsimonious explanatory principles. This shows in the insistence on micro foundations, in the avoidance of "ad hoc" explanations, and in the expansion of the explanatory endeavors of economics beyond its traditional disciplinary boundaries. (Mäki 1990b, 2001a, 2002b, 20079a; Kincaid 1997) For a long time, the ideal of *intra*-disciplinary unification has motivated and constrained practices of theorizing and explanation within economics, exemplified by Paul Samuelson's 1947 book *Foundations of Economic Analysis* and by the later doctrine of rational expectations. In the course of the last half a century, *inter*disciplinary explanatory expansion has become increasingly popular, as in Gary Becker's "economics imperialism." Explanatory unification may be based on more abstract explanatory principles and have a more universal reach, such as in the practice of insisting on rational choice micro foundations in economics, sociology, and political science. Or it may be less abstract and have a more local or regional reach, such as in using increasing returns and monopolistic competition for unifying (the phenomena explained by) location theory, trade theory, growth theory, and so on (Mäki & Marchionni 2009).

Explanatory unification is a generally respectable ideal of scientific theorizing. However, unification is neither uniform nor uniformly praiseworthy. Scientific realism can be taken to imply a constraint on preferred kinds of unification. If the accomplishment is mere *derivational unification* by way of deriving a large number of *explanandum* sentences from a parsimonious set of *explanans* sentences or from a compact sentential scheme, this as such is not yet to be celebrated. The realist will hail an accomplishment that makes claims about the real world, not just about logical relationships between sentences. The goal and achievement should be *ontological unification,* whereby an explanatory theory unifies what previously appeared to be different kinds of phenomena by establishing an ontic unity between them, by showing that they are of the same kind after all. Ontic unity between phenomena may be due to being constituted in the same way (all matter is made of atoms), or to being caused by the same causal mechanisms (falling apples and planetary motions are governed by the force of gravity). (Mäki 1990b, 2001a, 2002b, 2009a)

It is one thing to be able to derive sentences about prices and price levels, wages and unemployment, marriage and politics, crime and addiction, from other sentences about constrained optimization or interactive rational choices in a market. It is quite another thing to establish a unity between these phenomena by showing that they all are manifestations of such choices in the real world. Meeting the latter challenge may benefit from derivational achievements, but mere derivational connections are insufficient for ontological unification. Mere derivational unification without ontological grounding gives rise to justified suspicions of the unifying models being mere substitute systems. This much is at stake when judging whether Samuelson's and Becker's achievements are comparable to those of Newton.

13. Commonsensibles and the Way the World Works

The ontological constraints on economic theories and models are shaped by the peculiar ontology of economics as a social science. Physical sciences view the world as populated by quarks and photons, magnetic forces and black holes. The world as depicted by theoretical physics cannot be observed by human senses nor is it part of our familiar everyday world of ordinary experience. The ontology of physics departs from the commonsense world of stones and trees, chairs and tables. No similar ontological departure from the commonsense realm takes place in economics. Economics views the world more ordinarily, largely comprising familiar entities of folk psychology and commonsense social observation. The world of economics is the ordinary world of firms and households, preferences and expectations, money and prices, wages and interests, contracts and conventions, inflation and unemployment, imports and exports. Economic models refer to a world furnished with what I have coined *commonsensibles,* thus they do not postulate unobservables in the same sense that much of physics does (Mäki1990b, 1992b, 1996b, 1998a, 2005a).

In economic theorizing and modeling, commonsensibles are theoretically *modified* (selected, isolated, idealized, abstracted, simplified, aggregated): firms and households as strictly maximizing units without internal organization, complete and transitive preferences, infinitely lived agents, 2x2x2 economies, two-player games, zero transaction cost economies, and so on. Enabled by their modifications, commonsensibles are also *rearranged* concerning how their inter-relations are conceived. Rearrangement amounts to revising the commonsense understanding and replacing it by a theoretical picture of the causal structure of the world. A commonsense picture is replaced with a scientific picture that economists hope will get the causal and other dependencies right—such as in arguments for trade, against protectionism, and in dealing with collective action dilemmas—or generally by postulating various invisible-hand mechanisms between intentional action and unintended aggregate or collective outcomes. What from a commonsense point of view appears as paradoxical is turned less so by making the mediating mechanisms transparent. Realism about economics is a combination of commonsense realism and scientific realism (Mäki 1990b, 1996b, 1998a, 2005a; but see Ross 2005).

The fact that economic models are about commonsensibles has epistemological consequences. Classics in economic methodology, such as John Eliot Cairnes and Lionel Robbins, believed that economics is in a better position than physics in having more or less direct access to the basic constituents and causes of economic phenomena. This judgment is in need of elaboration. There may be commonsense access to the realm within which those constituents and causes reside. But the common sense alone is unable to identify them *as* the basic constituents and causes. Economic theory and inquiry is needed for this. (Mäki 1990c) Nevertheless, what remains significant is that the concepts, theories, and models of economics are strongly constrained by economists' commonsense intuitions, including intro-spection. This is only natural; after all, economists live their lives as observing and interpreting agents in the economies they model.

This idea of theories and models being constrained by background beliefs can be extended beyond mere common sense. Economists generally hold, at least implic-itly, ideas or visions of *the way the world works* (*www*). The sources of information contributing to the contents of the *www* conception are various, ranging from com-monsense experience and empirical data to academic education, scientific theories, metaphysical convictions, political and moral ideologies. The contents of this world-view deal with human behavioral dispositions (the role and degree of rationality, selfishness, sociality, morality), functioning of market mechanisms (whether they are predominantly negative or positive feedback mechanisms), boundaries of the economic realm (whether the economic realm is sharply separate from the realms of biology and sociology, for example), and many other things. The important point is that the *www* conception operates as an *ontological constraint* on economic theories, models, and explanations. The constraint mainly functions negatively: proposed theories, models, and explanations that do not meet the *www* constraint will be considered unfavorably—or will not be considered at all—by those holding the respective *www* conviction (or "intuition"—to use a popular phrase). This is how the ontological constraint starts playing an epistemological role, ruling out ideas not worthy of belief, acceptance, or further exploration. Much of disagreement and criticism between economists of different persuasions boil down to differences in their respective *www* convictions. Therefore, those disagreements cannot be understood or resolved by way of empirical testing only; the call is for ontological investigation and argument. (Mäki 2001b, 2008b)

14. Folk Psychology and Predictive Progress

My suggestion that economics is about (modified and rearranged) commonsensibles can be seen as an extension and modification of Alex Rosenberg's favorite idea that economics is formalized folk psychology. Folk psychology is the commonsense conceptualization of human action in terms of intentions and beliefs, desires and expectations, hopes and fears—all these familiar mental terms that humankind has kept using for millennia. Economic models formalize selected parts of folk psychology in terms of preferences and subjective probabilities, maximization, and rational expectations, etc.

Rosenberg (1992) believes this is a weakness and a source of failure of economics as an aspiring empirical science. His criterion of scientificity is predictive progress. Economics fails in generating predictive progress. The reason for its failure is its dependence on folk psychology. This is the reason because folk psychology fails to capture the deeper causes of human behavior. As long as economics is committed to the folk psychological framework, it cannot become a science.

I have not been a fan of this diagnosis (Mäki 1996a). I believe progress can be generated by way of further modifications and rearrangements of commonsensibles, including folk psychological items. One may make progress by moving from certainty to uncertainty in decision making, from unbounded to bounded rationality, from maximization to satisficing, from symmetric to asymmetric information, from fixed learning rules to evolving learning rules, from emotionally cold to emotionally ordinary agents, from asocial and amoral agents to ones with social and moral awareness, and so on. Such modifications among the commonsensibles pertaining to agents prompt further modifications among the social and institutional commonsensibles (including their inclusion in the models), such as firm structure, market structure, constitutional structure, incentive structure, and so on. Given that "predictive progress" can take on a variety of forms (that Rosenberg does not analyze), many such changes may amount to progress of some such forms. For example, a move from symmetric to asymmetric information or from zero to positive transaction costs in one's model may predict the emergence of an institutional structure that was beyond the horizon of previous models.

15. Realism and the Reality of Rhetoric

Rhetoric is real, and it matters. This is what a realist has to acknowledge in order to be realistic about actual science. Rhetoric is a matter of communication and persuasion, of an agent conveying meanings and beliefs to an audience. This is part of the social dimension of inquiry that is also built into my account of models. The presumed background beliefs and anticipated deliberations and responses of an audience—or several audiences—constrain the construction and use of models, their form and contents. Since a model had better be received as comprehensible and persuasive by the relevant audiences to be of any relevance to scientific inquiry and perhaps to policy purposes, the model is shaped by its anticipated and actualized reception. Note that the notion of an audience can be generalized so as to comprise the "internal audience" of the economist himself. Indeed, the economist carries out a lot of pretesting of his model in his private mind before submitting it to the verdict of external audiences. In both cases, the model is judged for its intelligibility and plausibility (Mäki 1992c, 1993b).

Much of what economists do is done with the purpose of persuading an audience or is done in a way that persuades an audience. There are many kinds of audience to be addressed directly or indirectly: colleagues in the same research field, students, journal editors and referees, department chairs and university administrators, other social scientists, lay people, the media, politicians. These audiences are persuaded to adopt this or that belief, such as of the scientificity or topicality of a theory or technique, of the efficacy of a piece of policy advice, of the excellence of the expertise of the author. Various rhetorical ploys are employed to persuade audiences, such as the use of accessible (sometimes inaccessible) language, illuminative metaphor, appeal to academic authority and trendiness, exhibition of mathematical brilliance, appeal to "intuition" and commonsense experience.

In McCloskey's (1983, 1994) seminal work on the rhetoric of economics, these ideas have been used for downplaying the ideas of objective reality and objective truth. (Arjo Klamer [2007] seems recently to have retreated from such an antirealist position.) What there is in the world and what is true of it becomes nothing but results of rhetorical persuasion. Truth *is* persuasiveness, so truths are collectively constructed in a rhetorical conversation. Truths are *made* amongst those who are eligible to participation in the conversation, namely, the well-educated and well-behaved economists, those who abide with the *Sprachethik,* subscribing to canons such as, "Don't lie; pay attention; don't sneer; cooperate; don't shout; let other people talk; be open-minded; explain yourself when asked; don't resort to violence or conspiracy in aid of your ideas." These canons define the notion of honest conversation in McCloskey's image of economics. Economics is made better by persuading economists to observe the *Sprachethik* and to raise their self-awareness of the rhetorical character of their activities, not by imposing methodological rules on their conduct.

In my alternative realist account of rhetoric, the world and truths about the world are not dependent on persuasion amongst economists and their audiences. I reject the presumption that the occurrence of rhetorical persuasion alone rules out the possibility of attaining and communicating persuasion-independent truths about economic reality (Mäki 1988, 1993a, 1995, 2000a, 2004c). We need to distinguish between *what is true* and *what counts as true* (in some culture or group, or at a certain time), or between *truth* and *plausibility*. Although what is plausible and what counts as true can be manipulated by rhetorical persuasion, what is true cannot. The same applies to what is real. We do not have to think that the *reality* of the connection between minimum wage and employment or the *truth* of our theory of it is a function of rhetorical persuasion, even if we think that our *belief* in its reality and in the truth of our theory of it can be influenced by rhetoric. A model—or a statement made in using it—is not made true (false) by being found persuasive (unpersuasive) by a cohort of economists with a certain educational background, academic incentive structure, and moral standards. Background beliefs and the institutional structure of economic inquiry play a very important role in what is found persuasive and in what counts as true at any given time. They also shape the likelihood of successfully tracking truths about the world by a community of inquirers. But they have nothing to do with what is and is not true. This is implied by my rhetorical realism.

An extreme line in resisting rhetorical realism and supporting antirealism could suggest that economics as it is currently practiced is *nothing but a rhetorical game of persuasion,* perhaps one that systematically violates the *Sprachethik,* that economics is not in the business of generating truthful information about the real world. It may be solely preoccupied with the study of the substitute worlds of theoretical models, whereas the so-called empirical tests would be just rhetorical exhibits. Empirically, I would respond by saying that even if this gloomy picture were correct about some parts of current economics, it is unlikely to be true about all of it. And normatively, the natural remedy would be to preach not just rhetorical self-awareness and the *Sprachethik,* but to preach them *together with realism.*

16. Economics of Economics

Economists customarily describe their scientific activity in terms of building and modifying models, and testing them by checking their refutable implications against empirical data. This portrays the activity as conforming to the canons of what is supposed to be the scientific method. The initiative to study the rhetoric of economics questions these traditional philosophical portrayals, but the attack from rhetoric is not in terms of economics itself—but neither are those traditional portrayals! Recently, some economists and many others, including a few philosophers of science, have started using economic ideas in depicting scientific activity itself—another imperialistic extension of economics as it were. The earlier simplified description of good science was in terms of disinterested scientists thrown in an institutional vacuum, and pursuing nothing but truthful (or otherwise epistemically adequate) information about the world. Now, scientists are portrayed as being driven by self-seeking desires in a competitive scientific market: they seek to maximize their own fame and fortune, credibility and prestige, and other such noncognitive personal utilities. This trend is taken by some to imply dispensing with traditional issues in scientific methodology, replacing it with a social science of science. (See Hands 2001.)

Although I do not think that traditional issues in methodology are dead at all, I am rather fascinated by these new developments toward expanding the domain of economics. Perhaps the most intriguing perspective is provided by what I have called the *economics of economics,* the attempt to look at economics itself in economic terms. Depending on one's choice of economic theory in depicting economics itself, the consequences may be dramatic (Mäki 2005b). One of my own contributions has been to look at Coasean transaction cost economics in its own lights (Mäki 1999). This is in line with Ronald Coase's own advice of doing methodology as an exercise in economics; indeed, he is all in favor of economics of economics. The result appears paradoxical.

Coase dislikes what he calls "blackboard economics," which is detached from real world issues, or economics that deals with models as substitute systems only, as we could say. Coase would prefer economics to engage in case studies so as to generate information about the details of real economies. But a higher-order application of his own transaction cost accounts to the study of economic science reveals the embarrassing result that blackboard economics is more transaction cost efficient than Coasean transaction cost economics: the intellectual and academic transaction costs of measuring and monitoring scientific performance are likely to be lower in formalized work examining substitute systems on the blackboard than in less standardized case studies of the complexities of real-world situations. Therefore, on Coasean grounds, blackboard economics is to be preferred—an outcome Coase flatly rejects!

In my view, the tension must be resolved by way of institutional design guided by realist tenets. The proposal would be to redesign academic institutions so as to shape the (production and transaction) cost structure of economic inquiry in a way that fortifies those academic incentives that function in support of efforts to build models as surrogate systems with the ambition of revealing significant truths about real-world economies.

17. How (Not) to Criticize Economics

What the foregoing observations reveal is that economic model building is driven and constrained by a variety of factors. It is actually constrained by principles, standards, ideals, conventions, and incentives that economists explicitly or implicitly accept as honorable. There are trade-offs between some of the constraints, thus choices have to be made such that not all constraints will be equally met by a given model or style of modeling. These trade-offs must be interpreted and choices be made in a justifiable manner. In my philosophy of economics, there is a super constraint entailed by a commitment to realism that should not be easily compromised. Here is a summary of what this means.

Economists build and use unrealistic models with unrealistic assumptions aiming at isolating possible mechanisms that also unify much while persuading various audiences. Model building is constrained by factors such as available data, mathematical tractability, theoretical tradition, rhetorical conventions, intellectual production and transaction costs, academic power relations, and other institutions of economics, as well as intellectual milieu and moral and political ideologies. These goals and constraints do not yet guarantee that the models are more than just fictional substitute systems.

Further rules are needed to ensure that the aforementioned sorts of constraint serve as favorable rather than unfavorable means in pursuing truthful information about the world. These include ideas such as the desirability of ontological (instead of mere derivational) unification; accepting any particular consideration of mathematical tractability only temporarily, not as a permanent constraint, and not as suppressing major ontological convictions; epistemically significant persuasiveness being dependent on a sufficiently open and democratic structure of the institutional conditions of rhetoric; and more. On such conditions, some of these constraints may serve justificatory functions. It is in the form of such rules that my realist methodology becomes more broadly normative.

From my realist point of view, there is no general problem with unrealistic models with unrealistic assumptions or the method of isolation by idealization. This means that the locus of appropriate criticism of any chunk of economics does not mostly lie at the level of general philosophical description of method, but rather at the level of how the method is used and how its use is constrained and what results it produces. For example, there may be worries about the contents of any particular *www* constraint, which should prompt ontological argument about the general worldviews driving and constraining economic modeling. There may be worries about particular methods being inappropriate or being inappropriately used in economic investigation, resulting in some systematic distortion or neglect of major facts about the social world. And there is a chance that the various pragmatic constraints, such as tractability and rhetorical conventions, or academic incentive structures, more generally, shape or suppress some appropriate *www* constraint in undesirable ways. The issues are mostly about realisticness, not about realism. (Mäki 1994b)

So one has to examine the social conditions under which economics makes claims about the world. The institutional-industrial organization of economics contributes to shaping the models and styles of modeling that are favored or are out of favor. Sometimes one may feel that it is easier to point out flaws in the social structure of economic inquiry than in that inquiry itself directly, by arguing that the institutional-industrial structure does not meet the ideal conditions of epistemically virtuous and successful science. This may be taken to have consequences for our assessment of its epistemic strategies and achievements: because economic theories, explanations, and policy advice are produced in institutionally imperfect conditions, we may expect those products to be imperfect as well. The academic and other reward structures may encourage epistemically low-ambition research in encouraging quantitative productivity (but on the other hand, normal science is supposed to be pretty much like this). They may encourage dogmatism and arrogance while suppressing critical and deviant voices (but on the other hand, a suitable degree of dogmatism is supposed to be a precondition for cumulative research). Once one starts listing such possible flaws, and is then reminded of the other side of the coin, things become more complicated again.

This is where the challenge lies—and it is a double challenge. We want to have economic models that provide us with truthful information about the real world. In order for economics to be capacitated and disposed to produce such models, economics had better operate in institutionally ideal conditions. In order for us to describe such ideal conditions and to estimate the distance between the actual and ideal conditions, we need another set of (metascientific) models of those conditions, capable of conveying truthful information about them. But if the former set of models are built in institutionally imperfect conditions, it is likely that the latter set of metamodels—models of modeling—will also be produced under imperfect conditions. Our judgments about the institutional conditions required for economics to produce truthful models of social reality, therefore, seem to be on no firmer ground than the economists' models themselves (Mäki 1993b, 1999, 2005b).

There is no reason for despair or nihilism. This is just what science is like, including the scientific and philosophical investigation of science itself—an imperfect human endeavor. The chance of error is there, particularly pronounced in sciences dealing with very complex subject matter; and science itself is a very complex socio-epistemic system, thus the possibility of error in making metalevel claims about science is also considerable. My scientific realist philosophy of economics entertains *epistemic ambition and optimism*, but—as any reasonable realism should—also subscribes to *fallibilism* as the superrule. This rule suggests that a systematic investigation of its possible errors be put on the research agenda of economics. Any discipline should openly recognize and examine its characteristic imperfections. Honesty and modesty is power. Arrogant and pretentious overconfidence would be an expression of weakness.

REFERENCES

Bhaskar, Roy (1975/1978). *A Realist Theory of Science*. Hassocks, England: Harvester Press.
Bhaskar, Roy (1979). *The Possibility of Naturalism*. Brighton, England: Harvester Press.
Blaug, Mark (2002). "Ugly Currents in Modern Economics." In *Fact and Fiction in Economics. Models, Realism, and Social Construction*, U. Mäki, Ed., 35–56. Cambridge, England: Cambridge University Press.
Cartwright, Nancy (1983). *How the Laws of Physics Lie*. Oxford: Clarendon.

Cartwright, Nancy (1989). *Nature's Capacities and their Measurement*. Oxford: Clarendon.

Friedman, Milton (1953). "The Methodology of Positive Economics." In his *Essays in Positive Economics*. Chicago: University of Chicago Press.

Guala, Francesco (2005). *The Methodology of Experimental Economics*. Cambridge, England: Cambridge University Press.

Hands, Wade (1994). "The Sociology of Scientific Knowledge." In *New Directions in Economic Methodology*, R. Backhouse, Ed., London: Routledge. 75–106.

Hands, Wade (2001). *Reflection without Rules. Economic Methodology and Contemporary Science Theory*. Cambridge, England: Cambridge University Press.

Harré, Rom (1970). *The Principles of Scientific Thinking*. Chicago: University of Chicago Press.

Hausman, Daniel (1981). *Capital, Profits, and Prices. An Essay in the Philosophy of Economics*. New York: Columbia University Press.

Hausman, Daniel (1992). *The Inexact and Separate Science of Economics*. Cambridge, England: Cambridge University Press.

Hindriks, Frank (2005). "Unobservability, Tractability, and the Battle of Assumptions." *Journal of Economic Methodology* 12: 383–406.

Hindriks, Frank (2006). "Tractability Assumptions and the Musgrave-Mäki Typology." *Journal of Economic Methodology* 13: 401–423.

Kincaid, Harold (1997). *Individualism and the Unity of Science*. Lanham: Rowman & Littlefield.

Klamer, Arjo (2007). *Speaking of Economics. How to Get in the Conversation*. London: Routledge.

Kuorikoski, Jaakko, Lehtinen, Aki, and Marchionni, Caterina (2008). "Economics as Robustness Analysis." (unpublished).

Lawson, Tony (1997). *Economics and Reality*. London: Routledge.

Lehtinen, Aki and Kuorikoski, Jaakko (2007). "Unrealistic Assumptions in Rational Choice Theory." *Philosophy of the Social Sciences* 37: 115–138.

Lipsey, Richard (1971). *An Introduction to Positive Economics*. London: Weidenfeld & Nicolson.

McCloskey, D.N. (1983). "The Rhetoric of Economics." *Journal of Economic Literature* 31: 434–461.

McCloskey, D.N. (1994). *Knowledge and Persuasion in Economics*. Cambridge, England: Cambridge University Press.

Mäki, Uskali (1986). "Rhetoric at the Expense of Coherence: A Reinterpretation of Milton Friedman's Methodology." *Research in the History of Economic Thought and Methodology* 4: 127–143.

Mäki, Uskali (1988). "How to Combine Rhetoric and Realism in the Methodology of Economics." *Economics and Philosophy* 4: 89–109. Reprinted in *The Philosophy and Methodology of Economics*, Bruce Caldwell, Ed. Aldershot, England: Edward Elgar.

Mäki, Uskali (1989). "On the Problem of Realism in Economics." *Ricerche Economiche* 43: 176–198. Reprinted in *The Philosophy and Methodology of Economics*, Bruce Caldwell, Ed. Aldershot, England: Edward Elgar.

Mäki, Uskali (1990a). "Methodology of Economics: Complaints and Guidelines." *Finnish Economic Papers* 3: 77–84.

Mäki, Uskali (1990b). "Scientific Realism and Austrian Explanation." *Review of Political Economy* 2: 310–344.

Mäki, Uskali (1990c) "Mengerian Economics in Realist Perspective." *History of Political Economy*, Annual Supplement to Vol. 22: 289–310.

Mäki, Uskali (1992a). "On the Method of Isolation in Economics." *Poznan Studies in the Philosophy of the Sciences and the Humanities* 26: 319–354. Reprinted in *Recent Developments in Economic Methodology*, J. Davis, Ed. Cheltenham, England, Elgar.

Mäki, Uskali (1992b). "Friedman and Realism." *Research in the History of Economic Thought and Methodology* 10: 171–195.

Mäki, Uskali (1992c). "Social Conditioning of Economics." In E. de Marchi, Ed., *Post-Popperian Methodology of Economics*, 65–104. Dordrecht, The Netherlands: Kluwer Publishers.

Mäki, Uskali (1992d). "The Market as an Isolated Causal Process: A Metaphysical Ground for Realism." In *Austrian Economics: Tensions and New Developments*, B. Caldwell & S. Boehm, Eds., 35–59. Dordrecht, The Netherlands: Kluwer Publishers.

Mäki, Uskali (1993a). "Two Philosophies of the Rhetoric of Economics." In *Economics and Language*, W. Henderson, T. Dudley-Evans, & R. Backhouse, Eds., 23–50. London: Routledge.

Mäki, Uskali (1993b). "Social Theories of Science and the Fate of Institutionalism in Economics." In *Rationality, Institutions and Economic Methodology*, U. Mäki, B. Gustafsson, & C. Knudsen, Eds., 76–109. London: Routledge.

Mäki, Uskali (1994a). "Isolation, Idealization and Truth in Economics." In *Idealization in Economics*, B. Hamminga & N. de Marchi, Eds., special issue of *Poznan Studies in the Philosophy of the Sciences and the Humanities* 38: 147–168.

Mäki, Uskali (1994b). "Reorienting the Assumptions Issue." In *New Directions in Economic Methodology*, R. Backhouse, Ed. London: Routledge. 236–256.

Mäki, Uskali (1995). "Diagnosing McCloskey." *Journal of Economic Literature* 3: 1300–1318. Reprinted in *Recent Developments in Economic Methodology*, J. Davis, Ed. Cheltenham, England: Elgar.

Mäki, Uskali (1996a). "Two Portraits of Economics." *Journal of Economic Methodology* 3: 1–38.

Mäki, Uskali (1996b). "Scientific Realism and Some Peculiarities of Economics." In *Realism and Anti-Realism in the Philosophy of Science*, R.S. Cohen *et al*, Eds., Dordrecht, The Netherlands: Kluwer. 425–445.

Mäki, Uskali (1998a). "Aspects of Realism about Economics." *Theoria* 13: 301–319. Reprinted in *Recent Developments in Economic Methodology*, J. Davis, Ed. Cheltenham, England: Elgar.

Mäki, Uskali (1998b). "Mechanisms, Models, and Free Riders." In *Economics and Methodology. Crossing the Boundaries*, R. Backhouse, D. Hausman, U. Mäki, & A. Salanti, Eds. Macmillan. 98–112.

Mäki, Uskali (1999). "Science as a Free Market: A Reflexivity Test in an Economics of Economics." *Perspectives on Science* 7: 486–509. Reprinted in *Recent Developments in Economic Methodology*, J. Davis, Ed. Cheltenham, England, Elgar.

Mäki, Uskali (2000a). "Performance Against Dialogue, or Answering and Really Answering: A Participant Observer's Reflections on the McCloskey Conversation." *Journal of Economic Issues* 34: 43–59.

Mäki, Uskali (2000b). "Kinds of Assumptions and Their Truth: Shaking an Untwisted F-twist." *Kyklos* 53: 303–322.

Mäki, Uskali (2001a). "Explanatory Unification: Double and Doubtful." *Philosophy of the Social Sciences* 31: 488–506.

Mäki, Uskali (2001b). "The Way the World Works (www): Towards an Ontology of Theory Choice." In *The Economic World View. Studies in the Ontology of Economics*, U Mäki, Ed. Cambridge, England: Cambridge University Press. 369–389.

Mäki, Uskali (2001c). "Models." In *International Encyclopedia of the Social and Behavioral Sciences*, Volume 15, 9931–9937. Amsterdam: Elsevier.

Mäki, Uskali (2001d). "Realisms and Their Opponents." In *International Encyclopedia of the Social and Behavioral Sciences*, Volume 19, 12815–12821. Amsterdam: Elsevier.

Mäki, Uskali (2002a). "Some Non-reasons for Non-realism about Economics." In *Fact and Fiction in Economics. Realism, Models, and Social Construction*, U. Mäki, Ed. Cambridge, England: Cambridge University Press. 90–104.

Mäki, Uskali (2002b). "Explanatory Ecumenism and Economics Imperialism." *Economics and Philosophy* 18; 237–259.

Mäki, Uskali (2003). " 'The Methodology of Positive Economics' (1953) Does Not Give Us *the* Methodology of Positive Economics." *Journal of Economic Methodology* 10: 495–505.

Mäki, Uskali (2004a). "Theoretical Isolation and Explanatory Progress: Transaction Cost Economics and the Dynamics of Dispute." *Cambridge Journal of Economics* 28: 319–346.

Mäki, Uskali (2004b). "Realism and the Nature of Theory: A Lesson from J.H. von Thünen for Economists and Geographers." *Environment and Planning A* 36: 1719–1736.

Mäki, Uskali (2004c). "Some Truths about Truth for Economists, Their Critics and Clients." In *Economic Policy-Making under Uncertainty: The Role of Truth and Accountability in Policy Advice*, P. Mooslechner, H. Schuberth, & M. Schurtz, Eds. Cheltenham: Edward Elgar. 9–39.

Mäki, Uskali (2005a). "Reglobalising Realism by Going Local, or (How) Should Our Formulations of Scientific Realism Be Informed about the Sciences." *Erkenntnis* 63: 231–251.

Mäki, Uskali (2005b). "Economic Epistemology: Hopes and Horrors." *Episteme: A Journal of Social Epistemology* 1: 211–220.

Mäki, Uskali (2005c). "Models are Experiments, Experiments are Models." *Journal of Economic Methodology* 12: 303–315.

Mäki, Uskali (2008a). "Unrealistic Assumptions and Unnecessary Confusions: Rereading and Rewriting F53 as a Realist Statement." In *The Methodology of Positive Economics. Milton Friedman's Essay Fifty Years Later*, U. Mäki, Ed. . Cambridge, England: Cambridge University Press.

Mäki, Uskali (2008b). "Scientific Realism and Ontology." In *The New Palgrave Dictionary of Economics,* 2nd edition. London: Palgrave Macmillan.

Mäki, Uskali (2008c). "Method and Appraisal in Economics, 1976–2006." *Journal of Economic Methodology* 15, forthcoming.

Mäki, Uskali (2009a). "Models and the Locus of Their Truth." *Synthese*, forthcoming.

Mäki, Uskali (2009b). "MISSing the World. Models as Isolations and Credible Surrogate Systems." *Erkenntnis*, forthcoming.

Mäki, Uskali (2009c). "Economics Imperialism: Concept and Constraints." *Philosophy of the Social Sciences*, forthcoming.

Mäki, Uskali & Marchionni, Caterina (2009). "On the Structure of Explanatory Unification: The Case of Geographical Economics." *Studies in the History and Philosophy of Science*, forthcoming.

Marchionni, Caterina (2006). "Contrastive Explanation and Unrealistic Models: The Case of New Economic Geography." *Journal of Economic Methodology* 13: 425–446.

Mayer, Thomas (1993). *Truth versus Precision in Economics.* Aldershot, England: Elgar.

Morgan, Mary (2005). "Experiments Versus Models: New Phenomena, Inference and Surprise." *Journal of Economic Methodology* 12: 317–329.

Musgrave, Alan (1981). " 'Unreal Assumptions' in Economic Theory: The F-twist Untwisted." *Kyklos* 34: 377–387.

Nowak, Leszek (1980). *The Structure of Idealization.* Dordrecht, The Netherlands: Reidel.

Rosenberg, Alexander (1976). *Microeconomic Laws.* Pittsburgh: University of Pittsburgh Press.

Rosenberg, Alexander (1992). *Economics: Mathematical Politics or Science of Diminishing Returns?* Chicago: University of Chicago Press.

Ross, Don (2005). *Economic Theory and Cognitive Science.* Cambridge MA: MIT Press.

von Thünen, Johann Heinrich (1910). *Der isolierte Staat in Beziehung auf Landwirtschaft und Nationalökonomie.* Jena: Verlag von Gustav Fischer.

CHAPTER 5

WHY THERE IS (AS YET) NO SUCH THING AS AN ECONOMICS OF KNOWLEDGE

PHILIP MIROWSKI

ONCE upon a time, say around the era of David Ricardo and Karl Marx, political economy was primarily concerned with the production of national wealth. This "classical" notion tended to hang on long into the twentieth century, well after the invention of neoclassical economics in the 1870s (Mirowski 1989, chapter 7). Nevertheless, there was no denying that within neoclassical economics, exchange had displaced production as the primary topic of interest; this informed the definition of economics articulated by Lionel Robbins that its proper subject was the "allocation of scarce means among given ends." But subsequently something rather extraordinary happened around the middle of the twentieth century, gaining momentum as the century waned. More and more, economics at the cutting edge (as opposed to in the textbooks) became relatively cavalier about treating trade as static allocation, and instead became all wrapped up in the image of the market (or the agent) as a processor of information or knowledge. I am not referring here simply to the phenomenon of the award of the Bank of Sweden Prize to George Akerlof, Michael Spence, and Joseph Stiglitz at the dawn of our millennium

(Stiglitz 2002), or to arcane disputes over something called "common knowledge" in game theory (Aumann 2000; Geanokoplos 1992; Samuelson 2004), or assertions that knowledge was the source of all economic growth (Romer 1990), or endless arguments over whether rationality is "bounded" or not (Conlisk 1996). I mean instead that, if your goal in life was to get published in a highly-ranked economics journal, you could no longer safely cast your analysis in terms of the old familiar trope of static allocation. As Kenneth Arrow (in Colander et al. 2004, 292) put it, "one of the biggest differences between 1950 and 2000 is the much greater role now given to the role of knowledge and information." Economists now bandy about the term *information* in their papers almost as freely as they had once resorted to the term *prices*. Clearly something epoch-making had happened to economics, but what precisely was it? Had the avant-garde imperiously consigned all that had gone before to a bonfire of the vanities? Sometimes the more impetuous among the cognoscenti wrote as though it did:

> There is no single new Law of Economics...The world is not convex; the
> behavior of the economy cannot be described as if it were solving a (simple)
> maximization problem; the law of supply and demand has been repealed
> (Stiglitz 1985, 22)

In other instances, various notables hastened to reassure the rest of us that nothing had really changed at all, and that, contrary to most impressions, the info-fascination was just a minor variation on the age-old wisdom of neoclassical economics: (Shapiro & Varian 1999; Varian 2002; Kreps 1997). Both stories were equally implausible; and this ushers us toward the nub of the present philosophical perplexity. How can it be that everyone seems to believe that there has been some sort of Great Transformation of Economics into a Science of Knowledge, and yet be utterly incapable of producing even a spare consensus on the hallmark doctrines of the New Order?[1] Risking ridicule, one can't help but wonder: How do they *know* that knowledge has become central to the discipline? This paradox will lead us into an even deeper question: How is it possible that a neoclassical economic theory, committed to a thoroughly ahistorical noncontextual theory of equilibrium (and notoriously weak on how that equilibrium is attained), could provide an adequate account of the process by which knowledge is gained, interpreted, and understood? At minimum, one might expect that such expert economic epistemologists could inform us about how they managed to arrive at such an important breakthrough—but there is no such rendition anywhere to be found. Instead, what we are proffered are a motley of just-so stories about how novel mathematical tools caused the scales to fall from their eyes, or else a fable about how some prophetic scholars woke up to the fact that the neoclassical tradition had been neglecting psychology for over a century, or else a foible of entirely vacuous appeals to the natural progress of science.[2] Hasn't it become apparent that something is awry with these Wizards of the Knowledge Economy? With each subsequent attempted dismissal of the question, the weasel reveals more of his glinting tooth. Never was there a greater need for philosophical reflection, even in a discipline that spurns philosophy as a matter of course.

Here I will put forth the proposition that there has been no such thing as a cogent "neoclassical" explanation of the recent ambition to propound a neoclassical Economics of Knowledge.[3] It suffers from the bad habit of presuming what it cannot demonstrate. The very notion that austere utility maximization could induce economists to develop a naturalized epistemology and a rich cognitive psychology smacks too much of magic realism. Yet many economists find it perfectly natural to shrug off such paradoxes of self-reference: they have yet to suffer the consequences of their insouciance. To the modern economist, philosophers appear to constitute about as much danger to their prognostications as do literary critics. Therefore, I shall also endeavor to point out that all major existing modern traditions of the Economics of Knowledge have encountered their comeuppance *solely from within,* leading various economists to concede (if not entirely acknowledge) that their own constructions of the epistemology of the agent were structurally incoherent. If I am correct about this, then the widespread contemporary conviction that our science possesses a glittering new toolkit in the form of an Economics of Knowledge is all the more puzzling, and requires further serious explanation.

I shall then press against the grain by suggesting that this phenomenon will never be adequately understood by disembodied analysis alone—that is, by the kind of arguments most frequently found in the philosophical literature. The fact that the contemporary neoclassical orthodoxy stands proud of a nonexistent achievement cannot simply be reduced to the temporary self-deception of the isolated rational agent, or the satisficing outcome of costly ratiocination, or else some sort of focal point causing every strategic scientist to converge upon a Nash equilibrium. A purely decision-theoretic conception of philosophy stands helpless before this phenomenon, even though we shall argue later that specific traditions within philosophy can help illuminate the reasons that various analytical options have hit intractable roadblocks. At the end of the day, the looming question remains: How can so much intellectual effort have shown such paltry results?

Economics as a discipline subsists as one science within an ecology of neighboring sciences, one species within a deme, and is not comprised of a single pure breed of representative agent. This alone renders the pretence of a unique economics of knowledge hard to comprehend. The effulgent diversity of theories, schools, and doctrines, even within a discipline that appears monologically intolerant of dissent to outsiders, dictates that the movement and interplay of ideas and inducements must be tracked through time, as collective phenomena. This type of explanation can only be adequately prosecuted through historical research. Here I endeavor to make this case for the transformation of neoclassical economics from a self-conception as being concerned with allocation to a discipline besotted with epistemic questions about the agent, and insist upon historical determinations as emanating from both inside and outside economics. Once that is gotten out of the way, we can then explore the proposition that the Shopkeeper of Information parades about in the buff.

I should also signal that many of the various models of the epistemic agent described later also appear in the work of many philosophers, but this chapter is solely concerned with the problems they have encountered *within economics*. The larger implications for philosophy will have to be postponed to some other venue.

1. Cognopolis: The Conditions that have Promoted the Existence of an Economics of Knowledge (or, Economic History for Philosophers)

As Dan Schiller perceptively queried almost two decades ago, "Why wasn't the status of information a major topic in economic theory in 1700, 1800, or 1900? Why was it only in the postwar period that the economic role and value of information took on such palpable importance?" (1988, 32) The easy retort that it was inadvertently overlooked until WWII simply will not stand up to scrutiny. Rather, there were very specific historical conditions that stood as necessary prerequisites for the seeming inevitability of the spectacle of economists blithely placing knowledge on a par with knishes or narcotics. There was something overdetermined about the epistemic turn in economics, which needs to be situated in a larger frame, if only to invest our eventual negative verdict with a greater degree of plausibility.

Our initial point of departure is the phenomenon of the "cognitive turn" or "cognitive revolution" taken in most social and natural sciences in the period immediately following WWII in America, as outlined in detail in (Mirowski 2002; Baars 1986; Gigerenzer & Murray 1987; Capuro & Hjorland 2002). The immediate implication of such a dramatic shift was the heightened likelihood that economics would be caught up in the enthusiasm, as indeed it was. "Information" became a topic of mathematical models starting in the 1920s, and had begun to spread throughout the *natural* sciences in WWII. Claude Shannon's "information theory" started off as an attempt to theorize cryptography (Mirowski 2002, 68–76), and it rapidly became conflated/confused with a formal theory of intelligence. A concern over military intelligence led to the founding of a science of military decision theory, carried out under the rubric of operations research. This development was crucial for all of the social sciences, full of implications for the ontological status of information vs. knowledge, but we must merely take it as given here. The other development we may provisionally treat as exogenous was the construction and stabilization of the first electronic digital computers in WWII. The physical instantiation of machines that think (whatever was intended by such locutions) provided irresistible metaphors for cognitive activities, many of which would be taken up to various degrees in all of the social sciences in the postwar expansion of academic research. These physical traditions concerning the sciences of information set the stage for a later reconstruction of economics, rendering some attempt at accommodation nearly inevitable. However, there also subsisted conditions peculiar to economics that definitively shaped the way that these ideas would be understood within the expanding program of neoclassical economics.

Perhaps the next most significant event for economics was a dispute that originated within the Austrian tradition, namely, the "Socialist Calculation Controversy."[4] Starting in the 1920s, a stellar array of economists (and even some philosophers, such as Otto Neurath) began to argue for or against the proposition that socialist planning was impossible in principle, due primarily to epistemic considerations. A few salient aspects of the Controversy are useful to remember when it comes to discussing the economics of knowledge. The first is that almost every figure whom we shall cite in Section 4 made a point of insisting upon the relevance of their favored informational approaches to reconsideration of the ultimate verdict of the socialist calculation controversy. In other words, whatever you personally believed about the economics of knowledge, there was no gainsaying the fact that everyone knew the topic was freighted with profound political implications, with consequences that stayed relatively close to the surface in the work of those covered here. The second fact is that two of the major protagonists in the calculation controversy then went on to facilitate development of two of the primary characteristic doctrines of the modern cognitive regime in economics: Oskar Morgenstern played a crucial supporting role in the invention of game theory;[5] and Friedrich Hayek engineered the incubator for the modern neoliberal versions of the "marketplace of ideas."[6] Thus the Controversy had reverberations down throughout the annals of postwar modern microeconomics, far beyond the narrow confines of comparative systems or the economics of planning.

The Socialist Calculation Controversy was the event that began, ever so slowly, to shift the prevailing image of the function of The Market among all persuasions of neoclassical theorists. Due to the fallout of the Controversy, it began to be less fashionable to concentrate too intently upon the supposed nature of welfare outcomes to the neglect of what it was the agent supposedly knew. One of the very few histories of twentieth-century economics to take note of this phenomenon, Nicola Giocoli's *Modeling Rational Agents* (Giocoli 2003), suggests that pre–WWII theorists were driven by the dual motives to escape from psychological commitments and abjure assumptions of "perfect knowledge," but that these motives were contradictory, prompting postwar economists to opt for a desiccated redefinition of rationality as formal consistency of static plans and preferences. While the uneasy relationship of neoclassical economics to academic psychology has been (and continues to be, e.g., Bruni & Sugden 2007) an important boundary condition for the modern definition of the economics profession, Giocoli's narrative suffers from an excessive reading of the postwar cognitive concerns back into the prewar welfare concepts: in economics, the prewar dependence upon supposed "perfect knowledge" was rather, in practice, the banishment of any formal conception of knowledge whatsoever. *Knowledge* might get mentioned in passing in pre-WWI economic commentary, but it had no palpable instantiation in the neoclassical models themselves. *Welfare* was hidden and inaccessible, lodged within the recesses of the intrinsically unknowable mind of the agent. People were treated a monads, requiring neither communication nor agent interaction. The delayed elevation of game theory to canonical status in microeconomics was one reaction to this *idiot savant* of an economic agent, but as we shall describe in detail below, the set of proposals was far more diverse than Giocoli ever admits. Indeed, as Hands (2006) has argued, Giocoli partakes of the conventional internalist narrative that the "ordinalist revolution" from "utility" to revealed preference over the course of the century stripped the agent to bare logical essentials, and managed to render neo-classical economics simultaneously both more observable and less beholden to any cognitive commitments; but this conventional wisdom is historically unsupported and conceptually weak. Not only do I wholeheartedly agree with Hands' account;[7] I will venture even further to point out that neoclassical economists circa 1950 managed the near-miraculous feat of seeming to dispense with psychology while endowing their agents with prodigious epistemic powers. This is a balancing act worthy of *Cirque du Soleil,* one that can set the audience's head spinning, and needs an instant replay in slow motion to appreciate the careening prestidigitation. It is the slow-motion map of that activity that this paper seeks to provide in subsequent sections.

In philosophy, one tends to treat questions of knowledge as timeless; but in economics, this would lead to confusion and worse. It was not merely intellectual jousts like the Socialist Calculation Controversy, but also distinctly material developments within the advanced industrial economies, something one might call the "economic history of knowledge," that also summoned forth the postwar fascination with an economics of knowledge. These tended to materialize somewhat later, after 1980.

The worldly philosophers with their epistemic ambitions were administered two quick jolts by events in the real world. The first was the progressive de-industrialization of the older developed economies, which gained momentum after the fall of the Berlin Wall; and the second was the across-the-board neoliberal[8] push to commercialize science and privatize education on a global scale. These dual phenomena could not help but transform the context for the debut and persistence of an Economics of Knowledge, as well as deflect its trajectory.

The United States had been losing net manufacturing employment to production facilities overseas since 1989 (Burke, et al. 2004). Some pundits sought to try and impose a positive spin on the phenomenon, by suggesting that advanced economies were becoming increasingly weightless, or would graduate to a third stage of capitalism consisting almost exclusively of the service sector, or indeed disengage from gross physical production processes altogether. Of course, most people recognized that much of that talk bordered on delusional, but nevertheless managed to appear sensible by engaging in locutions such as "The Information

Society" or "The New Knowledge Economy."[9] For the reader, these terms may seem impossibly quaint, but that would discount the extent to which these notions have become entrenched as second nature among bureaucrats and the denizens of business schools. As Walter Powell put it, "If the knowledge economy is measured by the rise in knowledge management services among consulting firms or by the rapid growth in intellectual property as a legal specialty, then its growth has been considerable" (Powell & Snellman 2004, 199). For those in search of cognpolitan career paths, the contemporary options must seem like Hobson's choice, with the future consisting either of slinging hamburgers at minimum wage or else becoming a Knowledge Worker in some urban office building. Lest the reader think this merely the airy froth of the chattering classes, let us quote a recent Nobel economist:

> The scientific revolution of the past century has resulted in the systematization of change itself...Knowledge and information is being produced today as cars and steel were produced one hundred years ago...the standard theorems of welfare economics, which underlay the presumption of the efficiency of the market economy, *assume* that information and knowledge is unaffected by any action taken by any participant. Thus standard economic theory has little to say about the efficiency of the knowledge-based economy...We are slowly shedding the limitations of Matter to unleash the expansiveness of non-rivalrous Ideas. (Stiglitz 1999)

However much the siren song of "Pure Transcendent Idealism" managed to bewitch economics at the end of the millennium, or however much it was in the nature of the Capitalist Spirit actually to slip the surly bond ratings of Earth, it seems fairly clear that neoclassical economics was coming under heavy pressure to claim that it could analyze knowledge as well or better than it could analyze cars or steel. The fact that it had only sporadically attempted to do so in a desultory manner prior to the 1980s was not seen as some insurmountable obstacle: Indeed, the inducements to sing encomia to the Knowledge Economy fructified possible analytical options when it came to neoclassical economics. Readers should keep this fact in mind when they are confronted with multiple analytical versions of the economics of knowledge in subsequent sections.

The other salient development in the world of commerce was the broad-based corporate push to commercialize science, education, and intellectual property in general in the period following 1980 (Mirowski, forthcoming). In the legal and business literature, this is now regarded as one of the major watersheds of recent modern economic history.[10] The fact that this information enclosure movement is not confined to the United States and Europe, but is in intent and execution a global trend, speaks volumes about how the status of knowledge has become a ubiquitous source of naked political controversy in the modern world.[11] Once again, for the purposes of this paper we must take this phenomenon as exogenous and given, and yet it is difficult to overstate its importance for our present topic. Yet this modern appropriation of science and its accoutrements takes the syllogism one step further: If knowledge is to be deemed the ultimate source of economic success, then it should by all rights itself be subject to the greatest degree possible to market organization and discipline, or so say the promoters of the New Enclosure of the Knowledge Commons. Of course, if economics had turned out to have had nothing much to say about knowledge, than this entire neoliberal project would have had to find its rationale and slogans elsewhere. But such an opportunity would never be passed up so imperiously—and, therefore, the Economics of Knowledge finds itself poised in the thick of one of the most consequential battles of the day: the dispute over whether the process of intellectual inquiry itself qualifies a market process on all fours with the shilling of movies or shelling of peas.

In the latter half of the twentieth century, there was no sanctioned unified response coming from within the community of economists to these linked challenges. Hence the first fallacy we seek to dispel in this paper is the pretence that there now exists a *single tradition of the orthodox economics of knowledge*.[12] The neoclassical program was born into a state of epistemic agnosticism (Mirowski 1989) and, therefore, came equipped with no privileged definition of knowledge ideally suited to *homo economicus*. This should go without saying, except for the fact that almost every major figure we shall encounter, from Kenneth Arrow to Gary Becker, from Robert Lucas to Larry Samuelson, from Joseph Stiglitz to Robert Aumann, from Fritz Machlup to Paul Romer to Dominique Foray, persists in writing as though it were the case. Here the banishment of history from the training of modern economists has begun to take its toll. It is certainly true that enthusiasts for one recent version of Nash game theory have tended to curry their own favored epistemic approach, as do the heirs to the Chicago School or members of that broad church shared by the high priests of the metempsychosis of the nonexcludable "public good." Yet none of these can be conceptually reduced to any of the others.

The cognopolitan building sites where the different versions of the economics of knowledge were forged would include: the military-induced school of decision theory; the tradition of game theory fostered within the incubator of operations research (Mirowski 2002); the field of mechanism design (Lee 2006); the movement massed under the banner of "rational expectations theory" (Sent 1998); the disparate variants of the "economics of information" (Macho-Stadler & Perez-Castrillo 2001; Phlips 1988); the promiscuous inquiry dubbed the "economics of innovation" (Foray 2004); organization theory (Antonelli 2005; Amin & Cohendet 2004); the burgeoning area of the "economics of science" (Mirowski & Sent 2002); the economics of intellectual property (Landes & Posner 2003; Scotchmer 2004) and extends even into nascent areas such as so-called behavioral economics and neuroeconomics (Glimcher 2003; Camerer *et al* 2005).

There are undoubtedly others as well.[13] This paper would be foolish to aspire to describe, categorize, and taxonomize every single branch and rhizome of neoclassical theory that has ever displayed pretensions to pronounce on knowledge—such an encyclopaedia still does not exist at this late date, itself a significant fact.

Instead, we will provide an overview of what we claim are the three main modalities by which knowledge has been conceptualized and portrayed within all these diverse subfields of neoclassical theory.

2. EVERY DOGMA HAS ITS DAY: THE MARKETPLACE OF IDEAS AS HAYEKIAN PRELUDE

In the beginning, neoclassical economics sought to explain the prices of tangible commodities—what the market was supposed to be busily churning out. Whatever it was that the traders involved believed about those goods, or each other, or indeed about the market itself, might conceivably have had some bearing on the trading outcome; figures such as Edgeworth, Marshall, Pareto, and others all conceded this point at one time or another. Some Europeans seemed more exorcized about the problem than most American economists (Giocoli 2003). Nevertheless, they all subscribed to the conviction that the operation of the market was effectively separable from questions of epistemology, and that such questions could be safely left to others.[14] This status quo began to change early in the twentieth century.

Neoliberal intellectuals love to point to early prewar instances anticipating the metaphor of the marketplace of ideas, especially those found in the realm of American jurisprudence.[15] However, they rarely admit that such metaphoric flights were nowhere to be found in formal neoclassical economics, at least until they began to surface, not in America, but rather in the writings of the later generations of the Austrian School. The fruits of the intellectual ferment in Vienna for philosophy and economics, from the positivism of the Vienna Circle to the mathematical innovations of the *Mengerkreis,* are well known in the historical literature. What has been less explored is the role of the Austrian school in elevating the notion that the fundamental role of the market was, not the static allocation of things, but rather the processing and conveyance of knowledge: In other words, the "marketplace of ideas" was not merely a *façon de parler,* but a very real phenomenon.

The pivotal protagonist in this transmutation was Friedrich Hayek. At one time, it was commonplace to portray Hayek as a figure who was defeated in midcareer by John Maynard Keynes, and consigned to exile outside the legitimate economics discipline; but recent research has reversed this verdict.[16] Not only is Hayek now regarded as the godfather of the rise of the neoliberal movement, and the entrepreneur behind the establishment of the Chicago School of economics; but he is also now conceded to be the locus of real intellectual inspiration behind the cognitive revolution in American neoclassical economics. The marketplace of ideas constitutes the fire within and the fuel behind the three versions of the economics of knowledge described later in Section 3, and hence it becomes crucial to understand the extent to which it was intimately bound up with the establishment of Neoliberalism in social science in America and Europe. The origins of the marketplace of ideas in such postwar Hayekian projects as the Society for Freedom in Science, the Mont Pelerin Society, the University of Chicago economics department, Chicago law and economics, and his connectionist theory of mind, will provide some indication of the political valence of the catallactic approach to knowledge.

Neoliberalism, as it developed after WWII, diverged from classical liberalism in a number of ways; it renounced the passive notion of a *laissez faire* economy in favor of an activist and constructivist approach to the spread and promotion of free markets.[17] The starting point of neo-liberalism is the admission, contrary to classical liberalism, that their political program will only triumph if it becomes reconciled to the fact that the conditions for its success must be *constructed,* and will not come about on its own in the absence of concerted effort. This had direct implications for the neoliberal attitude toward the state, as well as toward political parties and other corporate entities that were the result of conscious organization, and not simply unexplained organic growths. In a phrase, the market could not be depended upon to naturally conjure up the conditions for its own continued flourishing. As Milton Friedman once joked in a letter to Friedrich Hayek, "our faith requires that we are skeptical of the efficacy, at least in the short run, of organized efforts to promulgate [the creed]" (in Hartwell 1995, xiv). The ultimate purpose of institutions such as the Mont Pelerin Society and the Chicago School was not so much to revive a dormant classical liberalism as it was to forge a neoliberalism better suited to modern conditions. The conundrum of the right-wing intellectual in the Depression and in WWII was to explain why people in general could not comprehend the political truth of the dangers of a planned economy, and thus reconcile their dismay with their commitments to personal freedom. Hayek's response to the conundrum was to insist that intellectuals were at fault: they were secondhand dealers in ideas, and had promulgated false and misleading images of what the market was and what it did.

It may seem incongruous, but the resolution of Hayek's problem situation was eventually to be found in the promotion of the idiom of the marketplace of ideas to pride of place in neoliberal theory. As he wrote in his much-quoted 1945 address "The Use of Knowledge in Society":

> The economic problem of society is thus not merely a problem of how to
> allocate 'given' resources...It is rather a problem of how to secure the best use
> of resources known to any of the members of society, for ends whose relative
> importance only those individuals know...it is a problem of the integration of
> knowledge which is not given to anyone in its totality. (1948, 77–8)

This revision of "the economic problem" was the seed from which both Neoliberalism and the quest for an economics of knowledge would germinate, but at this early stage Hayek himself could not foresee all its progeny; nor indeed would he subsequently accept patrimony for each and every pretender. Nevertheless, this insistence that the market first and foremost dealt in knowledge rather than more mundane physical stuff was immensely suggestive, at least in part because the exact semantic referent of the problem was left relatively vague in Hayek's writings. Did his claim refer to human nature, or to the market as a discrete entity, or to the products of cognition, or to something about society as a whole? Sometimes he treated the market as a *processor* of information, inspired by his own early work on psychology, and amplified by the fascination with the postwar computer and cybernetics that surrounded him in America. Sometimes he shifted register to suggest that ideas were things that were conveyed through market processes, as in his disparagement of the second-hand dealers whom he sought to displace. Sometimes he jumped levels to have it inform a philosophical thesis about what could and could not be known by humans in principle. Although it is true that Hayek himself never resorted to the explicit terminology of a "marketplace of ideas," and kept his distance from some acolytes at Chicago who did, there is no denying that, in the coterie of conservative intellectuals associated with Mont Pelerin, the University of Chicago and their fellow-travelers drew the inference that it was their locution of choice when promoting their novel vision of the efficacy of market organization.[18]

Hadn't conservative liberalism already proffered its wares in this agora of the mind, and failed to find a buyer? But this was emphatically *not* the lesson extracted by Hayek and his followers. On one level, Hayek believed the correct apprehension of the nature of the market had not as yet been put on the auction block; all that had been previously available were debased and tawdry wares, such as rationalism, Marxism, and (yes) static neoclassical equilibrium analysis. The primary task for his neoliberal cadres was, therefore, to produce a novel set of doctrines, including a more valid economic theory. Another would be an attack upon the state-dominated structure of education, which would better approximate the ideal marketplace of ideas if it were privatized.[19] On a different and more disturbing level, Hayek posited that no one would ever be capable of fully grasping the operation of a marketplace of ideas *by its very definition*. A marketplace of ideas processed information in ways that any human mind would be stymied in attempts to imitate, such that no central planner could ever mimic its operation. Consequently, participants would always languish unsatisfied. Neoliberalism preached "the necessity of the individual submitting to the anonymous and seemingly irrational forces of society...the understandable craving for intelligibility produces illusory demands which no system can satisfy" (Hayek 1948, 24). This was just another instance of the neoliberal insistence on how the market could not be left to its own devices to buttress its own successful operation.

It is worthwhile spending a little time on Hayek's route to the marketplace of ideas, if only to clarify which aspects were picked up by subsequent neoclassical models of knowledge, and which portions were quietly bypassed in the interests of downplaying any conflict with the neoclassical tradition. Hayek struggled throughout his life to reconcile some seemingly contradictory elements of his heritage, which included the Austrian advocacy of subjectivism as a philosophical presupposition; his early rejection of contemporary schools of psychology; the preservation of Austrian capital theory (which is often forgotten was Hayek's other prewar preoccupation); his disparagement of "scientism;" the problem of the treatment of expectations within economic theory; and the Socialist Calculation controversy. Yet wherever he looked at other disciplines, such as philosophy or psychology, there seemed very little in the way of useful resources to help him resolve these tensions. For instance, he had a visceral adverse reaction to Viennese positivism, probably due to a personal distaste for the antics of Otto Neurath. Behaviorist psychology was another anathema, as were many of the natural scientists who sought to apply their theories and methods to the social sciences. One of the very few natural scientists for whom he felt an affinity was Michael Polanyi. Polanyi was another Viennese thinker, a chemist turned philosopher, who set out to diagnose the philosophical maladies of the age, which he also equated with socialism and the planning mentality. Although there was still much on which they would differ, Polanyi's conception of an ineffable "tacit knowledge" located at the very heart of the scientific process would stand as one unacknowledged subtext to the neoliberal marketplace of ideas as developed by Hayek.[20]

Hayek's neoliberalism circa 1955 was comprised of a number of theses, most of which had direct bearing on the treatment of knowledge in economics. For purposes of comparison with the fate of the subsequent economics of knowledge, we simply provide a telegraphed list, with dates of their first published appearance in brackets:

(A) Jettison the conception of knowledge of the future (impossible in any event) as an ideal condition found in previous economics, and replace it with an equilibrium condition of agreement and coordination between the prospective plans of economic agents [1937]. The market is therefore first and foremost a cognitive phenomenon.

(B) The later Hayek flirts with various cybernetic approaches to the philosophy of mind, and in particular, his *Sensory Order* is regarded as one precursor to connectionism in cognitive science [1952]. Every individual's impressions of the world are distinctly different, due to his or her own idiosyncratic set of neural connections. Hayek's model of the mind was a projection of his own earlier model of Austrian capital theory (1982, 291).

(C) Although individualism is still the *sine qua non* of all economic explanation, rationality is in fact social, brought about by the operation of the market [1946]. The original metaphor is now inverted: The market is just the model of the individual mind blown up to global scale.

(D) Individuals are preternaturally cognitively weak, and cannot in any sense comprehend the whole of human knowledge; perhaps *hoi polloi* can't even get past first base. Sometimes this insight is expressed as a peculiar version of knowledge, which exists as stuff that is so thermodynamically dispersed that no one can possess it in its entirety [1945]. Later on, this is expressed as the precept that no mind can completely know itself.[21]

(E) Although there is really no such thing as an expert (recall intellectuals are a part of the problem in the neoliberal playbook), some bureaucratized forms of the pursuit of knowledge leave room for social activities where agents do not simply accept the conventional wisdom (or market signals) passively, but change knowledge through active critique. The natural sciences are the premier case of this alternative to the marketplace of ideas [1945].[22] However, "scientific knowledge is not the sum of all knowledge" (1948, 80). Thus philosophers (like the logical positivists), who take scientific knowledge as the paradigm instance of human knowledge, have gotten the situation backwards. Scientific knowledge, properly understood, should be subordinate to the market, not vice versa.

(F) Historical knowledge is a category mistake. [1943] The marketplace of ideas treats the genealogy of thought just like sunk costs: bygones are bygones.

(G) It is an error to portray the knowledge conveyed by markets as consisting entirely of expectations about future prices (1948, 51). Price expectations comprise a very small subset of human knowledge. Prices cannot themselves embody all relevant knowledge, since it is of utmost consequence that much knowledge cannot be encoded by any means whatsoever [1945].

(H) The philosophical school[s] which suggest that human agency is a developmental notion, where changing your mind is tantamount to you changing your intrinsic identity, and freedom is the ability to assert your will, is a German sickness [1945], and pernicious (1948, 26). The marketplace of ideas is not about subjecting your preferences or ideas to critique and reconceptualization; it is concerned with the public expression of your current preferences/ideas and learning to gracefully acquiesce in the acceptance or rejection of your preferences by the marketplace as a whole. Hence, the line between ideas and preferences are thus comprehensively blurred [1946]. Consequentially, truth is relativized, but not reduced to convention, since it is still held that the market produces optimal outcomes but configurations that transcend the ability of any individual human to understand them.

Perhaps the most fascinating aspect of Hayek's quest for a neoliberal doctrine concerning knowledge is the way in which his legacy was embraced by those who came after. The characterization of the marketplace of ideas grew to be central, even indispensable, to almost all subsequent developments that occur under the rubric of the economics of knowledge, but it happened in such a way that so many of Hayek's specific epistemic theses become undermined, or dispensed with altogether. Many modern economic epistemologists set off down their career paths burning with a desire to disprove or otherwise refute Neoliberalism (if not Hayek personally); but the real moral of our tale turns out to be that Neoliberalism may have proven more powerful than any of their fervent intentions. At one time, only the most avid Hayekian would have written:

> As almost any thinker has experienced, the free and open competition of ideas does tend to lead, more directly than any other path, to the advancement of knowledge. And thus the institution known as the market, to the extent it involves such competition, seems to be an appropriate model for trying to understand how knowledge, as well as other forms of wealth, increases. (Bartley 1990, 26)

But these days this could come from any randomly selected instance of the popular press or any random academic outlet. Who will now volunteer for the thankless task to prove that the marketplace of ideas is little more than collective illusion? The goal of the Mont Pelerin Society was to reconstitute a *Weltanschauung* more powerful than the passing fads and fancies of the intellectuals; we leave it to the reader to gauge the extent of their success.[23]

3. THE THREE FACES OF KNOWLEDGE
IN POSTWAR NEOCLASSICAL ECONOMICS

At the beginning of this paper, I insisted upon the irreducible diversity and complexity of the postwar orthodoxy, as a necessary prerequisite to understanding the sheer incongruity of the across-the-board watershed in economics in the twentieth century from advocates of static allocation to wizards of epistemology. Here we make good on that assertion, by citing some of my earlier work with Wade Hands on the three main schools of postwar American neoclassical microeconomic theory.[24] Since I am also going to claim there were essentially three conceptual approaches to the economics of knowledge in this period, it might seem as though I will have to fill in all nine cells of the 3 × 3 permutations. Luckily, the actual historical situation was not quite so promiscuous, although neither was it so cut and dried that each school advocated one and only one analytical approach to knowledge. Rather, as happens so often in the history of science (Pickering 1995; Collins 2004), the entire virtual space of intellectual possibility was not explored, but neither did everyone converge to a single conceptual option.

It is of paramount importance to observe that no single discrete doctrine served as an all-purpose 'litmus test' for neoclassical orthodoxy in the immediate postwar era. In particular, each of the following 'core' theses was rejected by some substantial subset of card-carrying postwar academic economists in good standing: utility functions exist and are real, demand curves slope downwards, income effects are significant considerations, it is intrinsic to human nature to maximize something, markets excel in optimizing something, governments are inevitably deleterious to the harmonious functioning of markets, monopoly is detrimental to the successful functioning of markets, supply equals demand, human beings are rational. Rather, interlocking configurations of positions with regard to these and other questions became stabilized into three competing 'schools' in America, whose acolytes would vie with one another for adherents and intellectual credibility within an arena of a small set of designated journal outlets; otherwise they served to exclude some other economists as not meeting 'neoclassical' standards.[25] This fostered a situation in which neoclassical economics possessed almost no uniform core creed. It was all the more noteworthy, and served to further obscure matters for outsiders, that two of the three schools were initially physically located at the same geographical location, namely, Chicago. The nascent orthodoxy thus began small and local; but the burgeoning American higher educational system, along with the pervasive abundant military funding of science, served to expand their representation with unprecedented speed.

The numerous ways in which the schools both differentiated their doctrines and sought to co-opt the propositions of their rivals is far too complex to be adequately covered here. Instead, we simply telegraph the tenets most relevant to a history of American microeconomics in sections A–C.

A. Chicago School

Organized 1946.[26] Initial members were recruited from the wartime "Applied Mathematics Panel," an operations research (OR) unit located at Columbia and Princeton. Core set: Milton Friedman, Allen Wallis, Aaron Director, George Stigler, and Gary Becker. Demand curves were deemed real and guaranteed to slope downwards, but all the concerns elsewhere about "underlying true determinants" of demand were treated as dispensable. Slutsky equations and integrability conditions were regarded as a minor distraction. Income effects don't matter. Chicago built up (an historically inaccurate) self-account where its origins were purportedly located in Marshallian doctrine. The major determinant of local orthodoxy was the construction of a neoliberal political doctrine; this dictated strident resistance to Keynesian enthusiasms and denial of the pervasive character of monopoly and market failure. Aggregation problems were treated as irrelevant, and so was imperfect competition. One of their achievements was the promulgation of a workable empiricism, based upon partial equilibrium analysis and simple ordinary least squares regression analysis. Models were kept modest and tractable. Major sources of funding are corporations and politically motivated private foundations, particularly the Volker Foundation.

B. Cowles Commission

Although Cowles as an organization long predated the neoclassical triumph, its special approach to price theory congealed around new orthodoxy, circa 1948 (Mirowski 2002), when Tjalling Koopmans took over the research directorship from Jacob Marschak. The core set of protagonists were Koopmans, Marschak, Kenneth Arrow, Gerard Debreu, Leonid Hurwicz, and Roy Radner. It was mostly comprised of trained natural scientists moving into economics later in their careers. Cowles was driven from Chicago to Yale in 1954 by rancorous disputes with the Chicago school. In this period Cowles underwent a research shift from earlier attempts to empirically verify Walrasian systems of demand, in favor of treating Walrasian general equilibrium as the Bourbakist "mother-structure" of all economic theory; this was anointed the Arrow-Debreu model. Slutsky conditions were transformed from empirical propositions needing verification to abstract statements of pervasive interdependence of equilibrium conditions. An alliance with the military (and RAND in particular) strengthened the project of providing an abstract decision theory in a context of technology of planning for optimization, and it linked Cowles economists to the pervasive military organization of science in America. A left-leaning inclination to plan the economy was justified by insisting upon the ubiquity of market failures, defined as divergences from Pareto optima. Demand curves were thought to not really exist; only demand systems existed, which are nearly impossible to empirically verify. The econometric estimation of theory was eventually forsaken in favor of treating the economic agent as a miniature econometrician. Fascination with planning alternative abstract systems of exchange led to the innovation of mechanism design (Lee, 2006). Cowles was also the first of the three schools to seriously engage with game theory (Mirowski 2002).

C. MIT (Often Includes Harvard Faculty)

Technically founded in 1941, effectively in 1945, the core set of protagonists were Paul Samuelson, Robert L. Bishop, Hendrik Houthakker, Robert Dorfman, Robert Solow, George Akerlof, and Joseph Stiglitz.

A major problem in the philosophy of economics has been the general lack of awareness of the shape of this school, relative to the others, due to the overwhelming presence of Samuelson (1998) in seeking to control his own legacy and portray his *Foundations* as representing orthodox neoclassicism as a whole. The consequence for economists has been to overrate the importance of the doctrine of revealed preference to the detriment of the larger picture. Revealed preference for MIT purportedly did away with problems of verification of demand curves, which were simply presumed to exist. Problems of interrelated demand functions, such as complementarity, were played down; integrability conditions reappear as the Strong Axiom of Revealed Preference. This school stood as the major champion of models of imperfect competition, which helps explain the relative disinterest in Walrasian general equilibrium. MIT was partial to stories in which demand did not equal supply. One major determinant of MIT orthodoxy was the reconciliation of left-liberal statist impulses with imperative to repudiate socialism: Keynesian macroeconomics was seen as the 'middle way.' Yet the distinction between macroeconomics and microeconomics was elided in numerous ways. Partly this straddle was achieved through an ironic stance toward both the existence of utility and the importance of general equilibrium, which instead promotes pragmatic or toy models (two agents, two goods, two states, etc.) illustrating principles that cannot be logically demonstrated as inevitable generic covering laws. Nevertheless, Marshallian partial equilibrium was openly derided.[28] Empiricism was also treated in a relatively ironic manner; facility with advanced econometric techniques often trumped robust simple estimation. (For instance, Samuelson himself never engaged in any econometric empiricism, but he wrote extensively on the agent as econometrician *manqué*.) However, the early success of Samuelson's *Principles* enshrined the MIT approach as the public face of the orthodoxy for decades.

Because the three schools differed so much in their orientation about what constituted the sanctioned content of legitimate neoclassical price theory, it was essentially a foregone conclusion that they would each comprehend the neoliberal notion of the marketplace of ideas in a very divergent fashion. The Chicago department was situated at ground zero of postwar neoliberalism in America, and hence it was perhaps the quickest to pick up on Hayek's notion and develop it, primarily by scrubbing it clean of any overt Austrian taint, and reconcile it with their empirical Marshallian-style portrait of the market. The distance from Hayek's "Economics and Knowledge" (1937) to Friedman's *Capitalism and Freedom* (1962) and Stigler's "Economics of Information" (1961) provides a short but bracing introduction to the rapid domestication of the neoliberal program within one precinct of American economics. It may not have been what Hayek intended, but by 1960 he was no longer a player in the stabilization of American neoclassical economics. The reaction of Cowles was, by contrast, a cacophony of options concerning how one might begin to upbraid and refute Hayek. However, the hunters got captured by the game: the more they felt compelled to engage with Hayek, the more they also took on board the conceptual framework of a marketplace of ideas.[29] Of the three postwar schools, MIT was the slowest to take up the gauntlet. It seems possible that much of the delay could be attributed to Paul Samuelson's strident position that one could do scientific neoclassical economics devoid of any commitment to cognitive principles whatsoever; but there is the curious contrary fact that Samuelson was the first to envision a neoclassical science policy, which implicitly presumed certain commitments concerning the treatment of knowledge. Whatever the cause, MIT was soon to join the crowd with its own special version of the cognitive marketplace by the late 1960s.

Now we finally arrive at the technical problem faced by each of the three schools in the postwar American context. What would it mean for economists to endow their agent with a capacity for knowledge? After all, one could not seriously dissect the validity of a marketplace of ideas until one registered some commitments about what knowledge was, and how agents processed it. Here we must insist that *nothing in the previous neoclassical tradition had provided solid dependable guidance about the appropriate treatment of knowledge in neoclassical economic models.*[30] There were hints scattered here and there, to be sure, but the urgent imperative to grapple with the marketplace of ideas brought the utter disarray of any epistemic approach in neoclassical economics out in the open. Furthermore, no one seemed willing or able to boldly adopt Hayek's positions A–H (in Section 2) wholesale. Yet, ultimately, economists did not concoct their ontologisms from scratch. Rather, in each case, they depended heavily upon the kindness of strangers, in the person of the external natural sciences,[31] to suggest the foundations upon which they might erect their mathematizations of knowledge. Out of the myriad of possibilities, postwar neoclassicals settled upon three gross analytical options, which are outlined in Table 5.1.

I. Information as a Thing/Commodity

If a dominant heuristic of postwar economists was "do as little as possible to revise or alter the neoclassical theory handed down from our forebears" when discussing the operation of the marketplace of ideas, then one can readily appreciate why this option would have initially appeared so attractive. If information was a thing-like object, then it could just be subtended to the commodity space as one more good, and nothing need be changed about the standard maximization model whatsoever. Moreover, a thing-like information absolved the theorists of having to confront whatever model of mind was supposedly inherent in the utility function. Playing fast and loose with commodity space was a popular pastime in postwar

Table 5.1 Three Paradigms of Neoclassical "Information"

Information is:		
a thing (Shannon)	an inductive index (Blackwell)	symbolic computation (Turing)
Cognition is:		
irrelevant	intuitive statistics and epistemic formal logic	symbol manipulation
Learning is:		
purchase of a commodity	statistical inference	algorithm augmentation
Communication is:		
same as exchange	signaling	information transmission

economics—think of the way Gerard Debreu deformed it in order to model uncertainty, or Kelvin Lancaster contorted it to capture qualities. Therefore, editing in information seemed a snap.

The problem immediately arose about how to measure or quantify this kind of information, and that is where Claude Shannon's "information theory" entered the picture. Shannon had developed an argument that suggested information could be treated just like entropy in physics, comparing it to an enumeration of the number of ways a stochastic microdynamics of symbols could make up a measurable macrostate of messages. Shannon then used the measure to derive theorems about efficient coding procedures to maximize transmission (through telephones, telegraph wires, and other channels) in the presence of noise. I will not reprise the tedious and protracted disputes that broke out in the 1950s and 1960s concerning the attempts by social scientists to co-opt the Shannon definition for their own purposes.[32] A concept fashioned to discuss mechanical obstacles to communication channels may turn out to be utter nonsense when used to discuss the semantics of communication, as many soon came to realize. In most American social sciences, explicit recourse to Shannon information theory disappeared from the theoretical journals by the 1970s; most sophisticated readers of the literature had come to realize that it was not the philosopher's stone, and it wasn't even very impressive as an intuition pump. But that did not exhaust its significance for economics. The Shannon mania of the first two postwar decades had the unintended consequence of bolstering the general impression that scientists could and should treat information as a quantifiable thing, and even as a *commodity*. In practice, it became quite common to conflate the embodiments and encapsulations of knowledge in objects and artifacts as mere epiphenomenal manifestations of a generic thing called information. It was a reification based largely upon a misapprehension—but it still had untold consequences. One suppressed implication was the bogey of self-reflexivity: "I do not suppose that the information content of this essay could ever be quantified" (Dorfman 1960, 585).[33]

Nevertheless, once knowledge was identified as a good, then arguments could begin over just what special sort of good it might be. Perhaps it resembled a capital good, but one capable of metempsychosis, like human capital. Or, perhaps its special conditions of production dictated its status as a public good? Here this version of the economics took a perilous turn, from which it has yet to recover. If you could get people to accept that knowledge was a good, it helped if you then began to endow it with all sorts of peculiar qualities. Starting with Samuelson (1954) and Arrow (1962), knowledge was claimed to be a weird sort of thing whose use by one person did not prevent its use by another (in the jargon: 'non-rivalrous'); but also something from which it was intrinsically difficult to prevent another from enjoying the benefits once you bought it (in the jargon: 'non-excludable'). This created all sorts of problems for mathematical modeling, but more to the point, was used in the 1960s–1980s to justify state subsidy and provision of this marvelous commodity. But upon the neoliberal turn identified earlier in Section 2, a curious scholastic argument was subsequently made (Romer 1990; Warsh 2006) that the previous characterization had been mistaken, and that knowledge was only partially excludable, and distinctively different from human capital, rendering it an even more special category beyond public goods. This ontological slipperyness of what, after all, is supposed to be a physical given to the model, is the first symptom of an indeterminacy in this particular approach to an economics of knowledge (Mirowski, 2007).

The arguments over the precise economic character of this good have not yet subsided, and they are often the starting point for outsiders to the economics profession who seek to comment upon the economists' approach to knowledge (Marginson 2007).

II. *Information as an Inductive Index and/or the Stochastic Object of an Epistemic Logic*

With the development of mathematical statistics, there had been efforts early in the twentieth century to link intuitions of a good statistical sample to the amount of information it contained, particularly in the tradition of R.A. Fisher. However, none of these proposals amounted to much outside a small coterie of statisticians. By constrast, in the postwar period, an interesting phenomenon arose in which the statistical tools of inductive inference (having spread throughout the social sciences) began to get conflated with models of the mind (Gigerenzer & Murray 1987). Since the story of psychology in the early twentieth century consisted of a series of frontal assaults on the conscious mind as executive in charge of rationality, a revanchist movement resorted to the theory of probability to stem the tide.[34] The situation changed rather radically when mathematical statisticians were brought together with operations researchers and game theorists at the RAND Corporation in the early 1950s. There, especially in the work of David Blackwell, a practice of equating information with measures defined over partitions imposed upon an exhaustive enumeration of states of the world, both actual and virtual, became established.[35] Crudely, how much a procedure (it was harder to phrase this in terms of real people) knew about a world was a function of how finely or coarsely it could divide up the possibilities and thereby assign probabilities to eventual outcomes, and the sensitivity with which its detectors could discriminate which of the possibilities had actually obtained. The necessity for game theory to divide and discriminate strategies according to states of the world was an immediate inspiration, but quickly the formalism was rapidly developed in two relatively separate directions: one, as the framework for modern definitions of one version of inductive inference, and the other, as the scaffolding used to assign semantic relations to a modal logic.[36] In an alliance with artificial intelligence, it became the basis for formal models of an important class of machine logic.

The formalism of matrices of sharply divided partitions defined over a full enumeration of possible states of the world was an artifact of its origins in the statistics of linear estimators and the matrix algebra of game theory, and so it was essentially a foregone conclusion that postwar economists, many of whom had econometric backgrounds and some of whom had studied game theory, would become intimately acquainted early on with the state space characterization of information. Decision theorists also deemed it a flexible framework within which to couch von Neumann-Morgenstern expected utility. However, there was very little about the formalism that recommended itself as a portrait of *cognition*. Under this description, knowledge was a rather all-or-nothing affair: "Although you may have false beliefs, you cannot know something that is false" (Fagin et al. 1995, 32). Indeed, it was much better attuned to be recruited as one narrow component of a mechanical inference algorithm, but one where there was no such thing as surprises or unanticipated change, not to mention learning, and issues of interpretation were banished. Some took to discussing mechanical alterations in the underlying partitions as being due to signals emanating from nature or other agents, but this was a rather cavalier and careless treatment of communication and the implementation of language. Even under such desiccated circumstances, the Blackwell formalism did not prove quite so powerful as some had hoped; for instance, it was shown that a simple one-dimensional index of a certain partition being more informative than another over a given set of states of the possible worlds was generally unavailable, given that the partitions imposed only a partial ordering over finite information structures (McGuire & Radner 1986, 108–119). It was, thus, a portrayal of knowledge "from the outside," so to speak, preserving more than a tinge of the behavioralist presumptions popular back in the 1950s.[37] It can be used to discuss a very narrow range of interactions between agents, but only interaction in which the underlying enumeration of states is completely and comprehensively shared. Here, we find the source of the excessive literature in economics journals on the causes and consequences of common knowledge. For these and other reasons, it would be a mistake to treat the state space formalism as a uniquely credible or comprehensive approach to knowledge. One frequently finds that philosophers and computer scientists admit this, but I have *not once* come across a comparable admission in a text written by an economist:

> We don't feel the semantic model…is the unique 'right' model of
> knowledge…We do not believe there is a right model of knowledge. (Fagin et al.
> 1995, 8)

III. Information as Computation

This version of knowledge owes the greatest debt to the postwar development of the computer and the theory of computation, but curiously enough, has proven over time to be the least palatable to the vast majority of neoclassical economists. It predominantly travels under the banner of "computationalism," which tends to identify mental states with the computational states found in (either abstract or tangible) computers (Scheutz 2002). Computationalism is comprised of many competing visions, ranging from formal symbol manipulation to connectionism to machine cognition; but economists have rarely been sensitive to these controversies within artificial intelligence and cognitive science.

To simplify our exposition, here the processing of information will be equated with symbol manipulation by automata of various computational capacities, with the Turing machine occupying the highest rung on the computational hierarchy. The importance of the computational hierarchy is that it permits the proof of impossibility theorems concerning what can and cannot be computed on machines falling within a particular computational class. Computational approaches have had the prophylactic virtue of ruling out all sorts of physically and mathematically impossible procedures from falling within the purview of a Promethean conception of rationality. Treatment of infinities assumes much heightened significance; implementable algorithms are more highly regarded than in-principle proofs. Furthermore, actual experience with computers have provided all manner of heuristic suggestions about how to approach cognitive science. Indeed, as one Clark Medal recipient has admitted, "if you try and do psychology at MIT, you study computers, not humans" (Matthew Rabin in Colander et al. 2004, 141).

Early on, the computational metaphor of mind proved a mixed blessing for economists. If one were to seriously entertain the notion of a marketplace of ideas, the problem became where in the economy one would situate the computer. Was each agent a Turing machine, or perhaps an automaton of less exalted capacity? The von Neumann architecture did seem a bit removed from human cognition, and then there were the interminable disputes of the 1960s–1990s over what humans could do that computers could not. Most would admit computers could contain information, but could a computer be seriously thought to be knowledgeable? Or perhaps edging closer to Hayek's vision, the marketplace itself should be treated as one vast Turing machine, with agents simply plug-compatible peripherals of rather diminished capacities? This problem was compounded by the patrimony of the original neoclassical model, located as it was in noncomputable N body mechanics (Mirowski 1989). Perhaps some aspect of the neoclassical model was shown to be Turing noncomputable? The temptation was then to shift the location of the computer to another ontological level in order to evade the unsavory implications. One way to summarize the uneasy love/hate relationship of postwar economists with the computer was that it could not be ignored, but perhaps computer science might be gingerly overlooked. Nevertheless, time and again, issues of computability were conceded to be germane to an economics of knowledge (Mirowski 2002).

If economists were poised circa 1950 to become junior epistemologists, whichever of the three schools they inhabited, then you might have presumed that they would at least have engaged in a clarifying discussion or two about what they believed knowledge was and how people achieved it. By and large, this did not happen[38]—hardly a propitious start for our Great Watershed. Instead, many economists boldly set forth, confidently asserting all manner of theses about information and the market, but when they were forced to get more specific for the purposes of their mathematical models, they tended to adopt their concepts wholesale from elsewhere, usually locations where serious discussions of information had previously been going on.

Of the many surveys of the economics of information that started appearing over a decade ago, one in particular began, "Imagine that modern decision theory began, not with perfect rationality and imperfect information, but their opposites?" (Conlisk 1996, 691). Other than making an excessively vague appeal to an entirely unspecified notion of perfection, the question simply reveals how limited was the author's grasp of the relevant literature. Not only was there more than a single research foray whose trajectory one might track in making such a generalization; more significantly, there still is no consensus over the extent to which an orthodox economics of knowledge would permit extensive cognitive amendments to the supposedly standard neoclassical model. Economists such as Conlisk probably thought that von Neumann-Morgenstern expected utility was the alpha and omega of decision theory in the postwar period, but that misrepresents both von Neumann's own position (Mirowski 2002, 127–129) and the actual historical record of the three-school interaction.

Our taxonomy of thing/inductive index/computation begins to explain why the disarray has perdured seemingly invisible to the participants. Time after time, important figures often left misleading markers on the trails to their own contributions, sowing confusion. Students picking up economics texts with *information* in their titles got little better for their troubles than a random subset of analytical alternatives. To counteract this absence of structure, we now turn to situate them within the writings and contexts of the three postwar schools of economics.

4. Vestiges of the Economics of Knowledge

Imagine a generic neoclassical economist poised at the brink of their academic ascendancy within economic discourse circa 1950; let's call her Maxine Mum. She comes equipped with a commitment to the maximization of utility, but not much more in the way of guidance about how to render the marketplace of ideas a viable doctrine. Perhaps she is aware of Hayek's philosophical challenge; but more likely, Maxine harbors little more than a vague second-hand impression of it. There are some intellectual resources from external disciplines at her disposal, outlined in the previous section. There are also raging disputes over whether neoclassicals should pay any attention at all to psychology, not to mention *which* version of psychology might be relevant, and suggestions to wait for the whole notion of the relevance of information to economic process to blow over, as so many other intellectual fads evaporated over the subsequent decades. Maxine's own local reference

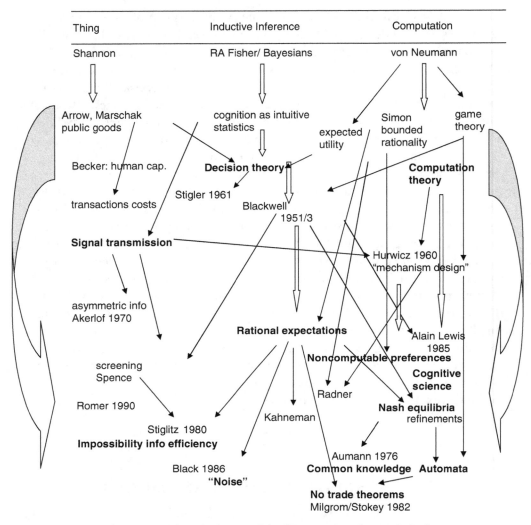

Figure 5.1. Historical Map of the "Economics of Knowledge"

group has tutored her in what it means to do "good scientific economics," but that still leaves her appreciable room to tinker and amend the tradition.

What one would expect Maxine to produce under those circumstances is a diverse set of contradictory proposals, with denizens of a particular school tending to cluster around one particular resource, but nevertheless accompanied by a fair amount of dispersion and cross-fertilization and, not to put too fine a point on it, rank confusion. We seek to impose a little order on what looked suspiciously like a free-for-all by providing a map of various economic doctrines that made use, to a greater or lesser degree, of the three possible paradigms of information schematized in our historical Figure 5.1. The "Historical Map of the Economics of Knowledge" is intended neither

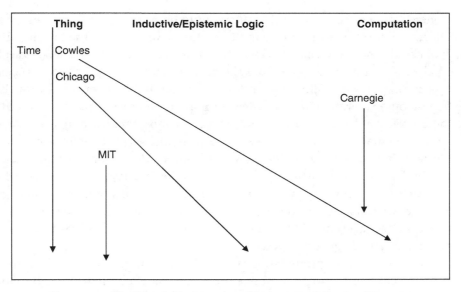

Figure 5.2. The Rough Trajectories of Important Schools of Postwar
Economics through Information Space

to be comprehensive nor strictly chronological, although there is a tendency for later papers to be located further down the map. Indeed, it would be better if the map were not a flat plane but were rolled up as a cylinder (with time as the axis of symmetry), so that the arrows would not appear as such a thicket but would rather reveal the ease with which one paradigm could bleed into the other, without the economists in question even noticing it. The map locates individual economists and their papers in the temporal process, although in many instances (e.g., rational expectations economics, mechanism design, Nash equilibrium refinements) it is better to think of each entry as representing a scholarly community of shifting membership. A few individuals on the map (e.g., Kenneth Arrow, Roy Radner, Leonid Hurwicz) tend to occupy alternative positions on the economics of knowledge throughout their careers, so it is misleading to always equate a position on the map with a particular economist. If one were enjoined to trace the rough centers of gravity of the trajectories of our three schools, even though this is a poor representation of actual events, it would look something like the vectors in Figure 5.2. Cowles begins early on to explore the possible incorporation of knowledge as thing into neoclassical theory, but rapidly becomes disillusioned with it, opting then for something approaching cognition as inductive logic. However, the increasing interaction with game theory ushered some Cowles figures toward epistemic logic, while others began to explore computational themes. The path of Chicago was simpler, with many of their figures starting off favoring a thing-like knowledge; but as the school became more mathematically formal, they moved toward a vision of cognition as inductive logic. MIT, curiously enough, has proven the least promiscuous of the three schools, generally sticking to knowledge as commodity, modulo a little inductive window dressing.

There was one more school that turns out to be significant for our story, but we must omit it from our narrative in this section primarily because for the early days of its existence, it wasn't neoclassical; and when it finally turned neoclassical, it expelled its main protagonist from the economics department. The Carnegie School, an important offshoot of Cowles, turned out to be the prime site for the self-conscious exploration of knowledge as information processing, due primarily to the influence of Herbert Simon.[39] Simon was the most prominent figure to take up Hayek's denial of the omniscience of the economic agent, only to turn it into a theory of bureaucratic rationality, an anathema to the neoliberals. "Bounded rationality" became a theme song of Carnegie in the mid-1950s, right around the same time that Maxine began to entertain her own versions of an economics of knowledge; what matters for our current purposes is that when it was appropriated by neoclassical economists in our three schools, it did not at all resemble what Simon had originally intended (Klaes & Sent 2005, 49).

Given the effulgent proliferation of theoretical innovations, and the multiform ways economists sought to differentiate their own products, it will become important for the major thesis of this paper to hew to the generalizations inscribed in these tables about the three primary paradigms of information economics. However, the reader should keep in mind that this is a device for making a philosophical argument, and not a comprehensive description of all of postwar economics. After describing some of the actual contributions located on the map in this section, we shall then proceed in the next and final section to argue that each paradigm has found itself stuck in a cul-de-sac by century's end, at least as far as the original program of the reconciliation of neoclassical theory with the formal modeling of information is concerned.

A. The Chicago School

As explained in (Mirowski & van Horn 2009), Friedrich Hayek was instrumental in consolidating the Chicago School in 1946 and, therefore, might have been forgiven for expecting that his call for a fundamental reconceptualization of the essence of the market as information conveyance device be pioneered at Chicago; but that is not quite how things turned out. As is well known, Hayek was turned down for a position in the economics department, and had to accept the consolation prize of a professorship at Chicago on the Committee on Social Thought. This ostracism extended to Hayek's conception of cognition; the early figures of the Chicago school simply presumed that epistemological innovation was superfluous in neoclassical economics, particularly given Friedman's notorious doctrine of "as if" maximization of utility in his 1953 *Essays in Positive Economics*. Instead, Friedman took the position that simple price theory could already explain knowledge as well as any other commodity, and he made no effort to delve into the fine points of epistemology. His neoliberal instincts told him that the free market of ideas would sanction the privatization of most educational institutions (1962, chapter 6), and that patents simply didn't qualify as illegitimate monopolies (1962, 127). In this, he resembled Gary Becker, who took vague metaphoric appeals to knowledge as human capital and turned them into a protean neoliberal celebration of thing-like knowledge as the pivotal analytical innovation within labor economics. The appeals to knowledge as commodity were even more pervasive in the Chicago Law School, with first Aaron Director (1964) and then Ronald Coase (1974) simply taking the discrete vendibility of ideas as an axiom and using the putative symmetry between the markets for ideas and commodities as a stick with which to beat left-leaning academics over their own lack of consistency. The appeal to competition as justification for any set of ideas that neoliberals wished to promulgate was taken to its extreme in the later work of Richard Posner (2005). Even though he was never a faculty member at Chicago, it is our contention that Fritz Machlup (1962; 1980) should be included in this group as well. Chicago also nurtured an attempt to produce neoliberal sociology of science with roots in the Mertonian tradition, exemplified in the work of Joseph Ben-David (1991, 11), who had been informed by Friedman's economics in arguing that state organization of science actually had stunted its development in Europe.

Over time, Chicago began to inch toward a more quasi-cognitive approach by linking questions of information to inductive inference. George Stigler entered the lists for the Chicago School in (1961) with an interpretation of cognition as simple statistical sequential search for the lowest price for a given good, which he considered "[his] most important contribution to economic theory" (Stigler 1985, 79–80). His orientation was informed by his experience with the development of sequential analysis at the Applied Mathematics Panel during the war (Wallis 1980; Klein 2000), even though he did not avail himself of the full statistical technique. Instead, the model simply posited a stopping rule for visiting a stochastic distribution of stores, and then purchasing the item with the lowest realized price known to the agent. This was a characteristically Chicago partial-equilibrium story, since the mere violation of the law of one price would vitiate the microeconomics that Chicago had championed. Full recourse to sequential analysis would not posit a fixed sample size, as Stigler did. Minor improvements along these lines were suggested by Nelson (1970), but by and large, the model did not capture the fancy of the larger profession. One reason might have been the obvious disjuncture between the limited treatment of uncertainty and the larger problem of the role of uncertainty in neoclassical dynamics. It is a Chicago hallmark that this sparse limited form of cognition superimposed upon unchanged static utility maximization neither altered their preferred partial equilibrium analysis in any significant way nor did it address larger ambitions to treat the market as an information processing device.

The next big Chicago development was a further move in the direction of cognition as inductive inference, but only after a newer generation of neoliberal theorists had suffered a run-in with serious cognitive science during their apprenticeships at the fledgling Carnegie School (Sent 1998, 2002). This was the infamous "rational expectations" movement, which began as a proposition about microeconomics (Muth 1961), but really caught the attention of economists when it was turned into a weapon to undermine and destroy Keynesian macroeconomics. Figures such as Robert Lucas and Thomas Sargent (1981) adapted the well-established tradition of recasting the cognitive agent as a little econometrician from decision theory (and Cowles), and augmented it with the stricture that said agent should also use the "best" theory of price determination in forecasting price movements. It was more than hubris that caused the rational expectations movement to project neoclassical price theory into the recesses of the cranium of the agent; it also permitted the fixed point equilibrium concept to be extended to another area of economics, this time having to do with knowledge. In an unacknowledged bout of reflexivity, neoclassical theory was declared to be the "best" theory of the economy available to the agent (but how did she *know* that?), and therefore also the "best" theory of cognition for that agent. However, there was concomitantly an indirect embrace of Hayek's original neoliberal notion of the market as information processor in the guise of the "efficient markets hypothesis," namely, the proposition that the market managed to incorporate all relevant information into the existing current price, and thus would convey to all participants all that they needed to know in order to make rational economic decisions. Yet the divergence from Hayek was also notable, since the epistemology of the Chicago-style agent never ventured beyond simplistic models of inductive inference.

We should also take note of a curious development in growth theory (and a retrograde movement back to information as thing) which by current criteria should be included under the rubric of the Chicago School (Warsh 2006; Mirowski, 2007). After a hiatus in the 1970s, growth theory was revived in the late 1980s by supposedly dealing with the scandal that knowledge was believed to be the ultimate source of all economic growth, but was treated as unexplained manna from heaven in Solow growth theory. Paul Romer wed the MIT macro fascination with knowledge as a thing with the Chicago advocacy of the commodification of human capital, and produced a model of knowledge as a partially excludable nonrival commodity. For Romer, "knowledge enters production in two distinct ways... [as] a new good that can be used to produce output... [and which] increases productivity of human capital in the research sector" (1990, 584). While the mathematical model was a bit awkward, the promise to both "endogenize" the causes of economic growth and simultaneously to justify the concurrent privatization of intellectual property caused this paper to be one of the all-time citation classics in the field of economics.

B. The Cowles School

The advent of information processing at Cowles was a much more complex set of events, and cannot be adequately summarized in a few sentences.[40] A crude gloss would point to the fact that Jacob Marschak, Kenneth Arrow, and Leonid Hurwicz were all heavily influenced by contemporary developments within cybernetics, but that they all began (under the influence of Claude Shannon and RAND) by treating information as a fungible commodity—"Uncertainty usually creates a still more subtle problem in resource allocation; information becomes a commodity" (Arrow 1962, 614)—but only to rather rapidly back off from this option (although never entirely renouncing it), and transfer allegiance to conflating information processing with statistical induction. This move was closely related to their retreat from a full-blown econometric empiricism (for which they had originally gained recognition) in favor of models of the economic agent as himself portrayed as a miniature econometrician. At that point, the original Cowles team fragmented into various unrelated research programs into the economics of information, as the allure of epistemic econometrics palled, and the significance of game theory grew more insistent. Eventually, however, Cowles members in various combinations would explore all three paradigms of information analysis enumerated in the previous section.

There are a number of things to keep in mind about Cowles when observing them foraging about for an economics of knowledge. First, because of their intimate connections with RAND, they were in much closer physical proximity to key natural scientists engaged with innovating new approaches to information than were the other schools. For instance, John von Neumann had made a number of overtures to Cowles economists in the late 1940s (Mirowski 2002, chapter 3). Kenneth Arrow in particular was a close colleague of David Blackwell; Leonid Hurwicz and Stanley Reiter enjoyed close collaborations with various computer scientists. Secondly, many Cowlesmen explicitly admitted that their motivation in the 1940s–1960s in discussing information was to refute Hayek (also at Chicago from 1950 onwards), and thus to show that information economics need not have neoliberal implications. Nevertheless, it seems apparent in retrospect that the hunter got captured by the game, in that the frame tale of the omniscient marketplace of ideas came to dominate much of their own work in mechanism design, asymmetric information, "failures" of expected utility theory, "incomplete markets," and a host of other innovations. Finally, it is significant that it was various renegade Cowles members (such as Herbert Simon, Alain Lewis, Roy Radner, and Gerald Kramer), and *not* members of the other schools of economics, who came to the realization that tinkering with the utility framework was just too timid a response to the challenge, and struck out to construct a more full-blooded cognitive model, often based upon the computationalist paradigm, in order to introduce an agent-friendly version of information to buttress the edifice of an economics of knowledge.

Some members of Cowles started out believing that the existing Walrasian model was sufficient in and of itself for refutation of Hayek's proposed revision of the marketplace of ideas. Tjalling Koopmans adopted the position that the Walrasian model actually showed that agent cognition was effectively unnecessary, because the individual agent only needed to know his own preferences and parametric prices in order for equilibrium to obtain.

[O]ne can in particular interpret the proposition as a statement of conditions under which the simplicity of incentive structure and the economies of information handling characteristic of a competitive market organization can be secured without loss of efficiency of allocation...The price system carries to each producer, resource holder, or consumer a summary of information about the production possibilities, resource availabilities and preferences of all other decision makers. Under the conditions postulated, this summary is all that is needed to keep all decision makers reconciled with a Pareto optimal state once it has been established. (Koopmans 1957, 53)

The other members of Cowles were not quite so publicly confident that the heritage of Walrasian models adequately addressed this exquisite economy of information: Marschak and Arrow were especially insistent. Much of this discussion within Cowles sought to bundle together the various worries onto the procrustean bed of "uncertainty," and one can observe that by the mid-1950s Koopmans first floated the trial balloon of blaming this on "missing markets":

Here, perhaps the most crucial kind of uncertainty...arises from the lack of information on the part of any one decision-maker as to what other decision-makers are doing or deciding to do. It is a puzzling question why there are not more markets for future delivery through which the relevant information about concurrent decisions could circulate in an anonymous manner.[41]

Koopmans was not quite so daunted by these problems as Marschak, about whom "on many occasions during the 1950s and 1960s we heard economists question whether Marschak had not actually left economics for other disciplines, such as psychology [or] information science" (McGuire & Radner 1986, viii). Marschak tried out various paths to his grail of an economics of information (and he was one of the earliest American economists after Hayek to use the term), but none of them seemed to pan out. First, he struggled with subjecting Shannon information to a supply/demand framework, and then he entertained the Blackwell formalism, only to reject it (Marschak 1968); then he dallied with the idea of transactions costs as capturing informational issues; he also pioneered a computer/organization metaphor, which was later to thrive under the rubric of "mechanism design" in the format of his "team theory," which itself also failed to catch on. He was among the first to participate with professional psychologists in experiments designed to test the limits of decision theory, at a time when that was still an anathema in the economics profession. The failures of Marschak (particularly when compared to the relative success of Arrow) to command the attention of neoclassical economists are perplexing, even in retrospect. Perhaps it had something to do with the fact that the models he explored were embarrassingly progressively removed from the Walrasian general equilibrium that Cowles had come to champion: how to do justice to information in a partial equilibrium framework? Or maybe it had something to do with his level of skepticism over the explanatory power of game theory? Or perhaps it was his relative disaffection from the Bourbakism, which had become all the rage at Cowles?

In any event, it was Kenneth Arrow who became the Cowles poster boy for an economics of information, and indeed, any of the themes covered in this paper can be found there at one time or another: knowledge as commodity, information as public good, missing markets, cognition as intuitive statistics, tacit knowledge in the guise of learning-by-doing, decision theory as ersatz psychology, the Blackwell formalism, asymmetric information and moral hazard, bounded rationality, complexity theory, and even cognition as computation. If one does not look too comprehensively at his *oeuvre,* one can find some modicum of support for just about any late twentieth century orthodox approach to the economics of information one might care to promote; and this may account for some of Arrow's popularity within the profession. The irony of this eclecticism is that at one juncture or another, he has repudiated each and every one of them.[42] The pattern seemed to be that, once a particular research line threatened to invalidate some critical aspect of the neoclassical program or other, Arrow would repudiate the research line, and not the primary notion that neoclassical models were the appropriate vehicle to express the primacy of the marketplace of ideas. This may explain some his most recent crotchety statements, such as:

> The idea that people have difficulty computing the system has a long history; you can see it in Veblen, for example. But nothing followed from this insight. Herb Simon was a great apostle of this view. He's a great figure, and his work did lead to a research program, but in my view, it fizzled out....As I think more about complexity theory, I become more convinced that there is some sense we will never know how the economy operates. (Arrow in Colander et al. 2004, 293, 298)

In many ways, the less famous Cowlesmen were more inclined to follow down the consequences of the alternative paradigms to their bitter conclusions. Leo Hurwicz sought to incorporate communication into the Walrasian tradition with his initiation of the program of "mechanism design" (Lee 2006), if only to better define what neoclassicals meant by the "decentralization of information." For this he received a Nobel in 2007. Roy Radner sought to ponder even more seriously the implications of cognitive science for the Walrasian program. He explored the consequences of the observation that no agent should be presumed to engage in a trade that depends upon information not available to him at that juncture, and insisted that a Pareto optimum could only be defined relative to a given structure of information, a stricture that, if heeded, would destroy most of the models that today pass under the banner of a neoclassical economics of information. Contradicting Arrow, he insisted that the separation between informational and computational considerations was entirely artificial, and wrote, "The Arrow-Debreu world is strained to the limit by the problem of choice of information. It breaks down completely in the face of limits on the ability of agents to compute optimal strategies" (Radner1968, 35). Radner's insights have been subsequently ignored for the most part, but will play an important role in the arguments of the next section.

In the modern orthodoxy, the lasting visible heritage of Cowles came with their latching on to the "state space" formalism as plug-compatible with their general equilibrium orientation; first pioneered at RAND by David Blackwell (1951), it was now treated in some quarters as the standard model of information in economics (Samuelson 2004). Although Cowles as an institution left Chicago in 1955, the program it started was continued at RAND, Stanford, Israel, Louvain, and wherever else operations researchers gathered together under military auspices. An important component of OR was the further development of game theory, which was treated as though it were continuous with the neoclassical program.[43] Game theory was intimately related to the state space formalism and its inductive offshoots, since they were essentially developed simultaneously at RAND, and therefore when strategic cognitive considerations were invoked, it tended to become the paradigm of choice in the treatment of knowledge. However, this rapidly conjured a seeming paradox:

> [I]n the long run, you cannot use information without revealing it; you can use information only to the extent that you are willing to reveal it. A player with private information must choose between not making use of that information— then he doesn't have to reveal it—or making use of it, and then taking the consequences of the other side finding it out...sometimes, in a non-zero-sum situation, you may *want* to pass information to the other side...The question is how to do it so that you can be trusted, or in technical terms, in a way that is incentive-compatible. (Aumann 2004, 15)

Notions of strategic mendacity thus entered the pristine marketplace of ideas, like the proverbial serpent in paradise. Robert Aumann was the high priest of this particular theodicy, which attempted to reconcile the ways of Mammon to Man through the instrumentality of what became known as "common knowledge rationality." Aumann's flash of inspiration, which came in the early 1970s at Stanford (Aumann 2004, 19), was that the inductive inference version of Blackwell's formalism dictated that if the probabilities of two people for a particular event are common knowledge, then they must be equal. Combine this with the epistemic logic strand of Blackwell, and one arrived at the notion that it would be irrational for two agents to disagree in a fully effective marketplace of ideas. Economists had been slinging around notions of asymmetric or "private" knowledge for decades, but maybe they just had not taken the lessons of cognition to heart. Or, as Aumann 2004, 19 puts it, "Correlated [Nash] equilibrium is nothing more than just common knowledge of rationality, together with common priors." It would be hard to conceive of a more neoliberal doctrine than that—so much for the original Cowles ambition to repudiate Hayek.

The temptation for all three schools throughout the last half-century has been to elide or slur the distinctions between the three paradigms of information, if only to disguise the ease with which they slid from one modeling tradition to another. Cowles was often most guilty of this, given it covered the most landscape in information space in the postwar period, but perhaps precisely for that reason, it equally produced scholars who warned against the promiscuity:

> Information can be measured, knowledge cannot...There is also an important distinction between 'knowledge theory' and 'information theory.' The former refers to partition models of knowledge, the syntax of knowledge, common and mutual knowledge, axiomatics, and so on...On the other hand, 'information theory' deals with information transmission, noisy channels, entropy and so on. Though related, the two are really quite different. (Aumann 2005, 89)

C. MIT School

The path to an economics of information trod by the MIT school looks very different than the road taken by their rivals. For instance, it was only in the late 1960s when some of their foot soldiers began to take up one of the three paradigms of the treatment of information. But the published record hides a more surreptitious innovation, which dates from the immediate postwar period. Paul Samuelson (2004, 531) has recently admitted that he helped ghostwrite the postwar bible of American science policy, Vannevar Bush's *Science—the Endless Frontier* (1945). One reads therein that,

> Basic research leads to new knowledge. It provides scientific capital...New products and processes do not appear full-grown. They are founded on new principles and new conceptions, which in turn are painstakingly developed by research in the purest realms of science. (1945, 11)

In retrospect, it seems clear that this so-called "linear model" of innovation was the precursor to Samuelson's celebrated analytical construct of the "public good" (1954), rather than the other way around. Due to a quirk of fate, Arrow (1962) got credit for the idea that there was something characteristically odd about knowledge that prevented the marketplace of ideas from churning out enough of it, but Samuelson and MIT were the true progenitors. Samuelson and his colleagues were casting about for an economic justification for the state to subsidize the postwar production of knowledge—again we observe the imperative to upbraid Hayek and Chicago on the one hand, but also to rationalize (if not openly endorse) the military control of science on the other (Hounshell 2000)—and the thought that they might hitch it to their advocacy of *macroeconomics*. Knowledge was said to be a prerequisite for economic growth, but there were these curious aspects of nonrivalrousness, uncertainty, and zero marginal cost that impeded the marketplace from sufficient investment to guarantee the expansion of the system as a whole. Note well that the MIT approach simply begins with the presumption that knowledge is a commodity without any explicit justification or discussion, trots out the production function, and then lets rip. The capstone to the position was Robert Solow's famous (1957) paper on the sources of technical change, which elevated knowledge to the position of the mysterious "residual," which explained the preponderance of American growth. This combination of linear model, public good, production functions, and national macrostatistics became the only game in town for discussing science policy in the postwar period (Godin 2005), and bureaucratic knowledge economics in particular, or at least until it was unceremoniously dissolved by the neoliberal tide.

This vision of the economics of knowledge as a kind of accessory to activist Keynesianism can help explain why the MIT school only got with the larger program of subscribing to one of the three paradigms of knowledge once their Keynesian macroeconomics came under severe attack. We can date their entry into the information sweepstakes with the famous "Lemons" paper by George Akerlof (1970). That paper has an MIT-style toy model that was used to argue a different rationale for government intervention, namely, that asymmetric information (as in the used-car market) would cause only faulty cars to be offered on the market, because good cars were constrained to be sold at the same (blue book) price. The bottom line that no cars would be sold at all had (of course) no relationship to the real-world used-car market; but that was not the point of the exercise. As Akerlof argued in his Nobel lecture:

> [T]he study of asymmetric information was the very first step towards a realization of a dream. That dream was the development of a behavioral macroeconomics...The modeling of asymmetric information was to price theory what the modeling of putty-clay, vintage capital and learning by doing had been to growth theory. (2002, 411, 413)

Characteristically, these models were used to support political intervention in the marketplace, but this is where things got sticky. MIT (plus Harvard) thought it was bequeathing the profession a previously overlooked wealth of hidden information, secrets ,and ambiguous actions, a Kabuki tragedy behind every transaction, but when you looked closely at their models, they really were not all that interested in game theory, which was supposed to be the modality of choice when discussing evasion, mendacity, and strategic behavior. In any event, the Aumann wing of Cowles (discussed earlier) was busy undermining their simplistic notions of "private" information and "hidden" action. The MIT minions believed they had been savaging the Hayekian marketplace of ideas, but all the while they were amazingly oblivious to most of the critical epistemological issues; all subtlety appeared lost on these wizards of Mass Ave. mentalism. For instance, the MIT School was noticeably unconcerned with the problems of the curse of dimensionality as a barrier to cognition (strangely, given their ambivalence about full general equilibrium), and they were seemingly uninterested in relevant developments in cognitive science only a few buildings away on the MIT campus. When neuroeconomics caught on with a subset of economists at the turn of the millennium, it bore a "not made at MIT" trademark.[44] Perhaps this was a symptom of their sustained agnosticism about belief in the existence of utility.

The most prominent representative of the modern MIT School of the economics of information is Joseph Stiglitz. Although he has been trumpeting the advent of a "new economics of information" for years now (as we noted previously), what is most incongruous about his work is the way it simply ignores almost everything else going on in neoclassical economics, as well as the Blackwell and Turing-inspired paradigms. Whatever else one might think of Cowles and Chicago, it is indisputable that they were intermittently entertaining the pros and cons of different conceptions of knowledge and their consequences for neoclassical theory. But MIT has held itself to different standards:

> [I]t seemed to me the most effective way of attacking the paradigm was to keep within the standard framework as much as possible...While there is a single way in which information is perfect, there are an infinite number of ways that information can be imperfect. One of the keys to success was formulating

> simple models in which the set of relevant information could be fully
> specified...the use of highly simplified models to help clarify thinking about
> quite complicated matters. (Stiglitz. 2003, 613, 583, 577)

What are the lessons that MIT thinks it has derived from this procedure? As
Stiglitz summarized in his Nobel lecture:

> When there is no noise, prices convey all information, and there is no incentive
> to purchase information. But if everybody is uninformed, it clearly pays some
> individual to become informed. Thus, there does not exist a competitive
> equilibrium. (2002, 395)

It would be something noteworthy if Stiglitz or his co-workers had provided a general impossibility theorem, along the lines of Gödel's incompleteness theorem or
Turing's computability theorem, but Stiglitz has repudiated Cowles' stress on general
equilibrium (2003, 580, 620), Chicago's resort to transactions costs (573), and doesn't
even seriously consider the game theorists' versions of strategic cognition. Indeed,
it seems rather heroic to derive any general propositions whatsoever from any of
his individual toy models. Stiglitz himself admits this in when he is not engaged in
wholesale promotion of his information program.[45] Instead, it is possible that "simple" models serve mainly to confuse the issues that beset the quest for an economics
of information.

Take, for instance, the famous Grossman-Stiglitz model (1980). The text starts
out by positing information as a commodity that needs to be arbitraged (393), but
claims in a footnote (397) that the model of knowledge therein is tantamount to
the Blackwell formalism (recall the Aumann quote above), and defines its idiosyncratic notion of equilibrium as equivalence of expected utilities of informed and
uninformed agents. Of course, for simplicity all the agents are posited identical; how
this is supposed to relate to any vernacular notions of divergences in knowledge is
something MIT has never been forced to address. When Grossman offered his own
interpretation of their joint effort, he took the position that the rational expectations model was identical to the approach in Hayek (1948) (we remind the reader of
Section 2), that their little toy model had refuted it, that "when the efficient markets
hypothesis is true and information is costly, competitive markets break down," and
that "We are attempting to redefine the Efficient Markets notion, not destroy it"
(Grossman 1989, 108).

5. Why There Is Not Yet a Credible
Economics of Knowledge

One lesson we can glean from our survey thus far is that the orthodox "economics
of knowledge" literature has been far less concerned with developing a clear position

on epistemology than it has been with one of two objectives: (a) to reconcile the bequeathed model of the constrained optimization of utility with something a qualified representative of the natural sciences (but not psychology proper) claims is a scientific treatment of information; and (b) to reprimand Hayek and his followers on their vision of the marketplace of ideas and thus promote the favored politics of the particular school, while still treating human cognition as though it resembled a neoclassical market. (It is important to appreciate that *adoption of the marketplace of ideas* is *the* crucial analytical move, and not any nominal pro- or anticapitalist politics of the individual economist in question.) It is our argument that the bulk of the literature we have cited in Section 4 fails on both counts, and this is the root of our contention that there is not yet an economics of knowledge that deserves the name.[46] The culmination of a half-century of development of each of the three paradigms of information has led to a situation in which each is revealed individually incompatible with the core neoclassical price theory.

Why are the "Fundamental Theorems of the Economics of Information" conspicuous by their absence? Why, indeed, does the locution "The Economics of Knowledge" strike many as an oxymoron?[47] Armed with the taxonomy of Section 3 and the roster of actual economic models of Section 4, we can begin to proffer a systematic answer to those questions. In this section, we start by suggesting some basic philosophical obstacles, but then, because economists tend to despise philosophy, we shall point out how they have undermined their own case in the standard orthodox economics literature. In short, we maintain that there are fundamental logical obstacles to equipping the neoclassical agent with a consensus technology to take knowledge on board. Furthermore, the neoclassicals have themselves discovered this over the last three decades, even though they remain loathe to admit it.

We shall proceed by first enumerating four generic contradictions that seem to bedevil all three schools of American neoclassical economics. They are generic in the sense that they do not depend upon the particular paradigm of information (as defined earlier in Table 5.1) that the economist in question adopts. In one way of thinking, they are the hidden ontological obstacles to a serious economics of knowledge.[48] To make them a bit more vivid and less abstract, we shall dub them: (i) the impossibility of having your cake and eating it, too; (ii) the curse of the schizophrenic agent; (iii) the Wizard of Oz effect; and (iv) the broken bootstrap. Once we have gained some appreciation for the ontological obstacles, we can then point to the ways in which they have made themselves manifest in actual models found in the orthodox economics literature. We shall accomplish this by running through the tripartite taxonomy once again: information as thing, information as inductive inference, and information processing as computation. Perhaps through this exercise we can render the obscure objects of desire just a bit less obscure, but not in the vain hope that neoclassical economists will proceed to fix their models as a consequence; they have long shown their disdain for any assistance from philosophers or historians. Rather, our ultimate objective is to provoke some serious alternative economic analysis of modern developments that economists have so

far underestimated, such as the corporate takeover of the university, the privatization of science, the naturalization of cognition, and globalization of the neoliberal
regime of the organization of knowledge.

(i) The Impossibility of Having/Eating Cake

The ontological maladies begin, as might be expected, with the history of the commitment to the supposedly non-negotiable precept that the agent comes equipped
with a fixed and well-behaved set of preferences. This, along with a commitment
to ubiquitous maximization, is what gets you your union card as a neoclassical
economist in good standing. The story thus imparted as you sat at the feet of your
graduate microeconomics instructor in pursuit of that certification is that we once
believed in utility as a palpable psychological entity, but Paul Samuelson helped us
leave that all behind, and now our minimalist Protestant catechism consists of a
few axioms of revealed preference, which boil down to the injunction of consistency
in choice, perhaps combined with von Neumann-Morgenstern expected utility as
a convenient appendage. It matters little for our present purposes whether anyone
actually conforms to this catechism in practice;[49] all we need note here is that you
must publicly testify your faith in this version of 'rationality' in order to enter the
portals of the Elysian fields of ranked economics journals.

The first ontological contradiction is that the credo effectively militates against
the further augmentation of this minimalist wispy agent with whatever cognitive
capacities are deemed requisite to solve the problems inherent in models of information (which are the preferred *topoi* of those very same economics journals that
enforce the neoclassical creed). Here is where the trouble really begins. The assertion of agency defined as a fixed, invariant, and comprehensive set of preferences
devoid of all psychological content, combined with the assertion of agency as an
arbitrary complement of cognitive mechanisms allowing the processing of information and the alteration of beliefs/ideas, comes close to the simultaneous assertion of A and not-A (which may account for much of the modern polymorphous
perversity of the neoclassical agent).[50] These fundamental modeling procedures
are inherently incompatible. Nevertheless, this practice has become so pervasive
yet so unconscious in late neoclassicism that it is difficult to get the average practi-
tioner to even see there is a problem, much less acknowledge it.

Since this really is hard for an orthodox economist to appreciate, let us entertain a brief example. It is well known that most uncontaminated experimental
subjects do not play a Nash equilibrium in the (ultimatum) game of "divide
the dollar." One interpretation suggests that this means they are irrational, but
other defenders of Nash, such as Ken Binmore (1999), insist that subjects need to
repeat the game a few times to learn to be 'rational'. However, that is an unavail-
ing defense, because any specification of Nash equilibrium must include both the
knowledge and the cognitive learning capacities of the subjects at the outset and,
therefore, should be "always already" incorporated in the Nash calculation. Any

attempt to introduce knowledge to save a version of rationality innocent of psychology changes the fundamental constitution of the original model of the agent and, therefore, is no longer merely based upon uncontaminated invariant preference. As Bruni and Sugden have recently put it:

> Conventional theory describes the behavior of individuals *who know which actions best satisfy their preferences*. The theory abstracts from the processes by which individuals discover how to satisfy their preferences...So, if preference consistency is interpreted merely as a matter of formal rationality, it is hard to explain the context-independence attributed to discovered preferences. (2007, 163, 170)

To give this complaint a Continental accent, the neoclassical agent is about being, not about becoming. Or, in a more flat Midwestern accent, this is like trying to have your cake and eat it, too.

Living the contradiction, a modern economist can sneer at psychology as an inferior social science due to its amorphous orthodoxy, and yet become enthusiastic about so-called behavioral economics as somehow rectifying the empirical flaws of neoclassical economics (Wolfe, 2008). Embracing the void, the economist can point to papers that mathematize lexicographic orderings or dispense with the axiom of independence in expected utility theory, but turn around and reject papers for publication that might turn such alternatives into the basis for a general model of the economy. Reveling in the heady air of paradox, the economist can become reconciled to "bounded rationality" emanating from within the Carnegie School by insisting that it is nothing more than constrained maximization applied to the very act of constrained maximization itself (because costly optimization leads to suboptimization).

Of course, one cannot blithely convict the economist for wanting to stuff incompatible principles together into a single orthodox model—lots of sciences seek a similar grail. Consider the repeated baroque attempts to reconcile classical and quantum mechanics. The point we are making here instead is merely that the shotgun marriage of thin invariant preferences with thick cognition will never lead to any foundational model of agency, because any revision or alteration of the one will legitimately be deemed arbitrary from the perspective of the other. The neoclassical agent will always be an unstable compromise between invariant preference field and dynamic information processor.

(ii) Curse of the Schizophrenic Agent

The original neoclassical model from 1870–1940 was first and foremost a model of static allocation of physical goods, based upon the metaphor of a mass-point coming to rest in a field of force (Mirowski 1989). Equilibrium, although not completely specified (with economics lacking the equivalent of a Hamiltonian dynamics) was more or less straightforward: goods moved around between people through the medium of exchange until the maximum of a utility gradient ensued. What the agents thought about the process, if indeed they could be said to think at all, made no difference whatsoever. There was a single index of success or failure of the market, namely, maximum utility. It was a clean causal story, with a sharp separation of agency from the environment.

But then along came the computer, and with it the attendant ambition for an economics of information, and things changed. By endowing the agent with some semblance of cognitive capacities, the very notion of equilibrium began to undergo subtle transformation. In effect, the agent now exhibited *two* distinct motives for exchange: conventional allocative efficiency, and the new notion of cognitive equilibration. It became conceivable that trade could come to a halt before transactors were content with what they knew or believed about their activities. Divergent beliefs or knowledge might potentially result in trades that would *not* have occurred under the simple regime of static allocation. This was an obvious implication of changing the analytical purpose of the market to be conceived as an information processor.

The disturbing aspect of these developments was that the whole class of phenomena roughly characterized as "problems with information" was not simply being superimposed as a second-order improvement upon the unchanged core neoclassical orthodoxy (as in the burgeoning literature on asymmetric information, risk analysis, etc.), but those problems were tending to subvert the coherence of the foundations of the theory of demand. This prospect really only began to loom large with the displacement of the Walrasian model by game theory as the prime mathematical technique of choice of the orthodoxy.[51] The illusion of continuity within the orthodoxy had been fostered largely as a function of the allegiance pledged by the 1980s to the Nash equilibrium concept, which maintained a foundation in previous utility theory, as well as the idiom of constrained maximization. However, the Nash equilibrium shifted the emphasis to cognitive concerns of what the agent knew about others and their motives, including what the rival knew about what the protagonist knew, and *ad infinitum*..., something generally abjured in the prior Walrasian tradition. A truly prodigious literature arose concerning the true meaning of common knowledge, a prerequisite of Nash equilibrium that blurred the boundaries between individual and collective cognition. The position championed by the followers of Herbert Simon that all the aforementioned models only dealt with substantive rather than procedural rationality,[52] only served to exacerbate the problem of founding a dynamics upon the basic static neoclassical model.

The simple ontological point to be made is that once the neoclassical agent was endowed with some epistemic abilities, then he/she/it now came equipped with *at least two separate motives* for exchange, and these motives did not need to reinforce one another; in fact, in general, they might instead conflict. This did not bode well for the neoclassical program, which had invested its tough-minded prescriptivism and integrity in their being only a single version of equilibrium (and one that was unique and stable to boot, although these qualities proved elusive) to which market prices were thought to converge. Our survey of the three paradigms of information, in Figure 5.1 reveals how equilibrium notions fragmented, once caught in a pincers between the dual motives for exchange. Even Hayek never adequately confronted the possibility that allocation and information might be at odds.

(iii) The Wizard of Oz Effect

The key departure for postwar neoclassical theory was to essentially buy into the tale of the existence of a marketplace of ideas, even though the details might not end up looking very much like Hayek's version of that catallactic universe. Indeed, the earliest way to upbraid Hayek was to insist that the marketplace of ideas was identical to the neoclassical market model, and that the market could allocate ideas in the same manner that it allocated widgets. This led to all manner of strange claims being made that neoclassical general equilibrium theory had managed to demonstrate that the market was the most efficient and parsimonious mechanism in terms of information usage relative to all alternative possible mechanisms of resource allocation.[53] For instance, one version of this argument, attributable to Jordan (1982), asserts that competitive equilibrium requires a "message space" (itself an artifact of the Blackwell formalism) of dimension $n(m-1)$, where n is the number of agents and m is the number of goods, and that any other mechanism requires a message space of higher dimensionality. In a sense, this was a reformulation of Koopmans' original argument at Cowles. Putting aside quibbles over whether this dimension captures anything of real economic significance, arguments of this ilk are entirely misleading.

The trick to such arguments is to deal entirely with models of static equilibrium, and then paint the neoclassical model as a wonderful embodiment of the parsimonious marketplace of ideas. This conveniently ignores the fact that there is (still) no general theory of dynamic convergence to equilibrium, either for Walrasian general equilibrium or Nash game theory. What should concern economists within this tradition is not only how informationally demanding the presumed mechanism is when the state of equilibrium occurs, but also how much information is required to get us there in the first place. The fruit of decades of effort along these lines has not been reassuring. For instance, the mathematician Steven Smale (1976a,b) proposed a "Global Newton Method" of dynamical adjustment for the Walrasian model that did guarantee stability, but only at the price of a truly prodigious informational requirement. In an important paper, Saari and Simon (1978) asked whether they could find "locally effective price mechanisms" that use less information than Smale's Global Newton Method, and they answered in the negative. One way to read the Saari/Simon paper is to suggest that any adjustment process leading to an equilibrium from any arbitrary price vector would require an infinite amount of information in a truly general neoclassical world.

Our purpose here is not to dissect the fine points of models of dynamical price adjustment, but rather to make a basic philosophical point—you cannot paint the marketplace of ideas as a marvelously parsimonious and magnificently efficient model of cognition if you can't even demonstrate mathematically that the internal production of neoclassical market equilibrium does not bear information requirements that outstrip any other known algorithmic process. Strip aside the curtain, and you discover to your dismay that the all-powerful wizard is just as weak and flawed as you and me, and that we had been kept in his thrall by some garden-variety *son et lumière* effects.

(iv) The Broken Bootstrap

Suppose, for the sake of argument, that the marketplace of ideas actually manages to price information in such a way that all relevant considerations are somehow embodied in the price data it emits. But then, for the neoclassical economist, the market must be essentially indistinguishable from the cognitive processes people use to process information, although it may differ in details. If that were true, then what precisely is it that induces agents to resort to the market to conduct their cognitive processing rather than just doing it all themselves? Why not outsource most cognition to the mighty marketplace of ideas? Convenience might be the convenient answer: the market is just *cheaper and easier* than sitting down to think things through from first principles. Sometimes this is phrased using the terminology of "transactions costs." But that way lies Bedlam, not Enlightenment.

There are at least two contradictions that arise from this line of reasoning. The first is that, no doubt, we do rely upon others for all manner of assistance, and perhaps even the kindness of strangers, when it comes to accumulating knowledge, but that is because epistemology is inescapably *social or communal,* and not because of the efficacy of any market phenomena as such (Kusch, 2002). The neoclassical model rules out social epistemology as a matter of course by the way it specifies agency,[54] only to reintroduce it as a *deus ex machina* to extricate itself from paradoxes of positing the neoclassical marketplace of ideas as a superior information processor. This is clearly illegitimate.

The second contradiction arises from paradoxes of self-reference. The posit of "transactions costs" clearly implies the existence of a metamarket that can set the prices of various formats of market exchange, but that easily leads to an infinite regress. Who sets the prices of resort to the market to get the right prices? When we shift to an information notion, the paradoxes become more insistent. The market as information processor must itself be priced for us to think about it, but are those prices set within the very same market, or are they banished to some meta-epistemic sphere? In the same way that the Cantor diagonal argument leads to formally undecidable propositions, the price of the marketplace of ideas leads to formally undecidable market prices.

Now, earlier contradictions (i-iv) are of the character of in principle objections, the sort that a philosopher might propose. Postwar neoclassical economists have not had much time for philosophical argument (think of Samuelson sneering that real economists do economics, whereas methodologists just chatter), so one would not expect them to be daunted by anything so flimsy as a mere in-principle contradiction. That is why it becomes important to round out this section by demonstrating that each of the three paradigms of the treatment of information in postwar economics have individually come to grief over the postwar period in a purely internalist sense: that is, reputable orthodox economists using orthodox mathematical models have played out the contradictions in their own programs, resulting in the fact that, by the millennium, no version of the economics of information has emerged unscathed.[55] The landscape, far from being crowded with monumental theorems and general models, is merely dotted with abandoned half-finished shells. This is the effective content of the claim that there is (as yet) no such thing as an economics of information.

Perhaps one of the greatest ironies of the entire situation is that economists have become so very insulated from the culture of which they are nominally a part that they just don't see how absurd the situation looks from outside the walls of their cozy club. One of the recipients of the 2001 Bank of Sweden Prize, given for information economics, had the temerity to reveal this insularity in his Prize lecture:

> I was asked recently by a somewhat incredulous questioner (actually a journalist) whether it was true you could be awarded a Nobel Prize in Economics for simply noticing that there are markets in which certain participants do not know certain things that others in the market do know. I thought it was pretty funny. (Spence 2002, 435)

Let us decide for ourselves whether the history of the economics of information has been a laughing matter. To do so, let us revert back to our historical map in Figure 5.1.

a. Information as a Thing

Speaking of the Nobel, one of the many incongruities of the 2001 award was that one of the recipients had essentially deconstructed the legitimacy of the entire project of treating knowledge as a commodity. To reprise the quote from Joseph Stiglitz:

> When there is no noise, prices convey all information, and there is no incentive to purchase information. But if everybody is uninformed, it clearly pays some individual to become informed. Thus, there does not exist a competitive equilibrium. (2002, 395)

While Stiglitz was unable to provide a general theorem based upon a sufficiently generic model, this nevertheless seems a reasonable restatement of what we have called the "broken bootstrap." Stiglitz was honored, it seems, for asserting that "informational efficiency" of the marketplace of ideas is self-contradictory. His papers were published in all the sanctioned orthodox journals. The lessons he prefers to draw from modeling information as a thing is that markets don't need to clear, that the two fundamental welfare theorems don't hold, that there subsists no law of one price, and that in general, supply does not equal demand. I should think the rest of the profession has drawn the rather more obvious conclusion, that one should cease and desist treating information as a simple commodity if one wishes to remain a neoclassical economist in good standing.

There was one further reason to reject the thingification of knowledge, at least if one were a partisan of the Cowles School. The more that one declared adherence to Nash game theory, the more it became apparent that the construct of knowledge as a thing you could hoard and keep private was becoming implausible, since your implacably rational opponent could supposedly divine what you did and did not know from your observable market behavior. From the strategic viewpoint, there were no distinct individuals with their little discrete private bits of fungible knowledge tucked away in the recesses of their craniums populating the marketplace of ideas; there was just common knowledge, and the return of the Germanic Group Mind, where no one possessed the capacity to agree to disagree. This may be one reason why Cowles explicitly repudiated the Shannon formalism by the 1970s. MIT, never really much enamored of game theory, never quite felt the full force of this objection.

Nevertheless, the thinglike conception of knowledge was still quite prevalent in the popular culture, especially in an era of ever-fortified intellectual property rights, so there were a few economists, primarily in business schools and science-policy units, who sought to find some accommodation between neoclassical theory and the thing paradigm. Paul David, its main representative, has insisted that, "Acknowledging the peculiar character of information as an economic commodity is [the] necessary point of departure ..." (David 2003, 1). The single most common characteristic of this group was a fascination with tacit knowledge.[56] The idea here was that only some knowledge was codifiable, as they liked to put it; the rest was intangible, and passed along outside of marketplace interactions. These economists seemed to believe the tacit/codifiable dichotomy would constitute an escape from the broken bootstrap, or at least the Stiglitz version, since some information just couldn't be purchased. However, (David & Dasgupta 1994) still argued that maximization held sway, since the problem then became one of choosing the optimal mix of tacit and codifiable information in any given circumstance. This argument became quite popular in the last decade as a neoliberal defense of the privatization of the university and the enclosure of the information commons, even though David later admitted, "we cannot really hope to derive either theoretical propositions or empirical measures regarding whether of not the relative size of the codified portion [of knowledge-P.M.] must be secularly increasing or decreasing" (Cowan et al. 2000, 230).

I agree with (Nightingale 2003) that this only appears to rescue the neoclassical tradition by further undermining it. Seriously entertaining the tacit character of knowledge raises its embodied, social, and procedural aspects to the fore, and has been more amenable to constructivist rather than objectivist approaches. It, therefore, exacerbates the "cake" contradiction explained earlier. It is, therefore, indicative that there are no serious formal models of tacit knowledge within the contemporary neoclassical tradition.

b. Inductive Inference/Epistemic Logic

The most telling instance of the philosophical contradiction of the schizophrenic agent has come with the internal development of the Blackwell conception of knowledge, which has been the mathematical economist's epistemic model of choice. It took only a little while after the first specification of the concept of common knowledge for theorists to realize that in a situation in which traders are risk-averse, have the same priors, and the market clears, then it is also common knowledge that traders expected monetary gain, given their information must be positive in order for them to be willing to trade. Hence the mere fact that one trader has information that induces him or her to want to trade at the current price would imply other traders should rationally be unwilling to trade with him or her: he or she knows something they apparently do not. Once that happened, it became possible to see that, even in the case where conventional gains in static allocation were possible, informational considerations might serve to stymie any trade (Samuelson, 2004, p.369). This was first mooted by a "no-trade theorem" (Milgrom & Stokey 1982), which has subsequently been broadened substantially. Furthermore, it was quickly demonstrated that the paradox was not due to any quirk of the original model, but was a direct consequence of the state space model of epistemic logic.[57] It would seem a tragedy for the neoclassical program that the entire market system would freeze up, just because they had augmented their rational agent with some serious epistemic capabilities. Thus it grew unclear whether the shift to an economics of information from the previous static allocation paradigm was really functioning to bolster the orthodoxy, or instead was further weakening it.

A similar, but equally damning implication came from Fischer Black,[58] the famous progenitor of Black-Scholes theory of the pricing of financial derivatives. In an important paper (Black 1986), which wonderfully exemplifies the philosophical contradiction of having your cake and eating it, too, Black deconstructed the version of the "Efficient Markets Hypothesis" that descended from the "Rational Expectations" tradition. He was aware of the no-trade argument that, if all traders were strategically rational in the neoclassical sense, then prices would embody all relevant information, but that no one would voluntarily take the other side of a proffered trade. However, the volume of trades in financial markets suggested that this portrayal of events could not be correct. Indeed, what most insiders believed is that most financial exchanges were populated by a substantial proportion of "noise traders," that is, people who mistake noise (or their own deluded estimations of their abilities) for real information, and execute trades on that basis. But noise trading renders prices less informative than the ideal posited by rational expectations theory; indeed, the participation of noise traders drives prices away from any conventional notions of economic fundamentals. Nevertheless, noise traders perform a valuable function of creating the conditions for a thick market: They keep the smart insiders in business, so they can provide new information to the marketplace. Therefore, there is no way that prices could convey information in the way proponents of the marketplace of ideas had claimed.

In some respects, Black's noise resembled Stiglitz's impossibility, but with a much better sense for how the real world seemed to work. Perry Mehrling (2005, 239) asserts that Black did not lose faith in equilibrium, but merely circumvented the schizophrenia of individual rationality by presuming the market as a whole was still rational—in other words, Hayekian neoliberalism without the Hayekian epistemic commitments. But (evoking the broken bootstrap) for that, who needs neoclassical microtheory?

c. Information as Computationalism

The contradictions of the first two paradigms of information were made manifest by honored and revered neoclassical economists; the curiousity of this third case is that the proofs of contradiction were due to more obscure figures.[59] A number of outsiders to the economics profession, from Michael Rabin to Gerald Kramer to Stephen Kleene had realized that, if one modeled the neoclassical agent as a Turing machine, then it would be possible to show that many aspects of neoclassical economics could be shown to be noncomputable in the sense of formal computational theory. The person who made this case in detail was the student of Kenneth Arrow and RAND mathematician Alain Lewis. Lewis (1985), who showed that no finite automata could make the choices that Arrow's choice function formalism had presumed he could accomplish: "It is obvious that any choice function C that is not *at least computationally viable* is in a very strong sense *economically irrational*…the choices prescribed by a *computationally nonviable* choice function can only be implemented by computational procedures that do one of two things: either (a) the computation does not halt and fails to converge, or (b) the computation halts at a nonoptimal choice" (1985, 45–46). In later papers, Lewis extended the indictment to include the infamous fixed point theorems of Walrasian general equilibrium, the convergence of the core to Walrasian equilibrium, Nash equilibrium, Hurwicz allocation mechanisms, and much else besides. This is the best instantiation of what we have called the Wizard of Oz effect that can be found in the archives of the economics profession.

It seems that few have appreciated just how devastating these results are for the entire program of the economics of information. If the marketplace of ideas is thought to operate like a computer, and then one insists upon neoclassical economic theory as the correct and appropriate model of the market, then economists are dealing in delusion, since they regularly endow the market with capacities that *no existing computer can or ever has possessed*. Although it is not a popular opinion in the contemporary profession, it seems hard to escape the implication that neoclassical economics and computers are just incompatible. One may wish (as Hayek did) to portray the entire market institution as resembling a computer, but to do so, one must relinquish any commitment to the neoclassical orthodoxy.

6. CONCLUSION

I suspect that for many, the arguments contained herein may seem Pyrrhic. Everyone seems to believe that knowledge is the key to economic success, and yet our most-developed schools of economic thought are mired in the most frightful muddles when it comes to modeling knowledge in an economic setting. The implicit moral is that economists may believe they have left philosophy behind with their high-tech methods, but this is nothing but *hubris* born of isolation and a lack of appreciation for how difficult the problems of knowledge and its comprehension really are.[60]

NOTES

1. Fifteen year on, Kreps' (1990, 578fn) warning is still good advice: "The terms of information economics, such as moral hazard, adverse selection, hidden action, hidden information, signaling, screening and so on are used somewhat differently by different authors, so you must keep your eyes open when you see any of these terms in a book or an article…As a consumer of the literature, you should pay less attention to these labels and more to the 'rules of the game'—who knows what when, who does what when." The only codicil one might add is to replace "consumer of the literature" with "epistemically challenged member of the economics community," which better captures the repressed paradox.

2. One lame excuse will have to suffice here: "Many scientific discussions focus on knowledge, as researchers have become aware of its importance for value creation on the firm level and wealth creation on the societal level. Yet, there is little common understanding about the special economic properties of knowledge…" (Gruber 2005, 595).

3. This point was admirably raised in Hands 2001, Chapter 7.

4. For background, see Lavoie 1985, Thomsen 1992, O'Neill 1996, Hayek 1948, Caldwell 2004.

5. Morgenstern's prescient concerns over the epistemic limits to economics, promoted well before any other significant figure in economics, including Hayek, are discussed in Mirowski 1992, 128–132; Innocenti 1995; Caldwell 2004, 211–212.

6. This is argued in greater detail in Mirowski & van Horn 2009; the argument in spare outline is presented later in Section 2. I would like to acknowledge here that Hayek

himself never used the specific terminology of the *marketplace of ideas*, but that his work summoned the concept in an amazing range of contexts, and so needs to be understood as its major progenitor.

7. "Now it seems obvious that having a continuous demand function for all bundles of goods in R_n is no more obvious than having a utility function for those same commodities; at least a utility function is only one function of n variables...There is no obvious reason that such a theory should be considered to be more observable, empirical, or reduce choice to mere consistency" (Hands 2006). It is beyond the scope of our present task to explore the functions that this myth has served in the history of postwar neoclassical economics.

8. 'Neoliberalism' is defined later in Section 2, but in greater detail in Mirowski & Plehwe, 2009.

9. For some economic examples, see Danny Quah in Vaitilingham, 1999; Shapiro & Varian, 1999; Joseph Stiglitz, 1999; Houghton & Sheehan, 2000; Powell & Snellman, 2004; Cooke, 2002; Feldman & Link, 2001. A Google search on the term *knowledge economy* in February 2007 produced an amazing 1,170,000 hits.

10. See, for instance, Drahos & Braithwaite 2002, Delanty 2001, Eisenberg 2001, Nelson 2004, Mowery et al. 2004, Washburn 2005, Slaughter & Rhoads 2004.

11. Some of the authors that address the globalized character of the contemporary transformation of the economy of knowledge include Drahos & Briathwaite 2002; Drori et al. 2003; Apple 2003, 2006; David 2004a; Economist Intelligence Unit 2004; Pels 2005; Mirowski, forthcoming.

12. The alert reader will recognize that this is a proposition characteristic of the social studies of scientific knowledge, applied to the sciences in general (Pickering 1995; Galison 1997); we simply extend it here to the history of economics.

13. The possibilities proliferate if we admit writers who might not qualify as neoclassical under a stringent construction of that term: say, Austrians like Israel Kirzner; or Institutionalists like Brian Loasby; or even indeed evolutionary economists such as Sid Winter. Since contemporary economists spend most of their coffee breaks over fine distinctions about who qualifies as being in and out of real economics, we opt in this paper to restrict attention to those who would be thought of as neoclassicals in good standing.

14. For those who know some history of economic thought, this proposition can be rendered in a more precise manner. I am *not* claiming that early neoclassical economists did not write on epistemic issues. Indeed, here the example of William Stanley Jevons looms large, since he wrote an entire book on epistemic issues in the philosophy of science (1905) and even was notoriously predisposed toward a mechanical theory of mind. Rather, I am pointing to the undeniable fact that Jevons (and others) were never able to reconcile or otherwise incorporate their various philosophical theses into the mathematical models of the agent that they placed at the center of their price theory. For instance, in the case of Jevons, *nothing* he wrote about induction was ever incorporated in his model of the maximization of utility. This is also true of philosophically sophisticated mathematical theorists such as Edgeworth. On the latter, see Mirowski 1994.

15. See, for instance, Director 1964; Coase 1974; Ingber 1984; McCloskey 1994, 368. As far as I am aware, no one has adequately traced these early locutions back to the pragmatist school of philosophy and explicated the role that they played there. If and when this happens, we may find that it had very little resemblance to the postwar neoliberal conception. A good start on this project can be found in Peters 2004.

16. Some instances of this revaluation are Caldwell 2004 and Mirowski & van Horn 2004.

17. The history of neoliberalism is a burgeoning topic in its own right, and would require a separate survey. The interested reader might consult Hartwell 1995, Mirowski & van Horn forthcoming b, Harvey 2005, Mirowski & Plehwe 2009.

18. One can observe this in the enumeration of appearances of the term *marketplace of ideas* in the *New York Times* reported in Peters (2004, 73). The Janus-faced character of the term, which "drips with nostalgia for the town square," even while it evokes the high-tech future of computerized interaction, was extremely important for the conservative movement from the 1950s onward.

19. While Hayek never openly attacked public education in this immediate postwar period, his comrade Milton Friedman did; see Friedman 1962, Chapter 6. Indeed, Friedman went so far as to praise a highly skewed distribution of income as a prerequisite for a free market in ideas (ibid. 17). For more on these issues, see Apple 2006 and Marginson 2007.

20. The intellectual relationship of Polanyi to Hayek is covered at greater length in Mirowski 2004, chapters 2 and 3. Polanyi's concept of tacit knowledge shows up at many different junctures in the postwar economics of knowledge.

21. The contemporary that most assiduously took to heart this insistence on the limits to cognition was in fact Herbert Simon, although he both inverted the political valence, and married his own version of the story much more inseparably to the computer, the method of experimentation, and to the natural sciences in general. See Crowther-Heyck (2005).

22. Hayek's ongoing relationship to Karl Popper is operative here. On this, see Hacohen 2000 and Uebel 2000.

23. The fact that the marketplace of ideas gained a foothold in American culture only as a consequence of the neoliberal project is nicely illustrated in Peters 2004, 73, where a keyword search on the term in the *New York Times* reveals that the term only began to spread in the 1950s, especially in the context of anticommunist controversies.

24. The primary sources are Mirowski & Hands 1998, 2006; Hands & Mirowski 1998. For those seeking a road map through the present argument, simplifying the trajectory of postwar economics through the thickets of knowledge, subsequent footnotes will identify the key points in the current text as numbered propositions. The three-school division of neoclassical market theory enumerated herein is Proposition 1.

25. Each school began with its own in-house journal, thus readily overcoming the problem of how to break into the prewar discussion and begin boundary maintenance. Chicago had the *Journal of Political Economy,* Cowles had *Econometrica,* and MIT found a friendly outlet down Massachusetts Avenue in the *Quarterly Journal of Economics.* The broader-based *American Economic Review* was definitively captured by the neoclassicals only in the later 1950s.

26. The actual conditions surrounding the founding of the Chicago School are highly contested. See Reder 1982 and Mirowski & Van Horn forthcoming. The differentiation of the schools discussed in Hands & Mirowski 1998 possibly downplays the significant rupture in Chicago price theory in 1946.

27. While this complaint might be launched against otherwise perceptive commentaries such as Wong 1978; Houthakker 1983, it can equally be seen as a fault of Mirowski & Hands 1998. Although revealed preference has become the preferred means of both affirming and denying the centrality of utility functions in the American

orthodoxy, it did not provide much in the way of heuristics as to the correct use of demand theory. Many of the obstacles to understanding the MIT/Harvard school come from the inaccessibility of primary archives to researchers, in contrast to the Chicago and Cowles situations. This has particularly blocked research into the patrons of the MIT School.

28. One non-Samuelsonian quote will have to suffice: Marshall "...was probably without peer in the delicate art of not letting his inadequate theory get too much in the way of his sensible view of reality" (Bishop 1964, 35). On the history of the importation of Cowles-style general equilibrium in the MIT graduate curriculum, see the Duncan Foley interview in Colander et al. 2004, 191.

29. An attempt to trace how the individual figures such as Arrow, Marschak, Hurwicz and Koopmans responded over time to the problem of information in their models is Mirowski 2002, chapters 5, 6.

30. Previous experience with various audiences has convinced me that this must be deemed Proposition 2. Too many *ex cathedra* pronouncements, especially by Nobel Prize winners, seem to have driven this fact from the minds of most contemporary trained economists.

31. The work of Shannon is surveyed in Mirowski, 2002, pp. 68–76; the role of Blackwell at RAND is briefly covered in Mirowski 2002, 379–389 and the contributions of Turing are described in Mirowski 2002, 80–88. Actually, the role of John von Neumann in introducing all three paradigms into economics was substantial, and his legacy is the subject of the book cited. The identification of these three particular theories as primary sources for the subsequent evolution of the economics of knowledge within neoclassicism is Proposition 3.

32. On the inappropriateness of the measure for economic and other purposes, see Tribus in Machlup & Mansfield 1983; Floridi 2004, 46–57; Mirowski 2002, 73–76; Arrow in McGuire & Radner 1986.

33. The notion that those devious relativists who thrive in science studies are the only cadre who are susceptible to the perils of reflexivity is one of the sillier arguments made by modern philosophers.

34. "History has witnessed the attempt to make probability theory coherent with what was believed to be rational thought, and it has seen efforts to reduce rational thought to probability theory. For instance, what was believed to be rational judicial and economic thought actually determined the way in which probability theory developed mathematically" (Gigerenzer & Murray 1987, 137).

35. The historical background to this development is covered in Mirowski 2002, 380–386. A nice introductory analytical treatment from the standpoint of epistemic logic is Fagin et al. 1995.

36. In this latter case, we observe one of the few instances where professional philosophers played a significant role in the development of a notion of knowledge that later became important in economics. The reason this happened was that many of the philosophers in question were also active at RAND in their other capacity as operations researchers. The story begins with Rudolf Carnap (1947), and reaches a high level of development with Saul Kripke (1963).

37. "Our notion of knowledge [herein] in a multi-agent system is best understood as an external one, ascribed by, say, the system designer to the agents. We do not assume the agents compute their knowledge in any way, nor do we assume they can necessarily answer questions based on their knowledge" (Fagin et al. 1995, 9). This quote reveals that

this state space conception is far removed from the computational conception described later.

38. Machlup 1962 was clearly one attempt, but actually ended up avoiding most of the thorny epistemological issues, as well as missing out on contemporary developments. In any event, it was roundly ignored by theorists.

39. However, see Sent (2001), Klaes & Sent (2005), Egidi & Marris (1992) and the recent biography by Hunter Crowther-Heyck (2005).

40. For a detailed summary, see Mirowski 2002, 370–389. Even there, many important Cowles initiatives are left unexplored.

41. "Comments in Thursday afternoon session" Conference on Expectations, Uncertainty and Business Behavior, Pittsburgh, Oct. 27–29, 1955, Box 5 folder 81, Tjalling Koopmans Papers, Sterling Library, Yale University. Note that, even though Koopmans was close to von Neumann in this era, he did not entertain the notion that game theory was a better formalism for addressing these questions.

42. For the repudiation of the Shannon concept, see Arrow in McGuire & Radner 1986. For the admission that his models had little to do with cognitive information processing, see Arrow 1984, 200. "There is no general way of defining units of information" Arrow 1996, 120. For Arrow's role in suppressing the work of Alain Lewis, which plays an important role in the next section, see Mirowski 2002, 427–436.

43. In fact, only a small part of game theory was developed in conformity with neoclassical models, but since that subset (primarily involving Nash equilibrium theory) later grew to such dominance in the economics profession, we shall restrict ourselves to that tradition for the purposes of this paper.

44. One might observe this by noting that the survey article on neuroeconomics by Camerer et al. 2005 might be seen as a laundry list of all the ways in which revealed preference theory is flat out wrong.

45. "Unfortunately, we have not been able to obtain a general proof of any of these propositions. What we have been able to do is analyze an interesting example" (Grossman & Stiglitz, 1980: 395).

46. This explicit rendering of the problematic of postwar neoclassical economics is Proposition 4.

47. Here, of course, we refer to the opinions of *outsiders* and not to those of card-carrying members of the economics profession in good standing. Some examples of those we have in mind are Boyle 2000, Apple 2006, andMarginson 2007.

48. The assertion and enumeration of these generic ontological obstacles to a viable economics of knowledge is Proposition 5.

49. Again we point to Hands 2006 as a perceptive theological deconstruction of actual events.

50. This has long been the complaint of philosophers critical of behaviorist psychology, coming from an appreciation for the literature of Continental philosophy. Here we might mention Charles Taylor, Alisdair MacIntyre, Michel Foucault, and Ian Hacking.

51. See, for instance, Peyton Young: "game theory challenged a basic tenet of classical economics because it called attention to situations in which individuals acting in their own self-interest do not necessarily arrive at a social optimum. Previously these situations had been perceived as exceptional or peripheral; game theory showed that they are ubiquitous" in Colander et al. 2004.

52. On Simon, see Sent 2001, Klaes & Sent 2005, and Crowther-Heyck 2005. It has since been noted that one culprit in this regard was the Blackwell "state space" formalism, which effectively banished procedural questions (Samuelson 2004, 400).

53. These papers began with the Cowles doctrine of Koopmans cited earlier in Section 3, and continued with the tradition of mechanism design associated with the names of Hurwicz and Reiter. For further considerations of this literature, see Costa 1998, Lee 2006, and Kirman 2006.

54. I am aware there are many philosophers who call themselves social epistemologists and yet make direct use of neoclassical models of the agent, such as Philip Kitcher and Alvin Goldman. Since I have critiqued their work in detail elsewhere (Mirowski 2004), I will here merely reiterate that the implications of the current critique of information in economics have more far-reaching consequences for some philosophers than previously allowed.

55. The tracing of each paradigm of the postwar treatment of information in economics found in Table 5.1 to its culmination in its own antithesis is Proposition 6.

56. The concept originated with Michael Polanyi; but these economists rarely read Polanyi, much less acknowledged the subtleties of his position (Mirowski 2004, Chapter 2). For the purposes of this paper, we shall identify Paul David (David & Dasgupta 1994, Cowan *et al* 2000) and Dominique Foray (2004) as representatives of this tendency. Paul Nightingale (2003) provides a wide-ranging critique of this position; see also Ancori et al. 2000.

57. This is explained in Fagin et al. 1995, 184. See also Samuelson 2004 and Sent 2006.

58. For historical background on Fischer Black, as well as a pellucid explanation of this paper, see Merhling 2005.

59. A more elaborate history of these contributions may be found in Mirowski 2002, 422–436.

60. The author would like to thank the following for their invaluable comments and input: Bruce Caldwell, Wade Hands, Harold Kincaid, Steve Turner, and participants at "History of the Human Sciences" conference at the University of Pennsylvania, May 2006, and the audience for the plenary address at the Philosophy of the Social Sciences Roundtable, Tampa FL March 2007.

REFERENCES

Ancori, B., *et al* (2000). "The Economics of Knowledge: the Debate about Codification and tacit Knowledge." *Industrial and Corporate Change* 9: 255–287.

Akerlof, G. (2002). "Behavioral Macroeconomics and Macroeconomic Behavior." *American Economic Review* 92: 411–433.

Akerlof, G. (1984). *An Economic Theorist's Book of Tales*. New York: Cambridge University Press.

Akerlof, G. (1970). "The Market for Lemons." *Quarterly Journal of Economics* 84: 488–500.

Amin, Ash & Cohendet, Patrice (2004). *Architectures of Knowledge*. Oxford: Oxford University Press.

Antonelli, C. (2005). "Models of Knowledge and Systems of Governance." *Journal of Institutional Economics* 1: 51–73.

Apple, M. (2006). *Educating the Right Way.* 2nd ed. London: Routledge.

Apple, M., ed. (2003). *The State and the Politics of Knowledge.* New York: RoutledgeFalmer.

Arrow, K. (1996). "The Economics of Information: An Exposition." *Empirica* 23: 119–128.

Arrow, K. (1984). *The Economics of Information.* Vol. 4 of Collected Papers. Cambridge: Harvard University Press.

Arrow, K. (1962). "Economic Welfare and the Allocation of Resources for Invention." In Richard Nelson, ed., *The Rate and Direction of Inventive Activity.* Princeton: Princeton University Press.

Aumann, R. (2005). "Musings on Information and Knowledge." *Economics Journal Watch* 2: 88–96.

Aumann, R. (2004). "Interview with Sergiu Hart." http://econ.tepper.cmu/md/uploads/05m103R.pdf

Aumann, R. (2000). *Collected Papers, vol 1.* Cambridge: MIT Press.

Aumann, R. (1976). "Agreeing to Disagree." *Annals of Statistics* 4: 1236–1239.

Baars, B. (1986). *The Cognitive Revolution in Psychology.* New York: Guilford Press.

Bartley, W.W. (1990). *Unfathomed Knowledge, Unmeasurable Wealth.* La Salle, Ill: Open Court.

Ben-David, J. (1991). *Scientific Growth.* Berkeley: University of California Press.

Bender, T., & Schorske, C., eds. (1997). *American Academic Culture in Transition.* Princeton: Princeton University Press.

Binmore, K (1999). "Why Experiment in Economics?" *Economic Journal* 109: F16–24.

Bishop, R. (1964). "The Impact of the General Theory," *American Economic Review,* 54:33–43.

Black, F. (1986). "Noise." *Journal of Finance* 41: 529–43.

Blackwell, D. (1953). "Equivalent Comparisons of Experiments." *Annals of Mathematical Statistics* 24: 265–272.

Blackwell, D. (1951). "Comparison of Experiments." In Jerzy Neyman, ed., *Proceedings of the Second Berkeley Symposium.*

Boyle, J. (2000). "Cruel, Mean or Lavish? Economic Analysis, Price Discrimination and Digital Intellectual Property." *Vanderbilt Law Review* 53: 2007–2039.

Bruni, L. & Sugden, R. (2007). "The Road not Taken: How Psychology was Removed from Economics." *Economic Journal* 117: 146–173.

Burke, J.; Epstein, G. & Minsik, C. 2004. "Rising Foreign Outsourcing and Employment Losses in US Manufacturing, 1987–2002," Univ. Massachusetts Working Paper No.89.

Bush, V. (1945). *Science-the Endless Frontier.* Washington: Government Printing Office.

Caldwell, B. (2004). *Hayek's Challenge.* Chicago: University of Chicago Press.

Camerer, C., Loewenstein, G. & Prelec, D. (2005). "Neuroeconomics: How Neuroscience can Inform Economics." *Journal of Economic Literature* 63: 9–64.

Capuro, R. & Hjorland, B. (2002). "The Concept of Information." *Annual Review of Information Science and Technology* 37: 343–411.

Carnap, R. (1947). *Meaning and Necessity.* Chicago: University of Chicago Press.

Coase, R. (1974). "The Market for Goods and the Market for Ideas." *American Economic Review, Papers and Proceedings,* May: 384–391.

Colander, D., Holt, R. & Rosser, J.B., eds. (2004). *The Changing Face of Economics.* Ann Arbor: Univ. of Michigan Press.

Collins, H. (2004). *Gravity's Shadow*. Chicago: University of Chicago Press.

Conlisk, J. (1996). "Why Bounded Rationality?" *Journal of Economic Literature* 34: 669–700.

Cooke, P. (2002). *Knowledge Economies*. London: Routledge.

Costa, M. (1998). *General Equilibrium Analysis and the Theory of Markets*. Cheltenham: Elgar.

Cowan, R., David, P. & Foray, D. (2000). "The Explicit Economics of Knowledge: Codification and Tacitness." *Industrial and Corporate Change* 9: 211–253.

Crowther-Heyck, H. (2005). *Herbert A. Simon: The Bounds of Reason*. Baltimore: Johns Hopkins University Press.

David, P. (2004a). "Understanding the Emergence of Open Science Institutions: Functionalist Economics in an Historical Context." *Industrial and Corporate Change* 13 (4): 571–89.

David, P. (2004b). "Can Open Science be Protected from the Evolving Regime of IPR Protection?" *Journal of Institutional and Theoretical Economics* 167: 1–26.

David, P. (2003). "The Economic Logic of Open Science and the Balance between Private Property Rights and the Public Domain in Scientific Information." In J.M. Esanu & P.F. Uhlir, eds., *The Role of Scientific and Technical Data and Information in the Public Domain*. Washington: National Academies Press.

David, P. & Dasgupta, P. (1994). "Toward a New Economics of Science." *Research Policy* 23: 487–521.

Delanty, G. (2001). *Challenging Knowledge: The University in the Knowledge Society*. Buckingham: Open University Press.

Demsetz, H. (1969). "Information and Efficiency: Another Viewpoint." *Journal of Law and Economics* 12: 1–22.

Director, A. (1964). "The Parity of the Economic Market Place." *Journal of Law and Economics* 7: 1–10.

Dorfman, R. (1960). "Operations Research." *American Economic Review* 50: 575–623.

Drahos, P. & Braithwaite, J. (2002). *Information Feudalism: Who Owns the Knowledge Economy?* New York: New Press.

Drori, G., Meyer, J., Ramirez, F. & Schofer, E. (2003). *Science in the Modern World Polity: Institutionalization and Globalization*. Stanford: Stanford University Press.

Economist Intelligence Unit (2004). *Scattering the Seed of Invention: The Globalization of Research and Development*.

Egidi, M. & Marris, R., eds. (1992). *Economics, Bounded Rationality, and the Cognitive Revolution*. Aldershot: Elgar.

Eisenberg, R. (2001). "Bargaining over the Transfer of Research Tools." In R. Dreyfuss, H. First, & D. Zimmerman, eds., *Expanding the Boundaries of Intellectual Property*, 223–249. Oxford: Oxford University Press.

Engelbrecht, H. (2005). "ICT Research, the New Economy, and the Evolving Discipline of Economics: Back to the Future?" *The Information Society* 21: 317–320.

Fagin, R., Halpern, J., Moses, Y. & Vardi, M. (1995). *Reasoning about Knowledge*. Cambridge: MIT Press.

Feldman, M. & Link, A., eds. (2001). *Innovation Policy in the Knowledge-Based Economy*. Boston: Kluwer.

Floridi, L., ed. (2004). *Blackwell Guide to the Philosophy of Computing and Information*. Oxford: Basil Blackwell.

Foray, D. (2004). *The Economics of Knowledge*. Cambridge: MIT Press.

Friedman, M. (1962). *Capitalism and Freedom*. Chicago: University of Chicago Press.

Fuller, S. (2005). "Knowledge as Product and Property." In N. Stehr & V. Meja, eds. *Society and Knowledge*. 2nd ed. New Brunswick: Transaction.

Fuller, S. (2002). *Knowledge Management Foundations*. London: Butterworth.

Galison, P. (1997). *Image and Logic*. Chicago: University of Chicago Press.

Geanakoplos, J. (1992). "Common Knowledge." *Journal of Economic Perspectives* 6: 53–82.

Georgescu-Roegen, N. (1975). "The Measure of Information—A Critique." In J. Rose & C. Bilciu, eds. *Modern Trends in Cybernetics and Systems* 3: 187–217. Berlin: Springer Verlag.

Gigerenzer, G., & Murray, D. (1987). *Cognition as Intuitive Statistics*. Hillsdale, NJ: Erlbaum.

Giocoli, N. (2003). *Modeling Rational Agents*. Cheltenham: Elgar.

Glimcher, P. (2003). *Decisions, Uncertainty and the Brain: The Science of Neuroeconomics*. Cambridge: MIT Press.

Godin, B. (2005). *Measurement and Statistics on Science and Technology*. London: Routledge.

Grossman, S. (1989). *The Informational Role of Prices*. Cambridge: MIT Press.

Grossman, S., & Stiglitz, J. (1980). "On the Impossibility of Informationally Efficient Markets." *American Economic Review* 70: 393–408.

Gruber, M. (2005). "Review of Foray (2004)." *Journal of Evolutionary Economics*.15: 595–8.

Hacohen, M. (2000). *Karl Popper: The Formative Years*. New York: Cambridge University Press.

Hands, D. W. (2006). "(Continued) Reconsideration of Individual Psychology, Rational Choice and Demand Theory: Some Remarks on Three Recent Studies." *Revue de Philosophie Economique* 13: 3–48.

Hands, D. W. (2001). *Reflection without Rules*. New York: Cambridge University Press.

Hands, Wade & Mirowski, Philip (1998). "Harold Hotelling and the Neoclassical Dream." In Roger Backhouse, D. Hausman, U. Maki, & A Salanti, eds., *Economics and Methodology: Crossing Boundaries*, 322–397. London: Macmillan.

Hartwell, R.M. (1995). *History of the Mont Pelerin Society*. Indianapolis: Liberty Press.

Harvey, D. (2005). *A Short History of Neoliberalism*. New York: Oxford University Press.

Hayek, F. (1982). "The Sensory Order after 25 Years." In W. Weimer & D. Palermo, eds. *Cognition and the Symbolic Process*. Hillsdale: Erlbaum.

Hayek, F. (1952) *The Sensory Order*. Chicago: University of Chicago Press.

Hayek, F. (1948). *Individualism and Economic Order*. Chicago: Regnery.

Hayek F. (1937) "Economics and knowledge." *Economica* 4(13): 33–54.

Hirschleifer, J., & Riley, J. (1992). *The Analytics of Uncertainty and Information*. New York: Cambridge University Press.

Houghton, J., & Sheehan, P. (2000). *A Primer on the Knowledge Economy*. Melbourne: Victoria Centre for Strategic Studies.

Hounshell, D. (2000). "The Medium is the Message." In T. Hughes & A. Hughes, eds., *Systems, Experts and Computers*. Cambridge: MIT Press.

Houthakker, H. (1983) "On Consumption Theory," in E.C. Brown and R.M.Solow, eds., *Paul Samuelson and Modern Economic Theory*. New York: McGraw-Hill.

Ingber, S. (1984). "The Marketplace of Ideas: A Legitimating Myth." *Duke Law Journal* (February): 1–91.

Innocenti, A. (1995). "Oskar Morgenstern and the Heterodox Possibilities of Game Theory." *European Journal of the History of Economic Thought* 17: 205–27.

Jevons, W. S. (1905). *The Principles of Science.* 2nd ed. London: Macmillan.

Jordan, J.S. (1982). "The Competitive Allocation Process is Informationally Efficient Uniquely." *Journal of Economic Theory* 28: 1–18.

Kirman, A. (2006). "Demand Theory and General Equilibrium: Down the Wrong Road." In P. Mirowski & D. Hands, eds., *Agreement on Demand.* . Durham: Duke University Press.

Klaes, M. & Sent, E. (2005). "A Conceptual History of the Emergence of Bounded Rationality." *History of Political Economy* 37: 27–60.

Klein, J. (2000). "Economics for a Client: Statistical Quality Control and Sequential Analysis." In Roger Backhouse & Jeff Biddle, eds., *Toward a History of Applied Economics.* Durham: Duke University Press.

Koopmans, T. (1957). *Three Essays on the State of Economic Science.* New York: McGraw-Hill. [reprint Augustus Kelley, 1991]

Kreps, D. (1997). "Economics—the Current Position." In T. Bender & C. Schorske, eds.,). *American Academic Culture in Transition.* Princeton: Princeton University Press.

Kreps, D. (1990). *A Course in Microeconomic Theory.* Princeton: Princeton University Press.

Kripke, S. (1963). "A Semantic Analysis of Modal Logic I," *Zeitschrift fur Mathematische Logik und Grundlagen der Mathematik,* (24): 323.

Kusch, M. (2002). *Knowledge by Agreement.* Oxford: Oxford University Press.

Landes, W., & Posner, R. (2003). *The Intellectual Structure of Intellectual Property Law.* Cambridge: Harvard University Press.

Lavoie, D. (1985). *Rivalry and Central Planning.* Cambridge: Cambridge University Press.

Lee, K. (2006). "Mechanism Design Theory Embodying an Algorithm-Centered Vision." In P. Mirowski & D. Hands, eds., *Agreement on Demand,* 283–304. Durham: Duke University Press.

Lessig, L. (2001). *The Future of Ideas.* New York: Random House.

Lewis, A. (1985). "On Effectively Computable Realizations of Choice Functions." *Mathematical Social Sciences* 10: 43–80.

Lucas, R., & Sargent, T. (1981). *Rational Expectations and Econometric Practice.* Minneapolis: University of Minnesota Press.

Machlup, F. (1980). *Knowledge: Its Creation, Distribution and Economic Significance.* 3 vols. Princeton: Princeton University Press.

Machlup, F. (1962). *The Production and Distribution of Knowledge in the US.* Princeton: Princeton University Press.

Machlup, F. & Mansfield, U. eds. (1983). *The Study of Information.* New York: Wiley.

Macho-Stadler, I. & Perez-Castrillo, D. (2001). *An Introduction to the Economics of Information.* 2nd ed. Oxford: Oxford University Press.

Makowski, L. & Ostroy, J. (2001). "Perfect Competition and the Creativity of the Market." *Journal of Economic Literature* 39: 479–535.

Malone, C. & Elichirigoity, F. (2003). "Information as Commodity and Economic Sector." *Journal of the American Society for Information Science and Technology* 54: 512–520.

Marginson, S. (2007). "The Public/Private Divide in Higher Education: A Global Revision." *Higher Education* 53: 307–333.

Marschak, J. (1968). "Economics of Inquiring, Communicating, Deciding." *American Economic Review* 58: 1–18.

Marschak, J. (1954). "Towards an Economic Theory of Organization and Information."
    In R.M. Thrall *et al.*, eds., *Decision Process.* New York: John Wiley.
McCloskey, D. (1994). *Knowledge and Persuasion in Economics.* New York: Cambridge
    University Press.
McGuire, C.B., & Radner, R., eds. (1986). *Decision and Organization.* Minneapolis:
    University of Minnesota Press.
Mehrling, P. (2005). *Fischer Black and the Revolutionary Idea of Finance.* New York:
    Wiley.
Milgrom, P. & Stokey, N. (1982). "Information, Trade and Common Knowledge." *Journal
    of Economic Theory* 26: 17–27.
Mirowski, P. (forthcoming). *SciMart: The New Economics of Science.* Cambridge:
    Harvard University Press.
Mirowski, P. (2007) "Did the (Returns to) Scales Fall from their Eyes?" *Journal of the
    History of Economic Thought*, December, 29:481–494.
Mirowski, P. (2004). *The Effortless Economy of Science?* Durham: Duke University Press.
Mirowski, P. (2002). *Machine Dreams.* New York: Cambridge University Press.
Mirowski, P., ed. (1994). *Edgeworth on Chance, Economic Hazard and Statistics.* Lanham:
    Rowman & Littlefield.
Mirowski, P. (1992). "What Were von Neumann and Morgenstern Trying to
    Accomplish?" In E.R. Weintraub, ed. *Toward a History of Game Theory.* Durham:
    Duke University Press.
Mirowski, P. (1989). *More Heat than Light.* New York: Cambridge University Press.
Mirowski, P. & Hands, D. W., eds. (2006). *Agreement on Demand.* Durham: Duke
    University Press.
Mirowski, P. & Hands, D. W., eds. (1998). "A Paradox of Budgets." In M. Morgan
    & M. Rutherford, eds., *From Interwar Pluralism to Postwar Neoclassicism,* Annual
    Supplement to Volume 30, History of Political Economy, 260–292. Durham: Duke
    University Press.
Mirowski, P. & Plehwe, D., eds. (2009). *The Road from Mont Pelerin: the Making of the
    Neoliberal Thought Collective.* Cambridge: Harvard University Press.
Mirowski, P. & Sent, E. eds. (2002). *Science Bought and Sold.* Chicago: University of
    Chicago Press.
Mirowski, P. & van Horn, R. (2009). "The Road to a World Made Safe for Corporations:
    the Rise of the Chicago School." in (Mirowski & Plehwe, 2009).
Mirowski, P. & van Horn, R. (forthcoming). "Neoliberalism." In Ross Emmett, ed., *Elgar
    Companion to the Chicago School of Economics,* forthcoming.
Mirowski, P. & van Horn, R. (2005). "The Contract Research Organization and the
    Commercialization of Science." *Social Studies of Science* 35: 503–548.
Mowery, D., Nelson, R., Sampat, B. & Arvids, Z. (2004). *Ivory Tower and Industrial
    Innovation.* Stanford: Stanford University Press.
Mowery, D. & Rosenberg, N. (1998). *Paths of Innovation.* New York: Cambridge
    University Press.
Muth, J. (1961). "Rational Expectations and the Theory of Price Movements."
    Econometrica 29: 315–355.
Nelson, P. (1970). "Information and Consumer Behavior." *Journal of Political Economy* 78:
    311–329.
Nelson, R. (2004). "The Market Economy and the Scientific Commons." *Research Policy*
    33: 455–471.

Nightingale, P. (2003). "If Nelson and Winter are Only Half Right about Tacit Knowledge, Which Half?" *Industrial and Corporate Change* 12:149–183.

O'Neill, J. (2003). "Unified Science as Political Philosophy," *Studies in the History and Philosophy of Science* 34: 575–96.

O'Neill, J. (1996). "Who Won the Socialist Calculation Controversy?" *History of Political Thought* 17: 431–442.

Pels, D. (2005). "Mixing Metaphors: Politics or Economics of Knowledge?" In N. Stehr & V. Meja, eds. *Society and Knowledge*. New Brunswick: Transaction.

Peters, J. D. (2004). "Marketplace of Ideas: History of a Concept." In Andrew Calabrese & Colin Sparks, eds., *Toward a Political Economy of Culture*, 65–82. Lanham: Rowman & Littlefield.

Phlips, L. (1988). *The Economics of Imperfect Information*. Cambridge: Cambridge University Press.

Pickering, A. (1995). *The Mangle of Practice*. Chicago: University of Chicago Press.

Porat, M. (1977). *The Information Economy*. Washington: Dept. of Commerce.

Posner, R. (2005). "Bad News." *New York Times Book Review,* July 31.

Powell, W. & Snellman, K. (2004). "The Knowledge Economy." *Annual Review of Sociology* 30: 199–220.

Radner, R. (1968). "Competitive Equilibrium under Uncertainty." *Econometrica* 36: 31–58.

Reder, M. (1982). "Chicago Economics: Permanence and Change," *Journal of Economic Literature* 20: 1–38.

Riley, J. (2001). "Silver Signals." *Journal of Economic Literature* 39: 432–478.

Romer, P. (1990). "Endogenous Technical Change." *Journal of Political Economy* 98: S71–S102.

Rothschild, M. (1973). "Models of Market Organization with Imperfect Information: A Survey." *Journal of Political Economy* 81: 1283–1308.

Saari, D. & Simon, C. (1978). "Effective Price Mechanisms." *Econometrica* 46: 1097–1125.

Samuelson, L. (2004). "Modeling Knowledge in Economic Analysis," *Journal of Economic Literature* 42: 367–403.

Samuelson, P. (2004). "An Interview with Paul Samuelson," *Macroeconomic Dynamics* 8: 519–542.

Samuelson, P. (1998). "How Foundations Came to Be," *Journal of Economic Literature,* 36:1375–1386.

Samuelson, P. (1954). "The Pure Theory of Public Expenditure." *Review of Economics and Statistics* 36: 387–389.

Scheutz, M. (2002). *Computationalism: New Directions*. Cambridge: MIT Press.

Scotchmer, S. (2004). *Innovation and Incentives*. Cambridge: MIT Press

Sent, E. (2006). "The Tricks of the (No-) Trade (Theorem)." In P. Mirowski. & W. Hands, eds., *Agreement on Demand*, 305–321. Durham: Duke University Press.

Sent, E. (2002). "How (Not) to Influence People: The Contrary Tale of John Muth," *History of Political Economy* 34: 291–319.

Sent, E. (2001). "Sent Simulating Simon Simulating Scientists," *Studies in the History and Philosophy of Science A* 32: 479–500.

Sent, E. (1998). *The Evolving Rationality of Rational Expectations*. New York: Cambridge University Press.

Shapiro, C. & Varian, H. (1999). *Information Rules*. Cambridge: Harvard Business School Press.

Shannon, C. (1948). "The Mathematical Theory of Communication." *Bell System Technical Journal* 27: 379–423; 623–656.

Shi, Y. (2001). *The Economics of Scientific Knowledge*. Cheltenham: Elgar.

Shiller, D. (1988). "How to Think about Information." In V. Mosco & J. Wasko, eds. *The Political Economy of Information*. Madison: University of Wisconsin Press.

Slaughter, S. & Rhoades, G. (2004). *Academic Capitalism and the New Economy*. Baltimore: Johns Hopkins Press.

Smale, S. (1976a) "A Convergent Process of Price Adjustment and Global Newton Methods," *Journal of Mathematical Economics*, 3:107–120.

Smale, S. (1776b) "Dynamics in General Equilibrium Theory," *American Economic Review*, 66:288–294.

Solow, R. (1957). "Technical Change and the Aggregate Production Function." *Review of Economics and Statistics* 39: 312–320.

Spence, A. M. (2002). "Signaling in Retrospect and the Information Structure of Markets." *American Economic Review* 92: 434–459.

Spence, A. M. 1974. "An Economist's View of Information." In C. Canadia, A. Luke & J. Harris, eds. *Annual Review of Information Science and Technology* 9: 57–78.

Stigler, G. (1985). *Memoirs of an Unregulated Economist*. New York: Basic Books.

Stigler, G. (1961). "The Economics of Information." *Journal of Political Economy* 69: 213–225; reprinted in *The Organization of Industry*. Homewood: Irwin [1968].

Stiglitz, J. (2003). "Information and the Change in Paradigm in Economics. ." In R. Arnott, B. Greenwald, R. Kanbur & B. Nalebuff, eds. *Economics in an Imperfect World*, 569–639. Cambridge: MIT Press.

Stiglitz, J. (2002). "Information and the Change in Paradigm in Economics." *American Economic Review* 92: 460–501.

Stiglitz, J. (2000). "The Contributions of the Theory of Information to 20th century Economics." *Quarterly Journal of Economics* 140: 1441–1478.

Stiglitz, J. (1999). "Knowledge in the Modern Economy." In Romesh Vaitilingham, ed., *The Economics of the Knowledge Driven Economy*, 37–57. London: Department of Trade and Industry.

Stiglitz, J. (1993). "Reflections on Economics." In Arnold Heertje, ed., *Makers of Modern Economics, vol. 1*. Hemel Hempstead: Harvester Wheatsheaf.

Stiglitz, J. (1985). "Information and Economic Analysis." *Economic Journal—Conference Papers* 95: 21–41.

Thomsen, E. (1992). *Prices and Knowledge*. New York: Routledge.

Uebel, T. (2000). "Some Scientism, Some Historicism, Some Critics." In M. Stone & J. Wolff, eds., *The Proper Ambition of Science*, 151–173. London: Routledge.

Vaitilingham, R., ed. (1999). *The Economics of the Knowledge Driven Economy*. London: Department of Trade and Industry.

Varian, H. (2002). "A New Economy with No New Economics." *New York Times*, Web version, January 17.

Wallis, W. A. (1980). "The Statistical Research Group." *Journal of the American Statistical Association* 75: 320–330.

Warsh, D. (2006). *Knowledge and the Wealth of Nations*. New York: Norton.

Washburn, J. (2005). *University, Inc.* New York: Basic Books.

Wolfe, A. (2008) "HedonicMan," *New Republic*, July 9.

Wong, S. (1978). The Foundations of Paul Samuelson's Revealed Preference Theory. Boston: Routledge and Kegan Paul.

Woolgar, S. (2004). "Marketing Ideas." *Economy and Society* 33: 448–462.

Zappia, C. (1996). "The Notion of Private Information in Modern Perspective." *European Journal of the History of Economic Thought* 3: 107–131.

PART II

MICROECONOMICS

CHAPTER 6

....

RATIONALITY AND INDETERMINACY

....

CRISTINA BICCHIERI

1. INDETERMINACY

....

MUCH of the history of game theory has been dominated by the problem of indeterminacy. The very search for better, more encompassing versions of rationality, as
well as the long list of attempts to refine Nash equilibrium, can be seen as answers,
or attempted solutions, to the indeterminacy that has accompanied game theory
through its history. More recently, the experimental approach to game theory
has attempted a more radical solution: by directly generating a stream of behavioral observations, and thus controlling some crucial parameters, one hopes that
behavioral hypotheses will be sharper, and predictions more accurate. I shall look
at several attempts to address indeterminacy, including the shift to evolutionary
models. However, because my goal is to establish whether rational choice models
are inescapably doomed to produce indeterminate outcomes, I will pay much more
attention to the experimental turn in game theory, the difficulty it encounters, and
the promising results obtained by more realistic models of rationality that include
a social component. The sophisticated reader should bear with some initial review
of familiar ideas for the sake of following the historical (and logical) thread, from
early attempts to address indeterminacy out to novel ideas and solutions.

There are at least two kinds of indeterminacy we may want to distinguish.
One, which I will dub *epistemic indeterminacy*, is something we all have to live
with. Our knowledge of the world is limited, and the outcomes of our choices

usually are not deterministic; instead, any choice corresponds to several possible outcomes, each tied to the occurrence of a particular state of the world. Though we cannot predict which outcome will occur, we can assess the probability with which the corresponding state of the world will occur and can choose on the basis of this probabilistic assessment. Rational choice in this context simply means maximizing expected utility, where the subjective utility of an act is the weighted sum of the desirability of its consequences, and the weights are the probabilities we assess for each of the possible consequences. Decision theory formalizes all this: It tells us which strategies are rational, that is, coherent with the subject's preferences with respect to certain and uncertain outcomes, and with her beliefs about all the variables that are relevant to choice but that she cannot control.

Though we live with epistemic indeterminacy, some form of *predictability* in the context of individual decision making is still possible. By predictability I mean the ability of a third party to predict what sort of action an individual will take. For example, suppose there are reliable statistical data available and we know our subject knows them, we know his preferences, and have every reason to believe he is both practically and epistemically rational.[1] In this case, we can in fact predict what this person will choose. The prediction becomes a little more complicated in case there are no objective probabilities to rely on, but suppose again that we happen to know a person's subjective probabilistic assessments. In this case, provided again that we know that person's preferences and have every reason to believe such individual is both practically and epistemically rational, we can predict his choice.[2]

This simple model of rational choice has been criticized as too abstract and demanding: on one end, the amount of knowledge required for third-party predictability is quite extreme, and on the other end, the decision maker is often unable to even imagine all the possible consequences of her actions, calculate the probabilities, maximize as the rationality recipe recommends, and so on. What I want to stress here, however, is not our obvious condition as cognitive misers. Instead, I want to draw attention to the fact that, even if we were perfect cognitive machines and/or perfect predictors, there are contexts in which rationality may not help us make a choice or predict what another's choice will be. Such contexts are very common; whenever we interact with other individuals and the outcome of such interaction depends upon the joint actions of all the parties, we face *strategic indeterminacy.*

To act rationally in a strategic context is much more difficult because the consequences of an action depend upon what *all* the parties involved do. That is, outcomes are jointly determined by the parties' independent actions. The interactive decision problem of an agent can be represented in general terms as follows: The agent will choose a plan of action considering that the consequences of his/her choice also depend on a combination of unknown and uncontrollable variables, including other agents' plans of action. Rephrasing the problem in terms of decision theory, we may say that the agent is *rational* if she maximizes her expected

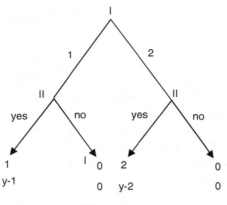

Figure 6.1.

utility, calculated by assigning subjective probabilities to the possible values of all the relevant variables she cannot control, and taking into account her present information. The fundamental difference between decision theory and game theory is that the latter tries to *explain subjective beliefs using strategic reasoning.*

For example, think of a two-player bargaining game in which player I moves first, and can sell to player II a good for a low price ($1) or a high price ($2). Player II can accept (yes) or reject (no) I's proposal; if II rejects, both get 0 (Figure 6.1). I's problem is one of maximizing expected utility (in this case, expressed in terms of money), given what he knows (or believes) about II's knowledge, preferences, and beliefs.

Note that how much information is possessed by the players is crucial in determining the outcome, and our knowledge of such information is equally critical in determining the possibility of predicting what the players will do. Suppose that the rules of the game and players' rationality are *common knowledge.*[3] If II is known to be rational, then I can *infer* that II will refuse if the price is greater than y, and accept if the price is lower than y. However, without knowing the value of y, player I would still be unable to predict II's response to his offer. If we also assume that payoffs are common knowledge, then I would know the value of y, *predict* how II will react to each offer, and choose accordingly.[4] In our case, if I knows that $y > 2$, then he expects II to accept both prices. If instead I knows that $1 < y < 2$, then he expects II to accept only the low price.

Notice that I's subjective beliefs about player II's choices are *endogenous.* He infers them from his knowledge of the structure of the game, of player II's payoffs and rationality. In sum, in a strategic context, what is rational for a player to do depends upon what he expects other players will do, which in turn is inferred from the knowledge that a player has about other players and the structure of the game. *Each party to a strategic interaction is at the same time a chooser and a predictor of other parties' choices.* In this case, epistemic and strategic indeterminacy are entwined.

2. Nash Predictions

An easy solution to the problem of strategic indeterminacy would be to collapse it into epistemic indeterminacy: if players' subjective beliefs were treated as *exogenous* to the game, other players' choice profiles would become states of the world that have a given probability of occurring, and one might just try to maximize expected utility with respect to those states, bypassing the fact that such states are determined by what other players believe their counterparts are going to choose. Is this an interesting solution to strategic indeterminacy? Not if we think that the notion of *Nash equilibrium* is important.

Nash equilibrium (Nash 1951) is the standard solution concept for noncooperative games. Informally, a Nash equilibrium specifies players' actions and beliefs such that (a) each player's action is optimal given his beliefs about other players' choices; (b) players' beliefs are correct. Thus, an outcome that is not a Nash equilibrium requires either that a player chooses a suboptimal strategy, or that some players misperceive the situation. More formally, a Nash equilibrium is a vector of strategies $(\sigma_1^*, . ., \sigma_n^*)$, one for each of the n players in the game, such that each σ_i^* is optimal given (or is a *best reply* to) σ_{-i}^*.[5]

Nash equilibrium is an appealing solution concept for noncooperative games for several reasons.[6] It captures an important feature of individual rationality, that is, that being rational means maximizing one's expected utility under the constraint represented by what one expects other individuals to choose. It is supported by correct beliefs, in the sense that, if players are in equilibrium, their beliefs about each other's strategy choice are correct. Finally, the concept of Nash equilibrium depicts the idea of a self-enforcing agreement. Were players to agree in preplay negotiation to play a particular strategy combination, they would have an incentive to stick to the agreement only in case the agreed upon combination is a Nash equilibrium. There are many real-life situations in which there is no third party available to monitor and enforce compliance with an agreement: many transactions are conducted with a handshake in the expectation that the parties will fulfill their promises. Indeed, when this happens it means that it is in the parties' interest to fulfill the terms of the agreement, that there is no incentive to unilaterally deviate from it. It means, in other words, that the agreement is a Nash equilibrium.

Game theorists typically assign a predictive value to Nash equilibrium. In a well-known passage of their book, *Theory of Games and Economic Behavior* (1944), von Neumann and Morgenstern said that rational players who know (i) all there is to know about the structure of the game they are playing, (ii) all there is to know about the beliefs and motives of the other players, (iii) that every player is rational, (iv) that every player knows (i)–(iii), (v) that every players knows (i)–(iv), and so on, will be able to infer the optimal strategy for every player. In that case, each player will behave rationally by maximizing his expected utility conditional on what he expects the others to do. This states what could be rightly called the central dogma of game theory: that rational players will always jointly maximize their expected utilities, or play a *Nash equilibrium.*

Ken Binmore (1987/1988) has argued that there are two possible interpretations of Nash equilibrium. According to the *evolutive* interpretation, a Nash equilibrium is an observed regularity. Players know the equilibrium, and test the rationality of their behavior given this knowledge acquired from experience. The players (and the game theorist) can accordingly predict that a given equilibrium will be played, since they are accustomed to coordinate upon that equilibrium and expect (correctly) others to do the same. According to the more commonly adopted *eductive* interpretation, instead, a game is a unique event. In this case it makes sense to ask whether players can deduce what others will do from the information available to them. The players (and the game theorist) can predict that an equilibrium will be played just in case they have enough information to infer players' choices. The standard assumptions game theorists make about players' rationality and knowledge should in principle be sufficient to guarantee that an equilibrium will obtain. The customary assumptions are:

C(SG + PF). The structure of the game (SG) and players' preferences (PF) are common knowledge among the players;

C(Rat). The players are rational (Rat) and this is common knowledge.

When a game has a unique Nash equilibrium, we can predict that it will be played if we are able to show that players, armed with common knowledge of rationality and of the structure of the game, will infer the Nash solution. If players have dominated strategies, C(Rat) entails that they will eliminate them, and this is common knowledge (we assume that the consequences of C(SG + PF) and C(Rat) are common knowledge, too). Often, after we have eliminated strictly dominated strategies for one player, we may find that there are now strictly dominated strategies for another player, which will be eliminated as well. This process of successive elimination can continue until there are no more strictly dominated strategies left. If a unique strategy remains for each player, we say the game has been solved by *iterated dominance.* It is easy to prove that a strategy profile thus obtained is a Nash equilibrium (Bicchieri 1993).

Common knowledge of rationality, preferences, and strategies may thus facilitate the task of predicting an opponent's strategy but, as I argued elsewhere (Bicchieri 1993), it does not guarantee that the resulting prediction will be correct. This is because the concept of Nash equilibrium embodies a notion of individual rationality, since each player's equilibrium strategy is a best reply to the opponents' strategies, but unfortunately it does not specify how players come to form the beliefs about each other's strategies that support equilibrium play. Beliefs, that is, can be internally consistent but fail to achieve the interpersonal consistency that guarantees that an equilibrium will be attained. Bernheim (1984) and Pearce (1984) have argued that assuming players' rationality (and common knowledge thereof) can only guarantee that a strategy will be *rationalizable,* in the sense of

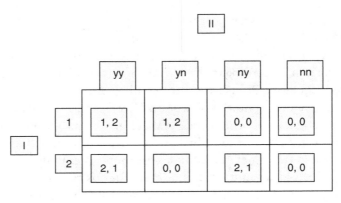

Figure 6.2.

being supported by internally consistent beliefs about other players' choices and beliefs. Yet a combination of rationalizable strategies may not constitute a Nash equilibrium. On the other hand, the fact that a Nash equilibrium is always a combination of rationalizable strategies is of no help in predicting it will be played.

Consider for a moment the normal form representation of the Figure 6.1 game:

I am assuming here that I knows II's payoffs, and that $y=3$. Player II has four strategies: always accept (yy), always reject (nn), accept if \$1, reject if \$2 (yn), and reject if \$1 and accept if \$2 (ny). For player II, nn is strictly dominated by yy, so C (Rat) allows I to exclude it (and II knows it). However, all three other strategies of player II are rationalizable, as well as the two strategies of player I. Moreover, there are three pure strategy Nash equilibria of this game: $(2,yy)$, $(1,yn)$ and $(2, ny)$, and no way to predict, by C(Rat) and C(SG+PF), which of them, if any, will be played.

The *refinements of Nash equilibrium* program is precisely an attempt to eliminate some equilibria as being unreasonable. If we consider again the extensive form game of Figure 6.1, we can imagine player II threatening to reject if I asks a high price. This threat is embedded in the equilibrium $(1,yn)$, but is it a credible threat? Player I knows that $y=3$ and that II is rational, hence I knows that, faced with a choice between 0 and 1, II will always choose 1, that is, will always accept the high price. Thus the $(1,yn)$ equilibrium should be eliminated as unreasonable. In this case, we have applied the simplest refinement of *subgame perfection*. Briefly, a Nash equilibrium s^* is perfect if it remains an equilibrium in every proper subgame of the original game G. In our simple example, we can calculate the final result by backward induction: We take the subgames starting at II's decision node and look at the optimal choice for player II. If $y=3$, the optimal choice for II is to accept at both subgames. Knowing that, player I will always choose to set a high price. Another way to look at the same problem is to perturb the game by assuming that every strategy has a very small probability of being chosen (Selten 1975). So in the equilibrium (1,*yn*) player II is indifferent between *yy* and *yn* simply because II is certain that I will choose 1, the low price. However, if there is a small probability that I, by mistake, chooses the high price, then *yy* gives II a higher utility than *yn*.

The problem with the refinements literature is that it lacks a coherent interpretation of deviations from equilibrium play (Bicchieri 1988, 1993). A deviation may be a mistake, but it may also be a signal. There is no general model of belief revision that would include different refinements as special cases of some general, substantive criterion of belief change. Moreover, in order to predict a specific equilibrium outcome, it must be assumed that players share (and have common knowledge that they share) the same "reasonable" principles. Multiplicity of equilibria only aggravates a problem already present in cases in which the equilibrium is unique: the equilibrium depends on parameters that are not known to an external observer trying to predict the outcome of the game. Note that, in this case, the players themselves are external observers of their interactive environment who have to guess what their opponents will do, which in turn depends upon the opponents' expectations about other players' choices, and so on.

3. Evolution and Learning

One way to solve strategic indeterminacy is to think in terms of evolution. Evolutionary models describe aggregate dynamics, without explaining in great detail how such dynamics are generated by individual behaviors. In fact, individuals in such models are often represented as strategy bearers whose choices are fixed or, when they have the possibility of shifting strategies, such shifts are not determined by what they expect others to do but rather by how well they have done in the past. In such models, a Nash equilibrium is no longer interpreted as a unique event; it is instead conceived as an observed regularity, of which we want to know how it was reached and what accounts for its stability. When multiple equilibria are possible, we want to know why players converged to one in particular and then stayed there. In this case, the selection process is not the result of complicated, multistage reasoning; it simply results from some form of natural selection.

Evolutionary theories are inspired by population biology (e.g., Maynard Smith & Price 1973). These theories dispense with the notion of the decision maker, as well as with best responses/optimization, and use in their place a natural selection, "survival-of-the-fittest" process together with mutations to model the frequencies with which various strategies are represented in the population over time. In a typical evolutionary model, players are preprogrammed for certain strategies, and are randomly matched with other players in pairwise repeated encounters. The relative frequency of a strategy in a population is simply the proportion of players in that population who adopt it. The theory focuses on how the strategy profiles

	D	H
D	B/2	0
H	B	B-C/2

Figure 6.3.

of populations of such agents evolve over time, given that the outcomes of current games determine the frequency of different strategies in the future. As an example, consider the symmetric game in Figure 6.3 and suppose that there are only two possible behavioral types: hawks and doves.

A hawk always fights and escalates contests until it wins or is badly hurt. A dove sticks to displays and retreats if the opponent escalates the conflict; if it fights with another dove, they will settle the contest after a long time. Payoffs are expected changes in fitness due to the outcome of the game. Fitness here means just reproductive success (e.g., the expected number of offspring per time unit). Suppose injury has a payoff in terms of loss of fitness equal to C, and victory corresponds to a gain in fitness B. If hawk meets hawk, or dove meets dove, each has a 50% chance of victory. If a dove meets another dove, the winner gets B and the loser gets nothing, so the average increase in fitness for a dove meeting another dove is $B/2$. A dove meeting a hawk retreats, so her fitness is unchanged, whereas the hawk gets a gain in fitness B. If a hawk meets another hawk, they escalate until one wins. The winner has a fitness gain B, the loser a fitness loss C. So the average increase in fitness is $(B-C)/2$. The latter payoff is negative, since we assume the cost of injury is greater than the gain in fitness obtained by winning the contest. We assume that players will be randomly paired in repeated encounters, and in each encounter they will play the stage game of Figure 6.3.

If the population were to consist predominantly of hawks, selection would favor the few doves, since hawks would meet mostly hawks and end up fighting with an average loss in fitness of $(B-C)/2$, and $0 > (B-C/2)$. In a population dominated by doves, hawks would spread, since every time they meet a dove (which would be most of the time) they would have a fitness gain of B, whereas doves on average would only get $B/2$.

Maynard Smith interpreted evolutionary games as something that goes on at the phenotypic level. The fitness of a phenotype depends on its frequency in the population. A strategy is a phenotype, and a player is just an instance of such a behavioral phenotype. In our example, we have only two behavioral phenotypes: hawk and dove. Evolutionary game theory wants to know how strategies do on average when games are played repeatedly between individuals who are randomly drawn from a large population. The average payoff to a strategy depends on the composition of the population, so a strategy may do very well (in term of fitness) in one environment and poorly in another. If the frequency of hawks in the population is q and that of doves correspondingly $(1-q)$, the average increase in fitness for the hawks will be $q(B-C)/2+(1-q)B$, and $(1-q)B/2$ for the doves. The average payoff of a strategy in a given environment determines its future frequency in the population. Strategies that, on average, earn high payoffs in the current environment are assumed to increase in frequency, and strategies that, on average, earn lower payoffs are assumed to decrease in frequency. If the average payoffs of the different strategies are the same, then the composition of the population is stable. In our example, the average increase in fitness for the hawks will be equal to that for the doves when the frequency of hawks in the population is $q=B/C$. At that frequency, the proportion of hawks and doves is stable. If the frequency of hawks is less that B/C, then they do better than doves, and will consequently spread; if their frequency is larger than B/C, they will do worse than doves and will shrink.

Note that if $C > B$, then $(B-C)/2 < 0$, so the game in Figure 6.3 has two pure-strategy Nash equilibria: (H, D) and (D, H). There is also a mixed strategy equilibrium in which Hawk is played with probability $q = B/C$ and Dove is played with probability $(1-q) = C-B/C$. If the game of Figure 6.3 were played by rational agents who *choose* which behavior to display, we would be at a loss in predicting their choices. We know that from C(SG + PF) and C(Rat) the players cannot infer that a particular equilibrium will be played; moreover, since there are no dominated strategies, all possible outcomes are rationalizable. In our hawk/dove example, however, players are not rational and do not choose their strategies. So if an equilibrium is attained, it must be the outcome of some process very different from rational deliberation. The process at work is natural selection: High-performing strategies increase in frequency whereas low-performing strategies diminish in frequency and eventually go to zero.

The mechanism is quite simple: the bearer of a successful behavioral trait will have more offspring than the bearer of a less successful trait, and each of the descendants will display the same behavioral trait, hence the frequency increase. This is an extremely simplified and probably wrong story of how behavioral traits are transmitted among humans. We have no evidence for the genetic transmission of behavioral traits such as altruism, selfishness, or the tendency to escalate conflicts. There is instead evidence that such traits are culturally transmitted, and a realistic model of how a specific behavioral pattern becomes dominant in a population should therefore include a description of how individuals learn behavioral patterns and imitate those who are successful.

We have seen that in a population composed mostly of doves, hawks will thrive, and the opposite would occur in a population composed mainly of hawks. So, for example, if hawks dominate the population, a mutant displaying dove behavior can invade the population, since individuals bearing the dove trait will do better than hawks. The main solution concept used in evolutionary game theory is the *evolutionarily stable strategy* (ESS) introduced by Maynard Smith and Price (1973). A strategy or behavioral trait is evolutionarily stable if, once it dominates in the population, it does strictly better than any mutant strategy, hence it cannot be invaded. To formalize this concept, let me first make a brief digression. In a symmetric game like hawk/dove, we have a finite set of pure strategies S and a corresponding set Δ of mixed strategies. A population state is equivalent to a mixed strategy $x \in \Delta$. Note that the evolutionary model gives a natural interpretation to mixed strategies as the proportions of certain strategies (or traits) in a population. A state in which each individual plays a pure strategy and the proportion of different strategies correspond to x is called a polymorphic state. Alternatively, we may interpret the population state x as monomorphic, in the sense that each player plays the mixed strategy x. In a two-player game, being matched against a randomly drawn individual in population state x is equivalent to being matched against an individual who plays the mixed strategy x. Hence the average payoff of playing strategy y in population state x is equal to the expected payoff to y when played against the mixed strategy x, that is, $u(y,x)$. The population average in this case is equal to the expected payoff of the mixed strategy x when matched against itself, that is, $u(x,x)$.

In a symmetric, two-player game, x is an ESS if and only if, for all $y \in \Delta$ such that $y \neq x$,

(1) $u(x,x) > u(y,x)$

or

(2) $u(x,x) = u(y,x)$, and $u(x,y) > u(y,y)$.

Condition (1) tells us that strategy x is a unique best reply against itself. If the bulk of the population consists of type x and a small number of mutants of type y enters the population, if x does better against x than y does against x, y will be less fit and disappear. However, if x is a mixed strategy, we know (1) does not hold. In this case, for x to be an ESS (2) must hold. If both x and y perform equally well against x, then y will be less fit than x if x does better against y than y does against y.

In the hawk/dove game, neither of the two pure behavioral types is evolutionarily stable, since each can be invaded by the other. We know, however, that a population in which there is a proportion $q = B/C$ of hawks and $(1-q) = C-B/C$ of doves is stable. This means that the type of behavior that consists in escalating fights with probability $q = B/C$ cannot be invaded by any other type, hence it is an ESS. To show that the mixed strategy $x = (B/C, C-B/C)$ is an ESS, we have to show that condition (2) is satisfied. Indeed, $u(x,y) - u(y,y) = 1/2C \ (B-Cq)^2$ is greater than zero for all $q \neq B/C$.

An ESS is a strategy that, when it dominates the population, is a best reply against itself. Therefore, an evolutionarily stable strategy such as $(B/C, C-B/C)$ is a Nash equilibrium. Though every ESS is a Nash equilibrium, the reverse does not hold; in our stage game, there are three Nash equilibria, but only the mixed strategy equilibrium $(B/C, C-B/C)$ is an ESS. However, when a strategy is a *unique* best reply to itself, it is both an ESS and a *strict* Nash equilibrium. In this special case, the reverse also holds: Every strict Nash equilibrium is an ESS. In a strict equilibrium, there exists no other strategy that is an alternative best reply to the equilibrium strategy, and this guarantees noninvadability.

The prior examples show how evolution can at least partially solve the problem of equilibrium selection without imposing heroic cognitive requirements on players. An ESS is, in fact, not just a Nash equilibrium but also a perfect and proper equilibrium (Van Damme 1987). Furthermore, an evolutionary account of how a Nash equilibrium is achieved provides an explanation of the dynamics of the selection process, something which the refinement program cannot do. In the hawk/dove example, we have assumed that the success of a strategy depends on the outcome of pair-wise random matches. It is often the case that a strategy's success depends not on the strategy played by a particular opponent, but on the population-wide frequencies of strategies. When examining behavior in a *population game,* we adopt the concept of an *evolutionarily stable state* (also ESS) (Hofbauer & Sigmund 1998).

Suppose the game has N pure strategies, with an $N \times N$ symmetric expected payoff matrix $A=(a_{ij})$. There is an infinite number of players, and each player initially commits to playing exactly one of the N pure strategies. Let p be the $N \times 1$ vector denoting the population-wide proportion of each of the N strategies (player types) in the population at a given time. Let

$$f_i(p) = \sum_j a_{ij} p_j = A_i p$$

denote the fitness of strategy i and let $\sum_i f_i(p) = Ap.$ denote the population-wide payoff. The population-wide weighted average fitness value is $p^T Ap$. We say that $\hat{p}$ is an *evolutionarily stable state* if for any $p \neq \hat{p}$ in the neighborhood of $\hat{p}$, we have:

$$\hat{p}^T Ap > p^T Ap$$

This captures the idea that the population-wide payoff under $\hat{p}$ is higher (locally) than for any other vector p.[7]

The definitions of evolutionarily stable strategies or states are static. To describe the dynamic process that leads to a certain distribution of strategies in a population, we have models of the selection dynamics that express the growth rate of a strategy i in population state p as a function of i's average payoff in p relative to the average payoff to other strategies in p. ESS does not refer to a specific dynamic, but biologists and evolutionary game theorists frequently use deterministic *replicator* dynamics (Taylor & Jonker 1978) of the form:

$$(*) \quad p_i(t+1) = \frac{p_i(t) A_i p(t)}{p^T(t) Ap(t)},$$

where $p(t)$ denotes the population-wide proportions at time t, the denominator is a measure of average strategy fitness in the population at t, and the numerator measures the fitness of strategy i at time t. Strategies with above-average fitness see their proportions increase, and those with below-average fitness see their proportions decrease.[8]

ESS are asymptotically stable fixed points of this replicator dynamic, though the converse need not be true (see, e.g., Samuelson 1997). A similar relationship holds between the replicator dynamic and Nash equilibria: if $\hat{p}$ is a Nash equilibrium of the symmetric NxN game with expected payoff matrix A, then $\hat{p}$ is a stationary state of the replicator dynamic.

In evolutionary theory replication, variation and heredity are the basic assumptions. Any entity capable of replicating itself with differential success will be subject to an evolutionary process. Differential success, in turn, is related to hereditary variations. In biology, replicators are genes and in genetic evolution, variation is provided by random mutations and recombinations of gene sequences. Behavioral patterns can be replicators, too, in the sense that behavioral trait x is replicated when a gene x that predisposes its carriers to behave according to this pattern replicates itself. This means that bearers of gene x will behave in ways that make them reproductively successful, so that in the next generation there will be more copies of x. To the extent that behavior x promotes the replication of its predisposing gene, we are correct in saying that the behavior is replicating itself. Individuals are just bearers of such genetic material, hence they are born with fixed behavioral traits. Variation of competing strategies is provided by random mutations and recombinations of gene sequences.

When we think of strategies, however, we usually refer to behaviors that are not genetically inherited. In economic and political applications of game theory, actors can be firms, political parties, nations. Even when actors are individuals, their strategies have a strong cultural component. Evolutionary models can still be applied to explain how Nash equilibria are attained and whether they are stable, but selection mechanisms in this case work through processes of cultural transmission such as learning and imitation. Learning and imitation are subject to mistakes, and new strategies may enter the population either by random mistake or by purposeful innovation. For example, we tend to imitate successful individuals, where success is measured in terms of some shared values. Since it is usually difficult to point to one particular behavior as responsible for successful performance, what is imitated will often consist of a set of behavioral rules, and this in turn may generate mistakes. Payoffs in this case cannot represent fitness changes, but if we give them a utility interpretation, we must provide for interpersonal comparisons of utilities. Indeed, to imitate a more successful individual, one must be able to compare one's payoffs with the payoffs of others, but traditional von Neumann-Morgenstern utilities do not allow for such comparisons.

Evolutionary games provide us with a way of explaining how agents that may or may not be rational and—if so—subject to severe information and calculation restrictions, achieve and sustain a Nash equilibrium. When there exist evolutionarily stable strategies (or states), we know which equilibrium will obtain, without the need to postulate refinements in the way players interpret off-equilibrium moves. Yet we need to know much more about processes of cultural transmission, and to develop adequate ways to represent payoffs, so that the promise of evolutionary games is actually fulfilled.

An alternative to a traditional evolutionary model is a learning model. By learning we mean a mechanism by which a player's present choice depends on previous experience, which in interactive environments includes the choices made by other players. In learning models, players may be endowed with small or large memories, and be as sophisticated as we want them to be. Some such models assume that players only look at past actions and outcomes, and choose more frequently those actions that are associated to higher payoffs. In this case, we are far from the traditional model of rational choice, and the problem of strategic indeterminacy does not arise. Other models, however, assume that players are also forward-looking; at every stage of the game, players make probabilistic conjectures on the opponents' strategies, and then maximize expected utility on the basis of such conjectures. Though players are usually assumed to ignore the effects that their own choices have on their opponents' future choices, they are endowed with belief-revision capabilities, and modify their conjectures on the basis of their observations of how the opponents have played. It can be proved that, in the long run, if a learning dynamics converges (and thus players' subjective probabilistic assessments coincide with the observed frequencies), the limit is a Nash equilibrium (Fudenberg & Levine 1998). Clearly, in any learning model observation of other players' choices is crucial. But what does a player observe? Suppose a simultaneous-move game is played repeatedly. After each stage game, since actions and strategies coincide, what a player observes are the opponents' strategies (single uncontingent actions). It is worthwhile to note that in such models one need not assume complete information or common knowledge of rationality. What is important to assume is that players are epistemically rational in a weak sense: their beliefs must be internally consistent, and belief revision is done according to Bayes rule. Strategic indeterminacy seems to be resolved in that, when a successful learning process will lead the players to a Nash equilibrium, such equilibrium can reproduce indefinitely, and thus players' predictions about each other's actions turn out to be accurate.

The problem with these kinds of models is that most of the interactions we want to represent are *dynamic* ones. In a dynamic game, players only observe the terminal nodes that are reached in that play of the game, not the parts of their opponents' strategies that specify how they would have played at information sets in unreached parts of the tree. Thus players cannot observe their opponents' strategies since, in this case a strategy does not coincide with an action. Note that a strategy is a complete, contingent plan of action that tells a player how to behave in all sorts of circumstances (i.e., at every information set). In a dynamic game, it is impossible to tell how an opponent *would have* played in circumstances that did not occur; all that can be observed are the actions performed during the game. The problem here is that a conjecture can be compatible with what is observed, but it may be wrong. Consider again the game in Figure 6.1. Suppose player I believes, for whatever reason, that player II would only buy for a low price. In this case, the optimal choice for player I would be to ask for a low price, and if II accepts, players will be locked in the outcome $(1, y)$. Player I will have no reason to change his initial conjecture, and will never be able to know how II would have reacted to a higher price. In this case, the outcome $(1, y)$ is compatible with the Nash equilibrium $(1, yn)$, but yn might not be the strategy chosen by II.

What we are facing here is an interesting twist: Players can learn to correctly predict the outcome of the game, and thus reproduce it indefinitely, even if they are wrong about each others' strategies. In fact, players can even generate stable outcomes that are incompatible with Nash equilibrium. Fudenberg and Levine (1998) did show that there are situations in which each player chooses a best reply to her conjecture, and that conjecture is compatible with the pattern of play she observes, but the *self-confirming equilibria* thus obtained are not Nash equilibria.

The conclusions we can draw for strategic indeterminacy are not reassuring. On the one hand, we have seen that, in the context of common knowledge of SG, PF and Rat, strategic indeterminacy can be resolved only by endowing players with an unrealistic load of extra information (and common knowledge thereof). For example, players would have to have common knowledge of how to interpret deviations from the equilibrium path, have a common understanding of how to prioritize within a hierarchy of possible interpretations, have common priors about players' types, and so on. Note that in this case we resolve strategic indeterminacy by completely eliminating epistemic indeterminacy. Only in these circumstances Nash predictions can be made by the theorist *and* the players. If instead we abandon full rationality and information in favor of an evolutionary approach, Nash equilibrium can be justified as the outcome of a process of natural selection. In this case, we have completely bypassed the problem of strategic indeterminacy, since players have no need to *reason to* an equilibrium. Finally, learning models cast doubt on the possibility of predicting Nash equilibria. Limited observability of players' actions may prevent convergence to a stationary state, and even with observability, dynamic games may converge to stable and stationary states that are not Nash equilibria.

3. EXPERIMENTS

As we shall see next, the experimental approach, by controlling the rules of the game, the monetary payoffs, and the amount of knowledge players have about these parameters, seems at first sight a viable solution to the problem of indeterminacy. Observations about players' behavior are generated in the laboratory, where the experimenter can control the game description, the order of moves, players' information about earlier moves, the outcomes and their relation with players' moves, as well as players' knowledge of all of the above. However, since players' preferences over outcomes cannot be easily controlled, the experimenter will have to make hypotheses about players' preferences, and about players' knowledge about each other's preferences. Only in this case we will be able to make predictions about the outcome of the game. When experimental economists started testing the prediction that players converge to a Nash equilibrium, the default auxiliary hypotheses were that players only have selfish preferences over monetary outcomes, and that this fact is common knowledge among them. The falsification of many such predictions in a variety of games has led some to claim that Nash equilibrium theory has been falsified, but all that was falsified are the auxiliary hypotheses about players' preferences and common knowledge thereof. The challenge now is to make new, better hypotheses about players' utilities, hypotheses that are general enough to explain the results of a variety of experiments, and are specific enough to allow for meaningful predictions. To illustrate the difficulties and potential pitfalls of the new approach, as well as the consequences for the indeterminacy problem, I shall now turn to a well known experimental game that has engaged both theorists and experimentalists in an attempt to make sense of the unexpected results.

In 1982, Guth, Schmittberger and Schwarze published a study in which they asked subjects to play what is now known as an Ultimatum bargaining game. Their goal was to test the predictions of game theory about equilibrium behavior. Their results instead showed that subjects consistently deviate from what game theory predicts. To understand what game theory predicts, and why, let us consider a typical Ultimatum game. Two people must split a fixed amount of money M according to the following rules: the proposer (P) moves first and offers a division of M to the responder (R), where the offer can range between M and zero. The responder has a binary choice in each case: to accept the offer or to reject it. If the offer is accepted, the proposer receives $M-x$ and the responder receives x, where x is the offer amount. If the offer is rejected, each player receives nothing. If rationality (and self-interest) are common knowledge, the proposer knows that the responder will always accept any amount greater than zero, because Accept dominates Reject for *any* offer greater than zero. Hence P should offer the minimum amount guaranteed to be accepted, and R will accept it. For example, if $M = \$10$ and the minimum available amount is 1 cent, the proposer should offer it and the offer should be accepted, leaving the proposer with $9.99. This is the result predicted by *perfect equilibrium* theory.

Experiments find, however, that nobody offers 1 cent or even 1 dollar. Note that such experiments are always one-shot and anonymous. That is, subjects play the game only once with an anonymous partner and are guaranteed that their choice will not be disclosed. The absence of repetition is important to distinguish between generous behavior that is dictated by a rational, selfish calculation and genuine generosity. If an Ultimatum game is repeated with the same partner, or if a player suspects that future partners will know of her past behavior, it may be perfectly rational for players who are only interested in their material payoff to give generously, if they expect to be on the receiving side at a future time. On the other hand, a responder who might accept the minimum in a one-shot game might want to reject a low offer at the beginning of a repeated game, in the hope of convincing future proposers to offer more.

In the United States, as well as in a number of other countries, the modal and median offers in one-shot experimental games are 40% to 50% of the total amount, and the mean offers are 30% to 40%. Offers below 20% are rejected about half the time.[9] These results are robust with respect to variations in the amount of money that is being split, and cultural differences (Camerer 2003). For example, we know that raising the stakes from $10 to $100 does not decrease the frequency of rejections of low offers (those between $10 and $20), and that in experiments run in Slovenia, Pittsburgh, Israel, and Tokyo, the modal offers were in the range of 40% to 50% (Hoffman et al. 1998; Roth et al. 1991).

If we go by the default assumption that players only value their monetary outcomes, then we must conclude that the prediction that players will choose the perfect equilibrium has been falsified. However, as I already mentioned, what has been falsified are the auxiliary hypotheses about players' preferences (and their common knowledge of such preferences). Individuals' behavior across games suggests that money is not the sole consideration, and instead there is a concern for fairness, so much so that subjects are prepared to punish at a cost to themselves those that behave in inequitable ways.[10] A concern for fairness is just one example of a more general fact about human behavior: we are often motivated by a host of factors of which monetary incentives are one, and often not the most important. When faced with different possible distributions, we usually care about how we fare with respect to others, how the distribution came about, who implemented it, and why. The variety of reasons we have for behaving one way or another should be incorporated into a utility function, and economists have recently started to develop richer, more complex models of human behavior that try to explain what we have always known: We do care about other people's outcomes. Thus a better way to explain what is observed in experiments is to provide a richer definition of rationality: People still maximize their utilities, but the arguments of their utility functions include other people's utilities.

In what follows, I will look at two possible explanations for the generous distributions we observe in Ultimatum games. There is no room here to provide a detailed account of how to test these explanations against some interesting variations of the game, and the reader is referred to the relevant literature.[11] I want only to note that such testing is not always easy to conduct. The problem is that we still have quite rudimentary theories of how motives affect behavior. And to test a hypothesis about what sort of motives induce us to act one way or another, we have to be very specific in defining such motives, and the ways in which they influence our choices. In the Ultimatum game, the uniformity of responders' behavior suggests that people do not like being treated unfairly. That is, if subjects perceive an offer of 20% or 30% of the money as unfair, they may reject it to "punish" the greedy proposer, even at a cost to themselves.[12] One possible hypothesis we may make is that both proposers and responders are showing a *social preference* for fair outcomes, or an aversion to inequality.[13] If we make this hypothesis, we can still explain the experimental results with a traditional rational choice model, where the agents' preferences take into account the payoffs of others.

In models of inequality aversion, players prefer both more money and that allocations be more equal. Though there are several models of inequality aversion, perhaps the best known and most extensively tested is the model of Fehr and Schmidt (1999). This model intends to capture the idea that people may be uneasy, to a certain extent, about the presence of inequality, even if they benefit from the unequal distribution. Given a group of L persons, the Fehr-Schmidt utility function of person i is

$$U_i(x_1,...,x_L) = x_i - \frac{\alpha_i}{L-1}\sum_j \max(x_j - x_i, 0) - \frac{\beta_i}{L-1}\sum_j \max(x_i - x_j, 0)$$

where x_j denotes the material payoff that person j gets. α_i is a parameter that measures how much player i dislikes disadvantageous inequality (an "envy" weight), and β_i measures how much i dislikes advantageous inequality (a "guilt" weight).[14] One constraint on the parameters is that $0 < \beta_i < \alpha_i$, which indicates that people dislike advantageous inequality less than disadvantageous inequality. The other constraint is $\beta_i < 1$, so that agents do not suffer terrible guilt when they are in relatively good positions. For example, a player would prefer getting more without affecting other people's payoff, even though that results in an increase of the inequality.

Applying the model to the Ultimatum game I just described, the utility function is simplified to

$$U_i(x_1, x_2) = x_i - \begin{cases} \alpha_i(x_{3-i} - x_i) & \text{if } x_{3-i} \geq x_i \\ \beta_i(x_i - x_{3-i}) & \text{if } x_{3-i} < x_i \end{cases} \qquad i = 1,2$$

Obviously if the responder rejects the offer, both utility functions are equal to zero, that is, $U_{1reject} = U_{2reject} = 0$. If the responder accepts an offer of x, the utility functions are as follows:

$$U_{1accept}(x) = \begin{cases} (1+\alpha_1)M - (1+2\alpha_1)x & \text{if } x \geq M/2 \\ (1-\beta_1)M - (1-2\beta_1)x & \text{if } x < M/2 \end{cases}$$

$$U_{2accept}(x) = \begin{cases} (1+2\alpha_2)x - \alpha_2 M & \text{if } x < M/2 \\ (1-2\beta_1)x + \beta_2 M & \text{if } x \geq M/2 \end{cases}$$

The responder should accept the offer if and only if $U_{2accept}(x) > U_{2reject} = 0$. Solving for x, we get the *threshold for acceptance: $x > \alpha_2 M/(1+2\alpha_2)$*. Evidently if α_2 is close to zero, which indicates that player 2 (R) does not care much about being treated unfairly, the responder will accept very mean offers. On the other hand, if α_2 is sufficiently big, the offer has to be close to half to be accepted. In any event, the threshold is not higher than $M/2$, which means that hyper-fair offers (more than half) are not necessary for the sake of acceptance.

Note that for the proposer, the utility function is monotonically decreasing in x when $x \geq M/2$. Hence a rational proposer will not offer more than half of the money. Suppose $x \leq M/2$; two cases are possible depending on the value of β_1. If $\beta_1 > 1/2$, that is, if the proposer feels sufficiently guilty about treating others unfairly, the utility is monotonically increasing in x, and his best choice is to offer $M/2$. On the other hand, if $\beta_1 < 1/2$, the utility is monotonically decreasing in x, and hence the best offer for the proposer is the minimum one that would be accepted, i.e. (a little bit more than) $\alpha_2 M(1+2\alpha_2)$. Lastly, if $\beta_1 = 1/2$, it does not matter how much the proposer offers, as long as it is between $\alpha_2 M(1+2\alpha_2)$ and $M/2$. Note that the other two parameters, α_1 and β_2, are not identifiable in Ultimatum games.

As noted by Fehr and Schmidt, the model allows for the fact that individuals are heterogeneous. Different α's and β's correspond to different types of people. Although the utility functions are common knowledge, the exact values of the parameters are not. The proposers, in most cases, is not sure what type of responders they are facing. Along the Bayesian line, her belief about the type of the responder can be formally represented by a probability distribution P on α_2 and β_2. When $\beta_1 > 1/2$, the proposer's rational choice does not depend on what P is. When $\beta_1 < 1/2$, however, the proposer will seek to maximize the expected utility:

$$EU(x) = P(\alpha_2 M/(1+2\alpha_2) < x) \times ((1-\beta_1)M - (1-2\beta_1)x)$$

Therefore, the behavior of a rational proposer in the Ultimatum game is determined by her own type (β_1) and her belief about the type of the responder. The experimental data suggest that for many proposers, either β is big ($\beta > 1/2$), or they estimate the responder's α to be large. The choice of the responder is only determined by his type (α_2) and the offer. Small offers are rejected by responders with a positive α.

The positive features of the Fehr-Schmidt utility function are that it can rationalize both positive and negative outcomes, and that it can explain the observed variability in outcomes with heterogeneous types. One of the major weaknesses of their model, however, is that it has a consequentialist bias. Players only care about final distributions of outcomes, not about how such distributions come about. However, recent experiments have established that how a situation is framed matters to an evaluation of outcomes, and that the same distribution can be accepted or rejected depending on "irrelevant" information about the players or the circumstances of play (Bicchieri 2006; Camerer 2003). Another difficulty with this approach is that, if we assume the distribution of types to be constant in a given population, then we should observe, overall, the same proportion of fair outcomes in Ultimatum games. Not only this does not happen, but we also observe individual inconsistencies in behavior across different situations in which the monetary outcomes are the same. If we assume that individual preferences are stable, then we would expect similar behaviors across Ultimatum games. If instead we conclude that preferences are context-dependent, then we should provide a mapping from contexts to preferences that indicates in a fairly predictable way how and why a given context or situation changes one's preferences. Of course, different situations may change a player's expectation about another player's envy or guilt parameters, and we could thus explain why a player may change her behavior, depending on how the situation is framed. In the case of Fehr and Schmidt's utility function, however, experimental evidence implies that a player's *own* β (or α) changes value in different situations (Bicchieri 2006, Chapter 3). Yet nothing in their theory explains why one would feel consistently more or less guilty (or envious) depending on the decision context.

4. Norms and Expectations

To make clear what I mean, let us consider the results of a questionnaire distributed to 100 Carnegie Mellon undergraduate students that depicted three situations in which the payoffs were the same, but the descriptions of the situation significantly differed.[15]

1. Imagine you must choose how to allocate $10 between yourself and person Y, whom you don't know. You must allocate the money in one of two ways:

   A. You and person Y both get $0
   B. You get $2 and person Y gets $8

82% of the students choose B, (2, 8).

2. In this scenario, you can offer whatever you want, but Y lets you know that she wants to be offered more than $5. Y announces that you must offer $8 (and keep $2) or she will reject the offer. To prove this to you, Y takes a "commitment pill" that will biologically compel her to reject any offer of less than $8.

   A. You keep more than $2 of the $10 for yourself and Y rejects—both you and Y get $0
   B. You offer to keep only $2 of the $10 and Y accepts—you get $2 and Y gets $8

Only 49% of the students choose B (2, 8).

3. In this scenario, Y wants to be offered more than $5. Y lives on an island with a different culture, but where the people are of similar wealth to you. In Y's culture, the "last mover" is perceived as the person who controls this game, and is expected to get more of the money. An anthropologist, who will phone your offer to Y, informs you that in Y's culture, any offer less than $8 is viewed as insulting. If you do not offer the split $2, $8, Y will reject your offer. The anthropologist tells you that if the roles were reversed, Y would offer you $8. There is no anthropologist telling Y what you think is fair.

   Here 63% of the students choose B (2, 8).

Note that all these choices are consequentially equivalent: either both parties get 0, or we have a (2,8) distribution. As I argued before, most models of social preference are consequentialist, but the results I am reporting show that people assign a value to the process through which the outcome is obtained.[16] The (2,8) outcome in the "commitment pill" choice is clearly less attractive; here the responder is rejecting potentially fair offers and, by taking the pill, has given herself an unfair advantage.[17]

In the anthropologist scenario, the responder obeys a different rule, and doesn't know you don't know it. Moreover, it is clear that the rule is symmetrical: Were the responder in the proposer's role, he would just keep $2. If we consider the three cases, and the students' responses, it seems that what makes the difference is the presence (or absence) of social norms that can be violated, and violation consistently elicits a negative reaction in a majority of participants.

The first case presents a simple choice. Only a person with a strong aversion to inequality would choose the (0, 0) outcome, and lose $2. Such people exist, but their number is quite small. Because there is no clear rule about how to behave, the (2, 8) outcome seems the obvious choice. The second case instead is one in which Y is patently unfair, and the majority of students choose to punish him, at a cost to themselves. The last case is one in which a different norm is at work, and thus the receiver who expects $8 is not seen as greedy or manipulative.

If a person has a strong aversion to inequitable outcomes, the number of rejections should stay the same, irrespective of the description of the situation. But the above examples and many experimental results show that this is not the case; most people are extremely sensitive to the way a situation is framed, and when fairness is at stake, many will choose to punish transgressions at a cost to themselves.[18] Preferences, that is, are conditional on the decision context. But what exactly *maps* a context into a specific interpretation that involves, among other things, expectations, beliefs, and causal attributions about other people's motives and future behaviors? I have argued elsewhere (Bicchieri 2006, Chapter 2) that we interpret any situation we are in, and especially new ones, according to scripts that represent stored, generic knowledge about classes of situations. We have scripts that describe what happens at parties, lectures, family reunions, party meetings, and so on. Such scripts contain roles, sequence of actions rules, beliefs and expectations regarding individuals' roles, as well as prescriptions for unexpected occurrences. Scripts are typically shared within a given culture and, indeed, what is apparent from a variety of experiments is that individuals share a common understanding and interpretation of the experimental situation and the kind of behavior that is most appropriate in those circumstances.[19] Social norms, I have argued, are embedded into scripts. In the typical Ultimatum game, once a fair division script is activated, players will have definite beliefs about what the proposer should offer, especially if they do not have any specific information about him. If a fairness norm is prompted, not only will one expect to get a fair share, but one will be ready to attribute an unfair share to the greediness of the proposer, feel outraged, and retaliate.

Since script activation involves activation of the appropriate expectations and beliefs, the *expectations* subjects have about what others do in the same situation, as well as about what they believe is expected of them, play an important role in guiding their choices. The majority of individuals do not show a consistent disposition to behave in a cooperative, trusting, or fair way. People do not punish transgressors in all circumstances, nor do they positively reciprocate in all cases in which reciprocation is a possible choice. Rather, individuals change their behavior according to the way the situation is framed, which in turn generates very different expectations about what other individuals similarly situated would do, as well as beliefs about what one is expected to do in such situations. Experimental data show that such expectations, when elicited, are interpersonally consistent, and I want to argue that the social norms that generate them are key to understanding experimental behavior and can offer a solution to the indeterminacy problem.

My definition of social norm (see Appendix) is different from the traditional sociological ones, in that I understand a social norm to be a behavioral rule that is supported by (and consists of) the empirical and normative expectations of those who abide by it. People, I have argued, have a *conditional preference* for following a norm, provided their expectations are met (Bicchieri 2006, Chapter 1). In an Ultimatum game, for example, the proposer will have an incentive to be fair if she believes the responder expects a fair share, and in the absence of any other information that is precisely what most proposers expect. Note that I am not assuming the proposer *wants or prefers* to be fair, unconditionally. Surely there are such individuals, but we need not count on them to have fair distributions. It is enough to assume that most individuals conditionally prefer to be fair given that they believe that (a) others typically behave in a fair way, and (b) they are expected to choose a fair division. Whether their motive is fear of retaliation or just the recognition of others' legitimate expectations is not relevant to the present discussion.

The norm-based utility function I introduced in (2006) can now be applied to the Ultimatum game. Let π_i be the payoff function for player i. The norm-based utility function of player i depends on the strategy profile s, and is given by

$$U_i(s) = \pi_i(s) - k_i \max_{s_{-j} \in L_{-j}} \max_{m \neq j} \{\pi_m(s_{-j}, N_j(s_{-j})) - \pi_m(s), \ 0\}$$

where $k_i \geq 0$ is a constant representing i's sensitivity to the relevant norm. Such sensitivity may vary with different norms; for example, a person may be very sensitive to equality and much less so to equity considerations. The first maximum operator takes care of the possibility that the norm instantiation (and violation) might be ambiguous in the sense that a strategy profile instantiates a norm for several players simultaneously (as would be the case, for example, in a social dilemma with three players). The second maximum operator ranges over all the players other than the norm violator. In plain words, the discounting term (multiplied by k_i) is the maximum payoff deduction resulting from all norm violations.

In the traditional Ultimatum game, the norm usually prescribes a fair amount the proposer ought to offer. The norm functions that represent this norm are the following: N_1 is a constant N function, and N_2 is nowhere defined.[20] If the responder rejects, the utilities of both players are zero.

$$U_{1reject}(x)=U_{2reject}(x)=0$$

Given that the proposer offers x and the responder accepts, the utilities are the following:

$$U_{1accept}(x)= M-x-k_1\max(N_1-x,0)$$
$$U_{2accept}(x)=x-k_2\max(N_2-x,0)$$

where N_i denotes the amount player i thinks he should get/offer according to some social norm applicable to the situation, and k_i is non-negative. Note that k_1 measures how much player 1 dislikes to deviate from what he takes to be the norm. To obey a norm, sensitivity to the norm need not be high. Fear of retaliation may make a proposer with a low k behave according to what fairness dictates but, absent such risk, his disregard for the norm will lead him to be unfair. I assume here it is common knowledge that $N_1 = N_2 = N$, which is reasonable in the traditional Ultimatum game. Again, the responder should accept the offer if and only if $U_{2accept}(x) > U_{2reject} = 0$, which implies the following *threshold for acceptance: $x >$* $k_2 N/(1+k_2)$. Notice that an offer larger than the norm dictates is not necessary for the sake of acceptance.

For the proposer, the utility function is decreasing in x when $x \geq N$, hence a rational proposer will not offer more than N. Suppose $x \leq N$. If $k_1 > 1$, the utility function is increasing in x, which means that the best choice for the proposer is to offer N. If $k_1 < 1$, the utility function is decreasing in x, which implies that the best strategy for the proposer is to offer the least amount that would result in acceptance, that is, a little bit more than the threshold $k_2 N/(1+k_2)$. If $k_1 = 1$, it does not matter how much the proposer offers, provided the offer is between $k_2 N/(1+k_2)$ and N.

It should be noted that k_1 plays a very similar role as that of β_1 in the Fehr-Schmidt model. In fact, if we take N to be $M/2$ and k_1 to be $2\beta_1$, the two models agree on what the proposer's utility is. It is equally apparent that k_2 in this model is analogous to α_2 in the Fehr-Schmidt model. There is, however, an important difference between these parameters. The αs and βs in the Fehr-Schmidt model measure people's degree of aversion toward inequality, which is a very different disposition than the one measured by the k's, that is, people's sensitivity to different norms. The latter will usually be a stable disposition, and behavioral changes may thus be caused by changes in focus or in expectations. A theory of norms can explain such changes, whereas a theory of inequity aversion does not.

It is also the case that the proposer's belief about the responder's type figures in her decision when $k_1 < 1$. The belief can be represented by a joint probability over k_2 and N_2, if the value of N_2 is not common knowledge. The proposer should choose an offer that maximizes the expected utility

$$EU(x) = P(k_2 N_2 / (1 + k_2) < x) \times (M - x - k_1(N_1 - x)).$$

If we now apply the above utility function to the questionnaire we just discussed, it is reasonable to assume that in the Ultimatum game the norm prescribes (5, 5) offers, and the proposer should thus never expect to keep less than 5. Her choice in the pill scenario is whether to induce rejection or accept $2:

$$U_{1reject}(x) = 0$$

$$U_{1accept}(x) = 2 - k_1(5 - 2)$$

If $k_1 > 2/3$, *reject* is the utility-maximizing choice. In the anthropologist scenario instead, the conditions for obeying the (5, 5) norm fail: the responder neither knows the rule nor expects the proposer to follow it. Actually, the relevant norm is (2, 8). The discounting term drops out and it is again preferable to offer 8.

Consider once more the game in Figure 6.1. Let us suppose that it represents a situation in which, for whatever reason, low price is the norm. In this case, even if player I does not know the value of y, she knows that player II will reject an offer of 2 for any $y > 2$ *and* $k_{II} > 1$.[21] Player I is thus playing a Bayesian game in which player II can be one of different types.[22] However, his prior probabilities are influenced by the norm's existence. The norm points to the equilibrium (1, yn) and, in case the norm is de facto followed in the population, player I will have good reason to assess a high probability to $k_{II} > 1$. Note that assessing the k of player II is crucial even if I were to know the value of y. For example, if $y = 3$ and in the absence of a norm, player I would most certainly choose the high price. The presence of a norm, however, drastically changes the situation, since now player I has to assess the probability that II cares about the norm. In this case, it is better for player I to choose the low price, even if he personally does not care that much about following the norm. Expectations, in other words, are crucial to our decision to obey norms.

I said before that norms are a way to solve the indeterminacy problem, and I have argued elsewhere (Bicchieri 2006) that established norms are equilibria. However, since social norms often go against our self-interest, especially when we narrowly interpret self-interest as a desire for material incentives, a social norm need not be an equilibrium of an ordinary game in which payoffs represent self-interested preferences. Thus, for example, a cooperative norm cannot be a Nash equilibrium of a Prisoner's Dilemma (PD) game. If such a norm exists and is followed, however, the original PD game would be transformed (at least for the norm-followers) into the subsequent, very different game:

In the traditional PD, each player's preference ranking is $DC > CC > DD > CD$. B in Figure 6.4 stands for best, S for second best, and so on. In the symmetric coordination game instead, each norm follower's preference ranking is $CC > DD > DC > CD$.[23] That is, the players who follow a cooperative norm will do it because their empirical and normative expectations have been met, hence they *prefer* to obey the norm. The new coordination game has two *strict* Nash equilibria, one of which is Pareto superior to the other.[24, 25] When a norm of cooperation exists and is

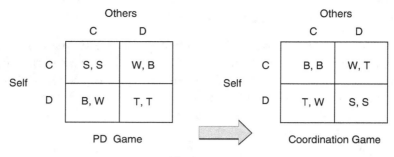

Figure 6.4.

obeyed, a game like the PD above is *transformed into a coordination game:* Players' payoffs in the new game will differ from the payoffs of the original game, since their preferences and beliefs will be as in conditions 2, 2(a) and 2(b) or 2(b') in the Appendix. Indeed, if a player knows that a cooperative norm exists and expects a sizeable part of the population to follow it, then, provided she also believes she is expected (and maybe also prefers) to follow such norm, she will have a preference to conform to the norm in a situation in which she has the choice to cooperate or to defect. Note that what I am saying implies that a social norm, unlike a convention, is never a solution of an original coordination game, though it is an equilibrium of the new, transformed game it *creates.*

More formally, and to further illustrate the norm-based utility function introduced above, consider the PD we are discussing. The norm-based function for either player is defined at C and undefined at D. The utility function for player 1 is then the following:

$$U_1(C,C)=\pi_1(C,C)-k_1(\pi_1(C,C)-\pi_1(C,C))=\pi_1(C,C)$$
$$U_1(D,D)=\pi_1(D,D)-k_1(\pi_1(D,D)-\pi_1(D,D))=\pi_1(D,D)$$
$$U_1(C,D)=\pi_1(C,D)-k_1(\pi_1(C,C)-\pi_1(C,D))$$
$$U_1(D,C)=\pi_1(D,C)-k_1(\pi_2(C,C)-\pi_2(C,D))$$

Player 2's utility function is similar. The game turns out to be a coordination game with two equilibria when $U_1(D,C) < U_1(C,C)$ and $U_2(D,C) < U_2(C,C)$, that is, when[26]

$$k_1 > \frac{\pi_1(D,C)-\pi_1(C,C)}{\pi_2(C,C)-\pi_2(C,D)}$$

$$k_2 > \frac{\pi_2(D,C)-\pi_2(C,C)}{\pi_1(C,C)-\pi_1(C,D)}$$

Otherwise it remains a PD.

It is important to note that my definition of social norm does not entail that *everybody* conforms. In fact, the definition (see Appendix) says that a social norm may exist and not be followed. For some, the PD in our example is never trans-

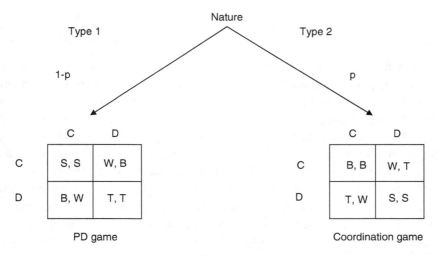

Figure 6.5.

formed into any other game. And even a person who starts playing a coordination game like the one described above may revert to playing the regular PD if she realizes that *empirical expectations* have been violated. Let me clarify this point with a simple example. Suppose an actor is faced with a finitely repeated PD, and suppose the situation is such that a cooperative norm is primed. The player knows there exists a cooperative norm that applies to this kind of situation. The player also knows that there are several types of players, some of whom would not see the game as he does. To make matters easy, suppose there are two types of players, those who simply see the game as a PD, and those that follow a cooperative norm.[27] In this case we may model the choice situation as a Bayesian game (Figure 6.5) in which Nature picks a player type with a given probability, so that with prior probability p the opponent one faces is playing a coordination game, and with probability $(1-p)$ he is playing a PD. If a norm-follower assesses a sufficiently high probability to being matched with a similar type, he will cooperate.[28]

Note that, when faced with a defection, a player will reassess his probabilities, and possibly revert to playing the equilibrium strategy (defect) for the traditional PD. Thus, one might say that the *existence* of a norm always presents a conditional follower with a Bayesian game: If the normative and empirical expectations conditions are fulfilled, she will attach a higher probability to being matched with a similar player type (a norm follower), and act accordingly. But she must also be prepared to revise her probabilistic assessment in case experience contravenes her previous expectations.[29] Note that the existence of a social norm facilitates equilibrium selection in the Bayesian game faced by the conditional norm followers. If the probability of being matched with a similar type is high enough, C,C is the selected equilibrium. Otherwise D,D will be selected.

5. Conclusions

The search for better, empirically grounded theories of how agents make decisions has led experimental economists to make many new assumptions about what motives guide us, and to incorporate these motives in utility functions. We are a long way from designing utility functions that are general enough to capture the richness of experimental data available. A promising way to proceed is to include a truly social component into utility functions. An example is the introduction of social norms, since their existence shapes our choices through the expectations they generate. We can maintain a traditional rational choice model, but make more interesting and realistic auxiliary hypotheses about preferences and motives. Epistemic indeterminacy is mitigated by the existence of social norms since, as I have argued, norms come in packages that include beliefs, expectations, causal attributions, and so on. Strategic indeterminacy is mitigated, too, since the existence of a norm points to a specific equilibrium, allowing players to coordinate on it. I use the term *mitigate* because players still have to assess their opponents' sensitivity to the relevant norm, and their choice will depend on this assessment. Experimental evidence, however, points to the fact that players, when a norm applies to the situation they are in, tend, *ceteris paribus,* to have quite uniform expectations of their opponents' caring about it (they are expected to care) and act accordingly in a uniform way.[30] Bringing more empirical data of this kind into our models is the only way I can see to solve the indeterminacy problem that has plagued otherwise excellent choice models for too long.

Appendix: Conditions for a Social Norm to Exist

Let R be a *behavioral rule* for situations of type S, where S can be represented as a mixed-motive game. R is a social norm in a population P if there exists a sufficiently large subset $P_{cf} \subseteq P$ such that, for each individual $i \in P_{cf}$:

Contingency: i knows that a rule R exists and applies to situations of type S;

Conditional preference: i prefers to conform to R in S on the condition that:

(a) *Empirical expectations: i* believes that a sufficiently large subset of P conforms to R in S;

and either

(b) *Normative expectations: i* believes that a sufficiently large subset of P expects i to conform to R in S;

or

(b′) *Normative expectations with sanctions: i* believes that a sufficiently large subset of *P* expects *i* to conform to *R* in *S*, prefers *i* to conform and may sanction behavior.

A social norm *R* is *followed* by population *P* if there exists a sufficiently large subset $P_f \subseteq P_{cf}$ such that, for each individual $i \in P_f$, conditions 2(a) and either 2(b) or 2(b′) are met for *i* and, as a result, *i* prefers to conform to *R* in *S*.

NOTES

1. By *practical rationality* I mean that an agent will choose that action that best fulfills her goals, given her beliefs about the situation. By *epistemic rationality* I refer to the rationality of an agent's beliefs. This may simply mean that probabilistic beliefs obey the axioms of probability calculus, but it may also mean that an agent will use all the statistical data that are available to her (see Bicchieri 1993, Chapter 1)

2. In fact, we can even *infer* a person's utility by looking at a sequence of choices she made, provided we assume she is consistent. F. P Ramsey (1931) was the first to show how, by observing a series of bets an individual is prepared to make, it is possible to infer both her preferences and probabilistic beliefs.

3. An event *p* is *common knowledge* among the players if all the players know that *p*, all know that all know that *p*, and so on. (Lewis 1969; Aumann 1976).

4. When players have common knowledge of the rules of the game and of their mutual preferences, the game is one of *complete information*. In our example, if I does not know *y*, or if I knows *y* but he does not know that II knows that, then the game is one of incomplete information (Harsanyi 1967–1968).

5. Note that optimality is only conditional on a fixed σ_{-i}, not on all possible σ_{-i}. A strategy that is a best reply to a given combination of the opponents' strategies may fare poorly vis a vis another strategy combination.

6. One important virtue of Nash equilibrium is that for games with a finite number of pure strategies and finitely many players, a Nash equilibrium always exists, at least in mixed strategies (Nash 1951).

7. By contrast, $\hat{p}$ is a symmetric *Nash equilibrium* if $\hat{p}^T A \hat{p} \geq p^T A \hat{p}$ for all feasible *p*.

8. Note that (*) is a deterministic system which allows some strategies to become extinct, in the sense that $p_i(t) = 0$ for some *i,t*. To prevent extinction, mutations are added, but a discussion of how to modify (*) to include mutations and how to interpret the latter would take us too far from the present topic. For an analysis of stochastic models, see Foster and Young (1990).

9. Guth et al. (1982) were the first to observe that the most common offer by proposers was to give half of the sum to the responder. The mean offer was 37% of the original allocation. In a replication of their experiments, they allowed subjects to think about their decision for one week. The mean offer was 32% of the sum, which is still very high.

10. We know that responders reject low offers even when the stakes are as high as three months' earnings (Cameron 1995). Furthermore, experiments in which third parties have a chance to punish an unfair proposer at a monetary cost to themselves show that (moderately) costly punishment is frequent (Fehr & Fishbacher 2000).

11. See Camerer (2003, Chapter 3) and Bicchieri (2006, Chapter 3).

12. Note, again, that the experiments I am referring to were all one-shot, which means that the participants were fairly sure of not meeting again; therefore, punishing behavior cannot be motivated as an attempt to convince the other party to be more generous the next time around. Similarly, proposers could not be generous because they were expecting reciprocating behavior in future interactions.

13. By *social preference* I refer to how people rank different allocations of material payoffs to self and others.

14. The term max $(x_j - x_i, 0)$ denotes the maximum of $x_j - x_i$ and 0; it measures the extent to which there is disadvantageous inequality between i and j.

15. The questions were devised by Jason Dana and Daylian Cain, who were taking my course on social norms.

16. I have extensively discussed this point in Bicchieri (2006, Chapter 3)

17. T. Schelling (1960) presents several cases of 'commitment strategies' that help one of the parties to get the upper hand in negotiating an agreement.

18. See, for example, Fehr et al. (2003), Dana, Weber *et al* (2003), Frey and Bohnet (1995), Hoffman, McCabe et al. (1994), Bicchieri and Chavez (2007).

19. Bicchieri and Chavez (2007).

20. Intuitively, N_2 should proscribe rejection of fair (or hyperfair) offers. The incorporation of this consideration, however, will not make a difference in the formal analysis.

21. Note that for $1<y<2$, I knows II will only accept the low price.

22. When players are uncertain as to the type of player they are facing, they will assess some probability that the other player is of a certain type. Typically, the list of all possible types and their prior probability of occurring in the population are taken to be common knowledge among the players (Harsanyi 1967, 1968).

23. For a justification of this ranking, see Bicchieri 2006, 16–19.

24. In a strict Nash equilibrium each player's strategy is a unique best reply to the other players' strategies. This means that a strict Nash equilibrium cannot include weakly dominated strategies.

25. A coordination game is a game in which there are at least two Nash equilibria in pure strategies, and players have a mutual interest in reaching one of these equilibria (*CC* or *DD* in our game), even if different players may prefer different equilibria (which is not the case in the above example).

26. Note that $U_1(D,C)$ stands for the utility of player 1 when 1 plays D and 2 plays C. Analogously, $U_2(D,C)$ stands for the utility of player 2 when 1 plays C and 2 plays D.

27. In a finitely repeated game, even a selfish player may want to cooperate for a while, if it is not common knowledge that all players are rational and selfish (Kreps et al. 1982). This consideration, however, has no bearing on my argument, since until a defection is observed a player cannot distinguish between a forward-thinking selfish type and a true cooperator.

28. If players use an availability heuristic to come to this probability assessment, the probability of playing a coordination game might initially be much higher. That is, if a player is the type who follows a cooperative norm, that player tends to believe there is a high probability that others are like him or her.

29. Recent experiment I conducted showed that, even if subjects do not particularly care about a (fairness) norm, their expectations about their partner's sensitivity to it drive their choices (Bicchieri & Chavez 2007). Moreover, we also discovered that subjects are very sensitive to what other people in their situation have done, and when there is conflict between normative and empirical expectations, the latter always win (Bicchieri & Xiao 2007).

30. Bicchieri and Chavez (2007), Bicchieri and Lev-on (2007).

REFERENCES

Aumann, R. (1976). "Agreeing to Disagree." *Annals of Statistics* 4: 1236–1239.

Bernheim, D. (1984). "Rationalizable Strategic Behavior." *Econometrica* 52: 1007–1028.

Bicchieri, C, (1993). *Rationality and Coordination.* Cambridge: Cambridge University Press.

Bicchieri, C. (1988). "Strategic Behavior and Counterfactuals." *Synthese* 76: 135–169.

Bicchieri, C. (2006). *The Grammar of Society: The Nature and Dynamics of Social Norms.* Cambridge, England: Cambridge University Press.

Bicchieri, C. & Chavez, A. (2007). "The Fragility of Fairness: How Beliefs Affect Behavior in Ultimatum Games." Discussion paper, Goldstone Research Unit, University of Pennsylvania, May 2007.

Bicchieri, C. & Lev-on, A. (2007). "Computer-Mediated Communication and Cooperation in Social Dilemmas: An Experimental Analysis." *Politics, Philosophy and Economics* 6 (2): 139–168.

Bicchieri, C. & Xiao, E. (2008). "Do the Right Thing: But Only If Others Do So." *Journal of Behevioral Deasion Making,* 21: 1–18.

Binmore, K. (1987, 1988). "Modeling Rational Players I and II." *Economics and Philosophy* 3: 9–55, and 4: 179–214.

Camerer, C. (2003). *Behavioral Game Theory: Experiments on Strategic Interaction.* Princeton: Princeton University Press.

Cameron, L. (1995). "Raising the Stakes in the Ultimatum Game: Experimental Evidence from Indonesia." *Working paper, Princeton Department of Economics—Industrial Relations Sections* 345.

Dana, J., Weber, R. & Kuang, J. (2003). "Exploiting Moral Wriggle Room: Behavior Inconsistent with a Preference for Fair Outcomes." *Carnegie Mellon Behavioral Decision Research Working Paper* 349.

Fehr, E. & Fischbacher, U. (2003). "The Nature of Human Altruism." *Nature* 425: 785–791.

Fehr, E. & Schmidt, K. (1999). "A Theory of Fairness, Competition, and Cooperation." *The Quarterly Journal of Economics* 114 (3): 817–868.

Foster, D., & Young, H.P. (1990). Stochastic Evolutionary Game Dynamics. *Theoretical Population Biology* 38: 219–232.

Frey, B. & Bohnet, I. (1995). "Institutions Affect Fairness: Experimental Investigations." *Journal of Institutional and Theoretical Economics* 151 (2): 286–303.

Fudenberg, D. & Levine, D.K. (1998). *The Theory of Learning in Games.* Cambridge, MA: MIT Press.

Guth, W., Schmittberger, R. & Schwarze, B. (1982). "An Experimental Analysis of Ultimatum Bargaining." *Journal of Economic Behavior and Organization* 3: 367–388.

Harsanyi, J. (1967–68). "Games with Incomplete Information Played by 'Bayesian' Players." Parts 1, 2, and 3. *Management Science* 14: 159–182, 320–332, 468–502.

Hofbauer, J. & Sigmund, K, (1998). *Evolutionary Games and Population Dynamics.* Cambridge: Cambridge University Press.

Hoffman, E., McCabe, K.A,. Shachat, K., & Smith, V. (1994). "Preferences, Property Rights, and Anonymity in Bargaining Games." *Games and Economic Behavior* 7: 346–380.

Hoffman, E., McCabe, K.A. & Smith, V. (1998). "Behavioral Foundations of Reciprocity: Experimental Economics and Evolutionary Psychology." *Economic Inquiry* 36: 335–352.

Kreps, D., Milgrom, P., Roberts, J., and Wilson, R. (1982). Rational Cooperation in the Finitely Repeated Prisoner's Dilemma. *Journal of Economic Theory* 27: 245–252.

Lewis, D. (1969). *Convention: A Philosophical Study.* Cambridge, MA: Cambridge University Press.

Maynard Smith, J. & Price, G. (1973). "The Logic of Animal Conflict." *Nature* 246: 15–18.

Nash, J. (1951). "Non-cooperative Games." *Annals of Mathematics* 54: 286–295.

Pearce, D. (1984). "Rationalizable Strategic Behavior and the Problem of Perfection." *Econometrica* 52: 1029–1050.

Ramsey, F.P. (1931). "Truth and Probability." In R. B. Braithwaite, Ed., *The Foundations of Mathematics and Other Logical Essays.* London: Routledge and Kegan Paul.

Roth, A.E., Prasnikar, V. Okuno-Fujiwara, M. & Zamir, S. (1991). "Bargaining and Market Behavior in Jerusalem, Ljubljana, Pittsburgh, and Tokyo: An Experimental Study." *American Economic Review* 81 (5): 1068–1095.

Schelling, T. (1960). *The Strategy of Conflict.* Cambridge: Harvard University Press.

Selten, R. (1975). "Re-examination of the Perfectness Concept for Equilibrium Points in Extensive Games." *International Journal of Game Theory* 4: 22–55.

Taylor, P.D. & Jonker, L.B. (1978). "Evolutionary Stable Strategies and Game Dynamics." *Mathematical Bioscience,* 40: 145–156.

Van Damme, E. (1987). *Stability and Perfection of Nash Equilibrium.* Berlin: Springer.

Von Neumann, J. & Morgenstern, O. (1944). *Theory of Games and Economic Behavior.* Princeton: Princeton University Press.

CHAPTER 7

EXPERIMENTAL INVESTIGATIONS OF SOCIAL PREFERENCES

JIM WOODWARD

1. INTRODUCTION

THIS article surveys some of the philosophical issues raised by recent experimental work on so-called social preferences.[1] More broadly, my focus is on experimental explorations of the conditions under which people behave co-operatively or in a prosocial way or, alternatively, fail to do so. These experiments raise a number of fascinating methodological and interpretive issues that are of central importance both to economics and to social and political philosophy. It is commonly claimed that the experiments demonstrate that (at least some) people not only have selfish preferences concerning their own material payoffs, but that they also have preferences concerning the well-being of others—that is, social preferences. (More concretely, it is claimed that some subjects have well-behaved utility functions in which monetary payoffs to others, as well as to themselves occur as arguments) Moreover, the contention is not just that some subjects have such social preferences, but that these can have large and systematic effects on behavior, both in the experiments under discussion and in real life contexts outside the laboratory.

These experimental results are thus taken to show the falsity or limited applicability of the standard *homo economicus* model of human behavior as entirely self- interested. For example, Henrich et al. write, in the opening paragraph of the "Overview and Synthesis" chapter of their 2004 book:

> The 1980's and 1990's have seen an important shift in the model of human motives used in economics and allied rational actor disciplines....In the past, the assumption that actors were rational was typically linked to what we call the *selfishness axiom*—the assumption that individuals seek to maximize their own material gains in the interactions and expect others to do the same. However, experimental economists and others have uncovered large and consistent deviations from the predictions of the textbook representation of *Homo economicus*...Literally hundreds of experiments in dozens of countries using a variety of experimental protocols suggest that, in addition to their own material payoffs, people have social preferences: subjects care about fairness and reciprocity, are willing to change the distribution of material outcomes among others at a personal cost to themselves, and reward those who act in a pro-social manner while punishing those who do not, even when these actions are costly. Initial skepticism about the experimental evidence was waned as subsequent experiments with high stakes and with ample opportunity for learning failed to substantially modify the initial conclusions. (8)

Other economists have challenged this interpretation of the experimental results, contending that they may be accounted for entirely in terms of selfish preferences and conventional game theory assumptions. In addition, even among those who agree that the experimental results cannot be fully accounted for just in terms of selfish preferences, some deny that the invocation of social preferences provides an illuminating explanation of behavior. They urge instead that the experimental results should be accounted for in some other way—for example, by appeal to *social norms*. In support of this position, it is observed that the behavior in the games, which is taken to be evidence for social preferences (and *hence* the preferences themselves), often seem to be highly context dependent and nonrobust, in the sense that a large number of different changes in the experimental set up lead to different behavioral results. Economists who invoke the notion of social preferences typically assume (or argue) that such preferences are not only well behaved in the sense of satisfying the usual axioms of revealed preference theory, but also that they are sufficiently stable that we can use them to predict behavior across some interesting range of contexts. (This assumption is more or less explicit among those who think of experimental games as ways of *measuring* social preferences). If this stability assumption is not true, one might well wonder whether whatever accounts for nonselfish behavior is usefully conceptualized as a social preference rather than in some alternative way. This issue will also be explored below.

If it is true that the behavior exhibited in the games discussed below cannot be fully accounted for by selfish preferences, then, whatever the positive explanation for the behavior may be, a number of other questions arise. What is the evolutionary history of such prosocial behaviors (as we will call them) and the preferences/motivations that underlie them? To what extent are these behaviors and motivations innate, or genetically specified, and to what extent do these reflect the influence of learning and culture? How much variability with respect to prosocial behavior/motivations is there among people within particular societies or groups and how much variation exists across groups? To the extent that people exhibit prosocial behavior and motivations, what is the content of these—are (many) people unconditional altruists, conditional co-operators or reciprocators of one or another kind, norm followers, or some mixture of all of these? Experimental investigations of social preferences have little directly to say about the first of these questions but are at least suggestive about many of the others.

My plan is to proceed as follows. I begin with an overview of some the experimental results (Section 2) and then turn to issues about their robustness and the implications thereof (Section 3). Section 4 explores the possible role of neurobiological evidence in addressing issues of robustness and discriminating among alternative explanations of experimental results. I next turn to a more systematic comparison of different approaches to explaining the experimental results, considering in turn explanations that appeal to social preferences (Section 5), explanations that appeal to selfish preferences, and explanations that appeal to norms (Section 6). I will conclude with some very brief remarks about the implications of all of this for normative social and political theory.

2. Some Experimental Results

In an ordinary *ultimatum game* (UG) a proposer (P) proposes a division of a monetary stake to a responder R. That is, if the stake is n, P may propose any amount x up to n for himself, with $n-x$ going to R. R may then either accept or reject this offer. If R accepts, both players get the proposed division. If R rejects, both players get nothing. The identities of both P and R are unknown to one another. If the game is one-shot and both players have entirely selfish preferences, the subgame perfect equilibrium is that P offers R the smallest possible positive amount of money (e.g, one cent if the stake is divisible down to pennies), and R accepts. This is not what is observed experimentally in any population. In most populations in developed countries, Ps offer an average of 0.3–0.4 of the total stake, and offers under 0.2 are rejected half the time. Offers of 0.5 are also common.

Dictator games (DGs) are like UGs except that the responder has no opportunity to reject: the proposer (dictator) unilaterally decides on the allocation. If the dictator has only self-interested preferences, he will allocate the entire amount to himself. Instead, in DGs in populations in developed countries, the mean allocated is 0.2 of the total stake, although there is considerable variance with many allocations of 0 and also many of 0.5.

In a *public-goods* game, each of N players can contribute an amount c_i of their choosing from an initial endowment that is the same for each player. The total amount Σc_i contributed by all players is multiplied by some factor m ($m< 1/N$) and divided equally among all of the players, regardless of how much they contribute. In other words, each player i's endowment is changed by $-c_i + m\Sigma c_i$. In this game if players care only about their own monetary payoffs, the dominant strategy is to contribute nothing—that is, to free ride on the contributions of the other players. In one-shot public-goods games in developed countries, subjects contribute on average about half of their endowment, although again there is a great deal of variation, with a number of subjects contributing nothing.

In repeated public-good games, subjects begin with substantial mean contribution, which then significantly declines under repetition. If a costly punishment option is introduced, which allows subjects to punish noncontributors but at a cost to themselves, a number will do so, even in the final round, in which punishment cannot influence future behavior. Introduction of this option prevents the decline in contributions with repeated play. Allowing discussion also boosts contributions.

In trust games, the trustor has the opportunity to transfer some amount X (from an initial stake) of the trustor's own choosing to a second party (the trustee). This amount is increased by the experimenter by some multiple $k>0$. (e.g., X may be tripled). The trustee then has the opportunity to transfer some portion of this new amount kX back to the trustor. In a one-shot game, a purely self-interested trustee will return nothing to the trustor and, recognizing this, the trustor will transfer nothing to the trustee in the initial step. Subjects in developed societies tend to transfer around 0.4–0.6 of their stake, and the rate of return by trustors is around 0—that is, trustors return approximately the result transferred but no more.

Cross-Cultural Results

In the experimental results described so far, subjects were drawn from developed counrties (United States, Europe, etc.) and there was considerable uniformity of behavior across these subject pools. However, in a fascinating series of cross-cultural experiments (described in Henrich et al. 2004), in which such games were played in a number of different small-scale societies in Asia, Africa, and South America, there was considerably more variation in results. For example, among the Machiguenga in Peru, one-shot UG offers had a mean 0.26 and mode of 0.15 (far lower than mean and modal offers in developed societies), and almost no offers were rejected. In contrast, among the Lamerela in Indonesia, offers in excess of 0.50 (hyperfair offers) were common and there was frequent rejection, even of hyperfair offers. A similar variation was found in public-goods games and trust games.

Moreover, in at least some cases, these results appear to correlate with features of social life in the societies in question. For example, the Machiguenga are described as "socially disconnected" by anthropologists, with economic life centering on the individual family and little opportunity for anonymous transactions. By contrast, the Lamerala are a whaling society in which there is a high degree of cooperative hunting and food sharing, and in which it is common for people to reject gifts out of concern that this will place them under a large obligation to reciprocate. The Orma in Kenya make relatively high contributions in public goods games (both in comparison to many other small scale societies and the contemporary United States: 0.58 of their endowments). Participants in this game associated it with a *harambee*, "a Swahili word for the institution of village level contributions for public goods projects such as building a school" (Ensminger 2004, 376), and, in fact, a harambee collection was going on at the time the public-goods game was played. It seems plausible that the relatively high level of contribution was at least in part a reflection of the willingness of the participants to think of it as an instance of this practice.

3. Three Notions of Robustness

It was noted earlier that one of the issues I raised by this experimental work concerns the fragility/robustness of the behavior detected and of whatever explains it. To motivate this issue, it will be useful to distinguish three different notions of robustness that can be of interest in experimental investigation.

Detection Robustness

This has to do with whether we can we detect (or triangulate in) on the same phenomenon in different ways within a specific experimental or nonexperimental context, by using different detection or measurement techniques of procedures. As a physical example, suppose that we attempt to measure the melting point of lead under fixed experimental conditions. Detection robustness has to do with whether different techniques or instruments for measuring the melting point (e.g., different thermometers of different design) yield the same or closely similar results for the melting point. To the extent that there is such agreement, it provides some reason to think that the phenomenon we are claiming to detect is real (or the measurement result accurate), rather than an artifact of the particular measurement technique we happen to employ. The usual motivation for this claim is that different detection and measurement techniques are likely to have different sources of error associated with them. Although any one technique may involve unknown errors, if a number of techniques agree, it is unlikely that errors are present in each in such a way that each leads to the same result even though that result is mistaken.

Phenomenon Robustness

Phenomenon robustness has to do with whether we continue to detect the same phenomenon as we alter the experimental conditions in various small ways or under small alterations in background conditions in nonexperimental contexts. Under what conditions does the phenomenon of interest change? For example, under the same atmospheric pressure, does lead melt at the same temperature both here and on the surface of Mars? Does lead melt at the same temperature under different atmospheric pressures? Obviously, issues of this sort are very important when we come to talk about the "external" or "ecological validity" or "exportability" of experimental results.

Relational Robustness

Assuming that the phenomenon of interest shows variation across some changes in experimental and background conditions, relational robustness has to do with whether we find other factors that co-vary with it in a robust way. That is, is the *relationship* between the phenomenon (or some feature of it) and some other condition robust in the sense that this relationship continues to hold as other conditions vary? For example, does the melting point of lead systematically co-vary with variations in atmospheric pressure, even as other conditions (e.g., location) vary?

Applied to claims about prosocial behavior /social preferences, these distinctions lead to the following conceptions of robustness:

Detection Robustness in Experimental Games

Behavior in experimental games is often taken to be evidence for the existence of preferences with certain characteristics—for example, rejection of low offers in a UG is taken to show that responders have a taste for negative reciprocity, and cooperative behavior is often taken to show that subjects have preferences for positive reciprocity. Detection robustness in this context has to do with whether we can also detect such preferences in other ways, at least within the context of some particular game or relatively similar game.

Phenomenon Robustness in Experimental Games

Suppose that subjects drawn from a certain pool exhibit certain behavior in a particular version of some game. Phenomenon robustness in this context has to do with how stable or robust this behavior and the preferences that underlie lie it are under changes that are relevant and potentially important from the point of view of economics. For example, does the same behavior persist under changes in the subject pool, under (apparently) small changes in instructions, under changes in the monetary stakes, under changes in anonymity or information conditions? More ambitiously, one may ask whether the same behavior is exhibited in, say, both the extensive and normal form of the game, under use of the strategy method, under different ways of framing or labeling the alternatives in the game or when the game is repeated or preceded by a training or learning period. Even more ambitiously, one may ask whether preferences and motivations that are claimed to be at work in one kind of game are also at work in other related games—for example, do subjects who make relatively generous offers in dictator games also behave cooperatively in prisoner's dilemmas or public good games?

In practice in experimental economics, the distinction between detection and phenomenon robustness may not be entirely sharp. Consider the issue of whether proposer behavior in ultimatum games reflects a self-interested fear of rejection by the responder or a social preference of some sort for the welfare of the responder or some combination of these. By itself, merely observing proposer behavior in an ordinary UG cannot discriminate among these hypotheses. However, one common argument that is made in this connection is the following: if we compare proposer behavior in UGs and DGs, we see that proposers make more generous offers in UGs. (Proposer play in a DG is completely non-strategic since there is no possibility of responder rejection). This (it is argued) makes it reasonable to assume that proposer play in a DG reflects or measures the proposer's pure, non-strategic, "altruistic" preferences for generosity and fairness. If we assume that proposers in a UG also have altruistic preferences, then this suggests that proposer play is the net upshot of two kinds of influences: a non-strategic preference to be generous and in addition a self-interested fear of rejection. Thus, by comparing UGs and DGs, we may detect or decompose the preferences underlying behavior in the UG—something that would not be possible if we just looked at the UG alone. Notice, though that this argument about detection rests on a strong assumption about the (phenomenon) robustness of altruistic preferences—that the same altruistic preferences that are apparently present in a DG continue to be operative under the different conditions of the UG. It certainly seems possible that this assumption might be wrong—that the DG and UG are different enough that they trigger or engage very different preferences or norms, with even subjects who are generous in the former, behaving (and thinking it OK to behave) in a purely strategic way in the latter.[2]

Relational Robustness in Experimental Games

In the context of experimental investigations of social preferences, relational robustness has to do with what else such preferences stably correlate with in the field, in daily behavior, and in institutions and practices outside the lab The existence of such correlations is another way of providing reassurance that the phenomenon one is apparently detecting in experiment has some sort of existence outside the laboratory. For example, the correlation found in the Henrich et al. study between the size of offers in the UG among the Machiguenga and the Lamerela and features of their societies provides some reason to think that in these societies the UG is a way of measuring or detecting more general features of their social life.

Why Robustness Matters

Investigation of the conditions under which a phenomenon is robust (or not) is important for a number of reasons. First, as remarked earlier, it is one source of information about external validity. If a phenomenon appears to exist under very specialized conditions in the laboratory but substantially changes or disappears under variations in those conditions and there is reason to believe that those variations are common outside of the laboratory, then this may provide some prima-facie reason to doubt that the phenomenon is widespread or important outside the laboratory. For example, if people exhibit apparently prosocial behavior in certain one-shot laboratory games but (as some economists contend) such behavior disappears when subjects play repeated versions of the same game, and if in real life (outside the laboratory) most interactions are repeated rather than one shot, this may provide some reason to think that the behavior exhibited in the lab (and any prosocial preferences associated with it) is unlikely to be common or important outside of the lab.

Second, issues about robustness are important because they can constrain the possible explanations of the prosocial behavior seen in laboratory games. If prosocial behavior is highly nonrobust—for example, if subjects who exhibit prosocial behavior in the context of one game fail to do so in other games, under small changes in context, under repetition and so on, this may cast down on explanations of that behavior that appeal to the idea that people have social preferences that are stable across different contexts.

Third, issues about phenomenal robustness are very important if we wish to use the results of experimental investigations for the design of social mechanisms or institutions or for the purposes of normative moral and political theory, since in most cases we need to build these around behavior and motivations that are stable and robust rather than fragile. For example, as noted above, introduction of a costly punishment option boosts contributions in laboratory public-goods games, and this suggests the possibility that allowing people to sanction one another in certain ways might help to solve certain public-goods problems in real life (while merely exhorting them not to free ride may be relatively ineffective.) However, one of the many questions we would like answered before adopting any such proposal is whether willingness to sanction, even at cost to oneself, is robust in the sense of occurring under various conditions that occur outside the laboratory, whether such sanctions are as effective at boosting contributions under a variety of conditions that occur outside the lab, and so on.

4. Neural Mechanisms

I turn now to some brief remarks about the role of neurobiological evidence in investigations of social preferences and behavior. This is a hot area of current research that has evoked both widespread interest and considerable skepticism. Some of this skepticism focuses on particular experiments or on imaging techniques such as functional Magnetic Resonance Imaging (fMRI), which I will not try to address. There is, however, a more general source of skepticism, which simply put is this: It is completely uncontroversial that in all of the experiments under discussion, something goes on in subject's brains. It may be of interest to neurobiology to learn which neural regions are differentially activated when, for example, subjects reject low offers in ultimatum games. But (the skeptic argues) why is this of any interest to economics or social science? What matters for the latter sciences is simply how subjects behave (both in different experimental situations and outside the laboratory).

The contrary view is that a better understanding of the neural mechanisms that underlie behavior in experimental games can be of great relevance and importance to social science. In particular, information about neural mechanisms can be used to address some of the issues about the various forms of robustness of prosocial preferences described earlier. For reasons described in the following section, this second view strikes me as more plausible.

Underdetermination and Triangulation

First, as we have already noted, often behavioral evidence by itself cannot fully discriminate among a number of different hypotheses about the social preferences (or whatever) that underlie behavior in experimental games. In other words, one faces an underdetermination problem. Neural evidence can help to resolve this indeterminancy and to provide an alternative means of triangulation on underlying causes, such as subjects' motives and preferences. As an illustration, several explanations (described in more detail later) have been proposed for the willingness of subjects to behave co-operatively in a one-shot game in which the choice that maximizes their expected monetary payoff is to behave uncooperatively. One of these (in addition to the hypothesis that subjects have prosocial preferences) is that subjects have only self-interested preferences regarding their own monetary payoffs, but that such preferences can lead to cooperative play in repeated games. If subjects import habits and heuristics associated with such repeated play into one-shot games, they will play cooperatively even in one-shot games. Although there is additional behavioral evidence that is relevant to discriminating among these competing explanations (again, see later discussion), it is unlikely to be fully persuasive by itself. The following imaging experiment of Rilling et al. 2004, (see also Rilling et al. 2002), provides an additional source of evidence. These authors imaged subjects in a one-shot sequential PD. They showed that the outcome in which there is mutual cooperation generates higher activation in the dorsal striatum (a brain system known to be centrally involved in reward processing) than the activation that results when a human subject knows that he or she is playing against a computer that also plays cooperatively, generating the same monetary payoff for the subject. Moreover, the mutual cooperation with a human partner also generates higher activations than earning the same amount of money in an individual decision-making task. A further study showing that the mere viewing of faces of people who previously cooperated in a social dilemma game activates reward-related areas (Singer et al. 2004). A natural (although admittedly not the only) interpretation of these results is that subjects get an additional reward (over and above whatever reward they receive just from the monetary payoff) when they are involved in a cooperative venture with another human being. Indeed, it appears they get such a reward when they merely view cooperators.

Although one may quibble about whether the preferences involved in such cooperative behavior are genuinely unselfish,[3] the imaging experiments do seem to suggest two points. First, the subjects apparently have preferences for something more or different from their own monetary payoffs, regardless of whether one decides to call such preferences unselfish. Second, such preferences may well play a role in explaining cooperative behavior in one-shot interactions or in circumstances in which actors are unsure whether cooperative behavior will be reciprocated.

As a second illustration of the role of neurobiological evidence, consider responder behavior in a UG. As we noted, many responders in societies like the contemporary United States reject low offers. However, this behavioral evidence fails to discriminate among several different hypotheses about why rejection occurs—for example, responders may reject simply because they dislike receiving much less than proposers (inequality aversion) or they may reject because they have a "taste for negative reciprocity"—that is, they feel angry or indignant at proposers who make low offers and wish to punish them. On the first hypothesis, subjects care only about outcomes and in particular about how their payoff compares to that of the proposer. On the second hypothesis, responders respond negatively to choices or intentions that they perceive as hostile or unfair by punishing proposers. In an attempt to discriminate among these alternatives, Sanfey et al. (2003) used fMRI to image second movers in one-shot ultimatum games with $10 stakes. Some subjects played against humans who followed a predetermined algorithm in making offers. Others played against a computer that was programmed to make an identical set of offers. Both sets of subjects were informed about whether they were playing against a human or a computer. Unfair offers from human partners were associated with higher activation in several brain areas, including the anterior cingulate cortex, dorsolateral prefrontal cortex, and anterior insula, with higher levels of activation being positively correlated with decisions to reject. Anterior insula is known to be associated with negative emotional states, including anger and disgust. This by itself does not show that the rejections were motivated by negative reciprocity rather than a general aversion of some kind to unequal splits. However, two additional pieces of evidence from this study provide at least some support for the negative reciprocity thesis. The first is that unfair offers by humans were rejected at a significantly higher rate than identical offers by the computer. The second is that unfair offers from human partners show significantly higher activation in these brain areas than identical offers from the computer. Taken together, these results suggest that second movers respond not just to the offered split itself but to the intention that is taken to lie behind the split and that they are willing to punish or exhibit negative reciprocation toward splits that are taken to reflect an unkind intention. So at least in this context, there is evidence that negative reciprocity is present.[4]

Neural Evidence and Phenomenon Robustness

A second way in which information about neural mechanisms can be relevant is that it may cast light on the likely phenomenon robustness of various sorts of behavior. That is, understanding the mechanisms underlying various behaviors may give us some insight about the conditions, if any, under which the behavior is likely to change, its plasticity under learning, under changes in incentives, and so on. This is particularly true if the neural structures in question are damaged in some way. For example, there is considerable evidence that damage to orbitofrontal or ventromedial cortex in early childhood can lead to sociopathic behavior that is apparently virtually uncorrectable by learning or training—the normal functioning of these structures in early life appears to be essential for normal moral and social development, and when they are seriously damaged, no alternative brain areas are able to compensate. (This stands in striking contrast to the more common pattern in which recovery of other cognitive functions is more likely when neural damage occurs early in life).

Different Behavior in Similar Games

A closely related point is that information about underlying neural mechanisms may also help us to understand why what seem to be (from the point of view of existing theory) very similar or identical games or decision problems elicit very different behavior—the explanation may be that the brain uses rather different mechanisms or processes or exploits different information in dealing with these problems. As an illustration, consider the contrast between choice under conditions of risk (when subjects are confident about the values of probabilities for various possible outcomes) versus conditions involving uncertainty/ambiguity (when subjects are not confident or lack information about such probabilities). A number of well-known thought experiments (such as the Ellsberg paradox) as well as other empirical investigations show that many subjects respond differently to situations involving risk and ambiguity that classical decision theory implies are equivalent. A recent imaging study by Hsu et al. (2005) shows that different neural circuits appear to be involved in choice under risk and choice under uncertainty: choice under ambiguity is positively correlated with differential activation in the amygdala and orbitofrontal cortex, and negatively correlated with striatal activation. By contrast, areas activated during the risk condition relative to ambiguity include the dorsal striatum, but not the orbitofrontal cortex or amygdala. Moreover, striatal activity correlates positively with expected reward. The involvement of these different neural structures in choices involving risk and ambiguity both helps to explain why subjects treat these two kinds of choices so differently and also may have implications for how easy or likely it is for subjects to learn to treat the two sorts of choices in the same way, as many normative versions of classical decision theory tell us to do. To the extent that the brain is wired up to distinguish these two sorts of choices, it may not be so easy for subjects to learn to treat them as equivalent.

5. SOCIAL PREFERENCES

I turn now to a discussion of some general strategies that have been employed by economists for explaining the behavioral results observed in the experiments described earlier. The first such strategy (the *social preference* strategy) has already been alluded to: Players have relatively stable social preferences—that is, utility functions/dispositions to behave, which include payoffs to others and which are at least somewhat stable across both across small changes in particular games and across different but related games. That is, these preferences and the associated behavior exhibit a fair degree of phenomenon-robustness.

The Fehr-Schmidt Model

One of the best known examples of a theory of this type is the "inequality aversion" model of Fehr and Schmidt (1999). Suppose that $X = x_1 . . x_n$ represents the monetary allocation among each of n players. Fehr and Schmidt propose that the utility of the ith player for this allocation is

$$U_i(X) = x_i - a_i / n - 1 \sum \max[x_j - x_i, 0] - b_i / n - 1 \sum \max[x_i - x_j, 0]$$

where the summations are for $j \neq i$ and $b_i \leq a_i$ and $0 \leq b_i \leq 1$. The utility of the ith player is thus a function of the monetary payoff he receives (this represents his selfish preferences) and two other terms. The first reflects how much i dislikes disadvantageous inequality, where this is measured by the difference between his payoff and the payoff received by the best-off individual, discounted by an individual sensitivity parameter a_i. The second term reflects how much i dislikes advantageous inequality, again discounted by an individual sensitivity parameter b_i. The assumption that both a_i and b_i are non-negative but that $b_i \leq a_i$ means that the players do not like inequality for its own sake, but that they dislike disadvantageous inequality more than they dislike advantageous inequality. a_i, b_i are taken to be stable characteristics of individuals—that is, for the same individual they are constant across some range of variation in the conditions of play for individual games of the same type and also across some range of games.

If we are willing to assume that subjects have such preferences with stable a_is and b_is, it will make sense to use one-shot games to measure or identify subject's utility functions, and then use these to predict/explain behavior across games. This is what Fehr and Schmidt try to do. Their strategy is to estimate subjects a_is, and b_is from their behavior in an ordinary ultimatum game and then use this information to predict behavior in other games, such as an ultimatum game with responder competition, and public goods games with and without punishment. However, in doing this, Fehr and Schmidt do not (as one might expect) employ information about the behavior of subjects in one game and then use this information to predict the behavior of the *same subjects* in other games. Instead, the games with which they are concerned involve different subjects, who are apparently assumed to come from a common pool or distribution of types. That is, what Fehr and Schmidt do is to gather information about the distribution of the coefficients a_i and b_i in UGs for certain subjects and then, on the assumption that the same distribution will hold among the different subjects who play other games, determine if their aggregate behavior in new games can be predicted from this distribution.

Criticisms of the Fehr-Schmidt Model

Although Fehr and Schmidt claim some predictive success in this enterprise, their work has been subjected to a detailed critique by Shaked (2007) who argues that they provide little evidence for stability of the coefficients across different games and that no real prediction is achieved. Instead, Shaked claims that, at best, what Fehr and Schmidt accomplish is a kind of curve–fitting: They are able to show there are some choices of values for the coefficients that are consistent with the aggregate behavior of the subjects across several different games, but they do not succeed in estimating precise values for these coefficients in one set of games and using these to predict behavior in other games. More specifically, Shaked shows that the data from UGs that Fehr and Schmidt employ can be used to pin down the coefficients a_i and b_i only to coarse intervals. For example, all that can be inferred from proposers who offer an even split in the UG is that their b_is ≥ 0.5. Moreover, nothing can be inferred about the joint distribution of a_i, b_i since each player is either in the role of a proposer or a responder but not both. For proposers who offer an even split, Fehr and Schmidt make the specific assumption that $b_i = 0.6$, but provide no theoretical rationale for this choice of value. This choice does yield a prediction about behavior in ultimatum games with responder competition that fits the data well, but other theoretically allowed assumptions about b_i (that is, assumptions consistent with $b_i > 0.5$) yield predictions at variance with the data—for example, $b_i = 0.84$ yields the prediction that 50 percent of groups with responder competition will be at competitive equilibrium rather than the observed 80 percent.

As another illustration, Fehr and Schmidt's attempted explanation of behavior in public goods games with punishment again requires the special choice of value $b_i = 0.6$ and additional assumptions as well—among them, that a_i and b_i are strongly correlated, which as we have seen, does not come from the data. For other games, either they provide no predictions or yet more special assumptions are required—for example, behavior in the DG is explained by a model in which the fitted utility functions are nonlinear rather than the linear form originally proposed by Fehr and Schmidt.

Other Variables Affecting Social Preferences

On reflection, these limitations of the Fehr-Schmidt model are unsurprising because we know from other evidence from other games that subjects' behavior can be quite sensitive to many other variables that are not represented in the Fehr-Schmidt utility functions. These include framing and labeling/property rights; anonymity; perceived intentions; and group identification, all discussed in the following sections.

Framing and Labeling/Property Rights

The way in which choices are described or labeled can affect behavior. For example, Hoffman et al. (1994) found that when an ultimatum game is described as an exchange, with the proposer described as a seller and the responder as a buyer, the mean offer falls by about 10 percent. A similar change occurs if the proposer earns the property right to his position by winning a contest.

Anonymity

In an ordinary DG, the identities of the players are not known to one another, but the experimenter knows the amount allocated. In a double-blind DG, the experimenter does not know the amount allocated, and the mean contribution falls to 0.1 (from 0.2 in an ordinary DG). On the other hand, providing information about the recipient boosts the amount allocated to an average of 0.5 of the stakes. Dictators also allocate considerably more when they have the opportunity to allocate to a charity such as the Red Cross rather than to an unknown individual. However, the effect of anonymity does not seem to be stable across different sorts of games—for example, in a double blind UG, proposers do not significantly reduce offers.

Perceived Intention

We have already noted (in connection with UGs and sequential PDs) that the intentions with which subjects are perceived to act can substantially affect the behavior of other subjects toward them. In general subjects seem to care not just about the monetary payoffs that they and others receive, as in the Fehr-Schmidt utility function, but also about how those outcomes come about and what the alternatives are that were not chosen, both of which affect whether outcomes appear to be the result of hostile or cooperative intentions.

Group Identification

There is at least some evidence that manipulation of group identification and solidarity affects cooperative behavior. For example, Dawes et al. 1989 artificially created distinct groups and then conducted public-goods experiments with similar payoff structures in which subjects either had an opportunity to provide contributions to their own group or to the other group. Contributions were much higher in the former condition.

Rabin and Fairness Equilibria

The Fehr-Schmidt model is just one of many treatments of social preferences in the literature—other models include Bolton and Ockenfels 2000, Rabin and Charness 2002, Falk and Fischbacher 2006, and Rabin 1993. The latter is one of the most ambitious attempts to model preferences regarding fairness in a psychologically realistic way. Space precludes detailed discussion, but the basic idea is that subjects care not just about outcomes but also about the motives and intentions with which other players act. Players wish to reciprocate positively when others act kindly toward them and to reciprocate negatively or retaliate when others act hostilely. More specifically, suppose that player i chooses strategy a_i and that b_j is i's belief about the strategy that will be chosen by j. Let, c_i be i's belief about j's belief concerning i's choice of strategy. Player i's choice will result in an allocation to player j which will depend on a_i and on the strategy chosen by j, which defines a set of possible payoffs to j. Let $\pi_j^h(b_j)$ be the highest possible payoff for j in this set, $\pi_j^{min}(b_j)$ the lowest possible payoff, and define the equitable payoff $\pi_j^e(b_j)$ as the average of the highest and lowest possible payoffs, excluding Pareto dominated payoff pairs. Then player i's *kindness* toward player j is given by $f_i(a_i, b_j) = \pi_j(b_j, a_i) - \pi_j^e(b_j)) / \pi_j^h(b_j)) - \pi_j^{min}(b_j)$. Player i's *belief* about player j's kindness toward him is given by $f_j^*(b_j, c_i) = \pi_i(c_i, b_j) - \pi_i^e(c_i) / \pi_i^h(c_i) - \pi_i^{min}(c_i)$

Each player then chooses so as to maximize his or her expected utility, which is given by

$$U_i(a_i, b_j, c_i) = \pi_i(a_i, b_j) + f_j^*(b_j, c_i)[1 + f_i(a_i, b_j)]$$

In other words, players care about their own payoffs (the first term), whether they are treated kindly (the second term) and about reciprocity (the third term, which is positive when players respond to kindness with kindness and hostility with hostility). Rabin then employs an equilibrium concept for the game (called a "fairness equilibrium") in which players maximize their utilities, and their beliefs correspond to what actually happens in the game.

Rabin's model has the great merit of incorporating the fact that subjects care not just about their monetary payoffs but the motives and intentions with which other players act. In this respect, it is superior to models (like Fehr-Schmidt) which allow only information about outcomes into player's preferences. On the other hand, while Rabin (1993) applies the model to examples involving monopoly pricing, and to gift exchange views of employment relationships, there is, to my knowledge, no systematic attempt to show that it can explain behavior in a wide range of experimental games. If the model is to do this, all the varieties of non-self-interested behavior described earlier and the effects of anonymity, framing, group identification, and so forth on such behavior must be captured by the last two terms of the player's utility functions in Rabin's model. It is at least not obvious that it is possible to do this. Rabin's model also has the disadvantage that in many games there will be many different fairness equilibria, depending on the beliefs players happen to have. In such cases the model has limited predictive power (cf. Bicchieri 2006, 111–112). In addition, the model also does not apply to games in which there is asymmetric information about payoffs. So despite its elegance, it seems unlikely that the model will provide a completely general account of social preferences.

Preliminary Conclusion

What then can we conclude about attempts to explain behavior in games by appeal to social preferences? I have discussed only a few of the many models presented in the literature, and it may be that the apparent instability and context-dependence of social preferences reflect only the limitations of these models. That is, it may turn out that, with a more adequate parameterization/representation of social preferences, these will turn out to be relatively stable and robust across different situations. On the other hand, in the light of the results already discussed, it seems entirely possible that what we call social preferences will turn out to be rather non-robust in the sense of phenomenon robustness—that is, in any tractable model, both prosocial behavior and preferences will exhibit a relatively high level of sensitivity to contextual variables like those described earlier. In some cases, it may also turn out that it is difficult to devise different detection procedures that might be used to triangulate on the same underlying preferences in different ways. As suggested earlier, both sorts of failure of robustness raise the issue of exactly what we are measuring—stable preferences or something else?

How Much Stability at the Individual Level?

In this connection, it is striking how little appears to be known about even qualitative stability of type (with respect to prosocial behavior) at the individual level. For example, little is known about whether, as one might expect (and as social-preference approaches suggest), subjects who are likely to reject low offers in UGs are also those who tend to punish in public-goods games, whether those who contribute generously in public-goods games also behave cooperatively in one-shot prisoner's dilemmas, and so on. It seems to me that it might be worthwhile to first investigate whether there is such qualitative consistency of type before attempting detailed parameterizations of social preferences. This, of course, would require evidence about the play of the same subjects across different games.[4]

Which Game?

I turn now to another problem with the project of measuring social preferences, which has been discussed by Binmore (2007) and Samuelson, 2005, among others: When the experimenter has his subjects play a game that he intends to be taken as one-shot, can we really be sure that the players model it as a one-shot game? Binmore and Samuelson ask us to consider the following possibility: Most or at least a very great deal of real-life social interaction (especially in small scale societies) is best modeled as a repeated game. Thus, when subjects play a one-shot game in the laboratory, what they typically do is to import patterns of behavior, heuristics, or norms that derive from their experience in playing some repeated game that looks similar. In other words, they (perhaps consciously, perhaps tacitly[6]) model the laboratory game as some familiar repeated game for which they have acquired some relevant pattern of behavior.

If this is correct, it creates problems for the whole project of using one-shot games to measure social preferences. As a simple illustration, suppose that subjects are presented with a one-shot game in which monetary payoffs to each player (not necessarily their utilities) have the structure of a PD. Suppose that many subjects cooperate. One explanation is that the subjects have social preferences that make cooperation an optimal strategy for each—they care about the payoffs to the other player as well as their own and act so as to maximize their expected utility. However, there is another possibility: Suppose the subject's experiences in real life are with iterated PDs. As is well–known, in an iterated PD game of indefinite length, cooperative strategies such as a mutual choice of tit-for-tat are one possible Nash equilibrium, even if subjects selfishly care only about their own monetary payoffs. Thus, if subjects tacitly model one-shot PDs as repeated games and automatically import strategies like tit-for-tat that are successful in repeated games into the one-shot game, we can explain their behavior without any appeal to other-regarding social preferences.[7] A similar observation applies to other one-shot games that are often taken to show the existence of social preferences. This is one of several considerations that lead Binmore to conclude that it is "unparsimonious" to assume the existence of anything but selfish preferences in explaining behavior in one-shot games.

Even if we do not follow Binmore all the way to this conclusion, he seems to have identified a potentially serious methodological problem with the use of games to measure social preferences. The problem is simply that the experimenter may not have full control over which game is being played. The experimenter may assume and intend that the game be a one-shot PD but in fact subjects may be playing an iterated PD (or something else). Obviously, using games to measure subject's preferences requires knowing which game is being played. Ideally, what one would like is a theory of how subjects model games and the ability to detect which model the subject employs. However, we are very far from having such a theory.

Do Subjects Import Norms from Repeated Games?

When subjects play one-shot games, do they import behavior from some repeated game in the manner that Binmore and Samuelson suggest? The empirical evidence bearing on this question is complex and equivocal in some respects. The Henrich et al. 2004 cross- country study certainly suggests this sometimes happens. Thus, as we noted, it seems to be a plausible conjecture that the willingness of the Lamerela to make hyperfair offers in the UG is connected to the fact that theirs is a society in which there is a great deal of cooperative behavior and competitive gift giving, the generous contributions of the Orma in a public-goods game are connected by the players themselves to their Harambee institution and so on. Indeed, if there was no importation or transfer of behavior that is common in everyday life into one-shot games, one might well wonder what such games measure, and about their external/ecological validity, and their phenomenon and relational robustness. However, as we have observed, it is arguable that this sort of external/ ecological validity may come at the expense of control over which game is being played.

Consider, on the other hand, a very strong form of what I will call the norm importation thesis according to which subjects always and automatically transfer strategies appropriate for some repeated game they have experienced in real life into one-shot games in a behaviorally inflexible way—that is, they always play one-shot games as though they are repeated games. This is inconsistent with a substantial amount of behavioral evidence (admittedly largely from subjects in developed societies) suggesting that even naïve subjects play differently in repeated and one-shot games of the same type and that they modify their behavior in the latter depending on the play of their opponents and on considerations having to do with reputation formation. For example, Fehr and Fischbacher (2003) (also described in Camerer & Fehr 2004) conducted a series of UGs in two different conditions, each involving subjects playing a different opponent in each of ten different iterations. In one condition, proposers knew nothing about past play of responders, so responders had no opportunity to build a reputation by rejecting low offers. In the reputation condition, proposers knew about the past play of responders. It was found that the great majority of responders increase their threshold for the lowest offers they will accept in the reputation condition as opposed to the no reputation condition. This suggests that they understood the value of reputation formation and along with it, the contrast between one-shot and repeated play.

Robustness of Behavior and Preferences under Repetition

A distinct but related issue concerns the phenomenon stability/robustness of behavior and preferences under repetition of a game. Suppose, for the sake of argument, that subjects do sometimes exhibit non-self-interested behavior in one-shot games, at least when they have had little experience with such games. Suppose, however, that the following claims are also true. (i) Under repetition of the game, either with the same opponent or with strangers or both, the behavior of such subjects changes. they learn different behaviors and instead converge on an equilibrium that is a Nash equilibrium of the repeated game on the assumption that they have entirely self-interested preferences. (ii) Suppose also that, in most ecologically realistic circumstances outside the laboratory, people's interactions are best modeled as a repeated game. Then, even if inexperienced subjects seem to exhibit other-regarding behavior in some one-shot games, this will tell us very little about why (or the conditions under which) cooperative behavior occurs in real life, since under real-life conditions, repetition will lead to preferences and behavior that are different from those exhibited in the one-shot game. For the purposes of explaining behavior in real life, what will matter is what happens when games are repeated with knowledgeable subjects who are given ample opportunities for learning. Laboratory investigation should thus focus on such games, rather than on one-shot games with inexperienced subjects.

An argument along these lines is advanced by Binmore (2007). In support of (i) he appeals to empirical results about how behavior changes under repeated play. For example, as we have already noted, in a one-shot public-goods game, subjects initially contribute an average of 0.4–0.6 of their endowments. However, when subjects repeatedly play such one-shot games with different pools of players (so-called stranger rematching), contributions fall substantially, although a small core continues to contribute substantially. The generous initial contributions in the one-shot game are thus not robust under repetition even of one-shot games with other players, still less under repetition of play with the same other players. To the extent that in real life subjects generally have extensive experience with repeated play in public-goods games, one might wonder whether the high level of initial contributions has anything of interest to tell us about why cooperation occurs or does not occur in public goods games outside the laboratory.[8]

How Common Are One-shot, Anonymous Interactions?

Among other things, these issues about the relationship between behavior in one-shot and in repeated games also raises empirical questions about which there seems to be surprisingly little consensus—questions about the relative frequency of one-shot vs. repeated games/interactions (and relatedly, anonymous vs. non-anonymous interactions) in ecologically realistic circumstances, both in developed and small-scale societies. Economists like Binmore (e.g., 2007) hold that, as a matter of empirical fact, subjects in both developed and small scale societies are rarely involved in one-shot, anonymous interactions, and that the overwhelming majority of their experience is with repeated games or at least with games in which others are able to observe their play and hence in which they have incentives to establish a reputation. According to Binmore (2007), this is why subjects have difficulty playing in an adaptive way in one-shot laboratory games, at least initially, and why experimental investigations should focus on repeated games played by subjects with ample opportunities for learning. A contrary view is that one-shot interactions (e.g., between buyers and sellers who are not involved in any ongoing relationship) in which the outcomes are not observed by third parties are fairly common in large societies with extensive markets like the contemporary United States or at least that such interactions are far more common in developed societies than in many small- scale societies.

In this connection it is interesting to recall that one of the general results of the Henrich et al. (2004) study is that there is *more* cooperative behavior in one-shot laboratory games in countries with large levels of market integration than in small-scale societies that lack such integration. If the experiences of subjects from small-scale societies is overwhelmingly with repeated games that can foster cooperation even with selfish preferences, (and if such subjects have little experience with one-shot games), why aren't they the *most* likely to import cooperative patterns of play into one-shot laboratory games? In fact, both the experimental results and a reading of the ethnographic evidence reported in Henrich et al. seem to suggest that people from small-scale societies in which there are very limited opportunities for one-shot anonymous interactions (and who behave cooperatively at least in part because of this) have no difficulty changing their behavior to act more selfishly when they are placed in changed real-life circumstances in which more one-shot interactions and anonymity are possible—for example, when they move to much larger villages.[9]

By contrast, one would expect that subjects from developed societies have at least some experience with anonymous one-shot interactions as well as repeated games and hence should find it easier than subjects from small-scale societies to distinguish the two. If such subjects have only selfish preferences, one would think that they would be more likely play noncooperatively in one-shot games, which again is the opposite of what is observed. Instead, it appears that subjects in developed societies with market integration are more likely to have *learned* to behave cooperatively in one-shot, anonymous interactions.

Let me add, however, even if one rejects the claim that players in one-shot games automatically import behavior from repeated games, so that behavior in one-shot games tells us little or nothing about social preferences, another of Binmore's central challenges remains. This is that social preferences are highly unstable, nonrobust, and context dependent, varying both across situations, and under learning and repetition, even for the same individual. If, because of this instability, social preferences can't be used to predict much, what good are they?

6. BICCHIERI ON SOCIAL NORMS

These concerns about the instability of social preferences is one of several considerations that can be used to motivate an alternative approach, developed by

Cristina Bicchieri in a series of papers and her recent book, *The Grammar of Society* (2006). Rather than attempting to explain behavior in social games in terms of social preferences, Bicchieri instead proposes to explain it in terms of social norms and the preferences subjects have for following such norms. For reasons of space, I will not attempt to describe Bicchieri's full account of norms in any detail, but I will, instead, sketch her views in what I hope is an intuitive way.

Bicchieri's characterization of what it is for a norm to exist in a group is complex; it includes the idea that there is a sufficiently large subset of people in the group who are aware of the existence of some behavioral rule R in the group, prefer to conform to R conditional on their belief that others conform, and either believe that a sufficiently large subset expects conformity to R (normative expectations) or believe this and, in addition, may sanction behavior that is contrary to R (normative expectations with sanctions). In principle, a norm might be very general and context-independent—for example, always propose an equal division in UGs or any other two-person game involving division of a surplus. However, norms can be (and in fact very often are) sensitive to contextual factors like framing and intentions. They thus may offer a better way of explaining, or at least describing, behavior in games in which context matters. As an illustration, suppose that different social norms in our society govern the sharing of resources over which one has earned clear ownership or property rights and the sharing of resources that one acquires as a windfall or purely by chance. The norms are that one is required to share less of the resource in the former case than in the latter. This would explain why treatments that establish property rights for proposers lead to less generous offers in dictator and ultimatum games than in games in which the position of proposer is awarded randomly by the experimenter. Different contexts or frames trigger different norms in otherwise similar games.

In thinking about this idea, it will be useful to distinguish two different ways of conceptualizing norms. One approach (again associated with Binmore) is to think of a norm (or behavior conforming to a norm) as simply a Nash equilibrium in some repeated game. With this approach, the norm (or a preference for conforming to the norm) does not enter directly into a subject's utility function. Rather, subjects have certain preferences (which may be self-interested, although presumably one could tell a structurally similar story with non-self-interested preferences), and people's conformity to the norm is explained (or partly explained) by appealing to these preferences and the structure of the game. In other words, the existence of the norm (or at least its persistence) is conceived of as something that needs to be explained (an explanandum), and not as part of what does the explaining (the explanans).

Bicchieri's approach is very different—for her the norm enters into the subject's utility function. It figures in the explanation for the subject's behavior. More specifically, let us suppose that the strategy set for a group of n players involved in some game is $s = (s_1, . . s_n)$. Let S_{-j} be the set of set of strategy profiles for all the players except j. The utility for the ith individual deriving from the strategy profile s is given by an expression of the form

$$U_i(s) = \pi_i(s) - k_i \max \max\{\pi_m(s_{-j}, N_j(s_{-j})) - \pi_m(s), 0\}$$

where $._i$ is the self-interested (or at least non-norm based) payoff to i, and k_i is said to be a constant measuring the sensitivity of i to the relevant norm. The second term in the utility function is meant to capture the payoff reduction i experiences resulting from all norm violations. (I note for future reference that although k_i is described as a constant, it is plausible that at least in some cases, the same subject will be more sensitive to some norms than to others. In such cases, the value of k_i will depend on which particular norm N is of concern—that is, it will be a function of N as well as of i. It is of course an empirical question to what extent subjects who are sensitive or not to one norm will also be sensitive to others.)

According to Bicchieri's view, when a subject begins conforming to a norm, not having previously done so, the subject's preferences will be different—the subject will now have a preference for conforming to the norm. This contrasts with the first approach to norms described earlier, which postulates no such change in preferences.

Problems Facing Norm-Based Accounts

In my view, the norm-based approach is a very interesting alternative to the social preferences account that deserves further development. However, in its present form it raises some obvious issues that need to be addressed. One set of concerns is similar to the concerns raised by the social-preference approach. Is the norm-based account able to successfully predict new behavior? For example, can we estimate the crucial parameters in a norm-based utility function from behavioral data from one set of games and then use this information to predict behavior in new situations (rather than retrospectively choosing parameter values that merely rationalize or fit already observed behavior?) To what extent can we identify (independently estimate the values of) individual payoff, norm violation, and sensitivity variables on the basis of behavioral data? How stable are the values of these variables across different games and situations?

To illustrate some of these issues, consider Bicchieri's treatment of a variant of a UG involving asymmetric information. In this game, the resource (chips) that the proposer is to divide are worth three times as much to the proposer than it is to the responder, and this is known to the proposer but not to the responder. The observed behavior in this game is that the proposers offer approximately half the chips—a division that, in terms of number of chips, is a bit more generous than what responders receive in an ordinary UG but that corresponds to a monetary division that is far more unequal than the modal offer in a ordinary UG. The rejection rate for such offers is low.

What accounts for the change in proposer behavior in this new (asymmetric information) game? In her book, Bicchieri (2006) models the new game by assuming that proposers are now guided by a new norm N_2 that is different from the norm N_I that influences proposers in the original UG. Her rationale for this is that "proposer's perception of the fair amount or her interpretation of the norm may have changed due to her awareness of the informational asymmetry" (2006, 120).

In more recent correspondence, however, Bicchieri has suggested instead that one might model behavior in the asymmetric information UG as a norm evasion phenomenon—that is, to the extent the proposer is influenced by a norm, it remains the same as the norm N_I in original UG but the informational asymmetry enables the proposer to behave in a more self-interested way without fear of rejection. It is not clear how best to represent this in terms of Bicchieri's framework. One obvious possibility is to suppose that the proposer's utility function does not change at all but that the proposer simply assigns a lower probability to the responder's rejection of an offer of a given monetary value in the asymmetric information form of the game (since the responder will be unaware of the value of the chips to the proposer). The proposer then maximizes expected utility given this belief. If so, the proposer is not really more willing to evade the norm governing the game in the asymmetric information condition than in an ordinary UG. Rather the proposer has a weak attachment to the norm in both games, her behavior being dominated by self-interest. Self-interest mandates different play in the two games because of the informational differences.

An alternative (perhaps equally intuitive) possibility for modeling norm evasion is that the sensitivity parameter k_i changes when the informational asymmetry is introduced—proposers are less sensitive to whatever fairness norms govern the UG when they think that they can violate these norms in a way that will go undetected by the responder. (This of course would violate the constraint that the k_is be constant, but there may be independent reasons for relaxing this constraint—see later discussion). Yet another apparently different possibility is that the payoff to self term π_i (s) changes when the informational asymmetry is introduced—perhaps in the ordinary UG this term reflects both the monetary payoff to self and whatever disutility proposers get from seeming to be unfair to responders (angering responders, etc.) when they make low offers. In the asymmetric information condition, there is no such disutility, because responders don't know that they have been treated unfairly. Obviously, however, allowing this sort of disutility to figure in the payoff-to-self term (and to vary across different contexts) complicates the estimation of the value of this term.

What sort of empirical evidence might be used to distinguish these various possible models for proposer behavior in the asymmetric information UG? More generally, how do we tell when a change in behavior reflects a change in norm and when is it to be explained in some other way? How do we disentangle the effect of a norm on behavior from the effect of the parameter k_i which measures sensitivity to the norm? Presumably, one way to accomplish this would be to engage in some sort of quasi-anthroplogical investigation of what subjects take to be norms governing the behavior in question. For example, one possibility would simply be to ask subjects about their beliefs about what norms govern play in the asymmetric information version of the UG. An inconsistency between a subject's expressed belief about the operative norm and the subject's actual behavior in the game might then be taken to reflect a low k_i. If people generally agree that, say, the same norm governs play in both an ordinary UG and the asymmetric information UG, and that this norm mandates an equal monetary division of the stakes, then behavior in the asymmetric information game will be best explained by some model in which subjects evade this norm rather than a model in which the norm itself changes between the two games.[10]

As already noted, an appeal to norms seems very plausible in accounting for some influences on play in experimental games—for example, the role of labeling and framing effects. However, it is arguable that not all influences on behavior are plausibly explained by an appeal to norms. Consider the role of anonymity in dictator game. Subjects give less in the double-blind condition than in an ordinary DG and, in this case, the change in behavior cannot be explained in terms of a change in belief about the probability of responder rejection. Can this change in behavior be explained in terms of a change in the applicable norm—that is, is there a norm that says that one should give less in the double- blind condition? This is an empirical question, but my guess would be that, to the extent it admits of a definite answer, there is no such norm, at least in developed countries. Within Bichierri's framework, the most obvious alternative way of explaining behavior in the double-blind DG is to appeal to the idea that the anonymity condition makes whatever norm governs, both ordinary and double-blind DGs, less salient, as reflected in the value of the sensitivity parameter k_i.[11] However, if one takes this route, k_i will not be a stable feature of individual and norm, but rather will vary with the information condition present in the game (and perhaps with other contextual features as well). This may limit the ability of the norm-based approach to generate genuine predictions across games.[12]

This is not to say, however, that the norm-based approach generates no distinctive predictions in comparison with the social-preferences approach. Presumably one distinctive prediction one might associate with a norm-based theory like Bichierri's is that (at least for many plausible assumptions about the distribution of the k_is) there should be more variability of individual behavior in games in which it is not clear (for the subject pool) what the relevant norm is or in which there are competing norms than in games in which there is a single governing norm. In the latter case, one should see a very substantial fraction of behaviors that conform to this norm—a spike at the norm as well as perhaps another spike at whatever behavior corresponds to self-interested play. When there are a small number of competing norms, this should show up in a somewhat discontinuous frequency distribution of behaviors that cluster around the competing norms, with lower frequency of behavior between norms—that is, bimodal or polymodal distributions. In general, variability in behavior should decrease as more context is supplied, which plausibly can be regarded as cueing a particular norm. To the extent that behavior in a game is norm governed, one would also expect to be able to relate this behavior to norm-governed behavior in real life, as in the case of the relationship between Orma play in public-goods games and the harambee institution.

On the other hand, to the extent that even rather similar-looking games are governed by different norms, there will be no obvious general reason, according to the norm-based approach, to expect individuals to play in a similar way across such games—that is, to exhibit some recognizable consistency of type across games. For example, if the norms governing play in a UG are different from those governing play in a DG, then unless there is some independent reason to think that both norms require generous behavior on the part of proposers (and proposers who are sensitive to one norm are likely to be sensitive to the other), there will no general reason to expect proposers who make generous offers in one of these games to do so in the other. A similar conclusion will follow if there is no obviously relevant norm in the DG.

As concrete illustrations of some of these points, it is arguable that in societies like the contemporary United States, the norm or norms that apply to DGs are weaker or less obvious than those that apply to UGs—indeed, some would say that unless further context is provided there are no clear norms for proposer behavior in a DG. If this is correct, then with a norm-based approach, one should expect (*ceteris paribus*, of course) more variability in proposer behavior in a DG, than in, for example, a UG. On the assumption that one of the norms that influences behavior in a UG mandates an equal split, one should see a number of proposer offers at this value. On the other hand, on a norm-based approach, there is no particular reason to expect offers of, for example, 0.45 of the stake, since presumably there is no norm that suggests this division. If such a division is observed, this will be because the proposer just happens to weigh payoff to self and the utility of norm violation in such a way as to generate this result. In fact, one does observe an increased frequency of offers around 0.5 in UGs in developed societies (although there are intermediate offers as well) and more variance in DGs than in UGs. Similarly, on the assumption that a UG corresponds to something like a take-it-or-leave-it offer in real life, one might expect that there will be clearer norms governing such offers in societies that have substantial experience in bargaining, trade, and market exchange than in societies lacking such experience. If so, and such norms influence behavior in UGs, one would expect less variance in proposer offers in the former societies than in the latter. A number of the papers in Henrich et al. report just this pattern.[13]

By contrast, a pure social-preference approach (according to which social preferences alone are sufficient to explain behavior) will have something like the opposite profile. As noted earlier, there is no particular reason to expect everyone to have the same social preferences—indeed advocates of the social-preference approach typically deny that there is such uniformity. So even within a single game where there is an opportunity to express social preferences, there should be considerable variation in subject behavior. Although advocates of the social-preference approach have had relatively little in general to say about what distribution of types of preferences we should expect (presumably because they regard this as an empirical matter), there is no obvious theoretical reason (at least absent additional assumptions) why this distribution should be discontinuous or clumpy rather than relatively continuous. Thus, there is no obvious reason why, in a UG, many more subjects should have degrees of inequality aversion that lead them to offer 0.5 rather than 0.45 of the stake. On the other hand, there should be some nontrivial consistency of type at the individual level across games—so that one can use behavior in ultimatum games to predict behavior in other games, as Fehr and Schmidt attempt to do.

7. Conclusions Regarding Social Preferences, Norms, and Self-Interest

What can we conclude from this survey of experimental results and attempts to explain them? Clearly, there is a body of very interesting and suggestive behavioral results from games like UG, DG, and such. These results exhibit considerable qualitative stability in the aggregate (e.g., in mean subject behavior) when experiments are repeated under the same or very closely similar conditions (same subject pool, etc.). However, behavior is also influenced by a large number of disparate factors—subject pool/culture, information/anonymity conditions, perceived intentions, faming and labeling effects, and so on. There is also a great deal of individual variation in behavior. My assessment is that the evidence that many subjects exhibit behavior that is not narrowly self-interested (they care about other things than their own monetary payoffs) and that this can sometimes exert a major influence on aggregate outcomes seems fairly compelling, but that attempts to offer systematic, non-adhoc explanations of this non-self-interested aspect of behavior have so far been not been very successful. Unsurprisingly, it is easier to provide evidence against the hypothesis that we are purely self-interested than to construct a convincing account of why and when deviations from self-interest occur.

One (messy) possibility is that behavior in the games discussed in this survey, and in real life as well, reflects the combined influence of *all* the various factors (norm adherence, social preferences, self-interest, etc.) considered earlier, with these factors varying in influence both across different contexts and for different subjects. That is, subject behavior is the upshot of social preferences of various sorts (inequality aversion; positive and negative reciprocity; perhaps, more rarely, pure altruism) that differ substantially among people but perhaps exhibit some stability across contexts for individuals *and* of influences that reflect norms drawn from experience with repeated play in the larger society that are more context specific. Moreover, subjects also differ in the weight that they give to self-interested preferences in comparison with social preferences and preferences for norm adherence.

At least some of the apparent context dependence and instability of social behavior and the social preferences (or whatever) that underlies it may reflect the fact that these are the upshots of a number of such disparate influences. Of course, this does not rule out the possibility that, at some time in the future, investigators will be able to decompose the influences on such behavior into a small number of well-behaved underlying causes (with such and such a contribution from self-interest, such and such a contribution from inequality aversion, and so on). However, it is also true that nothing assures us that we will be successful in doing this. It may be that it is simply wrong to think that individuals possess stable, context-independent characteristics like "degree of inequality aversion," which then combine with other similarly stable characteristics—for positive and negative reciprocity, self-interest, and so forth—to produce overall behavior. However, even if this turns out to be the case, there still will be much to learn from experimental games: Researchers can continue to investigate qualitative facts about robustness (or not) of behavioral patterns under changes in information, repetition, and so on, to investigate facts about the extent of individual variation and so on. This information will be highly relevant to economics and to moral and political philosophy.

Section 8. Implications for Moral and Political Philosophy

I suggested earlier that results from experimental games may have important consequences for normative moral/political philosophy. This is obviously a very large topic, and I have space only for some brief remarks. I begin with one initial source of resistance to any claims along these lines, which is that they must run afoul of some version of the naturalistic fallacy, namely, that experimental studies can at best *describe* how people behave in various situations. They cannot tell us how people *ought* to behave.

Moral Motivation

There are a number of possible responses to objection. First, many historically important normative moral and political theories (e.g., those of Hobbes, Locke, Hume, Marx, Bentham, Mill) do appeal to more or less explicit descriptive assumptions about human behavior and motivation. They do so for the obvious reason that most theorists have supposed that normative recommendations that require behavior and motivation that most people rarely or never exhibit are unlikely to be very effective or useful. More generally, the range of motives and behavior that people actually exhibit or can be made to exhibit in practically achievable circumstances is an important constraint on normative theorizing. For example, Hobbes and contemporary Hobbesians like Kavka (1986) suppose that humans are at least predominantly self-interested and use this supposition to restrict the space of useful normative theories in various ways. If, as the evidence reviewed earlier suggests, this supposition is wrong and, non-self-interested behavior is possible for significant numbers of people in some contexts, this opens up a different set of possibilities for normative theorizing. Similarly, one of the reasons that Rawls (1971) rejects utilitarianism as an acceptable normative theory (or a theory that would be chosen in his original position) appeals to what he calls "the strains of commitment." Rawls's argument is that utilitarianism permits highly unequal distributions, and that people who are among the sharply disadvantaged under such distributions will find it impossible to adhere to or be guided by utilitarian principles. Obviously this is an empirical claim about human behavior and motivation, as is Rawls's contention that people will find it easier to conform to the requirements of his own theory than to utilitarianism.

As another illustration, consider that many of the normative theories found in the philosophical literature suppose that, to the extent that there are principles mandating concern for the welfare of others and accompanying preferences or motivations, these will be (at least at the most fundamental level) unconditional and purely outcome oriented. That is, it is supposed that these principles will not assign any fundamental moral significance to whether the others to whom goods and bads are provided are behaving cooperatively on noncooperatively toward others or the decision maker, will not assign any fundamental moral significance to whether these others are participating in a shared system of reciprocation with the decision maker, and so on. The results discussed earlier suggest, on the contrary, that, to the extent that people are not self-interested, their most strongly operative motives have to do with conditional cooperation and positive and negative reciprocity, rather than unconditional altruism. If so, normative theories should be sensitive to these facts about motivation.

Reflective Equilibrium

A second way in which descriptive information about human behavior can be relevant to normative theorizing invokes the common idea that the appropriate moral methodology is one that involves appeal to reflective equilibrium or that attempts to articulate some set of moral commitments that we all share. To the extent that this is the appropriate way of proceeding in moral theory, empirical information about people's actual moral judgments and commitments is again highly relevant, and presumably these are expressed both verbally and in nonverbal behavior.

With this as background, consider some common claims in the normative literature. Many theories of justice and fairness are naturally viewed as committed to the claim that there is some shared conception of justice that can be captured in terms of a few highly general principles that underlie all our more particular judgments—whether these principles be those of utilitarianism, Rawls's theory, or whatever. The task of the normative theorist is then to articulate these principles. Although I don't claim that empirical results about the apparent context dependence and individual variability of social preferences straightforwardly refute this claim, they do put some pressure on it. If it turns out that, as an empirical matter, there is no simple, context-independent common structure to most people's social preferences, why suppose that they share some common set of normative commitments, captureable by means of a few general principles, which the moral theorist can articulate? If, as an empirical matter, what is shared is instead more naturally conceptualized as a complex set of situation-specific norms, as Bicchieri claims, this seems to provide prima facie support for the views of normative theorists like Walzer (1983) and Elster (1991) according to which the rules of justice are far more local and domain specific. If behavior and preferences are even more context-dependent in such a way that even the norm-based approach is of limited usefulness, this may provide prima-facie support for some version of "moral particularism" in the sense of Dancy (2004).

Consequentialism and Deontology

I conclude with a remark about the debate in moral theory between consequentialists and deontologists. The behavioral evidence reviewed here shows that, just as deontologists claim they should, people care about more than just outcomes, whether for themselves or others; they also care about the intentions with which actions are performed, about motives and about the processes by which outcomes produced. These concerns in turn can exert powerful influences on behavior. To the extent that the task of moral theory is to articulate underlying shared normative commitments, it seems likely that these will have at least some of the features emphasized by deontologists. Moreover, even consequentialists, who reject this conception of the task of moral theorizing, should nonetheless pay attention to these deontological features in their normative recommendations. This is because these features will influence people's behavior and hence the real-life consequences that will result from the consequentialist's normative recommendations. It may be, from a consequentialist perspective, irrational for people to get more disutility from and react more hostilely to bad outcomes that are the result of intentional choices than those that result in some other way, but, given that people *will* react in this way, sophisticated consequentialists will need to take this into account in their calculations.

NOTES

1. Thanks to Ken Bimmore, Francesco Guala, Dan Hausman, and Jiji Zhang for helpful comments and conversations.

2. For example, if subject play is primarily to be explained in terms of adherence to social norms (see later), then it seems entirely possible that subjects may see the dictator game as governed by some norm of sharing or altruism, as when one gives money to a charity or homeless person, while the ultimatum game may be seen as governed by bargaining norms, as when one bargains over a used car, with the convention being that is entirely appropriate to drive the hardest bargain possible, with generosity or altruism playing no role. To the extent this is the right analysis, it would be wrong to simply assume that the DG measures a preference that is also present in the UG.

As Camerer, 2003 notes, one way of getting at this issue empirically is to compare offers in UGs with the offers that would maximize expected utility given the actual pattern of rejection in these games. If these are the same, this suggests that proposers are behaving in a purely strategic self-interested way (and perhaps also in accord with some norm that says this is permissible in a bargaining situation). In fact, the most recent evidence is that offers are larger than the payoff maximizing offers, given plausible assumptions about risk aversion. This suggests that proposers are not behaving in a purely self-interested way, and that they exhibit some generosity and/or are influenced by some sharing norm. The general point, however, is that we need some reason to think that this is true before taking a comparison of proposer behavior in UGs and DGs to be a measure of the influence of proposer generosity in DGs.

3. One response to the imaging experiments I have heard from some economists is that even if the foregoing interpretation is accepted at face value, the subjects are still behaving selfishly—it is just that they are acting for the pleasure or "warm glow" they get from cooperation. Of course this argument recapitulates familiar philosophical disputes about psychological egoism: If we stipulate that, whenever subjects' reward systems are activated, they are acting selfishly, then since arguably all intentional or purposeful action involves such activation, all such actions will be selfish. One may doubt, however, whether this is a very useful stipulation, because, given the empirical facts about the ubiquity of the reward system, it effectively defines unselfishness out of existence.

4. Additional evidence for this interpretation comes from experiments conducted by Falk, Fehr, and Fishbacher, 2003. The authors had subjects simultaneously enter choices for each of four mini-ultimatum games (MUGs). In each game, one of the choices for the proposer is (8,2), but the other option varies from (10,0), (8,2), (5,5), (2,8). Unsurprisingly, Falk et al. (2003) observe that responders' behavior is strongly influenced by the alternatives available to the proposers. For example, rejections are much more common when the proposer chooses (8,2) when the alternative is (5,5) than when the alternatives are (10,0) or (2,8). This is exactly what one would expect if second movers detect and respond to first movers' intentions, since intentions depend on alternatives that are not chosen as well as those that are chosen, with choice of (8,2) over (10,0) revealing a kinder intention than the choice of (8,2) over (5,5). By contrast, if responders care only about outcomes, they should reject the choice of an (8,2) split at a constant rate across these games.

5. Two additional observations are relevant here. First, it is entirely possible that the degree of consistency of type itself varies across individuals. That is, it may be that some individuals exhibit considerable consistency of type or behavior across different situations and others do not. Second, other sorts of measures besides behavior in games may be useful (as part of a triangulation strategy) in detecting whether there are consistent types. For example, Smith et al. (2002) administered a personality test designed to measure degree of "Machiavellian Intelligence"—that is, the extent to which subjects were willing to flout cooperative norms (to lie, cheat, etc.) in order to secure self-interested ends—and then had subjects play repeated trust games. There was little correlation between play in these games and test scores except for subjects with very high scores. These "high Machs" were much more likely to behave in an uncooperative way in trust games. It would be interesting to see if these same subjects were also more likely to contribute little or nothing in public-goods games, defect in PDs, etc. As another illustration, consider recent imaging experiments by Singer et al. (2004) on the neural basis of empathy. These researchers found that subjects who had high scores on standard empathy test questionnaires also had activation in neural areas (insula, anterior cingulate) thought to be involved in empathy in empathy-related tasks. This at least suggests the possibility that there may be types of people who are more or less empathetic. It would be interesting to see whether scores on empathy questionnaires and physiological measures correlate with play in for example,various versions of the DG.

6. Experimenters go to considerable lengths to make sure that subjects understand (at a conscious level) the rules of the game that they are playing, including whether it is one-shot or repeated. I take it that what is being suggested is that despite their intellectual recognition that the game is one-shot, subjects may nonetheless import (as a result of unconscious processing or implicit learning) patterns of play from repeated games with which they have experience.

7. This general strategy of appealing to the possibility of cooperative strategies emerging in repeated games with entirely selfish players to explain observed cooperation raises a number of interesting issues that are beyond the scope of this essay. Very briefly: (i) games like repeated PDs have many Nash equilibria, a large number of which involve noncooperative play. Whether subjects converge on a cooperative or a noncooperative equilibrium depends on many additional factors, including, perhaps, accidents of history as well as more systematic influences. (ii) In a repeated PD as well as a number of other games considered in this chapter, interaction is bilateral and information about payoffs and past behavior is fully known. One might think that many real-life situations in which cooperative behavior is present are not like this; many players rather than just two are involved, and subjects have very incomplete information. For a variety of reasons, it appears to be much more difficult for purely selfish players to sustain cooperation in such situations (cf. Gintis, 2006). To the extent this is so, results about repeated games involving selfish players may not provide satisfactory explanations of either cooperative behavior observed in one-shot games or more generally in nonlaboratory contexts.

8. This point seems independent of the issue of why contributions decline in public-goods games under repetition. It may be, as some claim, that subjects are mainly self-interested but require some experience to learn that contributing nothing is an optimal strategy. Alternatively, many subjects may be conditional cooperators who eventually decide to contribute nothing after repeated experience with non-cooperative play by other selfish players. Either way, it remains true that contributions decline with repeated play.

9. See, for example, Marlowe 2004.

10. It is worth noting, however, that empirically determining which norm (or norms) are operative in any particular context may be far from straightforward, given the complexity of Bicchieri's characterization of norms. Recall that, among other things, the existence of a norm requires a sufficiently large subset of subjects with beliefs about how others will behave, preferences about conformity to the norm conditional on the behavior of others, beliefs about other's expectations regarding conformity to the norm, and so on. Thus, the norms that subjects think govern play in a UG or a DG will depend, among other things, on their beliefs about how others are likely to play the game, what others expect of them given facts about how others will play, and so on. As a result, it isn't clear that one can get at the question of which norms govern a game simply by asking subjects what sort of behavior is fair in the game, since subjects may well interpret this question as, for example, a question about how they should play in circumstances in which most others are behaving fairly, but also believe most others will not behave fairly. In this case, subjects presumably believe there is no norm in Bicchieri's sense.

As a concrete illustration of this difficulty, suppose that many subjects say that an equal monetary split is fair in the asymmetric information version of the UG but that a substantial number of subjects also believe that a substantial number of subjects will offer much less than half the monetary value of the stakes in this game, believe that others believe or expect that this will happen, and so on. What then is the norm governing the game?

11. Another alternative would be to regard the payoff-to-self term as varying across the two versions of the DG—perhaps on the grounds that the dictator gets disutility from having his or her stinginess known to the experimenter in the usual version of the DG but not in the double-blind game. As noted earlier, this move complicates the problem of determining the value of the payoff-to-self term and raises the question of how we can distinguish a change in the value of this term from a shift in k_i.

12. Camerer and Fehr (2004, 78) raise another issue for appeals to norms to explain behavior. This is that subjects change their behavior (and their willingness to conform to norms) in response to changes in payoffs. To the extent that such changes involve changes in payoffs to self, Bicchieri's account appears to be able to capture this phenomenon, since according to her view, subject's behavior is influenced by personal payoffs as well as preferences for conforming to norms. However, it is arguable that a more problematic set of cases for an account like Bicchieri's involves trade-offs among different sorts of other-regarding preferences. Consider a DG where the dictator D can contribute some portion of her stake to each of two subjects, A and B, where D knows no identifying information about either subject. To the extent that there is a norm governing this allocation, it presumably mandates that A and B receive the same amount (x,x), whatever that may be. Suppose that D reserves d for herself. Now consider cases in which D is still able to allocate d for herself but faces choices of the form $(x-k_1, x+k_2)$ for the allocations to A and B, where $k_2 > k_1 > 0$. Presumably for some values of k_1 and k_2 many dictators will prefer an unequal split and this will become more likely as $k_2 - k_1$ becomes larger. For example, a dictator might prefer (5,5) to (6,4) but (15, 4) to (5,5) even though the latter violates the norm of equality. Presumably, different dictators will favor different rates of trade-off between equality vs. maximizing the sum of A's and B's payoff. It seems unlikely that this trade-off rate will itself follow any generally accepted norm; instead if it reflects anything systematic, it will reflect the relative strength of D's social preferences for equality and for maximizing the total pay-off. The general point is that some social choices will reflect trade-offs among different social values, where the trade-off rate is not itself prescribed by some norm.

13. Also relevant in this connection are results reported in Guth (1995) He finds that in a MUG, proposers choose highly unequal splits much more often when an even split is replaced with a slightly uneven one. For example, given a choice between (17, 3) and (10,10), proposers choose (10,10) half the time. When the (10,10) option is replaced with (9,11), responders choose (17, 3) two-thirds of the time. A natural interpretation of this result is that proposers are influenced by an equal split norm when conformity to it is possible, but that there is no obvious norm that tells them they should prefer (9,10) to (17,3). In a social-preference approach, there must be an (unexplained) sharp discontinuity between proposer's attitudes toward (10,10) and (9,11).

REFERENCES

Bicchieri, C. (2006). *The Grammar of Society: the Nature and Dynamics of Social Norms*, Cambridge, England: Cambridge University Press.

Binmore, K. (2007). *Does Game Theory Work? The Bargaining Challenge*. Cambridge, MA: MIT Press.

Binmore, K. (2005). "Economic Man-or Straw Man." *Behavioral and Brain Sciences* 28: 23–24.

Bolton, G. & Ockenfels, A. (2000). "ERC—A Theory of Equity, Reciprocity, and Competition." *American Economic Review* 90: 166–193.

Camerer, C. (2003). *Behavioral Game Theory: Experiments in Strategic Interaction.* Princeton, NJ: Princeton University Press.

Camerer, C. & Fehr, E. (2004). "Measuring Social Norms and Preferences Using Experimental Games: A Guide for Social Scientists." In J. Henrich et al., Eds., *Foundations of Human Sociality: Economic Experiments and Ethnographic Evidence from Fifteen Small-Scale Societies,* 55–95. Oxford: Oxford University Press.

Dancy, J. (2004). *Ethics without Principles.* Oxford: Clarendon Press.

Dawes, R., Caporael, L. & van de Kragt, A. (1989). "Selfishness Examined: Cooperation in the Absence of Egoistic Incentives." *Behavioral and Brain Science* 12: 683–699.

Elster, J. (1991). *Local Justice: How Institutions Allocate Scarce Goods.* New York: Russell Sage.

Ensminger, J. (2004). "Market Integration and Fairness: Evidence from Ultimatum, Dictator, and Public Goods Experiments in East Africa." In Henrich et al., Eds., *Foundations of Human Sociality: Economic Experiments and Ethnographic Evidence from Fifteen Small-Scale Societies.* Oxford: Oxford University Press.

Falk, A. & Fischbacher, U. (2006). "A Theory of Reciprocity." *Games and Economic Behavior* 54 (2): 293–315.

Falk, A., Fehr, E. & Fischbacher, U. (2003). "On the Nature of Fair Behavior." *Economic Inquiry* 41(1): 20–26.

Fehr, E. & Fischbacher, U. (2003). "The Nature of Human Altruism." *Nature* 425: 785–791.

Fehr, E & Schmidt, K. (1999). "A Theory of Fairness, Competition, and Cooperation." *Quarterly Journal of Economics* 114: 817–868.

Gintis, H. (2006),."Behavioral Ethics Meets Natural Justice." *Politics, Philosophy and Economics* 5: 5–32.

Guth, W. (1995). "On Ultimatum Bargaining Experiments—A Personal Review." *Journal of Economic Behavior and Organization* 27: 329–344.

Henrich, J., Boyd, R., Bowles, S., Camerer, C., Fehr, E. & Gintis, H. (Eds.). (2004). *Foundations of Human Sociality: Economic Experiments and Ethnographic Evidence from Fifteen Small-Scale Societies.* Oxford: Oxford University Press.

Hoffman, E., McCabe, K., Shachat, K. & Smith, V. (1994). "Preferences, Property Rights and Anonymity in Bargaining Games." *Games and Economic Behavior* 7: 346–380.

Hsu, M., Bhatt, M., Adolphs, R., Tranel, D. & Camerer, C. (2005). "Neural Systems Responding to Degrees of Uncertainty in Human Decision-Making." *Science* 310: 1680—1683.

Kavka, G. (1986). *Hobbesian Moral and Political Theory.* Princeton: Princeton University Press.

Marlowe, F. (2004). "Dictators and Ultimatums in an Egalitarian Society of Hunter-Gatherers: The Hadza of Tanzania." In Henrich et al., Eds., *Foundations of Human Sociality: Economic Experiments and Ethnographic Evidence from Fifteen Small-Scale Societies.* Oxford: Oxford University Press.

Rabin, M. (1993). " Incorporating Fairness Into Game Theory and Economics." *American Economic Review* 83: 1281–1302.

Rabin, M. & Charness, G. (2002). "Understanding Social Preferences with Simple Tests." *Quarterly Journal of Economics* 117(3): 817–869.

Rawls, J. (1971). *A Theory of Justice.* Cambridge: Harvard University Press.

Rilling, A., Sanfey, A., Aronson, J., Nystrom, L. & Cohen, J. (2004). "Opposing BOLD Responses to Reciprocated and Unreciprocated Altruism in Putative Reward Pathways." *NeuroReport* 15 (16): 2539–2543.

Rilling, J., Gutman, D., Zeh, T., Pagnoni, G., Berns, G. & Kilts, C. (2002). "A Neural Basis for Social Cooperation." *Neuron* 35: 395–405.

Samuelson, L. (2005). "Foundations of Human Sociality: A Review Essay." *Journal of Economic Literature* 43: 488–497.

Sanfey, A., Rilling, J., Aronson, J., Nystrom, L. & Cohen, J. (2003) "The Neural Basis of Economic Decision-making in the Ultimatum Game." *Science* 300: 1755–1758.

Shaked, A. (2007) "On the Explanatory Value of Inequity Aversion Theory." http://www.wiwi.uni-bonn.de/shaked/rhetoric/. Accessed September 25, 2007.

Singer, T., Kiebel, S., Joel S., Dolan, J. & Frith, C. (2004). "Brain Responses to the Acquired Moral Status of Faces." *Neuron* 41: 653–662.

Smith, V., Gunnthorsdottir, A. & McCabe, K. (2002) "Using the Machiavellianism Instrument to Predict Trustworthiness in a Bargaining Game." *Journal of Psychology and Economics* 23: 49–66.

Walzer, M. (1983). *Spheres of Justice*. New York: Basic Books.

CHAPTER 8

COMPETING CONCEPTIONS OF THE INDIVIDUAL IN RECENT ECONOMICS

JOHN B. DAVIS

1. INTRODUCTION

In the last two decades, the economics research frontier has been significantly transformed by the emergence of a collection of new approaches that criticize traditional neoclassical assumptions, and whose origins lie largely in other sciences.[1] If changes in the research frontier herald future changes in economics (Davis 2006b), that the new methods and concepts being adopted in economics come from other sciences strongly suggests that economics will be substantially different in the future. This invites us to inventory the traditional neoclassical assumptions that have been the target of these recent critiques, and ask what alternative assumptions are being proposed as their replacements. Here I focus on one of the most fundamental commitments of neoclassicism under question, the conception of the individual human being as an economic agent. The traditional assumption under challenge is that of the human individual as an atomistic being, *Homo economicus*. But rather than there being one single alternative conception of the individual on the agenda in the new work on the research frontier, there are a variety of different conceptions and elements of conceptions of individuals under investigation as befits the different origins of the new ideas in economics in different sciences. The task before us, then, is to distinguish these different conceptions and evaluate their prospects within economics.

Why is the conception of the individual in economics a matter of central importance? First, since the conception of what an individual is underlies the conception of an economic agent, failure to adequately articulate the former leads to ambiguity regarding what agents are as well as regarding how cause-and-effect processes operate in economic life. Second, the conception of the individual economic agent constitutes an ontological anchor for economic analysis, such that failure to develop an adequate conception of the individual jeopardizes the realism of economic analysis. Third, on the assumption that economics is about human individuals, having an adequate conception of the individual is important for the human relevance of economics.

One way to begin is to identify the principal weaknesses of the *Homo economicus* conception. Despite its long-standing appeal, systematic examination of the conception, as I have pursued using personal identity analysis (Davis 2003b), shows that the conception neither allows us to individuate human beings in the sense of showing them to be distinct agents, nor allows us to re-identify them across change in the sense of showing them to be enduring agents. The first criterion is synchronic, or oriented toward phenomena considered within limited time frames, and the second is diachronic, or oriented toward phenomena considered over periods of time. Note, then, the following three points: First, that the neoclassical *Homo economicus* conception satisfies neither criterion means that any alternative conception of the individual can at least improve upon it by satisfying one of the two criteria without yet being entirely satisfactory in addressing them both. Second, that the conception of the individual is generally not the primary focus in the new research programs in economics means that there is often limited sensitivity to the need to address both synchronic and diachronic dimensions. Third (and most importantly for what follows), that the new research programs can generally be differentiated according to whether they emphasize synchronic or diachronic concerns means that they are more disposed to and more likely successful in making better cases for conceptions of the individual satisfying the criterion that coheres best with their general orientation.

These points suggest that we should not expect full-blown, comprehensive conceptions of the individual to be associated with the new research approaches in economics, but should rather expect to find a set of arguably incomplete conceptions arranged along a spectrum of synchronic or diachronic concerns. At the same time, it seems only realistic to suppose that any reconciliation or integration of potentially quite different strategies for conceptualizing individuals in the new programs on the research frontier will depend on many other fundamental concerns regarding the redirection of economics other than how one understands the nature of individuality. Here, then, my object is to explore the different research programs' possible "resistances and accommodations" to one another on the subject of how one conceptualizes individuals (Pickering 1995) in the context of their respective strategies for bringing about change in the nature of economics. These "resistances and accommodations," moreover, need to be seen from the perspective of the outside-inside dynamic of change on the research frontier that is driving a process of change *in* economics generated by science concerns arising *outside* economics.

I take the leading postneoclassical research approaches to be classical game theory, evolutionary game theory, behavioral game theory, evolutionary economics, behavioral economics, experimental economics, neuroeconomics, and agent-based computational or complexity economics. They can be shown to collectively share the idea that human individuals are not isolated, atomistic beings, but they also differ significantly in how they understand this critique, according, I will argue, to whether they emphasize synchronic or diachronic frames of explanation. Indeed, I will argue that those that adopt the former frame lend themselves more to a microeconomic sort of view, whereas those that adopt the latter frame lend themselves more to a macroeconomic sort of view. Thus, what mutual accommodation and integration might transpire between these different approaches is very much a matter of how these broadly different frames of thinking are re-organized in economics as a result of the importation of new science contents from outside economics.

The idea that human individuals are not isolated, atomistic beings can be explained by saying they are socially embedded (Davis 2003b). This concept has many interpretations, but a basic Cartesian understanding provides an initial intuition. Descartes is famous for his *cogito, ergo sum* proposition. The equivalent proposition for the embedded individual conception is *cogitamus, ergo sum*. That is, when individuals act in social contexts, for example, by expressing themselves in first person plural terms, and thereby (normally) bind themselves to the content of their shared assertion, they individuate themselves relative to those to whom the assertion applies. Generally, that is, individuality arises out of relations to others rather than isolation from others. Thus, at issue in the new approaches in economics is how individuality arises out of social interaction, or how individual behavior depends upon aggregate behavior.

To organize the discussion that follows in the next three sections, I characterize the *Homo economicus* conception in terms of three linked properties that are central to it as an atomist conception. On the standard view, individuals: (1) have exogenous preferences, (2) interact only (or almost only) in an indirect manner with one another through the price mechanism, and (3) are unaffected in these two respects by the aggregate effects of their interaction with one another. As we will see, the new research programs differ in how objectionable they find each of these properties, as befits their different commitments to synchronic or diachronic forms of explanation. Thus, another way to see the issue of mutual accommodation and possible adjustment of these new programs to one another with respect to their respective conceptualization of the individual is in terms of the relative significance these three properties have in the different programs according to their respective emphases on synchronic and diachronic concerns.

The discussion that follows these three sections then reviews the role of synchronic and diachronic types of explanations in the possible emergence of a new general research program, discusses embedded individual microfoundations for that general program, and closes with speculations regarding the role of thinking about individuals in a future synthesis of the new research programs.

2. Exogeneity Under Attack

The exogeneity assumption underpins neoclassicism's account of how individuals are distinct agents in terms of the idea of each necessarily having only his or her own preferences. Aside from the problematic and circular character of the idea of one's own preferences,[2] there are two related ways in which the exogeneity assumption has been challenged in the recent new approaches: (1) nonsubjective factors are shown to influence individual preferences via framing effects, and (2) preferences are seen to reflect the kind of environment the individual or agent occupies. In both cases, preferences cease to be strictly the agent's own preferences, effectively becoming socially embedded rather than atomistic. However, the way in which this occurs differs according to whether the approach is more synchronic (or microeconomic) or more diachronic (or macroeconomic), and this has implications for the kind of embedded individual conception developed. I discuss the first case in connection with the rise of behavioral economics and behavioral game theory and the second case in connection with the rise of one version of computational economics, namely, agent-based computational economics.

Behavioral Economics and Behavioral Game Theory

There have long been doubts in and out of economics about the realism of the exogeneity assumption, but since Maurice Allais's (1953) discovery of common consequence and common ratio effects at odds with expected utility theory's independence axiom, and subsequent experimental evidence of preference reversals in the choice of lotteries showing how orderings depend on preference elicitation procedures (Lichtenstein & Slovic 1971), doubts about exogeneity have been focused on the independence axiom. The independence axiom states that, given the choice between two things, an individual's preference for one over the other is unaffected by the introduction or presence of a third thing. Behavioral economics, particularly as it has emerged from the work of Daniel Kahneman and Amos Tversky, has made abandonment of the independence axiom central to a new view of the individual that adds a procedural element to choice behavior in supposing that individuals rely on a variety of decision heuristics or rules sensitive to context to frame their choices. Thus, in Kahneman and Tversky's prospect theory

(1979), choice is a two-phase process with prospects "edited" in the first phase using different decision heuristics, such that choices are then made in the second phase from a restricted or reformulated class of prospects. This two-phase analysis makes it possible to look at gains and losses relative to reference points, and ultimately introduces well-observed phenomena at odds with standard framework predictions, such as *status quo* bias and loss aversion (Tversky & Kahneman 1992). More generally, prospect theory opens the door to the investigation of a variety of descriptive and procedure invariance failures that cast doubt on the traditional idea that individuals possess stable and coherent preferences.

Thus, with this view, preferences are malleable and dependent on the context in which they are elicited (Camerer & Loewenstein 2003), and choice involves processes whereby individuals effectively construct their preferences (Payne, Bettman & Johnson 1992; Slovic 1995). Defenders of the traditional exogeneity assumption, in contrast, have argued for a "discovered preference hypothesis," as coined by Charles Plott (1996; also cf. Smith 1989; Harrison 1994; Binmore 1999), which assumes that individuals have coherent and stable preferences, and though those preferences are not necessarily immediately revealed in their decisions, they can be discovered to underlie their apparent preferences, should individuals engage in information gathering, deliberation, and trial-and-error learning. But the case for "discovered preferences" is by no means a simple one, and in any event has not been persuasive to many who favor a more empirically based behavioral approach to economics (Cubitt, Starmer & Sugden 2001).

One particularly clear application of these conclusions lies in behavioral game theory research. In a widely replicated experiment, laboratory subjects engage in a form of interaction called the ultimatum game, and experimenters test the hypothesis that individuals might act out of a motivation contrary to their self-interest, namely, a sense of reciprocity or a desire to respond in kind to the actions of others, whether for good or bad, depending on the context or institutional framing of their interaction. The self-interest postulate is reflective of the exogeneity assumption, because many neoclassical economists take it to be tautologically true on the belief that individuals necessarily act on their own preferences. Experimental researchers have found, however, that laboratory subjects behave consistently or inconsistently with the self-interest hypothesis according to context and institutional framing (Fehr & Gächter 2000; cf. Samuelson 2005). This result has been experimentally generalized to a variety of other types of games, such as the public-goods game, and has subsequently given rise to a new area of investigation called social-utility/social-preferences research (Camerer & Fehr 2004).

The general conclusion of behavioral research on these subjects is that non-subjective factors influence individuals' preferences via various types of framing effects. But while framing reflects the way the world is presented to an individual, so that the behavioral conception of the individual is an embedded rather than an atomistic one (and presumably, therefore, one of the individual as socially embedded), the behavioral treatment of *social* is so flat and parsimonious that it includes practically nothing more than the idea that individuals are (or must be) influenced by other individuals. For contrast, and to anticipate what follows, we might note that any conception of individuals that takes them through some sort of developmental or evolutionary process requires a stronger conception of *social*, because it makes the understanding of the individual depend on changing interaction with others, which expands the idea of *social* to include social structure. But although some behavioral experiments involve repeated play, the experimental set-up lacks the degree of structural detail in the agent-based approach to computational economics.

Agent-based Computational Economics and Complexity Accounts

To understand the nature of social embedding in agent-based approaches to computational economics (agent-based computational economics or ACE), we need to first distinguish an earlier version of computational thinking in economics that has grown out of neoclassical economics, which, in a quite opposite manner, disembeds cognition from individuals. This more traditional form of computational economics derives from postwar artificial intelligence (AI) theory, now known as classical AI. Classical AI, in contrast to later connectionist and neural network AI theory, treats cognition as any (serial) symbol-processing activity understandable in computational terms. Drawing on the computation concept of a Turing machine,[3] Noam Chomsky's generative grammar idea,[4] and the view that the brain itself is merely a computing device,[5] classical AI is functionalist in supposing that cognition may be equated with any and all computations made possible by a given set of functional operations. As functional operations are by nature immaterial, they can, accordingly, be realized or instantiated in a variety of different physical forms. This "multiple realizability thesis" implies that cognition need not be exclusively associated with human beings (or any other particular kind of entity), and thus provided a basis for early AI theory, at least in the weak AI version that seeks to locate cognition in nonhuman physical forms, without supposing they replicate human intelligence.

This early view is adopted in postwar formalist neoclassicism, which, although not explicitly termed a computational economics nonetheless was functionalist in character, gave rise to computational general equilibrium theorizing.[6] Thus the optimization algorithms generated in the development of the Arrow-Debreu-McKenzie axiomatic general equilibrium rational choice models (and later rational expectations models), though originally thought to reflect human reasoning, came to be seen as purely functional in nature, leading to their "disembedding" from human individuals, and instantiation in any number of other types of agents.[7] In this economics version of the multiple-realizability thesis, then, preferences have no special relation to human beings, and accordingly are neither no longer subjective phenomena, nor serviceable for uniquely distinguishing human individuals, since any imaginable agent—human or nonhuman, individual or group, subpersonal agent or whole agent—could be said to have preferences as defined by that agent's objective function.

For a number of reasons, however, doubts developed about classical AI's functionalist commitment. Particularly influential was John Searle's (1980) Chinese room argument, which concluded that symbol manipulation lacked meaning without a concept of understanding, or that syntax does not suffice for semantics.[8] Semantics concerns the nature of meaning, and since meaning is always intentional, it presupposes a vantage point from which things take on an "aspectual shape" (Searle 1992, 157). But this meant for Searle that the functionalist disembedding of the mind from the brain is incoherent, because it identified cognition with immaterial operations.

Much of later AI has followed this lead, and assumed that some system of symbol grounding is needed to explain cognition, and that symbol systems are "grounded-up" in nonsymbolic systems (Harnad 1987, 1990). The sort of view this involves—generally termed connectionism, and developed in terms of neural networks and parallel distributed processing—is that cognition is not simply symbol manipulation, but rather involves a nonsymbolic/symbolic dynamic process operating on a multilevel basis. The idea that cognition is "grounded-up" has also been expressed as "bottom-up design" and "situatedness" (Brooks 2002). Essentially the idea is that cognition depends on sensory classification systems, which cannot be separated from an entity's place in the world.

In economics, then, though the use of computational methods for solving the Arrow-Debreu-McKenzie axiomatic general equilibrium models continues the early AI functionalist tradition (cf. Amman et al. 1996), an ACE has subsequently also emerged" which explicitly employs a bottom-up type of analysis that models agents in specific environments (cf. Tesfatsion & Judd, 2006).[9] That is, ACE modeling captures the "ground-up" idea of connectionist AI by adopting a "culture-dish" approach to the study of economies seen as complex adaptive systems. The modeler computationally constructs an economic world comprising multiple interacting agents, where each agent is "an encapsulated piece of software that includes data [about the agent] together with behavioral methods that act on these data," and where agents are both economic agents and represent other social and environmental phenomena (Tesfatsion 2006). After specifying an initial state of the economic system, the economy is allowed to evolve to simulate the dynamics of real-world systems.

Individual behavior, then, is seen to not only reflect the kind of environment the individual or agent occupies, but also to undergo adaptation as changes in that environment feedback to the individual. For example, in Leigh Tesfatsion's simulation model of the labor market, a small number of work suppliers and employers of different types repeatedly interact, each keeps "separate track of his interaction with each potential worksite partner," and continuously updates his or her behavioral rules for different worksites based on what is remembered about past payoffs in past interactions (Tesfatsion 2001, 9). The analysis embeds individuals in a social structure, defined in terms of an array of possible labor market interactions, and generates a dynamic account of the behavior of individuals and social structure in which each acts upon the other. This contrasts with the more modest social embedding of individuals in behavioral economics research, where these reciprocal effects are largely absent. The difference may partly be explained in terms of the different methods of investigation—experiment vs. simulation— with the former lending itself more to synchronic analysis and the latter lending itself more to diachronic analysis. But there is also a difference in terms of the way that the social is built-in to the ACE approach. Behavioral economics essentially asks where and how the atomistic conception of the individual breaks down, whereas the ACE approach begins with a situated agent, and never so much as entertains the old atomistic conception.

3. Interaction Revisited

The standard view is that individuals interact only (or almost only[10]) indirectly with one another through the price mechanism. Classical game theory, of course, originates in the rejection of this assumption. Individuals are interdependent in the sense that they know (or have beliefs about) each other's utility functions, know the rules of the games they play with each other, and have common knowledge of this.[11] They are thus able to take the actions of others into account in making their own decisions, rather than simply responding to price signals. Within this framework there is a wide range of accounts of interdependence and its effects that socially embed individuals in games, though they generally share the restriction that individuals' preferences remain exogenous, and assume that individuals employ traditional expected utility reasoning. Evolutionary game theory, in contrast, puts both exogeneity and standard rationality theory to the test by explaining individual strategies as best responses to selection pressures, such that individuals are effectively only the bearers of strategies that are themselves in competition. Interaction in dynamic game-theoretic contexts thus further embeds individuals, indeed so such so that they arguably lose their status as economic agents. Finally, ACE network theories offer yet a third view of interaction between individuals by supposing that individuals interact both directly and indirectly with other individuals in structures of interaction.

Classical Game Theory

Here I focus on the contribution of John Harsanyi in light of his explicit elaboration of an alternative conception of the individual as being of a certain type (cf. Davis

2003a). Harsanyi proceeds by adopting two stratagems required to make use of the Nash equilibria framework. First, he argues that games of incomplete information should be treated as a new kind of game of complete information: "the new game G^* will be one with *complete* information because its basic mathematical structure will be defined by the probabilistic model for the game, which will be fully known to both players" (Harsanyi 1995, 295). Second, though he assumes that players employ pure strategies (since this seems more plausible than randomization), they appear to other players to be using mixed strategies if we suppose these apparent mixed strategies are other players' best guesses or conjectures about which pure strategy a player is playing (Harsanyi 1967/1968). He then argues that although a complete information game (or C-game) is always analyzed on the assumption that "the centers of activity" are particular individuals, incomplete information games (or I-games) are more clearly formulated as having types of players as their "centers of activity" (Harsanyi 1995, 295).

With this conception, facts about players not known to all players are replaced by probability assessments regarding players' characteristics that are known to all players. Players are represented as types because they may be represented in terms of certain sets of characteristics. Broadly speaking, they may be represented as being certain types, because of "causal factors" or "social forces" in the world that determine what characteristics different individuals are likely to possess (Harsanyi 1995, p. 297).[12] Harsanyi also assumes that players know which type they themselves each represent—"know their own identities" (296)—and rely on this information to assess the probability that other players are of certain types. This makes each player's assessment that another player is of a certain type a conditional probability assessment, one conditional, that is, on knowing one's own type. All players make such assessments and, consequently, any given player (player 1) will act "so as to protect his interests not only against his unknown *actual* opponent...but ... against all M types of player 2 because, for all he knows, *any* of them could now be his opponent in the game" (299). Thus, each player's expected payoff depends not just on the strategy of the actual unknown opponent, but also on the strategies of any one of M potential opponents.[13] Then, regarding types of players as "the real 'players'" and their payoff functions as the "real payoff functions, one can easily define the *Nash equilibrium*...of this C-game G^*" (300).

Harsanyi's intention to treat individuals as being of certain types involves a significant departure from the standard arm's-length, indirect-interaction view.[14] His "as if" complete information games not only knits individuals together in the pattern of their choices; it also gives them full accounts of one another, if in a probabilistic sense, in contrast to neoclassicism's assumption of them being inaccessibly subjective about one another. Consequently individuals are socially embedded in the games they play with one another in that their individuality depends on their interaction, in this instance in being recognized as individual types by one another. Despite this, classical game theory retains the standard exogeneity assumption, since interaction never changes individuals' payoff functions. This further step is undertaken in evolutionary game theory.

Evolutionary Game Theory

Evolutionary game theory (EGT) arose out the application of the theory of games to biological contexts, and the development of the concept of an evolutionarily stable strategy (Maynard Smith & Price 1973; Maynard Smith 1982). It took on direct economic application in Robert Axelrod's investigation of cooperation (Axelrod 1984), and gained a larger following in economics as a result of disenchantment with the equilibrium refinements project of classical game theory. The central assumption is that players adapt their behaviors in terms of the strategies they play over the course of repeated games. Payoffs represent fitness in some selection process that players achieve by adapting their strategies to the dynamics of competition. Interaction is, thus, both game theoretic and subject to evolutionary forces.

One of the more interesting aspects of EGT is its ambiguity regarding how the players of games are to be understood (cf. Ross, 2005, 194ff). If we see EGT as simply an extension of classical game theory, payers are the human individuals whose choices reflect beliefs about which strategies are the best replies to the strategies of others. But if we suppose that the selection process determines which strategies produce fitness, strategies themselves are the players, and individuals "are simply passive vehicles for these strategies, coming to play their brief hands and then dying off to be replaced by others who inherit their dispositions with modifications induced by mutation and, at the population level, by selection" (Ross 2005, 198; also cf. Sugden 2001).[15]

Thus, if in classical game theory, individuals are socially embedded in the games they play, EGT (arguably so) further embeds them in the dynamics of interaction so as to remove them as agents from the game altogether. That is, EGT effectively turns the standard exogeneity assumption on its head by making particular individuals irrelevant to selection. Here we find an especially clear difference between classical game theory's synchronic perspective and EGT's diachronic perspective.

ACE Network Theories

Network theory originates in mathematics and graph theory, and today is part of the study of complex systems and nonlinear dynamics. The analysis and study of networks exists in virtually every science (Strogatz 2001), and is an important foundation of ACE. Networks are structures made up of nodes, which can be individuals or groups of individuals, and the links or ties between them, which can vary in strength. In the case of economic networks, individuals can thus be said to have both strong ties to some individuals (interact directly) and weak ties to other individuals (interact only indirectly), such as in models of oligopoly firms surrounded by a competitive fringe. Alan Kirman has argued that assuming individuals interact in both ways represents an advance over both general equilibrium theory and game theory, which each assume that individuals interact in only one way—indirectly in the former and directly in the latter—associating this with the Sonnenschein-Mantel-Debreu problems of the former and the equilibrium selection problems of the latter (Kirman 1997; also cf. Rizvi 1994; Davis 2006a). Tesfatsion sees the need to combine direct and indirect interaction in models of markets as an implication of abandoning the artificial Walrasian auctioneer construct in explaining real world interaction between individuals (Tesfatsion 2006).

Distinguishing different kinds of ties and seeing them as interconnected in some way introduces structure into the analysis of individual interaction. Tesfatsion (2001), for example, develops a model of labor markets in which work suppliers and employers interact repeatedly at different kinds of worksites in prisoner's dilemma games. Thus individuals are not only embedded in games with other individuals, but are also embedded in games that are themselves embedded in a social structure. Whereas game theory explains the emergence of social structures in the form of norms and conventions, ACE network theory presupposes such structures in the analysis of games. Indeed, ACE network theory begins with a liberal view of the population of agents, including among them, "individuals (e.g., consumers, workers), social groupings (e.g., families, firms, government agencies), institutions (e.g., markets, regulatory systems), biological entities (e.g., crops livestock, forests), and physical entities (e.g., infrastructure, weather, and geographical regions)" (Tesfatsion 2006, 6). This larger cast of agents represents an even further departure from the standard view of interaction than one finds in neoclassicism.

4. Aggregate Behavior and Feedback

On the standard view, the relationship of individual behavior to aggregate behavior is unidirectional. Aggregate behavior has individual behavior as its basis, and feedback effects from aggregate behavior to individual behavior are assumed to be absent. Individuals' choice sets are parameterized by aggregate outcomes, but individual preferences remain unaffected and insulated from changes at the aggregate level. One well-known expression of this is the New Classical Macroeconomics microfoundations research program that aims at unifying microeconomics and macroeconomics by aggregating up to macroeconomic relationships strictly in terms of preferences, endowments, and technology. Here I review three challenges to this general view from behavioral game theory, neuroeconomics, and evolutionary economics/ACE complexity thinking. In different ways, all embed individuals in social economic frameworks by allowing for aggregate level feedback effects, which affect individual behavior.

Behavioral Game Theory

Behavioral game theory departs from classical game theory's rationality focus by applying experimental results from cognitive psychology to the study of individuals' strategic interaction in games (Camerer 2003). By creating complete, self-contained economies in the laboratory made up of agents and institutions, researchers are able to generate experimental data that allow them to test a variety of standard theory assumptions.[16] The kinds of games generally given the most attention are those that exhibit cooperative dilemmas with free rider problems such as the public-goods game (Fehr & Gächter 2000). The general problem encountered in these games is an equilibrium selection problem in that free-riding equilibria and cooperative equilibria can both exist according to the kinds of institutions (or instructions for experimental subjects) in place.[17]

In one recent examination of this problem designed to explain the effect of different institutions on individual behavior (Gürerk et al. 2006), an experiment was devised in which players repeatedly choose between two different institutions: one in which individuals chose a level of contribution to a public good, which was then augmented by the experimenter and divided among players, and a second in which the same arrangement applied, but there was also an opportunity for individuals to punish free riders. In initial rounds of the game, free riding prevailed in the no-punishment setup, leading to low payoffs, whereas free riding was punished in the setup in which this was available, leading to higher payoffs. But with repeated play, individuals migrated from the low- to the high-payoff game with the punishment institution.

What the experiment was interpreted to demonstrate was that individuals change their behavior in light of their appraisal of aggregate outcomes.[18] That is, individuals adopt one set of decision rules at the outset, observe their consequences in the aggregate, and then revise their decision rules in light of their observations. This in turn affects the character of overall aggregate behavior by virtue of the increased share of individuals participating in the punishment institution, suggesting that individual and aggregate behavior continuously interact in a cycle of mutual effects on one another. In contrast, in the standard (nonexperimental) framework, such feedback mechanisms do not operate in that rational individuals are always predicted to choose the free-riding institution.

Neuroeconomics

Neuroeconomics can be seen as an extension of behavioral economics' cognitive science-based revision of standard expected utility reasoning through use of neuroscience imaging techniques to more securely ground observed behavioral propensities in neurological phenomena, and thus as a strategy for making incremental changes in standard theorizing. It may also be seen as offering an alternative framework in the form of an altogether different set of theoretical constructs to explain behavior, and thus as a strategy for making radical departures from standard theorizing (Camerer, Loewenstein, & Prelec 2005). In the more radical approach, cognitive decision making is thought to employ both deliberative and automatic processes, and cognition and emotion are thought to both contribute to behavior. Taking these two dimensions together gives four possible combinations of neural functioning that can be employed to categorize kinds of human behavior that may operate in parallel, separately (seen as specialization), and in coordination. This implies that individuals are capable of a variety of different possible behaviors, whereas, in contrast, standard theory only allows for behavior explained exclusively in terms of expected utility maximizing.

One way of seeing the neural basis for human behavior, then, is to say that human intelligence is modularized or highly domain (or neuron) specific. This in turn implies that environmental triggers can call forth different types of neural activity. For example, in regard to time-preference, whereas standard theory assumes the same degree of time-preference for all intertemporal trade-offs, it can be argued that different contexts elicit different degrees of time-preference according to the deliberative, automatic, cognitive, and affective aspects of the neural processing involved. At the same time, neuroscience research does not support the conclusion that particular types of behavior are always associated with the same brain modules. Brain injury research shows a relatively high degree of plasticity or the ability of the brain to shift functions from one domain to another that has not been impaired. But the shifting of functions can also occur under normal circumstances, such as those associated with learning and experience. Thus reinforcement learning in normal form games has been explained as combining rapid emotional processing—reflecting sense of gain or loss—and a slower deliberative processing—reflecting grasp of counterfactuals (Camerer and Ho 1999).

What emerges from this are views of the brain, behavior, and the environment that involve response and adjustment in a complex array of different possible forms. It would thus be a mistake to say that neuroeconomics research follows the standard model's understanding of the relation of individual behavior to aggregate behavior.[19] Rather, while aggregate behavior is a product of individual behavior across many individuals, aggregate behavior also exercises feedback effects on individual behavior that it can, in principle, be traced to changes in individual neural functioning. Like behavioral economics and game theory research, much of neuroeconomics research employs laboratory experiments in which experimental subjects play repeated games during brain imaging. Repeated games allow researchers to track changes in behavior associated with experimental subjects' experience across games. Accordingly neuro-imaging offers the opportunity to replicate results arrived at in pure behavioral experiments, such as the choice-of-institutions game discussed in the previous section. The evidence produced thus far suggests that both sets of investigations support one another, and, therefore, that individual and aggregate behaviors have mutual effects on each other.

Evolutionary Economics/ACE Complexity Thinking

I combine these two different research programs here because they reach very similar conclusions with respect to the issue of individual and aggregate behavior.

Indeed, though the two programs have two separate sets of origins, they overlap on a number of counts that arguably reflect their shared diachronic orientations. Evolutionary economics is a research program concerned with the evolutionary analysis of long-run change that derives from evolutionary theory in biology and sociobiology, and efforts to extend and modify this form of analysis in connection with human social behavior and social-cultural evolutionary processes (Nelson 1995; Vromen 1995).[20] ACE/complexity thinking has similar origins, but adds an emphasis on the mathematics of nonlinear dynamic systems and simulation models as compared to evolutionary economics' preference for theorizing based on empirical research. Both assume that evolutionary theorizing rejects accounts of economic change that employ "mechanical analogies" (Nelson 1995, 53).

Evolutionary economics approaches in particular develop arguments about systems that are subject to processes of random variation but also exhibit selection processes that winnow those variations. Evolutionary systems consequently show both strong inertial tendencies working to preserve what survives selection and also continuous change as the introduction of new variety through random mutation modifies those systems. Thus behavior of a system in the aggregate is continuously affected by the behavior of its changing elements, which in turn are affected by the selection behavior of the system.

ACE/complexity thinking similarly emphasizes dynamic interaction between a system's elements and its structure. The behavior a system's elements exhibit produces aggregate patterns or structures in the system. Because this structure is emergent, the behavior of the system's elements then adapts to it. The system's structures are then further changed, the elements further adapt, and so on in a continuous process of change through time. A class example is W. Brian Arthur's El Farol bar problem (Arthur 1994). One hundred people independently decide whether to show up at the El Farol bar. If many predict the bar will be crowded, the bar ends up being empty. But should the bar be empty, they revise their prediction, then expecting it to be empty, and all go, but it ends up being crowded, leading them to then predict the bar will be crowded, and so on. Predictions thus depend on predictions, and no correct expectations model is available. In contrast, in rational expectations models, agents somehow know in advance what model is correct (and everyone knows that everyone knows this is the correct model), so that aggregate behavior is fully known in advance, and agents need never revise their behavior.

5. Synchronic and Diachronic Forms of Explanation

All the research programs reviewed earlier, then, adopt elements of an embedded individual conception, but, as should now be clear, they do so in quite different ways according to the different types of objections they make to the standard conception. To make the nature of that conception and its critique clear, these objections were organized according to which of its three (linked) properties they target: preference exogeneity, indirect interaction, and absence of feedback effects from aggregate to individual behavior. But under each objection I have also provided discussions of approaches that reflect either more synchronic or more diachronic concerns in order to emphasize the deeper differences between these approaches. In the discussion in this section, I further pursue these differences to examine what types of contributions they make to a general conception of the individual as an embedded agent.

As noted at the outset, conceptions of the individual can be evaluated according to two criteria needed to explain the (personal) identity of the individual (Davis 2003b). The individuation criterion requires that a conception of the individual show how individuals are distinct and independent from one another. Individuation is largely a synchronic concern. The re-identification criterion requires that a conception of the individual show how individuals can be shown to be the same separate entities across a process in which some or even many of their characteristics change. Re-identification is largely a diachronic concern. Note also, however, that neither framework is particularly well suited to addressing the other framework's natural focus. Because synchronic forms of explanation largely bracket through-time or through-process considerations to focus on the character of an entity or mechanism, they do not really address whether individuals are re-identifiable through change. Because diachronic forms of explanation emphasize change and process, they tend to ignore the status and individual credentials of particular entities. This suggests that the conceptions (or elements of conceptions) of the individual we find in the new research programs—to the extent that they offer essentially synchronic or diachronic forms of explanation—are likely to be incomplete, and that a complete conception of the individual satisfying both criteria will need to combine elements of both synchronic and diachronic research programs. Because the research programs with the more synchronic orientation are more "micro" in nature, and the research programs with the more diachronic orientation are more "macro" in nature, this further suggests that an adequate embedded individual conception, as might emerge from some combination of the new research programs in economics, needs to combine both micro and macro aspects.[21]

The research programs with synchronic forms of explanation, then, are classical game theory, behavioral economics, behavioral game theory, and neuroeconomics. Should these research programs move toward synthesis in the future or be increasingly accommodated to one another in Pickering's terms, then it seems reasonable to suppose that the rationality assumptions of classical game theory are most likely to be given up (or significantly modified), because they are contested in one way or another by all the remaining programs in this group. At the same time, that game theory has become central to behavioral, experimental, and neuroeconomics research suggests that it is likely to remain essential to synchronic forms of investigation. We might consequently label this synthesis *experimental game theory*, where this encompasses complimentary behavioral and neuroeconomics strategies.

The research programs with diachronic forms of explanation are EGT, evolutionary economics, and ACE/complexity economics. Here there are arguably greater barriers to mutual accommodation and synthesis by virtue of there being two quite different views of individual agents. On the one hand, EGT and evolutionary economics both subsume individual agents in evolutionary processes. With the more radical view of EGT, strategies are players, and individual agents "are simply passive vehicles for these strategies" (Ross 2005, 198), while in evolutionary economics individuals need not be human individuals and need not survive in any particular form through a given evolutionary process. On the other hand, ACE/complexity approaches, as ground-up, agent-based forms of investigation, presuppose individual agents (human and otherwise), and investigate how these particular agents adapt to dynamic processes. We might distinguish these two opposed kinds of views as *evolutionary-process* and *evolutionary-agent* strategies. Accommodation of these strategies to one another does not seem possible within the boundaries of the programs as they are currently pursued.

There accordingly seem to be two quite different possible future pathways available for the new research programs taken as a whole. If synchronic and diachronic forms of explanation are integrated, and micro and macro approaches are developed together in a shared framework, then the reconceptualization of individuals in an *experimental game theory* could be linked up with the *evolutionary-agent* approach in ACE/complexity accounts, because both frameworks emphasize individual agents. Alternatively, should *evolutionary-process* accounts prevail, synchronic and diachronic forms of explanation in the new research programs would likely not link up, thus tending to reproduce the current division between micro and macro in terms of two research programs largely opposed to one another on the place and significance of individuals in economic explanation.

One motivation for the first scenario is a preference for a unity of science view. But philosophers' and scientists' preferences may be irrelevant when it comes to how economics actually develops. A second, perhaps stronger motivation is grounded in the availability of critique. That is, when micro and macro explanations are not reconciled, proponents of each may argue for the reduction of the other to their own framework. This is the basis of neoclassical microfoundations reasoning, where the critique advanced is that the macro must ultimately be understood in terms of the decisions of individuals.[22] In the following section, however, I outline another microfoundations critique for a pathway the new research programs might take that favors the combination of *experimental game theory* and the *evolutionary-agent* approach. The difference between this argument and the standard microfoundations argument is that, whereas the latter as based on the atomist conception of the individual and is reductionist, the former argument, as based on an embedded individual conception, is not reductionist, and thereby has an appeal the standard view lacks.

6. EMBEDDED INDIVIDUAL MICROFOUNDATIONS

The standard case for microfoundations involves a transcendental argument that supposes macroeconomic relationships must be explainable in terms of the behavior of individuals. As individuals exist, and as macroeconomic relationships are aggregative and do not make reference to individuals, they must somehow be "reduced to" or re-interpreted in terms of individual behavior. At root in the argument, however, is the idea that individual behavior and aggregate behavior cannot be combined in a single representation, thus requiring one or the other. Should this view be given up, and individual behavior and aggregate behavior be seen as somehow related, the traditional reductionist project ceases to have meaning. This alternative view naturally finds support in embedded individual conceptions, which, by definition, combine individual and aggregate behavior. Thus, embedded individual conceptions short-circuit reductionism. At the same time, if individual behavior and aggregate behavior are represented as related and mutually determining, explanations of aggregate behavior that exclude explanations of individual behavior, such as arguably is the case in the *evolutionary-process* approach, make the same mistake as traditional microfoundations arguments, and are at best incomplete. An embedded individual microfoundations would accordingly incorporate an *evolutionary-agent* approach.

But how would such a view provide microfoundations were the project not reductionist? Essentially an embedded individual microfoundations project constitutes a focus of analysis rather than an interpretive substrate. Individuals remain a central concern (for the reasons set forth at the outset), but their investigation (also transcendentally) presupposes and simultaneously requires examination of the aggregative relationships they occupy. This type of investigation clearly demands attention to a balance between individuals' embeddedness and independence that is not needed in atomistic individual microfoundations arguments, which assume individuals to be always independent. This type of investigation also demands attention to whether embedded individuals are sustainably independent, because if they are not, they could arguably be said to drop out of our explanations, as in *evolutionary-process* approaches.

Here I do not attempt to set out such an explanation, since this task must presuppose the elaboration of particular substantive arguments about how the synchronic and diachronic research programs discussed earlier might be synthesized. But such an explanation, I suggest, can proceed in terms of two criteria, that is, by evaluating proposed individual conceptions according to whether they allow us to individuate and re-identify the economic agents they assume. Satisfying the re-identification criterion, it should be added, likely constitutes the more difficult task, since there is a clear debate in diachronic research programs regarding whether individuals are passive placeholders in evolutionary processes. Further, significant difficulties confront *evolutionary-agent* approaches regarding individual re-identification across change, because it is not clear how individuals' adaptations to changing social structures are compatible with their re-identification as self-same individuals.[23] Indeed, then, which of the two broad scenarios for the future of economics as it develops out of the new research programs transpires—a single unified program or reproduction of the division between micro and macro—depends on these issues.

7. CONCLUDING SPECULATIONS

It was noted earlier that the new research programs in economics have hardly made the conception of the individual their chief concern. Thus, their development is likely to be driven by other factors, and their adoption of particular conceptions of the individual to be more a by-product of other considerations. At the same time, most of the new research approaches in economics work implicitly with new conceptions of the individual, ones that I have argued all depart from the standard atomistic conception. This by itself may cause more attention to be paid to those conceptions, since it would seem ultimately to be bound to become clear to most practitioners that they are working with conceptions of the individual at odds with the conception that has been a pre-eminent marker of economics for over a century. Indeed, the standard view of the individual has long had more than scientific significance, since it is also one fixed in the popular understanding of economics, both on account of the way economics has long represented itself as a science of individual choice, and because economic micropolicy, which impacts the world, is formulated in terms of individuals. Moreover, already a vigorous debate over the implications of thinking about individuals as less than rational—because of (embedding) framing effects—has surfaced in regard to the discussion of paternalism vis-à-vis free market prescriptions (Camerer & Loewenstein 2003).

It might also be argued that it is in the nature of a transition from one dominant approach (neoclassicism) to another—where this specifically involves the import of other science technologies—that a kind of interregnum period is likely to prevail when technical questions are foremost in economists' effort to assimilate new methods.[24] Yet when method stabilizes, the trees slide into the background to reveal the shape of the forest. Then arguably the perennial questions re-emerge for philosophers regarding individuals, markets, and value.

NOTES

1. Thanks without implication go to Fredrik Hansen, Floris Heukelom, Harro Maas, Abu Rizvi, and Leigh Tesfatsion, and the members of the workshop.

2. I argue in Davis (2003b) that this conception of the individual as a distinct being is circular in that the individual is picked out in terms of the idea of 'own' preferences. The conception allows that two individuals could have identical preferences, but would still be distinct individuals by virtue of those preferences belonging separately to each. The concept of belonging presupposes that which is to be picked out.

3. For more on Alan Turing, see Mirowski (2002).

4. Noam Chomsky (1955 [1975]; 1965) held that language capacity involves information processing that relies on a "deep" generative grammar that could be understood as syntactic symbol manipulation, an elementary form of which would employ Boolean algebra.

5. Warren McCulloch, a physiologist, and Walter Pitts, a logician, supposed that the human nervous system could be understood as universal computing device. In their seminal 1943 paper, "A Logical Calculus of the Ideas Immanent in Nervous Activity," they showed that configurations of neurons could perform any calculations computable by a Turing machine, and generated a mathematical model of the neuron, in which collections of neurons acted as "logic gates," now known as the McCulloch-Pitts neuron.

6. The Sonnenschein-Mantel-Debreu results were a significant stimulus for this development (cf. Rizvi 1997).

7. See Davis (2003b, Chapter 5) for a discussion of the emergence of functionalism in postwar neoclassical economics in the work of Kenneth Arrow, Paul Samuelson, and others.

8. Searle also created the distinction between strong AI and weak AI, in which the former identifies the computer and mind, and the latter involves computational simulation of some aspects of mind.

9. Leigh Tesfatsion recalls that at a 1996 UCLA workshop she, Robert Axtell, Charlotte Bruin, and Axel Leijonhufvud "discussed naming the field 'agent based economics.' Consequently, this is why I called the website that I developed in late 1996 the 'agent-based economics website.' However, I soon discovered that many analytical microeconomists felt they were already doing 'agent-based economics' simply by means of having a utility maximizing consumer agent! So I changed the name of the website to the 'agent based computational economics' (ACE) website to try to indicate that we were referring to something quite distinct from current mainstream economics. This is the name I still use for the Web site [http://www.econ.iastate.edu/tesfatsi/ace.htm] today" (Testfatsion, personal communication, 5 May 2006).

10. Externalities constitute the exception.

11. "It is not enough that each player be fully aware of the rules of the game and the utility functions of the players. Each player must also be aware of this fact, i.e., of the awareness of all the players; moreover, each player must be aware that each player is aware that each player is aware, and so on ad infinitum. In brief, the awareness of the description of the game by all players must be a part of the description itself" (Aumann 1989, 473).

12. Drawing on game theory applications to the Cold War, Harsanyi's example distinguishes American and Russian types whose causal factors pertain to their locations in the United States and the Soviet Union.

13. These are labeled semiconditional payoff functions.

14. I say "intention," because it may be argued that Harsanyi's assumption that individuals know their own types inadvertently re-introduces elements of the standard view (cf. Davis 2003a).

15. An analogous but slightly different argument can be applied to the classical sequential-move or extensive form game (cf. Ross 2005, 201 ff).

16. A parallel anthropological game theory investigation relies on non-experimental field data to examine strategic behavior across cultures (Henrich et al. 2004).

17. Thus, Vernon Smith's famous slogan is, "institutions matter" (Smith 1989).

18. Also, that migration occurred over repeated play, or that players did not select the higher payoff institution on the first round(s) of the game, was interpreted to indicate that individuals lack rational foresight.

19. See the paper by Don Ross in this volume for this point (Ross 2007).

20. According to most commentators, EGT falls outside the evolutionary economics research program on account of its classical game theory origins, though it shares roots in biological theory.

21. In contrast, the atomistic individual conception, which might be characterized as an exclusively synchronic form of explanation, involves only a micro type conception.

22. There are of course also macrofoundations arguments for micro.

23. Thus, one ACE/complexity account of individual identity argues that individuals do not/cannot retain self-same identities across processes of change (Kirman & Teschl 2006).

24. Thus, some have defined the new approaches in economics in terms of tools rather than content as, for example, with David Colander's modeling characterization (Colander 2000), whereas dominant discourses appear to rather define themselves in terms of content (Robbins 1935 [1932]).

REFERENCES

Allais, M. (1953). "Le comportement de l'homme rationnel devant le risque: critique des postulats et axiomes de l'ecole americaine." *Econometrica* 21: 503–556.

Amman, H., Kendrick, D. & Rust, J., Eds. (1996). *Handbook of Computational Economics*, Vol. 1. North Holland: Elsevier.

Arthur, W. B. (1994). "Inductive Reasoning and Bounded Rationality." *American Economic Review* 84 (2): 406–411.

Aumann, R. (1989). "Game Theory." In J. Eatwell, M. Milgate & P. Newman, Eds., *The New Palgrave: a Dictionary of Economics*. London: Macmillan.

Axelrod, R. (1984). *The Evolution of Cooperation*. New York: Basic Books.

Binmore, K. (1999). "Why Experiment in Economics?" *Economic Journal* 109: F16–24.

Brooks, R. (2002). *Robot: The Future of Flesh and Machines*. London: Penguin.

Camerer, C. & Loewenstein, G. (2003). "Behavioral Economics: Past, Present, Future." In C. Camerer, G. Loewenstein & M. Rabin, Eds., *Advances in Behavioral Economics*. Princeton: Princeton University Press.

Camerer, C. (2003) *Behavioral Game Theory: Experiments in Strategic Interaction*, Princeton: Princeton University Press.

Camerer, C. and Fehr, E. (2004) "Measuring Social Norms and Preferences Using Experimental Games: A Guide for Social Scientists." In J. Heinrich et al., Eds. *Foundations of Human Sociality,* 55–95. Oxford: Oxford University Press.

Camerer, C. and Ho, T. (1999) "Experience-Weighted Attraction Learning in Normal Form Games." *Econometrica* 67 (4): 827–874.

Camerer, C., Loewenstein, G. & Prelec, D. (2005). "Neuroeconomics: How Neuroscience Can Inform Economics." *Journal of Economic Literature* 43: 9–64.

Chomsky, N. (1955 [1975]). *The Logical Structure of Linguistic Theory.* Cambridge: MIT Humanities Press, Microfilm. Re-issue New York: Plenum Press, 1975.

Chomsky, N. (1965). *Aspects of the Theory of Syntax.* Cambridge, MA: MIT Press.

Colander, D. (2000). "The Death of Neoclassical Economics." *Journal of the History of Economic Thought* 22 (2): 127–144.

Cubitt, R., Starmer, C. & Sugden, R. (2001). "Discovered Preferences and the Experimental Evidence of Violations of Expected Utility Theory." *Journal of Economic Methodology* 8 (3): 385–414.

Davis, J. (2003a). "The Conception of the Individual in Non-Cooperative Game Theory." Tinbergen Institute Discussion Paper, 2003–095/2, http://www.tinbergen.nl/home.html.

Davis, J. (2003b). *The Theory of the Individual in Economics.* London: Routledge.

Davis, J. (2006a). "Complexity Theory's Network Conception of the Individual." In A. Giacomin & C. Marcuzzo, Eds., *Money and Markets.* Cheltenham,England: Elgar.

Davis, J. (2006b). "The Turn in Economics: Neoclassical Dominance to Mainstream Pluralism?" *Journal of Institutional Economics* 2 (1): 1–20.

Fehr, E. & Gächter, S. (2000). "Fairness and Retaliation: The Economics of Reciprocity." *Journal of Economic Perspectives* 14: 159–181.

Gürerk, Ö., Irlenbusch, I. & Rockenbach, B. (2006). "The Competitive Advantage of Sanctioning Institutions." *Science* 312: 108–111.

Harnad, S. (1987). "Category Induction and Representation," in S. Harnad, ed., *Categorical Perception: The Groundwork of Cognition.* New York: Cambridge University Press.

Harnad, S. (1990). "The Symbol Grounding Problem." *Physica* D 42: 335–346.

Harrison, G. (1994). "Expected Utility and the Experimentalists." *Empirical Economics* 19: 223–253.

Harsanyi, J. (1967/1968). "Games with Incomplete Information Played by Bayesian Players." *Management Science* 14: 159–82, 320–34, 486–502.

Harsanyi, J. (1995). "Games with Incomplete Information." *American Economic Review* 85 (3): 291–303.

Henrich, J., Boyd, R., Bowles, S., Gintis, H., Fehr, E., & Camerer, C., Eds. (2004). *Foundations of Human Sociality: Ethnography and Experiments in 15 small-scale Societies.* Oxford: Oxford University Press.

Kahneman, D. & Tversky, A. (1979). "Prospect Theory: An Analysis of Decision under Risk." *Econometrica* 47 (2): 263–291.

Kirman, A. & Teschl, M. (2006). "Searching for Identity in the Capability Space." *Journal of Economic Methodology* 13: 299–325.

Kirman, A. (1997). "The Economy as an Interactive System." In W. B. Arthur, S. Durlauf & D. Lane, Eds., *The Economy as an Evolving Complex System II.* Reading, MA: Addison-Wesley.

Lichtenstein, S. & Slovic, P. (1971). "Reversals of Preference between Bids and Choices in Gambling Decisions." *Journal of Experimental Psychology* 89: 46–55.

Maynard Smith, J & Price, G. (1973). "The Logic of Animal Conflict." *Nature* 146: 15–18.

Maynard-Smith, J. (1982). *Evolution and the Theory of Games*. Cambridge, England: Cambridge University Press.

McCulloch, W. & Pitts, W. (1943). "A Logical Calculus of Ideas Immanent in Nervous Activity." *Bulletin of Mathematical Biophysics* 5: 115–133.

Mirowski, P. (2002). *Machine Dreams: Economics Becomes a Cyborg Science*. Cambridge, England: Cambridge University Press.

Nelson, R. (1995). "Recent Evolutionary Theorizing About Economic Change." *Journal of Economic Literature* 38: 48–90.

Payne, J., Bettman, J. & Johnson, E. (1992). "Behavioral Decision Research: A Constructive Processing Perspective. "*Annual Review of Psychology* 43: 87–131.

Pickering, A. (1995). *The Mangle of Practice*. Chicago: University of Chicago Press.

Plott, C. (1996). "Rational Individual Behavior in Markets and Social Choice Processes: The Discovered Preference Hypothesis." In K. Arrow, E. Colombatto, M. Perlaman & C. Schmidt, Eds., *The Rational Foundations of Economic Behavior*, 225–250. London: Macmillan and New York: St Martin's Press.

Rizvi, S. (1994). "Game Theory to the Rescue?" *Contributions to Political Economy* 13: 1–28.

Rizvi, S. (1997). "Responses to Arbitrariness in Contemporary Microeconomics." *History of Political Economy* 29: 273–288.

Robbins, L. (1935 [1932]). *An Essay on the Nature and Significance of Economic Science*, 2nd ed. London: Macmillan.

Ross D. (2007). "Integrating the Dynamics of Multi-level Economic Agency." *Philosophy of Economics Handbook*. Oxford: Oxford University Press.

Ross, D. (2005). *Economic Theory and Cognitive Science: Microexplanation*. Cambridge, MA: MIT Press.

Samuelson, L. (2005). "Economic Theory and Experimental Economics." *Journal of Economic Literature* 43: 65–107.

Searle, J. (1992). *The Rediscovery of the Mind*. Cambridge, MA: MIT Press.

Searle, J. 1980. "Minds, Brains, and Programs." *Behavioral and Brain Sciences* 3: 417–424.

Slovic, P. (1995) "The Construction of Preferences." *American Psychologist* 50: 364–371.

Smith, V. (1989). "Theory, Experiment and Economics." *Journal of Economic Perspectives* 3: 151–169.

Strogatz, S. (2001). "Exploring Complex Networks." *Nature* 410: 268–276.

Sugden, R. (2001). "The Evolutionary Turn in Game Theory." *Journal of Economic Methodology* 8: 113–130.

Tesfatsion, L. & Judd, K., eds., (2006). *Handbook of Computational Economics*, Vol. 2, *Agent-Based Computational Economics*. North Holland: Elsevier.

Tesfatsion, L. (2006). "Agent-Based Computational Economics: A Constructive Approach to Economic Theory." In L. Tesfatsion & K. Judd, Eds., *Handbook of Computational Economics Vol. 2: Agent-Based Computational Economics*. Amsterdam: Elsevier.

Testfatsion, L. (2001). "Structure, Behavior, and Market Power in an Evolutionary Labor Market with Adaptive Search." *Journal of Economic Dynamics and Control* 25: 419–457.

Tversky, A. & Kahneman, D. (1992). "Loss Aversion in Riskless Choice: A Reference-Dependent Model." *Quarterly Journal of Economics* 106 (4): 1039–1061.

Vromen, J. (1995). *Economic Evolution: On Inquiry into the Foundations of New Institutional Economics*. London: Routledge.

CHAPTER 9

INTEGRATING THE DYNAMICS OF MULTISCALE ECONOMIC AGENCY

DON ROSS

1. INTRODUCTION

This chapter is about the relationship between people, as modeled by the economist's concept of agency, and other entities modeled as agents in economics—in particular, sub-personal interests, as in models descended from Schelling (1978, 1980, 1984), and functional parts of people's brains, as modeled in neuroeconomics. This subject would not be very interesting if people and subpersonal interests reduced to or were simple additive functions of functional parts of their brains. However, for reasons that will unfold in what follows, I think that this common idea is untenable. The relationship between people, subpersonal interests, and brain systems is complicated, not simple. My objective here is to shed some light on it, on the basis of recent empirical research. I do not aim at stating a comprehensive theory of the relationship, which would be a premature ambition at this point in our collective knowledge.

Three recent book-length studies in the philosophy of economics (Mirowski 2002; Davis 2003; Ross 2005) have drawn attention to the fact that mainstream economic theory has consistently avoided commitment to any particular model of the person. This is the most significant respect in which economics has kept aloof from *part* of psychology. The widespread belief, on the other hand, that economists' attentiveness to the psychology of choice and decision had to wait for the Allais challenge and then for Kahneman and Tversky is a myth. It is true that, for a brief period after World War II, economists following Samuelson's lead tried to empirically (as opposed to just theoretically) operationalize personal choice as analytically derivative from observed consumption. This was a minor episode in the history of theory, which was abandoned after quick and stark empirical failure (Wallis & Friedman 1942). Ross (2005) argues that, if anything, mainstream microeconomics has been *more* sensitive to theoretical fashions in the psychology of choice than has been good for it, producing unwarranted instability in economists' (and their critics') evaluations of the adequacy of their modeling frameworks (see Ross forthcoming b for details).

This sensitivity to details of decision theory is an aspect of economists' abiding preoccupation with agency. To the extent that agency is grounded in the psychology of decision-making—as the subjective experience of weighing alternatives—then the basis of agency might be taken to be clear. Hence the attraction for Lionel Robbins (1935) of resting economic theory's foundations on putatively clear and universal knowledge of the experience of ranking subjective preferences. Alternative strategies for demarcating agents from nonagents, which one is forced to consider if one adopts a behavioristic viewpoint—or indeed just a sensible degree of Wittgenstein-style verificationism about reports due to putative introspective processes—lead into choppy philosophical waters.

Suppose one holds that agents are just those entities who turn out to be truly (or merely usefully, if one is a pragmatist) describable as consistently maximizing a specifiable function or class of functions over possible consumption bundles. The last four words in this formulation do no independent work, because what counts as a possible consumption bundle for an agent is determined by the function its behavior is taken to maximize. Then the mere claim that an agent is something that acts to maximize a function is not sufficient for fixing the scope of microeconomic theory, since everything that retains system integrity over detectable stretches of time—planets, rocks in gravitational fields, atomic nuclei—can be modeled in some sort of equilibrium dynamics. To be an economic agent, an entity to which a utility function can be imputed, a system must perform work to track environmental changes in order to try to maintain itself in equilibrium, and there must be nontrivial possibility of failure lest the tracking metaphor be empty. The metaphysical ideas underlying this conception are quite vague. Is a system that *always* loses equilibrating capacity after a time—e.g., every organism—a system that, by eventually failing to track its sources of utility (i.e., dying), thereby reveals its agency? This doesn't seem helpful, since in a dynamic and finite universe this criterion would again qualify everything as an agent. The most promising way to obtain restrictions is by reference to the core idea of post-Darwinian biology: require the possibility of local failure against a backdrop of system stability by identifying agency with units produced and shaped by some selection dynamics or other. Then organisms and species and firms and clubs are agents but rocks and planets aren't—or, if this still doesn't quite work because some sort of pan-selectionism holds in the limit (as in cosmological models taken seriously by some physicists such as Smolin 1997), then one can rule, for example, evolving galaxies off the table as economic agents by allowing that agency might be scale-relative and then adopting a pragmatic policy of restricting attention to particular (mid-range) scales.

Philosophers' eyes will roll at such slapdash ontology, but it is no looser than the implicit metaphysics characteristic of most sciences. In general, a science will resort to metaphysical or strictly logical individuation of types when and only when the relevant mathematics can't be induced to pull all the necessary weight for practical purposes. In their high-neoclassical phase, economists thought that mathematical relations borrowed from classical thermodynamics were adequate to the job; these days dynamic-systems theory is often suggested as providing foundations for those who need them—in particular who need them for an economics built on informational asymmetries, market inefficiencies, and increasing returns (Anderson et al. 1988, Arthur et al. 1997, Albin 1998, Blume & Durlauf 2005, Beinhocker 2006). The career of the critical historian of economics Philip Mirowski (see his 1989, 2002, this volume) can be summarized as a running campaign for the charge that in no period has economists' math done as much foundational work for them as they've imagined. Few economists accept Mirowski's allegation, though what they often offer as grounds for rejecting it is mainly indignant huffing and puffing (see Binmore 2004; Durlauf 2005).[1] Much of this is a battle over calling the glass half-full or half-empty. Because economists are constantly enlarging their mathematical toolkit, there is some sense in which their mathematics at a given time is *obviously* never sufficient to avoid tacit appeal to metaphysical assumptions in the uncleared patches of the conceptual jungle—we know from induction that there's always some new patch about to be cut. But since it is also true that economists never decide that some mathematical resources they once found significant are in fact irrelevant—the reader is invited to try to nominate even one important case of this—they can argue that, for any given area where concepts are not yet explicit, induction advises patience, while we wait for technique to advance into it, rather than dissipation of energy on frontal philosophical assault.

In this chapter, I will observe this pragmatic economist's attitude where the philosophy of agency is concerned. That is, I will assume cavalierly that, if we get nonredundant explanation and prediction of some system's trajectory through successions of states by regarding it as maximizing (or meliorating with respect to) a utility function,[2] then that system is an agent. My interest here is in general questions that persist *after* we agree to be cheerfully unphilosophical about agency. These questions arise precisely because aphilosophical pragmatism *does* have a price, even if it's a bargain. That price with respect to the concept of agency in economics is as follows. According to the pragmatic attitude, there is a wide variety of kinds of economic agents. Most people seem to be agents, or at least successions of them (as their utility functions change). Groups of people seem to be agents. For reasons I have explored in detail elsewhere (Ross 2005), both *functional aspects* and *some neurophysiological parts* of people seem to be agents. These various kinds of agents (among others) don't inhabit separate worlds, so a unified view of natural economic history must depict them as interacting. We can't rely on another science—say, psychology—to show us how to model their interaction, for in adopting cheerful pragmatism we decide to prefer a notion of agency tailored to specifically *economic* uses; thus we must not expect psychology to provide foundations for us. This is not a declaration of strict independence: of course we must pay attention to constraints arising from what neighboring sciences tell us is true about the world. (For example: which parts of people are agents, and what motivates these agents, is being discovered by neuroscience; see later sections 4 and 5). But the problem of how to apply our metaphysically sloppy but mathematically good-enough idea of agency to empirical processes that interest us as economists is all ours to deal with.

In this chapter I aim to make some progress on a few aspects of this problem, namely, What is the concept of a person in economic theory (if there is any role at all for such a concept)? Asked another way, the question is: What sort of economic agent is a person? And then: What, in general, is the relationship between personal agents and suprapersonal and subpersonal agents, the dynamics of which, I contend, explain why there are personal agents in the first place?

The chapter will be structured as follows. In Section 2, I will set the context for discussion a bit more precisely in current issues from the philosophy of economics. In Section 3, I will briefly give a high-level sketch of an approach to modeling people as production outputs of social dynamics, intended to explain why there are people. I confine myself to a sketch because I have defended this approach in detail and at substantial length elsewhere. Following a more detailed review of current foundational issues in subpersonal economics (picoeconomics and neuroeconomics), I will, in the most substantial part of the chapter, provide an extended example of modeling a behavioral phenomenon from this domain. The example in question will be the prevailing neuroeconomic model of addiction, which must be combined with picoeconomic insights to produce an understanding of why most people are not addicts and why most addicts eventually recover. In showing why it takes a person—and not just a brain—to overcome addiction, we will be provided with an illustration of why there is a role for the concept of the person in economic reasoning, and what sort of role this is. The final section will close with synthetic reflections on the earlier parts.

2. Philosophy and Pragmatism

Let us contrast two conceptions of economics which, I would argue, have contested for the soul of the discipline[3] throughout its history. On the first conception (1), economics is any body of theory or application of a body of theory that generalizes over maximizing, optimizing, or meliorating relationships among (i) utility functions, (ii) scarce production inputs, and (iii) reallocations of (ii) with reference to (i). This is equivalent in spirit to what Alex Rosenberg (this volume) calls a "nightmare" view of economics as consisting of any model or application of linear or dynamic programming[4]—I say "in spirit" because we clearly must add game theory to the technical set, but Rosenberg leaves it out. I think it is clear from Mirowski (2002) that he shares Rosenberg's attitude to this conception, which we might most accurately call "Debrevian." What contrasting pleasant dream might people who think Debrevian economics is a nightmare have in mind? Here is the alternative conception (2): economics is any body or application of theory that generalizes over the behavior of some specified class of people or their aggregates taking actions to optimize or improve their well being with respect to availability for use of scarce assets. This seems to be the conception embraced by Rosenberg in this volume.

I do not share Rosenberg's and Mirowski's attitude to nightmares and dreams. In my opinion, a great deal—the overwhelming majority—of misguided philosophy of economics over the years[5] has consisted precisely in criticism of approaches developed under conception 1 on grounds that they are not motivated by conception 2. By contrast, I maintain, the many useful exercises we find in economics that fit conception 2 are always best understood as special applications of models developed under conception 1.

My basis for this opinion is that part of what crucially makes an inquiry or enterprise scientific—in addition to devoted subservience to the authority of empirical measurement—is concern for *systematicity* under a formalizable framework that abstracts away from the parochial and mutually inconsistent folk ontologies inherited from human natural and cultural selection and built into the structures of natural languages. Scientific inquirers care about systematicity to the extent that they care about maximizing theoretical power for explanation and prediction. In economics, this concern is clearly manifest in the strong pressure to organize all historical data into either a linear programming model, a dynamic programming model, a game, or a complex combination of such models.

This point by no means applies only to data about people, but equally to data about institutional agents such as firms and countries. There are also interesting lessons to be learned from recent debates over how best to model putatively economic interactions among nonhuman animals. There has been a tendency to focus exclusively on game-theoretic approaches to such interactions, for reasons summarized by Bowles and Hammerstein (2003): animal markets (e.g., for mates) generally aren't anonymous and aren't set in institutional contexts with exogenous enforcement that could facilitate complete contracts. On the other hand, as Hammerstein (2003) points out, empirical data on interspecific mutualism show few cases of the sort of reciprocal altruism that abstract models based on evolutionary game theory often emphasize. The problem here is likely that reciprocity places strong demands on cognitive bookkeeping. However, production of capacities for this is rather a boutique industry for natural selection, however salient it might be to economists who happen to be members of Homo sapiens. Furthermore, as Hammerstein also emphasizes, game-theoretic models often implicitly restrict players' choices of interaction partners in ways that don't bind natural interactions. For both these reasons, nature is much stingier than game theorists in generating evolution of sophisticated strategic ploys for meta-exploitation and meta-meta-exploitation (and so on). Do economists respond to this situation by relying less on abstract models and more on natural history? Not at all. Bshary and Noë (2003), for example, show how lack of restriction on interaction-partner switching among cleaner fish and their clients on reefs promotes a preponderance of competition over non-parametric cunning. Members of species that cannot travel significant distances between reefs, and thus have reduced choice of cleaner services compared with more pelagic species, are more likely to have their scales nipped by cleaners and are made to wait in longer queues. The markets among these fish appear to be highly efficient, and they are elegantly captured by partial equilibrium models.

The point I want to make about these applications is not that anyone can know a priori that a given behavioral phenomenon among groups of animals must either yield to a game-theoretic model or to an aggregated optimization model. My point instead is that it is the discovery that one sort of model or the other applies usefully to a phenomenon that identifies the phenomenon in question as one partly governed by economics. If neither sort of model often yielded superior predictions and explanations of nonhuman interactions, then economists would (rightly) be dis-invited from the councils of ethology. Economists' domain of study is coextensive with the reach of their distinctive analytical technologies, not with an a priori conception of what constitutes an economic phenomenon. This is a sociological point, not a metaphysical one—but so, obviously, is Rosenberg's rival claim. The advantage of the first conception of economics is that it *correctly* describes the sociology. And then we can add the point that this sociology is maintained because it *works;* that is, game-theoretic models of interaction among animals with big brains yield powerful and successful generalizations, as do competitive models of mutualisms and other interactions among less cognitively well-armed organisms. Evolutionary game theory generates systematically useful models of longer-run interactions among lineages.

Defenders of conception 2 might try to reply by arguing that economic modeling of nonhuman agents is merely an extension of economic *methods* into another proper field (ethology). But for this reply to be convincing, it would have to be the case that economics provided a *superior* basis for understanding acquisitive behavior of people than of nonhuman agents. Otherwise, why would people be the base case and nonhuman animals secondary extension cases? However, it seems to me that critics such as Sen are partly right about one important claim, namely, that there aren't in fact many powerful generalizations to be had specifically about people as economic agents (qua economic agents). I say "partly" here because it turns out, as I will explain, that we *can* derive interesting ideas about the processes that *give rise to* people from applications of economics under conception 1. But with respect to the negative claim, the most directly relevant literature is that which records the history of devoted experimental efforts to determine whether people in microeconomic settings make choices according to expected utility theory, prospect theory, a host of specialized derivations from the matching law, or a grab bag of situation-specific heuristics. The best justified generalization to be drawn from this literature at present is: people are highly plastic and they make choices in all of these ways under subtly different circumstances. This is not the *kind* of conclusion that theorists who take for granted that people (whatever they're actually like) *must be* the paradigmatic economic agents want to admit. For them, it is the very point of behavioral economics to determine what properties distinguish these paradigmatic economic agents—and, *then,* by extension, all possible non-paradigmatic economic agents to at least some extent. For a leading example of this assumption at work, see the influential advanced text of Camerer (2003). We may state the assumption as follows: normal adult H. sapiens organisms, regarded as identical to people, are the basic, naturally occurring economic agents.

Elsewhere (Ross 2005, 2006a, forthcoming b), I defend an opposed view. According to this perspective, and to similar ideas discussed by Clark (1997), Rovane (1998) and Dennett (2003), people are not identical to H. sapiens organisms. The latter are products of genetic evolution. People, on the other hand, are normatively and socially regulated virtual constructs that arise out of complex dynamics operating at multiple interacting scales of observation and measurement. These scales *include* genetic-evolutionary dynamics, but also cultural-evolutionary dynamics, and information-processing dynamics at micro timescales both within the complex H. sapiens brain and at the scale where social signaling arises. There are powerful, systematic generalizations to be derived from models at each of these scales, some of which can be synthesized using the technologies of economics, namely, linear and dynamic programming and game theory (classical and evolutionary). Economics contributes to our understanding of people by designing, applying and testing such models. From a very abstract philosophical perspective, we can summarize what the synthesis shows us as follows: People are stabilization devices in social-evolutionary dynamics and, simultaneously, in picoeconomic and neuro-economic dynamics, who are recursively produced as outputs of games.

I cannot try to recapitulate the full argument for or explication of this claim, provided in the work of mine cited at the beginning of the previous paragraph. The next section will summarize its implications. For a critic who finds it novel to the point of unacceptable rashness, let me note that it has precedents of respectable vintage. It is, I suggest, substantially anticipated in the following remark by the early Darwinian psychologist James Mark Baldwin (1913): "The society into which the child is born is...not...merely a loose aggregate, made up of a number of biological individuals. It is rather a body of mental products, an established network of psychical relationships. By this the new person is moulded and shaped...He enters into this network as a new cell in the social tissue...He does not enter it as an individual; on the contrary, he is only an individual when he comes out of it...In the personal self the social is individualized." It surely did not cross Baldwin's mind that economic modeling tools might help to make this claim more rigorous; before dynamic game theory, these tools indeed couldn't do so, and under the strongly individualist spin attached to them by neoclassical spokesmen, such as Jevons and Robbins, they, in fact, encouraged its denial.

A principal conclusion of both Davis (2003) and Ross (2005) is that individualism *was* spin, not something that ever did serious work in the literal foundations of neoclassical theory. The very thin concept of agency in mainstream economics, from Jevons and Walras through the present, identifies agents with the gravitational centers of consistent preference fields. The theory incorporates no thesis about which empirical entities in particular implement such roles. Nor does it entail anything about how long their embodiment typically persists. Agents may be as transient as a modeler likes; so although agents may not change their preferences while remaining the same agents, people may do so and can simply be modeled as successions of agents. (This requires no denial that these successive agents have some special relationships to one another, including—possibly—economic relationships.) Davis, assuming that people *should be* the paradigmatic economic agents, puts the points I have just made to work in mounting a complaint against mainstream (neoclassical) economic theory. We can all agree with this up to a point: we would have grounds for disquiet if economic theory turned out to have no useful applications to human behavior. However, as Ross (2005) argues, it is a non sequitur to jump to such disquiet from the weaker claim (endorsed in Ross 2005) that insects are better exemplars of basic economic agency than people—while people approximate such agency from time to time in something like the way that countries do, shakily and imperfectly—or from the claim that economic theory attributes no distinctive properties to people. The main point for now is that the relationship between individual humans and economic agents remains open so far as the modeling technology is concerned.

I have been referring to mainstream economic theory. In Ross (2005), I follow most commentators in identifying this with neoclassical theory. This terminology is distracting to the extent that it encourages us to focus narrowly on a specific moment in the history of economics (from, typically, the first marginalists up to Hicks's and Samuelson's conversion to Keynesianism). In an effort to give substantive distinctions pride of place over primarily historical ones, I will here appeal instead to a comparative matrix offered by Leijonhufvud (2004). He distinguishes what he calls "classical" and "modern" economics as depicted in Table 9.1.

The idea behind this sorting is best illustrated just as Leijonhufvud does it, by reference to historical figures who instantiate each type. His examples of "classicals" are Ricardo, Marx, Marshall, and Keynes. It is clear, I suggest, that to this we could add

Table 9.1 Leijonhufvud's two eras of economics

	Classical	Modern
Objective of theory	Laws of motion of the system	Principles of efficient allocation
Individual motivation	Maximize utility or profit (intent)	Maximize utility or profit (performance)
Individual behavior	Adaptive Procedural rationality (often gradient climbing)	Optimizing choice Substantive rationality
Behavior and time	Backward-looking, causal	Forward-looking, teleological
Cognitive competence	Capable of learning Well-adapted locally	Unbounded
Role of institutions	Essential in guiding behavior, making behavior of others predictable	Problematic: Why use money? Why do firms exist?
Equilibrium concept	Constancy (point attractor)	Mutual consistency of plans

Hayek, Schumpeter, most contemporary behavioral and institutional economists, and Sen. The examples of "moderns" are Arrow and Debreu, Lucas, Sargent, and Prescott.

Hicks and Samuelson are cited by Leijonhufvud as "moving back and forth between the two [kinds of economics] as the problems they dealt with would dictate." Should we read this as meaning that Hicks and Samuelson were opportunists or merely transition figures? Let us take this not as a question about Hicks and Samuelson per se but about our way of organizing conceptions of economics. Leijonhufvud's matrix is not intended as an intervention in the history of thought but as an exercise in pedagogy for graduate economics students who don't know much history *or* methodology, and it is frankly driven by practicality and hindsight. Its interest to me in the present context derives from the fact that *all* the standard neoclassicals, except Marshall, are missing from the list of exemplars. Were nearly all the neoclassicals, then, "proto-opportunists," or was all of neoclassicism a transitional phase between classical and modern economics? This is a false dilemma, since both horns make valid points. Almost all economists in every generation, except those who work mainly to promote philosophical positions (for example, Hayek after the 1930s) have been and are opportunists in the sense attributed to Hicks and Samuelson. There are nearly forty economists on faculty in my department at the University of Cape Town. Exactly one consistently fits the profile of a modern in all of his work; but there is no one who never makes use of modern instruments or techniques. So these colleagues of mine join the early neoclassicals in not having clear columns on Leijonhufvud's matrix. In addition, the early neoclassicals don't fit because, indeed, they were transitional figures. But they were not transitional in the sense that classical assumptions were perishing in their era; in fact,the assumptions have not perished to this day. The neoclassicals were merely transitional in the sense that they anticipated important aspects of contemporary economics but didn't have the analytical tools to be fully modern.

An idea underlying the foregoing discussion is that philosophers and historians of thought, in trying to identify relationships among theoretical assumptions and preferences in economists, readily encourage themselves and their audiences to think of economists as more like philosophers—consistent developers and promoters of intellectual doctrine—then they really are. Economics, like all healthy sciences, is first and foremost a box of tools. There is no need to throw older tools away as newer ones are added to the kit. Excellence in economics consists mainly of well-trained and disciplined judgment in seeing how to fit tools to problems in ways that will generate explanatory insight.

In this spirit, I will in the remainder of this chapter drop all talk of methodological "isms" (though some philosophical isms not specific to economics will be featured here and there). The aim is simply to use items from the economist's toolbox to shed some light on the nature of people, in a manner different from that pursued by those who think that people manifest, in general, one or another distinctive kind of rationality, and who then quarrel among themselves over which kind of rationality this is.

3. People as Products of Cultural Macrodynamics

I said earlier that neighboring sciences will not tell economists how to model people as economic agents. However, it is to other disciplines—psychology, sociology, anthropology, evolutionary ethology and neuroscience—that we must turn to find out what people are in the first place. In Ross (2005) I argue that a crucial insight from the social, cognitive, and behavioral sciences is that a person is not identical to a biological organism with the DNA characteristic of H. sapiens. In particular, as Baldwin stresses in the quotation from him in Section 2, such organisms (or most of them) develop into people through processes of socialization and enculturation. The basis of a person's distinctiveness and coherence is *narrative:* a person is, fundamentally, an entity that can narrate a history of its dispositions, actions, tastes and motivations that other people will reliably interpret and respond to as a *biography.* (For similar ideas see Bruner 1992 and Hutto 2007). A biography is (roughly) a teleologically structured history of an entity whose behavior and manifest emotional expressions can be nonredundantly predicted and explained using *the intentional stance* (Dennett 1987), that is, the perspective that organizes behavioral data against a backdrop of attributed beliefs, desires, and similar representational states,[6] the so-called propositional attitudes. Psychologists study the process by which unenculturated individuals of the human species turn themselves into people under the rubric of "the social construction of the self." Therefore, I use the concepts of *person* and *self* interchangeably. In my terminology, then, *biological individual = pre-enculturated human ≠ self = person.* The former pair are theoretical constructs made for purposes of modeling, rather than kinds of entities we find running around, because human babies begin to be drawn into cultural personhood from the moment they can respond interactively to their parents.

Economic concepts and models can contribute to our understanding of both why and how humans are motivated to narrate selves and to pressure others to do so. As with any social species, humans are disposed by nature to seek gains from trade, including trade in labor and capital contributions to projects that require joint investment in order to be feasible. Achieving (relatively) efficient coordination equilibria in such games often requires strategic commitment by one or more parties, and stakes in reputations are the most basic commitment devices available among nonkin in typical ecological circumstances. In this context, narrative selves fuse two functions: (a) they provide structure that allows specific reputations to be encoded and remembered using pneumonic devices (standard story plots) biologically natural to humans; and (b) the coherence requirements that govern them embody strategic commitments—agents know that if they renarrate themselves too freely in order to allow more strategic flexibility, they risk being regarded as unpredictable (in everyday English, labeled *flighty* or *two-faced*) and to be excluded from potentially profitable relationships and projects. Supplementing these considerations is the fact that most games that are not strictly competitive have multiple equilibria. Relatively fine constraints on stability of selves (e.g., "She's the sort of person who puts more value in an exciting new experience than in security") facilitate joint equilibrium selection. To put it another way: Selves are sources of focal points in coordination games.

I noted in the previous section that the concept of agency incorporated into the formalism of mainstream economic theory encourages us to map agents onto transient stages of personal lives rather than onto whole personal biographies. Far from being the basis for an *objection* to mainstream theory (as in Davis 2003), this fact provides a natural way of factoring two (typical) standing empirical conditions in social life into economic models. The conditions in question are: (i) normal ecological cues for humans underdetermine which strategic moves in which games with which players are represented by any given human action; and (ii) people are expected by others (and hence by themselves) to dynamically revise their narratives, though within limits that leave them on equilibrium paths (point b in the previous paragraph), as they move through their life cycles. The fact that we are *not* forced to treat whole personal biographies as careers of single economic agents encourages us to make narrative revision endogenous, opening space for a new game-theoretic modeling domain I call game determination. I will very briefly explain this; readers who are puzzled by the concise account should consult Ross (2006a).

In consequence of fact (i) from the preceding paragraph, people engage in metagames over which games to play. These would be intractable in the framework of noncooperative game theory were it not for the constraints on narrative flexibility emphasized by fact (ii); bargaining among agents who have valuable reputations for being the sorts of people who keep their word allows noncooperative players to make binding promises in metagames that, thereby, simulate cooperative first stages relative to the games they determine—that is, that they generate as equilibrium outcomes. Game determination models the process by which narratives are revised as follows: Players of metagames bargain not just over immanent games in which they themselves, with their present utility functions, will be involved, but also with respect to expectations about the ranges of possible future agents, with new utility functions, who will face the consequences of present games. Present agents, that is, act with the likely circumstances of their descendent agents in consideration. Of course, sequences of agents that map onto the same person have many important properties in common (including a great deal of shared preference structure). These properties are no doubt crucial for grounding partiality of agents toward future stages of the person they share. However, we should bear in mind that many people are, in fact, deeply neglectful of their future personal utility. In addition, *most* people are also relatively ignorant about the utility functions of the future agents they will be, which is manifest in the fact that the matching law, which predicts standing tendencies for intertemporal preference reversals, more accurately describes human behavior than do models based on expected utility maximization by a single persisting agent (Herrnstein 1997; Ainslie 2001). The main factor that compensates for neglect and ignorance of the future in preserving the biographical unity we observe in people is the fact that their later stages inherit narrative constraints established by earlier stages, as a result of social expectations. (Institutions strongly reinforce this basic incentive; future agents associated with my body and social reputation will spend the money I earn and enjoy the security of the tenure I obtained. This gives me a special reason to be *interested* in these agents, and people tend, all else being equal, to favor the welfare of agents that interest them.) This explains my preference for making agent renarration endogenous in game-theoretic models of interaction, rather than for applying game-theoretic models only after psychological ones have been used to describe agent formation and stabilization.

Individual determining games are modeled using classical game theory, but these static games should be understood as abstractions from (or snapshots of) continuing evolutionary games among lineages of agents. In fully testing the applicability of a given game determination model, one would check to ensure that all equilibria of particular games corresponded to points in basins of attraction in plausible underlying evolutionary dynamics (see Cressman 2003 for techniques). The most important parameter in a determining game that must be chosen on the basis of empirical evidence (as opposed to modeling convenience or rigor, etc.) is the solution concept to be applied. The more foresight and concern for descendent agents is displayed by players of determining games, the stronger the restriction we can motivate on the relationship between a determining game and the games it determines. In the limit, where agents have perfect foresight and are perfectly altruistic with respect to their descendents, determining games will simply be stages in chains of extensive form games to be solved by finding sub-game-perfect equilibria. Institutional devices that strongly reward and reinforce time-consistent preferences, such as modern financial institutions, may push agents toward this limit. The economics appropriate to analyzing markets involving such agents will be Leijonhufvud's modern variant. Where players of determining games are altruistic about their descendents but information is incomplete, the appropriate solution concept might be sequential equilibrium (Kreps & Wilson 1982). At the other extreme, where players of determining games have little interest in and/or foresight about their descendents, outcomes of two-stage games, with determining games as first stages, might not even induce Nash equilibria in the determining stages. At this limit, construction of classical game-theoretic abstractions from the underlying evolutionary games would be pointless, and the economics we would usefully apply would be, in Leijonhufvud's terms, more classical in spirit than modern. It is doubtful that any actual people play determining games at either limit.[7] Where, between the limits, the games of a given actual set of people in a given circumstance fall must be discovered empirically by seeing which solution concepts yield outcomes that predict observations.

It might be regarded as an objection to the proposed modeling framework that it leaves so much open. However, I take it as simply a fact about people that their degree of intertemporal preference consistency is variable and highly sensitive to institutional and cultural contexts. This is a (massive) complication that any way of modeling them as economic agents must accommodate. I have discussed the implications of this variation in human economic behavior as a result of "top-down" influences in some detail elsewhere (Ross 2005, 2006a). In the present chapter, I will, therefore, leave this topic and concentrate instead on the source of variation from below. Not only are people not unified economic agents over time, they also only approximate unified agency *at* a time, in essentially the way that a country does. We can often usefully identify what a country wants (to reduce poverty, to win a war, etc.), but we recognize that such desires are complex functions of the interacting goals and beliefs of its citizens. Similarly, when we represent a person as an agent with consistent preferences, we perform an abstraction, suppressing attention to the fact that molar[8] behavioral dispositions are products of competitive and coalitional dynamics among subpersonal interests at the molecular scale (Schelling 1978, 1980, 1984; Ainslie 1992, 2001). In previous work on this theme (Ross 2005, 2006b), I claimed that this fact has its origins in the information-processing

complexity of the brain, arguing that, were all valuation performed at a single bot-
tleneck point, people would resemble mini Soviet Unions that would fail for the
same reason the big one did. However, I provided no evidence for or elaboration
of this claim based on neuroscience. In Section 5 of the chapter I aim to repair this
deficit by means of an extended example of the conflict among brain regions for
control of behavior that, in an unfortunate subset of people, leads to addiction. To
set this up, however, I must first provide background on the best developed general
approaches to modeling subpersonal economic processes.

4. People as Products of Neuroeconomic and Picoeconomic Dynamics

A well-known informal account of human molar behavior as a product of interaction among subpersonal agents is attributable to Ainslie (1992, 2001). Ainslie's
theory, which he calls picoeconomics, explains a range of common behavioral phenomena, including, among others, procrastination and neurosis. The theory's most
direct application is to difficulties people experience with impulse control, which it
explains by appeal to the equilibria of games played among hypothesized subpersonal
interests. The identities of such interests are directly inferred from commonsense
personal goals; thus someone might now be experiencing conflict between an interest in cleaning the sink and an interest in watching the rugby test. Picoeconomics
is not integrated with the more recent neuroeconomics that uses economic theory
to model the activity of functionally specialized groups of neurons (Montague and
Berns 2002; Glimcher 2003). It is, thus, an open question as to what relationship
picoeconomic interests might have to functional parts of the brain.

The virtual nature of Ainslie's interests leads many people's intuitions, in my
experience, to judge interests as not plausibly real forces or processes, but as, at best,
fictions constructed for modeling purposes. People with these intuitions generally
take a different view of the reality of interests if they are thought instead to be based
on independently discriminable brain regions. This reflects the intuitive reductionism of most scientists. However, in Ross (2006b) and Ross et al. (2008) I and
co-authors argue that such reduction of picoeconomics to neuroeconomics is not
in the cards. Ainslie (2005) agrees. Picoeconomic interests only do the explanatory
work required of them in Ainslie's model to the extent that they can be fleeting, persisting only for as long as the behavior they motivate. For example, as I write, I have
an interest in watching a baseball game, which has to this point been unsuccessful
in competition with a rival interest in making progress on this chapter. The first
interest will not outlast the baseball game, and the second interest will hopefully
have nothing further to do in a few days. Of course, I have a number of less fleeting,
related interests, such as in preserving a reputation for meeting deadlines; but this

is precisely *not* subject to overthrow by baseball games in the way that the interest in working *right now* is. Another of Ainslie's favorite examples is of an annoying interest in scratching an itch, which will fade entirely if even briefly ignored; unless the itch is caused by a foreign irritant, the interest in scratching *is* the itch. These examples should make clear that picoeconomic interests aren't subpersonal in the same sense as groups of neurons with specialist functions. The former are subpersonal in the sense that they have sharply limited projects that may not be endorsed by the whole person, but they are associated with *molar* phenomena—behavior of a whole ecologically embedded agent at a time. The agents of neuroeconomics, by contrast, are subpersonal in the sense of being molecular components of organisms. People who think picoeconomics is valuable science must defend it not be plumping for reductive vindication of the reality of subpersonal interests, but by resisting the widespread intuition that virtual entities are necessarily not fully real—a task for which good philosophical assistance is available (e.g., Dennett 1991).

What follows from this is not that neuroeconomics isn't important to the economics of the subpersonal, but that the relationship among neuroeconomics, picoeconomics, and microeconomics will be more complicated than a chain of intertheoretic reductions that model a parallel chain of ontological reductions. I will say more about the positive relationship between neuroeconomics and picoeconomics later in the chapter. First, however, some illustration is required of the complexities around reduction and other aspects of interpretation that arise *within* neuroeconomics.

Neuroeconomics is the application of economic theory to modeling the processes by which the brain allocates scarce resources of attention, evaluation, and motor-response preparation to competing stimuli. As a modeling approach, it is a statistical complement to the computational frameworks more familiar to cognitive scientists. If neuroeconomics were to have a bumper sticker, its best message might be the following quotation from Greg Berns (2003, 156): "The interaction of different pools of neurons in the brain may result in phenotypic behavior that appears to be irrational, but it is possible that the rational agents are the neurons, not the person." This should remind us of the earlier analogy between people and countries. We all know that countries often behave irrationally—erecting self-harming barriers to imports, for example—because of the interactions of rational citizens acting in pursuit of their parochial interests. I will illustrate expression of this same pattern in the case of the relationship between people and their neurons by focusing on some properties of the part of the brain that implements valuation and attentional allocation, the dopaminergic reward system, and its relations with other brain systems and with molar behavior. The reader is asked to bear with some rehearsal of modeling minutae here, for, as always in issues of conceptual foundations, the key motivating principles emerge from the details.

Neuroscientists individuate systems in the brain by identifying generic functional responses with relatively encapsulated neurotransmitter pathways. The reward system is distinguished as a pathway that transmits signals using the neurotransmitter dopamine. Activity in midbrain areas that people share with other vertebrates, the ventral tegmental area (VTA) and pars compacta of substantia nigra (SNpc), release dopamine in response to *surprising* magnitudes of *learned* contingencies. These signals project most directly to the ventral striatum (VS) and especially to the nucleus accumbens (NAcc). For reasons to be explained later, persistently high concentrations of dopamine in NAcc are a basic neural signature of addiction. The reward system's dopamine signal also projects to pre-frontal cortex (PFC), where it appears to produce, at least in nonaddicts, a serotonin signal that acts as an opponent process. I will have more to say about this opposition later.

Functional magnetic resonance imaging (fMRI) evidence (McClure, Daw & Montague 2003) strongly suggests that the reward system implements *temporal difference* (TD) *learning* (Sutton and Barto 1998). This denotes a family of functions that relate a situation at a particular time s_t to a time-discounted sum of expected rewards (idealized as numeric measures r of received utility) that can be earned into the future. Suppose, following McClure, Daw and Montague (2003), that t, $t+1$, $t+2$, etc. represent times on some arbitrary measurement scale. Then the TD equation is

$$V^*(s_t) = E[r_t + \gamma r_{t+1} + \gamma^2 r_{t+2} + \gamma^3 r_{t+3} + ...]$$

which we close by writing

$$V^*(s_t) = E[r_t + \gamma V^*(s_{t+1})]$$

This describes the procedure by which the reward-system learning algorithm continuously inputs new information to keep refining its estimate of V^* to get a particular stream of actual temporal valuations V. From this we can define a measure δ of the extent to which the value estimates of two successive states and a reward experienced by the system are consistent with one another:

$$\delta(t) = r_t + \gamma V(s_{t+1}) - V(s_t),$$

where δ is an error signal that pushes $V(s)$ toward better estimates as it gets more data. If $V(s_{t+1})$ turns out to be better than expected, then $\delta(t)$ will be positive, thus indicating that $V(s_t)$ needs to be adjusted upward. If $V(s_{t+1})$ turns out to be worse than expected, $\delta(t)$ will be negative and $V(s_t)$ will be adjusted downward. If $\delta(t) = 0$, then, of course, no learning occurs.

That the dopamine system implements TD learning is not presently controversial. However, there are different views among researchers as to the wider role of this learning. The reward system appears to integrate all the following functions: (i) learning environmental cues that predict reward, (ii) learning comparative values of rewards, (iii) focusing attention on cues that predict rewards, and (iv) motivating the system to act on the basis of these cues (thanks to projection from the dopamine system to motor neurons). However, it is not necessarily the case that TD learning is the source of the integration. In its basic form—and the form as just presented—TD learning does not predict a discovery due to Gallistel (1990), that conditioning outcomes in animal learning are timescale invariant. This means that responses from a given animal will be the same in two otherwise identical learning conditions if the interval durations between cues and rewards in one condition are a constant multiple of the durations of the other. In general, TD learning has generally been framed as a model of classical association conditioning, after Rescorla and Wagner (1972). By contrast with association models, Scalar Expectancy Theory (SET) (Gibbon 1977) and Rate Estimation Theory (RET) (Gallistel 1990), as unified in Gallistel and Gibbon (2000), are *timing* models of conditioning phenomena. According to such models, animals represent the durations of intervals and the rates of relevant events, and conditioned responding occurs as a function of the comparison of rates of reinforcement. Animals are drawn to environments with higher such rates by gradient climbing, rather than forming explicit associations between stimuli and conditioned responses. For ease of reference, I will call the unification of SET and RET "G-learning."

G-learning has attractive properties from the point of view of prospective unification of molecular accounts of learning with picoeconomics. In a recent reply to a panel of critics, Ainslie (2005, 667) welcomes Sanabria and Killeen's (2005) recognition that picoeconomics suggests "the opportunity to revise 'the hoary study of CRs [conditioned responses].'" He continues by affirming that "I judge such a revision to be among [my theory's] most important implications... [F]or the selection of responses, the potential of brief temporary preferences to lure organisms into responses that are aversive overall, could let us do without the *deux ex machina* of a second, 'conditioned' selective principle that is so often invoked to explain aversive, involuntary or maladaptive processes... The model of aversion as a rapidly cycling addiction comprising reward and inhibition of reward lets us add conditioned processes to the marketplace of rewarded processes." Sanabria and Killeen's (2005) specific remark that prompts this response of Ainslie's is: "A key property of signals of reinforcement is that they become both conditioned reinforcers, or CRs, and conditioned stimuli, eliciting approach... Is this the behavioral substrate of desire, of appetite? If so, then Ainslie's hyperbolic interests, Skinner's CRs, and Pavlov's CSs are the same entity. A theory of one is a theory of all" (661).

In this perspective, G-learning, to the extent that it applies directly to the reward system, would suggest a natural way of unifying the molar and the molecular accounts of entrapment by addictive targets. Ainslie's "rapidly cycling addictions" would simply be conceptualized as high-reward-rate environments that lure organisms' attention and approach, unless the dopamine system is opposed—as it appears to be, successfully in nonaddicts, by seratonergic and (probably) GABAnergic signals from PFC.[9] Gallistel likewise argues that classical and operant conditioning amount to the same thing. In addiction studies, there has been a long-running and unresolved debate over the relationship between supposedly classically conditioned cravings and apparently instrumentally conditioned preparations for consumption of addictive targets. Perhaps the debate has been inconclusive because these are one and the same process. But if G-learning is sufficient to provide neurocomputational foundations for Ainslie's molar account, then what is the role in choice, if any, of TD learning in the dopamine system?

A recent computational model of the reward system by Daw (2003) makes the two kinds of learning complementary. In this model, G-learning is taken to precede, and indeed to enable, TD learning. Suppose an animal has learned a function that predicts a reward at t, where the function in question decomposes into models of two stages: one applying to the interval between the conditioned and the unconditioned stimulus, and one applying to the interval between the unconditioned stimulus and the next conditioned stimulus. Then imagine that a case occurs in which at t nothing happens. Should the animal infer that its model of the world needs revision, perhaps to a one-stage model, or should it retain the model and regard the omission as noise or error? In Daw's account the animal uses G-learning to select a world-model: whichever such model matches behavior that yields the higher reward rate will be preferred to alternatives. Given this model as a constraint, TD learning can then predict the temporal placement of rewards ('when'-learning). This hybrid approach allows Daw to drop two unbiological features of the original Montague, Dayan and Sejnowski (1996) model of TD learning by the dopamine system: tapped-line delay timing and exogenously fixed trial boundaries (as can be justified only in the sparse and controlled setup of the laboratory). This is surely progress, as it is doubtful that anyone ever took these two properties for anything other than modeling conveniences. But at this point it can no longer be said to be clear what, if anything, is the canonical model of the role of TD learning in the dopamine system.

Fortunately for present purposes, at a slightly higher level of abstraction, this uncertainty about molecular mechanisms becomes less important. As noted earlier, there is increasing consensus that the reward system integrates reward prediction, valuation, salience, and approach, whether it does so by bolting together two learning algorithms, as in Daw's model, or by implementing a single more complex one, as in the Predictor-Valuation (PV) model of Montague and Berns (2002). Given the possibilities left open by present empirical knowledge, we can treat the latter either as a direct molecular account of one learning process, or as an account one level up in the molar direction of a function implemented by G-learning and TD learning together. The PV model is characterized as follows: Suppose $R(x,n)$ estimates the value of a reward distributed at various possible times $x, y, z, \ldots, n$ in the future, scaled according to the uncertainty attending to the intervals between the estimation point and each time, as in

$$R(x,n; D) = \int_{-\infty}^{+\infty} dy\, G(x-y, (x-n)D)r(y)$$

where $G(z,b) = (2\pi b)^{-1/2} \exp\{-z^2/2b\}$ and D is a constant. Then the value $F(n)$ that the brain attaches to getting a particular predictor signal at perceptual time n is given by:

$$F(n) = \int_n^{+\infty} dx\, e^{-q(x-n)} \int_{-\infty}^{+\infty} dy\, G(x-y,(x-n)D)\rho(y) = \int_n^{+\infty} dx\, \{e^{-q(x-n)}\}$$
$$\times\, \{R(x,n; D) = \int_n^{+\infty} dx\, \{\text{discount future time } x \text{ relative to perceptual time } n\} \times$$
$$\{\text{diffused version of reward estimate } \rho(x) \text{ for some } x \text{ and } n\}$$

Interestingly, as Montague and Berns point out, this functional form corresponds to the Black-Scholes model of portfolio option pricing. This helps to make vivid the *economic* character of the processes as modeled by neuroeconomics. PV is essentially a model of the reward system's estimate of the expected opportunity costs of attending to one stimulus rather than another and of preparing one motor response rather than another. (It seems that, in light of the brain's architecture, these opportunity costs can't be factored out separately.) Where there is an opportunity cost, there must be an underlying utility function. This, in turn, invites us to ask which natural entity we should associate as an agent with this utility function. Three possibilities might occur from a naïve perspective: that the utility function should be assigned to (i) the reward system, (ii) the brain as a whole, or (iii) the person.

It seems implausible that this question might reasonably be settled on any *general* ontological grounds of the sort that might be recommended by a metaphysical argument. The question asks for a pragmatic decision, though not one independent of the scientific facts. Different decisions will facilitate varying ways of modeling the relevant empirical phenomena. Deciding, for example, that it isn't helpful to model the reward system as an agent would be equivalent to concluding that it is a neurochemical system rather than a neuroeconomic one. This wouldn't amount to rejection of PV; it would be compatible with treating PV as a molar-scale description (from one of two scales—molar neuroscience if the whole brain is assigned a utility function, or behavioral if one assigns opportunity costs at no finer a scale than that of the person).

If we expected each of the three possible options under consideration[10] to be equally empirically adequate to the full range of phenomena up for prediction and explanation, then we would rightly regard the decision among them as having no objective basis; in making it, we would be in the domain of *pure* pragmatics. This situation is of course logically possible, but if it turned out to be actual this would be an astonishing coincidence. More seriously, if we don't think there is any hope for achieving an *integrated* scientific picture of the world—if, that is, we agree with Dupré (1992) and Cartwright (1999) that the best we can get from science is a disordered plurality of models of phenomena that can neither be unified nor pared down to a mutually consistent set on the basis of unambiguous criteria of preference—then the decision again leaves us in the domain of pure pragmatics. On Cartwright's picture, for example, we might write down both a neurochemical model and a neuroeconomic model of the reward system, and if each yielded nonredundant predictions good enough for some purposes, then *we would have no reason to ask* whether we should try to explain one in terms of the other (or, perhaps, both in terms of some third account). The reason we would have no reason is that, according to Cartwright, belief that there *is* a unified reality underlying the undisputed cacophony of models we find in science (Cartwright being right, in general, about the existence of such cacophonies) is "fundamentalism," and fundamentalism is just a metaphysical hankering.

However, on inductive grounds, I venture the following prediction about the future of neuroscience. Attempts will be (vigorously) pursued to provide a neurochemical explanation of the phenomena described by the PV model. If such attempts are *completely* successful, in the sense that a purely neurochemical model eventually explains everything the neuroeconomic model does (and, presumably, more besides), then we shall conclude that we've experienced an episode of intertheoretic (Nagelian) reduction and that attributing a utility function—that is to say, economic agency—to the reward system has been (as Dennett would put it) *discharged*. Alternatively, it may turn out that neurochemical facts constrain (in enlightening ways) the way PV is implemented in the reward system, but other aspects of PV can only be explained by reference to functional properties of neural learning more generally and perhaps by reference to ecological generalizations about the reward environments in which brains evolved and develop. In that case, the neuroeconomic model of the reward system will remain an irreducible part of our best scientific account of the world. And in *that* case there is no reason to hedge saying that the reward system has a utility function—is an agent—by using scare quotes or finger wiggles. The basic commitment of the naturalist, after all, is that the best scientific account of the world is the best account of the world, period. If that account assigns a utility function to the reward system, then it is true—in the one and only plain old sense of *true* that there is—that the reward system is an agent.

What seems to me very unlikely indeed is an outcome in which we get a decent neurochemical account of the reward system and a decent neuroeconomic account (i.e., answer presently open questions, such as whether PV describes integration of TD learning and G-learning, whether we need separate accounts of trace conditioning and delay conditioning within the PV or G-learning frameworks, etc.), and then nobody is interested in trying to tie them together. This expectation of mine, which I take to be well supported by induction on the general history of science, is why I think there is still some use for philosophy of science and why I think that Cartwright, despite her repeated powerful insights into the way science is carried out and models are put to use, is wrong about the importance of unification.

While we wait to find out what happens in the complex integration of neurochemistry and neuroeconomics, we can and should ask about the extent to which we get present explanatory payoffs from modeling the reward system as an agent. I contend that we do. In particular, I contend that the neuroeconomic account of reward prediction and valuation, when combined with behavioral insights due to picoeconomics, supports an elegant account of a widespread and important phenomenon, addiction, which has often been regarded as a leading counterexample to the rational agency model of economists as applied directly to people.

5. Case Study: A Neuroeconomic Account of Addiction

In trying to illuminate the highly abstract relationships among people, subpersonal interests, and functional brain systems—the first two of which are highly abstract entities to begin with—we do well to focus on a measurable behavioral phenomenon as an exemplar. In the context of modeling these concepts using economic agency theory, an ideal phenomenon is addiction. The reason it is ideal is that it directly challenges the core property required of an economic agent, namely, consistency in consumption preference. Famously, addicts simultaneously work to consume their targets of addiction and struggle to stop consuming them. They abstain and are proud, then relapse and express bitter resentment of themselves. Since an economic agent must be consistent, it is tempting to pronounce that the addicted person is *not* a proper agent. Perhaps, like a country, she is a squabbling *community* of subpersonal agents. Or perhaps the functional parts of her brain are at cross-purposes. Or perhaps these two suggestions amount to the same thing; perhaps conflicting subpersonal agents *are* different functional brain systems. Both the earliest (Schelling 1978, 1980, 1984) and the most elaborate (Ainslie 1992) models of people as products of economic bargaining among subinterests have been directly inspired by reflections on addiction. It is now empirically clear that, considered as a brain pathology, addiction is basically the consequence of over-dominance of the person by the midbrain reward system—the very system that, as modeled using economic theory, is the primary study target of neuroeconomics.

Let us begin by distinguishing two general ways in which one might conceptualize addiction. The first is behavioral: regard addiction as a pattern of compulsive or monomaniacal consumption of a particular class of reinforcers, in which the addict regrets the pattern but must pay large—in some cases unmanageable—costs to change it. The second is neuroscientific: regard addiction as a diagnosis of some or other distinctive neural properties of a person, where these are specifically linked to repeated exposure to some particular stream of environmental contingencies. In advance of empirical investigation, the neural properties in question could be neurotransmitter levels, neurotansmitter receptor distributions, neuro-connectivity patterns, abstractly characterized neural learning dispositions, or a combination of all these.

Why does it matter which of these approaches we use? The answer is that we want to know whether there are (i) general kinds of *causes* of addictions, which policies could try to interfere with, and (ii) general properties shared by all addicted people that interventions could try to change. (Note that scientific and clinical motivations here run in tandem.) Contrast these hopes for generalization with the skeptical possibility that addiction might just be a loose "folk" way of talking about people who are socially awkward because they do too much of one thing—drink, gamble, shop, eat—to be thought interesting or normal by others. There might be nothing more specific that all people called addicts have in common. In that case, we'd say that addiction was a social and cultural phenomenon rather than a psychological one.

It is often supposed that if addiction is a behavioral syndrome, it is reasonable to expect a wide variety of stimuli to be potentially addictive; whereas if it's a neurophysiological syndrome, only *substances* with particular chemical properties should be truly potentially addictive, with skepticism as just described applying to frequently labeled pop addictions (gambling, sex, shopping, etc.). However, the neuroeconomic model to be discussed below suggests that addiction is a general neurophysiological syndrome *and* that people become addicted to contingencies other than substances. Indeed, it suggests that substance addictions are special, complicated variations on the *basic* addictive syndrome that is best exemplified by pathological gambling. At the same time, it does not predict that all the pop targets of addiction—for example, sex—are genuinely addictive. (On the other hand, sweet and fatty foods probably are.) In my view this accords better with clinical experience than either of the simpler and more traditional perspectives.

Let us approach the neuroeconomic model by first refining the behavioral conception of addiction as a behavioral economist would, by reference to pathology of preference consistency. That is, let us stipulate that an addict is someone who consistently reverses their revealed preferences over their addictive target by spending nontrivial resources to try to "stay clean," and then *also* spending non-trivial resources on the target of addiction. The behavioral economics literature features two main mechanisms that might account for such a behavioral pattern: (i) people's intertemporal preferences are described by hyperbolic functions that become flatter with respect to rewards farther way in time from their reference points (Herrnstein 1981; Ainslie 1992, 2001), leading to preference reversals as rewards get closer to these reference points; (ii) people underestimate the cost of physiological withdrawal from addictions (Loewenstein 1999), leading them to spend more on addictive targets, and less on substitutes, than they intended. There is a great deal of direct evidence that both these conditions are generally true of people. Each of these facts raises a puzzle. The puzzle from (i) is: why don't *most* people display the addictive pattern with respect to their favorite consumption items? The puzzle from (ii) is: people who *do* manage to withdraw from addiction should be less likely to become re-addicted than people never addicted should be likely to become addicted. But the opposite is true: relapse, not difficulty in breaking through physiological withdrawal, is by far the greater problem in treatment of drug and gambling addictions.

Ainslie (1992, 2001) partly answers the first puzzle by appeal to "personal rules," devices by which people create assets they can lose immediately that are bundled with future rewards. A personal rule is a disposition of a person to predict her own future behavior on the basis of present ability to regulate impulsive choice by explicit scheduling principles. A successful personal rule prevents preference reversal, despite hyperbolic discounting, because a lapse in observing the rule carries a cost in *present* recognition that accumulated investment in the rule has been squandered *now*, where it might compete successfully with the impulsive stimulus, rather than only in the future where cost is steeply discounted. For example, when the person trying to quit smoking considers having an extra cigarette beyond what is allowed by her rationing rule, the cost directly relevant to her behavior isn't future health damage but the disappointment that a present asset, a rule predicting eventual success in quitting, will be destroyed now.

Many people find that this account of Ainslie's accords well with both heterophenomenology (Dennett 1991b) and clinical experience. However, the basic question underlying puzzle (i) isn't really addressed by it. Now we want to know why some people (addicts) are so much worse than most at finding and maintaining personal rules. The neuroeconomic model, I will argue, explains this picoeconomic regularity, and dissolves puzzle (ii) at the same time.

PV describes the reward system (at one or another of the two scales canvassed earlier) as essentially a consumer of *micro-scale novelty*—that is, of favorable contrasts in stimulus timing and magnitude relative to baselines established by regularities in experience. A useful image here is of a kitten pulled along by a string being dangled and jerked in front of its eyes (useful also for the point that the kitten would lose interest much more rapidly if the string jerked too metronomically—perhaps, in evolutionary terms, because this is indicative of the stimulus not being alive). Given the reward system's integration of so many basic inputs to behavior—attention, salience persistence, valuation, and motor priming—one is naturally led to raise a variant of puzzle (i) again at this scale of analysis: Why aren't most whole people driven by their dopamine responses to be myopic novelty seekers?

The answer, hinted at earlier, is that opponent systems with different utility functions usually prevent the reward system from seizing exclusive control of behavior. Circuits in orbitofrontal cortex (OFC) and possibly ventromedial prefrontal cortex (VMPFC) (though see Horn et al. 2003) appear to inhibit impulsivity through integration of cognition[11] (which suppresses hypothalamic input to VTA and SNpc) and emotion (especially fear of risk; Shiv et al. 2005). As noted previously, serotonin seems to be the neurotransmitter that carries the relevant signal, probably abetted by GABA neurons (Gulledge & Jaffe 2001; Yang, Seamans & Gorelova 1999).

The basic trigger mechanism for addiction seems to be that continuous floods of dopamine into NAcc depress serotonin levels in OFC and VMPFC and thereby reduce inhibition of impulse; in other words, the reward system is given greater influence over behavior. In the case of stimulant drugs (cocaine, amphetamines) extra dopamine is directly introduced in NAcc. Alcohol, nicotine, and opiates work on more indirect pathways that disturb neurotransmitter ratios and increase NAcc dopamine concentration by that mechanism. All these widespread addictive agents thereby crowd out salience of stimuli that don't predict drugs, and focus action on, enhance the perceived value of, and direct orientation toward stimuli that do (Koob, Paolo Sanna & Bloom (1998). The basic mechanism works as follows. In ventral striatum and VMPFC, neurons are normally held quiet by negative resting membrane potentials (called K+ currents) unless pushed into depolarized states by inflow from cerebral cortex and thalamus. When these neurons are depolarized, dopamine excites them; when they're polarized, dopamine dampens them further. Thus, motivation is sensitive to cognitive judgments (of course), but the reward system then amplifies these initial judgments if they're reinforced.

This describes the process by which the reward system simultaneously learns to pursue a target obsessively and increases the relative valuation of stimuli that predict it. However, it does not yet explain the steady state of addiction in which the addict finds difficulty pursuing alternative rewards, in particular the social ones associated with recovery, even when these are made intermittently salient enough to induce attempts at reform. (That is, we haven't yet resolved puzzle (ii)) Kalivas et al. (2005) report work that refines our understanding of behavioral attentional gating in addicts by separating its two underlying neurochemical substrates. Activation patterns in recovered rat cocaine addicts presented with cocaine-associated cues suggest that dopamine release in the projection from PFC to NAcc is responsible for strongly cueing the learned expectation of reward in response to the cues, while adaptations in glutamate synapses in NAcc reduce plasticity and impair the animals' abilities to learn to respond to alternative rewards. According to Seamans and Yang (2004) dopamine action gives rise to two possible states in VMPFC depending on which of two groups of receptors, D1 or D2, predominates. If D2 reception predominates, then multiple excitatory inputs promote VMPFC output to NAcc. If D1 reception predominates, then all signals below a high threshold are inhibited. In cocaine withdrawal, protein signaling to D2 receptors is reduced, thus inducing the animal to seek stimuli that can clear the high D1 threshold—namely, stimuli associated with cocaine. Here, then, is a neurochemical model of the mechanism by which withdrawal gives rise to cravings. A craving is nothing more or less than the phenomenology associated with the reward system's pulling attention back toward the addictive target and away from the alternative motivators on which cortical systems are trying to focus. Thus the reward system not only, as already stated, amplifies initial judgments that are reinforced; it also makes them difficult to behaviorally revise. Puzzle (ii) thus begins to dissipate.

Further details have come to light on the way in which dopamine and glutamate neurons complement one another in subserving reward learning and in generating addiction (Kelley 2004). Cells in NAcc and VMPFC, on which dopamine and glutamate neurons jointly synapse, act as coincidence detectors in associative learning. Essentially, an animal or person is motivated to act when dopamine and glutamate signals agree with one another in sending positive signals. Dopamine neurons respond to *global* saliences, that is, overall states of the world that suggest reward prospects. Glutamate, by contrast, responds to specific sensory information, and teaches the system to respond to new information with a similar profile. (As with any other neurotransmitter system, this teaching occurs by modification of synaptic potentials.) Glutamate thereby lays down episodic memories that are guides to subsequent actions, and so stamps in the dopaminergic response by modifying synapses to be alert to distinctive sensory predictors. Thus, the smoker cannot bear to finish a meal without lighting up, the drinker cannot pass the bar without going in, and the gambler experiences a compulsive rush when she hears jangling coins or sees flashing neon.

Powerful though the reward system is in regulating behavior, however, it is not normally in charge. Though dopamine concentration in NAcc is necessary for addiction, it is not sufficient for it; after all, stimulant drugs produce high concentrations of dopamine in NAcc of nonaddicts, and most people who are exposed to addictive substances or gambling do not become addicts. Goldstein and Volkow (2002) review a now substantial body of evidence that heavy consumption of drugs or gambling tips into addiction when *repeated* NAcc dopamine concentrations cause long-term changes in PFC circuits so as to impair inhibition of subcortical responses. One of the ways that some drugs do this is as directly as possible; stimulants, alcohol, and opiates physically destroy some prefrontal circuitry. More subtly, consumption of addictive substances appears to cause reformation of dendritic links as a result of which normal cortical inhibition of the amygdala is reduced (Robinson et al. 2001; Rosenkranz & Grace 2001; Miller & Cohen 2001). In effect, addiction not only hijacks the reward system, but sabotages the systems that might check its influence. The dissolution of puzzle (ii) is now complete.

Adding this evidence to that which we have reviewed on the dopamine-glutamate mechanism in NAcc, Goldstein and Volkow construct an integrated model of addiction that they call "impaired response inhibition and salience attribution" (I-RISA). This model links the neural processes underlying four distinct aspects of addiction to substances: intoxication, craving, compulsive drug administration, and withdrawal. The main distinctive general feature of intoxication is dopamine concentration in NAcc. Craving is then the learned association between the drug reward and various stimulus contingencies, based on modified synaptic potentials in amygdala, hippocampus, thalamus, anterior cingulate, and OFC. Compulsive drug administration is then the consequence of the reward system having learned to treat the addictive target as an overwhelmingly salient reward acting semi-autonomously in controlling behavior. Strong glutamate responses then support withdrawal, symptoms of which include dysphoria, anhedonia, impaired cognition, and irritability. As noted earlier, fear of withdrawal is almost certainly not the main factor in maintaining addiction. Instead, as a result of the resculpting of prefrontal circuits that reduces cortical inhibition of the midbrain, the cravings induced by the addiction-trained reward system, against which alternative rewards have difficulty competing, are often sufficient to provoke relapse after periods of abstinence. Because of the way in which the reward system learns, cravings are induced by any of the cues with which the target of addiction was associated during learning (Chiamulera 2004).

The focus of the past few paragraphs has been broadly hydraulic, a story told in terms of interacting functional systems. Though this allowed us to abstract away from biochemical details (which were merely referred to rather than described), the relevance of the neuroeconomic model may have faded from view. However, its importance becomes evident when we now ask why *some* but not *most* behavioral patterns that involve no introduction of exogenous chemical interferences, as with drugs, can trigger addictive response (that is, when we activate puzzle (i)).

Gambling is genuinely addictive for a minority of people; interpersonal sex is probably not potentially addictive for anyone.[12] Why?

The possibility of gambling addiction is bound to seem unlikely under any account of addiction that *begins* with drugs producing long-term changes in the brain as a consequence of the chemical properties of the introduced substances. As Wise (2002) argues, this point applies not just to traditional accounts that focus on chemical dependence and withdrawal but also to careless applications of the understanding of these processes in terms of neuroadaptations as described earlier. Wise emphasizes that rewarding properties of direct stimulants are learned extremely quickly; after as few as two or three electrical stimulations to hypothalamus, rats will begin frantically pressing levers for further such stimulation and ignoring food and water. Obviously, neuroadaptations cannot yet have occurred at the point where pursuit of the reward appears to be compulsive. "While it is clearly the case that brain changes associated with tolerance and dependence and brain changes associated with sensitization can develop under the right circumstances," Wise points out, "what remains to be determined is the degree to which either of these changes is necessary for motivational habits to become compulsive. The rapid onset of compulsive self-stimulation [in rats and primates] would seem to preclude any of these drug-induced long-term neuroadaptations as a necessary condition for compulsive drug-seeking" (233–234). And it seems quite implausible that sensitization to gambling causes compulsive gambling; almost certainly the causal relationship goes the other way around.

This is why the I-RISA model of the neurochemistry of addiction must be complemented by the neuroeconomic PV model discussed in Section 4. The distinctive properties of addictive targets are not chemical properties *in the first place*. Rather, the crucial requirement on an addictive target is that it trips the reward circuit into hysteresis: a self-amplifying causal process driven by positive feedback. In the case of drugs, their chemical influence on NAcc dopamine levels *happens to be* the mechanism by which hysteresis is induced. If this were the *only* mechanism for such hysteresis, then there would be no harm in our identifying addictive properties with intrinsic chemical properties. But the phenomenon of gambling addiction refutes this conceptual move. The intrinsic chemical properties of drugs are, in this sense, *distractions* from the elementary structure of addiction. They are of course important, and we should expect that they will greatly complicate development of neuropharmacological responses to addictive drugs. But sound method in both pure and applied science directs us to deal with basic cases of phenomena first and turn to complications later. These considerations suggest that gambling addiction should move to a position of central focus in addiction research. In their summary of the I-RISA model Goldstein and Volkow (2002) anticipate this point when they say that "a paradigm that simulates compulsive behavior (such as gambling when it is clearly no longer beneficial) might offer invaluable insight into the circuits underlying loss of control in addiction" (1645).

In an addiction science that takes gambling addiction as the template instance, neurochemistry does not supercede neuroeconomics (or neuropsychology) but complements it. Our attention is directed, in the first place, to understanding reward as a general process. Common sense is quite unfamiliar with this idea, since common sense identifies reward with receipt of a tangible benefit, often including shots of hedonic delight. However, as Wise stresses, rewards as neuroscience requires us to understand them are "unsensed incentives." The point of this phrase, in the context of reflections on targets of addiction, is that, although people sense the hedonic consequences of drugs, they are not directly conscious of their rewarding properties. (This is most obvious in the case of nicotine, which is strongly addictive despite the fact that its episodic hedonic properties are not vivid to experienced smokers.) In the case of addictive gambling, we are apt to wonder what it is that the gambler is getting that keeps attracting her to gamble more. Is it thrills or money or relief from boredom or what? It now seems that this is the wrong question to ask. Once we understand reward in the scientific—neuroeconomic—sense, then there is enlightenment in saying: *The problem with gambling is that, for some people, it is rewarding in itself.*

This statement will appear trivializing rather than illuminating if the reader does not yet appreciate how different the neuroeconomic concept of reward is from folk conceptions. As Wise points out, in neuroscience the distinction between a reward and a predictor of a reward is subtle, perhaps nonexistent. Rewards are units of information that "by association establish otherwise neutral stimuli as things to be approached" (233). The reward system is a device for leading animals to approach certain things rather than others, and it encodes no distinction between what is of ultimate benefit and what predicts an experience the animal is conditioned to repeat. In the case of animals that must adapt to changing environments, the system has a bias for—takes as rewarding—any predictor of *novel* experiences that are not aversive. People, furthermore, are the ultimate novelty seekers, our freakishly large brains signifying our status as the only animals in whom exaggerated drive for cognitive exploration is the basic species-specific adaptation. This emerges directly in the dopaminergic system's design; dopamine is not released by familiar stimuli but by positive surprises. Furthermore, as Wise reminds us, since the *sensed* properties of the reward, in the folk sense (i.e., the food in the mouth, the orgasm, the drug high, the receipt of the winnings at the window), are not typically surprising, the system becomes unresponsive to them. So saying as we do that the dopaminergic system responds to predictors of reward is actually a bit misleading. What we've been calling predictors of reward *are* (when positively surprising) the system's rewards.

What gambling fundamentally consists in is paying for the possibility of a surprise. This requires that odds in one's favor not be *too* high, and it may be important to the reward that they're negative. This doesn't imply that the gambler doesn't prefer winning to losing. All people who like gambling, and not just gambling addicts, want two things at once that they can't have both of: to win every bet, and to participate in processes where there's a high risk of losing. Should this really surprise us? How many people want, in general, exciting lives but lives in which nothing seriously threatens them? The gambler is literally paying to engage his or her reward system in the most direct and straightforward possible way. In light of this insight, we should now be able to see why, when people discover that there are institutions where they can buy such direct manipulation of the dopaminergic system, hysteresis is induced in some of them.

For the precise sense in which puzzles arise for neuroeconomists *before* the insight that what's rewarding to the reward system and what's rewarding to the person are two different kinds of things, consider a (2004) discussion by S.H. Ahmed. Reviewing Redish's (2004) neuroeconomic model of cocaine addiction, which directly applies associative TD learning following Montague, Dayan, and Sejnowski (1996), Ahmed points out that the model depends on the fact that cocaine directly causes dopamine release in NAcc, and so predicts strong reward regardless of any other contingencies. But then, Ahmed wonders, what about "addictions to ordinary rewards...which, unlike cocaine, produce a dopamine signal that can be accommodated" (1902)? The I-RISA model explains why, in a reward system that has learned to associate gambling cues with swift delivery of surprise, and that has disabled the capacity of forebrain circuits to interfere with its control of molar behavior, the dopamine signal resulting from engagement in gambling activity *cannot* be accommodated. Given what reward *means* in the midbrain, and given what gambling *is* from this point of view, it too is guaranteed to predict strong reward come what may. By contrast, the *person* gets what she regards as her reward from gambling—a cash win—only a minority of the time.

According to the account given here, then, addiction arises when the dopaminergic reward system hijacks the brain and, as a result, guides molar behavior according to its utility function rather than that of the person. Why, in general, is it bad for a person to be addicted? There are of course specialized answers for specific addictions, such as nicotine or alcohol, in terms of the health of cells and cellular systems. But, *in general,* the high costs of addiction are social—and this is the only kind of ultimate currency there is for people, given where they come from and what they're for, as described in Section 3. Being addicted isn't, in general, bad for the *reward system;* in gambling it finds a source of reward more reliable than socialization, and just as good with respect to *its* basic currency, surprise.

Recovery from addiction usually requires that other people assist the beleaguered frontal and prefrontal systems of the addict by helping them form Ainslie-type personal rules through incentive-compatible bargains with other brain systems, and by keeping the addict out of familiar environments so as to deprive the reward system of its prediction cues, thereby starving it of cheap dopamine and allowing prefrontal systems to reassert themselves. In sum, the reward system must be put at an economic disadvantage, its costs raised and its relative bargaining power lowered. This, in general, is how people must try to govern the subpersonal agents in their brains: not by issuing proclamations, but by facilitating internal logrolling among coalitions. Like other governments that can't rely exclusively, or even basically, on force, they're constrained by the utility functions of systems in their brains because they must satisfy a sufficient number of constituents to stabilize interneural bargains.

It is doubtful that individual people could successfully do this by themselves. If there were a casino on Robinson Crusoe's island (paying out in something more relevant to him than money), he might be helpless in the face of addiction. But people assist each other by forming coalitions against unruly interests in their brains. Not only do people, as virtual stabilization devices built from narrative expectations, make social stability possible; by a neat trick of multifunctionality, they also stabilize brains. No wonder, then, that most of us regard people as the center of the moral universe. But this has caused us to take a long time to recognize that they are highly derivative economic agents—derivative from social dynamics above and from subpersonal dynamics below. Economic modeling casts most light on them not by taking them as primitive atoms of acquisitiveness, but by showing us how various kinds of people and human behavior emerge from macroeconomic, microeconomic, picoeconomic, and neuroeconomic systems in dynamic interaction.

The picture I have painted here suggests that the core economic theory used to write down the models in all of these applications to different scales needs no significant revision, even to account for such apparently recalcitrant phenomena as addiction. It is true, as "heterodox" behavioral economists emphasize, that people only *approximate* economic agency. However, rather than mangle the formal concept of economic agency so that it maps onto people more reliably and accurately, we can use the *standard* theory to *explain* the merely approximate fit and the frequent departures. Subpersonal interests, invoked to explain molar patterns in personal behavior, are rational bargainers. Similarly, the reward system, properties of which account for regularities derivable from the molecular scale, maximizes the utility function natural selection built for it when it uses the person to capture as much blood hemoglobin from other systems as it can—damaging to the person though this may be if the reward system is too successful in its power struggle.

We need not choose, in an exclusive way, between Leijonhufvud's classical and modern economics. Because people only approximate economic agency, when we study their interactions in small groups, or when they confront novel problems, we often find that we require classical-style accounts. But then because contemporary institutions (at least in developed economies) put strong pressure on people to make themselves predictable to others—to make themselves, that is, reliable partners for coordination games—behavior comes to be ever more extensively dominated by effective personal rules. Economies populated by people in the strong grip of personal rules will tend, at the aggregate scale, to be well modeled using modern economics. (Thus, modern economics works *because of*, not *despite*, something emphasized by the classical perspective: the power of institutional constraints.) Finally, people behaviorally dominated by personal rules will, thereby, be more likely to avoid the dopamine surges in NAcc that can, in turn, cause the neuro-adaptations responsible for the power of addiction. And then, in nonaddicts and addicts alike, at the point of modeling the rational neural agents we re-encounter the valuation principles of modern financial economics. Thus, the benefit from acknowledging the complications in the relationships among people, subpersonal interests, and brain systems is directly that we minimize the new complications we need introduce into economic theory.

NOTES

1. Mirowski often seems to be criticizing economists for borrowing their mathematical tools from other sciences—first nineteenth-century thermodynamics, and more recently cybernetics. It is not obvious why this is a criticism. Would it be better for some reason if economists invented their own applied mathematics? Why? On the other hand, I think Mirowski is often read by economists as implying a more destructive kind of criticism than he intends or literally provides, just because he is fond of rhetoric that is far from the conventional bloodless style. His satirical tone is often motivated by some economists' tendency to *forget* that they didn't usually invent their own applied mathematics, a point that is clear from his writing, unless one fails to tune in his sense of humor.

2. By this I mean that we can't drop the imputation of utility responsiveness without losing information about some projectible generalizations. See Ladyman and Ross 2007, Chapter 4, for details about the philosophy of science underlying this.

3. Some people will find the idea that economics has a soul funny. In fact, most economists are at least for some part of their lives in love with the elegant reasoning patterns based on the concept of marginal opportunity cost. I still am.

4. I think it is clear from Rosenberg (1992) that he hasn't always regarded conceptions of this general sort as nightmarish. As he makes clear, the view of economics he defends in this volume is a view he has only recently come to.

5. I have in mind here both some respectable literature and some I regard as irresponsible populism. I will here cite only the respectable: my remark is intended to apply to, among others, Hollis and Nell (1975), Hausman (1992), and Sen (1987). For discussion of populist anti-economics and its relationship to serious criticism, see Ross (forthcoming a).

6. I here defer to standard usage in the philosophy of mind. However, as Mark Rowlands pointed out at a recent conference presentation, thinking of beliefs and desires as *states* has probably contributed to much confusion about the nature of mind. They are better thought of as *processes,* since their attribution, either by the subject herself or by another, labels and organizes a stream (however short) of behaviors and expected accounts and consequences of those behaviors.

7. In saying this, I indicate my opinion that rational expectations models of human agents are never maximally accurate. This doesn't imply that there might not be settings in which they are the most practically useful approximations for predicting values of some macroeconomic variables. Nor does it necessarily imply that central banks shouldn't design monetary policy as if rational expectations prevailed.

8. Behaviorist psychologists have traditionally distinguished between molar and molecular models of the causal processes thought to govern behavior. The distinction is pragmatic and context-sensitive in application, but useful and important all the same. The basic idea is that molar descriptions individuate kinds of behavior and kinds of influences on behavior, by reference to ecological effects that behaviors are implemented to bring about, whereas molecular descriptions individuate kinds of behavior and kinds of influences on behavior by reference to causal factors that can be located within the organism studied in isolation. The philosopher Jerry Fodor (1980), defending an imperialist version of cognitivism against (what he considers) residues of behaviorism in cognitive science, once promoted a principle he called "methodological solipsism." In the more widely used language of his foes, this amounted to a kind of exclusionary molecularism. A near-consensus view among recent philosophers (see Ross 1997), by contrast, is that only molar-scale descriptions are descriptions of *persons,* as opposed to parts of or processes in people that don't simply compose persons by aggregation. Persons, on this account, are embedded in (social) environments as part of their conception and basic ontology.

9. These might be the mechanisms for what Ainslie calls "personal rules;" see Section 5.

10. There might of course be others—I have given no argument for a strict disjunction of alternatives.

11. Especially, perhaps, cognition concerning the future; see Fellows and Farah (2004). Of particular interest in the present context is the fact that their results suggest that VMPFC activity has no effect on discounting, but instead promotes awareness of expected future contingencies. Note, then, this instance of a case for attributing different economic properties to different parts of the brain.

12. There is no shortage of popular, therapeutic, and nonneuroscientific social science discussion of, and practice oriented around, so-called sex addiction; but there is no neuroscientific evidence for it. Obviously, there are people who devote great time and energy to pursuit of sex. This is not evidence of addiction. Sex has a number of crucial disanalogies with targets of addiction. One of these is that fine manipulation of the reward contingency is not under an individual's own control. Admittedly, this objection does not apply to masturbation or devotion of attention to pornography. It is possible that there are masturbation and/or pornography addicts; but, again, I am aware of no neuroscientific evidence for this at present. Widespread belief in sex addiction is troubling. Neurochemical therapies for addiction are about to become common. There are grounds for concern that some people (especially minors) whose sexual behavior offends others' moral opinions will be inappropriately prescribed drugs that could damage their general motivational structures. This may be especially dangerous if, because they aren't really addicted to sex, adolescent victims of such moral paternalism (who are especially likely to be female) show little behavioral modification at normal doses.

REFERENCES

Ahmed, S. (2004). "Addiction as Compulsive Reward Prediction." *Science* 306: 1901–1902.
Ainslie, G. (1992). *Picoeconomics.* Cambridge, England: Cambridge University Press.
Ainslie, G. (2001). *Breakdown of Will.* Cambridge, England: Cambridge University Press.

Ainslie, G. (2005). "Precis of *Breakdown of Will.*" *Behavioral and Brain Sciences* 28: 635–673.

Albin, P. (1998). *Barriers and Bounds to Rationality*. Princeton: Princeton University Press.

Anderson, P., Arrow, K. & Pines, D. (1988). *The Economy as an Evolving Complex System*. Reading, MA: Perseus.

Arthur, W.B., Durlauf, S. & Lane, D. (1997). *The Economy as an Evolving Complex System II*. Reading, MA: Addison-Wesley.

Baldwin, J. (1913). *History of Psychology,* Volume 2. London: Wats.

Beinhocker, E. (2006). *The Origin of Wealth*. Cambridge, MA: Harvard Business School Press.

Berns, G. (2003). "Neural Game Theory and the Search for Rational Agents in the Brain." *Behavioral and Brain Sciences* 26: 155–156.

Binmore, K. (2004). "Review of Philip Mirowski, *Machine Dreams.*" *Journal of Economic Methodology* 11: 477–483.

Blume, L. & Durlauf, S., Eds. (2005). *The Economy as an Evolving Complex System III*. Oxford: Oxford University Press.

Bowles, S. & Hammerstein, P. (2003). "Does Marke Theory Apply to Biology?" In P. Hammerstein, ed., *Genetic and Cultural Evolution of Cooperation,* 153–165. Cambridge, MA: MIT Press.

Bruner, J. (1992). *Acts of Meaning*. Cambridge, MA: Harvard University Press.

Bshary, R. & Noë, R. (2003). "Biological Markets: The Ubiquitous Influence of Partner Choice on the Dynamics of Cleaner Fish—Client Reef Fish Interactions." In P. Hammerstein, Ed., *Genetic and Cultural Evolution of Cooperation,* 167–184. Cambridge, MA: MIT Press.

Camerer, C. (2003). *Behavioral Game Theory*. Princeton: Princeton University Press.

Cartwright, N. (1999). *The Dappled World*. Cambridge, England: Cambridge University Press.

Chiamulera, C. (2004). "Cue Reactivity in Nicotine and Tobacco Dependence: A 'Multiple-Action' Model of Nicotine as a Primary Reinforcement and as an Enhancer of the Effects of Smoking-Associated Stimuli." *Brain Research Reviews* 48: 74–97.

Clark, A. (1997). *Being There*. Cambridge, MA: MIT Press.

Cressman, R. (2003). *Evolutionary Dynamics and Extensive Form Games*. Cambridge, MA: MIT Press.

Davis, J. (2003). *The Theory of the Individual in Economics*. London: Routledge.

Daw, N. (2003). *Reinforcement Learning Models of the Dopamine System and Their Behavioral Implications*. Doctoral dissertation, Carnegie Mellon University, Pittsburgh.

Dennett, D. (1987). *The Intentional Stance*. Cambridge, MA: MIT Press.

Dennett, D. (1991a). "Real Patterns." *Journal of Philosophy* 88: 27–51.

Dennett, D. (1991b). *Consciousness Explained*. Boston: Little Brown.

Dennett, D. (2003). *Freedom Evolves*. New York: Viking.

Dupre, J. (1992). *The Disorder of Things*. Cambridge, MA: Harvard University Press.

Durlauf, S. (2005). "Dismal Science." *American Scientist Online*. Available at http://www.americanscientist.org/BookReviewTypeDetail/assetid/40753

Fellows, L. & Farah, M. (2004). "Dissociable Elements of Human Foresight: A Role for the Ventromedial Frontal Lobes in Framing the Future, but Not in Discounting Future Rewards." *Neurophyschologia* 43: 1214–1221.

Fodor, J. (1980). "Methodological Solipsism Considered as a Research Strategy in Cognitive Science." *Behavioral and Brain Sciences* 3: 63–109.

Gallistel, C. (1990). *The Organization of Learning.* Cambridge, MA: MIT Press.

Gallistel, C. & Gibbon, J. (2000). "Time, Rate and Conditioning." *Psychological Review* 107: 289–344.

Gibbon, J. (1977). "Scalar Expectancy Theory and Weber's Law in Animal Timing." *Psychological Review* 84: 279–335.

Glimcher, P. (2003). *Decisions, Uncertainty and the Brain.* Cambridge, MA: MIT Press.

Goldstein, R. & Volkow, N. (2002). "Drug Addiction and Its Underlying Neurobiological Basis: Neuroimaging Evidence for the Involvement of the Prefrontal Cortex." *American Journal of Psychiatry* 159: 1642–1652.

Gulledge, A. & Jaffe, D. (2001). "Multiple Effects of Dopamine on Layer V Pyramidal Cell Excitability in Rat Prefrontal Cortex." *Journal of Neurophysiology* 86: 586–595.

Hammerstein, P. (2003). "Why Is Reciprocity So Rare in Social Animals? A Protestant Appeal." In P. Hammerstein, Ed., *Genetic and Cultural Evolution of Cooperation,* 83–93. Cambridge, MA: MIT Press.

Hausman, D. (1992). *The Inexact and Separate Science of Economics.* Cambridge, England: Cambridge University Press.

Herrnstein, R. (1981). "Self-control as Response Strength." In C. Bradshaw, E. Szabadi & C. Lowe, Eds., *Recent Developments in the Quantification of Steady-State Operant Behavior,* 3–20. Amsterdam: Elsevier / North-Holland.

Herrnstein, R. (1997). *The Matching Law.* Cambridge, MA: Harvard University Press.

Hollis, M. & Nell, E. (1975). *Rational Economic Man.* Cambridge, England: Cambridge University Press.

Horn, N., Dolan, M., Elliott, R., Deakin, J. & Woodruff, P. (2003). "Response Inhibition and Impulsivity: An fMRI Study." *Neuropsychologia* 4: 1959–1966.

Hutto, D. (2007). *Folk Psychological Narratives: The Socio-Cultural Basis of Understanding Reasons.* Cambridge, MA: MIT Press.

Kalivas, P., Volkow, N. & Seamans, J. (2005). "Unmanageable Motivation in Addiction: A Pathology in Prefrontal-accumbens Glutamate Transmission." *Neuron* 45: 647–650.

Kelley, A. (2004). "Memory and Addiction: Shared Neural Circuitry and Molecular Mechanisms." *Neuron* 44: 161–179.

Koob, G., Paolo Sanna, P. & Bloom, F. (1998). "Neuroscience of Addiction." *Neuron* 21: 467–476.

Kreps, D. & Wilson, R. (1982). "Sequential Equilibria." *Econometrica* 50: 863–894.

Ladyman, J. & Ross, D. (2007). *Every Thing Must Go.* Oxford: Oxford University Press.

Leijonhufvud, A. (2004). "The Trento Summer School." In D. Friedman & A. Cassar, Eds., *Economics Lab,* 5–11. London: Routledge.

Loewenstein, G. (1999). "A Visceral Account of Addiction." In J. Elster & O.-J. Skog, Eds., *Getting Hooked: Rationality and Addiction,* 235–264. Cambridge, England: Cambridge University Press.

McClure, S., Daw, N. & Montague, P.R. (2003). "A Computational Substrate for Incentive Salience." *Trends in Neuroscience* 26: 423–428.

Miller, E. & Cohen, J. (2001). "An Integrative Theory of Prefrontal Cortex Function." *Annual Review of Neuroscience* 24: 167–202.

Mirowski, P. (1989). *More Heat Than Light.* Cambridge, England: Cambridge University Press.

Mirowski, P. (2002). *Machine Dreams*. Cambridge, England: Cambridge University Press.

Montague, P.R. & Berns, G. (2002). "Neural Economics and the Biological Substrates of Valuation." *Neuron* 36: 265–284.

Montague, P. R., Dayan, P. & Sejnowski, T. (1996). "A Framework for Mesencephalic Dopamine Systems Based on Predictive Hebbian Learning." *Journal of Neuroscience* 16: 1936–1947.

Redish, A. (2004). "Addiction as a Computational Process Gone Awry." *Science* 306: 1944–1947.

Rescorla, R. & Wagner, A. (1972). "A Theory of Pavlovian Conditioning: Variations in the Effectiveness of Reinforcement and Nonreinforcement." In A. Black & W. Prokasy, Eds., *Classical Conditioning II: Current Research and Theory*, 64–99. New York: Appleton Century Crofts.

Robbins, L. (1935). *An Essay on the Nature and Significance of Economic Science*, second edition. London: Macmillan.

Robinson, I., Gorny, G., Milton, E. & Kolb, B. (2001). "Cocaine Self-administration Alters the Morphology Dendrites and Dendritic Spines in the Nucleus Accumbens and Neurocortex." *Synapse* 39: 257–266.

Rosenberg, A. (1992). *Economics: Mathematical Politics or Science of Diminishing Returns?* Chicago: University of Chicago Press.

Rosenkranz, J., and Grace, A. (2001). "Dopamine Attenuates Prefrontal Cortical Suppression of Sensory Inputs to the Basolateral Amygdala of Rats." *Journal of Neuroscience* 21: 4090–4103.

Ross, D. (1997). "Externalism for Everybody." *Canadian Journal of Philosophy* 27: 271–284.

Ross, D. (2005). *Economic Theory and Cognitive Science: Microexplanation*. Cambridge, MA: MIT Press.

Ross, D. (2006a). "The Economic and Evolutionary Basis of Selves." *Cognitive Systems Research* 7: 246–258.

Ross, D. (2006b). "The Economics of the Sub-personal: Two Research Programs." In M. White & B. Montero, Eds., *Economics and the Philosophy of Mind*. London: Routledge.

Ross, D. (forthcoming a). "Economic Theory, Anti-economics and Political Ideology." In U. Mäki, Ed., *Handbook of the Philosophy of Science, Volume 13: Economics*. London: Elsevier.

Ross, D. (forthcoming b). "The Economic Agent: Not Human, but Important." In U. Mäki, Ed., *Handbook of the Philosophy of Science, Volume 13: Economics*. London: Elsevier.

Ross, D., Sharp, C., Vuchinich, R. & Spurrett, D. (2008). *Midbrain Mutiny: The Picoeconomics and Neuroeconomics of Disordered Gambling*. Cambridge, MA: MIT Press.

Rovane, C. (1998). *The Bounds of Agency*. Princeton: Princeton University Press.

Sanabria, F. & Killeen, P.R. (2005). "Freud Meets Skinner: Hyperbolic Curves, Elliptical Theories, and Ainslie Interests." *Behavioral and Brain Sciences* 28: 660–661.

Schelling, T. (1978). "Economics, or the Art of Self-Management." *American Economic Review* 68: 290–294.

Schelling, T. (1980). "The Intimate Contest for Self-Command." *Public Interest* 60: 94–118.

Schelling, T. (1984). "Self-Command in Practice, in Policy, and in a Theory of Rational Choice." *American Economic Review* 74: 1–11.

Seamans, J. & Yang, C. (2004). "The Principal Features and Mechanisms of Dopamine Modulation in the Prefrontal Cortex." *Progress in Neurobiology* 74: 1–57.

Sen, A. (1987). *On Ethics and Economics*. Oxford: Blackwell.

Shiv, B., Loewenstein, G., Bechara, A., Damasio, H. & Damasio, A. (2005). "Investment Behavior and the Negative Side of Emotion." *Psychological Science* 16: 435–439.

Smolin, L. (1997). *The Life of the Cosmos*. Oxford: Oxford University Press.

Sutton, R. & Barto, A. (1998). *Reinforcement Learning: An Introduction*. Cambridge, MA: MIT Press.

Wallis, W. & Friedman, M. (1942). "The Empirical Derivation of Indifference Functions." In O. Lange, Ed., *Studies in Mathematical Economics and Econometrics,* 175–189. Chicago: University of Chicago Press.

Wise, R. (2002). "Brain Reward Circuitry: Insights from Unsensed Incentives." *Neuron* 36: 229–240.

Yang, C., Seamans, J. & Gorelova, N. (1999). "Developing a Neuronal Model for the Pathophysiology of Schizophrenia Based on the Nature of Electrophysiological Actions of Dopamine in the Prefrontal Cortex." *Neuropsychopharmacology* 21: 161–194.

CHAPTER 10

METHODOLOGICAL ISSUES IN EXPERIMENTAL DESIGN AND INTERPRETATION

FRANCESCO GUALA

This chapter is organized around two topics: the first one is the methodology of *experimental economics,* a research program that is becoming increasingly influential in contemporary economic science.[1] The second one is *normative methodology,* an issue that has been widely debated by philosophers of economics over the last two decades.

A methodological discussion of experimental economics could simply aim at *describing* the methods used by experimental economists in their daily work, without asking questions of efficacy or justification. This would have the advantage of taking a detached, passive-observer attitude to scientists' work, like the attitude of an anthropologist studying the practices and rituals of an exotic society. The main limitation of the purely descriptive approach, however, is its ultimate irrelevance for scientists' methodological practices.[2] The "tribesmen" are usually fairly indifferent to the books that anthropologists write.

Another approach, the one that I will pursue in this chapter, is to take a more direct normative stance: instead of passively observing what economists do, the philosopher steps down in the arena of scientific debate and tries to issue some cautious advice on methodological matters. This has the advantage of engaging scientists in some of the very issues that are important and interesting for them, and in some cases it can even produce little improvements in methodological practice. It is not clear, however, how normative methodology should be done in the first place, so part of this chapter will try to clarify this (metamethodological) issue, using experimental economics as a case study.

The chapter is organized as follows: in the next section I will introduce by example some of the main methodological features of laboratory experiments in economics. In Section 2, I will return to the metamethodological theme and illustrate the framework that I will use to analyse the practices of experimental economics. Sections 3–6 will be devoted to an in-depth discussion of some methodological principles of experimental economics, from the most abstract to the most concrete rules that govern experimental design in the discipline. Section 7 will conclude with some general reflections.

1. Running an Economic Experiment: Public Goods in the Classroom

Experimental economics as we know it today is little more than half a century old. Like many methodological revolutions in science, the experimental turn in economics was primarily made possible, not by a change in philosophical perspective, but by a number of innovations at the level of scientific practice and theoretical commitment. Economists had traditionally been skeptical of the possibility of running controlled experiments, because of the great number of variables and the relative uncontrollability of the systems (the real-world economies) they wanted to study. In the middle of the twentieth century, however, economics was in the process of becoming a "tool-based" science (Morgan 2003); from the old, discursive "moral science" of political economy, it was changing into a discipline where models, statistics, and mathematics played the role both of instruments and, crucially, of *objects* of investigation. During this conceptual revolution, economists came to accept that the path toward the understanding of a real-world economy might have to go through the detailed analysis of "mediating" tools that bear only partial resemblance with the final target of investigation. Theoretical models and computer simulations entered the economists' basic toolkit first, with laboratory experiments following shortly after.[3]

An economic experiment observes the behaviour of real human beings performing an "economic" task in controlled laboratory conditions. Since not all readers will be familiar with controlled experiments of this kind, I will introduce briefly an example that can be used as a reference point throughout the chapter. It's a simple exercise that can be conducted in class, and I urge all readers to try it.[4]

1.1 Basic Setting

You can run this experiment with a set of playing cards, paper, and pencil. Distribute four cards of the same type to each student in the class (for example four aces, four twos, four kings, etc.). The numbers displayed on the cards do not matter, but their color does: each student will have two red (hearts and diamonds) and two black (clubs and spades) cards. At this point you will distribute a set of instructions that will read as follows:

> The exercise will consist of a number of rounds. When a round begins, I will come to each of you in order, and you will play *two* of your four cards by placing these two cards face down on top of the stack in my hand. Your earnings in dollars are determined by what you do with your red cards. In each of the first five rounds, for each red card that you keep you will earn four dollars for the round, and for each black card that you keep you will earn nothing. Red cards that are placed on the stack affect everyone's earnings in the following manner. I will count up the total number of red cards in the stack, and everyone will earn this number of dollars. Black cards placed on the stack have no effect on the count. When the cards are counted, I will not reveal who made which decisions. I will return your own cards to you at the end of the round by coming to each of you in reverse order and giving you the top two cards, face down, off the stack in my hand. To summarize, your earnings for the round will be calculated:
>
> Earnings = $4 times the number of red cards you kept + $1 times
> the total number of red cards I collect.
> (Holt and Laury 1997, 215)

Once the students have read the instructions carefully, ask them if they have any questions about the mechanics of the game, and remind them that they cannot communicate with each other during the experiment. Then tell them to put two cards face-down on their desk, and collect them. Count how many red cards there are in your stack, and write it on the blackboard. Encourage students to calculate their earnings (the instructions sheet will include a little table to facilitate such calculations); in the meantime, redistribute the cards (making sure that the right ones are returned to each student) and proceed to the next round.

If you have followed the procedures correctly, you have just performed a public-goods experiment in class. A public-goods game is basically a prisoner's-dilemma game with a higher number of players and strategies. Suppose there are 10 players with $8 each (i.e., $4 for each red card). The production function of the public good is .25 (each player receives $1 for every red card invested in the public account). If everybody invests one card in the public account, their revenue will amount to

$4 [from the private account] + ($1 × 10) [from the public account] = $14

In a classic public-goods experiment, all players play simultaneously and anonymously—at the moment of making a decision, each subject ignores the identity of the other subjects in the group, and how much they are contributing.

According to standard economic theory, the public good should not be produced; that is, there should be no contribution to the public project. This conclusion is reached by assuming that each player is indifferent to the others' payoffs, tries to maximize his or her own monetary gains, and is perfectly rational in the sense of Nash rationality.[5] Under these assumptions the best move—regardless of what the others do—is to contribute nothing. If the others do not contribute, why should one give one's own money, given that that player would get back only one quarter of the amount contributed to the project? If the others do contribute one card, it is still best not to give anything, and enjoy the fruits of the others' contribution plus one's own full endowment.

The Nash solution however is "Pareto-inferior" or suboptimal with respect to the outcome that would be achieved if everybody were willing to cooperate by contributing fully to the public account. Using the previous example, it's easy to calculate that the Nash solution (contribute nothing) gives each player an individual payoff of

$8 + 0 = $8.

The Pareto-optimal solution, instead, would have everybody contributing their full endowment to the public project, thus achieving

0+ ($2 × 10) = $20.

As a matter of fact, many experimental subjects (and your students won't be any different) contribute something to the public account. It is not unusual to observe average contributions in the area of 40 to 60 percent of the full endowment in the first round of a public goods game. In subsequent rounds, however, the average contribution usually begins to fall. If you repeat the game for five to ten rounds, it is likely that the contributions will reach a relatively low level, say about 10 to 20 percent of the endowment, and will be stuck there until the end of the game.[6]

1.2 Variations

At this point you may want to try something different. Holt and Laury (1997) suggest that you change the production function, from .25 to .50 (this can be done by reducing the value of keeping a red card, from $4 to $2). Once you have announced this change in the rules of the game, you will probably observe a resurgence of contributions. This is a well-known phenomenon, in fact a combination of two separate effects: a production function effect, and a restart effect. Neither of them can be explained by the standard theory: In a linear public-goods environment, the production function should not matter because the Nash equilibrium is always equal to zero contribution. And it is hard to see how merely interrupting the game for a few minutes and then restarting (with the same players and the same rules) should make people change their strategies. But that's what has been observed in a number of experiments.[7]

However, even in this new setting you will observe that, with repetition, the contributions will decline and converge toward Nash. Holt and Laury (1997) now suggest that you open a discussion session. Encourage your students to talk about what is happening and why. After they have diagnosed the problem ("I cannot trust that others will put both their red cards on the table" is a common explanation), ask them what can be done about it. If they do not propose it themselves, you may suggest that they should make a "pact" or "contract": each student should promise that they will put both red cards on the table. Someone might point out that there is no guarantee that the promise will be honoured, that in fact it is just "cheap talk" (this is likely to happen especially if your students have attended a game theory course). Ask them if they are willing to take the risk. If not, you continue the game as before. If they are, make them utter the promise and then play a few more rounds. It is not unlikely at this point to observe a big rise in contributions, up to 80 to 90 percent of the endowment. With repetition, this high level of contributions may survive for several rounds. If it flounders, however, it will decline quickly again toward Nash.[8]

1.3 Discussion

The decay of contribution in public-goods games is one of the most robust phenomena discovered by experimental economists since the 1950s. It is so robust that one can replicate it even with relatively slack design and control. It is also a sensitive phenomenon in the sense that the rate of contribution can be easily manipulated by changing some details of the design, as we have seen. In this sense, it is ideal for class experimentation. This classroom design, however, can be made more stringent by imposing some of the standard methodological principles of experimental economics.

First of all, unlike real experimental subjects, your students were playing for *fictional money*. In a real economic experiment, the subjects in contrast are incentivized by being paid real money, proportional to their earnings in the experiment. Secondly, your students probably have a history of personal interaction, and know each other quite well. They also know that they will continue to have interactions in the future, and this may lead them to behave strategically in order to maintain their reputation. Real experiments usually try to circumvent such problems by recruiting strangers and by dividing them randomly into different groups. As in your class experiments, there is usually complete anonymity regarding the choices and the earnings of each subject, but in real experiments more care is paid to isolate each subject using cardboard partitions or cubicles, and using a PC network to communicate decisions and receive feedback.

These are just some of the basic differences between a class demonstration and an experiment run for research purposes, but in this particular case they do not matter very much (in other cases they do). A class demonstration and a research experiment at any rate have at least one important feature in common. Both are based on the logic of *comparison and controlled variation*. At least two kinds of comparison are important in our public goods experiment. First, there is a comparison between the experimental results and the predictions of a theoretical model. I have said that standard theory predicts that nobody should contribute to the public account. In fact I have been a bit imprecise; strictly speaking, standard game theory doesn't predict anything of this sort. It just says that *if* people prefer more money to less and they are indifferent to others' earnings, *then,* assuming they are rational in the sense of game theory, they will contribute zero in a finitely repeated public-goods game.[9] In order to derive an unconditional prediction, we have to construct a more specific model by adding a selfishness assumption to the basic elements of game theory.

As we have seen, the behavior of real people does not quite resemble that of the agents in this theoretical model. A comparison between model and experiment tells us that something in the model does not capture what is going on in the experiment, even though we do not know exactly what that is.[10] A great deal of economic experimentation is, in fact, devoted to varying the initial conditions in order to identify the source of the mismatch between model and experimental setup. How do they differ? And are these differences robust to variations in the experimental conditions?[11] A second class of comparisons, then, concerns different experimental conditions: our class experiment, for example, taught us that an interruption in the middle of the game and a change in the production function can affect the level of contribution; and that an open discussion and a nonbinding agreement can do the same. In all such cases, we compare the pattern of contributions in one baseline condition with the pattern observed in another, different condition. In the jargon of experimental design, the variable that is being manipulated (the production function, say) is the treatment, and the baseline condition is a control.

2. NORMATIVE METHODOLOGY AS INSTRUMENTAL RATIONALITY

The design principles that I have briefly described—the use of monetary incentives and anonymity, for example—have evolved over the years and have been endorsed by economists for a variety of reasons. One is simply historical; some of the earlier experiments were designed in such a way as to implement these principles, and later experimenters have copied their designs, which have slowly become paradigmatic in the discipline. But this is not the whole story. Many of these design principles were carefully thought out and justified by methodological reasoning. The pioneers of experimental economics were, in most cases, engaged in a conscious project of methodological reform, where the use of the experimental method was aimed at improving the quality of the empirical evidence available to economists. The design principles (which in the meantime have become accepted by convention) *had* to have a normative justification, because the pioneers were probing an unchartered territory, and they were trying to overcome the limitations of more traditional methods of investigation.

One of the tasks for methodology may be precisely to dig out these rationales from the layers of conventional dust that has accumulated over the years, to formulate them rigorously, and check that they are still in line with the overall purposes of experimental research. But what are these more general goals or purposes? Unfortunately scientists tend to be much more casual about these wider issues than about the nitty-gritty of experimental design. They talk about them, of course, but much more briefly and in less depth than one would like (especially if "one" is a philosopher of science!). A cursory analysis of methodological discourse in economics reveals that there are broadly speaking three strata in experimenters' pronouncements:

- High-level discourse about theory, evidence, confirmation, falsification.
- Middle-level discourse about experimental design.
- Low-level discourse about the precepts of experimental economics.

At the *high level* we find the language and concepts of traditional philosophy of science. This is where we would expect to find a statement of the overall goals of experimentation. Most textbooks of experimental economics actually start with discussions of induction, falsification, and the relation between theory and evidence, which in many ways reflect the discourse of classic philosophy of science (à la Popper-Kuhn, to give an idea). These, however, are usually little more than vague gestures, and involve no strong commitment to a particular way of doing science—just something along the line that empirical evidence is used to test theories (sure: but how?) and that theory and data together are crucial for the advancement of science. These are hardly uncontroversial claims, but they are not very informative either.

As we continue reading an experimental textbook, we then encounter more specific principles of experimental design. These correspond to *mid-level* methodology, using the preceding scheme. Friedman and Sunder (1994) for example devote a few pages to illustrating the fundamental principles of randomization, classic 4×4 designs, and so forth, which are used in the experimental branches of psychology and the social sciences. The level of detail is much greater here, and one begins to hear the unmistakable tone of the expert preaching a fairly precise methodological doctrine. What is lacking, however, is a link between the high-level views of scientific progress and the more specific experimental designs illustrated in these sections.

We have not reached the most detailed and concrete level of methodological discourse in experimental economics yet. The methodological debates published in economics journals usually deal neither with high-level nor with mid-level methodological issues. Controversies tend to arise from much more specific issues of experimental design, such as the use of monetary incentives or the importance of repetition. These design principles are quite specific to experimental economics, and in many ways distinguish what economists do in the laboratory from the experimental practices that are prevalent in other sciences (psychology, for example). Such low-level principles receive a lot of attention in textbooks, too, but again there is typically little discussion of the relation between these practices and more general design principles at the mid and high level.

One important task for the methodologist, then, is to investigate how scientific practice and discourses cohere (if at all) moving back and forth across these three levels of analysis. This opens the possibility, not only of clarifying, but, also, of engaging in some internal criticism of the methods in use (or advocated) within the discipline. The normative edge in such activity is provided by a principle of *instrumental rationality:* A certain method or tool is justified if it is an effective means to reach a given end in given circumstances.

Following Giere (1988, Chapter 1), the instrumental approach can be contrasted with a *categorical* approach to normative methodology. According to the categorical approach, methodological rules have the form of "Do X (in C)," where X is a certain procedure or set of procedures, and C is a set of circumstances where the procedures are appropriate. (Ideally, one would like to have universal methodological rules that are appropriate in all circumstances.) The defining characteristic of categorical rules is the absence of an instrumental goal or purpose: one should do X—full stop—because X is the method of science. In contrast, *instrumental* rules have the form of "In order to achieve Y, do X (in C)," where the appropriateness of the rule is determined by its efficacy in relation to a certain set of goals (see also Laudan 1984; Rosenberg 1993, Chapter 1).

Philosophers of science have become increasingly sceptical about unconditional methodological prescriptions derived from highly abstract epistemological principles. Whether any of the great philosophers of science of the 20th Century ever subscribed to the categorical approach is open to question (Laudan 1984, Worrall 1989), but there is no doubt that whatever popularity this approach once enjoyed, it has become increasingly discredited in recent years. Recent proposals to abandon normative economic methodology altogether, such as D. Wade Hands's (2001), move from the presumption that normative methodology can only be done in the categorical mode. The instrumental approach, however, is not only a viable, but a more fruitful approach. It allows one to take scientific conventions and scientists' practical wisdom seriously, while retaining a critical edge. In the case of experimental economics, it allows one to achieve the following objectives:

1. To explain and understand how the three levels of methodological discourse are related to one another.
2. To outline the virtues and limitations of specific practices or methodological principles at each level of discourse.
3. To criticize specific practices or methodological principles if they are ill fitted to the overall goals of experimental economics.

3. Mid-Level Methodology: Models of Scientific Method

The instrumental approach falls under the umbrella of "naturalized philosophy of science" (Rosenberg 1996). A methodological rule X ought to be justified by checking whether it is effective in achieving goal Y in circumstances C. If it is not, then the methodologist and the scientist have the onus of finding another justification for the rule (by revising Y), redefining its domain of application (C), or replacing the rule with one that is more effective in achieving the original goal.

The simplicity of the instrumental approach, however, may be deceptive. As soon as we look at concrete scientific practice, things get more complicated—and interesting, too. A key tenet of the instrumental approach is that the means-goals relation is empirical, and thus methodology must be done a posteriori. As any econometrician knows, any given method of estimation (Ordinary Least Squares, say) works only if the data and the data-generating process have certain properties, or otherwise it will provide biased estimations. In general, whether *any* method is effective to achieve a given goal depends crucially on how the world is, and in this sense, there is continuity between scientific and methodological investigation.

It is generally recognized that most concrete scientific knowledge is conveyed in *models,* rather than high-level theories.[12] Similarly, most of our *methodological* knowledge is conveyed in *models of scientific method.*[13] Models of scientific method work in many ways like scientific models. Some are mainly heuristic or pedagogic devices;[14] others are supposed to be directly useful and applicable, but only when certain "happy" conditions hold. Since these conditions are typically rare, the models are mostly incomplete and difficult to apply in less-than-ideal circumstances.

3.1 Model Experimental Designs

At the beginning of many textbooks, you are presented with some *model experimental designs,* like those in Table 10.1. The symbols are to be interpreted as follows: R = randomization; X = treatment; O = observation. Each row of X's and O's represents an experimental group; some groups receive the treatment, others do not (the control groups). All subjects are assigned randomly to some group (R). After the treatment, you observe the level of some key variable (O), and draw an inference about the influence of X on O.

Each design presents in a schematic fashion a procedure aimed at solving a fairly specific experimental problem in ideal circumstances. Because the circumstances in which experimenters operate are seldom ideal, each model can be modified in order to fix a problem that the experimenter suspects might arise in a particular situation. A variation on the basic theme, however, often implies a

Table 10.1 Three model experimental designs

Posttest-only control group design	Pretest posttest control group design	Solomon four-group design
$X\ O_1$ R O_2	$O_1\ X\ O_2$ R $O_3\ \ O_4$	$O_1\ X\ O_2$ $O_3\ \ \ \ O_4$ R $X\ O_5$ O_6

trade-off in which one problem is solved at the cost of opening some other potential problems. Whether the new worry is worth taking seriously can usually be decided only on the basis of context-specific information about the experiment one is trying to make.

Consider the posttest-only design. The crucial assumption here is that randomization allows the creation of groups that are similar enough before the treatment. When this is questionable, the pretest-posttest design corrects the posttest-only model by introducing a measurement before the treatment is administered. Such a solution comes at a cost, because a measurement is itself an intervention that may affect the result of the experiment. A combination of posttest-only and pretest-posttest design can be used to control for this, in the so-called Solomon four-group design.

The logic should be familiar to theoretical economists: you start with a (semi-) ideal situation, try to figure out what could go wrong, and modify it accordingly (keeping the trade-off in mind, of course). Notice that all these models are based on the logic of comparison and controlled variation. The variation in the circumstances must be carefully planned and controlled; the groups ideally should be situated in conditions that vary with respect to just *one* parameter (the treatment). This is highlighted in particular by the simplest model, the posttest-only design. The other models are proposed as second-best when the uniformity of initial conditions across the two groups is in doubt. Then, it is worth specifying the ideal of the controlled experimental design in its purest form by amending the posttest-only design, as in Table 10.2.

The perfectly controlled design reproduces the essential characteristics of the posttest control group design, with some important differences. First of all, the letter R (for randomization) has disappeared. Randomization is functional to achieve uniformity of conditions across the groups, but in principle it is neither necessary nor sufficient for the success of an experiment. Despite its usefulness and popularity, it does not belong to the essence of the experimental method. Secondly, a new column for the background factors (K_i) to be kept uniform has appeared on the right-hand side of the table. I have used Ys instead of Os to represent measurements. This has the advantage of bringing the notation in line with the one that is

Table 10.2 The perfectly controlled design

	Treatment (putative cause)	Putative effect	Other factors (K_i)
Experimental group	X	Y_1	Constant
Control group	–	Y_2	Constant

commonly used to denote independent (X) and dependent (Y) variables in mathematical and causal modeling. The table assumes that X and Y are either present or absent, that is, that they are variables with just two possible values. But of course, it is possible to generalize and consider many-valued (even continuous) variables. The key is that we should be able to observe the difference that variations in X make with respect to Y.

4. High-Level Methodology: Causation

The discussion so far may have seemed arid and technical. However, this sort of detailed examination of scientific practice is necessary, once we endorse the instrumental approach to normative methodology. A less detailed analysis would carry the risk of misunderstanding the purposes and logic of experimental research. Let me mention an example: Alexander Rosenberg (1993) is well-known both for his endorsement of the instrumental approach and for his critique of the scientific ambitions of neoclassical economics. His critique, however, is exactly the sort of attack that does not do justice to real science. Rosenberg starts from the presumption that all good science should aim at the discovery of invariant universal laws. Then he shows that for various reasons—mostly drawn from the philosophy of mind—economists cannot hope to find such laws in the domain of individual choice. There is no need to investigate in detail the methods used by economists in their daily work. Such methods are bankrupt anyway, whatever they are, because the goals are unattainable. But the goals in this case have been *imputed,* rather than extracted from scientists' own commitments.

I will try to show that the methods of experimental economics are justifiable, if their objective is the discovery of *robust causal relations* rather than universal laws. In order to do that, we will have to step up one gear, from mid-level to high-level methodological discourse. The emphasis that I am giving to causation contrasts with a tradition that sees scientific experimentation as mainly aimed at theory testing.[15] I use *theory* here in a fairly specific way: a body of systematic, usually formalized claims derived from a set of axioms or principles. The sort of stuff that is routinely published in the *Journal of Economic Theory,* in other words. An informal guess or hypothesis does not count as a theory, in this sense, and not all theories describe causal mechanisms, although many do. Some of them simply describe associations between events (the principles of choice theory are a good example) or put forward possibility/impossibility claims, for example.

Of course many experiments are concerned more or less directly with the test of theoretical questions, but not all of them are. *All* experiments, in contrast (including theory-testing ones) make heavy use of the logic of controlled variation. The latter is ubiquitous, more fundamental, and is the hallmark of experimentation in all science, from physics to economics.[16] Consider a famous example from the history of natural science: Jean Perrin's experiments on Brownian motion were aimed at testing the theoretical hypothesis that Avogadro's number N (the number of molecules in a mole of any substance) is equal to 7×10^{23} as predicted by the Einstein-Smoluchowski theory. Perrin obtained the value of N by measuring the distribution of the observed displacements of gamboge grains (a substance similar to soap) from a population distributed according to a Gaussian model. One of the first experimental obstacles he faced was the demonstration that the displacement distribution was truly random, that is, that it did not result from some systematic hidden causal influence. This demonstration was crucial to establish that Brownian movement is due to forces that are "inside" the gamboge emulsion, so to speak. Perrin carefully varied the conditions of the experiment so as to show that factors like temperature, density and size of the grains, and external forces like vibrations of the glass containing the emulsion, made no difference to the values measured during the experiment. In doing this, he could also rely on the vast experience of previous experimenters who had investigated Brownian motion in a pretheoretical way. Another French experimenter, Leon Gouy, for example had worried that the displacements of the grains could be due to the vibrations caused by the passage of trams in the street below his laboratory. To check for this possible disturbing factor, he had carefully replicated his observations during the night and in the countryside, to make sure that it didn't make any difference for the observed values.[17]

This kind of reasoning takes place in all experimentation, including the public goods games illustrated in Section 1. Controlled variation is used to figure out which factors influence the level of contribution, and these factors can then be used to inform policy making. The theory for example suggests that no public good will be produced in a free-market environment. This pessimistic message has frequently inspired policies of state intervention (by providing centrally the missing goods), or of privatization (by imposing ownership rights on resources that were previously publicly shared). If the results of the experiments are to be trusted, however, in some situations public goods *can* be produced after all. It seems that public discussion and nonbinding agreements, for example, can go a long way toward improving the production of public goods. This knowledge can be used to support policies of democratization and public awareness, where the members of a community agree upon and oversee the production and consumption of public goods like fish, open fields, or clean air, that would otherwise be quickly spoiled by individualistic unconstrained fruition. The nice thing about experimentation is that it can be used to identify those variables that can be "surgically" manipulated to obtain certain desired effects.[18]

The perfectly controlled experiment plays a useful role in this conjunction. It is a useful abstraction precisely because it can be used to clarify the link between experimental design and the overall goals of economic science. Assuming that one such goal is to inform effective policy intervention, we can use the perfectly controlled design to facilitate the ascent to a higher level of methodological discourse—from experimental design to intervention and causation.

What sort of notion of causation is implicit in the model of Table 2? Intuitively, the treatment X is a causal factor that is being manipulated in an experimental situation, and the dependent variable Y is the putative effect. A literal translation of the perfectly controlled experiment would result in a definition of causation along these lines:

> *Causation (deterministic case)*: X causes Y if and only if they are constantly associated in causally homogeneous background conditions.

The homogeneous background conditions, K_i, are equivalent to what economists call *ceteris paribus* conditions. Since we know that the "other factors" are never perfectly homogeneous even in the lab, we try to catch the mistakes by some other means, for example, by randomization. One important issue about causation, which has been widely debated in the literature, regards the quantifier to be included in this definition: Should it say "in *all* homogenoeus K_i," or only in *some* of them? Some philosophers, like Cartwright (1983) and Humphreys (1989), have argued that it should be a universal quantifier (all). Others point out the oddity of this formulation: We have good evidence that my kicking caused the door to open even though we cannot show that the kicking opens the door in all background conditions (for example if the door is locked), but only in some (Dupré 1984, Hausman 1998). This is similar in spirit to the well-known INUS view of causation once defended by John Mackie (1974): A cause is one factor among many that jointly bring the effect about. By imposing the universality condition (a cause raises the probability of its effect in *all* homogeneous background conditions) we would divorce the metaphysics of probabilistic causation from the grammar of everyday (and scientific) causal explanation.

This also helps to retain the idea that causal claims can be tested in laboratory experiments: an experiment typically investigates the effect of manipulating a variable X on the background of a *single* set of K_i. The robustness of a cause-effect relation across different background conditions can then be investigated in a series of experimental investigations, but even then, it is rarely the case that *all* possible K_i are explored before making a causal claim (if it was possible at all).

Indeed, it is useful to distinguish—as most scientists do—between the existence of a causal relation and its *robustness* across changes in the background conditions (Woodward 2003).[19]

To sum up, we are left with the following characterization of causation:

Causation (deterministic case): X causes *Y* if and only if they are constantly associated in some causally homogeneous background conditions.[20]

A probabilistic version (to take into account the possibility of indeterminism) would go as follows (modified from Cartwright 1983):

Causation (indeterministic case): X causes *Y* if and only if $P(Y|X) > P(Y|{\sim}X)$ in some causally homogeneous background conditions.

This formulation highlights the context-specificity of causal inference: whether a certain experiment provides good evidence (or not) to test a certain causal hypothesis depends on the context, on whether the background conditions are "right." And this can only be discovered by empirical means. It also implies that generalizing from experimental data is ultimately an empirical task. A result obtained in a given set of experimental circumstances cannot and should not be extended automatically to situations where those conditions do not hold. That *X* causes *Y* in *C* does not imply in any way that *X* causes *Y* in *D*. We will return to this important issue later in Section 6.

5. Low-Level Methodology: Incentives, Anonymity, Repetition

Once properly reconstructed, there is a fairly tight match between mid-level experimental models and high-level methodological concepts of causation. Having a coherent package of mid- and high-level methodological principles is obviously an advantage, for it allows us to look critically from this vantage point at low-level methodological principles, which happen to be more controversial and hotly debated in experimental economics.

Lower-level principles play not only an important methodological role, but fulfill, also, various sociological functions. For example, they are associated with paradigmatic experiments, which have influenced the development of the field and continue to be used pedagogically for the training of young scientists. They are also often used to define the specificity of economic experimentation as opposed to experimentation as practiced in social psychology or cognitive science. And finally, low-level principles are used more or less explicitly as criteria to select what is published in economics journals. For these reasons it is difficult to appreciate low-level practices outside the context of their adoption.

5.1 The Precepts of Experimental Economics

The core low-level design principles that are commonly implemented in economics derive from the so-called precepts of experimental economics, formalized by Vernon Smith and his collaborators in the late 1970s (Smith 1976, 1982; Wilde 1981). The precepts were explicitly proposed for a particular category of experiments, namely, the market experiments run by Smith since the late 1950s. The main purpose of such experiments was to investigate the functioning of economic institutions, rather than the nature of individual preferences as is the case, for example, in public goods experiments. A market institution is typically a set of rules governing the exchange of goods. Neoclassical economic theory traditionally adopts an idealization—the Walrasian auctioneer—that coordinates trade in a perfectly competitive market, but we know from empirical observation that real-world markets use a variety of mechanisms that are sometimes very different from this ideal type. Are all such institutions equivalent, or do some work differently? In order to answer this question, the ability to *control* preferences is crucial. By controlling preferences, one can try to systematically vary the supply/demand schedules in a given market, and observe the results of such variations. Also, one can keep the preferences fixed "in the background" and observe the effect of using different institutions (an open-cry and a sealed-bid option, for instance) in a given environment (cf. Smith 1982b, 927). Both activities were at the core of Smith's research program, and the precepts of experimental economics were proposed as guidelines for the design of experiments of this kind.

The first four precepts are:

1. *Nonsatiation:* choose a medium of reward such that, of two otherwise equivalent alternatives, subjects will always choose the one yielding more of the reward medium.
2. *Saliency:* the reward must be increasing in the good and decreasing in the bad outcomes of the experiment.
3. *Dominance:* the rewards dominate any subjective costs associated with participation in the experiment.
4. *Privacy:* each subject in an experiment receives information only about her own payoffs.[21]

The rewards could be anything that satisfies the precepts—candies for children, mobile phone recharges for teenagers, or just the satisfaction of having done well in the experimental task. For a number of reasons, however, the use of monetary incentives has become de facto a universal methodological practice in experimental economics. Privacy or anonymity is, also, almost universally implemented, and indeed it would be difficult to publish in an economics journal the results of an experiment violating these two requirements. Recently, some influential economists have campaigned to include the *repetition* of a task among the fundamental precepts of experimental economics (Plott 1995, Binmore 1999). The important point is that such design principles are advocated for *all* experiments, well outside the intended domain of Smith's original precepts. It has even been proposed that they should be endorsed by psychologists, too, who traditionally have a much more eclectic approach to experimental design (Hertwig & Ortmann 2001). It is unclear, however, how such uniformity of practice at the low-level of experimental design is to be justified. Instrumental methodology can come to the rescue, by reminding us about the empirical character of methodological issues of this kind. In order to assess a proposed design principle, two crucial questions ought to be asked: What goals are the low-level precepts meant to achieve? And are they likely to achieve such goals?

5.2 Monetary Incentives

The main argument for using significant monetary incentives moves from the consideration that they reduce the variation in subjects' performance.[22] Incentives would improve performance by reducing the noise (deviations from the normative theory) due, for example, to lack of concentration or gaming. From their overview of empirical studies, however, Hertwig and Ortmann (2001) conclude that:

1. Deviations from the normative model of decision-making (EUT) are never completely eliminated by raising the incentives.
2. Variation is often reduced, but
3. Average performance is rarely significantly affected.
4. Moreover, in about 29 percent of experiments, higher incentives cause a *worsening* of performance.[23]

It is surprising, especially in light of 4, that experimenters currently do not have a good theory of why (and how) incentives might matter. Surely, if incentives are able to push subjects' performance in different directions depending on the context, then what we need is a systematic study and a theory of the effect of monetary incentives (Read 2005). Hertwig and Ortmann (2001) conclude that, until we achieve a better understanding of the ways in which monetary incentives work, a do-it-both-ways strategy (experimenting with and without monetary payoffs) may be the most reasonable approach to this particular design issue.

5.3 Anonymity

Restricting the range of interactions between subjects is another design practice that has become typical of experimental economics (as opposed to psychology, for example, where it is more often relaxed). The fourth of Smith's precepts (Privacy) imposes strict anonymity, and it is presented as functional to achieving full control of individual preferences in the laboratory. It is likely, in fact, that knowing the identity of other players and their earnings may trigger other-regarding behavior of some kind. Since Smith's experiments were aimed at studying institutions, it was reasonable to try to achieve control and uniformity on preferences by eliminating possible sources of disturbance.[24]

It is worth introducing, now, an important but often overlooked distinction between two types of privacy. *Full privacy* is obtained in particular in market experiments, where subjects not only ignore the identity of the other players, but are unaware of their earnings, too. Because each trader is assigned privately a reservation price, exchanging an item at a certain price does not automatically reveal one's earnings to the other party.[25] This sort of privacy, however, is not implemented in a wide class of experiments, including ultimatum and public-goods games. Here, because of the exact symmetry in the payoffs of all players, everyone is usually aware of the earnings of every other player in her group, even though it is impossible to attach a specific identity to them. Intuitively, this *weak privacy*—or "identity-privacy," as opposed to the full "identity and earning-privacy"—may be insufficient to induce completely self-interested preferences in experimental subjects and may trigger violations of the predictions based on standard self-interested models.[26]

Although (weak) anonymity has become de facto, a quasi-universal feature of economic experiments, some psychologists and economists have run experiments to test the effect of "proximity" with other players on behavior in social dilemma and ultimatum experiments (relaxing "identity-privacy," in the terminology introduced earlier). It is known, for example, that even a moderate amount of contact (like watching a photograph of the other player) increases significantly the amount of cooperation, with maximum levels reached under conditions of direct communication between the members of a group (Isaac and Walker 1988, Orbell et al. 1988). Although few economists engage in this sort of experiments, they are clearly most valuable to test the robustness of certain types of behaviour and anomalies.[27]

Anonymity is likely to be an important variable affecting economic behavior, in subtle ways that vary from context to context. Although there are good reasons to impose certain forms of privacy in *some* classes of experiment, we should be aware that no anonymity requirement is likely to be appropriate in *all* experimental circumstances. By imposing uniformity of design we would again prevent many important lessons to be learnt from experimental data.

5.4 Repetition

The importance of repetition is one of the earliest lessons taught by experimental economics. Smith (1962) highlights it in his first published article on experimental markets: double oral auction markets converge on efficient equilibria only after a series of repetitions. Similar results have been observed in repeated public goods games (the decay of contribution), and repetition has become a mantra of many economists and experimenters, recently backed up by the rise of evolutionary game theory.[28] As with incentives, however, there is little clarity on exactly why repetition matters. Almost everybody agrees that it allows some kind of learning to take place. But learning *of what?*

In a repeated game, subjects can learn about (1) the structure of the game (strategies, incentives, etc), or (2) the behaviour of the other players. If (1) is the case, repetition could play roughly a similar role to incentives, that is, they could facilitate understanding of the mechanics of the game and hence reduce variation (error) around the normatively correct strategy (Binmore 1999; Plott 1995). The empirical evidence, however, suggests that (2) accounts for the convergence toward Nash in an important class of experiments. Consider public-goods games again: A substantial portion of subjects in these experiments are conditional cooperators who make their decisions based on their expectations regarding the behavior of other players. In a standard experiment, the behavior of a minority of free riders frustrates conditional cooperators in the early rounds and triggers the decline of contributions toward Nash. Recent experiments show convincingly that if they are reassured that they are playing with other cooperators, most subjects are happy to continue to contribute until the end of the game (Burlando & Guala 2005; Gachter & Thoni 2005; Page et al. 2005).

Again, there seems to be no rationale for imposing repetition as a universal requirement of experimental design. Indeed by varying repetition and by studying its effects, one can learn a good deal about when and why it matters. But a design with repetition does not automatically guarantee or even improve the validity of an experiment.

6. EXTERNAL VALIDITY

Trying to solve what are essentially empirical issues by a priori methodological stipulation is always tempting. Unconditional rules are cognitively less demanding and easier to implement, to begin with. In some cases, one may even be able to build a rule-utilitarian justification for them, if the rules lead to positive consequences in the overwhelming majority of cases. But whether the consequences are overwhelmingly positive is itself an empirical issue, and as we have seen the evidence doesn't seem to point in this direction. "Aprioristic" tendencies can be found in another important methodological debate, concerning the generalizability of experimental results outside laboratory conditions. The "external validity" of experiments is one of the most sensitive and controversial issues in experimental economics. The common perception for a long time has been that the very possibility of the experimental approach in economics was at stake in this controversy, and, perhaps, for this reason both experimenters and their critics have been seeking universal a priori answers to the question of generalizability.

Call D_1 a set of conditions instantiated in a laboratory to establish a certain causal claim. Typically, such claim takes the form of "C causes E in D_1," where D_1 includes those causal factors and background conditions that experimenters consider relevant, given the body of scientific knowledge available at the time. Knowledge of D_1 (the "causal field," in Mackie's (1974) terminology) is typically incomplete at any given point in time because of practical and epistemic constraints. Call D_2 a set of nonlaboratory (real-world) conditions, which constitute a domain of prima facie applicability for the laboratory result. If D_1 includes a set of typical conditions instantiated in a public-goods experiment, for example, D_2 may include the behavior of donors to the Red Cross or of fishermen in the North Sea.[29] External validity sceptics deny that evidence collected in D_1 to support claims like "C causes E" also provide support for "C causes E" in D_2.

The standard reply to this challenge is known as the blame-the-theorist move: My experiment instantiates all the factors that the most advanced theory deems relevant for the occurrence of this effect. If something is missing from the experiment, it is missing from the theory too (Smith 1982, 268; Plott 1991). This reply is based on a view of science as a fundamentally theory-driven activity. In particular, it assumes that the inclusion of all the background conditions and factors in the causal field should be ideally included in the antecedent of a causal law. Following a terminology introduced by Jerry Fodor, let's call it the completer view of science. In previous work (Guala 2005, Chapter 7) I have criticized the completer view, for reasons that still appear compelling to me. Instead of repeating these reasons, however, let us take the completer view on board for the sake of the argument and see what it implies.

Suppose we have good experimental evidence in support of the claim that "C causes E in D_1." Whether this result extends to D_2 can be established only by looking at D_2, and checking whether the conditions listed in D_1 are instantiated there too. If they are, we can infer that the causal claim is likely to be valid in D_2, otherwise not. But this means that empirical evidence is required, at least to check what difference, if any, exists between D_1 and D_2. External validity is not a question that can be solved on a priori grounds.

Notice that this is *not* equivalent to shifting the burden of proof toward the sceptic. The experimenter cannot simply *assume* that the results of an experiment apply outside the laboratory, until a critic identifies a potentially relevant causal difference between the two domains. That would be equivalent to committing what Deborah Mayo (2006) calls "the fallacy of arguing from ignorance": Not having evidence against X is not equivalent to having evidence in favour of X. The absence of potentially relevant causal differences must result from a process of probing the relevant domains. It must result from a serious empirical inquiry, rather than from merely a lack of it.

But what if some potentially relevant difference is found? As we know, conditions in the laboratory are seldom, if ever, the same as those found in the field. We value the lab precisely because it is unlike the field, because we can manipulate, simplify, omit conditions that stand in the way of scientific inference in naturally occurring circumstances. When such differences are identified, the ball is in the experimenter's camp. Most alleged differences can be eliminated in the laboratory, and the hypothesis that they affect the main causal claim can be tested experimentally. External validity criticism of this kind is no enemy to the experimental approach, but rather a constant source of new hypotheses for testing (Starmer 1999, 9).

Contrary to what has been suggested (by, e.g., Siakantaris 2000) there is no vicious circularity in this dialogue between laboratory and field evidence. We can use methodology M_2 to confirm or extend a result obtained by means of M_1, if the results obtained with M_1 allow us to use M_2 more effectively than it would have been the case before M_1 was used in the first place. Field evidence can tell us more interesting stories if interpreted on the background of a body of experimental knowledge, and vice versa (Guala 2002b). As in the most advanced sciences, economists must build knowledge step by step, combining different methods of inquiry and exploiting their strengths when they turn out to be most useful in the course of a research program.

Thus a single experiment can be used only to back up a generic causal claim, a claim that "C causes E in D_1," accompanied by a more-or-less refined description of what D_1 amounts to. In a series of experiments, the robustness of the causal claim to a range of changes in D_1 can also be established,[30] but again no general inference to the validity of the experimental result can follow from that. Notice that this reluctance to go beyond the strict domain of empirical testing is not the consequence of a Humean anti-inductivist prejudice. We do not question this sort of inference because the laws of nature may change tomorrow for no particular reason; we worry that a result may not be projectible to a new domain for very good reasons indeed—because there may be relevant causal differences between the two domains. This cautious attitude is consistent with the empiricist commitment to accept in science only what has passed a severe empirical test, and to suspend judgment when we have insufficient evidence. This is extremely important, especially when we want to *act* on the basis of scientific knowledge: NASA does not design and launch space probes on the basis of laboratory data only. Because policy interventions based on economic knowledge are often much more costly and potentially deadly than the failure of a space probe enterprise, this is a maxim that economists should follow carefully too.[31]

7. CONCLUSION

Opponents of normative methodology often advocate a more empirical approach to the methodology of economics. However, it should be clear from this chapter that normative methodology in the instrumental mode is actually *extremely* empirically oriented. At the lowest level of analysis, most methodological issues (such as those raised by the use of incentives, anonymity, repetition) turn out to be straightforward empirical questions that can and ought to be solved by means of scientific investigation. Questions at the high and middle level of methodological analysis are also empirical, in the sense that they require an assessment of means-ends efficacy such as the one attempted in Section 4. Such assessment will involve a debate on the goals of scientific research, and so typically invoke fairly abstract concepts such as those that philosophers are traditionally accustomed to. But such concepts are introduced to make sense of scientists' real methodological practices and commitments, rather than to satisfy abstract epistemological or metaphysical desiderata.

The potential of this approach has not been fully exploited yet, at least by philosophers of economics. There are many more examples within experimental economics that I could have highlighted, and still more potential applications in other areas of economics in general. The instrumental approach calls for a careful analysis of scientific practice, at a level of detail that might put off those who see philosophy as flying high above the routines of laboratory science. But the gains may be considerable, especially if philosophers finally want to engage with the very issues that scientists find problematic in their own work. It is a price to be paid in order to be *relevant,* in other words, and irrelevance is the most depressing fate that an intellectual enterprise can possibly face.

NOTES

1. I should thank Harold Kincaid for several comments and suggestions that helped me to improve this chapter. This project was completed while I was supported by the ESRC grant RES-000-22–1591. The usual caveats apply.

2. Another, more fundamental worry is that a pure, value-free description of a set of social practices may not be possible even in principle. Since a proper discussion of this problem would lead me too far away from our topic, I ask the reader to take the descriptivist position in the text mainly as an ideal type.

3. We still lack a proper history of experimental economics, but bits and pieces can be found in Smith (1992), Roth (1995), Lee & Mirowski (2008), Fontaine and Leonard (2005), Moscati (2007), Guala (2007). Overviews of the main results of experimental economics are collected in Kagel and Roth (1995).

4. A fuller description of the experimental setup and some useful tips about how to run it in class can be found in Holt and Laury (1997), which is the main source for this section. For other class experiments, see Charlie Holt's excellent Web page (http://www.people.virginia.edu/~cah2k/teaching.html), as well as Bergstrom and Miller's (1997) textbook. Experiments are very useful pedagogic tools, and should be used more frequently especially in undergraduate and graduate courses in social philosophy or the philosophy of economics.

5. A Nash equilibrium is such that the strategy implemented by each player is the best move, given the strategies of the other players: in equilibrium, no player has an incentive to change her own strategy, in other words.

6. See Ledyard (1995) for a survey of the relevant experimental literature until the early 1990s.

7. See for instance Isaac, Walker, & Thomas (1984) for the production function effect, and Andreoni (1988) for a seminal study of the restart effect.

8. Orbell, van de Kragt & Dawes (1988) is a well-known study of promise making in public-goods experiments.

9. This point is often overlooked and leads to a lot of confusion in the interpretation of experimental results. See Hausman (2005) and Guala (2006) for discussions of this point and its implications for the way in which game theory models should be tested.

10. This is the well-known Duhem-Quine problem, which has been discussed extensively in the philosophy of science. For applications to experimental economics, see e.g. Mongin (1988), Guala (2005, Ch. 3–6), and Soberg (2005).

11. On the relation between models and experiments as tools for the investigation of economic reality, see Guala (2002a), Morgan (2005), and Mäki (2005).

12. See e.g., Cartwright (1983), Giere (1988), Morgan & Morrison (1998).

13. This idea should be familiar to people trained in classical statistics. In philosophy of science, it can be found in more or less explicit form in Cartwright (1995), Mayo (1996) and Hacking (2001).

14. Consider, for example, the hypothetico-deductive model: Few philosophers nowadays would claim that it gives an accurate representation of scientific reasoning, yet it is considered extremely useful for pedagogical purposes, for highlighting the main problems of confirmation and testing, and as a starting point to develop better (less idealized, more truthful) models.

15. Hacking (1983) provides several illustrations and a seminal critique of this tradition in the philosophy of natural science. Plott (1991) is an example of a theory-centered view of experimental economics. Recent critiques include Smith (2002), Guala (2005) and Reiss (2008, Chapter 6).

16. For some taxonomies of economic experiments, which include theory testing among various other goals, see, e.g., Smith (1994), Roth (1995), Sugden (2005).

17. See Perrin (1910). An excellent methodological analysis of Perrin's experiments can be found in Mayo (1996, Chapter 7).

18. On the link between experiments, causation, and surgical intervention, see Woodward (2003).

19. This discussion relates in various ways to the debate on so-called tendency laws that has been central in recent philosophy of economics (Cartwright 1989, Hausman 1992). Tendencies are, roughly speaking, super-robust causal relations, and postulating their existence would solve a lot of methodological problems, such as the problem of external validity that threatens many experimental results. My position is that the existence of economic tendencies is an empirical issue that should not be resolved by metaphysical *fiat* (see Guala 2002b, 2005, as well as later Section 6). On this issue, see also Siakantaris (2000), Alexandrova (2006), and Steel (2007).

20. Some philosophers add a time-order condition to avoid backward causation in time; Cartwright argues that once the background conditions are fully specified, cases of backward causation are taken care of, but since a proper discussion of this topic would lead me too far away, I will just gloss over it.

21. A fifth precept (Parallelism) is concerned with the external validity of experiments, and it plays a rather different function from the earlier ones. See later Section 6, as well as Guala (2005, especially Chapter 7).

22. Other arguments highlight the importance of testing economic theory in its own domain, e.g., where the assumption of self-interest is satisfied. Although this makes

sense for some market experiments, it is a confused piece of reasoning when applied to experiments aimed at *testing* the assumption of selfish preferences, like those on public goods. See Binmore (1999) and Hertwig & Ortmann (2001) for example.

23. See Smith and Walker (1993), Camerer and Hogarth (1999), Hertwig & Ortmann (2001).

24. It is also the case that many market interactions in real life occur between people who do not know each other, and each trader has little opportunity to learn about the profits made by the other party in the transaction. Since not all market interactions are of this kind, however, to claim that anonymity increases external validity in general is unwarranted. There is extensive evidence, for example, that reputation and reciprocity are very important for stock-market traders (see Abolafia 1996).

25. This is similar to not knowing the cost function of a product when we buy it from the producer. Without such information, one cannot calculate the profits of the seller. Although this is often the case especially with consumers' goods, it is well known that many firms like to share information about production costs with their clients in order to negotiate a "fair" price.

26. I'm indebted to Ana Santos for highlighting this distinction (see Santos 2006).

27. This is particularly important if behavior in ultimatum and public-goods games is to a large extent influenced by context-specific social norms (Bicchieri 2006). The framing of an experiment (with or without anonimity) may trigger different expectations about the norms of behavior that are in place—see the chapters by Jim Woodward and by Cristina Bicchieri in this volume for an extensive discussion of such issues.

28. Binmore (1999), again, is a good example. Evolutionary game theory models the dynamics of the propagation of a given strategy in a population playing an indefinitely repeated game. Clearly focusing on one-shot or finitely repeated interactions has little theoretical interest, from the evolutionary point of view, unless these interactions reveal those strategies that are at work in the long-term game of life.

29. To identify the "intended domain" of a given economic model is not always an easy task. A sophisticated discussion of this important and yet often overlooked problem can be found in Cubitt (2005).

30. This is roughly what Cartwright and Hausman call a "tendency claim" (see also footnote 19). On the importance of robustness (or "invariance") considerations see again Woodward (2003, Chapter 6).

31. And to an extent they are already following it. See for example the budding literature on "field-experiments" reviewed by Harrison and List (2004).

REFERENCES

Abolafia, M.Y. (1996). *Making Markets: Opportunism and Restraint on Wall Street.* Cambridge, MA.: Harvard University Press.

Alexandrova, A. (2006). "Connecting Economic Models to the Real World: Game Theory and the FCC Spectrum Auctions." *Philosophy of the Social Sciences* 36: 173–192.

Andreoni, J. (1988). "Why Free Ride? Strategies and Learning in Public Goods Experiments." *Journal of Public Economics* 37: 291–304.

Bergstrom, T.C. & Miller, J.H. (1997) *Experiments with Economic Principles: Microeconomics.* New York: McGraw-Hill.

Bicchieri, C. (2006). *The Grammar of Society: The Nature and Dynamics of Social Norms*. New York: Cambridge University Press.

Binmore, K. (1999). "Why Experiment in Economics?" *Economic Journal* 109: F16–24.

Burlando, R. & Guala, F. (2005). "Heterogeneous Agents in Public Goods Experiments." *Experimental Economics* 8: 35–54.

Camerer, C.F. & Hogarth, R.M. (1999). "The Effects of Financial Incentives in Experiments: A Review and Capital-labor-production Framework." *Journal of Risk and Uncertainty* 19: 7–42.

Cartwright, N. (1983). *How the Laws of Physics Lie*. Oxford: Clarendon Press.

Cartwright, N. (1989). *Nature's Capacities and Their Measurement*. Oxford: Oxford University Press.

Cartwright, N. (1995). "False Idealisation: A Philosophical Threat to Scientific Method." *Philosophical Studies* 77: 339–352.

Cartwright, N. (1999). *The Dappled World: A Study of the Boundaries of Science*. Cambridge, England: Cambridge University Press.

Cubitt, R. (2005). "Experiments and the Domain of Economic Theory." *Journal of Economic Methodology* 12: 297–210.

Dupré, J. (1984). "Probabilistic Causality Emancipated." *Midwest Studies in Philosophy* 9: 169–175.

Friedman, D. & Sunder, S. (1994). *Experimental Methods: A Primer for Economists*. New York: Cambridge University Press.

Fontaine, P. & Leonard, R., Eds. (2005). *The Experiment in the History of Economics*. London: Routledge.

Gachter, S. & Thoni, C. (2005). "Social Learning and Voluntary Cooperation among Like-Minded People." *Journal of the European Economic Association* 3: 303–314.

Giere, R.N. (1988). *Explaining Science*. Chicago: University of Chicago Press.

Guala, F. (2002a). "Models, Simulations, and Experiments." In L. Magnani & N.J. Nersessian, Eds., *Model-Based Reasoning: Science, Technology, Values*, 59–74. New York: Kluwer.

Guala, F. (2002b). "On the Scope of Experiments in Economics: Comments on Siakantaris." *Cambridge Journal of Economics* 26: 261–267.

Guala, F. (2005). *The Methodology of Experimental Economics*. New York: Cambridge University Press.

Guala, F. (2006). "Has Game Theory Been Refuted?" *Journal of Philosophy* 103: 239–263.

Guala, F. (2007). "History of Experimental Economics." In S. Durlauf & L. Blume. Eds., *The Palgrave Dictionary of Economics*. London: Palgrave-Macmillan.

Hacking, I. (1983). *Representing and Intervening*. Cambridge, England: Cambridge University Press.

Hacking, I. (2001). *An Introduction to Probability and Inductive Logic*. Cambridge, England: Cambridge University Press.

Hands, D.W. (2001). *Reflection without Rules: Economic Methodology and Contemporary Science Theory*. Cambridge, England: Cambridge University Press.

Harrison, G.W. & List, J.A. (2004). "Field Experiments." *Journal of Economic Literature* 42: 1009–1045.

Hausman, D.M. (1992). *The Inexact and Separate Science of Economics*. New York: Cambridge University Press.

Hausman, D.M. (1998). *Causal Asymmetries*. New York: Cambridge University Press.

Hausman, D. M. (2005). "'Testing' Game Theory." *Journal of Economic Methodology* 12: 211–223.

Hertwig, R. & Ortmann, A. (2001). "Experimental Practices in Economics: A Methodological Challenge for Psychologists?" *Behavioral and Brain Sciences* 24: 383–451.

Humphreys, P. (1989). *The Chances of Explanation*. Princeton: Princeton University Press.

Holt, C.A., & Laury, S.K. (1997). "Classroom Games: Voluntary Provision of a Public Good." *Journal of Economic Perspectives* 11: 209–215.

Isaac, R.M. & Walker, J.M. (1988). "Communication and Free-Riding Behavior: The Voluntary Contribution Mechanism." *Economic Inquiry* 26: 585–608.

Isaac, R.M., Walker, J.M. & Thomas, S. (1984). "Divergent Evidence on Free-riding: An Experimental Examination of Possible Explanations." *Public Choice* 43: 113–149.

Kagel, J.H. & Roth, A.E., Eds. (1995) *The Handbook of Experimental Economics*. Princeton: Princeton University Press.

Laudan, L. (1984). *Science and Values*. Berkeley: University of California Press.

Ledyard, J.O. (1995). "Public Goods: A Survey of Experimental Research." In J.H. Kagel & A.E. Roth, Eds., *The Handbook of Experimental Economics*. Princeton: Princeton University Press.

Lee, K. S. & Mirowski, P. (2008). "The Energy Behind Vernon Smith's Experimental Economics," *Cambridge Journal of Economics* 32: 257–271.

Mackie, J.L. (1974). *The Cement of the Universe*. Oxford: Clarendon Press.

Mäki, U. (2005). "Models Are Experiments, Experiments Are Models." *Journal of Economic Methodology* 12: 303–315.

Mayo, D. (1996). *Error and the Growth of Experimental Knowledge*. Chicago: University of Chicago Press.

Mayo, D. (2006). "External Validity and the Rational Scrutiny of Models of Rationality." Paper presented at the 2006 Philosophy of Science Association meeting in Vancouver.

Mongin, P. (1988). "Problèmes de Duhem en théorie de l'utilité espérée." *Fundamenta Scientiae* 9: 299–327.

Morgan, M.S. (2003). "Economics." In T. Porter & D. Ross, Eds., *The Cambridge History of Science, Vol. 7: The Modern Social Sciences,* 275–305. Cambridge, England: Cambridge University Press.

Morgan, M. S. (2005). "Experiments versus Models: New Phenomena, Inference and Surprise." *Journal of Economic Methodology* 12: 317–29.

Morgan, M. & Morrison, M., Eds. (1998). *Models as Mediators*. Cambridge: Cambridge University Press.

Moscati, I. (2007). "Early Experiments in Consumer Demand Theory: 1930–1970," *History of Political Economy* 39: 359–401.

Orbell, J., van de Kragt, A. & Dawes, R. (1988). "Explaining Discussion-Induced Cooperation." *Journal of Personality and Social Psychology* 54: 811–819.

Page, T., Putterman, L. & Unel, B. (2005). "Voluntary Association in Public Goods Experiments: Reciprocity, Mimicry and Efficiency." *Economic Journal* 115: 1032–1053.

Perrin, J. (1910). *Brownian Movement and Molecular Reality*. London: Taylor and Francis.

Plott, C.R. (1991). "Will Economics Become an Experimental Science?" *Southern Economic Journal* 57: 901–919.

Plott, C. R. (1995). "Rational Individual Behaviour in Markets and Social Choice Processes: The Discovered Preference Hypothesis." In K.J. Arrow, E. Colombatto, M. Perlman & C. Schmidt, Eds., *The Rational Foundations of Economic Behaviour,* 225–250. London: Macmillan.

Read, D. (2005). "Monetary Incentives, What Are They Good for?" *Journal of Economic Methodology* 12: 265–276.

Reiss, J. (2008). *Error in Economics: Towards a More Evidence-Based Methodology.* London: Routledge.

Rosenberg, A. (1993). *Economics: Mathematical Politics or Science of Diminishing Returns?* Chicago: University of Chicago Press.

Rosenberg, A. (1996). "A Field Guide to Recent Species of Naturalism." *British Journal for the Philosophy of Science* 47: 1–29.

Roth, A. E. (1995). "Introduction to Experimental Economics." In J. H. Kagel & A. E. Roth, Eds., *The Handbook of Experimental Economics,* 3–109. Princeton: Princeton University Press.

Santos, A. (2006). *The Social Epistemology of Experimental Economics.* Rotterdam: Erasmus University Ph.D. dissertation.

Siakantaris, N. (2000). "Experimental Economics Under the Microscope." *Cambridge Journal of Economics* 24: 267–281.

Smith, V.L. (1962). "An Experimental Study of Competitive Market Behavior." *Journal of Political Economy* 70: 111–137

Smith, V. L. (1976). "Experimental Economics: Induced Value Theory." *American Economic Review* 66: 274–277.

Smith, V. L. (1982). "Microeconomic Systems as an Experimental Science." *American Economic Review* 72: 923–955.

Smith, V.L. (1992). "Game Theory and Experimental Economics: Beginnings and Early Influences." In E.R. Weintraub, Ed., *Towards A History of Game Theory.* History of Political Economy Supplement, Vol. 24. Durham: Duke University Press.

Smith, V. L. (1994). "Economics in the Laboratory." *Journal of Economic Perspectives* 8: 113–131.

Smith, V. L. (2002). "Method in Experiment: Rhetoric and Reality," *Experimental Economics* 5: 91–110.

Smith, V.L. & Walker, J.M. (1993). "Monetary Rewards and Decision Costs in Experimental Economics." *Economic Inquiry* 31: 245–261.

Soberg, M. (2005). "The Duhem-Quine Thesis and Experimental Economics: A Reinterpretation." *Journal of Economic Methodology* 12: 581–597.

Starmer, C. (1999). "Experiments in Economics ... (Should We Trust the Dismal Scientists in White Coats?)," *Journal of Economic Methodology* 6: 1–30.

Steel, D. (2007). *Across the Boundaries: Extrapolation and Causality in the Biological and Social Sciences.* New York: Oxford University Press.

Sugden, R. (2005). "Experiments as Exhibits and Experiments as Tests." *Journal of Economic Methodology* 12: 291–302.

Wilde, L. L. (1981). "On the Use of Laboratory Experiments in Economics." In J. C. Pitt, ed., *Philosophy in Economics,* 137–148. Dordrecht, The Netherlands: Reidel.

Woodward, J. (2003). *Making Things Happen: A Theory of Causal Explanation.* Oxford: Oxford University Press.

Worrall, J. (1989). "The Value of a Fixed Methodology." *British Journal for the Philosophy of Science* 39: 263–275.

CHAPTER 11

PROGRESS IN ECONOMICS: LESSONS FROM THE SPECTRUM AUCTIONS

ANNA ALEXANDROVA
AND ROBERT NORTHCOTT

1. Introduction

The models of microeconomics are famously idealized and have a famously spotty predictive record. Yet recent years have seen some tremendous successes in using these models to construct reliable economic institutions. The focus of this chapter is one such institution, namely, spectrum auctions—now used all over Europe and North America to distribute licenses to telecommunications firms. This has been seen as a great triumph for game theory in particular. We shall explore the implications of this case for a venerable issue in philosophy of science, namely, the status of idealized models. What is the contribution of such models to empirical successes? We then use the lessons drawn from the spectrum auction to shed light, in turn, on a second venerable issue, namely, scientific progress. In particular, we explore the question, Is there progress in economics? And if so, what form does it take?

Previous analyses of these issues have often focused on theory in the abstract, or else on how models are used in academic discussions. But we believe there is much to be gained by examining the dirty details of how theory is actually applied when there is much at stake. Those details turn out to be revealing. They are especially revealing in a case of conspicuously *successful* application such as the spectrum auction, as such a case tells us much about how the gap between idealized model and messy world may actually be bridged.

Several well-developed philosophical accounts of models are now available. Auction design, meanwhile, is an instance of a larger branch of applied economics—institution design or, to use Al Roth's term, design economics. More and more, this is a principal arena for the application of microeconomic theory (Roth 2002), so it is desirable that any account of models speaks to it. Can our case study in design economics arbitrate between the different competing accounts? We believe that it can. In particular, even though the spectrum auction design is now a paradigmatic case of the use of microeconomic theory for policy making, we shall argue that none of the existing accounts can explain the role of models in it. We, therefore, propose a new account—models as open formulas—that, we claim, alone is able to do so.

The plan of the chapter is as follows: We begin in Section 2 by surveying existing work on scientific models, with an eye to the specific case of economics. We review four accounts in particular—the satisfaction-of-assumptions account, the capacities account, the credible-worlds account, and the partial-structures account. In Section 3, we tell the detailed story of the 1994 Federal Communications Commission (FCC) spectrum auction in the United States, highlighting the crucial role of experiment as well as theory. In Section 4, in the light of this case study, we present our own open-formula account of economic models.

We are then finally ready, in Section 5, to turn to the issue of economic progress. Our case study enables us to get clear on exactly what has been progressing, and on exactly what theory has—and has not—contributed to that. We shall conclude that we may *not* speak of empirical progress in economic *theory,* or at least that the success of the spectrum auction provides no warrant for doing so. Rather, progress is better seen as more akin to the worthy but piecemeal variety typical of *engineering.* This in turn has important implications for just what it is about economic theory that we should value.

2. Models in Science: A Brief Survey

The models we have in mind here are the rational choice ones of neoclassical microeconomics. These are idealized in that they posit perfectly rational agents never seen in real life, and in many other ways too. There exist a number of philosophical accounts of such models. (See Frigg and Hartmann 2006 for a general inventory of types of models in science.) The accounts we shall consider here focus on answering two questions: what sorts of claims do these models make? And how do these claims figure in the interventions (and explanations) that we might design on the basis of these models? In other words, what does the spectrum auction tell us about how, in cases of true success, economic models really work? Shortly, we shall review four such accounts.

It is important to distinguish these questions from others that philosophers of science have been concerned about, such as what kind of objects models are, how they represent, how they relate to theory, and more. Take for instance the debate about how models represent the world. Various accounts have been proposed: models have been said to represent by virtue of isomorphism (van Fraassen 1980), partial isomorphism (Da Costa & French 2003), similarity (Giere 1988), by generating inferences (Suarez 2004), or by satisfying descriptions (Frigg 2006). Interesting though the issue is, we do *not* think that a correct account of representation would answer the questions we are concerned about here. To illustrate why not, let us take a closer look at one of the accounts just mentioned—the partial isomorphism view, as recently defended by Newton Da Costa and Steven French (2003).

Partial Structures

According to the classic structuralist view, a model is a structure of the form $\{A, R_i\}_{i \in I}$, where A is a set of individuals in a given domain of knowledge and the R_i comprise a family of relations defined on A. In Tarski's schema, models provide interpretations of a language and we may talk about the truth of a sentence of this language by reference to a model that the sentence satisfies. Using this framework, philosophers of science have represented scientific theories by the structures or models that the linguistic formulations of those theories satisfy. Da Costa and French amend this idea in order to incorporate the incomplete and imperfect nature of scientific knowledge. To this end, they propose the notion of a *partial* structure, in which an n-place relation R_i is not necessarily defined for all n-tuples of elements in A. Then, such structures are true only of part of the domain that they model. The relationship between models and the world (the latter understood as a model of the true theory) is understood in terms of "relevant structural relationships, suitably weakened to include the more plausible similarity, rather than strict identity, and suitably broadened to cover similarities in both formal and material properties" (Da Costa & French 2003, 48). They dub such relationships partial isomorphism: One partial structure is partially isomorphic to another when certain relationships in the first structure stand in one-to-one correspondence to certain relationships of the second structure.

Da Costa and French take this framework to provide "an overarching account of models in science" (48). In their view, the notion of partial isomorphism can make sense of the use of idealization and approximation, the representative and heuristic functions of models, the autonomy of models from theories, and scientists' attitude toward models of partial or pragmatic acceptance.

Regardless of whether their account succeeds in these purposes, we do not think it succeeds in answering the questions we are interested in here. If economic models are to be represented by partial structures, then we need some account of how these partial structures are applied for explanation and intervention. More specifically, even if we grant that an auction model is partially isomorphic with reality, that fact is not very helpful in itself; such a model may still be dramatically inapplicable to the real world situations to which it is partially isomorphic, because there may be isomorphisms that do not tell us anything about the key processes involved. We need something extra to license interventions, that is, to distinguish between models that are useful and those that aren't. The critical question is whether a model is isomorphic to the part of the reality that actually matters. Da Costa and French's scheme does not tell us how to find out.

Credible Worlds

Another recent account views models as *credible worlds* (Sugden 2000, Gruene-Yanoff 2007). More particularly, and contrary to the Hausman satisfaction-of-assumptions account (see later), it denies that a model's assumptions describe the conditions under which causal relations hold in the world. Robert Sugden, in particular, worries that Hausman's logic is too restrictive because under it "we end up removing almost all empirical content from the implications of the models" (Sugden 2000, 17). Instead, economists' claims start to look like abstract theorems—*if assumption 1, assumption 2, . . . , assumption n are true, then such-and-such result follows*. But this is not how economists treat the conclusions of their models. Rather, they treat those models as making claims about the causal impact of one variable on another, holding fixed everything else. By itself, this is not a novel reading of models; what is novel is rather the justification that Sugden offers for it.

This justification lies in the notion of a credible world. A model is a sketch of a credible world to "the extent to which we can understand the relevant model as a description of how the world *could* be" (Sugden 2000, 24, original italics). Modelers construct imaginary worlds in which certain causal relations are shown to hold. To the extent that these relations cohere with our sense of how the actual world works, we come to view the world in the model as credible. A model is thus not a simplification of the existing world, but rather a parallel reality.

Unfortunately, the details of the account are unsatisfactorily underspecified. (Sugden notably does not connect it at all with the standard literature on the metaphysics of possible worlds.) Thus, for instance, how do we judge a world's credibility? Presumably, via background knowledge. But if so, judgments of credibility could not take us very far, in particular they could not take us *beyond* our background knowledge. In the case of the spectrum auction, *nobody*'s background knowledge could have told us which design would best distribute spectrum licenses. Of course, we can and do use judgments of credibility to decide which hypotheses we might admit into a pool of hypotheses to consider. But that is very far from showing that a particular piece of model-based knowledge is explanatory or is a reliable justification for policy. In the actual design of the auction, that crucial extra step required active experimental investigation, as we shall see, not mere informal judgments of credibility.

We conclude that the credible worlds view, although inspired specifically by microeconomic models and seeking to describe the conditions under which we can have confidence in them, turns out not to answer the questions that we are posing. It either fails to explain what makes models suitable bases for explanation and intervention, or else does not have that aim in the first place. However, there are other philosophical accounts of models that do clearly have that aim and that do give explicit answers regarding it. So we move on now to those.

Satisfaction of Assumptions

The first answer to these questions comes from an elaboration of the semantic view of theories defended by Ronald Giere (1988) and Daniel Hausman (1992). Hausman, applying the framework to economics, would argue that the equations in auction models, for instance, do not by themselves make empirical claims. Rather, they supply mere definitions, relating one mathematical entity to another. They only relate to the world via an additional hypothesis, namely that a real-world system satisfies some relevant class of the model's assumptions (Hausman 1992, 74–77). (A similar view of application appears to be endorsed by Morgan 2002.)

To see how this works, consider a standard auction theory model—say, one that claims that first-price auctions lead to bids lower than bidders' true valuations. To use this model to explain an actual first-price auction for, say, artwork, first the target system must satisfy the assumption that the auction is first-price. But that alone is not enough, because the model has many other assumptions, too, for instance that bidder's valuations have the right kind of statistical distribution, that bidders play according to Bayesian Nash equilibrium, that bidders are identical save for their valuations, etc. Should we, therefore, require that *all* the assumptions necessary for the derivation of the given result (i.e., bids below true valuation) be satisfied by the target system? This seems much too strict. No actual auction satisfies *all* the assumptions of a game theory model, for example, the assumption of perfect rationality. Rather, we need a criterion for distinguishing the relevant assumptions from the irrelevant ones.

One such criterion is supplied by the *de-idealization* approach (McMullin 1985). An assumption may be handled in two ways. First, the real-world system may satisfy it. Second, if it does not, then de-idealize by replacing the assumption with a more realistic one, while still preserving (to some degree) the predictions of the model relevant to explaining the target phenomenon. For example, if we have reason to believe that the real bidders are risk averse but our model assumes risk neutrality, then we add risk aversion into our model and check whether the derivation still holds. If it does, then the de-idealization process is successful and the model's result applies.

In such happy cases, we have the warrant to move from a claim in a model to a claim about a real-world target system. The fundamental problem with the strategy, however, is that, at least as far as economics is concerned, such happy cases may be hard to come by. In particular, problems arise when an assumption is not satisfied by the real-world system and yet cannot be relaxed, on pain of the model's derivation failing or on pain of us not being able to solve the model at all. For instance, in the actual spectrum auctions, bidders were not perfectly rational but all models assumed they were; hundreds of licenses were on sale, but there were hardly any multi-unit auction models at the time; models assumed no budget constraints, but real bidders most probably had those; and so on. Yet for none of these assumptions was de-idealization feasible. It was simply not possible, at least at the time, to build a model incorporating more realistic versions of the assumptions and to check the effect of these changes on the models' predictions. Indeed there simply was no *one* theoretical model capable of representing the actual auction as a whole, even at a very abstract level. This was known very well by the auction designers, who, as a result, had to use models in a more piecemeal manner, to be explained later.

Of course, the Hausman/McMullin account of model application may work better in other contexts. And, even in the case of auctions, we do know how to de-idealize *some* assumptions. But the important point for now is that de-idealization does not capture *all* that was actually going on in the spectrum auction design. A piece of the story is still missing.

Capacities

The last account is explicitly causal. On its view, models make claims about *tendencies* or *capacities,* notions proposed originally by John Stuart Mill (1843) and more recently elaborated by Nancy Cartwright (1989, 1998). For example, when we say that negatively charged bodies have the capacity to make other negatively charged bodies move away, we mean that they make others move away even in the presence of disturbing factors. Auction models, on this view, are built in order to investigate the canonical behavior of a capacity, that is, its operation in its pure form in the absence of interferences (Cartwright 1999). (A similar reading of economic models in terms of isolations is endorsed by Maki 1992.) For example, on the basis of a model, we may conclude that a first-price auction has the capacity to lower bids under the conditions of private values.

How might such models be applied? Following Polish philosopher Leszek Nowak, Cartwright argues that this occurs via a process of *concretization*. This involves adding back the factors (i.e., other capacities and disturbing factors) omitted by the model but present in the real-world situation. Unlike the previous account, concretization does not require that a model's assumptions be satisfied by the target situation for it to explain some feature of it. Capacities are supposed to be stable enough to allow us to move from what is true in a model to what is true in the real world. Of course, the various factors we introduce during concretization must correctly describe the disturbing factors. In particular, this means that de-idealization in the sense described earlier, although admissible, is not necessary. Concretization can proceed by correcting the model in accordance with our background causal knowledge in ways other than by construction of a great big model. Indeed, at some point we should expect theoretical tools to run out. For example, low-level facts that form no part of any theory, such as how different materials react to each other, prove necessary to correct theoretical models when constructing a laser (Cartwright 1989).

As we'll see shortly, the spectrum auction design required much more than theory. Knowledge of extratheoretical practicalities proved crucial, which tells in favor of Cartwright's concretization account. But it must still be demonstrated that economic models indeed supply genuine capacity claims, and this is a tough test to pass. Capacities, at least within a certain range of circumstances, are supposed to have stability in the face of other factors. That is, they are always 'attempting' to manifest themselves even when—because of disturbing factors—they do not actually do so. (For our purposes, we may ignore metaphysical qualms over the nature of this attempting, which is rooted in Cartwright's ontology of causal powers.) Yet, again as we'll see, that was certainly not the experience of the auction designers. Instead, they found interactions between causal factors more often than not, meaning that the postulated capacities were no longer operational, that is, they were no longer even attempting to manifest themselves. Consequently, the designers believed that the stability of causes was a poor working hypothesis.

More generally, in many contexts in special sciences, such as economics and biology, the stability of causal relations is precisely what is in question and cannot simply be assumed. (For more on whether there are capacities in economics, see Reiss, forthcoming.) And yet, even in such contexts, often theory can still be successfully applied. This suggests that something more is going on than is captured by the capacities account. We return to what that might be in Section 4. But first, it is time to tell the story of the spectrum auction in more detail.

3. THE STORY OF THE SPECTRUM AUCTION

Political Background

The radio spectrum is the portion of electromagnetic spectrum between 9 kilohertz and 300 gigahertz. Spectrum not needed for governmental purposes is distributed via licenses by the FCC. For a long time, most of these licenses were awarded on the basis of hearings in which potential users had to demonstrate the public interest of their proposed enterprise. Because these had tended to become highly politicized, in the 1980s Congress authorized the use of lotteries instead. Then, in 1993, the Omnibus Budget Reconciliation Act gave the FCC the right to use competitive market mechanisms such as auctions.

When taking office in 1992, Vice-President Al Gore viewed communications policy as key to his broader objectives. These were no less than to bring about an information revolution: deregulate the communications market, and thereby jump-start innovative technologies capable of bringing about genuine social change and empowerment. For instance, in one episode, the recently appointed FCC chairman Reed Hundt was in all seriousness lecturing Gerry Adams, the leader of the Irish republican party Sinn Fein (who had come to the United States hoping to have a meeting with Gore but instead had to make do with Hundt), that the Internet and cellular phones could bring peace to Northern Ireland (Hundt 2000). Less idealistically, Gore's team also saw an opportunity to weaken the big communications firms, who traditionally had been large Republican donors, by deregulating in such a way as to let new entrants take some of the industry's market share.

By the time the auctions were finally authorized by Congress, the Clinton administration was under siege, faced with Newt Gingrich's 1994 revolution in the House. The stakes were, thus, extremely high. If the auctions failed, the administration would lose credibility with regard to its communications policy and, with it, lose its ability to resist Congress. The FCC, as well as having to rethink its whole approach to spectrum distribution, would lose its bargaining power to extract concessions from the industry. In addition to the political stakes, there was also the considerable financial stake of the potential billions of dollars that could be raised for taxpayers.

Why Auction Design Matters

The best way to appreciate the importance of good auction design is to see what happens in its absence. In the early 1990s, the New Zealand government adopted a second-price design with no reserve price (i.e., no minimum bid). The results were deeply embarrassing because the high value of the licenses was widely known and publicized and yet the government ended up earning very little. Most notoriously, an Otago university student won a license for a small-town TV station by bidding just $5, actually paying nothing since nobody else submitted a bid. In Australia, the 1993 auction for satellite television licenses was a first-price sealed-bid auction, but with no deposit and no specific payment policy. An unknown outbid the big players such as Rupert Murdoch (which the government initially gave a good spin to), only to default on the payment with no punishment whatsoever (for which no good spin was available). A series of after-auction resales followed, which delayed the introduction of paid television for nearly a year (McMillan 1994).

More recently, Switzerland offered four licenses for sale in 2000 in an ascending auction and initially attracted nine bidders. However, the weaker bidders were put off by the competition from the incumbents, and, in addition to that, the government also allowed joint-bidding agreements, which gave two companies the right to agree on which license they'd each settle on without raising the price for each other—"officially-sanctioned collusion" in the words of Klemperer (2002a, 835). In the end, right before the auction, the number of bidders shrank to four, and it was looking increasingly likely that the four bidders would just pay the very low reserve prices. So the government tried to postpone the auction, only to be taken to court because it had not specified beforehand the right to cancel an auction in these circumstances. As a result, valuable licenses in one of the richest countries in Europe went for one-fifteenth of what the government had hoped (Wolfstetter 2003).

In contrast, the FCC's series of seven auctions from 1994 to 1996 were a remarkable success. They attracted many bidders, allocated several thousand licenses, and raised an inordinate amount of money—$20 billion—that surpassed all government and industry expectations (Cramton 1998). Even the first auctions went without a glitch and gave Reed Hundt the photo-opportunity of a lifetime when in front of TV cameras he presented to Bill Clinton a giant check made out to "American taxpayers" (Hundt 2000). The auctions' efficiency is harder to judge, partly because it is hard to observe bidders' valuations and hence hard to ascertain that the licenses went to those who valued them most. However, one positive sign is that similar licenses sold for approximately similar prices, suggesting that they were likely the market prices. Another is that many bidders were able, as desired, to purchase aggregations of licenses consistent with geographic synergies. Finally, there was little resale in the years following the auctions, which suggests that bidders still valued the licenses they purchased (Cramton 1998, 2006).[1] (Experimenters were also able to provide independent evidence of the auction's efficiency. See later.)

The Actual FCC Design

In the academic literature, the idea of using auctions to assign spectrum property rights dates from the 1950s (Herzel 1998, Coase 1998). The literature was revolutionized in the 1980s by a new generation of auction designs based on game theory. Nowadays, auctions have become a standard tool. Economic journals have published special issues on spectrum auctions (*Journal of Law and Economics* XLI (2) October 1998, *Journal of Economics and Management Strategy* 6, 1997), and the FCC hosts conferences in which economists discuss which designs are preferable for what purposes and what environments. The FCC Web site itself hosts records of papers and presentations on the topic by eminent scholars.

There was wide participation of economic theorists and experimentalists in the 1994 auction design. Several months in advance, the FCC solicited public comments. Many academics, hired either by prospective bidders or by the FCC itself, responded with recommendations. The constraints were set by government requirements: efficient and intensive use of the spectrum; promotion of new technologies; prevention of excessive concentration of licenses; and ensuring that some licenses go to favored bidders such as minority- and women-owned companies, small businesses, and rural telephone companies (McMillan 1994). Exactly what rules would reliably produce the desired outcome was a formidable puzzle for teams of economic theorists, experimentalists, lawyers, software engineers and policy makers.

To give a flavor of the intricacy of the final design, consider first that geographically the country was subdivided into 51 major trading areas, which in turn were subdivided into 492 basic trading areas, each of which had four spectrum blocks up for license. The auction mechanism finally selected was a simultaneous multiround auction. It put all licenses for sale *simultaneously,* as opposed to sequentially, and in an *open* rather than sealed-bid arrangement. Bidders placed bids on *individual,* as opposed to packages of, licenses they were interested in, and when a round was over, they saw what other bids had been placed. Then, the next round began, in which bidders were free to change the original combinations of licenses but had to increase their bid up to the level of the highest previous round bid plus a prescribed increment if they wished to hold on to a license. The process continued until no more bids on any license were received.

The bidding was regulated by a number of further rules:

Activity Rules: a bidder had to maintain a certain level of activity during each round, on pain of reduced eligibility in subsequent rounds. However, each bidder also got five waivers that allowed them to take advantage of five opportunities not to place a bid on a particular license in a round.

Minimum Bid Requirement: between rounds, the auctioneer specified the minimum bid increment (between 5 and 20 percent). The exact increment chosen depended on bidders' behavior—the more bidding, the larger the increment.

Designated Entities: companies owned by women, minorities, and/or small businesses, got 10–40 percent credits on specific licenses.

Spectrum Cap: no firm could own more than 45MHz of spectrum in any geographical area, hence could not bid on more than the corresponding number of licenses.

Payment Rules: the FCC required an upfront payment from which penalties were deducted if the bidder withdrew, or which got refunded if the bidder failed to win the license they were bidding for.

This is a very brief summary. The full statement of the auction rules takes over 130 pages (FCC 1994b). By rules, we mean the explicit and public instructions covering entry, bidding, and payment that all participants received and studied before the auction. But, as we shall see, in addition much work also had to be put into perfecting the precise material environment, that is, features such as the software, the venue and timing of the auction, and whatever aspects of the legal and economic environment the designers could control.

The critical question for us is what justified this final complex design—why this design rather than another? It would be convenient if the methodology could be read off uncontroversially from what the actors involved said and did, but matters are not so simple. This is not surprising given that the auctions were a hugely sensitive phenomenon that put at stake the fortunes of the FCC, the Clinton administration, and the telecoms industry, as well as the reputations of many economists. Two main competing accounts emerge—roughly, those of *theorists* and those of *experimentalists*.

The Theorists' View

John McMillan and Preston McAfee were economic theorists, at the time working, respectively, at University of California–San Diego and University of Texas–Austin, who became actively involved in the FCC auction design. McMillan was hired by the FCC itself, McAfee by the potential bidder Airtouch Communications. They are also the influential authors of the first two articles dedicated wholly to the FCC spectrum auctions, which appeared in the *Journal of Economic Perspectives* in summer 1994 and then winter 1996.

What is interesting about their version of the story is its emphasis on the role played by theory in settling the major design questions, and, hence, the conclusion that game theory deserves the major credit for the auction's success. The first paragraph of their joint article "Analyzing the Airwaves Auction" reveals this attitude: "Just as the Nobel committee was recognizing game theory's role in economics by awarding the 1994 prize to John Nash, John Harsanyi and Reinhard Selten, game theory was being put to its biggest use ever." They quote *Fortune* describing the auctions as the "most dramatic example of game theory's new power...It was a triumph, not only for the FCC and the taxpayers, but also for game theory (and game theorists)." Further on, *Forbes* is quoted again: "Game theory, long an intellectual pastime, came into its own as a business tool," as is the *Wall Street Journal*: "Game theory is hot" (all citations from McAfee and McMillan 1996, 159). What exactly was hot about game theory, according to McAfee and McMillan, was that the FCC "chose an innovative form of auction over the time-tested alternatives (like a sealed-bid auction), *because* theorists predicted it would induce more competitive bidding and a better match of licenses to firms" (1996, our italics).[2]

This is not to say that McAfee and McMillan accord *all* the epistemic credit to theory. Rather, on their account, various judgment calls were also required. Some examples of particular design issues will make clear their exact position:

> *Open or Sealed-Bid?* Theory suggests that an open auction, that is, one
>   in which all bids are public, reassures bidders that they have not
>   overestimated a license's value because the other bids give information

about rivals' evaluations. An open auction, therefore, should reduce bidders' fear of the winner's curse—the phenomenon in which the winning bid is the one that most overestimates the value of the object for sale. Therefore, an open auction should raise more revenue. However, other theory argues against open auctions, for example, because their greater information flow also makes undesirable bidder collusion easier and, thus, revenue *lower*. Therefore, theoretical advice was ambiguous, identifying two effects but not specifying which is the strongest. Which way to go, open or sealed bid? In the end, the designers chose an open auction. McMillan explains that the decision required a judgment call rather than a neat theoretical demonstration, but does *not* explain in any detail on what basis that judgment call was made.

Simultaneous or Sequential? Should all licenses be offered simultaneously, or instead auctioned off one by one, that is, sequentially? McMillan explains that the "debate pitted theoretical virtues against practical feasibility" (1994, 153). When several items are up for auction, the usual practice is to sell them sequentially. However, in the case of spectrum licenses, aggregation is important—companies wanted clusters of licenses that would work efficiently together. If these licenses were sold sequentially, a bidder would have to make guesses about the future prices of other licenses when bidding for current ones. Such uncertainty impacts not only on revenue raised but also on whether licenses get distributed efficiently, that is, to those who value them most.

These considerations argue in favor of a simultaneous auction. However, just imagine what it would be like to have literally thousands of licenses all up for sale at the same time! Would bidders be able to track an auction of such gigantic proportions? Would they be able to process that much information simultaneously? What if a small attention slip or clerical error turned into a disaster worthy of a court battle? Finally, would such an auction ever come to a stop?

To deal with these reasonable practical concerns while still holding on to the advantages of the simultaneous mechanism, the auction designers devised stopping rules and penalties for withdrawing bids. As for concerns about complexity, McMillan tells us, auction designers judged the problem manageable and hoped for the best.

Packages or Individual? Should bids for packages of licenses, as opposed to bids for individual licenses, be allowed? One argument in favor is *complementarity*. Two or more licenses are complementary if owning one increases the value of other. For example, a company might value a

Minneapolis license higher if it already owns Chicago rather than Atlanta. McMillan explains that it is easier to develop a customer base in adjacent geographical areas, to manage interferences, to establish roaming, and so on (1994, 150). The problem is that theory supports both package and individual bids, depending on the extent of complementarities, yet the exact extent of those was unknown. So arguments from sources other than theory must account for the adoption of one design rather than the other. In the end, package bidding was disallowed. (It is still officially considered by the FCC to be an option—it is listed as one of the two official auction designs on its Web site—but in the actual auction it was never permitted.)

Overall, when we look at the details, we can see the strength of McMillan's own admission that "theory has limits" (McMillan 1994, 151). Apart from anything else, none of the relevant models was remotely a model of the complete auction that the FCC was seeking to design. It is not clear that theory did any more than suggest possible issues for designers to take into account. This is no small contribution—but it does still leave one crucial factor unclear. Although we learn about the practical considerations and resultant judgment calls that were in play, we get no sense of what exactly *justified* those particular judgment calls that were eventually made.

The Experimentalists' View

We turn next to a very different perspective. Charles Plott, a prominent experimental economist from Caltech, worked on the FCC auctions from fall 1993 through the fall of 1994. He recounts his experience in Plott 1997. In experimental economics, laboratory environments are used to study people's decision-making processes. Many aspects of these environments, such as the subjects' characteristics, the information they receive, the rules within which they act, and so on, may be very carefully controlled. Such environments—or, as Plott calls them, *experimental test beds*—are treated as prototypes of more complex real-life economic situations. The test beds played many roles in the auction design. One was precisely to provide grounds (albeit retrospective ones) for the sort of judgment calls that McMillan talks about.

Initially, the experimental test beds were used to test broad aspects of the auction rules. Sometimes it was discovered that outcomes were very sensitive to unexpected features. For instance, in a sealed-bid auction in which the price is rising continuously and bidders drop out until only one remains, bidders had a tendency to stay in, rather than drop out, just to drive up the price for the competitor, even though this entails the risk of winning an unwanted item. The interesting fact is that the bubble created in this way is even bigger when bidders have access to information that rivals are still "in." Plott says that there "seems to be no theoretical foundation for this phenomenon, since expectations of the actions of others could cause the same behavior. Nevertheless, in experiments with the information removed such bubbles were less pronounced if they existed at all" (1997, 620, note 1).

In other words, experiment revealed something that could not have been known just from theory. Perhaps even more importantly for our purposes, Plott emphasizes that it also revealed "the sensitivity of the behavioral characteristics of the auction process to the environment in which it might be operating" (1997, 621). For instance, with regard to the bubble behavior just mentioned:

> Even if the information is not officially available as part of the organized auction, the procedures may be such that it can be inferred. For example, if all bidders are in the same room, and if exit from the auction is accompanied by a click of a key or a blink of a screen, or any number of other subtle sources of information, such bubbles might exist even when efforts are made to prevent them. The discovery of such phenomena underscores the need to study the operational details of auctions. (Plott 1997, 620)

Another example of these problems was *interactive* effects. Experiments showed that the impact of any particular auction rule tended to be dependent both on which *other* rules were included, and also on the details of the implementation. Theory alone was typically unable to predict these interactive effects, even those with respect just to other rules. So at later stages of auction design, experimental test beds were crucial to overcoming the difficulty. In Plott's phrase, the test beds enabled the "development and implementation of auction technology" (1997, 627). By "technology" he does not just mean the software that implemented the auction electronically. Rather, he means the overall set of rules governing bidding, activity, stopping, and so forth, *and* the material conditions such as the software. The experiments run at this stage enabled researchers to develop one technology, that is, one set of rules plus material environment, designed to generate the outcome desired by the FCC regarding speed, efficiency, income generation, and so on.

Plott's account shows the holistic nature of the auction design process. Individual rules do not have a stable effect across different environments, so the performance of any particular *set* of rules must be tested as a package, and moreover tested anew with every significant change in environment. This process of trying out different "wholes" was accomplished by a three-stage system of testing (Plott 1997, 630–631). First, Caltech undergraduates with experimentally induced preferences participated in auctions using the actual FCC software. Second, to make sure that the success of these mock auctions was not an accident, researchers then hired the same students to look for ways to derail the auction by various devious moves within the software (for example, withdraw but then start bidding again), in a process called debugging The students were paid for keeping diaries about their experience of playing the auction. Third, researchers implemented parallel checking, in which a program was fed the data from the experimental auctions and, on the basis of this data, it performed all the computations that the FCC program was to do. This allowed them to check the accuracy of the FCC programming and to reverse engineer the system when problems were discovered. The result of all this was the perfection of one piece of technology, that is, of one material environment in which the auction rules operated more or less as desired.

Therefore, it was *not* the case that the key design decisions were first made by theorists, and that the software was then developed to implement these decisions only afterwards. Rather, the two issues had to be settled simultaneously because, as the experiments showed, they were not independent of each other. (It is true though that Plott's team did not have total freedom here, because, by the time of the later experiments, the broad aspects of the auction design—for example that it would be open and disallow package bids—were decided.)

Next, the experimenters applied their understanding in the field, that is, at the actual auction itself. Plott was a member of the increment committee created by the FCC whose purpose was to advise on possible interventions into the first auction, held in July 1994. The FCC had reserved the right to intervene, for instance by speeding up rounds. Plott's team knew that the intervals between rounds did not make much of a difference to the efficiency of the design, so the increment committee was free to vary the length of the intervals (1997, 632–633). Thus, another function of the experiments was to teach researchers some of the ways in which it would be safe to perturb the final auction design.

The experimenters' final function was to check that the actual auction was running efficiently. In the laboratory, auction preferences are induced, that is, controlled by the experimenter. Subjects each receive a piece of paper informing them how much they are willing to pay for a license. This means that, at the end of such a mock auction, the experimenters are able to check whether the final price reached is an equilibrium price, that is, whether the winner is the bidder with the highest valuation. But in real auctions, this is impossible because bidders' preferences are unknown to outsiders. Francesco Guala explains how, nevertheless, it was possible to get some indication of whether the auction was efficient (Guala 2005). Prior to the real auction, a number of laboratory auctions were run that approximated its parameters as much as possible. Those parameters included the number of items for sale, rules, valuations (or guesses thereof), the extent of complementarities (or guesses thereof), and so on. The data from these auctions, such as their duration, price movements, existence of bubbles, and such, were meticulously collected. Similar data were then collected during the real auction, and compared to the laboratory data. Since the price trajectories achieved were very similar and since the laboratory prices were efficient, researchers were able to make an argument that the real auction prices were efficient too.

Lessons From the Spectrum Auction

How well do the four accounts of models face up to this detailed history? As noted earlier, unfortunately it seems that neither invoking a partial isomorphism between model and world, nor invoking the credibility of a model's world, sheds light on how the auction mechanism was constructed, nor on why it rather than some alternative mechanism was preferable. We shall reaffirm now why neither the satisfaction-of-assumptions nor the capacities accounts can do the job either, or at least why neither can give any more than an incomplete picture.

The theorists' and experimentalists' views emphasize different methods for giving warrant to the particular auction design adopted by the FCC. McMillan's narrative is most naturally read as endorsing the method of concretization, while Plott's, at least in part, isn't. Plott's narrative, however, is more successful at showing that the decisions that ended up being taken by auction designers were justified. So concretization does not seem to capture the true methodology of the auction design.

McMillan's history emphasizes the claim that the success of the FCC auctions consisted in the proper deployment of theoretical resources. Theoretical models allowed us to learn that open auctions encourage the flow of information, thereby reducing the winner's curse and increasing revenue; that package bids can be inefficient; that simultaneous auctions favor efficient distributions; and so on. The notion of capacity fits these claims nicely. For McMillan, theoretical results give us facts that are *stable* enough to employ for interventions, explanations, and predictions. At least sometimes, theoretical facts wear their policy implications on their sleeve. Thus the FCC auction design was successful *because* it harnessed the capacities of different design features properly.

Notice first that, contrary to the Hausman/McMullin satisfaction-of-assumptions account, this was not achieved by means of de-idealization. Assumptions in the auction models typically included, for instance, perfect rationality, no budget constraints on bidders, single units (as opposed to hundreds of spectrum licenses simultaneously on sale), and so forth. These assumptions were critical to the derivation of the models' results, yet no one had a model that yielded the consequences of relaxing these assumptions. Thus, as noted in Section 2, de-idealization was not feasible. Moreover, in the case of some other assumptions, even when a de-idealized theoretical treatment was available, the results were often discouraging, for example, proving that no competitive equilibrium is possible. All this, therefore, tells against the Hausman/McMullin account of model application being the full story in this case.

Since the language of capacities fits McMillan's own description of the theoretical arguments, turn lastly to the Cartwright/Nowak method of concretization. In the case of the auction, this would essentially amount to the process of combining together design features (i.e. auction rules) that have different capacities, in such a way as to ensure that the outcome is the one we want. This does seem to fit McMillan's history very well. For instance, simultaneous bidding, which is valued for its efficiency, also has the capacity to generate chaos by being too complex and by causing the auction to last too long. So we supplement it with various bidding and stopping rules that would prevent these effects.

Something like this story probably was the basis for constructing the mock auctions used *initially* by Plott's team. But a reason to include some rule in a preliminary test auction is not the same as a reason to include it in the final auction itself. In the first context we need only a defeasible reason, while in the second we need a solid justification. Plott reminds us again and again that experiments demonstrated interactions between different rules, in turn making it hard to draw any conclusions based only on models that understandably excluded messy real-world features, such as software details and small variations in rules. This is precisely what the experiments were for—they worked to reduce the uncertainty created by the interactions by revealing a single material environment in which the auction worked as desired. These are the experiments that supplied the needed justification for one design over another. Because of the interactions, Plott treats the material environments as *wholes* in which all elements together produce the result. No single feature of these environments on its own, such as the open design, can be said to be responsible for it.

This aspect of Plott's methodology suggests skepticism even about the capacities account. For example, while McMillan credits the open auction design with reducing the winner's curse effect, Plott remained entirely agnostic about how the winner's curse plays out when complementarities are in place (Plott 1997, 626). At the time, no model that incorporated complementarities even existed. In the experiments, more features were added specifically to defeat the winner's curse, namely, flexible minimum increments that made it more attractive to bid when activity was low, and also activity rules that required bidders to submit bids on pain of losing their eligibility. This does not demonstrate that the theoretical result was not taken seriously, but it does show that further justification was needed. Designers could not trust that the capacity of an open auction to defeat the winner's curse was stable enough to be relied on without further testing.

It would not be new to claim that theory alone cannot tell us the effects of features in any actual auction. Work on the role of models by contributors to (Morgan & Morrison 1999), by Cartwright (1983, 1989), and by a number of other philosophers of science, has already shown us how much extratheoretical knowledge is required to apply theory properly. However, Plott's methodology suggests a stronger conclusion: There was not even much knowledge of capacities at his disposal, and thus that the method of combination of causes was inapplicable. Regardless of whether auction designers did know any capacity claims, the methods they used to confirm the right set of auction rules and software were *not* that of concretization. For Plott, theoretical models were merely useful heuristics, generating categories in terms of which to start the design process. A new account of application is needed.

4. Models in Science Revisited: The Open-Formula View

Models as Open Formulas

How exactly does a model apply to a phenomenon, for example, when it yields its explanation? A common feature of the satisfaction-of-assumption and capacity accounts is that the recipe for identifying an explanatory claim involves the model *itself* in some essential way. On the former account, a model applies when some set of its assumptions are satisfied, and the explanatory claim can be obtained from the model by appropriately de-idealizing it. On the latter, a model applies if the causes it describes occur in the target situation. The associated explanatory capacity claim is thus stated by the model. But why should we assume that a model should necessarily provide such information? It might do so, but perhaps it is too restrictive to make that a requirement. We shall now propose that a model sometimes serves a different function, namely, that of a framework or heuristic for formulating causal hypotheses, but where it is those latter hypotheses—distinct from the model—that are explanatory. (For more philosophical detail about this approach than there is space to give here, see Alexandrova, forthcoming.)

In the experimental test beds of the spectrum auction, game theory models of auctions were used as suggestions for developing causal hypotheses that could then be tested by experiment. One such hypothesis might be: When values are private and some other conditions hold, first-price auction designs cause bids below true valuation. This hypothesis has the general form: Feature(s) $F(s)$ cause behavior(s) $B(s)$ under condition(s) $C(s)$. Note that not all the model's assumptions need appear in the specification of conditions $C(s)$. Rather, only those deemed salient are included. There is thus a distinction between such a causal hypothesis and the model proper. While the model plays an important role in formulating such a hypothesis, it does not fully specify it.

When a model is used in this way, we propose to conceive of it as an *open formula*, that takes the form:

1. In a situation x with some characteristics that may or may not include $\{C_1 \ldots C_n\}$, a certain feature F causes a certain behavior B.

where x is a variable, F and B are property names of, respectively, putative causes and effects in the model, and $\{C_1 \ldots C_n\}$ are the conditions under which Fs cause Bs in the model.[3] It is important to distinguish this from another claim:

2. There exists a situation S with characteristics $\{C_1 \ldots C_n\}$, such that in this situation a certain feature F causes a certain behavior B.

An open-formula 1, unlike an existential claim 2, makes no commitment about the existence of x, and does not make yet any claim about any situation under which Fs cause Bs since the features of x are not fully specified. Rather, x is a free variable that needs to be filled in, in order for the open formula to make such a claim. Once x is specified, we get a causal hypothesis of the form "an F causes a B in a situation S," where S is characterized by some conditions $C(S)$. Without closing the open formula by specifying x, 1 only gives us a template or a schema for a causal claim, rather than a fully fledged causal claim such as 2.

Advantages of the Open-Formula Account

What are the advantages of this new reading of models? First, it still allows us to pursue the old readings—when we so wish. Formally, one set of conditions C under which Fs cause Bs is just all of the model's assumptions. So if we have evidence to treat the model as a capacity claim or if we know how to de-idealize it, then we can use those methods. But we are also free to ignore some assumptions, and so in effect not to have to privilege the model's formal assumptions over other extratheoretical conditions under which the causal hypothesis might hold.

Thus we now have license to go ahead and build many different causal claims on the basis of one model. This freedom is particularly important in the circumstances that often exist in institution design. In the spectrum auction, sometimes it was simply not known whether some assumption, essential to a derivation in the model, was satisfied in the real world. For instance, many models assumed facts about the statistical properties of the distributions of bidder valuations, such as their shape, uniformity, continuity, and so on. But designers dealing with actual bidders have no way of ascertaining these facts simply because companies keep their valuations secret. In a situation like that, designers could not use the assumptions of the model as a guide to specifying Cs. So they hoped to find some other empirical conditions, not mentioned in the model, under which features F cause behaviors B.

Moreover, sometimes auction designers had no control over a condition C and so could not *make* the target system satisfy this assumption. This was the case with the assumption of Bayesian Nash Equilibrium, for instance. Auction designers knew that the flesh and blood first-time spectrum bidders they had to deal with in the actual auction could not be expected to have the sort of rationality that the models assumed. So allowances had to be made for lack of experience, for the fact that the auction was complex, and so on. In particular, new rules were added purely to push the bidders to behave as required to ensure efficiency. Formally, again, some set of conditions C, other than the one specified by the model, needed to be found in order to make Fs cause Bs in the real world.

Moreover, generally microeconomic models are often evaluated on their tractability, elegance, and, of course, deductive closure. But whatever their merits for other purposes, we see now that such criteria do not necessarily give us any assurance that a model explains and in fact may get in the way of explaining. They are thus all reasons that certain assumptions are included over and above the reason of merely stating the empirical conditions under which a result holds. In turn, this is why it often proves useful *not* to include such assumptions when formulating causal hypotheses about the real world.

These challenges indicate that we often cannot rely on models alone to tell us the vital conditions C. If so, then we need some other way. The open-formula view is set up precisely to accommodate the necessary contributions from beyond theory. However, such flexibility does not come free. For the older accounts, at least we have explicit procedures by which to guarantee that a causal claim derived from a model holds in the real world. More particularly, on the Giere/Hausman satisfaction-of-assumptions view, a successful de-idealization gives us warrant to assert that if the original model established a causal claim, then the de-idealized one does, too. Similarly, on the Mill/Cartwright capacity view, if a model makes a justified capacity claim, then that claim will still be true outside the model, provided that we have concretized successfully. In each case, if the original model tells us that an F causes a B in a situation S, then if the model also applies to a situation S^* according to the rules of the account, then the warrant to claim that an F^* causes a B^* automatically *travels* from the model to S^*. But on our open-formula view, such preservation of warrant cannot be sustained. Once we treat models merely as open formulas, the causal hypotheses we construct from them have to be confirmed in some other way.

There is, thus, a trade-off—the open-formula view gives us free reign to pick and choose the assumptions from the model that will figure in the final causal hypotheses we end up with, but the price is that we are left still needing a way to confirm those hypotheses. Nothing about the procedure of their formation guarantees that they will in fact hold; rather, that must be established anew each time. We think that unfortunately this price is in any case unavoidable because neither of the alternatives—de-idealization and concretization—is likely, for the reasons discussed earlier, to be available in many cases. Nevertheless, it does mean that we must now address how open formulas may be applied.

From Open Formulas to Explanations

A causal explanation of a real-world phenomenon requires that we make a true and justified claim about a real-world causal relation. With the open-formula account, we achieve this via a three-stage procedure:

> Stage 1: Construct an open formula by picking from a model's premises and conclusions the Fs and Bs of interest. These presumably will correspond to the putative causes and the putative effects at work in the real-world phenomenon of interest.
>
> Stage 2: Fill in x so as to arrive at a closed formula, that is, a causal hypothesis of the form "Fs cause Bs under conditions C" where Fs and Bs match some aspects of the target situation. The conditions C may or may not be described by the original model's assumptions.
>
> Stage 3: Confirm the causal hypothesis. We do that by finding a *material realization* of it, that is, a material environment in which an F indeed causes a B.

Stage 3 is obviously the difficult bit. That is why, in the case of the spectrum auction, so much work was needed in the experimental test beds. When we do achieve a material realization then we are entitled to say that the causal hypothesis inspired by the model is true, and, thus, that we have a causal explanation of B.

The features of the environment in which the causal hypothesis is true are what allow us to fill in the open formula, that is to specify fully the conditions C under which an F causes a B. Part of this specification may match the assumptions of the original model, but part of it may not.

How are material realizations specified? Answer: in the same way that we normally specify a claim about one set of sufficient causes of a phenomenon. (In the terminology of J.L. Mackie's INUS conditions, a material realization for a causal relation can be understood as one of the disjuncts of the overall INUS formula.) Thus, we do not just blindly list every feature of the material situation, such as the color of the bidders' eyes and so on. Rather, we only specify those conditions that are causally relevant.

Exactly what the conditions C must be like for Fs to cause Bs can be tricky to establish. We may *test* the causal relevance of Cs to Fs and Bs by drawing as convenient from the usual repertoire of methods—controlled trial, natural experiment, Mill's methods and variations on them, mark methods, Bayes Nets, and so forth. Whatever story philosophers of science and methodologists tell about causal inference generally, will presumably help to clarify how we may fill in models' open formulas.

This account of models, and of their application in terms of material realization, enables us to make sense of institution design. In particular, unlike the alternative accounts, it explains why the use of models in the design of the spectrum auction was justified, even though neither de-idealization nor extrapolation on the basis of capacities was always available. According to this view, the models of auction theory supplied researchers with a number of partially filled-in open formulas: "First-price auctions cause bids below true valuations under conditions...," "Open auctions defeat the winner's curse under conditions...," "Individual rather than package bids do not hinder efficient distribution under conditions..." and so forth. So at the beginning, there was a wide range of "F_i cause B_j in x" claims. After much work, what researchers ended up with was an explanation of the actual auction in the form:

3. A set of features $\{F_1 \ldots F_k\}$ causes a set of behaviors $\{B_1 \ldots B_m\}$ under a set of conditions $\{C_1 \ldots C_n\}$.

where Fs stand for features of rules, Bs for aspects of the auction's outcomes (i.e., its revenue generation, license distribution, speed, etc.) and Cs for the material conditions that the designers could control. The Bs were partially specified by the government. The trick was then to find the combination of Fs and Cs that would bring about those Bs. Some of the Fs, Bs, and Cs figured in the models of auction theory, others came from different sources of knowledge. Crucially, it was the experimental test beds that allowed auction designers to find one combination of rules and software such that when this combination was instantiated, the particular kind of open auction selected did indeed cause a speedy and efficient distribution of licenses.

5. PROGRESS IN ECONOMICS

At last, we are ready to turn to the question of *progress* in economics. Without the development of modern auction theory, the successful FCC auction design would not have been possible. In addition, there has also accumulated crucial practical know-how, so that the designers of the United States spectrum auction did not repeat the mistakes of their New Zealand and Australian predecessors, for instance. This suggests two distinct senses in which the successful FCC auction reveals progress in economics—first, purely theoretical development; and second, engineering development in how theory might be applied. Can both of these senses be sustained? The details of the auction case study now turn out to be very revealing. In particular, we shall argue, they endorse progress strictly only of the second engineering kind, in a manner to be explained. This has implications in turn for the role played in any progress by theoretical development, and, therefore, for just what it is about economic theory that we should value.

What Economic Progress Is Not

In order eventually to see the import of the spectrum auction case here, begin first with a brief detour into the literature on scientific progress generally. This has traditionally analyzed progress in terms of scientific theories. In particular, from the beginning it has been motivated primarily by the debate between scientific realism and antirealism. Because it is accepted that most, if not all, of our best theories are not literally true, a satisfactory account of approximate truth (or 'verisimilitude') has been seen as important, perhaps even essential, to the realist position (Putnam 1975; Newton-Smith 1981; Miller 1987; Boyd 1990; Psillos 1999). Scientific progress has then been seen in terms of successive theories achieving closer and closer approximations to the truth—convergent realism. For example, the sequence of Aristotelean, Newtonian, and finally relativistic mechanics is seen as one such convergence.

It has proven notoriously difficult to flesh out satisfactorily the needed notion of verisimilitude. One classic problem is language dependence: For any two false theories, any ranking of them by verisimilitude can be reversed simply by changing the choice of variables on which that ranking is defined (Miller 1974; Miller 1975). The problem is especially devastating because even were we to postulate a privileged one-true ontology—perhaps the natural kinds as revealed by an ideal science for instance—still that ontology would underdetermine choice of variables. For this and other reasons, it is currently dubious whether any authoritative sense can be made of a false theory's closeness to the truth. In turn, this has motivated some to be skeptical of global scientific progress at all (Laudan 1984).

This emphasis on realism and theories reflects the literature's concentration on fundamental physics and chemistry rather than the special sciences. For example, general relativity and quantum mechanics are plausibly taken to be literal descriptions of the world, and thus as potential candidates for being true and for being interpreted realistically. Or at least, so many realists have believed. Other positions, too, such as Van Fraassen's (1980) constructive empiricism, agree that such theories should be interpreted as literal descriptions. Theories in economics, by contrast, are agreed by all to be extremely idealized. Nobody thinks that *Homo economicus* is a literally true description of anyone. So the idea that economic theories could ever be literally true is clearly a nonstarter.

Nevertheless, this still seems to leave open a different sense in which economic theory could be progressing, namely, that it is becoming better at capturing particular aspects of reality. In particular, the thought runs, although auction models, for instance, are idealized descriptions and, thus, are not literally true, nevertheless they do successfully capture real patterns of strategic interaction between bidders. They are, thus, able to track regularities between, say, auction format and size of bids.[4] As we saw earlier, there are various ways in which more flesh has been put on this rather vague initial thought—by viewing economic theory as capturing causal capacities, as idealizations requiring only that their assumptions hold, as positing credible worlds, or as positing partial structures, and so on. We have argued that, in any case, the evidence of the spectrum auction does not support any of these interpretations. But bracketing that conclusion temporarily, how might those interpretations make sense of economic progress?

Unfortunately, a major problem remains even with this more modest conception of progress, in which theory becomes better merely at capturing particular aspects of reality. The problem stems ultimately from the continuing emphasis on theory in isolation. Like all idealizations, economic theory is good at capturing some things but less good at capturing others. For example, auction models capture patterns of strategic interaction between bidders but make no allowance for individual variations in agent psychology; for local details, such as software glitches or physical arrangement of bidders; and so on. How much do these omissions matter? An answer is surely vital to any assessment of how valuable a model is, and hence to whether that model represents progress relative to other models that capture other things. Yet the importance of any given omission will inevitably depend on the particular application in question. In some contexts the omission of variation in agent psychology, for instance, will matter more than in others. The point is that there is no univocal *general* answer about the seriousness of a given omission, independent of the local details. It follows that no context-general sense of theoretical progress can be sustained, for a model may simultaneously have progressed with respect to one application but not to another. An overall score for that model's progress could, therefore, only ever be a crude average of its scores over various particular applications, and would, therefore, carry no more weight than those applications' selection criteria.

For instance, on the capacities account, the importance of the capacities a model captures relative to those it omits will vary, case by case. The problem equally infects the other accounts, too. The degree of ease with which assumptions can be de-idealized, the degree of credibility of a world, and the degree of importance of the portion of the total domain that a partial structure captures—all of these, even assuming rigorous sense can be made of them, also seem bound to vary, application by application. The lesson is that, even when speaking of our more modest conception of it, we can only make sense of economic progress context-specifically. We can, therefore, *not* make sense of it for any theoretical model in isolation, such as a particular auction model, say. Rather, we can, at best, speak of that auction model representing progress with respect to a specific application.

Next, finally, turn to the new twist put on these matters by analysis of the spectrum auctions. Alas, the lesson of that analysis is that to speak even of application-specific progress is to be too optimistic. For, as we have seen, in the case of the spectrum auction at least, empirical warrant does *not* accrue to the theoretical model. The only confirmed causal claim is with respect to the mechanism as a whole (that is, claim 3). *That* causal claim is made only by the mechanism, of course, not by any of the auction-theory models. This is why the theoretical models garner no support here. Rather, support accrues only to the final mechanism used in the actual auction, and, thus, it is only that final mechanism that has a claim to be close to the truth. Because that mechanism was the result of extensive experimental tweaking independent of the theoretical model, it is a mistake to think that the success of the auction implies any progress toward the truth on the part of *theory,* even application-specifically. Thus, the contrasting experiences of the New Zealand and United States auctions, for instance, speaks to progress with respect to final mechanisms but not with respect to theoretical models. (Indeed, much the same theoretical repertoire was available in both cases.)

To sum up so far: The usual notion of scientific progress in the literature has been of successive theories approaching closer to the truth. This notion has proved problematic in general, for instance, because of language dependence. Even if we focus only on an agreed economic vocabulary, still economic theory is recognized by all to be highly idealized and, therefore, not a candidate for literal truth. A weaker claim is that economic theory nevertheless captures aspects or parts of the truth. But then we need to judge the relative importance of those aspects it captures and those it doesn't. Any such judgment must inevitably be application-specific, implying that theoretical models in isolation cannot be said to progress; rather, at best, they can be said to progress in capturing the truth about specific situations. Finally, the spectrum auction case suggests that even this last claim is not supportable, because the empirical warrant from successful applications in fact accrues only to final concrete mechanisms that cannot be derived directly from theoretical models. If we interpret progress in the traditional way as increasing closeness to truth, then, we have no reason to believe that economic theory is progressing.

Some Red Herrings

We shall offer a positive view, and address its implications for economic practice, shortly. Before that though, a little more negative work is required, in particular to dispose of some red herrings. First, a common fall-back defense of economic theory is that even if empirical warrant is elusive, still it provides 'insight' or at least is 'suggestive'. For instance, an auction model illustrates how the winner's curse comes about, or could come about, and thus increases our 'understanding' of that phenomenon. How are we to interpret the quoted terms? Can they carry any philosophical weight?

The most likely candidate for arguing so seems to be the view that theory provides *explanation*. In other words, auction theory explains why the winner's curse comes about, for instance. But on any standard account of explanation, for a theory to do this it must have empirical warrant, and, given the essential role of the experimental test beds, that is just what close analysis of the spectrum auctions casts into doubt. Thus, an auction model does not, in conjunction with initial conditions, entail the successful auction outcome, as would be required on the deductive-nomological view. Neither does it provide the cause or mechanism that produced that outcome, as only the final composite auction procedure achieves that. Neither finally does the theoretical model unify various phenomena, since on our view it does not on its own account for any phenomenon at all, let alone several different phenomena. The necessary empirical warrant is just what the theoretical models did *not* accrue in the case of the spectrum auction. Accordingly, we have no good reason to declare them explanatory of the auction's success. In lieu of some alternative interpretation (on which see later), therefore, and with apologies to Hume, in our view, vague talk of such models providing insight or understanding can contain nothing but sophistry and illusion.

Next, and more generally, it is easy just to declare after the fact that some real-world observation was explained by an economic model. The spectrum auction was different in that, it being a case of institution design, scientists faced the constraint of eventually having to actually run an auction and make it a success. This was, of course, a very different challenge to mere after-the-fact rationalization. And, although it might have looked casually as if, as the contemporary publicity claimed, the theoretical auction models indeed explained the outcome, as we have seen, the reality was more complicated. Judging by the example of the spectrum auction, therefore, there is ample reason to be cautious about attributions—after the fact and from a distance—of explanatory success to economic theory. When push came to shove and an actual working mechanism was required, it turned out not to be so.

A Positive Story—Economists as Engineers

We have seen the difficulty of making sense of any variety of purely theoretical progress. That was the negative story; what is the positive one? For that, consider,

again, the second option mentioned earlier, namely, that of understanding progress as progress in engineering know-how, that is, as progress in the practicalities of *applying* economic theory. We believe this turns out to be a much better
way to view the matter.[5] Moreover, such a view of economic progress, as well as
capturing the success of the spectrum auctions, also turns out to have normative
implications for the development of economic theory more widely. (Of course, we
do not mean to deny progress also in other applied economic tasks, such as measuring new data.)

A helpful analogy here is with the development of *racing cars*, for instance the
work of a Formula One team. The designers in such a team are faced with the challenge of maximizing a car's speed and reliability while constrained by regulations
concerning weight, tires, engine size, fuel capacity, and a host of other details. These
regulations typically change each championship season. There is of course a lot of
relevant theory to know and, for this reason, senior designers are highly trained
engineers. Yet theoretical knowledge alone is not enough. All teams also have huge
testing programs, analogous to the experimental test beds of the spectrum auction.
For example, new chassis designs are tested extensively in wind tunnels, while in-
house drivers take each new model for vast numbers of timed laps on private tracks.
Engineers on all teams are highly educated and presumably have very similar levels
of theoretical knowledge. Yet, of course, the final results of their efforts—that is,
each team's cars in the races—are far from very similar. On the contrary, some are
much more successful than others. And typically it is the teams with the biggest
development and testing budgets that end up producing the winning cars. That is,
within any one season, the quality of racing cars correlates with teams' development budgets rather than with their levels of theoretical knowledge.

Of course, theoretical knowledge is essential, too. No matter what the testing budget, presumably no team would be competitive without knowledge of
Newtonian mechanics, gas laws, the chemistry of fuel combustion, materials science knowledge of rubber and lightweight composites, and so on. But it does suggest that, just as the experimental test beds were essential to producing a successful
spectrum auction design, so are the wind tunnels and practice laps essential to
producing a successful racing car design. In both cases, abstract theory is necessary but not sufficient.

What does this tell us about progress? Within any one season, when regulations are constant, there exists progress in racing car design in that the cars become
faster and more reliable. Within that time span, the theoretical knowledge being
employed presumably does not change significantly. What does improve, rather,
is the ability to apply it effectively. That is, the development of better racing cars
through the season is due to the accumulation of new context-specific engineering
know-how. It is *not* due to any global nearing to the truth of our underlying theoretical picture of the world.

The context-specificity of such progress is reflected by its limited *exportability* to new contexts. The know-how that a racing-car team accumulates through

a season, just like the practical know-how that went into the spectrum auction design, is only exportable to a limited extent, or at least is not as exportable as the relevant theoretical knowledge. The success of one season's car does not guarantee success under new regulations in the next season, as the sporting record has demonstrated many times. Similarly, the successful design of a spectrum auction in the conditions and regulations of one country does not necessarily carry over to those of a new country (Klemperer 2002b). In both cases, the context has changed, and, thus, a new round of practical know-how must be acquired. For this reason, just as the winning racing-car team often changes from season to season, so a successful auction design in one country will not necessarily be successful in a different country. Thus, the spectrum auction in Switzerland was a comparative failure, despite being run six years after the successful FCC one. Of course, these are matters of degree, and there is exportability to some extent—thus racing-car teams learn from previous designs, just as U.K. spectrum-auction designers in 2000 learned from their U.S. predecessors. But the point is the asymmetry between on one hand context-specific practical know-how with limited exportability, and on the other hand context-general theoretical knowledge with great exportability.

Progress and Theory Revisited

In sharp contrast to the kinds of theoretical progress discussed earlier, this context-specific engineering progress is amply endorsed empirically. Thus, racing cars demonstrably do run faster and more reliably through the course of a season, just as the U.S. spectrum auction was demonstrably more successful than its predecessors. Nevertheless, as repeatedly emphasized, a necessary condition for engineering success is relevant theory, namely, in the case of the spectrum auctions, the new game-theory auction models. So we have an apparent paradox: Although there is no warrant for claiming theoretical progress in the sense of empirical success or increased closeness to the truth, still theoretical progress in *some* sense is necessary for the context-specific engineering progress for which there *is* warrant.

So what might this other, different kind of theoretical progress amount to? We must be careful to avoid yet another, final, red herring. In particular, one common thought is to view this different kind of theoretical progress as akin to progress in pure mathematics, a kind of internal progress of new concepts and categories, proofs and refinements, and so forth. For example, modern theory has seen the development of such concepts as multiple equilibria and asymmetric information effects, and in turn how these effects interact with other factors such as different auction procedures. No doubt, this is progress in some sense—but not progress for which the spectrum auction provides any empirical warrant. And without a clear connection to empirical progress, it is not clear why, as scientists (as opposed to pure mathematicians), we should value it. How is it to be measured, for instance? Was asymmetric information a more important conceptual breakthrough than new notions of equilibrium? What criterion could we use to decide – an aesthetic one? Any criterion encompassing empirical success would seem inevitably to run into the same difficulties that we discussed earlier, such as that the worth of these breakthroughs would be highly application-specific and dependent in any case on practical know-how, independent of theory.

We think the underlying problem here is again the attempt to define progress with respect to theory in isolation. To repeat: If the example of the spectrum auction is typical, then the only notion of progress in economics that is empirically warranted is of the context-specific engineering variety. Thus, the criterion for judging a new piece of theory should be: How much does it help economic engineers achieve empirical success? An expanding and dazzling theoretical repertoire of new methods, heuristics, and categories is, alas, of no empirical value *in itself*. Rather, it can only be valuable instrumentally. Nevertheless, this does at least finally yield us an indirect kind of theoretical progress, namely, that new theoretical development is progressive insofar as it generates useful new aids to the engineers.

The hard-nosed corollary is that theoretical developments that offer little prospect of being useable by economic engineers are of correspondingly little scientific value.[6] Of course, no one can ever know for sure in advance exactly which pieces of theory may eventually prove useful in this way. Readers will form their own judgment of the prospects for any particular example. Notice, however, that the issue is *not* the familiar one of pure versus applied research, wherein the former is damned by philistines as being perhaps noble in its pursuit of scientific truth but, alas, of no practical use. Rather, in the case of economics, the philistine argument is altogether stronger, namely, that the pure research cannot even be said to be pursuing scientific truth.

The design of the FCC spectrum auction is worthy of celebration. It was a tremendously sophisticated (and lucrative) piece of technology—on a par with, say, a laser or a jet airplane. Economic theory can be correspondingly proud of its contribution to this success. But the sting in the tail is this: that it is only through such contributions that theory partakes of scientific progress. Its only glory is via its utility to those working elsewhere.

NOTES

Authors' names listed in alphabetical order. The authors are equally and jointly responsible.

1. For an opposing view, see Nik-Khah (2008). He argues that in fact the auctions' only success was large revenues. Other objectives, such as decentralization of ownership and promotion of wireless technology in rural areas, were not met. Cramton 1998 and 2006 mostly disagrees. For our purposes, it is enough to say that the auctions were a more successful piece of technology than previous alternatives (such as the auction designs used in other countries, or nonmarket mechanisms).

2. Notice also the historical origin of McMillan's protheorist paper. McMillan was originally hired by the FCC as an independent advisor—independent in the sense that he was not at the same time employed by a potential bidder. His task was to help the FCC arbitrate between the conflicting advice received from game theorists employed by the different telecoms firms. As we shall see, game theory did not give a univocal answer to the question of which auction design would maximize efficiency. (It was through this hole that the telecoms companies were able to present their suggestions as being justified by considerations of efficiency when, in fact, the motivation was self-interest—Nik-Khah 2008.) In an attempt to explain the FCC's eventual decisions, McMillan produced a report that synthesized the debates that were taking place between the theorists (FCC 1994a). This report eventually turned into his 1994 paper. The primary purpose of the report might, thus, not have been to show what exactly theory can and cannot do for auction designers, but rather only to show that the FCC was aware of the conflict between different theoretical considerations and took that into account. So to this extent, McMillan's paper may, by political necessity, have been in part a public relations exercise.

3. Strictly speaking, we should not speak of Fs causing Bs "in the model." The causal dependence of Bs on Fs cannot simply be read off the deductive relations between the assumptions describing Fs and Bs. Rather, it is an interpretation given to the model using some background knowledge.

4. It may be disputed whether scientific progress is best viewed as progress toward truth or, instead, as progress only toward some lesser goal, such as better predictions, interventions, or empirical descriptions. None of our arguments turn on this general issue. We shall be emphasizing empirical success, but presumably such success would, in any case, be the best reason to believe in the metaphysically stronger claims of a model's truth or approximate truth.

5. Ken Binmore, chief designer of the extremely successful UK spectrum auctions of 1999 and 2000, sees his achievement as being akin to engineering in exactly this way (personal communication, one of the authors).

6. As mentioned in footnote 4, this remains true whether we understand *scientific value* to mean "closeness to the truth" or mere "empirical success". We are committed though to *scientific value*, implying something beyond mere mathematics-type, purely abstract theoretical development. Similar remarks apply to *scientific truth* and *scientific progress* below.

REFERENCES

Alexandrova, A. (forthcoming). "Making Models Count". *Philosophy of Science*.
Boyd, R. (1990). "Realism, Approximate Truth, and Philosophical Method." In C. Savage, Ed., *Scientific Theories*, 355–391. Minneapolis: University of Minnesota Press.
Cartwright, N. (1983). *How The Laws of Physics Lie*. Oxford: Oxford University Press.
Cartwright, N. (1989). *Nature's Capacities and Their Measurement*. Oxford: Oxford University Press.
Cartwright, N. (1998). "Capacities." In J.B. Davis, D.W. Hands, & U. Mäki, Eds., *The Handbook of Economic Methodology*, 45–48. Cheltenham: Edward Elgar Publishing.
Cartwright, N. (1999). *The Dappled World*. Cambridge, England: Cambridge University Press.

Coase, R. (1998). "Comment on Thomas W. Hazlett: Assigning Property Rights to Radio Spectrum Users: Why did FCC license auctions take 67 years?" *Journal of Law and Economics* XLI: 577–580.

Cramton, P.(1998). "The Efficiency of the FCC Spectrum Auctions." *Journal of Law and Economics* XLI: 727–736.

Cramton, P. (2006). "Simultaneous Ascending Auctions," In P. Cramton, Y. Shoham & R. Steinberg, Eds., *Combinatorial Auctions* 99–114. Cambridge, MA: MIT Press.

Da Costa, N. & French,S. (2003). *Science and Partial Truth: A Unitary Approach to Models and Reasoning in Science.* New York: Oxford University Press.

FCC (1994a). "Second Report and Order," 94–61, Washington, D.C.

FCC (1994b). "Fifth Report and Order," 94–178, Washington, D.C.

Frigg, R. (2006) "Scientific Representation and the Semantic View of Theories." *Theoria* 55: 49–65.

Frigg, R. & Hartmann, S. (2006). "Models in Science." *Stanford Encyclopedia of Philosophy,* http://plato.stanford.edu/entries/models-science/

Giere, R. (1988). *Explaining Science.* Chicago: University of Chicago Press.

Gruene-Yanoff, T. (2007). "Learning from Economic Models." Manuscript, Royal Institute of Technology, Sweden.

Guala, F. (2005). *Methodology of Experimental Economics.* Cambridge, England: Cambridge University Press.

Hausman, D. (1992). *The Inexact and Separate Science of Economics.* Cambridge, England: Cambridge University Press.

Herzel, L. (1998). "My 1951 Color Television Article." *Journal of Law and Economics* XLI: 523–527.

Hundt, R. (2000). *You Say You Want a Revolution.* New Haven: Yale University Press.

Klemperer, P. (2002a). "How (Not) to Run Auctions: The European 3G Telecom Auctions." *European Economic Review* 46: 829–845.

Klemperer, P. (2002b). "What Really Matters in Auction Design." *Journal of Economic Literature* 16 (1): 169–189.

Laudan, L. (1984). *Science and Values.* Berkeley: University of California Press.

Mäki, U. (1992). "On the Method of Idealization in Economics." *Poznan Studies in the Philosophy of the Sciences and the Humanities* 26: 319–354.

McAfee, P. & McMillan, J. (1996). "Analyzing the Airwaves Auction." *Journal of Economic Perspectives* 10 (1): 159–175.

McMillan, J. (1994). "Selling Spectrum Rights." *Journal of Economic Perspectives* 8 (3): 145–162.

McMullin, E. (1985). "Galilean Idealization." *Studies in History and Philosophy of Science* 16 (3): 247–273.

Mill, J. S. (1843). *System of Logic.* London: Parker.

Miller, D. (1974). "Popper's Qualitative Theory of Verisimilitude." *British Journal for the Philosophy of Science* 25: 166–177.

Miller, D. (1975). "The Accuracy of Predictions." *Synthese* 30: 159–191.

Miller, R. (1987). *Fact and Method.* Princeton: Princeton University Press.

Morgan, M. (2002). "Model Experiments and Models in Experiments." In L. Magnani & N.J. Nersessian, Eds., *Model-Based Reasoning: Science, Technology, Values.* New York: Kluwer Academic/Plenum Publishers.

Morgan, M, & Morrison, M, Eds. (1999). *Models as Mediators.* Cambridge, England: Cambridge University Press.

Newton-Smith, B. (1981). *The Rationality of Science*. Boston, MA & London: Routledge & Kegan Paul.

Nik-Khah, E. (2008). "A Tale of Two Auctions." *Journal of Institutional Economics* 4 (1): 73–97.

Plott, C. (1997). "Laboratory Experimental Testbeds: Application to the PCS Auction." *Journal of Economics and Management Strategy* 6 (3): 605–638.

Psillos, S. (1999). *Scientific Realism*. London: Routledge.

Putnam, H. (1975). "How Not to Talk about Meaning." In *Philosophical Papers, Vol. 1, Mathematics, Matter and Method*. Cambridge, England: Cambridge University Press. 250–269.

Reiss, J. (forthcoming). "Social Capacities." In Stephan Hartmann & Luc Bovens, Eds., *Nancy Cartwright's Philosophy of Science*. London: Routledge.

Roth, A. (2002). "The Economist as Engineer: Game Theory, Experimental Economics and Computation as Tools of Design Economics." *Econometrica* 70 (4): 1341–1378.

Suárez, M. (2004), 'An Inferential Conception of Scientific Representation.' *Philosophy of Science* 71 S: 767–777.

Sugden, R.(2000). "Credible Worlds: The Status of Theoretical Models in Economics." *Journal of Economic Methodology* 7 (1): 1–31.

Van Fraassen, B. (1980). *The Scientific Image*. Oxford: Oxford University Press.

Wolfstetter, E. (2003). "The Swiss UMTS Spectrum Auction Flop: Bad Luck or Bad Design?" In H-G. Nutzinger, Ed., *Regulation, Competition, and the Market Economy. Festschrift for C.C.v.Weizsäcker*, 281–294. Göttingen: Vandenhoeck & Ruprecht.

CHAPTER 12

ADVANCING EVOLUTIONARY EXPLANATIONS IN ECONOMICS: THE LIMITED USEFULNESS OF TINBERGEN'S FOUR-QUESTION CLASSIFICATION

JACK VROMEN

1. INTRODUCTION

For decades, if not for centuries, economists have been advancing evolutionary explanations.[1] These explanations have taken many different guises and are meant to serve different purposes (Vromen 2004). Some of them, such as evolutionary game-theory explanations of the convergence of populations on Nash equilibria, are meant to support traditional concepts in economic theory. Others, such as Robert Frank's evolutionary explanation of emotions as commitment devices, are meant to amend standard utility theory in a friendly revisionist way. Yet others, such as Nelson and Winter (1982)-type evolutionary economics, are meant to revolutionize economics. Orthodox economics, with individual maximization and aggregate equilibrium as two of its most central theoretical pillars, is to be superseded by an evolutionary theory of economic change, based on the twin evolutionary mechanisms of market selection and selective search.

The evolutionary explanations advanced and the understanding of what they do and do not achieve have not always been informed by possibly relevant insights gained in evolutionary biology. In particular, only recently have some economists with evolutionary leanings started to appreciate the relevance of Ernst Mayr's (1961) distinction between ultimate and proximate causes for a correct understanding of their own evolutionary approach. Ken Binmore (2005), for example, complains that critics of evolutionary game-theory analyses of human behavior mistake ultimate causes for proximate causes. And in his highly ambitious "A Framework for the Unification of the Behavioural Sciences" Herbert Gintis (2007) organizes his discussion of evolution and game theory along the lines of the distinction between ultimate and proximate causation (and between ultimate and proximate explanations). This is a welcome development. A clear understanding of Mayr's distinction might prevent economists from giving over-simplified evolutionary explanations. Early attempts at evolutionary theorizing in economics arguably suffered from sketching all too simple scenarios. It was assumed, in particular, that evolutionary theorizing implies that things similar to genes are in charge of behavior. With their routines as genes analogy, Nelson and Winter (1982) claimed that firm behavior is programmed by routines. Likewise, Binmore (1994) earlier on suggested that what really are in the driver's seat of individual human behavior are genes and memes. A clear appreciation of the distinction between ultimate and proximate causes might be an effective antidote against the misunderstanding that something like genetic determinism is implied in evolutionary theorizing.

In this paper, it is argued that Niko Tinbergen's (1963) four-question classification might be an even better antidote than Mayr's distinction against misunderstandings that hamper making headway with evolutionary theorizing in economics. Tinbergen's four-question classification, it is argued, can be seen as a further refinement of Mayr's distinction. Tinbergen's classification is used here as a sorting device. It is used not only to dispel misunderstandings of evolutionary theorizing and to warn against sketching all too simple evolutionary scenarios in evolutionary explanations as the ones alluded to above. Tinbergen's classification might also help in understanding what evolutionary explanations can and cannot explain. It might be instrumental in sorting out different sorts of questions that might legitimately be asked about behavior and that might call for different answers. Yet, despite all its merits some reasons are given in the paper for believing that even Tinbergen's classification might be too crude and too coarse-grained for some other purposes.

2. TINBERGEN'S FOUR QUESTIONS

Tinbergen's (1963) classification of four questions can be seen as a further refinement of Mayr's (1961) distinction between proximate and ultimate causes of behavior. Tinbergen's (1963) classification offers finer-grained distinctions within Mayr's (1961) distinction.

Mayr (1961) argues that behavior can be explained by reference either to ultimate or to proximate causes.[2] Consider the migrating behavior of warblers, for example. Sometime in late summer, warblers start flying southwards. Why do they do this? One explanation for this, Mayr argues, has to do with a drop in the number of hours of daylight (photoperiodicity) and with a drop in temperature. These extrinsic causes activate parts of the warblers' physiology (what Mayr calls "intrinsic physiological causes"), which in turn cause the warblers to fly southwards. Such extrinsic and intrinsic causes are called *proximate causes* by Mayr. Another explanation of the migrating behavior of warblers roughly runs as follows. In the course of the evolutionary history of their species, warblers have acquired a genetic constitution that induces them to respond appropriately to relevant stimuli from the environment. Ancestors of the present population warblers that acquired such a genetic constitution were reproductively more successful than other living competitors that had not acquired such a constitution. Natural selection working in evolutionary histories of species is called an *ultimate cause* by Mayr.

John Beatty summarizes the difference between proximate and ultimate causes as follows:

> The proximate causes of an organism's traits occur within the lifetime of the organism. They involve the expression of the information contained in the organism's genetic material, as mediated by the environment. The ultimate causes occur prior to the lifetime of the organism, within the evolutionary history of the organism's species. They involve the reasons why members of that species have come to have the genetic information that they do. (Beatty 1994, 334)

Proximate causes are constituent concurrent parts of the organism that contribute to the functioning of the organism as a whole during its lifetime. Proximate causes are referred to in attempts to answer *how* questions, like "How does something work?" and "How does the element contribute to the development of the larger capacity in question?" By contrast, natural selection is an ultimate cause that impinged on ancestors of the organism in question. Ultimate causes are referred to in attempts to answer *why* (in the sense of *how come*) questions, like "How come current organisms of a species have the genetic constitution that they have?"

Mayr argues that the two types of explanations are both legitimate. Even though they are clearly different, Mayr has often complained that in many papers the two are mixed up (Mayr 1994, 357). He also argues that they do not conflict. The two types of explanation are rather complementary, Mayr argues. For a full understanding of behavior they are both indispensable.

Ariew (2003) convincingly argues that Mayr himself subsumes and confounds two different sorts of processes under the heading of proximate causes. For Mayr, *proximate causes* refer both to the causes at work in the ontogenetic development of organisms and to the causes at work in the operation of adult, mature organisms. Yet it is clear that these are two distinct causal processes. The question "How do hearts come to develop out of embryonic cells?" is different from and calls for a different answer than the question "How do hearts contribute to circulation?" Ariew furthermore argues that Mayr's view that ontogenetic development is largely a matter of the decoding of genetic programs is outdated. Ariew suggests that instead of defining proximate causes in terms of the decoding of genetic programs, as Mayr does, proximate causes should be defined in terms of the causal capacities of structural elements.

Ariew also suggests that Mayr's view that natural selection is the sole ultimate cause in the evolutionary history of species is unduly restrictive. There are forces or mechanisms other than natural selection, such as migration, mutation, genetic recombination and drift, which might also influence how populations evolve. Ariew proposes to replace Mayr's concept of "ultimate cause" by the concept of "*evolutionary explanation*,"[3] which Ariew takes to be broad enough to accommodate all evolutionary forces (and not just natural selection).[4] Ariew also takes issue with Mayr's view that it is always historical questions that evolutionary biologists seek to answer. Again, Ariew argues that this is overly restrictive. Even if we confine our attention to evolution by natural selection, what evolutionary biologists might be (and actually are) interested in is not just how organisms in a particular species acquired certain traits, but also whether the trait is currently being maintained by natural selection. The question about the historical emergence of some trait might be different and may require a different answer from the question about its present persistence.

Apparently without knowing it,[5] Ariew thus reproduces the four questions that Niko Tinbergen, one of the co-founders of ethology (along with Konrad Lorenz), famously distinguished in his *On Aims and Methods of Ethology* (1963).[6] Tinbergen's four questions are often stated as follows:

1. What are the mechanisms that cause behavior?
2. What is the developmental trajectory?
3. What is the survival value?
4. How did it evolve?

It also has become standard to refer to these questions in terms of causation, development, function, and evolution, respectively (see, for example, Bolhuis & Verhulst

2005).[7] Causation relates to mechanisms in the mature organism, development covers the ontogenetic development of these mechanisms, function relates to the survival value that the behavior to be explained now has, and evolution relates to the phylogenetic history of the species in question.

With his four-question classification, Tinbergen can be said to refine Mayr's distinction between proximate and ultimate causes. The distinctions that Tinbergen makes are finer grained than Mayr's. Mayr's proximate causes are unpacked in Tinbergen's questions 1 and 2, and Mayr's ultimate causes are further differentiated in Tinbergen's questions 3 and 4. Like Mayr, Tinbergen argues that each of the four questions is legitimate in its own right, that each of them calls for a different sort of answer, that they are nonconflicting and complementary, and that they are all equally necessary in a fully rounded ethology.

The first two questions are about what Tinbergen calls the *behavior machinery* (Tinbergen 1963, 414). The second question addresses how the behavior machinery is built starting from embryonic cells, while the first question addresses how elements in a fully developed machinery are involved in the generation of the behavior to be explained. Rather than getting entangled in a debate about the extent to which behavior is innate or acquired, or instinctive or learned, Tinbergen urges ethologists to turn a close eye to how behavior actually develops (Manning 2005). When Tinbergen is talking about the behavior machinery, he is mostly referring to the level of (neuro)physiology. But he recommends studying the causation of animal behavior at all levels of integration, all the way down to molecular biology (Tinbergen 1963, 416).

Tinbergen also makes the interesting remark that his four-problem classification is pragmatic rather than logical (426). By this he means that the classification is based more on already established divisions and specializations within biology and ethology than on a neatly carved up total causal chain. There are overlaps between the fields covered by the questions (411). There are different systems of ontogenetic control and, instead of asking what the survival value or function of some behavior is (question 3), we could ask what the survival value or function of the different systems of ontogenetic control is. There is overlap also between the fields covered by questions 1 and 2. Individuals may continue to learn also after they acquired their mature shape. Another way of putting this is that ontogeny can continue beyond the period of growth to maturity (427). So a sharp and neat dividing line between causation and ontogenetic development cannot be drawn either.

When Tinbergen speaks of the survival value of behavior (question 3), he seems to have in mind *present* survival value, the value that some behavior now has. This allows him to say that whereas physiologists look at causes of current behavior, evolutionary biologists focus on their effects: "Both types of worker are, therefore, investigating cause-effect relationships, and the only difference is that the physiologists look back in time, whereas the students of survival value, so-to-speak, look "forward in time"" (418). But, following Lorenz, Tinbergen also reckons with the possibility that behavior patterns "misfire" (421). Behavior patterns that might be well-adapted to the natural environment in which they evolved might be ill-adapted to new, unprecedented or artificial surroundings.[8]

3. THE POTENTIAL USES OF TINBERGEN'S FOUR-QUESTION CLASSIFICATION

Both Mayr and Tinbergen were fulminating against what they saw as an unwelcome development within their profession: the rise to hegemony of physiological or physicist explanations of behavior. The prevailing view of the day was that evolutionary explanations, especially explanations that investigate the survival value of certain behavioral traits, are less amenable to the scientific method of observation and experiment than physiological accounts. Evolutionary explanations were widely considered to be speculative and to consist of uncritical guesses. Tinbergen reports of an incident in which he brought up the question of survival value but was firmly told by a zoology professor that this is the wrong sort of question to ask (417). The mere fact that questions of survival value focus on effects rather than causes of behavior, Tinbergen argues, does not make answers to these questions less scientific than answers to questions of causation. Both sorts of questions deal with a flow of events that can be observed repeatedly and which, thus, can be subjected to repeated observations and experiments.[9]

Like Tinbergen, Mayr was convinced that explanations by reference to ultimate causes not only differ from explanations by reference to proximate causes, but are also legitimate (in the sense of being scientifically respectable), complementary, and indispensable for a complete understanding of behavior. What Mayr wanted to counter in particular is the tendency of physiologically oriented biologists to assume that explaining by reference to proximate causes renders explanations by reference to ultimate causes superfluous. This tendency is seriously misguided, Mayr argues, for explanations by reference to ultimate causes answer a completely different type of question and hence give a particular sort of information that explanation by reference to proximate causes cannot possibly provide. The physiological answer to the question "Why do individuals behave the way they do?" thus cannot answer the question as it is understood by evolutionary biologists: "Why does (or did) the behavior have survival value?." This seems to generalize to Tinbergen's four questions. What is an adequate answer to one question need not be an adequate answer to another question. The forces or factors behind the evolution of some behavior (its emergence, as an answer to question 4) need not coincide with the forces and factors that now keep the behavior in place (its persistence, as an answer to question 3), for example. The function that the wings of birds initially served, for example, need not necessarily (and probably is not) flight (their present function). Tinbergen's four-question classification thus can serve as a reminder that there are several aspects of behavior that we might be interested in and that we should not take for granted from the outset, that we can have all-purpose explanations that address all the aspects equally well.

Tinbergen's classification might be instrumental also in alerting us to various ways in which the *simplest evolutionary scenarios* might get the actual causal story behind behavior wrong. Arguably, in the simplest evolutionary scenario, natural selection is the dominant (or only) evolutionary force at work. Furthermore, what is selected for ultimately coincides with what is "selected of" (Sober 1984) namely, genes. To be sure, natural selection never impinges directly on genes. Natural selection always impinges directly on phenotypic traits. But if there is genetic determinism, if ontogenetic development is under full control of genes, and if there also is a one-to-one mapping from genes onto relevant phenotypic traits, then what is ultimately selected for are genes. Finally, in the simplest evolutionary scenario possible, it is assumed that evolutionary pressures have remained the same. The same pressures that led to the evolution of the behavior in question now make the behavior persist.

To forestall possible misunderstanding, I do not take this simplest evolutionary scenario to be a faithful representation (not even approximately) of actual processes. On the contrary, it is meant to show that Tinbergen's classification can help in sorting out the various ways in which the simplest evolutionary scenario might go wrong as a representation of actual processes. First of all, as Ariew points out, natural selection might not be the dominant (let alone the only) evolutionary force at work (question 4). Furthermore, a more detailed study of how ontogenetic development actually proceeds (as Tinbergen pleads for, question 2) will point out that genetic determinism is at most approximately true for a few specific phenotypic traits. Consequently, behavior is not a matter of the decoding of genetic programs (question 1). Finally, the evolutionary environment might have changed considerably, so that the behavior's present survival value is unrelated to how the behavior evolved originally (question 3). In short, by zooming in on different parts of the total causal chain (Tinbergen 1963, 427), Tinbergen's classification directs our attention to the possibility that the actual total causal chain might be quite unlike the chain that is depicted in the simplest evolutionary scenario.

Until now I followed Mayr and Tinbergen in assuming that what explanations by reference to proximate causes explain (question 1, in particular) and what explanations by reference to ultimate causes explain (question 4, in particular) is the same, namely, behavior. But this does not seem to be quite right. The *direct* effects of evolution by natural selection are not behaviors but (changes in) gene frequencies in the population's gene pool. Recall that this is in line with how Mayr presents it. Mayr argues that what natural selection explains is why organisms of a certain species acquired the genetic constitution that they have now. In other places, Mayr argues that what natural selection explains is why organisms of some species have the internal physiological causes that they actually have. What all this suggests is that what explanation by reference to ultimate causes explains is not the behavior that organisms actually display but the proximate causes that they actually have. Another way of putting this is that natural selection does not produce behavior directly, but indirectly, via proximate causes (Sterelny 1992). Recall that an individual's genes and his physiological machinery can both be called proximate causes in that they either are involved in the development of (direct) causes of behavior (so only indirectly in the production of behavior), as with genes, or they are themselves direct causes of behavior, as in the case of internal physiological causes. If there were a one-to-one mapping of genes onto the relevant elements in the physiological behavior machinery, and if there is a one-to-one mapping of these elements to behavior, it does not matter a great deal whether we say that explanations by reference to ultimate causes explain behavior or that they explain proximate causes underlying behavior. But if such one-to-one mappings are lacking, it does matter. And in reality, the absence of such one-to-one mappings seems to be the rule rather than the exception. There are at least two principal reasons for this. First, the typical situation seems to be that more than one element feeds into the production of any particular instance of behavior (Sterelny 1992). And second, the elements seem to be of such a kind that what they produce individually is sensitive to prevailing environmental circumstances (including social circumstances).

If what explanations by reference to ultimate causes directly explain is not behavior but proximate causes, then explanations by reference to ultimate causes and explanations by reference to proximate causes do not have the same *explanandum*. The *explanandum* in explanations by reference to proximate causes is behavior (including the behavior of the growing, developing individual), whereas the *explanandum* in explanations by reference to ultimate causes are proximate causes. What are *explanantia* in the one sort of explanation, the explanation of behavior by reference to proximate causes, thus appear as *explananda* in the other sort of explanation, explanation by reference to ultimate causes. With this depiction of the relation between explanations by reference to ultimate causes and explanations by reference to proximate causes, the two types of explanations can still be said to be complementary. But it is a different sort of complementarity. The types are no longer complementary in that they provide different but compatible information about behavior. They complement each other in that what is doing the explaining in the one type is explained in the other type.

What is also suggested here is that there is a neat sequential order involved. Ontogenetic development in an organism takes place on the basis of its pre-evolved genetic constitution. Only after ultimate causes produced the embryo's genetic constitution, this genetic constitution, in turn, influences the organism's ontogenetic development, which, in turn, leads to the proximate causes of the mature individual. Although this depiction is not false, it is simplifying things considerably. It is not just (as already noted) that ontogenetic development, in the sense of learning, can continue after maturation. What is increasingly appreciated in evolutionary theory is also that how individuals develop ontogenetically and what proximate causes they develop can profoundly affect the courses that evolutionary processes take.[10] It is true that the pre-evolved genetic constitution may greatly influence ontogenetic development. But it is equally true that pre-evolved systems of ontogenetic control and pre-evolved mature proximate causes may greatly influence evolutionary processes. I will return to this shortly.

Evolutionary theorizing might also be instrumental in deciphering proximate causes. If we already have a solid understanding of what proximate causes underlie behavior, we just saw that evolutionary theorizing might help us explain why the organism in question has evolved these proximate causes. If we do not have such a solid understanding yet, evolutionary theorizing might help in acquiring a more solid understanding. Evolutionary theorizing might yield hypotheses about how the brain or mind is to be carved up in meaningful functional joints, for example. That is, evolutionary theorizing might serve a heuristic function in attempts to identify proximate causes. This is what evolutionary psychologists call function-to-form analysis (Buss 1999).

4. Dispelling Misunderstandings of Evolutionary Explanations in Economics

One of the possible uses of Tinbergen's four-question classification, we just saw, is that it can dispel common and sometimes tenacious misunderstandings of evolutionary theorizing. In this section, I show that this also applies to misunderstandings of evolutionary explanations in economics, misunderstandings that stood (and still stand) in the way of more widespread acceptance of evolutionary explanations in economics.

Bioeconomics

Although the bioeconomists Becker and Hirshleifer argued that there also is something to be learned for economists from evolutionary biology, bioeconomics has largely been a matter of promoting the use of (and actually using) standard economic theory in studying animal behavior (Vromen 2007). As such, bioeconomics can be called a form of economic (or economics) imperialism. What bioeconomists argued for in particular is that the "constrained maximization" framework of standard economic theory can also be fruitfully applied by evolutionary biologists. Thus, Tullock (1971) shows that the existing explanation of the coal tits' consumption of the eucosmid moth *Ernarmonia conicolana* in biology can be greatly simplified by treating coal tits as careful optimizing shoppers.[11] The assumption underlying this treatment of the coal tits' consumption behavior, Tullock argues, is that coal tits have inherited reasonably efficient patterns of behavior. To Tullock this assumption makes sense. For if their ancestors did not evolve reasonably efficient patterns of behavior, they would not have survived.

Tullock's treatment of the Coal Tits' behavior met incredulity in some quarters. Surely Tullock cannot possibly be serious in entertaining the thought that Coal Tits go through complex calculations before deciding what to consume? This reaction reflects a misunderstanding of what Tullock is actually arguing. Tullock is clearly not suggesting here that Coal Tits are actually doing the math that standard economic theory ascribes to them. The mental operations ascribed to them are not meant to give a realistic depiction of the proximate causes of the Coal Tits' behavior. Instead, what Tullock is arguing is that it can safely be assumed that natural selection, as the prime ultimate cause, produced Coal Tits that display reasonably efficient patterns of behavior. Only those Coal Tits survived that behave *as if* they were actually going through the mental operations ascribed them.[12] Tullock's suggestion that the behavior of current Coal Tits can be accurately described in terms of constrained maximization is grounded in the belief that constrained maximization accurately describes the outcomes of the working of the ultimate cause natural selection. It is not based on the belief that constrained maximization accurately depicts what is going on within the Coal Tits. On this latter issue, the issue of what proximate causes underlie the coal tits' behavior, Tullock has nothing to say.

Evolutionary Game Theory

Tullock's belief that evolutionary processes, driven by ultimate causes like natural selection, tend to converge on states that rational constrained maximizing individuals would also settle on seems to be supported by evolutionary game theory. Mailath argues that one of the main lessons from evolutionary game theory is that "…any asymptotically stable rest point of an evolutionary dynamic is a Nash equilibrium" (Mailath 1998, 1371). If some evolutionary dynamic, such as the so-called replicator dynamic,[13] drives a process in the direction of a rest point (a state that, once reached, is left unchanged by the dynamic), and if this point is asymptotically stable (which means that any path that starts sufficiently close to the rest point converges to that rest point), then this outcome of the evolutionary dynamic is a Nash equilibrium. As Binmore puts it, "An evolutionary process that adjusts the players' strategy choices in the direction of increasing payoffs can only stop when it reaches a Nash equilibrium" (Binmore 2004, 7). This makes many follow John Nash's own suggestion (made in his unpublished PhD dissertation, [Nash 1950]) that the concept of Nash equilibrium can be given an evolutionary (or, as Nash himself put it, a population-statistical) interpretation. Aumann (1997) argues that of the two interpretations that can be given of the concept of Nash equilibrium—a rationalistic (conscious maximization) and an evolutionary interpretation— the evolutionary explanation is the most fundamental one.[14] Hammerstein and Hagen likewise take the congruence of the end states of rational choice and of evolutionary processes to be the strongest conceptual link between economics and biology: "[Thus], although there are important exceptions, rational choice, evolution by natural selection, and learning often arrive at the same result" (Hammerstein & Hagen 2005, 608).

Thus, application of the Nash equilibrium concept need not imply that "hyper-rationality" is assumed on the part of the players. Yet this is how the Nash equilibrium is often understood, as requiring or presupposing hyperrationality. Once we grasp that many sorts of evolutionary processes, processes that involve less-than-fully-rational individuals, wind up in a Nash equilibrium (if they come to a rest at all), we see that this popular understanding is a misunderstanding. The existence of Nash equilibria is compatible with a multitude of different proximate causes. Replicator dynamic and other monotone dynamics posited in evolutionary game theory are also compatible with a multitude of different proximate causes. The only thing that replicator dynamic implies is that the frequency in the population of strategies with above-average fitness increases at the expense of the frequency of strategies with below-average fitness. There are many different proximate causes that can produce behavior consistent with this. This is one of the senses in which D'Arms et al. (1998) speak of the *flexibility* of what they call "generalist" evolutionary game-theory analyses. D'Arms et al. (1998) argue that "generalist" evolutionary game-theory analyses explain behavior by reference to ultimate causes and that there may be different proximate causes underlying the behavior to be explained.

Take for example Axelrod's (or actually Rapoport's) famous Tit for Tat (TFT) strategy. Tit for Tat seems to require quite sophisticated cognitive machinery on the part of individuals. For TFT to be a feasible strategy, it seems individuals must be able not only to discount future results but also to recognize opponents and to remember what those did in their last encounter. It seems only very few species are able to do all this. Yet Axelrod holds that TFT can be observed in many species. How can this be? Axelrod and Hamilton (1981, reprinted [in a slightly modified and abridged version] as Chapter 5 in Axelrod 1984) argue that this is because there can be, and actually are, (what they call) "substitute mechanisms" for the capacity to remember and recognize individuals/opponents that individuals interacted with before (continued association via, e.g., mutualisms, having fixed meeting places, territoriality) and for the discount rate (parameter w), namely, the chance that after the current interaction the two individuals will meet again. Having such substitute mechanisms suffices to be able to display TFT.

Robert Frank: Emotions as Commitment Devices

Frank's (1988) commitment model is also often misunderstood. The facts, first, that Frank shows that it pays in commitment problems to be emotionally committed to play cooperative strategies (rather than being able to choose flexibly what to do on the spot) and, second, that in the subtitle Frank speaks of *The Strategic Role of the Emotions* are taken to imply that what Frank is arguing is that it is rational for players to strategically choose to be emotionally committed. There are many things not fully clear about Frank's commitment model, but this understanding is plainly wrong. Again the fault is that ultimate causes are mistaken for proximate ones. The fact that Frank is arguing that emotionally committed players obtain better material results than emotionally uncommitted players is a crucial part in Frank's explanation by reference to ultimate causes of why emotional commitments could have survived tight selection pressures in the past. And emotionally committed ancestors have been able to obtain better results not despite but precisely because they could not opportunistically and strategically change strategies at any point in time. That emotionally committed players cannot do this figures in Frank's account of the proximate causes of behavior. That emotionally committed players reap superior material results because of their commitments figures in Frank's account of ultimate causes and their effects.

An indispensable element in Frank's account of the evolution of emotionally committed behavior is that emotional commitments are signaled to others and that others trust these signals. The crux in Frank's account arguably is that individuals that are emotionally committed to play cooperative strategies recognize each other and selectively only interact with each other. Frank is well aware of the fact that this creates a problem for his evolutionary account: How can such signaling systems have ever arisen while it is clear that signaling systems can only serve their signaling function if the system is already in place? It is clear why signaling systems can survive if they are fully in place. But how could the first pioneering signaling steps ever have survived before signaling systems were fully in place? Frank refers to Tinbergen's so-called derivation principle in arguing that the first pioneering steps must have brought the pioneers other evolutionary advantages. This can be translated into Tinbergen's four-question classification: in this case, the answer given to question 4 (How did the behavior evolve?) must clearly differ from the answer given to question 3 (What is the function of the behavior?).[15] Thus Frank displays a (for economists) unusual awareness of the finesses, specific demands of and possible pitfalls in evolutionary explanations.

Paul Glimcher's Version of Neuroeconomics

Due to the well-read overviews of Camerer et al. (2004, 2005), perhaps the dominant view is that neuroeconomics predominantly entails the accommodation of theoretical insights and empirical findings in (cognitive) neuroscience in economics. These insights and findings might help economists (and especially behavioral economists) understand better why standard economic theory does well in some settings while it does badly in others. This is not the only way in which neuroeconomics is practiced, however. Paul Glimcher is a neuroscientist who expects a lot from using expected utility theory and game theory in studying the workings of the nervous system. Glimcher advocates the reverse transfer of standard theories and approaches in economics to neuroscience. First attempts to implement this reverse transfer yielded stunning results. It turns out that at the level of individual neurons (or small groups of neurons) the firing rates seem to track changes in probabilities and values. Glimcher argues that the calculations ascribed to rational individuals in, for example, expected utility theory—first computing the relative desirability of each possible course of action and, second, selecting the most desirable one—are *literally* executed at the neural level.[16]

> Neoclassical theory has always made the famous *as if* argument: it is *as if* expected utility was computed by the brain. Modern neuroscience suggests an alternative, and more literal, interpretation. The available data suggest that the neural architecture actually does compute a desirability for each available course of action. This is a real physical computation, accomplished by neurons, that derives and encodes a real variable. The process of choice that operates on this variable then seems to be quite simple: it is the process of executing the action encoded as having the greatest desirability. (Glimcher, Dorris & Bayer 2005, 220)[17]

It might seem that what Glimcher et al. (2005) are arguing here is that neurons conduct the mental operations that, on a literal interpretation, expected utility theory ascribe to individuals, namely, that first desirabilities and probabilities of options are consciously computed and that subsequently the optimal choice is calculated. Given that most economists have long given up the idea that economic agents actually execute the computations that expected utility theory ascribes to them, this would be an astonishing result indeed; the computations are actually carried out by neurons inside economic agents!

Note first, however, that Glimcher et al. are not arguing here that neurons can always be assumed to perform these neoclassical computations. This can at most be assumed if there have been evolutionary processes going on long enough to produce these computations. Ultimate causes such as natural selection must have been working long and consistently enough for such computations to evolve. Glimcher's application of expected utility theory and game theory is inspired by Marr's (1982) computational approach. Any attempt to understand information-processing systems such as brains, Marr argues, should start with a specification of the task, or computational goal, that the system evolved to perform. This does not mean that Marr takes it for granted that individuals always actually attain this goal efficiently. Economic theory rather provides an indispensable benchmark (of optimality or efficiency) for further research into the brain (and into any information-processing system in general). It is a benchmark that possibly, and perhaps even probably, is not attained in actual behavior.[18] What is more, Glimcher suggests that adopting the economic approach is most useful in identifying neural mechanisms if the mechanisms in question fall well short of this benchmark. What is revealed then is that certain inherited and selected mechanisms that presumably worked well in the evolutionary environment in which they evolved do not perform well in the current environment. Mechanisms that were well adapted to the past environmental circumstances in which they evolved may well be maladapted to present circumstances. When activated in present circumstances, they misfire and produce suboptimal or inefficient results.[19]

Note also that Glimcher et al. are not postulating the existence of a little *homunculus* somewhere in the brain that collects the necessary information from two other groups of neurons about the desirability and probability of options and then consciously figures out what is the best option. Selection in the brain of the course of action that actually is displayed rather is taken to proceed in a purely mechanical way (in a winner-take-all fashion). So contrary to what a superficial and uninformed reading might suggest, what Glimcher et al. are *not* suggesting is that a literal interpretation of what expected utility theory says about the decision making of individual persons, namely, that they are actually consciously computing desirabilities and probabilities of options and then calculate the optimal choice, is literally true of what happens at the cellular level of neurons in the brain. What Glimcher et al. say about the firing behavior of neurons is supposed to tell us something about the behavior machinery within people. Firing neurons can be seen as proximate causes of behavior. How these proximate causes relate to folk-psychological notions like desires and beliefs is an intricate issue that will be discussed briefly at the end of this paper (see also Vromen 2007 for further discussion).

5. BLACK BOXING PROXIMATE CAUSES IN EVOLUTIONARY GAME THEORY

In two of the four examples just given, bioeconomics and evolutionary game theory, it is assumed that ultimate evolutionary causes directly produce behavior. In the other two examples given, Frank's emotions as commitment devices and Glimcher's version of neuroeconomics, it is assumed that what ultimate evolutionary causes directly produce are proximate causes of behavior; ultimate evolutionary causes here produce behavior only indirectly, via the production of proximate causes. Evolutionary explanations are used in these last two examples to open up and peer into the black box of proximate causes underlying behavior. Discussion of this is left to the next section. In this section, I discuss evolutionary game theory.

In evolutionary game theory, proximate causes are effectively black boxed. Evolutionary game theorists such as Binmore believe that what their models track are the workings and effects of ultimate causes only. Binmore argues that while studying behavior in terms of ultimate causes is relatively straightforward and has been pursued relatively successfully (in sociobiology, in particular), studying behavior in terms of proximate causes has proven to be difficult (Binmore 2005, 6). Fortunately there is no need to study proximate causes, Binmore seems to think, for we can successfully study behavior in terms of ultimate causes without going into its proximate causes.

The idea seems to be that, in giving evolutionary explanations of behavior, nothing really is said and nothing really needs to be said about the behavior's underlying proximate causes. It is believed that insightful evolutionary explanations of behavior can be given without paying attention to proximate causes of behavior. It is not that evolutionary game theorists necessarily deny that giving alternative explanations in terms of proximate causes can be interesting in their own right. But they maintain that in their own explanations of behavior no assumptions about specific proximate causes underlying the behavior need to be made and, moreover, that no such assumptions are actually made. And rightly so, for zooming in on proximate causes would only draw attention away from the remarkable general patterns that evolutionary explanations uncover. The potential drawback of focusing on the differences between the physiological and psychological mechanisms producing incest avoidance in humans and insects, for example, is that one loses sight of the fact that all these mechanisms evolved to solve the same evolutionary problem (avoiding malfunctioning or unfit offspring because of inbreeding; Sober 1993).

This idea seems to get some support from D'Arms et al.'s (1998) insightful discussion of evolutionary game-theoretic analyses of social contracts. D'Arms et al. argue that evolutionary game theorists can be justified in being agnostic about details such as proximate causes, if it is plausible to assume that there might be several possible proximate causes underlying the behavior to be explained.[20] This criterion of *flexibility,* as they call it, is clearly met in the example of incest avoidance just discussed.[21] In this case, we know that there are different proximate causes underlying incest avoidance in animals of different species. Invoking the criterion of flexibility seems to make sense especially if we are, as Binmore suggests, largely ignorant of the proximate causes behind behavior. Given this ignorance, if we were to advance an evolutionary explanation of behavior that can be produced by one proximate cause only, this dependency of the explanation on the existence of the proximate cause would not enhance the credibility of the explanation.

The preceding discussion of the various possible proximate causes that might underlie TFT furthermore suggests that it is perhaps safe to assume that the criterion in this sense is often met. Sometimes it might seem that the behavior explained could be displayed only by individuals with sophisticated proximate mechanisms. And it might be called into question that the individuals in question have such sophisticated mechanisms. But as the TFT case shows, there might be simpler substitute proximate mechanisms that can also do the job. It can be added, moreover, that if the behavior to be explained is actually observed, the individuals must have proximate mechanisms enabling them to display the behavior. After all, without suitable proximate mechanisms being in place and properly functioning, the behavior could not have been displayed in the first place![22] It thus seems that we should not worry too much that D'Arms et al.'s criterion of flexibility is not met. Most of the time the behavior explained in terms of ultimate causes seems to be multiply realizable by a number of proximate causes.

This does not establish that evolutionary game theorists are justified in remaining agnostic about proximate causes all at once, however. D'Arms et al.'s discussion concentrates on proximate causes of behavior that individuals display after they have fully gone through the evolutionary process. It is about different possible proximate causes that might be underlying "end-state behavior." But proximate causes do not make their first appearance only after evolutionary processes have come to a halt. Certain proximate causes must have been working already during evolutionary processes. I just argued that for any sort of behavior displayed there must be proximate causes underlying it. But this, of course, also holds for the behavior of individuals during evolutionary processes. Without there being any proximate cause already working, there cannot be "*during-the-process behavior*" in the first place. Individuals grow up and mature not only after evolutionary processes have converged on a stable rest point. The individuals involved in such processes also do so before evolutionary processes converge. The same holds for mature individuals.[23]

Now what implication does this have for the claim of "generalist" evolutionary game theorists that proximate causes can be safely disregarded? Can proximate causes underlying during-the-process behavior be as confidently disregarded as proximate causes underlying end-state behavior? Can generalist evolutionary game theorists claim that their models and analyses are completely silent about proximate causes underlying during-the-process behavior? Are their models and analyses perfectly flexible in the sense that they are consistent with all proximate causes that possibly could underlie during-the-process behavior? What I am going to argue for now is that this is highly unlikely. In their models and analyses, certain assumptions are (mostly implicitly) made about during-the-process behavior that at least conceivably are at odds with the proximate causes that were actually underlying during-the-process behavior. If the assumptions are widely off the mark in this respect, the evolutionary explanations proffered are deficient. They are deficient because their models and analyses are, as D'Arms et al. (1998) would say, not representative of the actual historical process that they purportedly study.

What specific proximate causes worked during the evolutionary process analyzed can make a real difference for the workings and effects of ultimate causes. Consider biological evolution. As McElreath et al. (2003) note, the trend in evolutionary theorizing is to acknowledge that the workings of ultimate causes cannot be studied without taking the workings of pre-evolved proximate causes into account: "Although the distinction between mechanism (proximate explanation) and function (ultimate explanation) is useful, it obscures the modern understanding that mechanisms have strong impacts on function." (McElreath et al. 2003, 126). It is increasingly appreciated in evolutionary theory that, even if we assume that natural selection holds sway here, different patterns of ontogenetic development and different mature proximate mechanisms may create markedly different selection environments. It is not just that differences in patterns of ontogenetic development and in mature proximate mechanisms may make for different social environments. The material parts of the environment may be different as well. As Laland et al.'s (2000) recent work on niche construction brings out so convincingly, for example, through their own behavior individuals often change the selection pressures to which they are exposed. So what is selected may depend crucially on what patterns of ontogenetic development and mature proximate causes there are.

If the workings and effects of ultimate causes depend on what proximate causes are at work during evolutionary processes, then the implication is that, by disregarding proximate causes in studying the workings and effects of ultimate causes, one runs the risk of analyzing models that are badly misspecified. The strategy set specified and the dynamic posited might fail to represent (even approximate) what actually happens in the evolutionary process. Or changes during evolutionary processes that would call for a different model might be missed (Vromen 2006). Evolutionary game theorists often simply assume or even take for granted that the models they analyze are not badly misspecified. But if proximate causes can make such a difference to the courses that evolutionary processes take, this assumption might well be too optimistic. Sometimes it is argued "... that one provide evidence of an underlying proximate mechanism supporting a choice in model construction...." (Alexander 2000, 497). Typically, however, this has more the character of a reminder than of a maxim for further action. No serious attempt is made to check whether there really are (or have been) proximate mechanisms that would justify the specific model constructed.

This complicates the story about the relationship between ultimate and proximate causes even further. Earlier, we saw that instead of assuming that explanations by reference to ultimate causes have the same *explanandum* as explanations by reference to proximate causes, it seems to make more sense to argue that proximate causes are the *explanandum* for explanations by reference to ultimate causes. Ultimate causes produce proximate causes. But now we see that proximate causes are also crucial parts in the workings of ultimate causes. This further complicates Tinbergen's depiction of the total causal chain. Tinbergen's depiction might be taken to suggest the following sequential order of events. The phylogenetic evolution of a species (question 4) has provided present newborn members of the species with some specific genetic material that control their ontogenetic development (question 2). Ontogenetic development, in turn, leads to the mechanisms in mature individuals that produce behavior (question 1). Their behavior, finally, has effects for how well the individuals can reproduce themselves (question 3). We saw that already Tinbergen himself recognized that the total causal chain cannot be carved up so neatly in separate parts. Tinbergen noticed that ontogenetic development, and especially learning processes, need not stop once an individual has matured, for example. What we just saw indicates that the depicted sequence might be oversimplified also in other respects. The specific factors and mechanisms that go into the ontogenetic development of immature individuals (question 2) and that go into the production of behavior of mature individuals (question 1) might greatly affect the course that evolutionary processes, also those of phylogenetic evolution (question 4), take. Indeed, one can go as far as to argue that selective forces (or selective pressures, or selective regimes) cannot be defined independently of such proximate causes (Sterelny 1996).

In short, if we want to analyze plausible models of the workings and effects of ultimate causes operating in evolutionary processes, we'd better make sure that we get the proximate causes underlying the behavior of the individuals involved in those processes at least roughly right. What about Binmore's remark that we do not and actually cannot know much about the proximate causes underlying behavior (especially those of individuals living long ago)? Parker (2006) argues that given the limited understanding of proximate mechanisms we once had, viewing individuals as "black boxes" was necessary for a while. But now that proximate mechanisms are gradually becoming better understood, it has become possible to develop more realistic evolutionary models (Parker 2006, 48).

How Does Cultural Evolution Fit In?

Until now, the focus of the discussion has been on biological evolution. Yet it seems safe to say that most evolutionary game-theory analyses (at least in economics) are about cultural evolution. What is the link between ultimate and proximate causes in cultural evolution? Binmore seems to think that evolutionary game theorists are justified in disregarding proximate causes also in analyses of cultural evolution. This view is untenable, I shall argue. In studying cultural evolution, there is even less justification for disregarding the proximate causes actually at work during evolutionary processes than in studying biological evolution. In cultural evolution, the distinction between ultimate and proximate causes gets blurred, or even breaks down. Ultimate causes become virtually indistinguishable from proximate causes. One could even say that in cultural evolution ultimate causes are proximate causes.[24]

To see this, let us have a glance at how evolutionary game theorists conceive of the main features of cultural evolution. Brian Skyrms (1996) is by no means the only one assuming that the replicator dynamic captures the essence, namely, differential replication (Skyrms 1996, x), of both biological and cultural evolution. What the replicator dynamic implies is that players' strategy choices adjust in the direction of increasing payoffs, as Binmore puts it (Binmore 2005, 7). Why are players' strategy choices adjusted in the direction of increasing payoffs in cultural evolution? That is because players are supposed to learn. It is *learning* that is assumed to drive cultural evolution. There are several accounts offered of learning in evolutionary game theory. In some accounts, individuals only learn from their own experience. Other individuals also learn "socially" from the experience of others in their neighbourhood. Young (1998) assumes that players pick best replies given their limited memory set. Whatever the specific learning and choice rules posited, there does not seem to be a way of denying that this is all about proximate causes of behavior. Each learning and choice rule posited either is a proximate cause or presupposes the workings of suitable proximate causes. If we choose to identify proximate causes at levels lower than that of psychological learning mechanisms, we could legitimately claim that each learning and choice rule is multiply realizable in various proximate causes. But it is clear that no matter what specific lower level we would choose, each specific learning or choice rule is not realizable in all (but only in some) conceivable proximate causes. Thus, no matter the level at which we identify proximate causes, what specific learning or choice rule is representative of some situation crucially depends on what specific proximate causes are at work.

In Skyrms's and Young's evolutionary game-theory analyses of cultural evolution, no attempt is made to link the choice of some particular dynamic with theoretical and empirical work on psychological (or cognitive) mechanisms working in individuals. Fixed (individual and social) learning rules are typically posited and then their implications are investigated in particular interaction structures. These rules allegedly have some psychological plausibility, but their specification is not informed by the now extant theoretical and empirical work on psychological and cognitive mechanisms. Yet it is clear that we cannot hope to understand actual processes of learning and imitation without having at least a rough idea about the psychological mechanisms involved. This latter insight is the point of departure in Dan Sperber's (1996) epidemiological account of cultural evolution. The basic idea in this account is that actually occurring processes of cultural transmission are, to a large extent, determined by pre-evolved psychological mechanisms of the individuals involved. Nichols (2004) follows Sperber in assuming that the cultural evolution of social and moral norms is biased by pre-evolved emotional attractors. Since psychological mechanisms are proximate causes of human behavior *par excellence,* proximate causes are crucial determinants driving cultural evolution in Sperber's and Nichols's accounts.

To an evolutionary biologist, learning belongs to ontogenetic development rather than to evolution, regardless of whether it is biological or cultural evolution that we are talking about (although Tinbergen's remark that learning can continue beyond maturation should be borne in mind here). To an evolutionary biologist, what is crucial in cultural evolution is the nongenetic transmission (or replication) of information. Most of the time it is assumed that cultural units spread in populations through imitation. What makes it an evolutionary process is that frequencies of cultural units change at the *population* level. To many, ontogenetic development is not an evolutionary process at all. Ontogenetic development is about changes at the *individual* level. Ontogenetic development may make for individual differences and idiosyncrasies. As we have seen, the causes driving ontogenetic development form a subset of proximate causes. Others (Skyrms 1996 included) argue that individual learning has the same abstract Darwinian structure of blind variation and selective retention (Campbell 1960) as biological evolution by natural selection. The selectiveness in retention might suggest that an ultimate cause like natural selection is at work in individual learning. But the selection is done here by the individual. Mostly it is assumed that an individual selectively sticks to lines of behavior that thus far produced satisfactory results. This clearly is driven by proximate causes within the individual. Or, more simply, this behavioral rule can itself be called a proximate cause. Anyway, regardless of whether learning is seen as an evolutionary process, there is no way of denying that learning rules either are proximate causes or are based on proximate causes. The upshot thus is that the course that actual processes of cultural evolution take is largely, if not completely, a function of what specific proximate causes are actually operating.

6. Peering into the Black Box: Identifying and Explaining Proximate Causes via Evolutionary Theorizing

Thus far, we looked at evolutionary explanations of behavior in economics that purportedly study the workings and effects of ultimate causes only. These explanations claim to be completely silent about proximate causes underlying behavior. Now we turn to attempts to identify proximate causes of behavior with the aid of evolutionary theorizing. The underlying idea here is that since proximate causes are the outcomes of prior evolutionary processes, evolutionary theorizing holds out the hope of generating interesting hypotheses about the sorts of proximate causes that might have evolved. Earlier, two attempts to identify proximate causes with the aid of evolutionary theorizing were already briefly discussed: Robert Frank's commitment model and Paul Glimcher's version of neuroeconomics. In this section, a few more attempts are discussed. The discussion focuses in particular on the issue of whether evolutionary theory gives any ground for believing that expected utility theory, literally understood, gives us a faithful depiction of what goes on within individuals during their decision making. In a literal understanding, expected utility theory is an idealization of "intentional (or folk) psychology," and is as such committed to the view that individuals go through a process of instrumental reasoning before they act. In the foregoing, however, we saw that on an alternative and common interpretation (popular especially, but not solely within circles of evolutionary theorists), expected utility theory is no more than a theoretical representation of observable patterns of behavior. With this interpretation, the theory is not committed to any particular view about the proximate causes producing the patterns. Thus understood, the theory says nothing about what happens within individuals before they display observable behavior. Results like those obtained by Glimcher might give some hope that something like instrumental reasoning, based on representations of desirabilities and of probabilities, is actually taking place within individuals. Is there reason to believe that there is something like instrumental reasoning, and possibly even utility maximizing, actually taking place somewhere in the behavior machinery?

It is not always clear what particular view on the behavior machinery is implied, even in evolutionary theories that purport to tell us more about cogs and wheels of the behavior machinery. Take Frank's commitment model again. It is clear that Frank argues that emotions (or "passions") are supposed to play a key role in the behavior machinery. But exactly what role they play is not entirely clear. Sometimes Frank suggests that emotions are in charge in some primary reward mechanism that determines the default operations in individuals. For deliberate choice to have a say in how individuals behave, it has to intervene in this primary mechanism. Emotions are likened to sensations of hunger and thirst here. People can deliberately decide to be on a diet, for example, but there is a continuous temptation to have high-calorie intake that they have to fight against. At other times, Frank suggests that emotions can be seen as basic preferences. Here, evolutionary theorizing is believed to impose an *adaptive rationality* standard: "In this framework, the design criterion for a preference is the same as for an arm or a leg or an eye: To what extent does it assist the individual in the struggle to acquire the resources required for survival and reproduction?" (Frank 2004, 48). Only if preferences meet this design criterion are theorists warranted in taking them up in utility functions. Whether Frank believes that utility functions thus derived actually play a causal role in the production of behavior is not clear.

Others are more straightforward on this issue. Aumann (1997) believes that the conscious-maximization framework of rational choice theory gives a faithful depiction of how people actually go about making decisions. The evolutionary interpretation of the concept of Nash equilibrium is supposed to refer to ultimate causes that have produced conscious maximization as the proximate causes behind human behavior. Thus Aumann leaves no doubt that he believes that the conscious-maximization framework is literally true of decision-making processes in humans (Vromen 2009). Robson (2001a, 2001b) likewise argues that evolutionary processes produced utility functions and utility maximizing in human beings (for a critique, see Vromen 2003). Werner Güth and other proponents of the so-called Indirect Evolutionary Approach (Güth & Yaari 1991, Güth & Kliemt 1998) also argue that what evolutionary processes directly produced are basic preferences and that people act rationally (either perfectly or boundedly) on them. Ben-Ner and Putterman (1998) refer to evolutionary psychology to make the same point: evolutionary theory facilitates the nonarbitrary identification of the basic preferences that people act upon.

This view, that evolutionary theory gives us reason to believe that individuals decide consciously and more or less rationally on the basis of their pre-evolved basic preferences, is contested within evolutionary theory itself. There is no shortage of alternative views about our internal behavior machinery (as Tinbergen called it) based on evolutionary theorizing. Gigerenzer et al. (1999) argue, for example, that evolution has endowed us, not with some sort of an all-purpose intelligence, but with fast and frugal heuristics. It is because we evolved a great variety of domain- and problem-specific heuristics and not because we avail of some jack-of-all-trades intelligence, Gigerenzer et al. maintain, that we often find solutions for problems rather effortlessly. These heuristics need not always bring us the best possible solutions. But on balance, when all relevant costs and benefits are factored in, they outperform an all-purpose mechanism particularly because they save on computation costs. Each heuristic evolved in some specific problem context and exploits simple relevant cues in the environment to produce results (this is called ecological rationality). A heuristic that evolved to perform well in the one sort of context (or environment) may perform poorly when it misfires in other contexts. This mismatch hypothesis is invoked to explain why heuristics fail to perform properly if problems are framed in a way that people are not accustomed to.

In all this, Gigerenzer et al.'s views on fast and frugal heuristics resemble evolutionary psychology's views on the massive modularity of the mind. Specific-purpose modules enable us to behave "better than rational," Cosmides and Tooby (1994) argue, because a massively modular mind has computational fitness advantages over a general-purpose mechanism like general intelligence. This massive modularity hypothesis has been challenged by many (cf. Samuels 1998). One of the things that are not clear is what modules (or psychological mechanisms, as they are now often called) precisely are and how they function. Some seem to take modules as behavioral dispositions. Others argue that they are to be understood as learning rules.[25] Note that the difference between these two could be that behavioral dispositions might pertain to mature individuals (Tinbergen's question 1), whereas the learning rules might belong to ontogenetic development (Tinbergen's question 2). It can make a huge difference whether the claim is that natural selection produced innate ontogenetic pathways or that natural selection produced mature behavioral dispositions. Nowadays the preferred interpretation among evolutionary psychologists themselves seems to be that natural selection produced particular developmental systems that reliably led to the development of certain modules as developmental targets. This is called design reincarnation theory (Tooby, Cosmides & Barrett 2003; Barrett 2006, 8).

Evolutionary psychology has also been criticised by many for its excessive nativism (Buller 2005). It is felt by many that the impact of culture and of cultural evolution is downplayed, if not downright neglected in evolutionary psychology. Theorists such as Fehr and Gächter (2002)and Gintis (2000) build upon Boyd and Richerson's (1985) gene-culture co-evolution theory in explaining what they call "altruistic punishment" and "strong reciprocity." What both notions aim to bring out is that people turn out to be willing to make substantial personal sacrifices in punishing cheaters. Fehr and Gächter (2002) and Gintis (2000) claim that altruistic punishment and strong reciprocity could only have evolved through cultural group selection. They also fulminate against the use that evolutionary psychologists make of the mismatch hypothesis to explain strong reciprocity

(Fehr & Henrich 2003). In their view, strong reciprocity cannot be treated as a remnant of the distant past that once was well-adapted to the then-prevailing circumstances, but that is now ill-adapted to present circumstances. When discussing the proximate causes underlying strong reciprocity, Fehr stresses the key role that emotions play. This he sees vindicated in experiments using functional Magnetic Resonance Imaging (fMRI) scans.

In their overviews of what economists could learn from neuroscience, Camerer et al. (2004, 2005) suggest that *dual processing theories* might be closest to the truth about how the human mind and brain work. After surveying relevant literature, Camerer et al. argue that automatic (that is, not consciously controlled) behavior is the default mode of operation in human behavior and that affect (rather than cognition) is primary in driving human behavior. In contrast to consciously controlled behavior, automatic behavior typically occurs without awareness, is accompanied by a subjective feeling of effortlessness, is reflexive (that is, not evoked deliberately), and is not introspectively accessible. Due to the latter feature, the causes behind most of our behavior elude us. Attempts to access these causes can be made and are often made, but are most likely to lead to spurious sense making (that is, we tend to posit particular, supposedly self-chosen reasons for our own behavior that are simply nonexistent). Attempts can also be made to override automatic, affect-driven behavior cognitively. But such attempts happen less frequently than we wish to think and are often not successful (like countering our longing for calorie-rich food in a diet).

Sterelny (2003) is perhaps the most sustained attempt to see what view of the internal behavior machinery is suggested by the latest state of the art in evolutionary theorizing. Sterelny argues that "...we have evolved wiring-and-connection features that are something like, but not perfectly like, beliefs and preferences as portrayed by intentional psychology" (10). We have evolved separate systems for representing preferences and beliefs, Sterelny argues, that are more sophisticated than just physiological drives or instincts and specific environmental triggers, respectively. Furthermore, the connections between the two systems are not fixed but flexible. Beliefs do not directly code for specific behavior, for example. That is why Sterelny speaks of decoupled representations. This seems to come close to how decision theory depicts human behavior. But Sterelny does not believe that decision theory is vindicated. What he takes from various experimental findings is that our motivations are not stable across different contexts (Sterelny 2004, 516–517). Decision theory is not able to account for this rather radical form of context sensitivity.

The preceding overview by no means exhausts all the hypotheses expounded about proximate causes based on evolutionary theorizing. Yet it suffices to show that the diversity in hypotheses offered is truly bewildering. It is not just that many different hypotheses are offered. It is not clear either how some of the hypotheses, like those of evolutionary psychologists, are to be interpreted. To complicate things even further, the hypotheses sometimes address mechanisms at different levels of analysis (or of integration, as Tinbergen put it). Proximate causes can be and *de facto* are identified at different levels of analysis. Just summing up now, among the candidate proximate causes that have been identified are the following:

- Genes (at the molecular level; cf. Mayr [1961])
- Neurons (at the cellular level; cf. Glimcher [2003])
- Brain areas (as lightning up in experiments with fMRI scans, for example)
- Emotions/affects and (cool) cognition (cf. Frank, Fehr, Camerer et al.)
- Desires (or preferences) and beliefs (or expectations) (cf. Sober & Wilson 1998 and Sterelny 2003)
- Psychological mechanisms/heuristics (cf. Gigerenzer et al.[1999] and evolutionary psychology)

This truly is a mixed bunch. It might be tempting to compare the situation here with Mayr's and Tinbergen's views about the different sorts of causes that can be identified and about the different questions that can be asked. Recall that Mayr and Tinbergen argued that the different questions and the different answers that they call for are legitimate, nonconflicting, complementary, and indispensable for a full understanding. The candidate proximate causes listed earlier can be seen as attempts to answer Tinbergen's question 1. Are further studies into each of these candidate proximate causes all legitimate, and are they nonconflicting, complementary, and indispensable for a full understanding of the mechanisms that cause behavior? Tinbergen argued that causation of animal behavior should be studied at all levels of integration, all the way down to molecular biology. Tinbergen presumably held that investigating proximate causes is legitimate at all levels of integration, and that the results obtained would be nonconflicting, complementary, and indispensable for a full understanding. But can the same be said about all the candidate proximate causes listed earlier?

While it seems to be clear that at least some of them (genes, neurons, and brain areas, for example) need not necessarily conflict with each other, this is not clear for all of them. One of the problems is that it is not clear whether all of these are to be located at different levels of analysis. Are evolutionary psychology's psychological mechanisms instinct-like behavior dispositions that contradict desire-belief folk psychology, for example (if so, they are to be located at the same level as desires and beliefs), or are these mechanisms to be located at a different level? Hagen and Hammerstein (2006) argue that evolutionary psychology's view of the mind as an assemblage of evolved, specialized mechanisms and the economists' implicit view of the mind (which they understand as an idealization of belief-desire folk psychology) are conflicting. This has significant consequences for how *framing effects* in experimental games are dealt with. As economists see it, frames can determine which preferences or norms subjects apply. The standard assumption is that, given the preferences and norms applied, subjects use their general-purpose optimizing engine to maximize utility. By contrast, evolutionary psychology takes frames to have the appropriate evolved strategy attached: "Framing, in this view, is a way for people to *avoid* the difficulties of optimizing by applying pre-established cognitive templates to problems" (Hagen & Hammerstein 2006, 346). If Hagen and Hammerstein are right, evolutionary psychology's mechanisms and economics' optimizing engine are rivals that are to be put at the same level of analysis.

Carruthers (2003) disagrees. He suggests that evolutionary psychology's mechanisms are to be located at a different level than folk psychology's desires and beliefs. In Carruthers's understanding, psychological mechanisms underlie changes in desires and beliefs. Evolutionary psychology does not contradict folk psychology. Evolutionary psychology rather complements folk psychology. What folk psychology itself cannot explain—when, why, and how desires and beliefs change—evolutionary psychology can. Note, though, that Carruthers's view differs from those who argue that evolutionary psychology's modules tell us what terms to include in the utility functions that people maximize. In Carruthers's understanding, rather than fixing stable preferences, evolutionary psychology might help us understand better when, why, and how preferences change over time.

Given all the different understandings, it is unclear whether the candidate proximate causes identified with the aid of evolutionary theorizing are nonconflicting and complementary. This only further strengthens the conclusion reached earlier that, as yet, it is not at all settled what specific hypotheses about the architecture and workings of the behavior machinery of humans are suggested by current state-of-the-art evolutionary theory.

7. CONCLUSIONS

Tinbergen's refinement of Mayr's distinction between ultimate and proximate causes is helpful in several respects. Above all, it shows that there are several legitimate questions to ask about behavior, that each calls for a different answer and that the answers need not conflict with each other. The forces that went into the evolution of some behavioral trait might be quite different from those that might keep the trait in place after it evolved, for example. In an economic context, a perfectly acceptable answer to the question of why some behavioral pattern emerged in the first place might be an incorrect answer to the question of why the pattern persists. Tinbergen's classification is also useful for dispelling and avoiding tenacious misunderstandings of evolutionary theorizing in general and of evolutionary theorizing in economics in particular. Often, the source of the misunderstanding is that ultimate causes are mistaken for proximate causes. Thus, when Tullock and other bioeconomists argue that the constrained-maximization framework can be fruitfully applied to study animal behavior, they do not assume that animals are in command of the calculus needed to solve the constrained maximization equations. Finally, Tinbergen's classification is suited to bring out the rather heroic assumptions made in the simplest evolutionary scenario possible. In such a scenario, genes (or some analogue) are not only the units that are selected but also the key players in the evolutionary process. Tinbergen's second question alerts us to the extreme assumption entailed here that ontogenetic development is under full genetic control.

We also saw that sometimes we should go beyond Tinbergen's classification. For some purposes, some further refinements may be needed. What use (if any) something now is need not coincide with the use it had when or after it evolved in the first place. Thus, we may add the question of what function (or survival value) something *now* has to the question about the function it once had (Tinbergen's third question). In the case of evolutionary game-theory analyses of cultural evolution, Tinbergen's classification does not seem to be very helpful. Because the driving force in these analyses is individual learning, and learning is (or is based on) proximate causes, the very distinction between ultimate and proximate causes seems to collapse here. Even though cultural evolution is entirely a matter of the working of proximate causes (as seen through the lens of evolutionary game theory), evolutionary game theorists hold that they afford an agnostic stance toward proximate causes. It has been argued that this stance is not warranted. It is increasingly appreciated that pre-evolved proximate causes may greatly affect the course that evolutionary processes take. This also holds for biological evolution. This calls for a further complication of Tinbergen's depiction of the total causal chain. Proximate causes are not only effects of the antecedent working of ultimate causes, as Tinbergen rightly notices, pre-evolved proximate causes are also at work in the working of ultimate causes, affecting the process and outcomes of the working of ultimate causes.

For a while, evolutionary theorists were pardoned to disregard proximate causes. Not much was known about proximate causes. But now, with our improved understanding of proximate causes at the molecular, cellular, and brain-area levels, we can do better. Luckily, the trend in evolutionary theory is to look for *integrating* what we now know about proximate causes in our analyses of evolutionary processes. Being better informed about proximate causes facilitates constructing more realistic evolutionary models (Parker 2006, 48). More realistic evolutionary models in turn might help to develop better hypotheses about proximate causes. It is encouraging to see more and more economists opening up to other disciplines and joining this search for more realistic evolutionary models and for better hypotheses about proximate causes.

NOTES

1. Helpful comments and suggestions from the participants of the Conference on Issues in Philosophy of Economics (May 19–21, 2006, Alabama: Birmingham), and especially from the two editors, Harold Kincaid and Don Ross, are gratefully acknowledged. The usual caveat applies.

2. Mayr was by no means the first biologist to have made this distinction. He was preceded in this by Shäfer and Thompson (see Beatty 1994).

3. This suggests that explanations by reference to proximate causes are not evolutionary at all. Sober (1993, 6) would agree with this.

4. Ariew also makes an interesting argument that evolutionary explanations are not causal but statistical explanations. I do not have space here to go into that.

5. In a footnote, Ariew thanks Sterelny for alerting him to the possible analogy of his own treatment with "Tinbergen's 4-way distinction between explanatory projects in biology" (Ariew 2003, 556), but he argues that this has to be worked out in a separate essay.

6. Somewhat surprisingly, it seems that Mayr and Tinbergen did not mutually influence each other (see Beatty 1994).

7. Tinbergen himself spoke of causation, ontogeny, survival value, and evolution (Tinbergen 1963, 411).

8. This is sometimes called the mismatch hypothesis.

9. In the meantime the table seems to have turned. As Manning (2005) argues, much more progress has been made with answering questions 3 and 4 than with questions 1 and 2. In the 1970s, sociobiology and behavioral ecology focused on question 3 (Parker 2006). To what extent Mayr's and Tinbergen's papers contributed to this sea change is hard to tell.

10. I am thinking here of "Evo-Devo" (Raff 1996), Development Systems Theory (Oyama et al. 2001) and theories of niche construction (Laland et al. 2000) in particular.

11. Note that Tullock is not arguing here that application of standard economic theory's constrained maximization framework in biology necessarily leads to different results or insights. The main gain envisioned is increased simplicity in explanation.

12. Several economists and philosophers of economics argue that the application of optimization models to *human* agents has a similar evolutionary rationale and should be given the same *as if* interpretation.

13. The replicator dynamic basically says that the growth rate of a strategy's share in some population is proportional to the degree in which it does better than the population's average. What is said here also holds for more general dynamics such as monotone dynamics.

14. Aumann's reason for believing that the evolutionary interpretation is more fundamental than the rationalistic interpretation seems to be that he takes natural evolution to be causally responsible for the capacity of people to engage in conscious maximization. See Vromen (2009) for further discussion.

15. Another famous case is the wings of birds. It is clear the function of fully evolved wings is flying. But what use is half a wing? Partly evolved wings may have had fitness advantages in terms of thermoregulation or in terms of facilitating wing-assisted incline running.

16. For a similar argument that expected utility theory and game theory are applicable directly at the level of neurons, see Don Ross's contribution to this Handbook.

17. See also: "...desirability is realized as a concrete object, a neural signal in the human and animal brain, rather than as a purely theoretical construction" (Glimcher & Rustichini 2004, 452).

18. It is "...more a hypothesis for testing rather than anything certain" (Glimcher 2002, 327).

19. This is similar to evolutionary psychology's point that psychological mechanisms that are adapted to the Environment of Evolutionary Adaptedness (EEA) are maladapted to present circumstances and to Gigerenzer's notion of ecological rationality.

20. Another detail that evolutionary game theorists may be justified in being agnostic about (if the contract to be explained is a global attractor) is initial conditions. See also Sober (1983) for an early illuminating account of equilibrium explanation.

21. D'Arms et al. (1998) discuss flexibility also in another sense: it must be plausible to assume that the specific dynamic posited in evolutionary game theory (such as *replicator dynamic*) can be understood to represent different possible processes (such as biological and cultural evolution).

22. Provided, of course, that the behavior to be explained is correctly identified. Stevens and Hauser (2004) argue, for example, that cooperative behavior in some primitive animal species that some identify as instances of reciprocal altruism are not really instances of reciprocal altruism because these animals lack the psychological machinery that is needed to display instances of reciprocal altruism.

23. Note that I am not arguing here that in studying long-run dynamics (produced by ultimate causes) we cannot afford to black-box short-run dynamics (produced by proximate causes). What I am arguing is that (long-run and medium-run) evolutionary processes might well have different dynamics and outcomes, depending on what specific proximate causes are working during these processes.

24. Recall that on Mayr's definition ultimate causes occur prior to the lifetime of individuals. Learning obviously takes place within the lifetime of individuals. Thus, on Mayr's understanding, learning cannot possibly qualify as an ultimate cause.

25. Yet others, such as Samuels et al. (2002), argue that evolutionary psychology's modules are perhaps best understood as (Chomsky-type) competencies. Gibbard (1990) argues that the species-specific psychological mechanisms that evolved in humans are the capacities to discuss the appropriateness of social norms and to be motivated to act according to the agreed upon norms.

REFERENCES

Alexander, J.M. (2000). "Evolutionary Explanations of Distributive Justice." *Philosophy of Science* 67: 490–516.

Ariew, A. (2003). "Ernst Mayr's 'Ultimate/Proximate' Distinction Reconsidered and Reconstructed." *Biology and Philosophy* 18 (4): 553–565.

Aumann, R. (1997). "On the State of the Art in Game Theory: An Interview with Robert Aumann (taken by Eric van Damme)." In W. Albers, W. Güth, P. Hammerstein, B. Moldovonu & E. van Damme, eds., *Understanding Strategic Interaction: Essays in Honor of Reinhard Selten,* 8–34. Berlin: Springer Verlag.

Axelrod, R. & Hamilton, W.D. (1981). "The Evolution of Cooperation." *Science* 211: 1390–1396.

Axelrod, R. (1984). *The Evolution of Cooperation.* New York: Basic Books.

Barrett, H.C. (2006). "Modularity and Design Reincarnation." In P. Carruthers, S. Laurence & S. Stich, Eds., *The Innate Mind: Culture and Cognition.* Oxford: Oxford University Press.

Beatty, J. (1994). "The Proximate/Ultimate Distinction in the Multiple Careers of Ernst Mayr." *Biology and Philosophy* 9 (3): 333–356.

Ben-Ner, A. & Putterman, L. (1998). "Values and Institutions in Economic Analysis." In A. Ben-Ner & L. Putterman, Eds., *Economics, Values and Organization*, 3–69. Cambridge, England: Cambridge University Press.

Binmore, K. (1994). *Game Theory and the Social Contract, Vol. I: Playing Fair*. Cambridge, MA.: MIT Press.

Binmore, K. (2004). "Reciprocity and the Social Contract." *Politics, Philosophy & Economics* 3 (1): 5–35.

Binmore, K. (2005). *Natural Justice*. Oxford: Oxford University Press.

Bolhuis, J.J. & Verhulst, S. (2005). "Evolution, Function, Development and Causation: Tinbergen's Four Questions and Contemporary Behavioral Biology." *Animal Biology* 55 (4): 283–285

Boyd, R. & Richerson, P. (1985). *Culture and the Evolutionary Process*. Chicago: University of Chicago Press.

Buller, D.J. (2005). *Adapting Minds: Evolutionary Psychology and the Persistent Quest for Human Nature*. Cambridge, MA.: A Bradford Book (MIT Press).

Buss, D.M. (1999). *Evolutionary Psychology: The New Science of the Mind*. Boston: Allyn & Bacon.

Camerer, C., Loewenstein, G. & Prelec, D. (2004). "Neuroeconomics: Why economics Needs Brains." *Scandinavian Journal of Economics* 106 (3): 555–579.

Camerer, C., Loewenstein, G. & Prelec, D. (2005). "Neuroeconomics: How Neuroscience Can Inform Economics." *Journal of Economic Literature* 43 (1): 9–64.

Campbell, D.T. (1987 [1960]). "Blind Variation and Selective Retention in Creative Thought as in Other Knowledge Processes." In G. Radnitzky & W.W. Bartley, Eds., *Evolutionary Epistemology, Rationality, and the Sociology of Knowledge*. 91–114. New York: Open Court. Originally published in *The Psychological Review* 67: 380–400.

Carruthers, P. (2003). "The Mind is a System of Modules Shaped by Natural Selection." In C. Hitchcock, Ed., *Contemporary Debates in the Philosophy of Science*. Oxford: Blackwell.

Cosmides, L. & Tooby, J. (1994). "Better Than Rational: Evolutionary Psychology and the Invisible Hand." *American Economic Review* 84: 327–332.

D'Arms, J., Batterman, R. & Gorny, K. (1998). "Game Theoretic Explanations and the Evolution of Justice." *Philosophy of Science* 65 (19): 76–102.

Fehr, E. & Gächter, S. (2002). "Altruistic Punishment in Humans." *Nature* 415: 137–140.

Fehr, E. & Henrich, J. (2003). "Is Strong Reciprocity a Maladaptation? On the Evolutionary Foundations of Human Altruism." In P. Hammerstein, Ed., *Genetic and Cultural Evolution of Cooperation*, 55–82. Cambridge, MA.: MIT Press.

Frank, R.H. (1988). *Passions within Reason*. New York: W.W. Norton & Company.

Frank, R.H. (2004). *What Price the Moral High Ground? Ethical Dilemmas in Competitive Environments*. Princeton: Princeton University Press.

Gibbard, A. (1990). *Wise Choices, Apt Feelings: A Theory of Normative Judgment*. Cambridge, MA.: Harvard University Press.

Gigerenzer, G., Todd, P.M. & ABC Research Group (1999). *Simple Heuristics That Make Us Smart*. New York/Oxford: Oxford University Press.

Gintis, H. (2000). "Strong Reciprocity and Human Sociality." *Journal of Theoretical Biology* 206: 169–179.

Gintis, H. (2007). "A Framework for the Unification of the Behavioral Sciences." *Behavioral and Brain Sciences* 30: 1–61.

Glimcher, P.W. (2003). *Decisions, Uncertainty, and the Brain: The Science of Neuroeconomics*, MIT Press.

Glimcher, P.W. & Rustichini, A. (2004). "Neuroeconomics: The Consilience of Brain and Decision." *Science* 306: 447–452.

Glimcher, P.W., Dorris, M.C. & Bayer, H.M. (2005). "Physiological Utility Theory and the Neuroeconomics of Choice." *Games and Economic Behavior* 52 (2): 213–256.

Güth, W. & Yaari, M.E. (1991). "Explaining Reciprocal Behavior in Simple Strategic Games: An Evolutionary Approach." In U. Witt, Ed., *Explaining Process and Change: Approaches to Evolutionary Economics*, 23–34. Ann Arbor: University of Michigan Press.

Güth, W. & Kliemt, H. (1998). "The Indirect Evolutionary Approach: Bridging the Gap between Rationality and Adaptation." *Rationality and Society* 10 (3): 377–399.

Hagen, E.H. & Hammerstein, P. (2006). "Game Theory and Human Evolution: A Critique of Some Recent Interpretations of Experimental Games." *Theoretical Population Biology* 69: 339–348.

Hammerstein, P. & Hagen, E.H. (2005). "The Second Wave of Evolutionary Economics in Biology." *Trends in Ecology and Evolution* 20 (11): 604–610.

Laland, K.N., Odling-Smee, J. & Feldman, M.W. (2000). "Niche Construction, Biological Evolution, and Cultural Change." *Behavioral and Brain Sciences* 23: 131–146.

Mailath, G.J. (1998). "Do People Play Nash Equilibrium? Lessons from Evolutionary Game Theory." *Journal of Economic Literature* 36 (3): 1347–1374.

Manning, A. (2005). "Four Decades on From the 'Four Questions.'" *Animal Biology* 55 (4): 287–296.

Marr, D. (1982), *Vision: A computational investigation into the human representation and processing of visual information,* San Francisco: Freeman.

Mayr, E. (1961). "Cause and Effect in Biology." *Science* 134: 1501–1506.

Mayr, E. (1994). "Response to John Beatty." *Biology and Philosophy* 9 (3): 357–358.

McElreath, R., Clutton-Brock, R., Fehr, E., Fessler, D., Hagen, E., Hammerstein, P., Kosfeld, M., Milinski, M., Silk, J., Tooby, J. & Wilson, M. (2003). "Group Report: The Role of Cognition and Emotion in Cooperation." In P. Hammerstein, Ed., *Genetic and Cultural Evolution of Cooperation*, 125–152. Cambridge, MA.: MIT Press.

Nash, J. (1950). "Non-cooperative Games." Unpublished Ph.D dissertation, Mathematics Department, Princeton University.

Nelson, R.R. & Winter, S. (1982). *An Evolutionary Theory of Economic Change.* Cambridge: Harvard University Press.

Nichols, S. (2004). *Sentimental Rules: On the Natural Foundations of Moral Judgment.* New York: Oxford University Press.

Oyama, S., Griffiths, P. & Gray, R., Eds. (2001). *Cycles of Contingency: Developmental Systems and Evolution.* Cambridge, MA.: MIT Press.

Parker, G.A. (2006). "Behavioral Ecology: The Science of Natural History." In J.R. Lucas & L.W. Simmons, Eds., *Essays on Animal Behavior: Celebrating 50 years of Animal Behavior,* 23–56. Burlington, MA.: Elsevier.

Raff, R.A. (1996). *The Shape of Life: Genes, Development, and the Evolution of Animal Form.* Chicago: University of Chicago Press.

Robson, A.J. (2001a). "The Biological Basis of Economic Behavior." *Journal of Economic Literature* 39: 11–33.

Robson, A.J. (2001b). "Why Would Nature Give Individuals Utility Functions?" *Journal of Political Economy* 109: 900–914.

Samuels, R. (1998). "Evolutionary Psychology and the Massively Modularity Hypothesis." *British Journal for the Philosophy of Science* 49: 575–602.

Samuels, R., Stich, S. and Bishop, M. (2002). Ending the rationality wars: how to make disputes about human rationality disappear, in R. Elio (ed.), *Common Sense, Reasoning and Rationality.* New York: Oxford University Press, 236–268.

Skyrms, B. (1996). *Evolution of the Social Contract,* Cambridge: Cambridge University Press.

Sober, E. (1984). *The Nature of Selection.* Cambridge: MIT Press.

Sober, E. (1993). *Philosophy of Biology.* Oxford: Oxford University Press.

Sober, E. & Wilson, D.S. (1998). *Unto Others: The Evolution and Psychology of Unselfish Behavior.* Cambridge: Harvard University Press.

Sperber, D. (1996). *Explaining Culture: A Naturalistic Approach.* Oxford: Basil Blackwell.

Sterelny, K. (1992). "Evolutionary Explanations and Human Behavior." *Australian Journal of Philosophy* 70 (2): 156–173.

Sterelny, K. (1996). "Explanatory Pluralism in Evolutionary Biology." *Biology and Philosophy* 11 (2): 193–214.

Sterelny, K. (2003). *Thought in a Hostile World: The Evolution of Human Cognition.* Oxford: Blackwell.

Sterelny, K. (2004). "Reply to Papineau and Stich." *Australian Journal of Philosophy* 82 (3): 512–522.

Tinbergen, N. (1963). "On Aims and Methods of Ethology." *Zeitschrift für Tierpsychologie* 20: 410–433. (Reprinted in *Animal Biology* 2005, 55 (4): 297–321).

Tooby, J., Cosmides, L. & Barrett, H. C. (2003). "The Second Law of Thermodynamics is the First Law of Psychology: Evolutionary Developmental Psychology and the Theory of Tandem, Coordinated Inheritances." *Psychological Bulletin* 129 (6): 858–865.

Tullock, G. (1971). "The Coal Tit as a Careful Shopper." *The American Naturalist* 105: 77–80.

Vromen, J.J. (2003). "Why the Economic Conception of Human Behavior Might Lack a Biological Basis." *Theoria* 48 (18): 297–323.

Vromen, J.J. (2004). "Taking Evolution Seriously—What Difference Does it Make for Economics?" In J.B. Davis, A. Marciano & J. Runde, Eds., *The Elgar Companion to Economics and Philosophy,* 102–131. Cheltenham, UK: Edward Elgar.

Vromen, J.J. (2007). "Neuroeconomics as a Natural Extension of Bioeconomics: How the Proliferation of 'Constrained Maximization' Backfires." *Journal of Bioeconomics* 9 (2): 145–167.

Vromen, J.J. (2006). "Depicting Social Contracts as Robust Equilibria: What is the Explanatory Power of Evolutionary Game-Theoretic Analyses?" EIPE working paper.

Vromen, J.J. (2009). "Friedman's Selection Argument Revisited." In U. Mäki, Ed., *The Methodology of Economics. Milton Friedman's Essay at 50.* Cambridge, England: Cambridge University Press.

Young, H. P. (1998). *Individual Strategy and Social Structure: An Evolutionary Theory of Institutions.* Princeton: Princeton University Press.

PART III

MODELING, MACROECONOMICS, AND DEVELOPMENT

CHAPTER 13

COMPUTATIONAL ECONOMICS

PAUL HUMPHREYS

1. INTRODUCTION

Computational economics is a relatively new research technique in economics, but it is inexorably taking its place alongside the more traditional methods of general theory, abstract modeling, data analysis, and the more recent experimental economics. Perhaps because of its relative newness, the term *computational economics* currently has no determinate meaning. In contemporary use, it refers to a heterogeneous cluster of techniques implemented on concrete digital computers ranging from the numerical solution of the Black-Scholes partial differential equation for pricing options:

$$\partial V/\partial t + \tfrac{1}{2}\sigma^2 S^2 \partial^2 V/\partial S^2 + rS\partial V/\partial S - rV = 0$$

through automated trading strategies to agent-based computer simulations of the evolution of cooperation.[1] Because of this heterogeneity, it is not possible to provide a comprehensive coverage of the topic in this article. Another reason for this restricted scope is that many of the methods used in computational economics have considerable technical interest but no particular philosophical relevance. For example, despite their practical importance, computationally assisted methods, such as solving agent pricing schemes using Lagrangian multipliers so that revenue is maximized for a seller faced with a buyer whose preference profile is unknown, introduces little that is methodologically new, because this is a familiar problem in the calculus of variations and the properties of the algorithms and implementations are well established. To partially compensate for the omissions, specific topics such as the application of computational techniques in neuroeconomics and the use of computers in experimental economics will be passed over in favor of methods that are widely employed and are characteristic of approaches used in the area. Moreover, those areas that are included will illustrate the fact that computational economics is not simply a subdomain of mathematical economics.

A core philosophical issue is the extent to which the methods of computational economics are peculiar to economics rather than consisting of cross-disciplinary methods that are drawn from or are applicable to other sciences. The division between the two methodological situations is not particularly neat, but in this author's view, one of the salient features of computational economics is that it is characterized primarily, although not exclusively, by the methods used and not by the subject matter to which it is applied. (An extended discussion of how subject-matter-specific content affects the construction and evolution of models and simulations can be found in Humphreys 2004, Chapter 3.) Although applying the Black-Scholes equation to European markets, for example, does require subject- matter-specific inputs in order to fit the model to the domain-specific content, the equation itself can be transformed into the familiar heat equation from physics. To take another example, many economic systems can be modeled by techniques drawn from the area of self-organizing systems, these methods also having important applications in biology. The domain of computational economics thus overlaps in important ways with the domains of computational biology, computational physics, and a number of other areas including the generic field of complexity theory. Because of this, posing the question of whether computational economics counts as a separate subdiscipline of economics is a question that in a certain sense misses the point. Just as many methods of econometrics are applicable to sociology, agriculture, and other areas, and indeed they must be in order to include variables from those areas in economic models of land use, for example, so too are the methods of computational economics. These cross-disciplinary aspects should not lessen the interest of these methods for economists.

2. WHY COMPUTATIONAL ECONOMICS?

There is no sharp divide between the precomputational era and the era of computational economics; nonlinear business cycles were studied in the 1940s and 1950s (e.g. Hicks 1950, Goodwin 1951, Tobin 1955; see Krugman 1996 for these and further references) and the first explicitly computable general equilibrium model was developed by Johansen in 1960. (Johansen 1960). Nevertheless, computational economics has gradually developed its own distinctive research methods that distinguish it from traditional mathematical economics, and one of the characteristic features of the approach is that it does not fit neatly into the traditional methodological categories of theory, observation, and experiment. A useful parallel to use in understanding the nature of the issues involved is the introduction of optical instruments into science. The invention of the telescope and the microscope forced scientists to face the possibility that they could acquire knowledge of phenomena that were not directly observable and that this knowledge required new kinds of representation and conceptualization in order to effectively understand the phenomena involved. In a roughly analogous way, most processes in computational economics and many of the outputs are not directly accessible to or verifiable by humans, and the need to develop new techniques to represent and understand them lies at the heart of many of the methodological issues peculiar to computational economics.

This representational issue is one aspect of a feature that runs through computational economics and which we can call the *interface problem*. The interface problem is familiar to us in other forms. In one version, the desire to distinguish between observables and unobservables in traditional philosophy of science is driven in part by the fact that it is the observable aspects of phenomena that constitute the interface between humans and the world, and the unobservable processes linking those observable phenomena are not directly accessible to humans. In another version, the need to present large data sets using representations that allow humans to identify structures embedded in those data poses a problem that has been around since the beginning of statistics. With the advent of ineliminable computational methods in parts of economic practice, another form of the interface problem presents itself, because in most cases the details of the intervening computational processes will not be directly accessible to us.

Underlying the interface problem is the assumption that science is human science and this assumption has driven, whether explicitly or implicitly, all previous philosophy of science. Although there are fascinating issues connected with the possibility of a completely automated science and some methods of automated trading come close to implementing it, for the foreseeable future humans will continue to play an important role in computational economics. This means that the epistemology of the input and output interfaces of computational economics must accommodate human limitations and abilities on the one side and those of the computational intermediary on the other.

With this in mind, let us call the methods of *traditional theoretical economics* (TTE) those modes of investigation that use unassisted a priori reasoning based on explicitly formulated, humanly accessible, theories and general principles of economics. As such, TTE forms the basis of much of traditional mathematical economics as well as constituting the principal method in political economy and related disciplines. We can call its counterpart that abandons this requirement of human accessibility *computational theoretical economics* (CTE).

An important distinction to make in this context is between representation and computation. Representation has been the main focus of the philosophical literature about theories and models, but for purposes of application, computation is at least as important. The desire for computational methods that will produce solvable representations of is one reason for the often mocked excessive idealization of economic models. Severe idealizations are needed in many cases, despite their lack of realism, in order to force the models into computationally tractable forms. Without such idealizations, TTE suffers from severe limitations on its domain of application. The most common limitation is that the mathematical model employed has no analytic solutions. There is no precise definition for the term *analytic solution* but two things are generally accepted: first, that the class of analytic solutions and the class of closed form solutions are the same; and secondly, that to have a closed form solution is to have a solution that is representable in terms of finite combinations of simple functions. The reason for this relatively casual treatment of such a commonly used term is important. The reference to simple functions—that is, those functions that appear simple to humans with their limited cognitive abilities—is once again a result of the interface problem and the accompanying desire within TTE to have exact, universal, results that are transparently comprehensible to suitably trained humans. Once one drops this emphasis on humans as the ultimate or sole beneficiaries of the models, some, although not all, of the motivation for emphasizing this restricted class of analytically solvable models disappears. CTE can provide approximate solutions to models that are analytically intractable and can graphically present solutions in ways that enhance our unaided mental representations.

I said not all the motivation disappears because, even within computational economics, analytic results are desirable, one reason being that they allow us to calibrate outputs from numerical simulations against the analytic results as a check on the validity of simulation outputs. In some cases, it is provable that no analytic solutions exist.[2] But even in the absence of such a proof, computational approaches constitute the only feasible methods in many areas such as sector economics because models that do produce analytic results are generally recognized as being too simple (See Kendricks 1996, 296).

To take another example, financial markets consisting of heterogeneous agents are very difficult to model analytically and one tactic used to circumvent this difficulty is to drop down to representative agent models (see LeBaron 2006), an approach that has been criticized (e.g., Hartley 1997) as failing to adequately address the Lucas critique. An alternative to introducing excessive idealizations in economic models is, thus recognize that what is complex to a human is not necessarily complex to an even moderately powerful computer and to trade exact solutions for approximate solutions and universal solutions for finite point-wise results. We thus have what we can call the *trade-off decision* in CTE: whether to achieve increased realism and increased scope at the cost of decreased epistemic transparency, a trade-off that has obvious parallels in the older debates about scientific realism. A trade-off decision is frequently required in social science simulations; as the model becomes more realistic, its complexity increases and at some point this complexity becomes counterproductive in terms of the model's intelligibility.

An inability to precisely predict states of a system frequently requires us to drop the insistence on exact quantitative representations of a system and to emphasize the importance of understanding the qualitative structure of a system. Dynamical systems theory has long conceded that point in physics by switching from numerically precise predictions to topological representations, and there is now a recognition that this can be beneficial in computational economics as well: "Phase space representations of dynamic systems are extremely common in modern economic analysis.... Before the mid-1970s, nearly all dynamic models in economics were globally stable; that is, the phase landscape was assumed to be like a bowl, a single basin of attraction in which all points drain to a single long run equilibrium. Since about 1975 it has become common also to work with models in which the phase landscape looks like a saddle—and in which some set of forward looking variables, such as asset prices, is determined by the assumption that the economy is always on the ridge that is the only path to long-run equilibrium." (Krugman 1996, 32)

There is one other representational aspect of the interface problem. Consider the way that theories and models are represented. There is no denying the importance of results showing what can and cannot be done in principle in various highly abstract languages, such as the lambda calculus or second-order logic. But the representational devices that computational economics uses are specific programming languages, and these have different strengths and weaknesses. MATLAB is proficient at matrix operations and numerical computation, and, thus, it is useful for such tasks as portfolio optimization; General Algebraic Modelling System (GAMS) is specifically designed for optimization problems; Mathematica is a general purpose numerical and symbolic processing language with excellent graphical capabilities, and so on. It is not simply that these high-level programming languages have different processing abilities; they can make a crucial difference in how models are conceptualized and developed. To take just one example, object-oriented programming environments such as Java require a different kind of conceptualization for a problem than does functional programming. Thus, in some applications of CTE, rather than conceptualizing the theory or model of TTE within traditional mathematical languages and then directly applying it to an economic system, the CTE model has to be translated into the intermediate framework of a specific software platform and its accompanying libraries or, in some cases, the CTE model is conceptualized directly within that framework. The considerations involved in these CTE constructions are so remote from the stylized syntax of traditional philosophy of science—let alone the even more austere apparatus of the semantic account of theories—that neither the usual syntactic nor the semantic account of theories comes close to capturing the reality of applying a model drawn from CTE.

3. COMPUTATIONAL COMPLEXITY AND TECHNOLOGICAL CONSTRAINTS

An important feature of computational economics is that informed applications of its methods require a more refined taxonomy of *computable* than is provided by the

traditional accounts of recursion theory.[3] Important as they are, the familiar categories of abstract computability, captured by well-known accounts in terms of general
recursion, Turing computability, and so on are not directly relevant to the concerns
of computational economics. Instead, there are two relevant issues that must be kept
clearly separate. The first is where a given problem falls within the various classes
of computational complexity. At present, there are hundreds of such classes, but the
most important are problems falling into the classes P, NP, and PSPACE. A problem
is in P if it can be solved in polynomial time; that is, if there is an algorithm that can
produce the correct answer (Yes or No) on a deterministic Turing machine for any
input string of length n in at most n^k steps, where k is a constant independent of the
input string. This must be the same algorithm for each n—it cannot vary with n.
The importance of this class is that it is widely considered to contain all those problems that can *realistically* be solved computationally when one is restricted to the
kind of computability captured by Turing machines. A problem falls into the class
NP just in case it is solvable in a number of steps that is a polynomial function of the
length of the input on a *nondeterministic* Turing machine. Unless P = NP, which is a
famous open problem in complexity theory (although the general view is that there
are NP problems that lie outside P), any problem that is in NP has instances that
will resist any realistic attempt at an exact computational solution.[4] These problem
classes are of more than theoretical interest to economists. For example, presented
with a game in extensive form, discovering whether it has an equilibrium in pure
strategies is an NP-hard problem[5] (see McKelvey & McLennan 1996, 115).

It is important to note that although the literature often informally talks of P and
NP problems in terms of the amount of time needed to compute their solutions, the
relation between the number of computational steps needed and the amount of actual
time needed inescapably adds technological considerations to these abstract classifi-
cations. The fact that a problem is P does not mean that it is feasible to compute it with
currently available resources and indeed computational load problems are a second
important constraint in many areas of CTE. This means that one of the distinctive
features of computational economics is that methodological issues are often insepara-
ble from technological considerations, so that the speed, memory capacity, and architecture of current computers are frequently inescapable constraints on what can be
computed in practice. And so, just as the limitations of a priori methods led to limits
on TTE models, these technological constraints force various degrees of simplification, idealization, and approximation even within CTE. One must, therefore, often
pay attention to the computational resources that are currently available, in addition
to economic theory and data, when constructing computational models. Finding all
the Nash equilibria in a finite N-person game for $N > 2$ is computationally intensive,
the methods that are effective for two-person games cannot be extended to the more
general case, and there usually exists a delicate balance between the global convergence
of a method for finding Nash equilibria and the speed of that process. (See McKelvey
& McLennan 1996, 106–107). To take a different type of example, within agent-based
models, a model society will often be significantly smaller in terms of the number

of agents it contains than is ideal to represent the population of a real society, the agents will have significantly fewer characteristics than do real agents, and increasing the topological connectivity of a fitness landscape will radically increase the computational demands of the model. Indeed, it is often the computational load issue for humans that forces the adoption of CTE techniques in the first place; simply consider that for Leontief input-output models with multiple industries, the impossibility of inverting the matrices by hand forces computational methods to be used.

These sorts of considerations are commonplace for computational economists, and they are mentioned here with a philosophical audience in mind because such practical considerations are viewed as irrelevant within traditional philosophy of science. For the purposes of understanding how computational economics is applied, however, we need to shift away from the highly idealized in principle a priori methods of traditional philosophy of science and toward approaches that take bounded computational resources seriously. This again makes the use of computational methods different from the introduction of a new mathematical technique. For example, is there a difference between, on the one hand, the inability at a given time to solve an open problem in mathematics using only traditional a priori methods because no human mathematician has yet been clever enough to invent a solution technique and, on the other hand, the inability to provide a solution to a model in mathematical economics because the necessary computational power is not currently available? If we are interested in the issue of scientific progress, yes, because it is possible to predict, often with a fair degree of precision, when the available computing power will become available—Moore's Law is simply the best known basis for such predictability—whereas it is not possible to make such predictions for human conceptual breakthroughs with anywhere near the same degree of accuracy.

And so it is worth considering the category of feasible computability (FC), where a function is feasibly computable, $FC(D,A,t)$, over domain D within time t just in case it is demonstrable that the estimated computing power needed to produce a correct output for the function in fewer than t steps using algorithm A at an arbitrarily chosen argument in D is technologically possible, even if not currently available.[6] Demonstrability can take the form either of a proof or of an empirical demonstration. Finally, we have current computability, $CC(D,A,t)$, where a function is currently computable over domain D using algorithm A within time t just in case $FC(D,A,t)$, and there currently exists a concrete computational device that produces the correct output from A for an arbitrary argument from D within time t. Humans form one such class of computational device.

4. Agent-based Modeling

An important component of computational economics is agent-based modeling, which is characterized by a direct modeling of the relationships between the economic actors. Within agent based models, there is ordinarily no global representation of the economy, and direct modeling of agent interactions rather than computational processing of antecedent theory is the focus.

Adapting the approach of Rasmussen and Barrett (1995), we can distinguish five objects of interest.

1. A real system **S** that is to be simulated.
2. A collection $\{S_i\}$ of models of subsystems of **S**.
3. An updating function f_i for each S_i together with an updating schedule U. The f_i can be a function of the internal state of S_i alone, or of the states of other systems S_j in addition to, or in place of, the state of S_i. The updating schedule can be simultaneous, sequential, random, etc. I assume here that the time t is the same for all S_i and for simplicity, I shall assume that the updating rules do not depend on the time t. So, let S_i, $i = 1, 2, \ldots, n$ be a collection of systems, which may or may not have internal structure. Each S_i has an intrinsic state $s_i(t)$ at time t. The dynamics for s_i are given by $s_i(t+1) = f_i(s_1,, \ldots, s_n, t)$, which involves transitions in the intrinsic state of s_i and interactions between s_i and other systems s_j.
4. A simulation *Sim* of **S** based on the models S_i.
5. The implementation of *Sim* on a concrete device C.

A major issue within this approach is the relation between the local dynamics of the subsystems and the global dynamics of the entire system. As Rasmussen et al. (1997) put it: '...in general no *explicit,* closed form function $F : X \rightarrow X$ exists that takes the current global state

$$X(t) = (s_1(t), \ldots, s_n(t)) \in X \tag{5}$$

and maps it into some other state in the state space X

$$F(X(t)) = X(t+1) \tag{6}$$

Such a function is only *implicitly* given through [the updating schedule]...Obviously, the classical dynamical systems which can be explicitly written in the form (6) are special cases...'

Roughly, the reason is this. A single time step in the simulation's dynamics has an explicit representation that will in general be a function only of the states of those other agents that are involved in direct relations with the given agent. But as the dynamics are iterated, the number of agents whose states indirectly affect the state of the focal agent will steadily increase. For example, suppose that agent A's assets are initially affected only by trades with agents B, C, and D. But at the next step, the assets of B, C, and D will have changed through their trades with E, F, and A itself and one has to calculate the step 1 values for those agents before performing the step 2 calculation for A. These calculations cannot be compressed in general because they are a function of the number of time steps involved. Thus, although we may have an explicit representation of the output from the economic system at any given time, this can be generated only by running the dynamics for the subsystems and there is never an explicit representation within the simulation for the dynamics of the economy as a whole.

Note that for the issue of realism, there is no basis on which to deny that the dynamics of the simulation *Sim* (and, therefore, perhaps, of the simulated system *S*) are real, even though we have no explicit representation of them. To put it in more familiar philosophical terms, if one wants to argue for the existence of specifically macroscopic economic mechanisms, some means other than representational realism will be needed. So any philosophical position, such as Quine's, that has as a sufficient condition for a realistic commitment, or even approaches realism through, an explicit formal representation is inapplicable and must be replaced by some other criterion. As in other areas, it is the dynamical aspects of simulations that are crucial in producing the states that contain candidates for realist claims as opposed to the static representational perspective of models and theories.

The need to introduce a new explicit representation into the simulation supports the idea that, at least conceptually, these kinds of simulations within computational economics give rise to emergent features. This has been argued for explicitly under the framework of "weak emergence" by Mark Bedau (1997 & 2003). One of the central techniques in this area is the investigation of self-organizing systems as a way to gain insights into invisible hand processes such as optimal pricing in markets resulting from many local interactions between economic agents. The emergence and persistence of structures in dynamic systems can be effectively explored with computational techniques in ways that are not possible using only traditional a priori methods. These structures, such as income distributions, or the persistence of a trade in a sector of a city, are often stable under the replacement of the individuals whose activities give rise to those structures and thus count as emergent under the commonly used criteria of novelty and autonomy. Thomas Schelling's famous segregation models were some of the first examples of this kind; other examples are patterns of land use within land markets (Parker, Evans & Meretsky 2001) and various market clearing prices (Epstein & Axtell 1996).

One philosophical interest of agent based modeling derives from what used to be called methodological individualism. Its goal is to replicate known phenomena and to discover previously unknown economic phenomena using only bottom-up mechanisms between individuals. and in this sense it is to be contrasted with results derived from models of top-down centrally planned economies. Results from agent based models can be used in two ways. The first is to use policy interventions based on the model. If a recognizable and stable economic structure or process emerges in the population of agents as a result of iterated interactions between the agents, such results can be used as a guide to generating that structure in a real economy assuming the structure is desirable, and avoiding it if not. The second use is explanatory and is much more problematical. The fact that a regularity or structure can be generated in this way within a model does not entail that the model accurately represents the way in which that regularity or structure is generated in real systems. Indeed, the ease with which computational models can be adjusted and refined in order to achieve a given output makes the underdetermination problem a pressing issue for computational economics. This is another reason why having a substantive, well-confirmed theory of the economic mechanisms behind the simulation is vital.

A third use of agent based models is for prediction. Rather than carry out a large-scale social experiment or extrapolate from a small controlled experiment, a computational model with the desired features can be used to simulate the dynamics of a society consisting of agents with specified characteristics under a new policy and one in which the consequences can be assessed. This use can be contrasted with the policy intervention approach. In the latter case, rather than making predictions from initial conditions and rule-based interactions as is done in predictive models, the goal is to find the appropriate kinds of interactions that will produce the state that the policy requires. (Because these models are usually statistical, the exact initial conditions are of less importance and indeed, are less often under the control of policy interventions.)

A fourth use involves the *exploratory use* of models. In this approach, the principal aim is gaining qualitative insight into broad structural features of an economy, including situations that are rarely if ever found in real societies. In exploratory uses, negative results can be as important as positive results, in the sense that one might identify characteristics of a society with undesirable economic characteristics and use the information to prevent such characteristics from finding their way into real social systems. In systems with multiple equilibria, for example, a question is why some of these possible states are not observed in real economic systems.

5. Normative and Descriptive Models

The distinction between descriptive models and normative models is a familiar one in economics, but it takes on a different form within computational economics. One of the original motivations for investigating models of bounded rationality was the experimental discovery that human agents violate prescriptive rules of rationality in their decision-making processes, whether those rules are decision theoretic, probabilistic, or based on some other criterion of rationality. Subjects often violate those rules and replace them with heuristic procedures that allow suboptimal choices developed within the applicable resource constraints, be they temporal, cognitive, or economic. To put the conclusions of that research crudely, people can't and won't do complex calculations in their heads. It takes too long, humans make too many mistakes, and exhaustive searches in the opportunity space cost too much. It must be kept in mind, however, that these results were motivated by psychological considerations and their universal validity as principles of inference has not been established.

Indeed, within certain areas of computational economics, the motivation for using these heuristics is largely irrelevant. For example, it can no longer be assumed that the other players in financial markets are humans. In 2005, 6 percent of the daily Nasdaq trades and 4 percent of the NYSE daily trades were made by a single automated trading company, Automated Trading Desk, LLC.[7] Within the area of algorithmic trading, the other agents routinely include automated traders using strategies that have been developed by genetic algorithms and institutional investors that have massive computational power at their disposal. Statistical arbitrage has also become a well-established technique in equity trading. This makes any evidence that various heuristic procedures have strategic benefits for humans compared to the use of unassisted a priori reasoning irrelevant, and it makes assumptions about one's opponent that are drawn from human evolutionary data ill advised.[8] This allows the vast literature on evolutionary and behavioral psychology, for example, to remain of interest to parts of the law and economics community, but of decreasing relevance to the investment community. We do not need to be limited by evolutionarily based abilities in the way that some contemporary accounts, based on evolutionary psychology, suggest.

So, appealing to an old philosophical maxim that *ought* implies *can*, what kinds of possibilities are relevant within computational economics as necessary conditions for what ought to be done? It is generally the complexity of the state space that forces constrained rationality. Although one might be interested in how simple strategies can exploit complex state spaces, if one can, instead, formulate a computationally implemented adaptive strategy that exhibits superior real-time performance, it would be irrational not to use it. There are definite limits to this superiority because one of the negative features of computational models is that their ability to deal with multiple parameters leads to very large-dimensional state spaces. Because of their size and the frequent inability to know a priori which areas of the state space to explore, exploratory research of selected parts of the state space plays a significant role in these approaches, and developing criteria for which parts to explore becomes critical. Once again, the use of substantive theory coupled with economic insight is important.

One issue that is brought out clearly by agent based models, although the conclusion does not require the approach, is the narrowness of views that consider economics to rest on a foundation of individual psychology. Within such models, there is an important difference between using agents that lack cognitive abilities—one example being regional economies— and the use of intelligent agents that can be not only individual economic actors but also companies and similar organizations exhibiting collective intelligence.

The difference between the two types of agent has an important effect on holistic features of the system. There are at least two levels of influence on agents: local interactions between the agents and global properties, such as unemployment rates, markets, social constraints, and such. Since agents interact pointwise within most agent based models, but at each stage the price for a commodity depends on all of the interactions in the society, there is feedback from the entire system to the individual agents. Whether this will have an effect depends upon the agents having cognitive access to the entire structure. Noncognitive agents will see only local features, whereas cognitive agents will have global information.

6. Data-based Models

Data-based modeling begins with time-series data or cross-sectional data drawn from real economies, and it is characterized by a much lower reliance on general theory. Most econometric models are data-driven in the sense that although the choice of variables and the plausibility of various causal connections may be guided by an appeal to theory, the generation and refinement of the model is primarily a result of structural features found in the data. Some areas of economics, such as financial markets, have access to massive data sets, often recording every trade made, and the quantity of data involved is impossible to process without the aid of computers. Furthermore, because these databases are directly encoded into machine readable form, they present themselves directly as information. Thus, unlike information-theoretic accounts of physics or of genetics, where the information results from the way physical or biological phenomena are represented, some economic data naturally occur as information.

It is sometimes claimed that the world itself is a computational device that computes its own successive states. While this claim is not immediately plausible for many areas, it is not unreasonable to think that financial markets, for example, are computational systems, with agents (whether human or otherwise) explicitly calculating optimal pricing and exchanging information. So as compared with information theoretic accounts of physics, this is plausibly realistic and not just representational. However, there is the issue of how the inputs should be represented. If there is a human intermediary between the data and the computation, then the information has to be presented to the human in a way such that he or she can decide which inputs will be fed to the machine. If there is no human, the task is somewhat simplified and raw data can be fed to the computer. However, simulations themselves generate vast quantities of data, far more than can be easily assimilated in raw form, and the need to present the output in a form that is comprehensible to humans is pressing. Yet again, we see the interface problem surfacing in this area.

The advantage of computational models in exploring the dynamics of economic systems in real time and in great detail is thus offset by the need to represent outputs consisting of extremely large data sets. It is here that the graphical abilities of modern computational devices and their real-time solutions of the models contribute to another shift in method—replacing understanding based on the syntactic representations of those outputs with a visual understanding. This is part of a more general issue of information compression, the need to construct new ways of presenting information so as to highlight essential content.

I used the expression *real economies* earlier to distinguish economic systems that exist in a laboratory or in the everyday world from those economic systems that operate entirely within the artificial worlds of computer simulations. The ease of generating simulated data raises two issues characteristic of computational economics. The first is the need to sharply separate claims based upon simulated data that are generated from explicit assumptions about the model from serious tests of a model based upon data gathered from real economic systems. Although the difference between the two is clear enough, a blurring of the difference can occur for a number of reasons. The advantages of using simulated data are striking: the properties of the data, such as the statistical distribution from which they are drawn, are known exactly and can be controlled; measurement error is largely nonexistent, and experiments can be replicated exactly with the same data points. Moreover, simulated data are cheap and much larger data sets can be used than is generally possible with sets of empirical data. Needless to say, they provide no test of the real-world adequacy of the assumptions governing the model. However, there is an essential difference in this regard between normative and descriptive economic models of the kind discussed earlier. With the former, simulated data are acceptable, whereas in the latter they are not. Rather differently, the problems associated with the empirical underdetermination of theories are magnified when simulated data are available. The vast number of possible mechanisms that can be explored using simulations often lead to intuitively plausible results being produced and the psychological attraction of assuming that the mechanisms underlying the simulation have captured the economic mechanisms producing the analogous real-world data can be irresistible. Without explicit caveats to counteract this (for an example of such warnings, see Axelrod [1997]) it is easy to come away with the impression that some result about real economies has been established. These exploratory investigations are best classified as *how-possibly* explanations rather than as answers to *Why* questions.

NOTES

1. I shall not discuss analog simulations here since they play no significant role in contemporary computational economics.

2. A well-known example is the nonexistence of a formula giving solutions in terms of radicals for an arbitrary fifth order polynomial with rational coefficients, the famous general quintic result.

3. It is worth emphasizing that *computable* does not mean "numerical." It includes algebraic computations as well.

4. A problem falls into the class PSPACE if it can be solved by a deterministic or indeterministic Turing machine using only a polynomial amount of memory, although it may need an unbounded number of steps. By Savitch's Theorem, the class of PSPACE problems is identical to the class of NPSPACE problems.

5. Informally, an NP-hard problem is one that is at least as hard as an NP decision problem.

6. Feasible computability is not relativized to a particular class of computational architectures, as, for example, are the various complexity classes.

7. http://www.atdesk.com. The received wisdom is that the conversion from fractional equity pricing to penny differentials aided the rise of automated trading.

8. The superiority of computer based methods is implicitly acknowledged by the development of procedures by internet chess groups and on-line poker rooms to detect such assistance.

REFERENCES

Axelrod, R. (1997). *The Complexity of Cooperation*. Princeton: Princeton University Press.

Bedau, M. A. (1997). "Weak emergence." *Philosophical Perspectives* 11: 375–399.

Bedau, Mark (2003). "Downward causation and autonomy in weak emergence." *Principia Revista Internacional de Epistemologica* 6: 5–50.

Epstein, J. M. & Axtell, R. (1996). *Growing Artificial Societies: Social Science from the Ground Up*. Washington, D.C.: Brookings Institution Press.

Goodwin, R. (1951). "The Nonlinear Accelerator and the Persistence of Business Cycles." *Econometrica* 19: 1–17.

Hartley, J. (1997). *The Representative Agent in Macroeconomics*. London: Routledge.

Hicks, J. (1950). *A Contribution to the Theory of the Trade Cycle*. Oxford: Oxford University Press.

Humphreys, P. (2004). *Extending Ourselves: Computational Science, Empiricism, and Scientific Method*. New York: Oxford University Press.

Johansen, L. (1960). *A Multisectorial Study of Economic Growth*. Amsterdam: North-Holland.

Kendricks, D. (1996). "Sectoral Economics." In H.M. Amman, D.A. Kendrick & J. Rust, Eds., *Handbook of Computational Economics, Volume 1*, 295–332. Amsterdam: Elsevier.

Krugman, P. (1996). *The Self-Organizing Economy*. Oxford: Basil Blackwell.

LeBaron, B. (2006). "Agent-Based Financial Markets: Matching Stylized Facts with Style." In David Colander, ed., *Post-Walrasian Macroeconomics: Beyond the Dynamic Stochastic General Equilibrium Model*. Cambridge: Cambridge University Press.

McKelvey, R. & McLennan, A. (1996). "Computation of Equilibria in Finite Games." In H.M. Amman, D.A. Kendrick & J. Rust, Eds., *Handbook of Computational Economics, Volume 1*, 87–142. Amsterdam: Elsevier.

Parker, D. C., Evans, T. P. & Meretsky, V. (2001). "Measuring Emergent Properties of Agent-Based Land-Use/Land-Cover Models Using Spatial Metrics." Paper presented in the *Seventh Annual Conference of the International Society for Computational Economics,* June 28–29th, New Haven, CT. (unpublished manuscript).

Rasmussen, S., & Barrett, C. L. (1995). "Elements of a Theory of Simulation." In F. Moran, A Moreno, J.J. Merelo & P. Chacon, Eds., *Advances in Artificial Life: Third European Conference on Artificial Life, Granada, Spain, June 4–6, 1995, Proceedings,* 515–529. Berlin: Springer.

Rasmussen, S., et al. (1997). "A Note on Simulation and Dynamical Hierarchies." In Frank Schweitzer, ed., *Self-Organization of Complex Structures,* 83–89. Amsterdam: Gordon and Breach Science Publishers.

Tobin, J. (1955). "A Dynamic Aggregative Model." *Journal of Political Economy* 63: 103–115.

CHAPTER 14

MICROFOUNDATIONS AND THE ONTOLOGY OF MACROECONOMICS

KEVIN D. HOOVER

1. THE IDEOLOGY OF MICROFOUNDATIONS

For more than fifty years, economic pedagogy has been structured around the division between macroeconomics and microeconomics.[1] Virtually every undergraduate economics major and graduate student begins his course of study with core classes in these two fields. Yet, in the conceptual schema of professional economists—surprisingly, perhaps, especially among macroeconomists—macroeconomics occupies an equivocal place.

The typical concerns of macroeconomics—such as national output, employment and unemployment, inflation, interest rates, and the balance of payments—are among the oldest in economics, having been dominant among the problems addressed by both the mercantilists and classical economists, such as David Hume, Adam Smith, David Ricardo, as well as even earlier writers. These concerns co-existed with ones that we now regard as characteristically microeconomic, such as the theory of prices exemplified in the labor theory of value of the classical economists or the theory of marginal utility of the early neoclassical economists. Questions about the relationship between these two groups of concerns could hardly be articulated until a categorical distinction between macroeconomics and microeconomics had been drawn.

Although John Maynard Keynes did not use the term *macroeconomics*, the category of macroeconomics entered the consciousness of economists as a result of the publication of Keynes's *General Theory of Employment Interest and Money* (1936).[2] *Macroeconomics* is used in at least two senses. First, Keynes (1936, 292–293) contrasted economic analysis that assumed that aggregate output was fixed and addressed the decisions of individual firms or workers and analysis that explained output as a whole, as opposed to the output of a particular firm. Second, macroeconomics has also been viewed simply as the economics of aggregate quantities— of GDP rather than cars, of the unemployment rate rather than the hiring decision, of the inflation rate rather than the price of Coca-Cola. These two characterizations of macroeconomics are different but not necessarily contrary. The interplay between them, indeed, explains some of the issues that arise in macroeconomics.

Once a distinction had been drawn—whether or not it was a crisp one—the question of the relationship between microeconomics and macroeconomics was immediately on the table (see Hoover 2002). Wassily Leontief (1936), in one of the earliest responses to the *General Theory,* attacked it for its inconsistency with a microeconomic account of general equilibrium. The Keynesian Lawrence Klein (1950, Chapter 3 and 192–199) saw the provision of microeconomic foundations for each of the main Keynesian functions (consumption, investment, and money demand) as part of the essential agenda of the Keynesian revolution.

Keynes himself analyzed the individual behavior that he understood to lie behind these functions. Yet, he also thought about how the behavior of the individual related to aggregate variables. For instance, Keynes's (1936, 169–172) account of the speculative demand for money depended on the individual's assessment of whether current interest rates are below or above the rate that he subjectively regards as normal. Individuals plunge into money when rates are below normal, since any return to normal implies a capital loss on holdings of interest-bearing bonds; whereas they plunge into bonds when rates are above normal in pursuit of the implied capital gain. Keynes argued that a smooth curve—rather than the knife-edge behavior of the individual—should relate aggregate money holdings inversely to interest rates, since subjective judgments about the "normal" interest rate vary among individuals.[3]

That economists had to think carefully about the differences between individual and aggregate behavior was once an article of faith and was clearly encapsulated into elementary textbooks (for example, in Samuelson's (1948) pathbreaking *Principles of Economics*) with reference to fallacies of composition. Yet seventy years after the publication of the *General Theory*, the reigning ideology of macroeconomists is that macroeconomics is secondary to microeconomics. Reflecting a common feature of ideologies, adherents of the reigning ideology have a variety of understandings of in what exactly the secondariness of macroeconomics consists and different degrees of allegiance to the ideology itself.

At least three broadly reductionist views of the relationship of macroeconomics to microeconomics are commonly encountered.

- One view holds that there is no useful distinction between macroeconomics and microeconomics. This is encapsulated in Robert Lucas's (1987, 107–108) desire to eliminate the distinction altogether.
- A second view defines macroeconomics, not by its methods or its conceptual scheme, which are no different from those of microeconomics, but by the range of problems to which it is addressed—for example, to monetary and fiscal policy. On this view, macroeconomics is distinct from other subfields in the same way that, say, industrial organization is distinct from labor economics, while both are subfields of microeconomics.
- A third view does admit different methods and approaches, but sees macroeconomics as only a pragmatic compromise with the complexity of applying microeconomics to economy-wide problems. This view asserts that macroeconomics reduces to microeconomics in principle but, because the reduction is difficult, we are not there yet.

These three views all contribute to the widespread belief that sound macroeconomics stands in need of *microfoundations.*

In referring to microfoundations for macroeconomics as an ideology, I use *ideology* both in the neutral sense of a more or less coherent set of beliefs guiding the collective activity of macroeconomic research and in its pejorative sense of false consciousness—a collective illusion shared by macroeconomists. My contention is that, even in its neutral sense, the ideology of microfoundations rests on a mistake about the ontology of the social world; whereas, in its pejorative sense, it shares the characteristic, common to political ideologies, of serving as a tool of persecution and intellectual repression. The ideologue searches for ideological purity. Since the consciousness is false, ideology in this sense is bound to be a muddle—but a deeply pernicious muddle.

The adherents of view 1 or 2 frequently also hold view 3 as well. And view 3 underwrites a kind of tyranny of the future, which is typical of totalitarian politics: a vision of heaven on earth justifies any misdeed today as long as it aims toward the future good, even when the path between the here-and-now and the future is obscure. I have elsewhere referred to this trope as *eschatological justification* (Hoover 2006a).

The reductionist impulse in macroeconomics is frequently referred to as *methodological individualism.* The term is not apt. Practical macroeconomics does not consist of true microeconomic models—that is, of models in which the behavior of macroeconomic aggregates is derived from the composition of the behaviors of individual economic actors. This would obviously be a very difficult way to approach the economy, posing problems of a similar nature to trying to explain the formation of hurricanes molecule by molecule, applying the established principles of Newtonian mechanics.

In practice, macroeconomists generally accept the representative-agent model as a workable microfoundation. The representative-agent model takes economy-wide aggregates (GDP and its components, price indices, average interest rates, and so forth) as if they were the equivalent to the similarly named variables associated with individual agents (the incomes of individual workers, the products of individual firms, the prices of those products, the interest rates at which an individual borrows, and so forth). The representative agent is just a microeconomic agent writ large. He maximizes utility subject to a budget constraint given by the national-income identity. He simultaneously maximizes profits subject to an aggregate production function. And the forms of these functions are identical to the forms that have proved tractable in microeconomic analysis.[4]

It is, in fact, microeconomists who have shown clearly that there is no valid reason to believe that the functional forms that apply to individuals will describe aggregates of individuals. For example, even if every individual is governed by Cobb-Douglas utility and production functions with individual goods as their arguments, it would be extraordinary for the macroeconomy to conform to Cobb-Douglas functional forms with aggregate consumption, GDP, capital, and labor as their arguments.[5]

Once we recognize that representative-agent models do not deal with individuals, we see that macroeconomics mimics the forms of microeconomics without successfully implementing an individualist methodology. This is so obvious that one must wonder in what the attraction of microeconomic forms consists. I conjecture that the real underlying motivation is not methodological but ontological. The ontological mistake of macroeconomics is to believe that the objects of macroeconomic analysis are not ontologically independent. Macroeconomists fear that they are not dealing with solid economic entities unless they can trace the route along which those entities reduce ontologically to intentional agents, individuals who make decisions in light of their preferences, goals, and beliefs. But, since this is an impracticable task, they emphasize the connection of the aggregate to the individual by aping the analytical forms of microeconomics.

The fears and strategies of economic reductionism are, then, quite different from those in other sciences. Many biologists, for example, are deeply afraid of functional or teleological explanations. They are not happy with explanations that rely on anything that attributes beliefs, goals, or other intentional states to individual organisms, much less to species. In contrast, the economist finds it hard to see any analysis as "economic" unless it deals in intentional states. The point of microfoundations is to recapture the teleology that appeared to be missing in macroeconomics.

A successful ontology of macroeconomics must recognize the fear that motivates the program of microfoundations. Macroeconomists are, of course, correct that there is an important sense in which macroeconomic behavior must emerge from microeconomic behavior. Macroeconomic aggregates are not free-floating Platonic forms or, as Searle (1995, 25) puts it, a "Hegelian world spirit." A successful ontology must provide an intelligible account of the connection between the individual and the aggregate.

I want, therefore, to turn to two questions: First, is there a successful ontology of macroeconomics? Second, what implications does (or should) this ontology have for practical macroeconomics?

2. On What There Is
in the Macroeconomy

2.1 Supervenience and Reductionism

I begin with my own earlier view of the ontology of macroeconomics (Hoover 1995; 2001a, Chapter 3; 2001b, Chapter 5). I argued that macroeconomics *supervened* on microeconomics. That is, while the conceptual structures of microeconomics and macroeconomics were distinct, any particular arrangement of microeconomic features would always generate exactly the same set of macroeconomic features.

Supervenience is usually regarded as a form of weak reductionism that aims to preserve the fundamental object of reduction of the macro to micro. For example, philosophers of mind who want to reduce the mental to the physical while recognizing that there is a gap between mental and physical concepts appeal to supervenience (Kim 1978). But just, as I previously noted, biologists seek reductions to purge their subject of intentionality whereas economists seek reductions to recapture intentionality, as an economist I sought to use supervenience in an antireductionist manner. The goal was not to reduce macroeconomics to microeconomics, but to show that macroeconomics could have an ontological anchor in the individual, while preserving ontological independence for causally interacting aggregates. The central idea was that, in moving from the microeconomic to the macroeconomic, we do not preserve, in Uskali Mäki's (1996) evocative term, the "ontic furniture" of the microeconomic world. The conceptual shift, I argued, was evident in the units of measurement. The price of goods has the dimension of dollars/unit of good, whereas the general price level, which is often thought to be analogous to a microeconomic price, has the dimension of current-period dollars per base-period dollar. Similarly, a real good has a physical unit, while the supposedly analogous macroeconomic quantity, real GDP, has only a monetary unit (base period-dollars). My argument, then, was that macroeconomic aggregates could be seen as emergent properties of the macroeconomy—ones that would not exist without the underlying microeconomic agents—but ones that, like mental properties emerging from physical properties—were ontologically distinct. But why should this relationship not be regarded as a species of reduction? Why should this distinction not be merely conceptual rather than ontological? In particular, why should we not just view the macroeconomic aggregates as (rather imperfect) summaries of the microeconomic data? Why should we regard them as "real" in the sense of existing *externally* (i.e., independently of any individual human mind) and objectively (i.e., unconstituted by the representations of macroeconomic theory) (see Hoover 1995, 236; 2001b, 109).

One argument against reduction of macroeconomics to microeconomics extends David Levy's (1985) argument that microeconomic actors necessarily employ macroeconomic concepts in their decision making. For example, anyone trying to calculate how much to put aside for his children's education needs to form expectations of the course of inflation, where *inflation* is a macroeconomic concept. Since these macroeconomic concepts are not those of an outsider who is observing and summarizing the microeconomic facts, but are those of individual agents who are making the microeconomic facts, it would seem that macroeconomic concepts are, in fact, constitutive of parts of microeconomic reality. A reductionist use of supervenience requires that the microeconomic and the macroeconomic belong to separate domains, but here they cannot be separated.

In addition to this argument against reductionism, I also tried to give positive arguments for the external reality of macroeconomic aggregates. First, I applied Ian Hacking's (1983, 22–24) manipulability criterion—"if you can spray them [i.e., electrons], then they are real"—to macroeconomics. A positive example of such a manipulation is the Federal Reserve's use of controlled movements in one macroeconomic aggregate—the real interest rate—to manipulate another—the yield curve. Second, I argued that the strategy of idealization in the construction of scientific models (see Nowak 1980 and Hoover 1994) can be successful empirically only if the models isolate the *essential* primary factors involved in causal processes. The success of an idealized model, therefore, amounts to an argument in favor of the existence of these primary factors. All successful macroeconomics, including any successful representative-agent models, trade entirely in macroeconomic aggregates. Despite their microeconomic trappings, the claims that representative-agent models are successful amount to implicit claims for the existence of macroeconomic aggregates. And *pace* Rosenberg (1992), I believe economics generally, and macroeconomics particularly, to have substantial empirical success.

2.2 A Critique of Supervenience

Julian Reiss (2004) argues that supervenience provides a poor framework for understanding the micro-macro relationship in a realist ontology of macroeconomics. He argues, first, that the classic applications of supervenience are reductionist and require that the concepts at the micro and macro levels be disjoint. An antireductionist twist to a supervenience argument, particularly one that argues that macroeconomic concepts are employed at the microeconomic level, is misguided to the point of triviality. All that is left of the original notion is that the there is a determinate many-to-one relationship between the individual and the aggregate, in which the same configuration of individual elements always fix the configuration of aggregate elements, although more than one configuration of individual elements might fix the same configuration of aggregate elements.

In part, Reiss's objection is that no one fails to accept that the macroeconomic behavior is ultimately the product of microeconomic behavior. He elaborates the objection, however, by challenging the ability of the microeconomic to fix the macroeconomic. He does so by appealing to Levy's observation that microeconomic agents use macroeconomic concepts. In particular, if agents use a price index to calculate real quantities or inflation rates that are salient in their individual decision making, and if, as is perfectly clear, there is no uniquely correct price index, then, the same set of background microeconomic facts might lead agents to make different decisions, depending on which price index they use, and consequently generate a different set of macroeconomic facts.

Reiss's argument that supervenience is inapplicable is offered constructively, in the sense that he supports a realist macroeconomic ontology and finds that an appeal to supervenience is a distraction that weakens the argument. Reiss misprizes the supervenience argument because he underestimates the ontological fears of macroeconomists. The lesson of the Lucas (1976) critique of macroeconometric models is that estimated relationships will be stable in the face of changing policy, and, therefore, useful in policy analysis, only when they capture the "deep parameters" of the economy, which we can appropriately translate into the "fundamental ontological building blocks of the economy." Lucas's assumption is that these deep parameters are necessarily microeconomic. The only way to calm the ontological fears of macroeconomists is to demonstrate that macroeconomic aggregates can stand in relationships governed by deep parameters without being severed from the microeconomic, for it is precisely the view that aggregates are not tightly connected to individual decision makers that drives the microfoundational ideology. Supervenience was offered as a balm—one way of clarifying that macroeconomic aggregates could be causally autonomous without becoming disconnected from individual behavior.

Reiss claims that the multiplicity of aggregation schemes (e.g., multiple price indices) undermines the supervenience account in the sense that he denies that the exact same micro facts must generate the exact same macro facts. The argument appears to be that, since the same micro facts can support different price aggregation schemes and each can be used to generate a different measure of inflation, then the micro facts have not "fixed" the macro facts about inflation. But this argument seems to hinge on the conflation of the measuring instrument with the thing measured and to appeal to a limited view of what constitutes the micro facts. Inflation as a category is something that we might measure through different schemes. One may be better than another, and yet, neither is perfect at capturing our theoretical conception. The claim about micro fixing macro is not about any particular imperfect measure, but about the object of measurement. The diversity of aggregate measures does not address the point at issue.

Further, even if the measures themselves disagree (inflation on the CPI is 3 percent per year, whereas on the GDP deflator it is only 1.5 percent per year), once we know what the measuring schemes are, they are still all fixed by the micro arrangements. If a particular micro configuration delivers CPI of 3 percent and GDP deflator of 1.5 percent, any repetition of that configuration would also deliver those same values. The values of these and other measures may all differ, but they differ in the same way for the same set of micro arrangements. And the distribution of assessments of macroeconomic quantities among different individuals is one of the pertinent microeconomic facts. It is only when we conceive of this distribution as not among the fixed facts that Reiss's argument gets any traction.

While Reiss underestimates the vital importance of meeting the ontological fears of macroeconomists, he may be correct that the effort to meet those fears with a nonreductive supervenience account is so alien to established usage that the term *supervenience* ought to be dropped. The point that macroeconomics can be causally autonomous without slipping its microeconomic moorings remains important nonetheless.

In retrospect, the argument that macroeconomic concepts are fundamentally involved at the microeconomic level may be too weak to support the status of macroeconomics. It may mistake an epistemological problem for an ontological one. Yes, any account of microeconomic behavior must recognize that individuals need to use aggregate concepts as a means of dealing with the complexity of the environments in which they make decisions. Consequently, there are no useful accounts of the microeconomic that do not involve aggregate variables. This can be true, however, without these variables existing independently of the representations of the individuals.

The first step in my attempt to establish the external reality of macroeconomic aggregates was to establish the independence of the conceptual framework of macroeconomics from that of microeconomics. To the degree that this was established through dimensional analysis of micro and macroeconomic quantities, it now seems to rest on too weak a reed. Dimensional analysis does point a genuine distinction between the micro and the macro, but it is the same distinction that can be found, for example, in the relationship between microphysical and macrophysical quantities, and does not point to consequences at the macro level for intentions that are the heart of economists' insistence on microfoundations for macroeconomics. Consider a physical example—the relationship between the momenta of molecules in a gas and the pressure as it figures in the ideal gas laws. In order to derive the ideal gas laws, the kinetic theory of gases makes use of deeply relational facts, namely, the assumed probability distribution of the momenta of the underlying molecules. Physicists tend to overlook the manner in which the assumption of a probability distribution adds a superindividual element into an erstwhile reductionist enterprise. The social elements in economics are relational facts among individuals. And analogous to physics, reductionist economics leaves out the characteristically social elements of economics. But as with the distributional assumptions in the derivation of the gas laws, we need to say something more about how these social relations work to generate macroeconomic phenomena. The question is whether we can provide a richer, but still intelligible account of the connection between the individual and the aggregate, which incorporates the specifically social features of economics.

2.3 The Construction of Social Reality

John Searle (1995) offers one such account.

The fundamental notion of microfoundations is that all macroeconomic facts ought to be shown to arise out of individual choice. Advocates of microfoundations see economic institutions, then, as lacking any independent ontological status; such institutions are, rather, essentially the epiphenomena or summary of the interactions of ontologically distinct individuals—"human molecules" in Tjalling Koopmans's evocative coinage (in excerpt from Koopmans in Hendry & Morgan 1995, 515; used as the title of Nelson 1992). The actions of such individuals are guided by their own beliefs, desires, and other intentional states, so that the intentions of another individual enter my own calculus only through my beliefs about what they might be.

An example shows how familiar this picture is to economists, as well as suggesting that there might be alternatives. Roger Guesnerie (1992, 1254) divides the justifications of the rational-expectations hypothesis into two types—*eductive* and *evolutive*. "Eductive explanations rely on the understanding of the logic of the situation by economic agents; they are explicitly or implicitly associated with the mental activity of participants aiming at 'forecasting the forecasts of others.'" Eductive rational expectations are the expectations of human molecules whose intentional states are radically isolated from the intentional states of others. In contrast, evolutive expectations are based on observations of economic behavior: "[e]volutive explanations put emphasis on the learning possibilities offered by the repetition of the situation; they are associated with the study of convergence or more or less ad hoc learning processes." The important point for us is not the *ad hoc* nature of the learning processes but the public nature of what is learned. Forming expectations on the basis of inductions about the process governing, say, prices puts little weight on an individual's intentional states and is, in principle, intersubjective. An eductive rational expectation is my own belief; an evolutive rational expectation is an attempt to characterize a fact in the world and could be something that I read in the newspaper. Even if I were to publish my belief, by the time that it is in print, it simply becomes an additional piece of information on which the holders of eductive rational expectations will ply their forecasting logic.

In opposition to the strictly individual intentionality of eductive rational-expectations, Searle tries to make sense of collective intentionality. As well as

"I believe" or "I intend," Searle argues that the states that "we believe" or "we intend" are part of the mental repertoire of every individual. The choice is not between strict reductionism and an untethered Hegelian spirit. Rather, individuals can possess individual or collective intentions, and collective action is one human possibility.

For example, when Exxon bought Mobile Oil, this was not an individual action in which the CEO's intentional state was "*I* intend to buy and believe that the chief financial officer and other parties intend to buy," and so for each relevant party. Instead, the intentional state of the CEO and the other parties was "*we* (i.e., Exxon) intend to buy." The intentions remain in the mind of each individual—no supermind is invoked. It is just that each individual intends to act collectively. The operative pronoun is *we*, not *I*. Each individual plays a particular role, and the intention is framed within the context of constitutive rules. If John Jones were the CEO, then a key intentional state belongs to John Jones, but it is meaningful to the purchase only because of his role as CEO and not because he is John Jones *per se*.

Another example: It is only within the constitutive rules of Major League Baseball that Barry Bonds can hit a home run, much less surpass Babe Ruth's or Hank Aaron's home-run records. And while in the 2006 season, Barry Bonds may have been the only one poised, to break these records, which makes his position seem individual, his role as the cleanup hitter for the San Francisco Giants could have been filled by other people. There is an independence between the role that an individual fills in a collective endeavor and the individual who fills it.

Searle rejects the notion of collective action as the complex outcome of the interactions of atomic intentionality—a form of intentionality for which eductive rational expectation provides a paradigm. First, while collective social facts exist only as the result of representations in some individual minds, typically no single mind is necessary or sufficient for their existence. In that sense, they are not subjective, but are experienced as objective facts not dissimilar to the facts about physical objects. Social objects (e.g., governments, money, or universities) are "placeholders for patterns of activities" (Searle 1995, 57). Collective intentionality is about ongoing activities and the possibility of more. And the patterns of activities themselves, such as a corporation or government, are different in kind from the individuals that play specific roles within them.

The independence of the collective level from particular individuals is also mirrored in physical sciences. Putnam (1975) argues that many physical explanations work only at a macro level. Why is it, for instance, that a square peg 15/16 inches on a side will pass through a square hole 1 inch on a side but not through a round hole 1 inch in diameter? The answer appeals to the microstructures of the peg and the board in which the holes are cut only to the degree that, whatever those structures are, they imply that the peg and board are rigid. No microanalysis can explain, in any general and, therefore, scientific manner, what is easily understood on the basis of macro-level geometry. Batterman (2001) uses a case study of rainbows to argue that scientific explanation quite commonly relies on higher level relationships that are indifferent to most of the fine details of the underlying microstructures.

Searle's second point is that the rules constitutive of social facts form a background, which is not maintained by conscious (or unconscious) intentions. A tyro baseball player may intend with each of his actions to follow the rules of baseball, but an experienced player simply intends various actions within the context of the game—bunting or stealing a base, for example. While the experienced player may be described as following the rules of the game, because his behavior conforms to the rules, he need not constantly intend to do so. The background framework of constitutive rules, not maintained by intentional states, accounts for the inert objectivity of social facts.

Searle finds many economic examples of social facts that are constructed through collective intentionality—money, for instance. Individual, engraved, green pieces of paper are nothing but paper except to the degree that they serve as markers in a set of constitutive rules involved in exchanging goods and storing purchasing power through time. In context, the paper serves as money only to the degree that a sufficient number of people believe that it serves those functions. Because the collective intentions are what give the paper its monetary character, it is also clear that the paper itself is dispensable. Metal or entries in a bank's computers might also serve as money, provided that people accepted them as markers in the set of constitutive rules. In this sense, money depends on the representations of individuals, but it does not depend on the representations of any particular individual.

Erstwhile paper money could become demonetized if a sufficient number of people ceased to believe that it could serve these monetary functions. Some of the police powers associated with state-issued money are aimed at removing the causes (such as counterfeiting) that might undermine people's belief or faith in the monetary character of the money tokens (paper or electronic).

Money, then, is epistemologically objective in that it exists independently of my representations, though not independently of all representations. And it is ontologically subjective—not subjective in the sense of not really existing, but in something more like the sense in which color is subjective. Colors are real; but without observers, light would have a frequency though not a color. Money, as anyone who has found himself "a day late and a dollar short" will attest, exists as a social fact. And while such a social fact depends on our representations and intentional states collectively, one encounters the possibilities of money or the constraints of a lack of money as palpably as one encounters the stone when building a wall or stubbing a toe.

Again, the literature on the microfoundations of money provides just the contrast case against which Searle argues. Search models of money (e.g., Jones 1976 or Kiyotaki & Wright 1989, 1993) seek to explain which objects become money and how they acquire their monetary properties with an appeal exclusively to individual intentionality. In a search model, an object becomes monetized through a process of each agent's individually regarding it as valuable, and believing that others also regard it as valuable, as an intermediate step in trade, one that reduces the expected costs of finding a suitable trading partner. Monetization is, therefore, closely related to the eductive justification of rational expectations in which the expectations are calculated as forecasts of the forecasts of others. Money in such accounts has no intrinsic value or, if it has intrinsic value because it is a real good like gold, its intrinsic value is not essential to its monetary character. Rather, its monetary character is sustained by all the agents in the economy solving a complex utility maximization problem in which the monetary character of the money good emerges as an equilibrium in which the particular good is the unique (or nearly unique) intermediary in all trades. Search models provide a paradigm for all microfoundational accounts of economic institutions.

Money as an institution is, on the microfoundational account, in need of perpetual intentional maintenance. Its status is fragile and would collapse easily if the optimizers shirked. In arguing that collective intentionality is exercised in a background of constitutive rules, Searle denies that economic institutions must be so persistently maintained by the right intentional states. Searle argues that ordinary economic actions are not the product of rational choice exercised through well-ordered preferences, but operations within internalized rules. The institution of money, on this view, need not be perpetually recreated by the decisions of economic agents in the manner of the search models, but can be taken as a given part of the background (objective relative to any particular individual), the context in which, say, individual shoppers decide to buy this or that particular good.

The problem of macroeconomic ontology has two levels. The first is to establish that there are social facts or institutions that ontologically transcend individual economic agents. The second is to establish that the macroeconomic aggregates are examples of such social facts and to determine their character. Searle's account so far addresses the first level. Social institutions are the product of collective intentionality, but they may form only the background that delineates the possibilities and constraints on individual actions. Can we use Searle's account to address the second level of the problem of macroeconomic ontology?

Searle (1995, 137–147) argues that, besides the mental causation and behaviorism ("billiard ball causation") familiar in much of social science, we should admit a third kind of causation, which recognizes the causal role that the background of constitutive rules plays in determining the actions and outcomes of individuals.[6] The argument amounts to recognizing that, in some cases, the particular intentional actions of individuals are less important to determining outcomes than the constraints that limit their behavior. The well-known argument of Stigler and Becker (1977) that, with no reference to utility functions, we know that demand curves must slope down because of the budget constraint illustrates how the background can determine the character of the outcome independent of intentional states. Similarly, Herbert Simon's (1957, Part IV, especially chapters 14 and 15) "bounded rationality" is in part driven by the role of constraints. Heiner (1983) argues that predictable behavior emerges from bounded rationality and background constraints essentially because something like Searle's background dominates individual preferences.

It is a small step to macroeconomic aggregates. Driven by constraints, the behavior of aggregates may sometimes be hardly related to the specific decisions of individual agents. Traffic flow or electricity demand can be characterized as aggregates, and the traffic engineer cares no more about the individual's car trip nor the electric company's load manager about the individual's decision to switch on the air conditioning than does the hydrologist about the individual water molecule. Not only would it be too hard to work from molecules (chemical or human) to the properties of the aggregates, it is beside the point (see Batterman 2001 for an extended treatment of physical examples).

And so, too, with the economy. Money regarded from the point of view of its large-scale movements in the national income or flow-of-funds accounts does not depend on any of its particular representations (i.e., on whether it takes the form of notes or coins in the cash register or of an ATM transaction), and the particular actions of individuals matter not at all relative to the average behavior of all individuals. While these characteristics are, in Searle's view, the product of the causal influence of the constitutive rules (e.g., that purchases are limited by the monetary resources of the individual), they seem to underwrite something quite like the "billiard ball causation" of physics, in the sense that individual intentions do not play any essential role in understanding the particular outcomes, even though intentional agents provide ineliminable substrate for the economic aggregates. The applicability of billiard-ball causation explains why a differential equation may characterize a traffic flow or the course of GDP growth.

That it is beside the point in certain sorts of causal analysis to inquire into the behavior of the individuals that constitute the aggregates is why I previously focused on dimensional analysis: The aggregate price level and the prices of individual goods are not the same and, indeed, not even commensurable (Hoover 1995). Although that characterization remains correct, it is not distinctively economic. The point applies equally to physical aggregation—the difference between the mechanics of molecules and the aggregate characteristics of pressure and temperature. But molecules do not have intentions. And with economic agents we have the extra obligations to explain what happens to intentions. Searle's account of social facts and a background of constitutive rules helps to explain the limited reach of individual intentions at the level of the aggregates and, therefore, supplies a piece that was missing in the earlier account.

Limited reach does not imply that individual intentions have no role to play in macroeconomics. To some extent, Searle may overstate the case in purging social institutions of a role for individual intentional states. Much of macroeconomics is about the interaction of policy makers with the aggregate economy, and, as Searle (1995, 138–139) agrees, the intentional actions of the policy maker may be pertinent to the macroeconomic outcome. An influential individual need not be a policy maker, but may be an opinion maker. If Bill Gates or George Soros or Warren Buffet takes a publicly observable action in response to an individual intentional state, it may have macroeconomic consequences, hardly different in character to policy actions directed by George Bush or Ben Bernanke.

But I would go further than this. The individual intentional state of the typical economic agent may have no noticeable effect on the aggregate. This is a version of the small-relative-to-the-market idealizing assumption that is frequently employed in microeconomics as perfect competition or in international finance as the small-country assumption. While no one agent may affect the outcome, collectively agents operating in more or less the same direction surely will.

The point is nicely made in a passage of Anthony Trollope's (1869, Chapter 25) novel *Phineas Finn*. In the novel, Phineas, a member of Parliament, tries to convince Mr. Bunche, a minor political operative, not to engage in a street demonstration in favor of a certain bill, on the grounds that his action, while possibly dangerous to himself and his family, could not possibly affect the outcome. Bunche replies:

> "Look here, Mr Finn; I don't believe the sea will become any fuller because the Piddle runs into it out of the Dorsetshire fields; but I do believe that the waters from all the countries is what makes the ocean. I shall help; and it's my duty to help."

Bunche's position is a direct retort to the economic analysis that concludes that it is irrational to vote, since the marginal vote cannot affect the result and, therefore, the expected benefits of casting a ballot are outweighed by even trivial costs of going to the polls. Mr. Finn goes on:

> "It's your duty as a respectable citizen, with a wife and family, to stay at home."

To which Bunche replies:

> "If everybody with a wife and family was to say so, there'd be none there but roughs, and then where should we be? What would the Government people say to us then? If every man with a wife and family was to show hisself in the streets tonight, we should have the ballot before Parliament breaks up, and if none of 'em don't do it, we shall never have the ballot. Ain't that so?"

Standard economic analysis of voting employs the model without collective intentionality. Mr. Bunche anticipates Searle in seeing that he can join with a group each to intend as a collectivity of voters. And what is more significant for us, the aggregate outcome, although it is not significantly altered by the individual identities of the voters, is determined by their collective intentional states.

In this respect, macroeconomic aggregates are importantly different from physical aggregates. How they relate to one another depends on the collective intentional states of underlying individuals, and explains why there are sources of instability in the relationships among economic aggregates not found in the relationships among physical aggregates. This is, of course, the insight behind Lucas's (1976) critique of macroeconometric policy analysis. Lucas argued that individual economic agents who understood the role of economic policy would make different choices and, therefore, would contribute to different aggregate outcomes as policy rules changed. As a result, the policy maker was not entitled to take the relationships among aggregates as a stable background that could be used reliably to predict the effect of a policy action.

The Lucas critique appears, then, to be compatible with a Searlean account of macroeconomic aggregates. The standard reaction to the Lucas critique, starting with Lucas himself, is to argue, first, that the only way to stabilize the relationships among macroeconomic aggregates is to base the analysis in the causal bedrock of "deep parameters" and, second, that those deep parameters are the ones that govern the tastes and technology of individual economic agents (Lucas 1980, 708–712; cf. Sargent 1981, esp. 233, 242). The second part of the reaction reflects the ideology of microfoundations and ignores the superindividual quality of economic facts and institutions based in collective intentionality. On the one hand, some of the social features that underwrite economic aggregates may be those for which the behavior of particular individuals is irrelevant, so that the deepest relevant parameters appear in institutional arrangements that form the background of constitutive rules in which individuals operate. On the other hand, macroeconomic aggregates sometimes may reflect the collective outcome of the intentional states of individuals operating within those rules. This second consideration implies that the analysis of what a typical individual might do may sometimes give insight into the collective outcome: The individual optimization problem is not wholly irrelevant to macroeconomics. But the first consideration undercuts the case that one can *deduce* the aggregate outcome from the behavior of a typical individual without regard to background of constitutive rules or economic institutions. There is no basis for the idea that a single agent or group of agents, just like one of the actual individuals but blown up to economy size, provides a legitimate basis for deducing the behavior of economic aggregates. The focus of early macroeconomists on fallacies of composition is warranted by the recognition that the collective intentionality generates a set of causal structures that is systematically distinct from the underlying individuals.

3. IMPLICATIONS FOR APPLIED MACROECONOMICS

At the end of Section 1, I posed two questions: First, is there a successful ontology of macroeconomics? Second, what implications does (or should) this ontology have for practical macroeconomics? If a macroeconomic ontology grounded in a Searlean account of collective intentionality permits us to answer yes to the first question, where does this leave us with respect to the second question?

Empirical economics from Davenant and King in the seventeenth century to today has largely dealt in aggregate quantities. It is only recently that detailed individual data or data from economic experiments has become available. Some eighteenth and nineteenth century economists (e.g., Tooke, Jevons) tried to use aggregate data to understand the causal structure of the economic world; yet, economists of the day were frequently skeptical. John Stuart Mill, for example, gave a detailed account of how to infer causation from experimental data with his canons of induction (Mill 1851), but he regarded the economy as too complex to be dealt with in an experimental manner. For Mill, the method of economics had to be a priori, based on the logic of the economic situation. Since deductions from theory led to conclusions about behavior in isolation from a huge range of complicating factors, they—at best—indicated *tendencies* of the economy. Economic statistics could illustrate these economic tendencies, but the failure of the data to conform to the theory could not provide evidence against the theory—too many complicating causes might explain away the deviations. Economics, for Mill, was an "inexact and separate science" (cf. Hausman 1992). Extreme versions of Mill's *apriorism* are found in such later economists as Robbins (1935) and Von Mises (1966). Their vision of economics as the science of the allocation of scarce resources to their optimal uses (optimization subject to constraints) provides the underlying vision of modern microeconomics.

Many nineteenth- and early twentieth-century statisticians and economists also doubted the applicability of statistics to economic data. Such data rarely appeared to conform to the laws of probability: They were not derived from controlled experiments and, when observational, rarely conformed to common probability models. They were, for example, almost never normal and frequently displayed trends or correlations between successive time-series observations.

Trygve Haavelmo (1944) initiated the modern period in econometrics with the idea that economic data could be divided into a systematic component (the economics) and an unsystematic component (the residuals). The residuals formed by conditioning the data on its systematic causes could be regarded as a random sample, conforming to the laws of probability, and be subjected to ordinary statistical analysis. The essential problem in Haavelmo's account of econometrics was to identify the systematic component. The identification problem had been recognized well before Haavelmo (see Morgan 1990, Chapter 6; Hendry & Morgan 1995, Section 3).

Supply and demand provide the classic illustration. Supply depends on price, and demand depends on price; the observed quantity and price are the intersection of the supply and demand curves. If all we observe are the prices and quantities at these intersections—even if, because of random shocks, these are not constant—how can we learn the shape of the supply and demand curves? If we happen to know that supply (say, of corn) depends on weather, as well as price, and demand depends on income, as well as price, and if weather and income are themselves variable, then variations in weather will shift the supply curve independently, tracing out the demand curve, and variations in income will shift the demand curve, tracing out the supply curve. In the argot of econometrics, the supply and demand curves are *identified conditional on the restrictions* that weather does not appear in the demand curve and income does not appear in the supply curve.

How—aside from common sense—do we justify these identifying restrictions? Haavelmo and later the Cowles Commission (Koopmans 1950 and Hood & Koopmans 1953) sought the source of the restrictions in economic theory. But economic theory, in their usage, was hardly more than organized common sense. It was not usually called upon to provide any detailed understanding of underlying causal mechanisms. Rather, it merely suggested a list of factors that might affect one aggregate function or curve but not another. And this list may or may not be suggested by a microeconomic model. The macroeconometric models of the 1950s and 1960s, identified in this framework, can be thought of as articulating "billiard-ball" causal relations among aggregates.

Liu (1960) was skeptical of what Sims (1980, 1) later referred to as "incredible" identifying restrictions. Both Liu and Sims suggested ignoring theory in favor of purely statistical characterizations of the data—a position that Sims later modified substantially (see Hoover 2006b). Although Sims's criticism had important practical consequences for macroeconometrics, it was the Lucas critique that sounded the knell for the first-generation macroeconometric models. Lucas's advocacy of microfoundations was essentially a reaction to the billiard-ball causality of the macroeconometric models, motivated by the desire to place intentional agents into empirical macroeconomics.

One reaction to the Lucas critique was to apply the representative-agent model to aggregate data. The optimization problem of the representative agent implies a set of restrictions—more complicated than the exclusion restrictions typically employed in earlier econometric models—that identify the equations of the optimization problem itself. This is an ideological response in the sense that, even within the terms of the individual intentionality of microeconomic theory, we know that aggregates do not conform to relationships that mimic, on a larger scale, microeconomic relationships (see Section 1).

What is more, if we take the representative-agent models seriously, then they imply more restrictions on the data than are needed for identification, and such overidentifying restrictions can be tested. For the most part, estimates using actual data reject the overidentifying restrictions. This would come as no surprise to Mill. And one camp of modern macroeconomists have adopted the Millian response of privileging a priori economic theory. The calibration methodology of Kydland and Prescott (1982, 1991) starts with economic theory, supplies values to key parameters of both the systematic and random components, and then simulates the model. The output of the models is then compared to the statistical characteristics of the actual data.

The calibration methodology has substantially more modest goals than the earlier macroeconometric methodologies. It is not generally used to explain or to predict the specific paths of observed variables. Rather it is used to explore the generic operating characteristics of a simulated economy, to explain what sort of tendencies might arise in an economy with, for example, different policy rules or different sources of random variation. In focusing on such generic characteristics, the calibrationists follow Mill: They hope that the models shed light on the actual data, but they do not regard the data as capable of falsifying the theory that informs the model.

Calibrationists use a representative-agent framework—in part, because it is tractable. The problem is not merely a technical one. Despite offering eschatological justifications for their models, their project of true microfoundations is hopeless. Consider a physical analogy. A hydrologist might model turbulence by constructing a computer simulation that models something on the order of 10^{27} to 10^{30} molecules (i.e., a billion billion billion to a billion billion billion billion) individual molecules according to the laws of mechanics. He sets the simulation running and observes what sorts of macrophysical outcomes are produced.[7] Why should the truly committed microfoundationalist not attempt the analogous exercise and create a calibrated model of individual agents?[8] Our ontological analysis suggests that such an exercise would not capture the features of the macroeconomy. It fails to make room for collective intentionality and its products, the background of constitutive rules that shapes the causal interactions of economic aggregates. Indeed, it would obscure the collective intentionality that lies behind the very phenomena that interest us when we pose macroeconomic questions. Individuals not only create social objects through collective intentionality, but they act and choose within the constraints of such structures. The ontological problem is that, contrary to the microfoundational ideology, physical things and individual actors are not all that exist independently.

The behavior of aggregates is driven both by the constraints of constitutive rules and by the collective intentionality of individual agents. Here I equivocate on *collective*, taking it both to refer to Searle's "we believe" and "we intend" and to the straightforward aggregation of the decisions guided by the intentional states of individual agents. The first sense helps to make aggregates different in kind from their microeconomic analogues; the second confirms the insight of the microfoundationalists that individual intentions do matter to aggregate behavior. I do not see any way that we can know a priori how to strike the balance between the relevance of individual intentions and constraints of collective intention. This is a question for empirical research in macroeconomics.

In Hoover (2006b) I distinguish between two methodological visions for empirical investigation in macroeconomics. The *Walrasian* method is the bottom-up approach of the engineer, who starts with the foundations in microeconomics and works to the superstructure of macroeconomics. No estimates of macroeconomic relationships can be secure unless they reflect the correct articulation of the economic structure. We have to start from first principles. The *Marshallian* method is the top-down approach of the archaeologist. Like the engineer, the archaeologist believes he is dealing with a well-defined structure, but his problem is literally how to *dis*cover it. He works down toward the foundations and sees no warrant for inferring what they must be like in advance of the investigation.

The Marshallian approach is not atheoretical. Nor is it opposed to micro-foundations, in the sense of looking for deeper structures behind the relationships of macroeconomic aggregates. It simply does not assume that the useful level on which to locate such structures is necessarily the level of the microeconomic agent. The Marshallian approach is, then, very close to what Auyang (1998, Chapter 1) refers to as "synthetic microanalysis." Early rational-expectations models provide an illustration of synthetic microanalysis (e.g., Sargent & Wallace 1975).

These models were essentially IS-LM-aggregate supply models, not representative-agent models claiming identification from microfoundational restrictions. The fundamental insights of such models are, first, that expectations should play a role in individual choice (for example, in labor supply or investment demand), and, second, that expectations that differed systematically from realizations would provide profit opportunities that individual agents could easily exploit. If we were truly dealing with individuals, we would want to understand the process of expectations formation, and we would want to model it in such a way that expectations would converge on actual realizations. But in these early rational-expectations models, this is not what is done. Instead, the aggregate implications of expectations are modeled in the form of a restriction that the mathematical expectation of a variable (X_t), conditional on available information (Ω_{t-1}), does not differ from the realization of that variable by more than a random error:

$X_t - E(X_t|\Omega_{t-1}) = \varepsilon_t$, where $E(.|.)$ is the conditional expectations operator and ε_t is an identically distributed, independent random-error term. A crucial assumption is that the information set (Ω_{t-1}) includes the structure of the model itself. This amounts to defining the expectation of X_t $(\equiv X_t^e)$ as the forecast of X_t that is generated by the model itself.

The variable X_t^e is not observable, except in the sense that we can back it out of the model. It is not the average expectation of individual agents nor even an aggregate, if by aggregate we mean something that is composed of smaller parts. Rather it is a system characteristic, the numerical manifestation of the restriction that neither the econometrician, the purveyor of the model, nor the policy maker, who might be a character in the model or a user of the model in the real world, can have a systematic informational advantage over individual agents. As such X_t^e does not possess causal capacities of the type championed by Cartwright (1989) that can be carried from one context to another. It is not a cause or effect, but a summary statistic without causal efficacy. The aggregate rational-expectations hypothesis is not the hypothesis that expectations are formed in any particular manner; rather it is the claim that the true causal variables of the macroeconomy are related to one another in a particular nonlinear manner, captured by what macroeconometricians refer to as *cross-equation restrictions*.

The rational-expectations hypothesis is an example of synthetic microanalysis because it begins with an insight into the macroeconomic implications of individual economic behavior. Like its closely related sister, the *efficient-markets hypothesis* of finance (Sheffrin 1983, Chapter 4), it conjectures that profitable or utility-improving options are not left unexploited. But it is a systems characteristic that operates on a plane distinct from individual choices. It in no way depends on the particular detailed economic histories of individual agents. We can, of course, compare the realizations of X_t^e to, say, individual reports or surveys of individual expectations. We would be surprised if the rational-expectations hypothesis were empirically verified at the macroeconomic level and, at the same time, movements in individual expectations failed to track X_t^e. Nevertheless, X_t^e does not directly characterize any individual expectation nor even their means or other statistical features. It is a feature of the macroeconomy that reflects the intentionality of individual economic agents without being reducible to their individual intentional states.

4. THE IRONY OF IDEOLOGY

Reductionism in physical and life sciences faces a number of challenges. There are causally significant macro features of the world that do not seem to depend on the details of the underlying micro arrangements. Reductionism in economics faces a similar challenge, albeit with additional complications. Economics is an intentional science. Whereas physical and life sciences fear anthropomorphic, teleological, or intentional explanations, economics would be denatured without them. As a human science, it demands that observed behavior be connected to goals, choice, and other intentional states. Economists are skeptical of billiard-ball causation because it omits the human side of human agents and their behavior. Recent economics embraces the program of microfoundations, which denies the independent existence of macroeconomic quantities. The challenge for any antireductionist macroeconomics is to provide an account that both assigns an independent ontological status to microeconomic individuals and to macroeconomic aggregates *and* provides an intelligible account of the connection between the intentional states of the individuals and the behavior of the aggregates.

We have argued that Searle's (1995) account of social facts as a background of constitutive rules created through collective intentionality and constraining the actions of individuals provides a rich understanding of the independence of super-individual economic structures from particular economic agents while preserving channels through which the beliefs, intentions, choices, and actions of individuals influence the behavior of macroeconomic aggregates. The irony of the program of microfoundations is that, in the name of preserving the importance of individual intentional states and preserving the individual economic agent as the foundation of economics, it fails to provide any intelligible connection between the individual and the aggregate. Instead, it embraces the representative agent, which is as close to an untethered Hegelian World (or Macroeconomic) Spirit as one might fear in the microfoundationalist's worst nightmare.

NOTES

1. Presented at the conference on Issues in the Philosophy of Economics, University of Alabama at Birmingham, 19–21 May 2006. Thanks to Paul Teller and Harold Kincaid for useful discussions on an earlier draft.

2. Fittoussi and Velupillai (1993) attribute the coinage of *macroeconomics* to Ragnar Frisch in 1931. But that is not right; Frisch used the term *macrodynamics*, albeit in a similar sense. A discussion on the History of Economics Society's listserv indicated that Böhm-Bawerk referred to the *microcosm* and the *macrocosm* of a developed economy in a sense quite similar to modern usage of *microeconomics* and *macroeconomics* as early as 1891; while the earliest use of *macro-economic* (with the hyphen) recorded on the *JSTOR* journal archive is in an article by J.M Fleming (1938).

3. LeRoy (1983) provides a persuasive reading of Keynes on the relationship between the individual and aggregate marginal efficiency of capital—the key to the investment function.

4. I have described a pure representative-agent model, which is in fact very common. But the point that I making applies equally to most so-called heterogeneous-agent models, in which a small number of types of agents are representative of large groups in the economy.

5. See Hoover (2001a, Chapter 3) and the references therein for a fuller discussion.

6. By "billiard ball causation," Searle (1995, 139) refers generally to nonintentional efficient causes.

7. I am not committed to this being workable research strategy for the hydrologist. Philosophers and physicists (e.g., Auyang 1998 and Batterman 2001) suggest reasons why the behavior of individual molecules, treated merely as interacting individuals, may not account for the features of the observed macrophysical data. However that may be, the problem for the hydrologist will not turn on the intentional states of the molecules.

8. In fact, agent-based simulation models have been constructed (e.g., Tefatsion 2006), though none with the scope of typical calibrated macroeconomic models and, to the best of my knowledge, none by the school of economists most committed to the ideology of microfoundations.

REFERENCES

Auyang, S. M. (1998). *Foundations of Complex-System Theory in Economics, Evolutionary Biology, and Statistical Physics*. Cambridge, England: Cambridge University Press.

Batterman, R. W. (2001). *The Devil in the Details: Asymptotic Reasoning in Explanation, Reduction, and Emergence*. Oxford: Oxford University Press.

Cartwright, N. (1989). *Nature's Capacities and Their Measurement*. Oxford: Clarendon Press.

Fitoussi, J.P. & Velupillai, K. (1993). "Macroeconomic Perspectives." In H. Barkai, S. Fischer & N. Liviatan, Eds., *Monetary Theory and Thought*. London: Macmillan.

Fleming, J.M. (1938). "The Determination of the Rate of Interest." *Economica* N.S. 5 (19): 333–341.

Guesnerie, R. (1992). "An Exploration of the Eductive Justifications of the Rational Expectations Hypothesis." *American Economic Review* 82 (5): 1254–1278.

Haavelmo, T. (1944). "The Probability Approach in Econometrics," *Econometrica* 12 (supplement): iii-iv, 1–115.

Hacking, I. (1983). *Representing and Intervening*. Cambridge: Cambridge University Press.

Hausman, D.M. (1992). *The Inexact and Separate Science of Economics*. Cambridge, England: Cambridge University Press.

Heiner, R.A. (1983). "The Origin Predictable Behavior." *American Economic Review* 73 (4): 560–595.

Hendry, D.F. & Morgan, M.S., Eds. (1995). *The Foundations of Econometric Analysis*. Cambridge, England: Cambridge University Press.

Hood, W. & Koopmans, T., Eds. (1953). *Studies in Econometric Method*, Cowles Commission Monograph 14. New Haven: Yale University Press.

Hoover, K.D. (1994). "Six Queries About Idealization in an Empirical Context." *Poznan Studies in the Philosophy of Science and the Humanities* 38: 43–53.

Hoover, K.D. (1995). "Is Macroeconomics for Real?" *The Monist* 78 (3): 235–257.

Hoover, K.D. (2001a). *The Methodology of Empirical Macroeconomics*. Cambridge, England: Cambridge University Press.

Hoover, K.D. (2001b). *Causality in Macroeconomics*. Cambridge: Cambridge University Press.

Hoover, K.D. (2002). "A History of Postwar Monetary and Macroeconomics." In J. Biddle, J. Davis & W. Samuels, Eds., *The Blackwell Companion to the History of Economic Thought*, 411–427. Oxford: Blackwell.

Hoover, K.D. (2006a). "A Neowicksellian in a New Classical World: The Methodology of Michael Woodford's Interest and Prices." *Journal of the History of Economic Thought* 28 (2): 143–149.

Hoover, K.D. (2006b). "The Past as Future: The Marshallian Approach to Post Walrasian Economics." In D. Colander, Ed. *Post Walrasian Macroeconomics: Beyond the Dynamic Stochastic General Equilibrium Model*, 239–257. Cambridge: Cambridge University Press.

Jones, R.A. (1976). "The Origin and Development of Media of Exchange." *Journal of Political Economy* 84 (4): 757–776.

Keynes, J.M. (1936). *The General Theory of Employment Interest and Money*. New York: Harcourt, Brace & World.

Kim, J. (1978). "Supervenience and Nomological Incommensurables." *American Philosophical Quarterly* 15 (2): 149–156.

Kiyotaki, N. & Wright, R. (1993). "A Search-Theoretic Approach to Monetary Economics." *American Economic Review* 83 (1): 63–77.

Kiyotaki, N. & Wright, R. (1989). "On Money as a Medium of Exchange." *Journal of Political Economy* 97 (3): 927–954.

Klein, L.R. (1950). *The Keynesian Revolution*. London: Macmillan.

Koopmans, T., Ed. (1950). *Statistical Inference in Dynamic Economic Models*, Cowles Commission Monograph 10. New York: Wiley.

Kydland, F.E. & Prescott, E.C. (1982). "Time to Build and Aggregate Fluctuations." *Econometrica* 50 (6): 1345–1369.

Kydland, F.E. & Prescott, E.C. (1991). "The Econometrics of the General Equilibrium Approach to Business Cycles." *Scandinavian Journal of Economics* 93 (2): 161–178.

Liu, T.C. (1960). "Underidentification, Structural Estimation, and Forecasting." *Econometrica* 28 (4): 855–865.

Leontief, W. (1936). "The Fundamental Assumption of Mr. Keynes's Monetary Theory of Unemployment." *Quarterly Journal of Economics* 51 (1): 192–197.

LeRoy, S.F. (1983). "Keynes' Theory of Investment." *History of Political Economy* 15 (3): 397–421.

Levy, D.M. (1985). "The Impossibility of a Complete Methodological Individualist: Reduction When Knowledge is Imperfect." *Economics and Philosophy* 1 (1): 101–108.

Lucas, R.E. (1976). "Econometric Policy Evaluation: A Critique." In Karl Brunner and Allan H. Meltzer (eds.) *The Phillips Curve and Labor Markets.* Carnegie-Rochester Conference Series on Public Policy, vol. 11, Spring, 161–168. Amsterdam: North-Holland. Reprinted in Lucas, *Studies in Business-Cycle Theory,* 1981, 104–130. Oxford: Blackwell.

Lucas, R.E. (1980 [1981]). "Methods and Problems in Business Cycle Theory." *Journal of Money, Credit and Banking,* 12 (4): 696–715.

Lucas, R.E. (1987). *Models of Business Cycles.* Oxford: Blackwell.

Mäki, U. (1996). "Scientific Realism and Some Peculiarities of Economics." In R.S. Cohen, R. Hilpinen & Q. Renzong, Eds., *Realism and Anti-realism in the Philosophy of Science,* 427–447. Dordrecht, The Netherlands: Kluwer.

Mill, J.S. (1851). *A System of Logic, Ratiocinative and Deductive: Being a Connected View of the Principles of Evidence and the Methods of Scientific Investigation,* 3rd. ed., vol. I. London: John W. Parker.

Morgan, M.S. (1990). *The History of Econometric Ideas.* Cambridge, England: Cambridge University Press.

Nelson, A. (1992). "Human Molecules." In N. DeMarchi, Ed. *Post-Popperian Methodology of Economics,* 113–134. Boston: Kluwer.

Nowak, L. (1980). *The Structure of Idealization: Towards a Systematic Interpretation of the Marxian Idea of Science.* Dordrecht, The Netherlands: Reidel.

Putnam, H. (1975). "Philosophy and Our Mental Life." In *Mind, Language, and Reality (Philosophical Papers, vol. 2),* 291–303. Cambridge, England: Cambridge University Press.

Reiss, J. (2004). "Review of Kevin Hoover's Methodology of Empirical Macroeconomics." *Economics and Philosophy* 20 (1): 226–233.

Robbins, L. (1935). *An Essay on the Nature and Significance of Economic Science.* London: Macmillan.

Rosenberg, A. (1992) *Economics—Mathematical Politics or Science of Diminishing Returns.* Chicago, University of Chicago Press.

Samuelson, P.A. (1948). *Economics, An Introductory Analysis.* New York, McGraw-Hill.

Sargent, T.J. (1981). "Interpreting Economic Time Series." *The Journal of Political Economy* 89 (2): 213–248.

Sargent, T.J. & Wallace, N. (1975). "Rational" Expectations, the Optimal Monetary Instrument, and the Optimal Money Supply Rule." *Journal of Political Economy* 83 (2): 241–254.

Searle, J.R. (1995). *The Construction of Social Reality.* New York: Free Press.

Sheffrin, S.M. (1983). *Rational Expectations.* Cambridge, England: Cambridge University Press.

Simon, H.A. (1957). *Models of Man: Mathematical Essays on Rational Human Behavior in a Social Setting.* New York, Wiley.

Sims, C.A. (1980). "Macroeconomics and Reality." *Econometrica* 48 (1): 1–48.

Stigler, G.J. & Becker, G.S. (1977). "De Gustibus Non Est Disputandum." *American Economic Review* 67 (2): 76–90.

Tefatsion, L. (2006). "Agent-Based Computational Modeling and Macroeconomics." In D. Colander, Ed., *Post Walrasian Macroeconomics: Beyond the Dynamic Stochastic General Equilibrium Model*, 175–202. Cambridge, England: Cambridge University Press.

Trollope, A. (1869). *Phineas Finn*.

Von Mises, L. (1966). *Human Action: A Treatise on Economics, 3rd. ed.* Chicago: Henry Regnery.

CHAPTER 15

···

CAUSALITY, INVARIANCE, AND POLICY

···

NANCY CARTWRIGHT

INTRODUCTION

···

This chapter has five aims[1]:

1. To explain the puzzling methodology of an important econometric study of health and status.
2. To note the widespread use of *invariance* in both economic and philosophical studies of causality to guarantee that causal knowledge can be used, as we have always supposed it can be, to predict the effects of manipulations.
3. To argue that the kind of invariance seen widely in economic methodology succeeds at this job whereas a standard kind of invariance now popular in philosophy cannot.
4. To question the special role of causal knowledge with respect to predictions about the effects of manipulations once the importance of adding on invariance is recognized.
5. To draw the despairing conclusion that both causation and invariance are poor tools for predicting the outcomes of policy and technology and to pose the challenge: What can we offer that works better?

1. A Puzzling Study of Health and Status

It seems being poor is not good for your health. Consider the following remarkable observation

> Travel from the southeast of downtown Washington DC to Montgomery county in Maryland. For each mile travelled life expectancy rises by about a year and a half. There is a twenty-year gap between poor blacks at one end of the journey and rich whites at the other.[2]

This striking quote is from an eminent epidemiologist, Michael Marmot, who argues that there is a social gradient in health: The higher your status the better your health; and the phenomenon is widespread, observed in the highly unequal United States, in more equitable Scandinavia, and even in the illustrious British civil service.

But how does Marmot know that it is *status* that is the cause of the health differences and not for example the reverse? I want to describe one attempt to answer this—a study by Adams, McFadden, et. al., a group of prominent economists (including a Nobel prize winner) who use econometric techniques to investigate the causal relations between socio-economic status and health among elderly Americans. What matters for our discussion here is the way the study tests for causality, in particular the fact that it uses two different tests.

The first test of the Adams, McFadden, et. al. (2003) study looks for

- Correlations between health and status, holding fixed other postulated causes of status.

The second looks for

- Invariance of the estimated correlation across the sample period. Is the correlation that obtains in one period the same as that in another?

My puzzle was, 'Why two tests?' My first thoughts were that the authors are cautious. They offer two tests for the same claim interpreted in the same way: Low status causes poor health. This suggestion has an initial plausibility. The first test is of a kind widely used throughout the social sciences; it is just what we would expect under a *Suppes*—or *Granger*–style (Suppes 1970; Granger 1969, 424–438) theory of probabilistic causality. As for the second, invariance is the central characterizing feature of causality under a number of contemporary accounts in both economics and philosophy. Since any single test is likely to be flawed, the cautious scientist will aim for the convergence of results across different tests for the same thing.

If this were the aim though, the specific strategy employed in the study would be a mistake. On a variety of current invariance theories of causality, it is easy to produce scenarios on which Suppes-style causality holds, but the requisite invariance does not, for the very reasons that economists from Mill to Lucas, including the founders of econometrics, have stressed: The underlying arrangements that give rise to economic regularities are often not stable across time and can be highly sensitive to interventions. So the two tests must be testing for different things, perhaps two different kinds of causality.

I now think we should interpret the use of two separate tests differently. The first is a genuine test for causation.[3] The second is a test to see whether the causal relations confirmed to occur in one period by the first test continue by the same test to be confirmed to hold in a second period. The authors themselves claim that the second serves as a weak test for the usefulness of the estimated correlation for policy prediction. We should like to know

> Will the correlations that occur in the data set (and thus the causal relations they indicate) be invariant across the envisaged policy changes?

It is a small indication in that direction that they are invariant at least across the period of the data.[4]

Following their lead, I think we should interpret the first as a test for causation and the second as a step toward showing that the established relation is useful for predicting outcomes of proposed policy. This interpretation gives rise to the central question of this paper: What makes causal relations especially useful for predicting the outcomes of future policy and technology?

2. INVARIANCE IN ECONOMICS AND PHILOSOPHY

This two-step process is not peculiar to the Adams, McFadden et. al. study. It is to be found in many other places in the current literature on causality, notably in the accounts of James Woodward (2003), Judea Pearl (2000), the Glymour-Spirtes group (1993), and in David Hendry's (2000) work. In each of these, it plays the same role as in the Adams, McFadden, et. al. study. Each of these provides an account—a different account—of what makes a set of relations *causal* relations. Causal knowledge is valuable because of its importance for policy and planning; we suppose some kind of tight connection between causal knowledge and the ability to predict the results of manipulations. In all these accounts, it is some kind of *invariance* assumption that secures this connection.

On the philosophy side, I shall focus on Pearl (2000), Woodward (2003), and the Glymour-Spirtes group (1993), both because invariance is an explicit demand in their links between causal knowledge and policy prediction and because the link is seldom made in other accounts. It is easy to see this point by looking first at an account of causation where we might have supposed the link to be immediate, David Lewis's counterfactual account (Lewis 1993 [1973]). For Lewis, *C* causes

E just in case if *C* had not occurred, *E* would not have occurred, where the change from *C* to ¬*C* is supposed to occur by miracle; that is, nothing changes except *C* and whatever is causally consequent on that. Suppose then that we know with certainty that *C* causes *E* in this sense. What does that tell us about the effects on *E* should we manipulate *C*? Nothing—unless we are in a position to perform miracles. No inferences about strategies can be drawn from the fact that *C* causes *E* on Lewis's account without making additional assumptions.

This is exactly what both Woodward and Pearl do. Both add the assumption—the *modularity* assumption—that miracle-like changes are always possible with respect to any factor that can genuinely be counted a cause. Both Woodward and Pearl discuss only systems in which the processes connecting causes with their effects are discrete: There is always one last set of causal factors (the 'direct' causes) that operate just before the effect is produced. This provides them with an analogue of Lewis's assumption that the miracle happens at the last instant, which avoids a host of counterexamples and inconsistencies. They suppose that *C* causes *E* only if the law connecting *C* with the last set of factors that produce it can be replaced with a new law that dictates ¬*C* while nothing else changes that is not causally consequent from that. So knowing that *C* causes *E* tells us at least this about manipulation: It is actually possible for *C* to change and only *C,* and if that happens the requisite change in *E* will follow.

To see this, let us look at Woodward's work. I concentrate on him because he is probably the most vocal champion of invariance. Both Pearl and Woodward focus on systems of linear equations of a familiar sort, which I call *linear deterministic causal systems with probability measures.* The same form is also compatible with the more general Glymour-Spirtes scheme.

A linear deterministic causal system with probabilities looks like this:

$$x_1 \; c= u_1$$
$$x_n \; c= \Sigma a_{ni} x_i + u_n$$
$$\mathrm{Prob}(u_1, \ldots, u_n) = \ldots$$

where the *u*'s represent quantities not caused by any of the *x*'s, and the symbol *c=* means that the left- and right-hand side are equal and that the factors on the right are the direct causes of those on the left. Different theories of causality place a variety of different constraints on $\mathrm{Prob}(u_1, \ldots, u_n)$. In characterizing a linear causal system with probabilities, I take a minimalist stand and include none of these constraints. The system is defined by its triangular form, which reflects a number of usual assumptions about causality, for example, that causality is irreflexive and asymmetric.

For Woodward, two demands must be fulfilled for equations like these to be properly labeled 'causal'.

- *Level invariance:* The equation must remain invariant under any changes on right-hand-side variables 'by intervention'. (An intervention on a factor changes the law linking that factor with its direct causes to a law that sets that factor at some specified value, with no other changes than those causally consequent on that.)

- *Modularity:* There must be some way to change the other causal relations in a system that leaves any genuine causal relation invariant.

Within a linear deterministic causal system, if we assume that any functionally true association derives from the basic causal principles of the system, it can be shown that being level invariant is a sufficient condition for a functionally true association to be one of the basic causal principles (Cartwright, 2007). So level invariance can be seen as a representation of the triangular structure of a causal system and the underlying facts about causality that it reflects.

What then of modularity? Both Woodward and Pearl demand not only that a system of causal equations be triangular in form but also that it be modular. Why do they build this additional demand into their characterization of causality? The effect of this requirement is that each variable in a system[5] can be changed (by changing the law that governs it) as if by miracle, without changing anything else except the effects of that variable. What justifies this as a condition on causality? Woodward and Pearl both give the same reason as Adams, McFadden, et. al:[6] This addition allows us to use the relation in question to predict what will happen under manipulation. That is, I take it, why Woodward calls his account of causality indifferently an "invariance" account and a "manipulability" account.

The special kind of miracle-like interventions envisaged by Lewis, Pearl, and Woodward are important for manipulability in Spirtes, Glymour, and Scheines (1993) as well. Spirtes, Glymour, and Scheines (1993) have a 'manipulation theorem' that tells how to calculate facts about the new probabilities that occur after one of these special interventions from facts about the probabilities and causal relations that obtain before (Spirtes, Glymour & Scheines 1993, 75–81). But they are more cautious in their claims than Woodward and Pearl, for they do not assume modularity—that is, they do not assume that such interventions are always possible. Rather, they show how to calculate what would follow were such an intervention to occur.

3. A More Useful Kind
of Invariance

Modularity thus secures a sure connection between causality and predictability under manipulation. But how satisfying is this connection? In fact it will allow us to use a given causal relation for very few policy manipulations. That is because the kind of manipulations under which it guarantees invariance—and hence predictability from the laws of the system—are very special. They are just the kinds of 'surgical incisions' that we would demand in a controlled experiment, and these are very unlike real policy changes.

First, in policy cases we have little guarantee that causal processes are discrete; and even where they are, we seldom are in control of the direct causes of a factor we consider manipulating to produce some desired effects. Second, when we do manipulate some factor we generally find ourselves changing far more than that single factor and its direct consequences. We usually end up changing a number of other factors relevant to the effect and very often we change the very principles by which these factors operate as well.

As I noted in Section 1, this is a problem that economists have been sensitive too from Mill (1994 [1884]) through the founders of econometrics (especially Haavelmo (1997 [1994]) and Frisch (1997 [1938])) to Lucas (1981 [1976]). Perhaps that is why it is in economics that we find accounts that connect causation with more realistic kinds of manipulations. Consider David Hendry (2000), who sometimes suggests that causes are super$X$, where super$X$ is a combination of X and invariance. Hendry's most developed example involves weak exogeneity and invariance.

Weak Exogeneity:

Given $P(Y\&X, \beta U\gamma) = P(Y/x, \beta)P(x, \gamma)$, x is weakly exogenous to a vector of outcomes Y if the parameters γ of the marginal distribution have no cross-restraints with the parameters β of the conditional distribution.

Weak exogeneity is a nice characteristic because it ensures that the marginal distribution can be ignored in estimating the conditional distribution. But it is not essential. If we envisage changing x to control the probability of Y, it is the conditional distribution itself that matters for our predictions independent of how we can learn about it. I follow Hendry in illustrating with a case where the variable (x) we envisage manipulating is weakly exogenous to the vector of outcome variables (Y) we care about because it makes very clear the importance of the additional invariance assumption.

Suppose we think of changing the distribution of x in order to affect the distribution of Y. It may seem that we can predict the outcome from the formula for the conditional distribution. But that is not so. Changing β changes the joint probability distribution, and there is nothing that ensures that the new distribution will still be the same. In the original distribution, β and γ may have no dependencies but that does not show what happens if the distribution is changed. So Hendry adds a constraint and defines: x causes Y if and only if the parameters of $P(Y/x)$ stay fixed as we vary the parameters of the distribution of x. In the case where x is weakly exogenous to Y, this gives us the notion of *super-(weak)exogeneity*.

Super-(weak)exogeneity

Suppose x is weakly exogenous for Y. Then x is *super-(weak)exogenous* relative to a proposed intervention (say a change in γ) if the parameters of interest (say β) for $P(Y/x, \beta)$ do not vary under the intervention.

I am going to discuss Kevin Hoover's account of causality. I note here that it shares with Hendry's an important advantage vis-à-vis strategy over the Pearl/Woodward/ Spirtes, Glymour, and Scheines approach. For Hendry, causation is characterized relative to a proposed intervention as that intervention will actually occur. His definition of causality requires that the relation we should like to use to predict the outcomes of our proposed manipulations be invariant under exactly those manipulations. The others insist, instead, on the invariance of the relation under highly artificial manipulations, manipulations that might occur in a controlled experiment to test for a causal connection but would hardly ever be ones we envisage for a real application, either in setting policy or in building a device or an institution. Unlike the earlier philosophical accounts, the accounts of causality that Hendry and Hoover offer show why causal knowledge is good for policy prediction, as we think it is, whereas these others do not show this.

Despite its nice connection with policy prediction, there is a difficulty with Hendry's account: It doesn't seem to be an account of causality at all. That's because of Hendry's focus on the conditional probability. A factor x we consider manipulating to affect Y will do so given Hendry's invariance assumption just in case Y is probabilistically dependent on x. But it is one of the truisms of causal theory that probabilistic dependence (correlation) is not causation.

It is easy to see these points by looking at a case with dichotomous variables. By the laws of probability

$$P(E)=P(E/C)P(C)+P(E/\neg C)P(\neg C).$$

In order to increase the probability of E, we consider a manipulation that takes the probability P to a new $P,'$ where P' has an increased probability of C. Under Hendry's invariance assumption, $P(E/\pm C)$ is to stay fixed. So

$$P'(E)=P(E\backslash C)P'(C)+P(E/\neg C)P'(\neg C).$$

So the strategy works just in case $P(E/C) > P(E/\neg C)$. From this I conclude that the X in Hendry's account (Causality (relative to G) = super$X$ (relative to G) (i.e., X + invariance of X under G)) can easily be probabilistic relevance. But that's odd because we all believe that probabilistic relevance is not causation and adding on that the relevance relations are invariant under some envisaged manipulation does not seem to make it so.

There is a similar difficulty with Hoover. Hoover distinguishes between parameters (represented by Greek letters, $\alpha, \beta, \gamma, \dots$), which we control 'directly', and variables (represented by Latin letters $x, y, \dots$), which we do not. He takes the notion of direct control by us to be primitive in his account and uses it to define causal relations between quantities we cannot directly control. The account is restricted to quantities whose values can be fixed, albeit indirectly, by manipulations we can perform. Let Par_z stand for the set of parameters that determine z. Hoover's definitions require that

Hoover causation: x causes y iff Par_x is a proper subset of Par_y.

So x (Hoover) causes y iff anything we can do to fix the value of x partially fixes the value of y but not the reverse. So Hoover's characterization ensures that know-

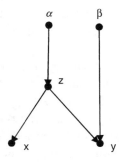

Figure 15.1.

ing causal relations allows us to predict the results of manipulations we might perform. But as with Hendry this characterization will sometimes count as causes factors that would usually be counted as mere correlates. Consider for instance the simple arrangement in Figure 15.1. Here the arrows are meant to represent relations that count as causal by whatever is your favourite other characterization of causality; we can for instance imagine building a machine with mechanical connections that fits the model in Figure 15.1.

We are thus faced with a trade-off. Hendry and Hoover connect causal knowledge with the predictability of the results of real manipulations, but they do not seem to be real causes; whereas Woodward, Pearl and Spirtes, Glymour and Scheines seem to connect real causes with manipulations, but they are not real manipulations.

4. CAUSALITY: WHAT IS THE USE OF IT?

Setting Hoover aside for the moment, there is another problem raised by the discussion of the approaches in the last section. Whether we start with real causation or some other relation and whether we end up with the ability to predict what happens under realistic or under miracle-like manipulations, what makes for the connection between the two is invariance. Woodward defines a causal relation as one that is invariant under miracle-like manipulations on right-hand-side variables. So clearly a Woodward-causal relation will predict accurately what happens under those kinds of exotic manipulations. The same is true for Pearl.[7] Hendry defines a causal relation as one that is invariant under various more realistic manipulations. So clearly a Hendry-causal relation will predict accurately what happens under those more realistic manipulations.

The logic is simple. We have an association. We assume it to be invariant under a particular kind of manipulation. So we are able to use that association to predict what happens under the specified kind of manipulation.[8] This logic works no matter whether the starting association is causal or not. Hendry's proposal is a case in point.

What good is causation then? It is generally supposed that there is some special connection between causation and policy prediction. Knowing the causal relation between two variables is supposed somehow to put us in a better position to predict what happens when we manipulate the first than simply knowing some arbitrary 'spurious' relation between them. But that does not seem to be the case.

Perhaps, despite my qualms in section 3), modularity is the answer after all. Both Woodward and Pearl insist that having the triangular form of a causal system is not enough to make a set of associations causal (with which I agree). There must in addition, they maintain, be some miracle-like manipulation possible on every variable in the system. Perhaps it is this very fact that makes causal knowledge so much more useful in general than knowledge of 'mere correlation'. I do not think so, for a number of reasons.

First, I do not think the claim is true. On the modularity thesis a relation is not causal unless there is some way to manipulate the cause, no matter how many other earmarks of causation the relation has. Nor is it enough that we be able to manipulate the cause, which may be hard enough; it must be possible to manipulate it in a very specific way—surgically, as if by miracle. I do not see any reason for believing this,[9] other than to satisfy the demand that causes should connect with strategies.[10]

My second worry is that the proposal does not do the job it is supposed to: It does not show what is special about causal relations over spurious ones. The modularity solution maintains that if a relation is causal, then there is always some manipulation of the cause that leaves that relation invariant, albeit an exotic manipulation. Suppose that is true. Then it is equally true for the spurious relation between joint effects of a common cause: There is always some manipulation on the first that leaves the relation between them invariant. Simply use the miracle-like manipulation hypothesized to be always available on the common cause to manipulate the first of the two joint effects. (For instance, in Figure 15.1 jiggle α to manipulate x by manipulating z.) This will change the second of the joint effects as well and leave the spurious relation between them invariant. Clearly, this manipulation will not itself be miracle-like on the first of the two related factors. But if the hope was to argue that causal relations are special because there is always at least some manipulation that leaves them invariant, miracle-like manipulations seem to have no special place.

This is indeed my third worry. Miracle-like manipulations of the kind under consideration are great for finding out about causal relations since they are the kinds of manipulations we would wish to make in a controlled experiment. But, as I urged in Section 3, they are not the manipulations we envisage in policy and technology. Yet we do think knowing causal relations is especially useful for planning. The possibility of invariance under miracle-like manipulations does not account for this.

An alternative to the modularity thesis that could explain the practical useful-ness of causal knowledge would be to argue that causal relations are more likely to be stable than are mere correlations. This might be supported by my own observa-tions that we often build both devices and institutions with shields to protect the structural arrangements from disruptions (Cartwright, 2007; 1989). But I cannot see how to use this to support the distinction I am looking for. Once a shield has been put in place to protect the internal arrangements of a structure, then causal relations and mere correlations may be equally stable. For instance, imagine that a shield is built around x,y,z, and β and their causal connections in Figure 15.1, allow-ing only the influence of α to penetrate. Then the spurious relation between x and y will be just as stable as that between z or β and y.

Conversely, one of the special worries in policy that we have noted is that causal relations are often not all that stable under manipulation. Not only is this the core of the famous Lucas critique; it was central to the philosophy of John Stuart Mill. It was, for instance, an important support for Mill's opposition to the subjugation of women. Mill admitted that, under the contemporary structure, putting women into positions of authority might well not produce good outcomes. But that, he maintained, would most probably change if the institutions of society changed to provide women the education and opportunity that would allow them to develop and exercise their native capacity for independent and creative thought (Guillin 2006).

In the end, the claim that causal relations are in themselves more stable than spurious ones seems too vague and too weak to serve as a defense of the vast effort we put into trying to secure causal knowledge. What seems true is that knowing causal relations is hugely useful for planning and prediction whenever we can add on the assumption that they will be stable. Nor is there anything wrong with an account of causation that needs to add this on. As Kevin Kelly[11] has pointed out, it is equally true of theories of mechanics (indeed, any theory for that matter) that they need what (following Wilfrid Sellars) I call *theory-exit assumptions* if they are to be put to use.

The problem is that this does not seem to distinguish between causal and non-causal relations. A simple kind of Humean view does better: If a causal relation is a universal association—it always holds whenever the cause occurs—then, clearly, causal relations are sure predictors. But this is not the case with any of our con-temporary theories of causality. It seems that causal relations will provide secure predictions about what happens under manipulations just in case they are invari-ant under those manipulations. But so, too, will noncausal relations. Why then do we take causal knowledge to be so much more useful than knowledge of other relations?

My worries here are not that we can find no difference between stable causal relations and other stable relations vis-à-vis manipulation. Consider a situation in which neither x nor y occurs but in which the principle "x causes y" holds. In this case, if we can change from not $\neg x$ to x, leaving the principle that x causes *y* unchanged, then we can ensure not only that *y* changes but also that it is *x* that changes it. This contrasts with the relation between *x* and *y* when the shield is erected in Figure 15.1 as described earlier. There if we change from ¬*x* to *x*, *y* changes as well. But the change from ¬*x* to *x* will not cause the change in *y*. We do not change *y* *through* changing *x*. This difference may be important ontologically. But it goes nowhere toward explaining why causal knowledge should be especially useful for prediction and control, worth buying at great cost.

5. ARE BOTH INVARIANCE AND CAUSALITY RED HERRINGS?

Sandra Mitchell (2003) points out that any true claim can be useful. Suppose we follow her lead. Perhaps causation and invariance are not the best keys to good prediction; they certainly are not the most direct. The simplest claim that will allow us to predict what will happen under manipulation is a true claim that describes just that.

This is in essence what Hoover-causation consists of. Causal claims, in Hoover's use of the term *causal,* describe what will happen under the manipulations we can perform. His account thus has the advantage over the other accounts discussed here. With Hendry it focuses on the kinds of manipulations we might actually carry out and does not restrict itself to miracle-like interventions. But it is more general. Hendry-causation secures prediction when a relation that predicts the outcome under current arrangements continues to occur under the proposed manipulation. Hoover-causation looks instead directly for information about what will happen given the manipulation. It does not depend on associations from the past continuing to hold across interventions.

Of course there is a sense in which this advantage is illusory. For nothing about Hoover-causation suggests how we are to come up with a Hoover-causal claim. But it can point us to an important lesson. Mill taught that economics cannot be an inductive science. Economic arrangements shift regularly in ways we generally cannot predict, and recent economics has made a point of how much more likely this is when interventions occur. Accounts that rely on invariance run just counter to Mill's cautions. Induction is what they offer, though with an explicit admission of Mill's worries, namely, use the associations of the past for future predictions, but use them only when they will continue to hold. We need something better.

Hendry himself is attentive to the fact that existing economic relations cannot be relied on to hold under manipulation. When it comes to forecasting, the use of causal models—even very accurate ones—can be dangerous, he warns, and for the very reasons that worried Mill: The arrangements correctly described in a causal model at one time are not likely to stay fixed across time. In his recent forecasting work Hendry develops a number of alternative modeling strategies that can be shown to give more accurate predictions across time if certain specified kinds of changes are occurring (Hendry & Mizon 2005; Andrews & Stock 2005).

What is surprising is that Hendry urges that these models may be good for forecasting but not for planning. Presumably that is because he imagines that the kinds of changes generally envisaged in planning are not the kinds that his strategies for forecasting deal with. What, then, do we do for planning? What kind of evidence will support policy and technology predictions and how is it to be marshalled and evaluated? That is the challenge, and it is an especially pressing one now that the call everywhere is for evidence-based policy. As methodologists we need to offer good counsel about just what counts as evidence when predictions about the effects of interventions are at stake, and about how to use that evidence. I do not think we have enough to say.

My conclusions in this chapter about the usefulness of causal knowledge are unfortunately negative. First, surprisingly, causation (at least under conceptions of it of the kind discussed here) seems irrelevant for reliable prediction in policy and technology planning. Causation without invariance will not do the job, and any invariant relation will provide reliable predictions regardless of whether it is causal. Second, invariance may be a good tool but, as Mill taught, it is altogether too rare and too unpredictable to do much for us. If we need to rely on invariance, we will not get very far, and the focus on it may distract attention from the fundamental challenge: to develop and understand methods—generally applicable methods—for evaluating policy and technology predictions.

In Sum

Overall my discussion raises a disturbing question. Causal knowledge is hard won. We spend a great deal of effort to achieve it. But what is the use of it once we have it? Invariance fares little better since it can generally not be relied on in economic policy considerations. What can we offer that is better?

NOTES

1. Research for this piece was assisted by the AHRC-sponsored project *Contingency and Dissent in Science*. I would especially like to thank Damien Fennell and Bengt Autzen for their help.

2. Marmot, 2004 , p. 2.

3. Because of my pluralist views about causality, I would more accurately say "a genuine test for one significant kind of causal relation."

4. Probably we shall really want to be exporting the conclusion to another population as well, not just to the same population under different policies, and that is clearly an even stronger move.

5. That is, any variable that appears as an effect in a law in the system of laws.

6. Actually, he gives the same reason—causes must be usable to manipulate their effects—for both level invariance and for modularity. I cite it only for modularity because level invariance does not provide manipulability unless modularity is added, and I, at any rate, have an alternative defense of level invariance.

7. Recall, Pearl demands of any equation in the causal system that it be invariant when the laws that determine the direct causes in that equation are replaced by laws that set the values of those direct causes at any arbitrary value.

8. A similar claim is true for Glymour, Spirtes, and Scheines, though their scheme is more complicated and provides more complicated inferences. (This is true, too, for Pearl when it comes to his full counterfactual account.) They begin with a mixed set of causal and probabilistic claims and then tell how to calculate what happens to various probabilities under certain miracle-like manipulations—but only supposing that the relations that support the calculation are invariant.

9. I argue for this more extensively in Cartwright (2001).

10. This indeed is how Pearl does defend it.

11. Kelly raised this point at my Center for Philosophy of Science lecture at the University of Pittsburgh, "Where Is the Theory in Our Theories of Causality," March 2006.

REFERENCES

Adams, P., Hurd, M., McFadden, D., Merrill, A., Ribeiro, T. (2003). 'Healthy, wealthy, and wise? Tests for direct causal paths', *Journal of Econometrics*, Volume 112, Issue 1: 3–56

Andrews, D.W.K. and Stock, J.H. (2005). "Inference with Weak Instruments," Cowles Foundation Discussion Paper No. 1530, 2005. Also in *Advances in Economics and Econometrics, Theory and Applications: Ninth World Congress of the Econometric Society*, Vol. III, (2006). R. Blundell, W.K. Newey and T. Persson (eds). Cambridge, UK: Cambridge University Press.

Cartwright, N. (2007). *Hunting Causes and Using Them*. Cambridge, England: Cambridge University Press.

Cartwright, Nancy D. (2006). 'Where is the Theory in our 'Theories' of Causality?' *Journal of Philosophy*, Vol. CIII, No. 2: 55–66. Also in Nancy Cartwright's *Hunting Causes and Using Them* (2007).

Cartwright, N. (2001). "Modularity: It Can—and Generally Does—Fail," in *Stochastic Causality (CSLI Lecture Notes)*, M.C. Galavotti, P. Suppes, & D. Costantini (eds), University of Chicago Press.

Cartwright, N. (1989). *Nature's Capacities and their Measurement*. Oxford: Clarendon Press.

Frisch, R. (1997 [1938]). "Autonomy of Economic Relations." In D.F. Hendry & M.S. Morgan, Eds., *The Foundations of Econometric Analysis*. Cambridge, England: Cambridge University Press.

Granger, C.W.J. (1969). "Testing for Causality and Feedback." *Econometrica* 37: 424–438.

Guillin, V. (2006). "Auguste Comte and John Stuart Mill on Sexual Equality: Historical, Methodological and Philosophical Issues." Ph.D. thesis, LSE.

Haavelmo, T. (1997 [1944]). "The Probability Approach in Econometrics." In D.F. Hendry & M.S. Morgan, Eds., *The Foundations of Econometric Analysis*. Cambridge, England: Cambridge University Press.

Hendry, D. F., & Mizon, G. E. (2005). "Forecasting in the Presence of Structural Breaks and Policy Regime Shifts." In D. Andrews & J. Stock, Eds., *Identification and Inference in Econometric Models: Essays in Honor of Thomas Rothenberg*. Cambridge, England: Cambridge University Press.

Hendry, D. F. (2000). *Econometrics: Alchemy or Science?* Oxford: Oxford University Press.

Lewis, D. (1993 [1973]). "Causation." In E. Sosa & M. Tooley, Eds., *Causation*. Oxford: Oxford University Press.

Lucas, R. E. (1981 [1976]). "Econometric Policy Evaluation: A Critique." In R.E. Lucas, Ed., *Studies in Business Cycle Theory*. Oxford: Basil Blackwell.

Marmot, M. (2004). *Status Syndrome—How your social standing directly affects your health and life expectancy*. London: Bloomsbury.

Mill, J. S. (1994 [1844]). "On the Definition and Method of Political Economy." In D. Hausman, Ed., *The Philosophy of Economics*. Cambridge, England: Cambridge University Press.

Mitchell, S. D. (2003). *Biological Complexity and Integrative Pluralism*. Cambridge, England: Cambridge University Press.

Pearl, J. (2000). *Causality: Models, Reasoning and Inference*. Cambridge, England: Cambridge University Press.

Spirtes, P., Glymour, C. & Scheines, R. (1993). *Causation, Prediction, and Search*. New York: Springer.

Suppes, P. (1970). *A Probabilistic Theory of Causality*. Amsterdam: North-Holland.

Woodward, J. (2003). *Making Things Happen*. New York: Oxford University Press.

CHAPTER 16

THE MIRACLE OF THE SEPTUAGINT AND THE PROMISE OF DATA MINING IN ECONOMICS

STAN DU PLESSIS

WHILE hard pressed in his second round with Tinbergen, Keynes played a trump: the Septuagint, he reminded Tinbergen, was produced by seventy translators working independently from the same Hebrew text and who emerged from their cells to find, miraculously, that they had produced seventy identical Greek translations of the Old Testament. And so the Septuagint was held to carry the (considerable) authority of independent confirmation. In modern econometric parlance, the Septuagint might be called a robust translation—a *believable* text for the Greek world—or it might simply have been the truth.

Turning on Tinbergen, Keynes (1939; 1940: 155–156) now wondered: "Would the same miracle be vouchsafed if seventy multiple correlators were shut up with the same statistical material?" and how else might we distinguish econometrics from "statistical alchemy"? It is a question that reveals unease with data mining: that rival and inconsistent models might proliferate; that design criteria might reveal the prejudices of the modeler, not the underlying economic structure; that parameter estimates might be biased; and that test sizes might be misleading. In short, data mining could compromise the believability of econometric models.

And yet there might not be an alternative to data mining if economics is going to be an empirical science practiced with the joint constraints of incomplete economic theory and nonexperimental data. We need data to complement our otherwise inadequate theoretical models, but because economic data is only rarely experimental, that means repeated use of the same data. This leaves modern econometricians to steer, as David Hendry (1997) said, between the Scylla of theory dependence and the Charybdis of data dependence.[1] Doing so with data mining seems to offend against norms of good conduct in econometrics; or at least, such norms were widely shared until recent advances in the theory of econometric modeling (Backhouse & Morgan 2000) and access to unprecedented computing capacity[2] had encouraged a revisionist literature in which the unhappy connotations of data mining have yielded to the view that data mining is a necessary part of a sensible modeling strategy. Indeed, data mining may even be a virtue (Hoover & Perez 2000). This chapter considers these developments and their implications for data mining in econometrics.

The organizing principle for this discussion of data mining is a philosophical spectrum that sorts the various econometric traditions according to their epistemological assumptions about the underlying data-generating process (DGP), starting with instrumentalism at one end and reaching claims of encompassing the DGP at the other; call it the DGP-spectrum. In the course of exploring this spectrum, the reader will encounter various Bayesian, specific to general (S–G) as well as general to specific (G–S) methods. A description of data mining and its potential dangers and a short section on potential institutional safeguards to these problems set the stage for this exploration.

1. SHARED EXPERIENCE

Chris Chatfield uses the term *data mining* to describe the situation in which "…models are not fully specified a priori, but rather are formulated, at least partially, by looking at the *same* data as those later used to fit the model" (Chatfield 1995: 426). This definition highlights the same features emphasised by Hoover and Perez (2000), that is the use of data to describe and estimate models on the one hand and the use of the same data to evaluate models against certain design criteria.

Both definitions emphasise the *dual use of data,* and this runs like a thread through the various habits associated with data mining in econometric modeling (Mayo 1996, Chatfield 1995, White 2000). Such dual use of data could manifest in more than one way, including (Spanos 2000): firstly, data snooping (including the visual inspection of the data), which occurs when the econometrician looks at the data in a more or less sophisticated way and allows such observations to influence model selection and model evaluation. Though endemic, at least in time series econometrics, according to White (2000), methodological concern over widespread data snooping dates back to Keynes's (1939) review of Tinbergen (1939) and even earlier to the concerns with stock market forecasting raised by Cowles (1933); secondly, an econometrician might select a sample or subsample iteratively to give acceptable parameter estimates. Keynes accused Tinbergen (1939) of this version of data mining when constructing time trends, leaving out or adding years at the endpoints of samples, which would have greatly influenced the slope of the trends.

A third variation of data mining occurs when an iterative process is followed to find a combination of explanatory variables (or regressors in a regression function) that satisfies some theoretical or other technical criterion. For example, an author might be investigating the potentially adverse impact of a tropical climate on per capita GDP growth. Levine and Renelt (1992) famously showed for data mining of this sort in cross-country growth regressions that depending on the combination of other regressors included in the model, the tropical effect might seem important or irrelevant to the long-run growth path. Finally, data mining also occurs when an author interprets the outcome of misspecification tests inductively, for example the non sequitur of interpreting observed autocorrelation in the residuals of a regression as evidence that the underlying population error has an autocorrelated structure. By respecifying his or her model with this amendment to the error structure, the econometrician will succeed only in hiding the evidence of model mis-specification uncovered in the preceding step.

The type of data mining at stake in this paper is this approach to modeling characterized by the dual use of data, not the branch of statistics, also called data mining, that studies the use of modern computer algorithms to search for patterns in large databases. Such statistical data mining is not an attempt to uncover any underlying DGP (Hand 1998). The boundary between this statistical study of local patterns in data and data mining as a tool of econometric modeling is not strict, though, indeed, econometrics at the instrumentalist end of the spectrum introduced earlier overlaps to an extent with data mining as a branch of statistics.

Data mining, at any point along the DGP spectrum, implies the repeated use of the same data. However, since so much economic data is nonexperimental (also called observational data) the repeated use of economic data is difficult, or even impossible, to avoid (White 2000; Spanos 1995). "Econometrics," so Schumpeter argued early on, "is nothing but the explicit recognition of this rather obvious fact" (Schumpeter 1933: 6).

The statistical considerations relevant to econometrics with nonexperimental data are different from those of experimental statistics (Hand 1998; Spanos 1995). Indeed, Spanos has argued that, given the inevitably widespread use of nonexperimental data in economics,[4] it would be more sensible to locate econometrics in the biometric tradition of statistics than in the experimental design tradition (Spanos 1995; 1999). A statistician operating in the experimental design tradition respects what Spanos calls a *predesignationist* rule that requires a specification of the relevant hypothesis before examining the data (Spanos 2000). In contrast, the biometric tradition was explicitly developed for settings where such rules are irrelevant.

The observational nature of much economic data implies an unknown sampling model, and this adds to the model uncertainty born from incomplete theoretical models. David Hendry (1995) provides a useful taxonomy of the levels of potential knowledge an econometrician might have about her model. At the first level the econometrician has complete knowledge of the probability structure of the event she is interested in, analogous to predicting the outcome of a fair die. But this level of knowledge is unobtainable for almost all econometric problems. At the second level of knowledge, the econometrician knows only that the die has six faces, but does not know whether the die is fair or not, that is, there is uncertainty about the probability structure. Econometrics becomes an estimation problem at this level, using observed frequencies to estimate the parameters of the underlying probability structure. But this level of knowledge is also unattainable in most econometric problems, since we do not know whether the die kept the same six faces, nor that it has precisely six faces.

Applied econometric research mostly occurs at a third level of knowledge, where our ignorance is extensive, in Hendry's (1995: 17) words: "we do not know how may faces the die has, how often the number 6 occurs on the faces of that die, whether it is biased, whether successive rolls are independent or are even conducted in the same way each time, and so on." At this level, we have a modeling problem where the observed data, past research and theory, must guide a speculative modeling strategy that is nevertheless disciplined by the data. Though much of econometrics occurs at Hendry's third level of knowledge, some of it pushes on into even less certain terrain where modeling is required for forecasting. At a fourth level of knowledge, the forecasting modelers are confronted with all the uncertainty of the third level as well as uncertainty about the invariance of the probability structure into the future. The model uncertainty assumed to be ubiquitous in econometrics is here understood to mean uncertainty at least at Hendry's third level.

This modeling challenge is particularly acute with small samples, since large samples show more variation in the variables allowing a more judicious choice of variables as well as allowing tests against hold-out samples (Pagan & Veall 2000). With large samples one might even appeal to White's theorem which guarantees the recovery, asymptotically, of the true DGP from an over-parameterised initial model as long as the initial over-parameterised model nested the true GDP (White 2005/1990).[5]

There is a widely held perception that data mining in the sense of a dual use of nonexperimental data in the context of model uncertainty is widespread (Greene 2000, Mayer 2000, Pagan & Veall 2000). Burger & du Plessis (2006) have measured the extent of data mining in applied econometrics by evaluating the modeling strategies employed in a random sample of papers drawn from academic journals in economics published in 2003. From the 75 papers in their sample 71 percent used nonexperimental data, and 89 percent showed explicit evidence of an iterative modeling strategy, of which the dual use of data associated with data mining is a common form.

For the remainder of this chapter, this combination of model uncertainty and observational data, which is associated with data mining in practice, will be treated as a shared experience for applied econometrics. While all the traditions considered here share this experience, they move beyond it with the guidance of different theories and techniques and in opposite directions. These traditions are often proponents of specific modeling strategies, and this is not by accident: a consequence of model uncertainty is that the modeler has no choice but to actively engage in model specification, which entails the following: formulating the model, estimating relevant parameters, and evaluating the model all of which occur in an "iterative and interactive way" (Chatfield 1995). But these "iterative and interactive" steps have to be taken with a watchful eye on the risks that are briefly explored in the following few paragraphs.

2. The Risks of Data Mining

The collection of research habits gathered under the heading of data mining has frequently furnished a stick with which to beat the econometric fraternity, and to cast doubt over the value of the considerable annual econometric output. It has also been used by proponents of specific econometric methods in their criticism of rival methods: Hendry (1997), for example, argued that Faust and Whiteman (1997a) had underplayed the "incipient 'data mining'" in the Real Business Cycle (RBC) and vector autoregression (VAR) methods, while Faust and Whiteman retorted that "every LSE-style paper reports extensive theory-free tailoring of the model that overwhelms any such alterations made in the RBC literature" (Faust & Whiteman 1997b: 192).

A recent example by Sullivan, Timmerman, and White (2001) show that these arguments are not just theoretical. Instead, they are based on the real risk that data mining might undermine the statistical inference at the heart of applied econometrics. In an investigation of calendar effects on the stock market, Sullivan et al. (2001) used a technique developed by White (2000) to evaluate the predictive power of different calendar-based trading rules, while accounting for the large number of potential rules among which the candidate rules would be selected. In this case, White's (2000) "reality check" is a procedure for finding consistent p-values to test the null hypothesis that the best calendar-based trading rule is no better than the expected performance of a benchmark of always being in the market.[6] The motivation for the technique is the risk—discussed in greater length in Section 2.1—that data mining changes the effective size of tests used in statistical inference, making it hard to distinguish between real effects and the outcome of chance and sampling error. Sullivan et al.'s (2001) results were startling: while a number of individual calendar effects were statistically significant, none of these remained so once the extent of data mining that had accompanied their discovery was factored in.

Stepping away from examples, the various risks posed by data mining could be divided into the following categories (Spanos 2000):[7] (i) selection of regressors; (ii) data and sample selection; (iii) diagnostic testing, and (iv) respecification. But these are only risks, and a framework is needed to understand when the risk is likely to lead to undesirable outcomes.

To that end, Spanos (2000) built on the econometric and philosophy of science literatures to derive a definition of "unwarranted" data mining. The latter occurs when a researcher (i) interprets data as evidence in support of a proposition (or theory or hypothesis), having (ii) searched either over the data to establish such evidence or having searched for data supportive of the proposition, and while (iii) the proposition would fail a severe test[8] on the same data. It is the combination of all three of these aspects that causes mischief. This is the definition of unwarranted data mining used throughout this chapter.

2.1 Searching for Regressors

The shared experience of data mining is the combination of model uncertainty and nonexperimental data. The risks posed by "searching for regressors" are closely related to model uncertainty while the nonexperimental nature of the data moves to the fore in the discussion of "data and sample selection" below. Due to model uncertainty, econometricians usually have considerable leeway in the choice of variables, the combinations of variables to be included, and the functional form of any estimable model.

The risk of unwarranted data mining looms large in this case, especially when the following iterative strategy is followed: Select combinations of potential explanatory factors iteratively until the coefficients of the model are statistically significant at a conventional level (such as 5 percent). In what has become a famous paper, Lovell (1983) used a Monte Carlo simulation to show that the probability of a type I error is much larger in such an iterative process than the 1 percent or 5 percent level reported for the final test.

For example, in the simple case where an econometrician had been searching for the "best" two regressors out of ten potential regressors—not an unusually large number for the empirical growth literature (e.g., Sala-i-Martin 1997)—in a simulation where the true DGP had precisely two regressors, Lovell found that the true significance level of a t-test with 5 percent nominal size was, in his simulation, a much higher 22.6 percent (Lovell 1983).

In this example the statistical tests conducted after a dual use of the data were no longer "severe" tests. There is a long literature in economics that explores estimation bias and implied changes to the size of tests from similar dual use of the data (Giles & Giles 1993; Granger, King & White 1995). Perhaps Leamer has articulated their collective concern most forcefully:

> This searching for a model is often well intentioned, but there can be no doubt that such a specification search invalidates the traditional theories of inference. The concepts of unbiasedness, consistency, efficiency, maximum-likelihood

estimation, in fact, all the concepts of traditional theory, utterly lose their meaning by the time an applied researcher pulls from the bramble of computer output the one thorn of a model he likes best, the one he chooses to portray as a rose. (Learner 1983: 36–37)

It is easy to see why an iterative modeling strategy would invalidate aspects of the traditional theory of inference, for example, the probability of at least one Type I error is 0.36 for 20 repeated tests on the same data where the size of each test was 5 percent and each null hypothesis was valid.[9] It would seem as if the probability of spurious results is very high in such cases (Hendry 2000). It is important to distinguish between the size of a single test and the size of a family of tests, and experiments, such as those of Lovell (1983) showed that the size of a family of tests rise sharply with a specification search in practice, just as in theory.

With the basis of traditional inference weakened, it becomes more likely that the final specification will show spurious relationships. This fear of spurious correlation is a prime reason for the professional suspicion of data mining in econometrics (Hoover & Perez 2000).

In response to this risk, one might follow Lovell's (1983) early recommendation that authors be required to state explicitly the extent of the search they conducted and to adjust the size of tests accordingly, for example, by using Bonferroni's correction for the family of tests or by using an equivalent single test as suggested by Godfrey and Veal (2000). Statisticians like Chatfield (1995) have argued along similar lines that the statistical report on parameter estimates remains incomplete until the model selection strategy is taken into account.

Section 4 returns to this recommendation, but as an empirical matter there is little evidence that it has had much impact on applied econometrics. Of the 67 papers that showed evidence of an iterative modeling strategy in Burger and du Plessis (2006), just 3 papers gave an indication of the extent of iterations involved, and only one of these allowed the extent of the iterations to influence the statistical inference. Further, the data mining of any one researcher working in a field of researchers represents only a fraction of the total number of searches (Denton 1985).[10] In such circumstances the appropriate adjustment to test size requires information about search paths in the entire literature. Uncovering such information is likely to run into severe difficulties given, *inter alia*, the observed reluctance of authors to publish an indication of their own searches.

2.2 Data and Sample Selection

A second variant of data mining is the iterative search for a data set. Such a search risks becoming unwarranted data mining when the modeler is willing to search over alternative data sets (differing in sample period, or nature, i.e., panel, cross-section or time series; frequency; or even different empirical measures of the same theoretical construct)[11] until the data yields an estimated model consistent with her theoretical priors.

This variant of data mining is unwarranted when the final model is offered as support for a theoretical proposition after following an iterative modeling strategy designed to confirm the theoretical proposition. The probability of a type II error is large in this case, as an estimated model contradicting the theoretical proposition is easily interpreted as evidence against the data, rather than evidence against the theory (Spanos 2000). For example, an econometrician might try out various interest rates and proxies of wealth until he or she finds a consumption function that satisfies his or her theoretical priors and which is then presented as the estimated version of a theoretical consumption function. But none of the failures encountered along the way were interpreted as evidence against the theory; rather they were interpreted as evidence that a particular interest rate (say) was inappropriate for the task at hand.

The use of "new data" is often mentioned as a potential safeguard against this variant of data mining (as it is also believed to be against other variants of data mining) (Granger 1999). "New data" might mean a new sample of the same population, or cross validation in cross-section data, or postestimation (hold-out) samples in time series, or a pure *ex ante* forecast.[12] The hope is that new data, especially when constructed by other researchers, would offer severe tests of the model at stake by introducing an element of objectivity in econometric modeling.[13]

It is especially for this reason that an *ex ante* forecast is sometimes thought to be the "gold standard" of model evaluation (Clements & Hendry 2005). However, Clements and Hendry have recently argued that this exaggerates the role that forecast performance can play in model evaluation (see also Sugden 1995). Their reasoning is based on eight dichotomies which, when taken together, undermines the view that forecast performance is a (or *the*) key test in model evaluation.

The themes of these dichotomies are: unconditional versus conditional models; internal versus external standards for forecast evaluation; checking constancy versus adventitious significance; *ex ante* versus *ex post* evaluation; one-step versus multistep forecasts; fixed coefficients versus updating; stationarity versus non-stationarity; and, finally, forecasting versus other objectives (Clements & Hendry 2005). Although this is not the place to discuss the details of these dichotomies, their collective impact is to undermine the (sometimes exaggerated) role given to a specific forecast performance in the process of model evaluation. Economists have to evaluate their projects carefully with respect to all eight of these dichotomies before making strong claims for the ability of an *ex ante* forecast to judge an econometric model.

It is possible to add an empirical observation to Clements and Hendry's (2005) theoretical caution, namely, new data is but little used to safeguard econometric models from unwarranted data mining. Burger and du Plessis (2006) found only 6 papers that used "new data" as a part of the model evaluation among the 75 papers examined by them.

2.3 Diagnostic Testing

Unwarranted data mining compromises not just estimation, but model evaluation too. Due to model uncertainty and the subsequent dual use of data, econometrics requires a discipline of postestimation model evaluation. But this discipline is poorly developed, as Clive Granger (1999) has lamented, with applied econometrics often reflecting greater concern with model inputs (for example, the estimation procedure) than with model outputs (for example, forecasts on new data).

Diagnostic testing is only infrequently an important criterion in model selection (Krämer et al. 1985),[14] and Burger and du Plessis (2006) found just 12 papers in their sample of 75 that included diagnostic testing in their modeling strategies. Kennedy (2003) has offered some reasons for the observed scepticism toward diagnostic testing, including that their validity depends on the validity of the estimated model, and that a series of such tests affects the sizes of these tests. These problems are compounded when the results of such tests are interpreted constructively in the respecification of the model, as discussed later.

These problems are not insurmountable and, for example, the G–S approach has a long literature arguing that the conditions required for informative diagnostic testing are crucial elements in a progressive modeling strategy.[15] But this confidence depends critically on the G–S goal of locating a statistically adequate model, which is congruent with the local DGP (LDGP) (Hendry 1995).[16] The other formal responses to data mining discussed later do not share this goal, and are, as a consequence, more circumspect about the potential safeguard from unwarranted data mining offered by diagnostic tests.

2.4 Respecification

Unwarranted data mining might also occur for a fourth reason, namely, the *ad hoc* adjustment of, say, the functional form of models in response to unfavorable output from statistical tests. In this way, the modeler uses the unfavorable statistical output inductively to respecify the model in such a way that, given the data, the same test is passed by the respecified model. It follows that the probability of passing this test with the respecified model is very high. But, by the same token, the severity of the test would have been greatly reduced (Spanos 2000).

Popper (2000/1959) had earlier argued that such ad hoc adjustments reduced the "empirical content" of a theory, where he defined the latter as the "class of potential falsifiers." He argued that any hypothesis could always be "immunized" against falsification by finite observations through the use of ad hoc auxiliary hypotheses. To avoid this he proposed a methodological rule, namely, that auxiliary hypotheses should increase, not decrease, the testability of the theory in question (Popper 2000/1959).

The dynamic specification of time series models has frequently served as a demonstration of this particular risk of data mining. An estimated macroeconomic time series model often shows evidence of residual autocorrelation, perhaps detected by the Durbin-Watson statistic. It is an easy step—though a *non-sequitur*—from this evidence to the conclusion that the stochastic error of the underlying DGP has an autocorrelated structure. A respecified model that corrects for this suspected autocorrelated error structure removes the evidence of autocorrelated residuals, even when no such structure exists for the errors of the DGP.

This is the danger of unwarranted data mining by respecification: the modeler shoots the messenger by eliminating the information content of statistical tests that were meant to warn the modeler that the estimated model conflicted with the data (Hendry 1980). Elsewhere, Hendry expressed the danger as follows:

> [*ad hoc* respecification] ensures that it [the model] matches where it touches—but otherwise leads to invalid inference...a revision process of gradually expanding a model and stopping at the first insignificant improvement maximises the initial contamination and hence the likelihood of false inferences. (Hendry 2000)

In summary, unwarranted data mining risks compromising the foundations of the associated statistical inference, especially by reducing the severity of tests.

In their recent reflection on data mining, Hoover and Perez (2000) suggested three possible attitudes toward the reality of data mining: First, don't do it, but if you must, then adjust the tests accordingly. Second, you can't avoid data mining, hence you should investigate and (somehow) report al possible model specifications. Thirdly, data mining is an essential part of reasonable econometrics, but needs to be implemented in the right way.

From the implicit data mining present in any examination of existing theories or existing data (Denton 1985, Greene 2000, Burger & du Plessis 2006) , and from the empirical investigation in Burger and du Plessis (2006), it is evident that the first response considered by Hoover and Perez (2000) is little practiced. This leaves the second and third attitudes to explore, but before turning to the various methodological responses entailed by those two attitudes, we take a short detour to consider possible institutional features, incentives, and disincentives, that might affect the risk of unwarranted data mining.

3. Institutional Considerations

The catalogue of risks associated with unwarranted data mining adds force to normative campaigns for appropriate reform to econometric method and practice. Nevertheless, and as Pagan and Veall (2000) recently observed, data mining remains ubiquitous despite decades of unease. Such persistence in the face of moral disapproval might encourage economists to investigate the positive causes of widespread data mining.

Following Pagan and Veall (2000) one could either argue that economists have revealed a preference for data mining or that data mining is a market outcome in the decentralized market for scholarly research and publication (Pagan & Veall 2000). Both interpretations open the way to an analysis of the incentive structure that supports data mining; that is, consideration of the formal and informal institutions of applied econometric research.

While such an analysis is beyond the scope of this chapter, the role that these institutions could play as a safeguard against unwarranted data mining is not. Editors, as intermediaries between the producers and consumers of econometrics, have the opportunity to impose standards that might facilitate the competitive evaluation of papers (Pagan & Veall 2000). To the extent that data is made available to referees, and the journal's audience, the direct feedback effect and the indirect feedback effect through reputation effect could strengthen safeguards against unwarranted data mining. Important results (especially with policy implications) might eventually be subjected to further tests, possibly by rival economists. In this way the passage of time (which creates new un-mined data) and the participation by rival researchers is likely to uncover fragile results.

The incentives created by editorial policies could also counter or nurture such critical evaluation of published work. For example, Denton (1985) warned of a "publication filter" whereby editors look more favorably on papers that report "significant" econometric results. Such a filter does not need formal or even informal enforcement by editors, as self-selection by potential authors who mine their models until they are able to report significant results, would achieve the same result[17] (Mayer 2000).

McCloskey and Ziliak (1996) recently updated their earlier study of applied econometric papers published in the *American Economic Review* during the 1980s with a similar study for the 1990s (Ziliak & McCloskey 2004). Their results suggest that Denton's "publication filter" might be more than a theoretical possibility even in leading journals. They found that no less than three-quarters of the papers published during the 1990s used statistical significance as the sole criterion for the inclusion of a variable (Ziliak & McCloskey 2004). Given such a standard, it is easy to see why an author might "self-select" not to submit a paper with "insignificant" coefficients.

Regrettably, the "publication filter" is not the only disincentive for evaluative work that might detect and discourage unwarranted data mining; there are few career rewards for such work, and, embarking on a replication might be read as a sign of sterile imagination by colleagues. Worse still, an attempted replication might then be viewed as a personal attack. Finally, repetition is hard, especially since the original data set and statistical algorithm is often hard to mimic[18] (Dewald et al. 1986).

In biology, a science where observational data is also regularly used in empirical investigations, it has long been recognized that such data places an extra burden on scientists to avoid misleading results. As the first editor of *Biometrika*, Francis Galton urged the distribution of data sets with papers, where practical, and the creation of a databank where such data may be accessed for critical reworking (Galton 1901). Ragnar Frisch matched Galton's sentiments when he announced, in the first edition, that *Econometrica* would, normally, publish "raw data" with applied papers to "stimulate criticism, control and further studies" (Frisch 1933).

While *Econometrica* has not, in the main, found it useful to implement the policy envisaged by Frisch, the *Journal of Money, Credit and Banking* launched the *Data Storage and Evaluation Project* in 1982 to facilitate the evaluation of econometric results.[19] But even there, Dewald, Thursby, and Anderson (1986) found it remarkably difficult to replicate published results, often due to errors, but also because data and programs had not in fact been stored.

The optimistic perspective of Pagan and Veall (2000) on the ability of replication and criticism in journals to expose and discourage unwarranted data mining should, therefore, be tempered with two observations: replication is difficult in economics and the incentives for such research may be weak. As a consequence, replication remains scarce and refutations scarcer still (Greene 2000).

Aris Spanos once claimed that he knew of no "economic theory that was ever abandoned because it was rejected by some empirical econometric test, nor was a clear-cut decision between competing theories made in lieu of the evidence of such a test" (Spanos 1986) and Lawrence Summers asked his readers to identify even a single "meaningful hypothesis about economic behaviour that has fallen into disrepute because of a formal statistical test" (Summers 1991). Because Summer's challenge came with no incentive to respond, Keuzenkamp and Magnus (1995) offered a prize[20] to any reader that was able to offer evidence to disprove Spanos and Summers. Nobody won.

Such claims are anecdotal though, and counter-anecdotes exist: Baumol's (1986) case for (an absolute version of) the convergence hypothesis suffered what appears to have been a conclusive refutation at the hands of DeLong (1988). Pagan and Veall (2000) offered further examples to strengthen their claim that the important hypotheses in economics are examined with vigor and sometimes overturned, such as one important claim by Alesina and the same sceptical Summers.[21]

Notwithstanding, there are few strong incentives and many practical hurdles for replication in applied econometrics. It is not surprising that the supply of such papers is modest, making it hard to have confidence that the critical discussion in economics will provide a strong safeguard against unwarranted data mining. Happily, recent developments in the theory and practice of econometric modeling might offer additional safeguards.

4. DEVELOPMENTS IN THE THEORY OF ECONOMETRIC MODELING

The four recent econometric responses to the challenge of data mining considered in this section move beyond a defense of prevailing practice, to build cases for progressive reform. I say *progressive,* because these are not calls for a return to stricter rules to avoid data mining. These are examples of the second and third response suggested by Hoover and Perez (2000), according to which data mining is seen as a crucial (or at least an inevitable) part of a sensible modeling strategy that uses the vast computing power offered by modern information technology (Hand 1998).

All four modern responses start from the common experience of grappling with model uncertainty and usually with nonexperimental data. However, the direction econometricians take from this shared experience depends on how they conceptualize the goal of econometric modeling. Specifically, the different positive approaches to data mining move apart from the shared experience in pursuit of different ontological and epistemological visions of the underlying data generating process (DGP).

Three of these are inductive strategies, the first of which is built on a radical ontology that rejects the very concept of a DGP (Section 4.1). The differences between the other three strategies are epistemological, with disagreement on the ability of the modeling process to discover the DGP. The DGP moves from the periphery to the center of the modeling exercise in the final response (Section 4.4). In that approach, the objective is to uncover the (local) DGP, and the beneficent data mining exercise proceeds deductively from a statistical model that the econometrician claims to be a valid reduction of the (local) DGP.[22] The four strategies are presented in turn, while moving along the DGP spectrum from the nihilistic extreme to the goal of encompassing the (local) DGP at the opposite pole.

4.1 A First Inductive Response: Robust Talk

Data mining poses not only a risk to the formal qualities of statistical inference in econometrics, but as a result thereof, also compromises the believability of particular models from the perspective of their consumers: other economists, policy makers and the broader public. Since the econometrician is uncertain about the appropriate model and has to discover the latter with observational data, the incentive for an applied econometrician who intends to persuade her clients of a model's veracity, is to select one (or a few) preferred estimation(s) iteratively and only to report these. More especially, the many specifications that yield results in conflict with the preferred model go unreported.

These incentives are understood by the customers of econometrics, too—or so argued *inter alia* Cooley and LeRoy (1981), Leamer (1983) and, more recently, Mayer (2000)—and these customers are correctly sceptical of applied econometric output, a strategic setting Cooley and LeRoy (1981: 826) described as "nearly a zero-communication information equilibrium. Researchers have the motive and opportunity to represent their results selectively, and the reader, knowing this, imputes a low or zero signal-to-noise ratio to the reported results." Their claim was followed by Leamer's emphatic assertion that "[h]ardly anyone takes data analysis seriously. Or perhaps more accurately, hardly anyone takes anyone's else's data analysis seriously" (Leamer 1983: 37). At stake is the quality of the scientific discussion in applied economics and not so long ago Peter Phillips saw a "huge credibility gap that exists between economic theory, empirical evidence and policy prescriptions" (Phillips 1988: 357).

This risk to the scientific discussion in economics is not simply theoretical, as survey evidence suggests that a large proportion of economists are sceptical of econometric output.[23] The first class of formal responses to the challenge of data mining discussed here is an attempt to shift econometrics out of this "zero-communication information equilibrium," that is, to improve the quality of scientific debate.

The recommendations in this class are so many attempts to remove the potentially deceptive aspects that might undermine applied econometrics. Mayer (2000), for example, sketches an "idealized—and simplified—picture of science" in which different econometricians, investigating the same hypothesis with the same data would emerge, in the manner of the legendary translators of the Septuagint, with the same model. The proliferation of models, and the doubtful power of applied models to conclusively reject empirical hypotheses in economics, shows that this idealisation does not obtain in economics. For this reason Mayer (2000) chooses to depict data mining as a communications problem and his proposed remedy is to encourage authors to report more than just the final specification, especially that they report specifications that conflict with the final model, as such information would be valuable to the reader.

Edward Leamer agrees with Mayer that data mining undermines the "atmosphere of econometric discourse" (Leamer 1983: 43). In a hierarchy of statements starting with "truth" at the top, followed by "facts," "opinions" and "conventions" at the bottom, Leamer (1983) argues that we rarely reach as high as "facts" and never in econometric modeling. We bring our opinions to the modeling exercise in econometrics, argued Leamer in this severe interpretation of model uncertainty, and these opinions are "whimsical." Consequently the consumers of econometric output have no confidence in any particular estimated model.

Since whimsical results fail to convince either economists or the public, Leamer argued, the focus in econometrics had to shift to producing more "robust" results, that is, results that do not depend on a narrow range of opinions. And to that end he recommended that the econometrician calculate the implications of many different possible models and then to report the "extreme estimates" of the estimates for particular variables, the width of which will indicate the fragility of inference based on individual models from the class considered. If we took our model uncertainty more seriously, as Leamer (1983) argued, we would uncover how fragile most of our estimates are, and the humble and transparent communication of these fragile results would clear the air that has been darkened by data mining.

Leamer recognizes the shared experience of model uncertainty and nonexperimental data identified earlier. But he combines this with a radical view of the purpose of econometric modeling, in which he rejects any attempt to uncover the underlying DGP. He argues that we do not know the underlying data generating mechanism, we will not discover it *en route* with our modeling, nor is it even useful to assume that such a thing as the "true" DGP exists (Leamer 1983). Woodward (2006) has recently argued that such a "radical subjectivism" about the DGP is necessary for the extreme-bounds approach to offer an attractive modeling strategy.[24]

This emphasis on robust correlates with the goal of improving communication follows an inductive argument, but it avoids running into the logical problems associated with induction by the very modesty of the goals; the underlying idea is to update the economist's (possibly whimsical) priors about the issue at hand by learning from the data.

Levine and Renelt (1992) implemented Leamer's strategy on one of the most heavily mined data sets in macroeconomics, the cross section data used in the empirical growth literature. They found, however, that very few of the usual suspects in the literature were robust correlates of cross-country growth.

But, Levine and Renelt made no allowance for the quality of the models they investigated; all of which were treated equally, as so many opinions. Building on their result, Sala-i-Martin (1997) suggested considering the whole distribution (across rival models) of a parameter by calculating the weighted average of the estimated parameter values and of their variances, across all possible models in which it occurs.[25] He then ran 2 million regressions to cover his conception of all the possible permutations of the growth regression. In this way he was able to identify 22 apparently robust variables.

More recently, and working with Doppelhofer and Miller (Sala-i-Martin, Doppelhofer, & Miller 2004), he used a technique between the OLS estimates of the 2 million regressions and a fully Bayesian model averaging called Bayesian Averaging of Classical Estimates (BACE). The assumptions about the DGP remains as agnostic as before, but they are able to report that: "When we examine the cross-country data usually used by growth empiricists using BACE, we find striking and surprisingly clear conclusions" (Sala-i-Martin et al. 2004). They found 18 significant correlates with economic growth out of a potential 67, and their emphasis remains on clarity of communication, without making any claim about the underlying DGP.

The modesty of their claim is clear from those variables identified as robust correlates of growth in both Sala-i-Martin (1997) and Sala-i-Martin et al. (2004). Of the 18 robust correlates in Sala-i-Martin et al. (2004) 3 had been assumed robust in Sala-i-Martin (1997), that is, the level of initial income, life expectancy at the start of the period, and primary school enrolment at the start of the period. Only 8 other variables were identified as robust by both studies, they were 3 dummy variables (Spanish colony, Latin America dummy, and Sub-Saharan Africa dummy), 3 religion fractions (fraction Confucian, fraction Muslim, fraction Buddhist) and 2 other variables (fraction of GDP in mining and the number of years as an "open" economy). This set is doubtless easy to communicate, but makes no attempt at uncovering anything that might be thought of as underlying causes, in the way that, for example, Acemoglu and Johnson (2005) have done. However, this is not a telling criticism against a radically subjectivist approach that aims only at improving the communication of econometric results in the face of the extensive data mining that is likely to result from model uncertainty and nonexperimental data.

4.2. A Second Inductive Response: The "Reality Check" and RETINA

Halbert White (2000) has been concerned with data mining in econometric models designed for forecasting, and has offered a rigorous test to reduce the risk of confusing skill and luck in such models. This reflects a concern with the risk posed by data mining to the usual process of statistical inference, especially of finding "significant" effects through data mining. A relevant hypothesis in exploring this question is whether the effect under investigation would outperform a benchmark model that would hold in the absence of the postulated effect. He calls this test the "Reality Check," and the challenge is to design a procedure for testing this hypothesis given the reality of data mining.

White's method starts with the construction of a statistic that captures the null hypothesis of "no predictive superiority over a benchmark model" for a set of k postulated effects. Identifying the most promising of these effects and comparing its outcome with the benchmark, without taking into account the specification search over many alternative effects, leads to the calculation of a naïve p-value for this hypothesis. White (2000) constructed a bootstrapping procedure for calculating the actual p-values relevant to the null hypothesis. This reality check yields dramatic results, for example White shows that the most promising among a class of stock-market prediction rules has a naïve p-value of 0.036, suggesting a statistically significant effect. But once the bootstrap reality check had been used to account for the specification search, the p-value associated with the most promising forecasting rule jumped to 0.204 (White 2000).

As stated, the DGP plays little role in White's reality check, but the DGP could be introduced along the following lines: White is concerned with identifying the "truly best" forecasting model, and this would match the DGP if the latter was simple enough and time invariant over the relevant data sample and forecasting horizon (not unlike the local DGP in section 4.4 below). However, this is not a step White (2000) felt compelled to take because his focus remained on forecasting performance.

The reality check is a systematic approach that protects econometricians from being impressed by spuriously accurate forecasts on mined data, such as the example by Sullivan et al. (2001) discussed in Section 2. Such a procedure could be automated and, indeed, White has suggested a relevant algorithm that combines the focus on forecasting with considerations such as flexibility in functional form (allowing for nonlinearities and interaction terms), and parsimony.

The algorithm is called Relevant Transformation of the Inputs Network Approach (RETINA) (White 1998) and has since become available for wider use (on GAUSS and MATLAB platforms) (Perez-Amaral, Gallo, & White 2003).

The four stages of the RETINA algorithm are discussed extensively in Perez-Amaral, Gallo and White (2003) and Castle (2005). Stage 1 entails preliminaries such as data transformation and a three way splitting of the data into subsamples. Stage 2 is a step-wise model search using only data from the first subsample, but tested in an out-of-sample forecast on the second subsample. This leads to a preferred model. Stage 3 uses the second subsample to search for a more parsimonious version of the preferred model, which will again be tested out-of-sample against the third subsample. Finally in stage 4 the algorithm repeats stages 2 and 3, but with the ordering of the subsamples reversed. The final preferred model will have the best forecast performance over the entire sample.

RETINA is a specific-to-general algorithm that selectively adds variables to a model with the goal of good forecasting ability within a parsimonious model. As such, it is another inductive approach to data mining; but, in contrast with the focus on better communication in the previous method, the emphasis here is on improving out-of-sample forecasts. It is an appeal to the old gold standard of econometric modeling, that is, forecasting, to show that the inevitable data mining yielded a "useful model." And though it would be possible to find a minor role for the DGP in this procedure, that would be step beyond what the proponents of the procedure feel comfortable to take; note, for example, how Perez-Amaral, Gallo and White describe RETINA's goal: "Identify a parsimonious set of (transformed) attributes likely to be relevant for predicting out-of-sample" (Perez-Amaral, Gallo, & White 2005).

4.3 A Third Inductive Response: Automated Model Selection with PIC

Peter Phillips and Werner Ploberger (1996) have developed a third inductive approach to data based model selection for which they have also created an automated modeling algorithm. The DGP takes an even more central role here, as a regulative idea,[26] even if the goal of the modeling exercise is not to uncover the DGP.

The statistical foundations for Phillips and Ploberger's approach is the earlier work on stochastic complexity by Rissanen (1986). Building on these foundations, Phillips and Ploberger are able to provide a useful (and consistent) modeling strategy as well an epistemological critique of what econometricians can hope to achieve given that "the true model for any given data is unknown and, in all practical cases unknowable"(Phillips 2003: C26).

Their agnosticism about the DGP is a tempered version of Rissanen's radical empiricism, about which he leaves little doubt when he expresses the wish to "remove the untenable assumption of data generating systems and 'true' parameters, we instead regard the class of models to provide a language in which to express the regular features in the data" (Rissanen 1986).[27] Phillips (1996) used this last extract from Rissanen to introduce his ideas on the DGP, and he has often referred favorably to the concept of a model providing a "language in which to express the regular features of the data".

But Phillips and Ploberger do not follow Rissanen all the way to an ontological rejection of the DGP.[28] In contrast, they use the DGP to derive limiting theorems for the ambitions of econometric modeling that determine quantitative bounds or limits to how close an actual econometric model can approach the DGP (also called the "proximity bound").[29] This limit is a positive function of the number of parameters in the initial model and a function of the nature of the data, for example, the proximity bound is wider for trending data (i.e. it is harder to find good models for trending data) (Ploberger & Phillips 2003).

The relevance of this theorem for data mining lies in the result that even with infinite data, a model cannot cross over the proximity bound; model uncertainty is not just a small sample problem in this conceptualization.[30] Phillips and Ploberger's large sample result implies the need for a yardstick with which to measure rival models in finite samples. To this end, they introduced a Bayesian information criterion, called the Posterior Information Criterion (or PIC), which is technically a posterior odds criterion that indicates which of the rival models are best supported by the data, after factoring in a penalty for the number of parameters in the model (Phillips & Ploberger 1994). The PIC has attractive small- and large-sample properties; for example, it is asymptotically equivalent to the more familiar Bayesian Information Criterion (BIC) (Phillips & Ploberger 1994) and it attains the proximity bound asymptotically (Ploberger & Phillips 2003).

It is this last result—that the PIC (and other Bayesian information criteria)—attains the proximity bound asymptotically, which provides a safeguard against unwarranted data mining. A model selected after an extensive specification search guided by the PIC is less likely to be spurious than models selected with less auspicious criteria, such as the coefficient of determination. Further, this model selection strategy can be automated and Phillips and Ploberger were pioneers in the field of automated model selection with the purpose of building good forecasting models, or what they have called "data based automation" (Phillips 2005). Their data-based automation uses the PIC to help the econometrician with difficult, but important decisions, such as the selection of an appropriate lag length, the inclusion or otherwise of an intercept, the specification of a trend, and the inclusion and timing of structural breaks (Phillips 1995). A very exciting prospect with this algorithm is its potential for offering a Web-based interface that would allow modelers to access the main algorithm via the Internet (Phillips 2005).

In addition to its use as a model selection criterion, the PIC has also been extended for purposes of comparing rival forecasting models, in which case it is called the forecast-encompassing PIC criterion (PICF) (Phillips 1995). Since the PICF is automatically available for each model specified in this way, it is also possible to combine the forecasts of various models by weighting their forecasts by their posterior likelihoods. This method is not only theoretically attractive, but practical too, as Phillips has demonstrated to encouraging effect with two well-known data sets in the macroeconometric literature (Phillips 1995).

Using an information criterion such as PIC as a model selection criterion is precisely how Granger, King, and White (1995) suggested the risk of unwarranted data mining might be diminished. They preferred an inductive model selection criterion based on a metric that measures the gap between the model and the DGP, to the deductive model selection criterion based on the theory of reduction, which is the topic of the next subsection and which is built around a set of criteria for an empirical counterpart to the (local) DGP.

4.4. A Deductive Response: Probabilistic Reduction

In the course of twenty-five years the G–S method (also called the LSE method, or sometimes the Hendry method) has risen to take a leading place among the rival methods for econometric modeling.[31] It is a tradition often associated with the London School of Economics, especially with David Hendry (though lately at Oxford) and collaborators. The core theoretical contribution of this method is the use of probabilistic reduction theory as a framework for empirical modeling, a theory that conceives of the entire modeling process as a series of reductions from the "unknown high-dimensional distribution" which is called the Data Generating Process (DGP), or alternatively the Haavelmo distribution (Spanos 1989). While probabilistic reduction theory is abstract, the G–S modeling approach is a practical analogue or embodiment thereof and designed to facilitate data-based econometric modeling (Campos, Ericsson, & Hendry 2005b).

The high dimensionality of the DGP implies that no econometric model could be its empirical counterpart, a view also shared by the three alternative approaches to data-based modeling discussed earlier. The differences between these approaches lie in the next step: While some discard the idea of the DGP and focus instead on clear communication, others decide to focus on forecasting, and Phillips and Ploberger propose a method for approaching the proximity bound defined relative to the DGP.

In contrast with those approaches, the G–S literature introduces a new concept to the debate, the local DGP (LDGP), which is a valid reduction of the DGP and is a smaller probabilistic model (a well behaved Haavelmo distribution) showing the parameters of the interest for the project at hand. Defining the parameters of interest for a particular project is, in fact, the first of ten steps in the reduction sequence. It is followed by data transformations and aggregation; sequential factorization; data partition; marginalization; mapping to stationarity; conditional factorization; constancy; lag truncation and functional form (Campos, Ericsson, and Hendry 2005b). A valid reduction path from the true DGP to a well-behaved LDGP entails no loss of information.

The econometric model will be a postulated empirical counterpart to this LDGP, and it is connected via the valid steps of reduction with the DGP itself.

Once the LDGP has been conceptualized, the implementation of G–S starts with an overparameterized general model (generalized unrestricted model or GUM), which is conjectured to nest the LDGP.

The next step is crucial in the G–S logic, and it is also the critical point where the G–S method tries to dispel concerns with unwarranted data mining. This critical step is to determine whether the GUM provides a statistically adequate approximation to the LDGP, that is, whether the GUM is a congruent description of the LDGP in Hendry's terms (Hendry 1995). A dominant (or encompassing) congruent model is one that accounts for the information in (i) the relative past; (ii) the relative present; (iii) the relative future; (iv) information from economic theory, which helps to define the parameters of interest; (v) information about measurements; (vi) information in rival models (again subdivided by relative past, present, and future) (Hendry 1995).[32]

A battery of mis-specification tests is used to establish the congruency of the GUM, and if the GUM is congruent, a series of simplifications are implemented to uncover a parsimonious econometric model without unacceptable loss of information. Each simplification is tested for a loss of information, and whether it leaves the simplified model congruent with the LDGP. These simplifications proceed deductively as a series of restrictions on the GUM, which is now treated as congruent with the LDGP. This series of deductive tests and the deductive reduction of the DGP to the LDGP explains why the G–S method is categorized as deductive in this chapter and contrasted with the various inductive approaches considered earlier.

Critics have raised a number of objections to G–S modeling, and the following paragraphs consider those that are relevant to data mining: First, the layers of testing in this explicitly iterative modeling strategy has exposed the G–S method to the suspicion of unwarranted data mining (Faust & Whiteman 1997a). Proponents of the G–S method have answered these concerns by, first, distinguishing warranted from unwarranted data mining (Spanos 2000) or distinguishing constructive from pejorative data mining (Campos & Ericsson 1999) and, second, arguing that the data mining in G–S is warranted or constructive.

The G–S argument that the form of data mining implicit in the G–S tradition is warranted is based on the following argument: The G–S authors allow that the validity of diagnostic tests depend on the validity of the estimated model. To establish the latter we need to draw a distinction between testing primary hypotheses on the one hand and mis-specification tests, on the other. Mis-specification tests are Fisher tests, that is, tests "without" the boundaries of the postulated model, while primary hypotheses are estimated "within" the bounds of a postulated model. The null-hypothesis under a mis-specification test is that the postulated model adequately describes the data while the alternative hypothesis is the non-null. A rejection of this null hypothesis does not provide any information about a reasonable departure from the null that might offer better description of the data (Spanos 2000).

Failed mis-specification tests are not treated constructively and are not used to redesign the GUM so as to immunise the GUM against a given test, a step that would have introduced concerns over the respecification bias (discussed earlier).

Instead a rejected GUM is discarded and the econometrician is required to rethink the model before formulating another estimable GUM (Spanos 2000).

Mis-specification tests are valid in this purely negative role of providing once-off tests of the postulated GUM, and they are explicit attempts to circumvent the dangers of data mining with diagnostic tests. "The valid aspect of econometrics is its destructive role" said Hendry and added "No sufficient conditions for validating models can exist in an empirical science; and failure to reject one of the necessary conditions does not establish that the model is invalid, but only that it is not demonstrably invalid" (Hendry 2000/1985: 275–276).

Second, Hoover and Perez (1999) raised the possibility that simplification of a congruent model might be path dependent. In principle the various endpoint models could be tested for encompassing, but given the tremendous labor involved in tracing even a single path given a fairly general GUM, this rarely happens in practice.

Third, the G–S method might lead to overfitting, by including variables that are opportunistically present in the GUM. And, finally, since the simplifications are performed iteratively on the same data set, the test statistics and especially the size of the tests cannot be interpreted in the standard fashion. Hoover and Perez (1999: 169) call the G–S test statistics Darwinian, that is, "the tests statistics for any specification that has survived such a process [of reduction] are necessarily going to be 'significant.' They are 'Darwinian' in the sense that only the fittest survive", but there is uncertainty over the size of such "Darwinian" test statistics.

This last criticism has been answered in theory and all three have been answered in practice. First, where theory is concerned the proponents of the G–S method have appealed to a theorem by Halbert White (2005) on the asymptotic size and power of a specification-based model selection procedure such as G–S. White (2005) shows that a general model that encompasses the LDGP will recover that DGP, with zero type I and II errors as the sample grows to infinity, a result that turns the table on the criticism of Darwinian test statistics. Hoover and Perez (1999) summarized this remarkable result:

> The critics fear that the survivor of sequential tests survives accidentally and, therefore, that the critical values of such tests ought to be adjusted to reflect the likelihood of an accident. White's theorem suggests that the true specification survives precisely because the true specification is necessarily, in the long run, the fittest specification. (Hoover & Perez 1999: 170)

White's theorem provides theoretical encouragement to a strategy based on a (probably) overparameterized unrestricted model as a starting point. But it also seems to contradict the theorem by Rissanen that Ploberger and Phillips used to derive a "proximity bound" between the an overparameterized starting point and the DGP, a boundary that cannot be crossed even as the sample size grows to infinity.

This contradiction between the theorems of White and Rissanen is striking, and it is surprising that it has not attracted much discussion on either side of the literature. The contradiction arises because White (and the G–S authors) assume that an econometric model could, in principal, nest the DGP, whereas Phillips and Ploberger reject the possibility of such nesting. As mentioned, the local DGP concept is critical for the G–S approach and now we see why: it is the reduction from the high-dimensional DGP to the relevant LDGP that facilitates both an specification-based strategy such as G–S and the applicability of White's theorem. The theoretical inconsistency between the ambitions of PIC and G–S originates in the theory of reduction.

However, using the theory of reduction and White's theorem to answer the theoretical concerns over Darwinian test statistics leaves unanswered the practical concerns about finite sample properties. To investigate this practical question Hoover and Perez (1999) translated the G–S method into an algorithm and automated the procedure on a computer. This allowed them to use Lovell's (1983) famous Monte Carlo setup to test the ability of G–S to discover the known DGP in Lovell's (1983) artificial economy. They could also evaluate the practical relevance of the following three criticisms of G–S: path dependency, overfitting, and unknown test size.

Hoover and Perez's (1999) results were encouraging; in contrast with the model selection criteria studied by Lovell (1983), the automated G–S algorithm recovered the DGP with considerable (though not nearly universal) success, and the size and power of t-test statistics in the final models were not much distorted by the iterative testing of the G–S procedure. Hendry and Krolzig (1999) responded to Hoover and Perez's (1999) simulation by introducing an automated G–S algorithm of their own, called *PcGets* (Hendry & Krolzig 2001), with which they were able to improve on Hoover and Perez's (1999) results. The data from Baba, Hendry, and Starr (1992) (a widely known earlier paper in the G–S literature) served as real world test for *PcGets,* and again the results were highly encouraging, with a final specification close to Baba et al.'s (1992), but reached within seconds instead of weeks or even months. From Hendry and Krolzig's perspective, a considerable merit of this powerful search algorithm is precisely that it affords the econometrician greater time and resources to "improving the theory, data measurement, and econometric specification underpinning the GUM" (Hendry & Krolzig 2004: 800).

In the G–S tradition, as in the other three traditions already discussed, recent advances in automated modeling have generated powerful tools that save time, search costs, and that should free more resources for the part of modeling where econometricians add more value. Though the automated G–S algorithms imply large numbers of iterative tests, there is no evidence yet, in theory or practice, that they expose the modeler to larger risks of unwarranted data mining.

5. Data Mining Races

The relatively easy access to the newly developed automated modeling algorithms have encouraged econometricians to pit them against each other in what may be described as "data mining races." Recent examples include: Hoover and Perez

(2004), Hendry and Krolzig (2004), Castle (2005), Perez-Amaral, Gallo, and White (2005). There is a sense in which this seems an obvious empirical test of the claims made for the various responses to the risk of unwarranted data mining. The proof of the pudding is in the eating, and with the automated versions of the implied algorithms readily available, the case for empirical trials seems compelling.

A typical example in this literature is Hoover and Perez's (2004) simulation based on Levine and Renelt's (1992) cross-country growth data set as the testing ground for two versions of Leamer's extreme-bounds analysis—those of Levine and Renelt (1992) and Sala-i-Martin (1997)—on the one hand and their own automated version of the G–S method on the other. They also ran Sala-i-Martin's (1997) method against their own G–S algorithm given Sala-i-Martin's (1997) original data set.

Hoover and Perez (2004) are well aware that the extreme-bounds approaches entails no concept of the DGP as a goal of the modeling exercise. Since they don't see any merit in the radical subjectivism of Leamer and others[33] they construct their data mining race as if this method was aimed at uncovering the true DGP. In contrast, the G–S method, which is the second competitor in their race, proceeds deductively once the modeler is satisfied on statistical grounds that the general model is congruent with the local DGP.

Hoover and Perez's (2004) results amplify the favorable evaluation of G–S in Hoover and Perez (1999), and this against two versions of extreme bounds analysis: Levine and Renelt's (1992) method is discovered to be too strict, because it eliminates many true variables, whereas Sala-i-Martin's (1997) is not strict enough, allowing too many opportunistic variables in the final specification. In contrast, the G–S method is "just right" in terms of both test size and power (Hoover & Perez 2004); a result confirmed by Hendry and Krolzig (2004) using their PcGets algorithm (Hendry & Krolzig 2001).

Although demonstrating the merit of the G–S approach with cross-section data adds important information to Hoover and Perez's earlier demonstrations in the time series context (Hoover & Perez 1999), it is less clear what we can learn from this race and the "future horse races against other search methodologies," which they eagerly anticipate (Hoover & Perez 2004: 790). The failures of extreme bounds analysis in their tests are not relative to successes that Leamer or other proponents of these methods seek. This same conclusion would have followed a discussion of most papers in this literature on data mining races, since the research question in these papers is not well defined.

6. Conclusions

Tinbergen and the other pioneers of modern econometrics already encountered the central features of our subject matter—model uncertainty and nonexperimental data—that opens the door to unwarranted data mining. And despite the pious intentions of Tinbergen's generation, the culture of repetition and criticism of applied econometrics has flourished only modestly. Indeed, there is little evidence of vibrant competition of that kind, at least where the journals are concerned.

But new hope springs from a number of exiting developments in the theory of economic modeling: This chapter surveyed four of these developments ranging from a radically subjective inductivism to a structural deductivism.

The subjectivist approach, associated especially with the work of Edward Leamer, regards data mining as a problem of communications in economic research and the proposed solution (EBA) is designed to expose the fragility of empirical results in econometrics. In contrast, Hall White's "Reality Check" and the RETINA algorithm deal with the risks of data mining by adjusting tests for all possible rival models and by using the gold standard of econometrics, new data, to test a model.

The DGP does not feature in either EBA or RETINA, but moves closer to center stage in the third approach discussed here, Phillips and Ploberger's PIC. This Bayesian criterion is a yardstick to guide a model search, given model uncertainty and nonexperimental data. Though the associated modeling strategy does not aim to uncover the DGP, it does aim for (and asymptotically reach) the proximity bound of the DGP. In contrast with the other approaches, G–S is a deductive approach with the explicit aim of encompassing the DGP. The risks of unwarranted data mining are avoided through the application of the theory of reduction; a once-off round of mis-specification tests on the general unrestricted model is followed by a series of deductive tests, the validity of which is based on the statistical adequacy (congruency) of the GUM. G–S, as well as PIC and RETINA can and have been automated and, especially the former, has built an impressive track record of applications.

If Keynes sent 70 modern Tinbergens into cells with data and laptops they could, following one of the various modeling strategies described here, conceivably emerge with similar models. And they would have done so rapidly using one of the automated algorithms mentioned earlier in this chapter. But would they have chosen the same algorithm, and which one is the fittest (if any)?

This question admits no easy answer: The experience of twenty years and the tremendous gain in computing power have introduced powerful tools that will reduce the cost of the slave-work in applied econometrics, but they have not reduced the importance of the first step in such a project—the research question.

A project's goal should still be the overriding factor in determining the appropriate research strategy (Granger 1999). Is it forecasting financial variables? Then RETINA looks promising. Or perhaps PICF? Is it a structural model for aggregate consumption? Then *PcGets* promises much. And in both cases the initial setup, including the data set, is critical, and there is as yet no algorithm to reduce that task. Indeed Hendry has consistently argued that these data-mining algorithms free the econometrician to labor at that end of the modeling task where he is most able to contribute (Granger & Hendry 2005).

Among the decisions that the econometrician cannot outsource to his data-mining algorithm is the philosophical question of his goal relative to the DGP. This issue turns on deeper questions in ontology and epistemology, the problem of induction, and the bridge between theoretical constructs and reality in empirical science. And the data-mining races of recent vintage between algorithms aimed at different kinds of answers to these questions are regrettably uninformative.

NOTES

1. Pagan (2003) uses the same tension between data dependence and theory dependence as an organizing principle for his survey of modern macroeconometric modeling methods.

2. The dramatic potential of modern computing power is transforming research in many fields (Glymour 2004), and there is optimism that it will do the same for applied econometrics (Phillips 2005).

3. *Instrumentalism* here means the ontological proposition that there is no underlying structure to which econometric models might be better or worse approximations. Edward Leamer is a leading proponent of this view, which he recently summarized as follows: "Models are neither true nor false. They are sometimes useful and sometimes misleading. *The goal of an empirical economist should not be to determine the truthfulness of a model but rather the domain of usefulness*" (Leamer 2004).

4. Schumpeter's well-known claim for economics as the "most quantitative" of all sciences is based on the nonexperimental nature of much economic data. In his words, from the first edition of *Econometrica* "There is, however, one sense in which economics is the most quantitative, not only of 'social' or 'moral' sciences, but of *all* sciences, physics not excluded. For mass, velocity current, and the like *can* undoubtedly be measured, but in order to do so we must always invent a distinct process of measurement... Some of the most fundamental economic facts, on the contrary, already present themselves to our observation as quantities made numerical by life itself. They carry meaning only by virtue of their numerical character... Econometrics is nothing but the explicit recognition of this rather obvious fact, and the attempt to face the consequences of it" (Schumpeter 1933: 5–6).

5. In the absence of such nesting of the underlying DGP, an alternative theorem attributed to Rissanen may be applied to show that the DGP will not be recovered, even asymptotically (Phillips 2003).

6. This benchmark represents a strong implication of the efficient market hypothesis (Sullivan et al. 2001).

7. For alternative discussions along the same lines, see Leamer (1978) and Chatfield (1995).

8. A "severe test" is here understood to have low size and high power. Hendry (2000) has shown that a better search algorithm in a modeling problem could both lower the size of inferential tests (the probability of Type I errors) and lower the probability of Type II errors.

9. If the size of each test was 5 percent and the null valid, then the probability of a Type I error (the probability of at least one rejection of the valid null) is given by:

$$P_{0.05} = (1-0.05)^{20} \approx 0.36$$

10. For Denton (1985) it is a fallacy of composition to argue that the risks of data mining would be diminished if everybody avoided data mining in their own research.

11. For example, searching over the various proxies for "institutional quality" to identify an institutional effect in a growth regression.

12. A hold-out sample is a subset of a time series (usually at the most recent end of the series) against which an out of sample forecast could be tested after the model was estimated on the remainder on the data set. Cross validation is technique whereby the original data is divided upfront into a number of subsets one of which will be set aside as a validation sample against which a forecast will be tested that was generated on the other subsets (called the training sets). In k-fold cross validation the exercise is repeated k times, with each of the k subsets serving once as validation data.

13. The objectivity of econometrics, as with other scientific activities depends *inter alia* on the intersubjective testability of the models. All econometricians, like all other scientists, are individually subjective in their treatment of theories and data, and the objectivity of the scientific exercise emerges, if at all, through the inter-subjective testing of these models by other econometricians and especially on new data (Popper 2000).

14. Krämer et al. (1985) found that an overwhelming proportion of published models in their sample failed standard diagnostic tests.

15. Hendry (2000) defines a "progressive modeling strategy" as one in which successive models account at least for the information in existing models, that is, the new model encompasses the existing models.

16. The local GDP is the joint distribution of the variables of interest for the problem at hand. It is derived from the all-encompassing DGP for the entire economy through a series of reductions. The term, Local DGP, has been attributed to Bontemps and Mizon (2003).

17. In the statistics and science literatures, this publication filter is often called the "file-drawer" problem, hinting at the unpublished results hidden in scientists drawers filter (Scargle 2000).

18. Dewald et al. (1986) found many authors unable to replicate their own results, notably when data or algorithms had been lost or when a research assistant was no longer at hand to explain her earlier work. In a group of 62 authors in their study, Dewald et al. (1986) found that only 22 provided the requested data and algorithms, while 20 made no reply, and the remaining replied that they were unable to comply.

19. The *Journal of Applied Econometrics* and the *Journal of Business and Economic Statistics* have taken similar initiatives (Pagan & Veall 2000).

20. The prize was an all-expenses paid week-long trip to the Center for Economic Research at Tilburg university.

21. Pagan and Veall (2000) refer to Alesina and Summer's claim that central bank credibility would lower the sacrifice ratio for monetary policy.

22. Pagan and Veall have elsewhere asked whether the emphasis on the centrality of the DGP in the G–S approach implies that "other approaches do not have a similar aim" (Pagan & Veall 2000)? This chapter answers Pagan and Veall in the affirmative, but with qualification: the G–S tradition emphasises the search for a local DGP—i.e. a reduction of the actual DGP that is adequate for the problem at hand (Hendry 2000)—while acknowledging that an inherently simply model could never provide a comprehensive specification of the DGP (Hendry 2000).

23. Mayer (1995) cited a survey that found 27 percent of economists were "quite sceptical" of econometric output published in journals with another 2 percent comprehensively sceptical and 56 percent "somewhat sceptical."

24. Woodward (2006) distinguishes "inferential" robustness (in the Leamer sense) from other potentially relevant concepts of robustness, such as measurement robustness, derivational robustness and causal robustness. Hoover and Perez (2004) showed in practice what Woodward (2006) showed in principle, i.e. that extreme bounds analysis is likely to overstate the "fragility" of econometric results. What is more, a correct model of the DGP is not expected to be inferentially robust against alternative specifications (Hoover & Perez 2004).

25. The weights are proportional to the likelihoods of the separate models, that is, models with higher likelihood receive a greater weight.

26. Even though this procedure is not intended to uncover the DGP, the merit of any particular model is defined relative to the unattainable DGP.

27. Rissanen (1986: 1092) expresses the same ideas elsewhere, for example: "In our general philosophy of modeling there are no data generating probabilistic systems nor 'true' parameter values."

28. Elsewhere Phillips (2003) explains his agnosticism with respect to the DGP: his central argument is that identifying a "formal statistical model whose variables are defined on a certain probability space" that "faithfully and completely represented" the DGP is unlikely because of the extreme complexity of the decisions represented by the DGP as well as endogeneities and dependencies that complicate the modeling process. But the pursuit of the DGP is not just futile, it is also misguided for Phillips, who sees an attempt at modeling the DGP as "...antithetic to the notion that a model itself is a simplified representation of a real world process" (Phillips 2003: C39).

29. Nevertheless Philips and Ploberger attribute the theorem that proves this proximity bound to Rissanen. They define the "distance" between the model and the underlying DGP in terms of the Kullback-Leibler (KL) distance. The DGP, therefore, plays a role in their conception of the limit to econometric modeling. Such a conception has no meaning in Rissanen's more radical empiricism, despite Phillips's (2003) claim that Rissanen has "asked how close on average (measured in terms of Kullback-Leibler distance) can we get to a true DGP using observed data." Rissanen's rejection of the KL distance is clear from the following: "The same is true about many other well-know model-selection criteria such as the AIC, where the objective is to estimate either a mean prediction error or the Kullback distance, both of which involve the expectation relative to an imagined and non existing 'true' distribution" (Rissanen 1987: 224).

30. In contrast, Pagan and Veall (2000) argued that the risks of data mining were largely small-sample problems and, more strongly, Hoover and Perez (1999) and authors in the G–S tradition, such as Hendry and Krolzig (1999) have used White's theorem to argue that their data mining algorithm would, asymptotically, uncover the DGP with a probability of one.

31. For early surveys see Pagan (1987) and Gilbert (1986), and more recently Campos, Ericsson and Hendry (2005b). Leading texts include Hendry (1995) and Spanos (1986), and a recent compendium of critical papers in the development of this method has appeared under the editorship of Campos, Ericsson, and Hendry (2005a).

32. Granger et al. (1995) preferred a model selection criterion based on a distance measure to the benchmark approach in the G–S approach, because they considered it problematic to select a particular set of qualifying criteria. It might be difficult to convince others that these are reasonable criteria.

33. Elsewhere, Hoover and Perez (2000) found Leamer's position on the DGP "barely coherent."

REFERENCES

Acemoglu, D. & Johnson, S. (2005). "Unbundling Institutions." *Journal of Political Economy* 115 (5): 949–995.

Baba, Y. D., Hendry, D. F. & Starr, R. M. (1992). "The Demand for M1 in the USA, 1960–1988." *Review of Economic Studies* 59: 25–61.

Backhouse, R. E., & Morgan, M. S. (2000). "Introduction: Is Data Mining a Methodological Problem?" *Journal of Economic Methodology* 7 (2): 171–181.

Baumol, W. J. (1986). "Productivity Growth, Convergence and Welfare." *American Economic Review* 76: 1072–1085.

Bontemps, C., & Mizon, G. E. (2003). "Congruence and Encompassing." In B. P. Stignum. Ed., *Econometrics and the Philosophy of Economics: Theory-Data Confrontations in Economics*. Princeton: Princeton University Press.

Burger, R. P. & Du Plessis, S. A. (2006). "Quantifying the Extent of Data Mining in Applied Econometrics." Stellenbosch, mimeograph.

Campos, J. & Ericsson, N. R. (1999). "Constructive Data Mining: Modelling Consumers' Expenditure in Venequela." *Econometrics Journal* 2: 226–240.

Campos, J., Ericsson, N. R. & Hendry, D. F., Eds. (2005a). *General-to-Specific Modelling*. The International Library of Critical Writings in Econometrics. Cheltenham, UK: Elgar Reference Collection.

Campos, J., Ericsson, N. R. & Hendry, D. F., Eds. (2005b). "General-to-Specific Modeling: An Overview and Selected Bibliography." Washington, Board of Governors of the Federal Reserve System, International Finance Discussion Papers, Number 838.

Castle, J. L. (2005). "Evaluating PcGets and RETINA as Automatic Selection Algorithms." *Oxford Bulletin of Economics and Statistics* 67: 837–880.

Chatfield, C. (1995). "Model Uncertainty, Data Mining and Statistical Inference." *Journal of the Royal Statistical Society, Series A* 158 (3): 419–466.

Clements, M. P., & Hendry, D. F. (2005). "Evaluating a Model by Forecast Performance." *Oxford Bulletin of Economics and Statistics* 67: 931–956.

Cooley, T. & LeRoy, S. (1981). "Identification and Estimation of Money Demand." *American Economic Review* 71: 825–844.

Cowles, A. (1933). "Can Stock Market Forecasters Forecast?" *Econometrica* 1 (3): 309–324.

DeLong, J. B. (1988). "Productivity Growth, Convergence and Welfare: Comment." *American Economic Review* 78: 1138–1154.

Denton, F. T. (1985). "Data Mining As an Industry." *The Review of Economics and Statistics* 67 (1): 124–127.

Dewald, W. G., Thursby, J. G. & Anderson, G. (1986). "Replication in Empirical Economics: The Journal of Money, Credit and Banking Project." *American Economic Review* 76 (4): 587–602.

Faust, J. & Whiteman, C. H. (1997a). "General-to-Specific Procedures for Fitting a Data-admissible, Theory-inspired, Congruent, Parsimonious, Encompassing, Weakly-exogenous, Identified, Structural Model to the DGP: A Translation and Critique." *Carnegie-Rochester Conference Series on Public Policy* 47: 121–161.

Faust, J. & Whiteman, C. H. (1997b). "Rejoinder to Hendry." *Carnegie-Rochester Conference Series on Public Policy* 47: 191–195.

Frisch, R. (1933). "Editorial." *Econometrica* 1 (1): 1–4.

Galton, F. (1901). "Editorial: The Spirit of Biometrika." *Biometrika* 1 (1): 3–6.

Gilbert, C. L. (1986). "Professor Hendry's Econometric Methodology." *Oxford Bulletin of Economics and Statistics* 48 (3): 283–307.

Giles, J. A. & Giles, E. A. (1993). "Pre-test Estimation and Testing in Econometrics: Recent Developments." *Journal of Economic Surveys* 7 (2): 145–197.

Glymour, C. (2004). "The Automation of Discovery." *Daedalus* Winter: 69–77.

Godfrey, L. G. & Veal, M. R. (2000). "Alternative Approaches to Testing by Variable Addition." *Econometric Reviews* 19: 241–261.

Granger, C. W. J. (1999). *Empirical Modeling in Economics.* Cambridge: Cambridge University Press.

Granger, C. W. J. & Hendry, D. F. (2005). "A Dialogue Concerning a New Instrument for Econometric Modeling." *Econometric Theory* 21: 278–297.

Granger, C. W. J., King, M. L. & White, H. (1995). "Comments on Testing Economic Theories and the Use of Model Selection Criteria." *Journal of Econometrics* 67: 173–187.

Greene, C. A. (2000). "I Am Not, Nor Have I Ever Been a Member of a Data-Mining Discipline." *Journal of Economic Methodology* 7 (2): 217–230.

Hand, D. J. (1998). "Data Mining: Statistics and More." *The American Statistician* 52 (2): 112–118.

Hendry, D. F. (1980). "Econometrics: Alchemy or Science?" *Economica* 47: 387–406.

Hendry, D. F. (1995). *Dynamic Econometrics.* Oxford: Oxford University Press.

Hendry, D. F. (1997). "On Congruent Econometric Relations: A Comment." *Carnegie-Rochester Conference Series on Public Policy* 47: 163–190.

Hendry, D. F. (2000). "The Success of General-to-specific Model Selection." In D. F. Hendry, ed., *Econometrics: Alchemy or Science? Essays in Econometric Methodology.* Oxford: Oxford University Press.

Hendry, D. F. (2000 [1985]). "Monetary Economic Myth and Econometric Reality." In D. F. Hendry, ed., *Econometrics: Alchemy or Science? Essays in Econometrics Methodology.* Oxford: Oxford University Press.

Hendry, D. F. & Krolzig, H. M. (1999). "Improving on 'Data Mining Reconsidered.'" *Econometrics Journal* 2: 202–219.

Hendry, D. F. & Krolzig, H. M. (2001). *Automatic Econometric Model Selection Using PcGets 1.0.* Harrow: Allstar Services.

Hendry, D. F. & Krolzig, H. M. (2004). "We Ran One Regression." *Oxford Bulletin of Economics and Statistics* 66 (5): 799–810.

Hoover, K. D. & Perez, S. J. (1999). "Data Mining Reconsidered: Encompassing and the General to Specific Approach to Specification Search." *Econometrics Journal* 2: 166–191.

Hoover, K. D. & Perez, S. J. (2000). "Three Attitudes to Data Mining." *Journal of Economic Methodology* 7 (2): 195–210.

Hoover, K. D. & Perez, S. J. (2004). "Truth and Robustness in Cross-Country Growth Regressions." *Oxford Bulletin of Economics and Statistics* 66 (5): 765–798.

Kennedy, P. (2003). *A Guide to Econometrics,* 5th edition. Oxford: Blackwell.

Keuzenkamp, H. A. & Magnus, J. R. (1995). "On Tests and Significance in Econometrics." *Journal of Econometrics* 67: 5–24.

Keynes, J. M. (1939). "Professor Tinbergen's Method." *Economic Journal* (September): 558–568.

Keynes, J. M. (1940). "On a Method of Statistical Business-Cycle Research. A Comment," *Economic Journal* 50 (197): 154–156.

Krämer, W., Sonnberger, H., Maurer, J. & Havlik, P. (1985). "Diagnostic Checking in Practice." *Review of Economics and Statistics* 67 (1): 118–123.

Leamer, E. E. (1978). *Specification Searches: Ad Hoc Inference with Nonexperimental Data.* New York: John Wiley.

Leamer, E. E. (1983). "Let's Take the Con Out of Econometrics." *American Economic Review* 73 (1): 31–43.

Leamer, E. E. (2004). "Are the Roads Red? Comments on 'Size Matters.'" *The Journal of Socio-Economics* 33: 555–557.

Levine, R., & Renelt, D. (1992). "A Sensitivity Analysis of Cross-Country Growth Regressions." *American Economic Review* 82 (4): 942–963.

Lovell, M. C. (1983). "Data Mining." *The Review of Economics and Statistics* 65: 1–12.

Mayer, T. (1995*). Doing Economics.* Aldershot: Edward Elgar.

Mayer, T. (2000). "Data Mining: A Reconsideration." *Journal of Economic Methodology* 7 (2): 183–194.

Mayo, D. G. (1996). *Error and the Growth of Experimental Knowledge.* Chicago: University of Chicago Press.

McCloskey, D. N. & Ziliak, S. T. (1996). "The Standard Error of Regressions." *Journal of Economic Literature* 34: 97–114.

Pagan, A. R. (1987). "Three Econometric Methodologies: A Critical Appraisal." *Journal of Economic Surveys* 1 (1): 3–24.

Pagan, A. R. (2003). "Reflections on Some Aspects of Macro-econometric Modeling." Stellenbosch, Keynote address delivered at the 8th annual AES Conference, July 2003, Stellenbosch, South Africa.

Pagan, A. R. & Veall, M. R. (2000). "Data Mining and the Econometrics Industry: Comments on the Papers of Mayer and Hoover and Perez." *Journal of Economic Methodology* 7 (2): 211–216.

Perez-Amaral, T., Gallo, G. M. & White, D. (2005). "A Comparison of Complementary Automatic Modeling Methods: RETINA and PcGets." *Econometric Theory* 21: 262–277.

Perez-Amaral, T., Gallo, G. M. & White, H. (2003). "A Flexible Tool for Model Building: The Relevant Transformation of the Inputs Network Approach (RETINA)." *Oxford Bulletin of Economics and Statistics* 65: 821–838.

Phillips, P. C. B. (1988). "Reflections on Econometric Methodology." *The Economic Record* (December): 344–359.

Phillips, P. C. B. (1995). "Bayesian Model Selection and Prediction with Empirical Applications." *Journal of Econometrics* 69: 289–331.

Phillips, P. C. B. (1996). "Econometric Model Determination." *Econometrica* 64 (4): 763–812.

Phillips, P. C. B. (2003). "Laws and Limits of Econometrics." *Economic Journal* 113 (March): C26–C52.

Phillips, P. C. B. (2005). "Automated Discovery in Econometrics." *Econometric Theory* 21: 3–20.

Phillips, P. C. B. & Ploberger, W. (1994). "Posterior Odds Testing for a Unit Root with Data-Based Model Selection." *Econometric Theory* 10: 774–808.

Phillips, P. C. B. & Ploberger, W. (1996). "An Asymptotic Theory of Bayesian Inference for Time Series." *Econometrica* 64: 581–413.

Ploberger, W. & Phillips, P. C. B. (2003). "Empirical Limits for Time Series Econometric Models." *Econometrica* 71 (2): 627–673.

Popper, K. R. (2000 [1959]). *The Logic of Scientific Discovery*. London: Routledge.

Rissanen, J. (1986). "Stochastic Complexity and Modeling." *The Annals of Statistics* 14 (3): 1080–1100.

Rissanen, J. (1987). "Stochastic Complexity." *Journal of the Royal Statistical Society, Series B* 49 (3): 223–239.

Sala-i-Martin, X. (1997). "I Just Ran Two-Million Regressions." *American Economic Review (Papers and Proceedings)* 87 (2): 178–183.

Sala-i-Martin, X., Doppelhofer, G. & Miller, R. I. (2004). "Determinants of Long-term Growth: A Bayesian Averaging of Classical Estimates (BACE) Approach." *American Economic Review* 94 (4): 813–835.

Scargle, J. D. (2000). "Publication Bias: The "File-Drawer" Problem in Scientific Inference." *Journal of Scientific Exploration* 14 (1): 91–106.

Schumpeter, J. A. (1933). "The Common Sense of Econometrics," *Econometrica* 1 (1): 5–12.

Spanos, A. (1986). *Statistical Foundations of Econometric Modeling*. Cambridge: Cambridge University Press.

Spanos, A. (1989). "On Rereading Haavelmo: A Retrospective View of Econometric Modeling." *Econometric Theory* 5: 405–429.

Spanos, A. (1995). "On Theory Testing in Econometrics. Modeling with Nonexperimental Data." *Journal of Econometrics* 67: 189–226.

Spanos, A. (1999). *Probability Theory and Statistical Inference*. Cambridge: Cambridge University Press.

Spanos, A. (2000). "Revisiting Data Mining: 'Hunting' with or without a License." *Journal of Economic Methodology* 7 (2): 231–264.

Sugden, R. A. (1995). "Discussion of the Paper by Chatfield." *Journal of the Royal Statistical Society Series A* 158 (3): 461–464.

Sullivan, R., Timmerman, A. & White, H. (2001). "Dangers of Data Mining: The Case of Calendar Effects in Stock Returns." *Journal of Econometrics* 105: 249–286.

Summers, L. (1991). "The Scientific Illusion in Empirical Macroeconomics." *Scandinavian Journal of Economics* 93 (2): 129–148.

Tinbergen, J. (1939). *Statistical Testing of Business-Cycle Theories I: A Method and its Application to Investment Activity*. Geneva: League of Nations.

White, H. (1998). "Artificial Neural Network and Alternative Methods for Assessing Naval Readiness." San Diego: NRDA technical report.

White, H. (2000). "A Reality Check for Data Snooping." *Econometrica* 68 (5): 1097–1126.

White, H. (2005 [1990]). "A Consistent Model Selection Procedure Based on M-Testing." In J. Campos, N. R. Ericsson & D. F. Hendry, Eds., *General-to-Specific Modeling Volume I*. Cheltenham, UK: Elgar Reference Collection.

Woodward, J. (2006). "Some Varieties of Robustness." *Journal of Economic Methodology* 13 (2): 219–240.

Ziliak, S. T. & McCloskey, D. N. (2004). "Size Matters: The Standard Error of Regressions in the American Economic Review." *The Journal of Socio-Economics* 33: 527–546.

CHAPTER 17

EXPLAINING GROWTH

HAROLD KINCAID

THE causes of economic growth have been a central preoccupation of economists since at least Adam Smith, and the topic has received considerable recent attention from contemporary economics.[1] Robert Lucas (1988) has said that "once you start to think about...economic growth, it is hard to think about anything else." In this chapter I look at two approaches to explaining growth: (1) neoclassical growth theory and related work that seeks a uniform equilibrium model of the determinants of growth and relies on cross-country regressions for evidence and (2) contemporary development economics that builds on microeconomic work on such things as information asymmetries, moral hazard, adverse selection, and market failure and detailed aggregate single-country case studies. These two trends have rather different assumptions about the nature of economic explanation of economic evidence and of the relation between economics and other social sciences in ways that are tightly interconnected. My goal is to tease out some implicit philosophy of science assumptions behind these different approaches with an eye to clarifying the debates and to understanding some of the complexities of economic science in practice. I argue that neoclassical growth theory rests on several untenable assumptions about evidence and explanation that render it of doubtful value, and that work in contemporary development economics avoids those assumptions and shows considerably more promise.

I approach this project with some philosophy of science assumptions of my own. The first is that no report of scientific research is a mere description of results observed. Every report is, instead, an argument designed to persuade. While the means of persuasion may sometimes not involve reasons supporting the truth of a conclusion, I doubt that this is generally the case. However, I do believe it is the case that the arguments given are often less than explicit and that they are just as frequently put in a guise that overstates the force they carry. In particular, there is a natural tendency to black box the methods used and to treat them as having a less contingent character than they may have by taking domain-specific empirical assumptions as universal and purely logical truths about good science.

A further assumption I make is that, in assessing scientific results, speaking of "the theory" in any scientific endeavor may oversimplify the actual practices of the field in various ways. Since Kuhn we have known (i.e., philosophers of science—scientists have known these things all along) that, in the first place, there is considerably more to science than theories or even theories and "the data." Skills and technologies are the most obvious further elements among many others. As a result, understanding the theories of a given area frequently involves understanding the context in which they are embedded. Moreover, what "the" theory in a given area actually comes to requires interpretation and often may have no uniform interpretation across the various individuals and communities involved. In the simplest case, the very same formalisms—equations usually—are shared, but the interpretations of what they mean vary. This arguably occurred in the first decades of quantum mechanics (Beller 2001), even after the Schroedinger and Heisenberg formulations had been shown to be equivalent. Furthermore, formalisms may differ within the same research tradition, for example, when different, nonequivalent modeling assumptions are made. Thus, identifying the theory of a given area requires a nuanced, nontrivial undertaking.

My project in this chapter will be to make explicit the kinds of arguments provided for evidence and explanations of the causes of growth, while paying some attention to the complexities and differences in interpretation of the models and data at issue. While my examples focus on growth, the practices I describe are common and not peculiar to work on growth. Along the way, I discuss such deep issues as the probability foundations of econometrics, the place of nonstatistical evidence, conceptions of economics as a separate science, and complex kinds of causality. The issues are big and hard ones, and I do pretend to provide a full assessment. However, at the end I hope to have clearer understanding of two important research traditions in economics and their relation to issues in the philosophy of science.

Neoclassical growth theory gets its seminal formulation in the 1950s in models described by Solow (1957). It begins with an aggregate production function for a country as whole described by

$$Y = AK^a L^{1-a}$$

where Y is total output, K is quantity of capital, L is quantity of labor, and A is productivity coefficient. Both a and $1-a$ are less than 1, indicating diminishing marginal returns, and $a + b = 1$, indicating constant returns to scale. Put in per capita terms, we get

$$y = Y/L = AK^a$$

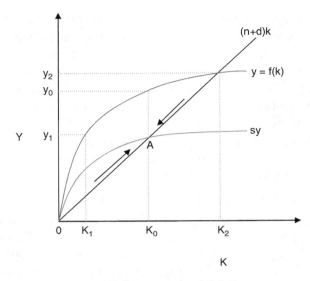

Figure 17.1. Solow growth model diagram

We add to this production function a simple function for investment

$I = sY,$

where s is the fraction of output saved. We also assume that

$y = f(n+d)$

where n is the growth rate of the population and d is the rate of depreciation of capital, and that at equilibrium

$(n+d)k = sy$, where k is per capita capital

Graphically, the basic model looks like Figure 17.1.

This is a basic form of the early versions of neoclassical growth theory. It is worth noting several things about it. The theory is, above all, a set of equations, and the information provided in the original articles and in textbook versions about what these equations mean is relatively thin. However, the model described here is advanced in a context of other understandings that may give it more content. The independent variables are called determinants, which is sometimes explicitly equated with cause and it is implicitly so equated whenever economists want to talk about policy implications. Those policy implications may not be explicitly discussed themselves, but a key purpose of the overall enterprise is policy advice (including the advice to do nothing).

More content comes when we ask what the theory is supposed to be explaining. The explicit explanadum is growth. However, historically, the models were advanced as supporting a neoclassical marginal product theory of the distribution of income between the factors capital and labor. That is a theory with considerably more content

than is expressed by the simple equations described earlier. The equations themselves, even when described as determinants or even causes, say nothing themselves
about the empirical referents of the terms or how they would be measured. Talking
about the marginal products of factors brings in the assumptions that the microeconomic model of the firm generalizes to the behavior of countries as a whole. Of
course, when marginal productivity is mentioned, there is sometimes the normative
context suggestion that marginal products are deserved. So the set of equations that
give us a very thin sense of a theory takes on much more content in this context.

There are now in the literature all kinds of additions and revisions to the basic
model outlined here. I note briefly two prominent approaches:

1. The first is the "augmented Solow model" (Mankiw 1995). It still takes
    technology as exogenous, but it divides up capital into physical and
    human capital. Doing so adds greater realism and also eliminates
    some unhappy implications of the initial neoclassical growth theory. It
    entailed that there should be large flows of capital from capital-intensive
    economies to the less developed, low-capital-intensity countries, where the
    marginal product of capital investments is higher. Flows of the required
    magnitude are not observed. Separating human capital from physical
    capital lowers the available capital to export (assuming human capital is
    not transportable as it were), and thus reduces the empirical puzzle.

2. Another set of revisions makes the level of technology and savings
    endogenous variables rather than ones set outside the model as they were
    in the Solow-Swann neoclassical growth theory. This work is sometimes
    called new growth theory, and seminal discussions come from Romer
    (1990, 1994). Technological change becomes explained in that there is
    a knowledge-producing sector that takes physical and human capital
    and existing knowledge as inputs and produces technological designs
    as output. This sector also introduces economies of scale and drops the
    assumption of perfect competition because it assumes that part of the
    knowledge produced is proprietary and produced by monopolies and
    that part of the knowledge produced becomes a public good. So we have
    the promise of explaining technological progress and doing so with a
    more realistic model that breaks with some general equilibrium theory
    simplifications found in the augmented Solow model.

Romer's models also include equations describing consumer and saving behavior. An intermediate sector takes designs and foregone consumer goods to produce durable (capital) goods. The consumer goods sector consists of one firm that
produces all output, owns no assets, and makes zero profits. Consumers own the
durable goods firms and receive net proceeds; consumers are treated as a single
Ramsay style infinitely lived representative agent. Because the production functions
in the consumer goods and durable goods sections are identical, consumers can

substitute a fixed number of consumer goods for production of capital good; they do so in a way that maximizes over the infinite future. The growth rate is, thus, determined in this way given the initial stock of capital, knowledge, and labor.

Attempts to provide evidence for neoclassical growth theory both adds to and decreases the complexity of the models. The increased complexity arises because yet another set of variables are added to the models described, namely, social variables such as the extent to which there is rule of law, the size of government, and so on. These are literally add-ons because they are not derived from neoclassical economic theory in any explicit sense, though there are economic stories to tell about why the enforcement of property rights and large government consumption have an influence on growth. Macroeconomic variables, such as inflation and openness to trade, are also added, and there are economic stories to tell about these as well. However, there is again an implicit theory in the background, and in the empirical work on neoclassical growth theory, social variables are almost always added in an unabashedly ad hoc way.

The empirical models tested are simplifications of the neoclassical growth models, at least insofar as they do not include all the relevant variables identified by those models. So technological change, the savings rate, the depreciation rate, the investment rate, the rate of technological diffusion and the population growth rate are, depending on the tester, not included in the regressions used to support neoclassical growth theory. Barro (2001), one of the most prominent defenders, admits all this and tests specifications using human capital, social variables, and macroeconomic variables such as inflation and openness to trade. Other tested models will include more of the traditional variables, but may impose values rather than test them. It is, for example, common practice to impose a constant depreciation rate for all cases studied (Pritchett 2003, Senhadji 2000) or to impose a factor share of one third for capital. In a similar vein, growth-accounting models will include the capital—physical and human—and labor-force factors of neoclassical growth theory but will have no direct measurement of technology (it is inferred as what is not explained by the factor variables) nor of its determinants, thus leaving out part of the neoclassical story in its more recent incarnations.

The two basic sorts of tests are of (1) conditional convergence, which says that all else being held constant, countries starting at lower initial per capita GDP will grow faster, a prediction of most neoclassical growth models, and (2) a correlation between per capita GDP as the dependent variable with measures of factor variables, social variables, and macroeconomic variables, depending on the specification. The evidence used in these tests is typically cross-country regressions. Regressions relate the variation in the values of the dependent variable to those of the independent variable. The size of that relation is described by the regression coefficient, which takes values from zero to one. Regressions are run on national data from as many countries as are available. The data are either for a specific year or, when multiple years are available, years are grouped into periods where averages are taken over the period. Final equations and regression coefficients are determined by tests of statistical significance—significant variables are regarded as well supported by the evidence, and nonsignificant ones as rejected.

There are a number of specific assumptions about explanation and evidence built into, or least strongly associated with, these general neoclassical approaches to growth. Let me start with the assumptions about explanation. They include at least:

1. An explanatory model is above all a set of equations describing functional relations between a set of variables. As we saw earlier, new growth theory often has a very thin interpretation beyond the presentation of a set of equations and their equilibrium conditions. Causal interpretations or observable equivalents of the variables may not be given at all—the set of equations itself is taken to be the proper scientific explanatory product. I should note that this practice is not at all unique to neoclassical growth theory, but it is standard practice in much of economics. *Show us the model* frequently means "give us the equations," not "show us a causal diagram connected to things we can measure."

2. Explanations come from citing regularities. Advocates of neoclassical growth theory generally eschew causal talk and provide no explicit causal models. Yet they do not take the instrumentalist line that they are not trying to explain but only to summarize observations, since their variables often have no obvious empirical counterpart at all. The neoclassical growth models clearly are supposed to be telling us something about how the world "works" — to explain the phenomenon of growth—and they do so by providing functional relations between variable, that is, regularities.

3. There is one set of regularities that determines the behavior of the many different national economies. This assumption shows up in different guises with different logical strengths in neoclassical growth theory. Yet the central practice of the empirical regression work is to estimate a single production function with a fixed set of variables and common coefficients on the regressors. This strong claim can be weakened, for example, by including regional dummy variables (e.g., including "sub-Saharan Africa") in the empirical models that are tested, but doing so is admitting explanatory defeat in a way that violates the spirit of the models being put forward.

4. The economic determinants of growth have their influence independently of each other and of social factors that might influence growth.

5. Social factors are minor in importance compared to the economic factors. The assumptions that the variables act independently as represented by the equations and that social variables are relatively unimportant as measured by the size of the relative coefficients is one way to formulate

the thesis that economics is a separate science that can be studied in relative isolation from sociology, politics, etc. This seems a considerably clearer formulation of economics as a separate science than that found in Mill's talk of "chemical" and "nonchemcial" causal relations and of economic factors "predominating" (the most explicit formulation in Hausman [1992]). The work in neoclassical growth concretely illustrates one thing the separateness of economics might mean.[2]

6. Aggregate economic entities can be treated as maximizing individuals. This assumption will be discussed in critical detail later, but its presence shows up in two places. One is the assumption that consumers can be treated as a single maximizing representative agent in those neoclassical growth models that include consumers such as Romer's. The other is in the use of aggregate production functions. Here it is assumed that the aggregate factors have well-defined marginal products, a clear scaling up of the maximizing conditions on firms. Solow (2000, p. xx) is explicit in seeing this as a key innovation on his part.

The assumptions about evidence in the neoclassical growth tradition are not as explicitly stated as some of the assumptions about explanation, but a look at the actual practice of providing evidence for neoclassical growth theory makes them clear. The overwhelming source of evidence comes from significance tests, with other statistical tests playing a supporting role. Embodied in this practice, I would argue, is a logic of science ideal. That ideal asserts that the relation between hypotheses and evidence is an a priori matter and that good methodology comes from specifying the formal rules that allow for valid inference from evidence to hypothesis. Significance tests seem to fit this bill perfectly. From the a priori truths of the probability calculus, we can deduce the probability of seeing the observed correlation, even if, in fact, there is no real relation between the variables. It is widespread practice to take statistically significant results as indicating that there is some real relation between the variables and nonsignificant results as showing there is no relation. Often the conclusion is the stronger one that the statistically significant coefficients measure the *magnitude* of the relation ("there is a relation" asserts less than "the relation is X."

We can get a greater feel for the depth of these various assumptions about explanation and evidence by noting that they were there at the beginning of the marginalist revolution and represented a decisive break from the classical tradition in economics. Of course establishing these historical points would be a project in itself, but I think that it is not hard to find some strong prima facie evidence for it.

So a quick story about key ideas in the development of classical economics and the marginalist revolution is as follows: Classical economics was strongly influenced by the image of science embodied in eighteenth- and nineteenth-century mechanics. That mechanics, however, admitted of two interpretations. One, with its locus in Britain, took Newtonian physics to be about identifying continuous causal processes, the trend culminating in the Maxwellian mechanical models that rejected in Fitzgerald's words "that old vomit of action at a distance" (Hunt 1991, 73). The other interpretation, centered in France, placed much greater emphasis on laws as mathematical universalities without any strong causal interpretation. The classical economists were, by and large, most influenced by the first, causal interpretation. So when Smith (Redman 1997, 233) says that science describes "the real chains which Nature makes us of to bind together her several operations," "invisible causes," "invisible Power," or "chain of invisible objects," he is expressing the continuous causal process picture of science. Likewise, Marx's laws of motion of the capitalist system are firmly about the causes of the development and transitions of modern capitalist system; his broad materialism was about vanishing spooky noncausal processes from understanding the social world. I take it as obvious that classes, institutions, and individuals in social roles are indispensable in Smith's and Marx's projects. Neither Smith nor Marx thus had any thought that economics was a separate science because the distinction was ontologically grounded; rather, economic and social phenomena are intrinsically intermixed and distinctions between them are piecemeal, pragmatic, and heuristic. Of course the classicals predated the rise of statistical thinking, so a commitment to the logic of science ideal was not a possibility. However, the kind of evidence they did provide relied on much less easily formalizable country historical comparisons, factory reports, and so on.

That the marginalists rejected this picture at every turn in favor of the ideals characteristic of neoclassical growth theory can be seen by looking at Jevons. In Jevons view:

1. Causes are suspect: "There is no particular difference between knowledge of causes and our general knowledge of succession (1874, 260)." Mill's methods for inferring causes are suspect. The final form of a theory is mathematical and makes no reference to causes.
2. Scientific inference is akin to the probabilistic problem of inferring a population trait from a sample trait, that is, from a logical problem. He sought to characterize an inductive logic of science.
3. Economics is about laws: Economics can produce laws that "apply, more or less completely, to all human beings of who we have any knowledge."
4. Marginalist explanations can be scaled up from the individual to the aggregate: "The principles of exchange are the same in nature, however wide or narrow may be the market considered. Every trading body is either an individual or an aggregate of individuals, and the law, in the case of the aggregate, must depend upon the fulfillment of the law in the individuals, (1888, Chapter IV, 20) or "the laws of economics are the same in the case of individuals and of nations" (1888, Chapter I, 21).

The vision of economic science found in Jevons thus differs markedly from the classicals; neoclassical growth theory shares those same differences.

This completes my discussion of neoclassical growth theory and the assumptions of its arguments. My next goal is to assess how these assumptions fare, and to describe alternative approaches to explaining growth that arguably do not rest on the neoclassical growth assumptions. These two processes will be intermixed because explaining alternative approaches will be pointing to phenomena that do not fit neoclassical growth assumptions.

Let me start with the general picture of explanation embodied in the neoclassical growth tradition. We saw that the dominant trend in neoclassical growth theory is to eschew causal talk for functional relations. However, a well-developed literature argues that appeal to regularities can be neither necessary nor sufficient to explain (Salmon & Kitcher 1989). Yet that does not mean that citing regularities is *never* explanatory. A reasonable case can be made that, in fundamental physics—quantum mechanics and general relativity—causal notions drop out in favor of functional ones (Ladyman & Ross 2007). If that is the case, it would be ill-motivated bullet biting to deny that physics does not explain rather than concluding that explanation by regularities is no explanation at all. However, the regularities in physics have two key characteristics that neoclassical growth accounts do not: universality and dynamics.

Put roughly, universalities are regularities that are invariant or stable insofar as they hold across a range of phenomena despite variation in the other factors involved (see Ladyman and Ross 2007 for a much more nuanced discussion). The regularities of physical theory provide a dynamic insofar as they describe the change in variables through state space. Neoclassical growth theory describes an equilibrium condition with some informal reasons to think that equilibrium might be stable once reached. It does not provide a dynamic for behavior far from equilibrium. Moreover, as we will see shortly, the models tested are positing a much simpler process than that proposed in neoclassical growth theory, and they do not model the causal processes involving savings and depreciation that might motivate stable equilibria. There is also little reason to think the regularities involved are invariant to any significant extent, especially the regularities that appear in the regression equations that are tested against the data. As I note later and in the discussion that follows of alternatives to neoclassical growth theory, the relation between factors involved in growth are likely to be quite context dependent.

Of course, we could take neoclassical growth theory as describing not just regularities but causes. After all, talk of "determinants" is ambiguous and, moreover, the main purpose of neoclassical growth theory is to look for policy variables that might be manipulated by policy. If neoclassical growth theory gave us the causes rather than regularities, then they would have a much stronger claim to actually be explaining.

However, if we look at the models actually tested in the cross-country regressions, they have the form depicted in Figure 17.2.

As should be obvious, this is a very simple causal model. It certainly is a possible model and, if well confirmed, would provide straightforward causal explanations. However, as we will see later, the evidence for it is seriously lacking.

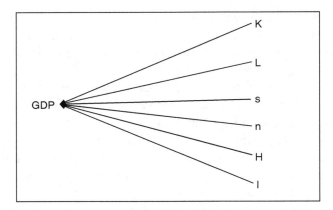

Figure 17.2. Causal model of cross country growth regressions

Taken as a causal model, the new growth theory provides a simple picture of causation for another reason. Generally ruled out as causal possibilities in such models are the following:

1. Necessary causes, that is, causes that are requirements for some outcome but on their own may not have any effect.
2. Contingent causes, that is, causes that may have influence only in specified background contexts that are not always present.
3. Causal influences that do not effect the variance of the variables being measured, for example, causes that effect levels.
4. Asymmetric causes, that is, causes where an increase in the value of variable may increase the value of the variable but a decrease may not produce a decrease or vice versa.
5. Causes that work only at a threshold.

Situations 1 and 4 are completely invisible to regression tests of causality, because regression is about variance and has no concept of necessary cause. Some evidence about the other kinds of causes can be gotten from multiple regressions—for example, for contingent causes by including interaction terms—but these are fairly crude tools that are hard to interpret and generally not employed in any case. These difficulties are nontrivial problems for neoclassical growth because, as we will see later, good work in development economics suggests that causes of these five types are common in the process of economic growth. These types of complex causality are in direct opposition to the neoclassical assumptions of independently acting causes and uniform regularities in the factors causing growth across countries.

The Jevonian assumption that aggregates can be treated as maximizing individuals is also problematic. We noted that this assumption shows up in at least two guises: in the uses of representative agents in some models and more fundamentally in the use of aggregate production functions. There is strong reason to think that representative agents make coherent sense in only very restricted conditions and this is generally recognized (Gallgati & Kirman 1999; Hartley 1997).

There are other, less appreciated problems surrounding aggregate production functions that relate in part to the Cambridge capital controversies in the 1960s and 1970s. That debate was often at cross-purposes, so it will be useful to keep in mind our earlier discussion of the different content that neoclassical growth theory might take on over and above the equations themselves. A fundamental worry in the Cambridge controversies was one about circularity. To produce an aggregate production function for an aggregation of diverse goods, such as that produced by a country, outputs and inputs have to be measured in value, not in physical terms. However, to have an aggregate value measure presupposes that there is already a price for capital and a given distribution of income. This looks like a short circle from what is to be explained to what is explaining. Solow's (1956) original article on neoclassical growth theory was locus classicus for this criticism.

Let us distinguish some of the different theses that might be involved:

1. Marginal productivity accounts of income distribution at any level are empty.
2. Aggregate production functions do not explain the relative shares due to capital and labor by virtue of their marginal productivities.
3. Aggregate production functions cannot tell us anything about the causes of growth.

The first claim is the strongest and was pushed by Robinson (1954) among others. It is uncompelling, since problems about aggregate production functions need not cast doubts on marginalist account of distribution at the microlevel (Fisher 1993).

The third thesis is also suspect because there are many different things one might want to say about the causes of growth that need not stand or fall together. One thing that cross-country regressions and related studies surely provide some evidence for is that greater capital intensity in a country means greater output, other things being equal. Of course that is not something we really need the elaborate machinery of cross-country regressions or growth accounting to find plausible. However, it is a thesis about the causes of growth that is logically independent from thesis 2, which goes on to explain the size of that contribution by aggregate marginal productivity.

The second thesis has more going for it. Solow clearly claimed that estimating an aggregate production function was providing evidence about the relative marginal productivities of the factors, productivities that explained the distribution of income between them. There are three fairly convincing reasons to be suspicious here. The original circularity problem remains because the aggregate production functions have to take the price of capital as given and, because in theory the price of capital depends on its marginal productivity, the latter is not being explained.

To put it simply, estimating aggregate production functions gives evidence about marginal productivities of aggregate factors only if we already have evidence that marginalist accounts apply at the aggregate level. The second problem is that there is no reason to think that aggregates behave according to marginalist analysis scaled up to the country level. There is no plausible story that I know of justifying treating entire countries as maximizing output in the way, for example, we might sometimes treat governments as maximizing a revenue function (in Ross's 2006 terminology, there is no "plausible intentional stance account"). Finally, Fisher (1993) has shown decisively that there should not be such a story, because the conditions under which firm-level production functions will combine to produce an aggregate production function of the standard sort are highly strict and very unlikely to be met in any real-world economy, even as an approximation.[3]

So there are serious doubts about neoclassical growth models insofar as they are supposed to be providing a causal explanation based on marginal productivities.[4] If the equations tested are just supporting the claim that there is some causal contribution and causal relation from the quantity of capital a country has at its disposal and the total output, then the doubts are less worrisome.[5] The equations themselves do not tell us which of these interpretations to impose (again, a model is not just a set of equations), but it is obvious that the advocates hope to be saying considerably more than this.

Explanatory assumptions 4 and 5 about economics as a separate science certainly seem suspect when it comes to explaining growth. The social factors such as norms and institutions are not always separable elements like so many beads on a string whose influence can be calibrated against a common metric. We will see some detailed evidence why this separation is implausible later when we discuss the alternatives to neoclassical growth provided by recent development economics.

Let's turn next to ask about the plausibility of the logic of science ideal as embodied in the cross-country regressions supporting new growth theory. No doubt there are some plausible a priori restrictions on acceptable inference, with not violating the probability calculus being the most obvious such restriction (though exactly what that comes to in dynamic belief change is controversial). However, the standards embodied in neoclassical growth theory in fact violate this most basic requirement. They do so by equating statistical significance with being well supported by the evidence. That this is an error should be common knowledge, but it is not, and economics is no exception in this regard. Here are the basics: a significance test, if reasonably based (more about this later), gives us information about seeing the results in question by chance if there is no real correlation involved. That means we get information about the plausibility of the competing hypothesis that our data is to be expected by chance alone. In short, it tells us about the $p(E/H=$no correlation and sampling error$)$. However, what we want to know is whether the hypothesis—say that growth and human capital are correlated—is well supported by the evidence at hand. That is asking about the probability that the hypothesis is true, given the evidence or $p(H/E)$. Statistical significance does not tell us that all by itself, and assuming it does is a well-known but widely ignored fallacy (Cohen 1994).

What else is needed if appeals to statistical significance are actually going to provide compelling results? What assumptions need to be added to turn the simple rhetorical appeal to statistic significance into an explicit and compelling argument? We need at the very least to have (1) some idea whether the data make sense if our hypothesis is true, as well as (2) if the data are consistent with other competing hypotheses, besides the possibility of chance effects.[6] Beyond this, standards are controversial to some extent. Bayesians will want to include the prior plausibility. However, one need not think that such things are available in any precise sense to see that if our background information tells us that the hypothesis at issue is really stupid, then its predictive success may not count much in its favor.

The standard evidence for neoclassical growth theory is questionable on both counts. In statistical terms, asking about how likely we are to see this data given the maintained hypothesis is asking about the power of the test—about the probability of a false negative which is 1- power. The evidence supplied for neoclassical growth theory (and most econometric studies) involves no attempt to calculate power. So when variables are rejected for lack of statistical significance, we do not really know what to conclude, despite the widespread practice of inferring that a correlation is weakly supported by the evidence if it is not statistically significant. There may be informal reasons for thinking that these tests have reasonable power, but they get little explicit discussion in presentations dominated by this logic of science ideal.

Two other errors are embedded in this statistical practice: not asking at what level the hypothesis *is* significant, and inferring that the observed values are the real values rather than that there is some correlation. That a correlation is significant at the .051 level is something a reasonable person would take as *some* positive evidence for a hypothesis, but that is precluded when variables are rejected if they are not significant at the .05 level. This seems especially true when models are offered as reasonable after detailed specification searches where significance levels change depending on what other variable are included in the equation. The second problem concerning inferring the magnitudes of correlations is that the significance tests, as typically used, tell us the probability of seeing the observed correlation when there is *no* correlation in the population. That is consistent with the true correlation being nonzero but different from the observed sample correlation. So the frequent fine judgments about which growth variables are "most important," based on rejecting the hypothesis of no correlation, have to be taken with a large grain of salt.

A final concern about this version of the logic of science ideal implicit in neoclassical growth theory is the basis for the probability claims made. This is, of course, a huge issue about much econometric work, viz., what are its probability foundations (see Kuzenkamp 2001). There are no random assignments or random samples from a population in the cross-country growth equations. In fact, the "sample" is the population. Haavelmo's solution to this problem is to take such data as a draw from a hypothetical population. However, his discussion is cryptic without any real account of how this assumption is justified. The most coherent story here, I think, is that we can try to show that the errors are randomly distributed.[7] If we can do this, then we have evidence for the claim that "if the data were generated by a process with a random component, then these kinds of error distribution would be expected." So statistical tests on errors are tests for this hypothesis. But note that this is only part of the evidence we need to know that it is reasonable to think that we have a random process. It would also be nice to know the plausibility of there being a random process in the first place. This is what a random assignment does and why an actual (not hypothetical) random sample or assignment will usually give a stronger argument than simply a probability calculation from a hypothetical sample.

However, this general defense of the probability foundations of econometrics is moot since there is very little error testing in the cross-country regressions (Barro 2001). Hendry and Krolzig (2004), for one, argue that specification searches of the type they favor on the cross-country data would find the true model if the probability assumptions of the model were met. However, they argue that there is no reason to think that the data in cross-country regressions satisfies those assumptions.[8]

All the aforementioned problems concern the extent to which we can reasonably believe the *correlations* described in the final models that rely essentially on significance tests are the real ones. However, one side of the new growth wants to go beyond correlations to causes. The evidence for the causal story is very dubious for two reasons, even if we had no doubts about what the correlations are: As we saw earlier, there is good reason to think that complex causality—necessary causes, thresholds, contextual causes, and such—abound in the real-world of developing economies. These are all ruled out by fiat in the cross-country regressions. The second problem is that the simple causal model proposed where growth is the dependent variable and is caused by a list of factors acting independently is not credible. There is good reason to think that growth itself influences the so-called independent variables to differing degrees and that there are causal relations among those variables, as some of neoclassical models explicitly acknowledge. The models tested, however, all make no allowances for such more complex causal models, testing only the simple model of Figure 17.2. But if we think mutual causation is at least logically possible between all the variables, then there are many, many other possible models to rule out, which the cross-country regressions certainly do not do.

To recap, we have so far traced out implicit assumptions about evidence and explanation of neoclassical growth theory and found them wanting. I turn now in the rest of the chapter to look at other work on growth that does not embody either the assumptions of formal accounts of explanation and evidence or of an ontologically ground separate science of economics. Instead, explanation is about causes where causes are complex in the ways already described, statistical results are only one kind of evidence and one needing an explicit argument for their applicability, and explaining growth is explaining a complex socioeconomic process that uses tools wherever it can find them.

There is a variety of recent work on growth and development that is quite different in spirit than the neoclassical growth models. Let me mention three bodies of work or approaches that overlap in various ways and are particularly interesting.

1. New institutional economics applied to growth issues. The focus is on situations in which price signals and efficiency do not suffice to explain because of things such as asymmetric information, moral hazard, varying consequences of different distributions of wealth, missing markets, and nonmarket institutions. Rural poverty and development have been prime areas for research (Hoff et. al 1993).

2. Single-country or regional analytic narratives. The term *analytic narratives* originates in recent literature from Bates' et al. (1998) use of game theory models to explain various institutional changes in economic history. They are narratives in the sense that they provide traditional historical accounts of how one event led to another. They are analytic in that explicit models constrain the narrative. Examples include Acemogula, Johnson, and Robinson's (2001) work on the role of institutions on economic growth, in general, and in Botswana, in particular, and Feenstra and Hamilton's (2006) work on the role of economic growth in Taiwan and South Korea. The former uses an explicit causal model relating early colonial institutions and current economic performance, and the latter uses monopolistic competition frameworks developed in industrial organization and international trade to explain the different business group structures found in Taiwan and South Korea.

3. Single-market or agent studies. Examples of the former are the numerous studies on rural credit markets in developing countries using survey data to examine the role of information asymmetries and nonmarket institutions to understand the supply and demand for credit (Siamwalla et al. 1993). Examples of the latter are numerous studies of the determinants of household behavior in developing countries. All are done with the goal of understanding their contribution to or detrimental effects on growth.

The aforementioned approaches to economic explanation may look disjointed compared to the models-as-equations vision of neoclassical growth theory and, correspondingly, thus look atheoretical. However, that need not be the case. As I have argued elsewhere (Kincaid 1996), there is a supply-and-demand argument strategy common in economics. That argument pattern lies behind all this work, which makes it systematic in a way that may not be obvious. Furthermore, pure economic theory has its place here, not in direct application to empirical phenomena, but as a hypothesis generator about possible mechanisms, causal factors, and causal processes. Let me explain.

The supply and demand argument strategy analyzes aggregate market phenomena. It works by:

1. Identifying the relevant commodity, buyers and sellers, and measure of price.
2. Explaining the market by identifying the relevant supply-and-demand curves and by explaining changes as either movements along curves or as shifts in curves.
3. Identifying the underlying causes of the slopes and shifts in slopes by looking at the assets, costs, and preferences of buyers and sellers, the paradigm case of which involves identifying substitutes and complements.

This kind of explanatory pattern is found over and over again in applied economics. Much other work, like that already described, consists of identifying the factors explaining shifts and slopes of supply-and-demand curves, including the degenerate but very important case in which there are no curves to be found because of missing markets, and shadow prices must be input, for example.

Two things to note about this broad supply-and-demand strategy. First, it need not and usually does not invoke individual utility functions. These are causal processes that can be described without any strong commitments beyond what aggregate processes are described. For example, as Becker (1978) showed, downward-sloping aggregate demand curves are consistent with random choices of individuals because of budget constraints. While aggregative in nature, the level of aggregation is very low, indeed, compared to the neoclassical production functions for entire countries, and it is at a sufficiently low level that approximate aggregate productions can be expected to exist. Second, there is a clear place for economic theory here, in the sense of the analysis of constrained maximization to suggest the relevant causal factors and relations in analyzing the determinants of supply and demand and their interaction in market and nonmarket outcomes. For example, models with increasing returns to scale have been very important in tackling developing economies. Game theory has been essential for formulating factors affecting household consumption and production. Thus, the alternative approach from recent development economics has systematic components.

Also in their favor is the fact that these approaches make frequent use of complex causality, and that many variables that occur in the neoclassical cross-country equations fall into these categories. The role of education, infrastructure, and inequality in growth are good examples. Literacy rates in Cuba are the highest in Latin America, but growth in Cuba is dismal. For education to have an influence, demand-side factors are essential—markets for labor in general and technological levels that can use the human capital investments come to mind. Infrastructure is another factor that is required for education to have an effect and is, arguably, a necessary requirement for growth. Well educated children of small farmers in an isolated rural outpost where production is almost entirely clan based are unlikely to make much difference for growth.

Single country narratives show that inequality may well be an important causal factor in some contexts. High inequality resulting from concentration of land in a ruling elite may mean that essential elements of growth, such as education, may not be forthcoming because it is in the interests of the powerful elite owning the land to prevent them. Cross-country equations do not find that inequality has an effect. This is taken to confirm the common neoclassical claim that distribution is a neutral factor when it comes to efficiency so long as property rights are well defined. This situation nicely illustrates how the causal assumptions embedded in neoclassical growth theory will make finding causes unlikely when the causes are complex. A factor that is necessary but not efficacious on its own or a factor that has causal effects when other factors must be present that vary across countries, will not show a consistent correlation with the effect. Inequality may have no influence in the cross-country regressions because it sometimes has an important effect and sometimes no effect at all.

These alternative approaches to neoclassical growth theory and the supply-and demand-strategy they embody also present a very different relationship between the social and the economic from that found in the strong separatist thesis embedded in neoclassical growth theory. Family ties, informal social networks, norms, caste structure, property-rights arrangements, interest groups, and so on are essential to the analysis and not a separable factor in explaining outcomes. Particularly important is the effort to include government and interest group rent seeking as an endogenous causal factor in explaining outcomes and in devising policy advice.

How is evidence provided for these kinds of accounts? Neoclassical growth theory seemed to have a simple, objective way to assess the evidence it provided—significance tests and the like. Of course, the moral of the earlier discussion of that kind of evidence was that it is often inadequate and not so objective and straightforward as it is often taken. Providing evidence is always providing an argument with a structure and assumptions, though that argument may be implicit as, I argued, is the case with appeals to statistical significance and probability. The advocates of the alternative approaches to neoclassical growth theory are much more aware that their evidence constitutes an argument with diverse elements that must be defended in diverse ways.

The most successful empirical work makes a multifaceted argument using various sorts of evidence to argue for an explicit causal model. Statistical arguments are certainly made, but they avoid elaborate data mining and are either based on actual known probabilistic mechanisms or are straightforward enough to have an interpretation as a ruling-out-chance argument. Crucial evidence for causal claims can be supported by cross-country comparison using variants of Mill's methods. Theoretical results are used to suggest possible causal mechanisms. Causal processes are traced in a continuous fashion, sometimes over a significant time period.

One standard kind of study that instantiates these tactics is the use of survey data in development economics. Here there are random samples, so we are on much stronger grounds for the inferences ruling out chance. The power of the tests is calculated, thus avoiding the troubling problem of trying to infer what lack of significance actually means. Detailed causal models based on the supply and demand argument strategy are supplied.

Detailed country studies are another route to providing well-specified evidential arguments. Let me illustrate with work on Mauritius (Subramanian and Roy 2003), one of the few African success stories. Between 1973 and 1999 Mauritius's GDP grew at an average rate of 5.9 percent, avoiding the effects of the financial crisis of the late 1990s. How is that growth to be explained?

Favorable initial conditions seem not to do the trick. Empirical work suggests that tropical climate, remoteness from markets, and commodity dependence are strongly associated with histories of slow growth. Yet Mauritius has among the worst scores on these items and thus the absence of those factors alone cannot be a necessary condition for growth. Openness to trade is another factor that we have good empirical and theoretical evidence to think can be a causal factor in growth, yet on International Monetary Fund measures Mauritius, in the early 1990s, ranked at the highest level of protection. Another possible cause—the government policy of establishing export process zones (EPZs) by itself cannot suffice, because multiple African countries have them without good growth.

Getting at the actual causes requires a more complex picture than can be captured by the search for single factors that are sufficient causes, and less aggregative measurements of possible causal factors are essential. The EPZs were not sufficient by themselves as the causal comparison illustrated suggests. However, there is substantial evidence that they were decisive for growth in combination with other causal conditions. The EPZ growth rate might have been simply due to government subsidies and not a net contributor to growth. However, growth accounting analysis during the relevant years shows that Mauritius' productivity growth in the EPZs was quite high, higher than the growth rate in the East Asian growth success stories. Making that growth possible were apparently at least two factors: favorable trade agreements in the sugar and textile industries with the United States and the European Union and the social and political institutions of Mauritius. The trade deals were actually part of protectionist policies in the United States and the European Union but worked to Mauritius advantage internally, and they made the export sector sufficiently profitable that it undercut the natural and growth-reducing tendencies of overinvesting in the highly protected domestic industries. So, in short, the variable "openness to trade" that is usually measured in the cross-country growth equations is too gross a variable to get at the real causal story.

The quality of institutions plays a role here as well in explaining why the export sectors worked. Mauritius ranks high compared to African and developing Asian countries on measures of institutional quality. The well-functioning and well-paid civil service probably reduced the amount of rent seeking and corruption in the administration of the EPZs. The health of the political system with functioning checks and balances helps explain why Mauritius did not go the standard African route of looting the most productive sectors by the government.

These are the arguments that Subramanian and Roy make. Note how they work: They use simple descriptive statistics on differences between countries to make causal arguments. They trace the steps in a causal process from the establishment of EPZs and the political system to the stages of growth. They do not involve simple causal relations between large-scale highly aggregated factors that are treated as independent causes. And, importantly, social factors, such as government rent seeking and the strength of the political system, are endogenous to the causal explanation.

So to conclude, this is surely a brief sketch of what alternatives to neoclassical growth theory look like as was the earlier discussion of probabilistic foundations, aggregation problems, and other complex issues in these debates. However, my stated goal was to trace out philosophy of science assumptions and the explicit and implicit arguments to shed some light on disputes about growth and development. I leave it to the reader to decide how bright that light has been.

NOTES

1. Thanks to Don Ross for helpful comments on this chapter.
2. Another distinct sense is to take economic theory as about constrained maximization with no commitment to the nature of the entities doing the maximizing as in Ross (2005).
3. Felipe and McCombie (2005) argue that aggregate productions that seem to fit the data well do so only because they are accounting identities. Fisher (1993) argues that their empirical fit results from the fact that relative shares of labor and capital have been constant. It is not clear to me the logical relationship between these two points.
4. One body of work related to the neoclassical model that I have not discussed in this paper is growth accounting. It is an interesting question that I do not have space to pursue: How do these aggregation issues bare on that work and its evidential value?
5. I am actually simplifying here, for there are options between providing good evidence for a full causal model and evidence only for some causal relation. Partial causal claims with restricted intent, for example, ones showing that the value of one variable is a limiting constraint on the value of some other variable, might be a case in point. It is an interesting question how Solow and related-type models might be used in making an argument about more complex causality than the models typically assume, and when the argument is about a single or few cases rather than a general model.
6. I am ignoring tough questions about whether the reported p values are believable that arise from performing multiple significant tests, sometimes millions (Sala-I-Martin 1997). Classical frequentist statistics imposes a penalty for multiple hypotheses tests and would find no meaning to p values asserted after indefinitely many specification searches (O'Brien & Fleming 1979). There are various brute force, empirical—that is, not logical deductions from the probability calculus—attempts to show what the p values would be for specification searches. However, it is probable that these empirical demonstrations make assumptions that are not satisfied in actual econometric practice. See Kincaid (2009) for discussion.

7. This corresponds to Spanos's (2000) idea that there are two quite distinct statistical enterprises, namely, testing the statistical model and using it to draw inferences.

8. One sometimes hears that, if we use generalized least squares, then we need not worry about correlated errors because GLS is still unbiased in this case. However, this misses the point—the unbiased holds only if we have a random sample, and the correlated errors argue against that.

REFERENCES

Acemoglu, D., Johnson,S., and Robinson, J.. (2001). "The Colonial Origins of Comparative Development. "*American Economic Review* 91: 1369–1401.

Bates, R., Grief, A., Levi, M., Rosenthal, J-L., and Weingast, B. 1998. *Analytic Narratives.* Princeton: Princeton University Press.

Barro, R. (2001). *Determinants of Economic Growth.* Cambridge, MA: MIT Press.

Becker, G. (1978). *The Economic Approach to Human Behavior.* Chicago: University of Chicago Press.

Beller, M. (2001). *Quantum Dialogue: The Making of a Revolution.* Chicago: University of Chicago Press.

Cohen, P. (1994). "The Earth Is Round (p < .05)." *American Psychologist* 49: 997–1003.

Felipe, J. and McCombie, J. (2005). "The Tyranny of the Identity: Growth Accounting." International Review of Applied Economics. 20: 283–299.

Fenstra, R, & Hamilton, G. (2006). *Emergent Economies, Divergent Paths.* Cambridge, England: Cambridge University Press.

Fisher, F. (1993). *Aggregation.* Cambridge, MA: MIT Press.

Gallegati, M. & Kirman, A. (1999). *Beyond the Representative Agent.* Oxford: Edward Elgar.

Hartley, J. (1997). *The Representative Agent in Macroeconomics.* London: Routledge

Hausman, D. (1992). *The Separate and Inexact Science of Economics.* Cambridge, England: Cambridge University Press.

Hendry, D. & Krolzig, H.(2004). "We Ran One Regression." *Oxford Bulletin of Economics & Statistics* 66: 799–810.

Hoff, K., Braverman, A. & Stiglitz, J. (1993). *The Economics of Rural Organization.* Oxford: Oxford University Press.

Hunt, B. (2005). *The Maxwellians.* Ithaca, NY: Cornell University Press.

Jevons, W. (1874). *Principles of Science.* London: Macmillan.

Jevons, W. (1888). *The Theory of Political Economy.* 3rd ed. London: Macmillan.

Keuzenkamp, H. (2001). *Probability, Econometrics and Truth.* Cambridge, England: Cambridge University Press.

Kincaid, Harold. (1996). *The Philosophical Foundations of the Social Sciences: Analyzing Controversies in Social Research.* Cambridge, England: Cambridge University Press.

Kincaid, H. (2009). "Naturalism and the Nature of Evidence in Economics," in Maki, U. *Handbook for the Philosophy of Science: Philosophy of Economics.* Elvesier.

Ladyman, J. and Ross, D. (2007). *Everything Must Go.* Oxford: Oxford University Press.

Lucas, Robert. (1988). "On the Mechanics of Economic Development." *Journal of Monetary Economics* 22: 3–42.

Mankiw, N. (1995). "The Growth of Nations." *Brookings Papers on Economic Activity* 25: 275–310.

O'Brien, P. & Fleming, T. (1979). "A Multiple Testing Procedure for Clinical Trials." *Biometrics* 35: 549–556.

Pritchett, Lance. (2003). "A Conclusion to Cross-national Growth Research: A Foreword To The Countries Themselves." In G. McMahon & L. Squire, L., Eds., *Explaining Growth: A Global Research Project*, 213–245. New York: Palgrave Macmillan.

Redman, D. (1997). *The Rise of Political Economy as a Science*. Cambridge: MIT Press.

Robinson, J. (1954). "The Production Function and the Theory of Capital." *Review of Economic Studies* 21: 81–106.

Roderik, D. (2003). In Search of Prosperity. Princeton University Press: Princeton, NJ.

Romer, Paul. (1990). "Endogenous Technological Change." *Journal of Political Economy* 98: S71-S102.

Romer, Paul. (1994). "The Origins of Endogenous Growth." *Journal of Economic Perspectives* 8: 3–22.

Ross, Don (2005). *Economic Theory and Cognitive Science: Microexplanation*. Cambridge, MA: MIT Press.

Sala-i-Martin, X. (1997). "I Just Ran Two Million Regressions." *American Economic Review* 87: 178–183.

Salmon, W. & Kitcher, P. (1989). *Scientific Explanation*. Minneapolis: University of Minnesota Press.

Senhadji, Abdelhak (2000). "Sources of Economic Growth: An Extensive Growth Accounting Exercise." *IMF Staff Papers* 47: 129–158.

Siamwalla, A., Pinthong, C., Satsanguan, P., Nettayarak, P., Minggmaneenakin, W. & Tubpun, Y. (1993). "The Thai Rural Credit System and Elements of a Theory." In K. Hoff, A. Braverman & J. Stiglitz, J., Eds., *The Economics of Rural Organization*. Oxford: Oxford University Press.

Solow, R. (1956). "A Contribution to the Theory of Economic Growth." *Quarterly Journal of Economics* 70: 65–94.

Solow, Robert. (1957). "Technical Change and the Aggregate Production Function." *The Review of Economics and Statistics* 39: 312–320.

Solow, Robert. (2000). *Growth Theory: An Exposition*. Oxford: Oxford University Press.

Spanos, A. (2000). "Data Mining Revisited: Hunting Or Without a License." *Journal of Economic Methodology* 7: 231–264.

Subramanian, A. and Roy, D. (2003). "Who Can Explain the Maurtian Miracle? Meade, Romer, Sachs, or Roderik?" In Roderik 2003, 205–244.

CHAPTER 18

SEGMENTED LABOR MARKET MODELS IN DEVELOPING COUNTRIES

GARY S. FIELDS

THIS chapter is about labor-market models.[1] The aim is to construct models that are as simple as they can be but as complicated as they need to be. Such models, if carefully done, can contribute to an understanding of observed labor market phenomena and to the formulation of sound labor market policies.

Some branches of economics work with models that assume that everybody who works participates in a single, undifferentiated labor market. I regard such models as grossly unrealistic. A better description, I would maintain, is that jobs differ in quality, these different groups being called segments or sectors. Thus, labor market segmentation is said to exist if (1) jobs for individuals of a given skill level differ in terms of their pay or other characteristics, and (2) access to the more attractive jobs is limited in that not all who want the better jobs can get them.

The notion of labor market segmentation can be stylized most simply by maintaining that there are two labor market segments. A realistic assumption is that all who participate in the labor market want the better jobs, but good jobs are available only for a fraction of the labor force. Those who do not get the good jobs must either take up a bad job or remain unemployed. Models with two labor market segments prove to be both tractable and insightful, and so are used here.

In this chapter, labor markets should be thought of as consisting not only of wage and salaried employment but also of self-employment. All who work or seek to work in labor markets are termed *workers*.

Why are labor markets important to economic development? Many individuals and institutions, including the World Bank and the regional development banks, seek "a world free of poverty." Broadly speaking, those who are poor are poor because (1) they earn little from the work they do, if indeed they have work at all, (2) the societies in which they live are too poor to provide them with substantial goods and services by virtue of their citizenship or residency, and (3) the poor are not permitted to move to richer countries. Thus, antipoverty efforts can be focused on (1) helping people as workers by creating more and better-paying employment, (2) helping people as citizens/residents through publicly provided goods and services, and (3) striving for freer movement of labor from poor to rich countries. This chapter is concerned with the first channel namely, helping improve labor market opportunities for workers.

The importance of labor markets for antipoverty efforts is underscored by research studies using decomposition methodologies. These studies have shown that labor income inequality is as important or more important than *all other income sources combined* in explaining total income inequality; see Ayub (1977) for Pakistan, Fields (1979a) for Colombia, and Fei, Ranis, and Kuo (1978, 1979) and Fields and O'Hara Mitchell (1999) for Taiwan. The reason that labor income is so important is, in the words of the 1990 *World Development Report,* that "the poor's most abundant asset [is their] labor." (World Bank 1990, 3). It follows that a very important factor in explaining family income inequality is that some people earn very large amounts for their labor while a great many earn very little. Thus, it is the inequality of labor incomes that accounts primarily for the inequality of total incomes.

Labor income also plays a predominant role in income mobility research. In much of this literature, economic welfare is gauged by household per capita income (PCI) or household per capita consumption (PCC). Research on changing PCI in Indonesia, South Africa, Spain, and Venezuela has shown that household per-capita income changes are determined much more by changes in household income (the numerator) than by changes in number of household members (the denominator) and that changes in labor income far outweigh changes in other sorts of income (Fields et al 2003).

This chapter approaches labor markets through segmented labor-market modeling. Such models start with the recognition that in many countries, the labor market consists of quite distinct segments that are linked with one another. When there are just two segments, these models are called dualistic labor-market models.

As explained below, segmented labor-market models are valuable because they can explain a number of phenomena that simply do not make sense in a single market setting. To develop a framework/typology and lay out the main issues in segmented labor-market modeling, the chapter proceeds in five stages.

The first main substantive section (Section 1) presents the essence of labor market dualism. I maintain that labor markets often consist of quite distinct segments and that a useful and insightful analytical approach is to start with just two.

The second main substantive section is on models of wages and employment in the formal economy. To be reviewed here are (1) the market-clearing labor-market model and the presumed equilibrating forces, (2) above-market-clearing wages set institutionally, (3) above-market-clearing wages set by efficiency wage considerations, and (4) above-market-clearing wages set by worker behavior.

The third main substantive section is on wages and employment in the informal economy. This section presents three characterizations of informal sector labor markets: (1) the informal economy as a free-entry sector that prospective workers enter only as a last resort, (2) the informal economy as a desirable sector that workers choose in preference to formal sector work, and (3) the informal economy with its own internal dualism, combining 1 and 2.

The fourth main substantive section is on formal-informal linkages. The models here are (1) the integrated labor-market model with full market clearing, (2) crowding models, and (3) the Harris-Todaro model.

Finally, the fifth main substantive section discusses five contributions that these models make to understanding and policy analysis. These issues are (1) why an increase in productivity might cause wages to fall, (2) why Taiwan's economic growth led first to falling unemployment at constant wages and then to economy-wide wage increases at full employment, (3) why the solution to urban unemployment in Kenya was not urban employment creation but rural development, (4) why poverty is so severe in the urban informal sector of many developing countries, and (5) why expanding formal sector employment sometimes improves labor-market conditions and sometimes does not.

Although the models presented here differ from one another in important respects, they all share certain common features of which the reader should be aware from the outset. First, firms in these models are assumed to be maximizing profits. This means that they hire workers, raise wages, and improve worker quality if and only if it is in their profit-maximizing interest to do so. Second, workers in these models are assumed to be maximizing utility. Especially in poor countries, in which large numbers of people value additional goods greatly compared to leisure, the utility-maximization assumption may often be fruitfully replaced by an income-maximization assumption. Third, the notion of market equilibrium used in this chapter needs to be clarified. Market equilibrium is a state toward which a market tends and, once there, it tends to stay. Market clearing is a state in which the quantity of a good or service supplied equals the quantity demanded. Some of the equilibria we shall deal with in this chapter are market clearing and others are not. And finally, the objective of this chapter is to make labor outcomes more understandable; much of what is understandable is not pretty.

1. The Essence of Labor Market Dualism

At the core of segmented labor-market modeling is the distinction between one part of the labor market and another. In the literature, one sector is alternatively called "formal," "modern," "industrial," "good jobs," or "urban," while the other is alternatively called "informal," "traditional," "agricultural," "bad jobs," or "rural." (At one point, I even called this latter one the "murky" sector.) Throughout this chapter, the formal/informal terminology shall be used.

Labor market dualism is a useful stylization of what has been called "labor-market segmentation" or "labor-market fragmentation." Dixit (1973, 325) explained why:

> The dual economy has, over the last decade, proved itself to be a useful conceptual framework for analyzing several problems of economic development...Dual economy models provide a significantly better description and understanding of the problems of development than any aggregate model...because the sectoral division chosen reflects several vital social and economic distinctions in the type of economy being analyzed.

Why have just two sectors? Basu (1997, 152) put it thus:

> The assumption of duality is merely for analytical convenience. If fragmentation—irrespective of the number of parts—in itself causes some problems and we wish to examine these, then the simplest assumption to make is that of dualism.

Unfortunately, international practice has been quite ambiguous about the feature distinguishing the two sectors. The International Labour Organization (ILO) and the Economic Commission for Latin America and the Caribbean have defined the informal sector as the sum of nonprofessional self-employed, domestic workers, unpaid workers, and workers in enterprises employing five or fewer workers. In Brazil, the formal sector consists of workers who hold labor cards entitling them to various benefits and protections and the informal sector of those who do not. In other contexts, the formal sector is distinguished according to whether the firm is registered with the government and pays taxes. Yet others equate the informal economy with drugs, prostitution, and other illegal activities. For alternative definitions and operationalizations, see ILO (2002) and Jhabvala, Sudarshan, and Unni (2003).

The distinguishing feature used by Nobel laureates Arthur Lewis (1954) and Simon Kuznets (1955) as well as other dual economy modelers is the fact that workers earn different wages depending on the sector of the economy in which they are able to find work. Lewis wrote (1954, 150): "Earnings in the subsistence sector set a floor to wages in the capitalist sector, but in practice wages have to be higher than this, and there is usually a gap of 30 per cent or more between capitalist wages and subsistence earnings." Lewis explained that although part of the gap is "illusory" because of the higher cost of living in the capitalist sector, there remained a real wage gap due to (a) the "psychological cost of transferring from the easy going way of life of the subsistence sector to the more regimented and urbanized environment of the capitalist sector," (b) the payoff to experience in the capitalist sector, and (c) "workers in the capitalist sector acquiring tastes and a social prestige which have conventionally to be recognized by higher real wages."

Kuznets (1955) further developed the model of wage dualism and intersectoral shifts by exploring how various measures of income inequality (including the income share of the lowest income quintile, the income share of the richest income quintile, and the range) would change as the high-income sector comes to employ an increasing share of the population. All of the inequality measures used by Kuznets (the income share of the poorest quintile, the income share of the richest quintile, and the interquintile range) exhibited an inverted-U pattern, which later came to be known as the "Kuznets Curve." Subsequent research examined inequality further (Knight 1976; Robinson 1976; Fields 1979a; Anand & Kanbur 1993) and also examined poverty (Fields 1979a; Anand & Kanbur 1985) in the Lewis-Kuznets process of intersectoral shifts.

Later writings on labor-market dualism were grounded in human capital theory as developed by Schultz (1961, 1962), Becker (1962, 1964), and Mincer (1962, 1974). This later literature on labor-market dualism stressed that for dualism to exist, different wages must be paid in different sectors to *comparable* workers. Subsequently, many researchers reported empirical evidence showing such dualism or segmentation for observationally equivalent workers.

The idea that different wages are paid to comparable workers has been incorporated, largely without question, into job-search theory. Since the late 1960s and early 1970s, a whole class of models has arisen in which a wide variety of wages exist in the labor market, and workers are presumed to search among employers for the best possible opportunities. See, for instance, the textbook treatments of job search in Ehrenberg and Smith (2003) and Cahuc and Zylberberg (2004) and also the work on equilibrium wage distributions by Stiglitz (1985) and Burdett and Mortensen (1998).

Dualistic labor-market models have been criticized on a number of grounds. One critique is that offered by Rosenzweig (1988). Noting that empirical studies often show that workers with given measured human capital characteristics have systematically different wages or earnings, depending on the type of employment in which they are working, he asked (756): "Do [these differentials] suggest barriers to mobility—noncompeting groups—or do they merely reflect compensatory differentials, rewards for unmeasured skills or compensation for unmeasured differences in the disutility of the workplace?" Favoring the latter set of explanations, Rosenzweig found the dualistic labor-market literature unconvincing.

Dualistic labor-market models, and segmented labor-market models more generally, have been criticized on other grounds as well. An Inter-American Development Bank report (IADB 2003) put it thus: "According to [the dualistic view of the labor market], the formal and informal economies operated in segmented labor markets and there is limited mobility between the two. Nothing could be further from the truth... In a given six-month period, about 16 percent of workers in Mexico and 11 percent of workers in Argentina move either in or out of an informal job." Nonetheless, the fact is that most workers *remain* in the sector in which they began.

These critiques notwithstanding, it appears to me that luck plays an important role in the sense that the very same individual with his or her own measured and unmeasured skills will do better or worse in the labor market over the long run if a job vacancy exists in a more attractive labor-market sector than if such a vacancy does not exist. Thus, labor markets are better characterized as being segmented in the sense of cumulative advantage and low-level traps (Nelson 1966, Merton 1968, Doeringer & Piore 1971, Boudon 1973, Meade 1976) than as being unified in the sense that the next-best employer is essentially indistinguishable from the current one.

To conclude this section, in most settings, I find that it is more useful to think of developing countries' labor markets as being fragmented or segmented than to think of all workers and firms in a country participating in one single labor market. When possible, Occam's Razor suggests limiting the analysis to two sectors. Labor market dualism was a most useful starting point for analyzing some economies when it was first presented decades ago, and it remains a useful characterization of some economies today. But when two sectors are simply not enough, three-sector or *n*-sector models can prove insightful, a point to be developed further in the sequel.

We turn now to the formal sector labor market, the informal sector labor market, and the interactions between them.

2. THE FORMAL SECTOR LABOR MARKET

This section presents four alternative models of wages and employment in the formal sector: the market-clearing labor-market model, models with wages set above market-clearing levels for institutional reasons, models with wages set above market-clearing levels for efficiency wage reasons, and models with wages set above market-clearing levels because of supply-side considerations.

A. The Market-Clearing Labor Market Model

The market-clearing labor-market model is so well known that it can be presented quite concisely. Figure 18.1 displays the three essential features. First, the amount of labor demanded is taken as a decreasing function of the wage, other things equal. The market labor-demand curve slopes downward because of diminishing marginal revenue product of labor, and the associated substitution and scale effects of a wage change. Second, the amount of labor supplied is taken as an increasing function of the wage, other things equal. The market labor-supply curve slopes upward because a higher wage induces workers to enter this labor market from

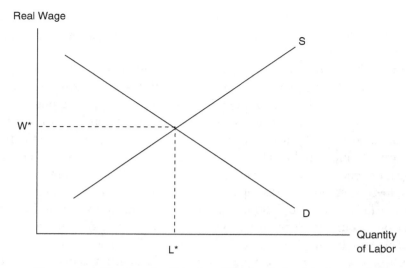

Figure 18.1. The Standard Market-Clearing Labor Market Model

other labor markets and induces nonworkers to enter the labor force. And third, the wage is set by supply and demand in order to clear the market.

According to the market-clearing model, three equilibrating forces operate: behavior of firms, behavior of workers, and behavior of wages. In the model, firms are free to hire workers or not, depending on what is in their profit-maximizing interest to do. If market conditions change, what is in their profit-maximizing interest to do will change accordingly, and firms are free to act on these changes. Similarly, workers are free to supply their labor in any given labor market or not depending on what is in their utility-maximizing interest to do. For them, too, if market conditions change, what is in their utility-maximizing interest to do will change accordingly, and they (workers) are free to act on these changes. And finally, if supply and/or demand conditions change, real wages are free to rise or fall accordingly. (In this chapter, wages should always be thought of in real terms.)

Let us now consider three groups of models with different causal structures and different market outcomes.

B. Above-Market-Clearing Wages Set Institutionally

An important class of models in the labor market literature holds that wages in the formal sector are set by a set of forces *different* from supply and demand. In the models reviewed in this section, the defining feature is heavy reliance on "institutional" forces. ("Institutional" forces are those other than the profit-maximizing behavior of firms and the utility-maximizing behavior of workers.)

It is useful to distinguish five institutional features that may be important in different settings (e.g., Fields & Wan 1989, Fields 1999). They are (1) minimum wages; (2) trade unions; (3) public-sector pay policies; (4) multinational corporations; and (5) labor codes.

Minimum wages aim to assure workers an "adequate" standard of living. Minimum wages have long been on the books throughout most of the developing world (Starr 1981, World Bank 1995, Inter-American Development Bank 2003), but their effects differ. In some countries, such as Bangladesh, Côte d'Ivoire, and India, minimum wages are said to be binding and enforced (World Bank 1995, 75). But in others, minimum-wage laws make little difference. South Korea introduced a minimum-wage system only in 1988, and the minimum-wage levels have been set so that they prove to be a binding constraint for only about 2 percent of Korean workers (Park 1991; Lee 2002). In the case of Taiwan, although a minimum-wage law has been in force for decades, no company has ever been fined for violating the law (Chang 1989).

Trade unions are often encouraged by government policy as a means of entitling workers to a "just" share of the fruits of their labor. One early theory of trade union behavior is that unions have a variety of objectives, including both higher wages and greater union membership (Dunlop 1944). More recent approaches have stressed that those already employed in unions (the "insiders") may be more concerned about raising their wages than about increasing membership (Blanchard & Summers 1986, Lindbeck & Snower 1988). Indeed, unions have raised the wages of their members by as much as 150 percent in Jamaica, 31 percent in Ghana, 24 percent in South Africa, and 20 percent in Malaysia (Tidrick 1975; World Bank 1995, Table 12.2; Aidt & Tzannatos 2002). By contrast, in South Korea and Taiwan, unions have been repressed and the union wage premium is at most two to three percent. (Lin 1989; Park 1991; Yoo 1995).

Public-sector pay policies often result in substantially higher wages being paid to government workers than to their private-sector counterparts. Costa Rica is an example of this, and as a result, "everybody" there tries to work for the government (Gindling 1991). In East Asia, the public sector pays what it has to in order to compete with the private sector—neither more nor less.

Multinational corporations frequently pay above-market wages in sub-Saharan Africa and elsewhere (Squire 1981). Wage levels and working conditions tend to be higher in export-oriented firms than in firms producing for the domestic market (ILO 1998, Moran 2002, Ghose 2003). Although export-oriented multinationals offer higher wages and better working conditions partly for efficiency wage reasons (see later subsection C), they also do this because some governments have "encouraged" them to do so by not so subtly threatening expulsion or expropriation if they do not (Eaton & Gersovitz 1984).

Finally, *labor codes* in some countries regulate hiring and firing, impose payroll taxes on firms, and mandate that employers provide certain benefits to their workers. Panama had such a labor code, and it was estimated to have raised labor costs by 90 percent (Spinanger 1985) before it was finally abandoned as unsustainable. Likewise, Bolivian employment legislation raises labor costs by an estimated 90–110 percent (Bravo 1995). Large firms in India and Zimbabwe are not permitted to dismiss workers; employment levels and economic efficiency have been found to be artificially low as a result (Fallon & Lucas 1991, 1993; Besley & Burgess, 2004).

Higher-than-market-clearing wages for institutional reasons in the formal sector are at the core of many economic models. They include the Keynesian macroeconomic model, Lewis's classical development model, Harris and Todaro's dualistic labor-market model, and many others. Virtually without exception, economic models regard formal- sector employment as being determined in a very neoclassical way: given the wage and the capital stock, employment is set according to the marginal revenue product of labor.

Ample research has shown that labor demand elasticities are significantly negative; Hamermesh (1993) provides a comprehensive review of the empirical literature. In South Africa, for example, various researchers have produced estimates of the wage elasticity of employment in that country's formal sector (Bowles & Heintz 1996; Fields, Leibbrandt & Wakeford 2000). Most estimates range from −0.5 to −0.7. While these studies differ in terms of their precise estimates, what they agree on is that (1) the wage elasticity of employment is significantly negative, and (2) the wage elasticity of employment is significantly less than one in absolute value.

Given significantly negative labor demand elasticities, higher-than-market-clearing wages would be expected to reduce formal sector employment below what it would have been otherwise. Unemployment will result in the economy unless all the workers not employed in the formal sector take up employment in the informal sector. Whether they do so or not is the subject of Section 4.

Given these research findings, the five labor market interventions reviewed above need to be considered carefully. Their aims are laudatory—to raise earnings and reduce poverty—and they do indeed benefit the workers who are fortunate enough to work in covered sectors of the economy. However, they appear to have had adverse employment and efficiency effects and to have contributed to the informalization of the economy, as employers evade the regulations by not engaging workers as regular employees or by not even appearing as official companies (DeSoto 1989, Turnham, 1993, Maloney 2003, Levy 2008). Helping formal sector workers may or may not be the best tool for fighting poverty in any given context.

C. Above-Market-Clearing Wages Set by Efficiency Wage Considerations

An old and well-established idea that commands nearly universal agreement, not only in economics but in human resource management, is that a firm can raise its labor productivity by paying a higher wage. Credit is usually given to Leibenstein (1957) for originating this idea in the economics literature. See also Stiglitz (1974, 1976), Mirrlees (1975), Bliss and Stern (1978), Shapiro and Stiglitz (1984), Akerlof and Yellen (1986), Dasgupta and Ray (1986), and Weiss (1990) for further developments. But it goes back much further than that to Henry Ford, who pioneered the radical practice a century ago of offering his workers $5 a day, which was twice the going wage at that time (Raff & Summers 1987).

Efficiency wage theory incorporates the proposition that higher wages can result in higher productivity but goes beyond it in a fundamentally important way. According to the core microeconomic model of firms, firms are trying to achieve higher *profits,* which may or may not be enhanced by higher *productivity.* Thus, the basic postulate of efficiency wage theory is that profit-maximizing firms will pay higher-than-market-clearing wages *if and only if the gains in productivity from doing so outweigh the costs, so that profits are increased.* In other words, it is not enough simply to maintain that paying a higher wage generates benefits. It must be that *the benefits exceed the costs.* Much that is written about "high road" labor relations practices ignores this fundamental truth; see, for example, Ulrich (1997) and Noe et al. (2000).

Efficiency wage theory has also contributed usefully to analyzing the mechanisms by which productivity gains are realized. These fall into two major categories.

One set of explanations is that higher wages enable firms to hire better-quality workers from a heterogeneous labor pool. They may, for example, hire workers who have more education and who, for this reason, are expected to be more productive. Alternatively, they may administer tests of potential job performance and hire those workers who perform the best on these tests.

The other set of explanations is that higher wages induce workers of a given skill level to perform in a more productive manner. The mechanisms analyzed here include better nutrition, improved morale, reduced shirking, lower labor turnover, reduced absenteeism, and greater discretionary effort.

Where the efficiency wage models come out, then, is that wages remain above the market-clearing level because firms in the labor market *find it in their profit-maximizing interest to keep wages above the market-clearing level.* Put differently, a firm that is paying efficiency wages would hurt its profits if it *lowered* wages.

As in the models reviewed in the previous subsection, when wages are higher-than-market-clearing for efficiency wage reasons, we also have unemployment as an equilibrium outcome. However, the unemployment that arises here occurs for a very different reason from the institutional wage case. In the efficiency wage models, it is *firms* that do not want to reduce wages, even though at least some of the unemployed would be willing to work for lower wages rather than remain jobless. This contrasts with the institutional wage case, in which it is *employed workers* who want the wage to remain where it is.

D. Above-Market-Clearing Wages Set on the Supply Side

Another explanation for wages remaining above the market-clearing level has been suggested and modeled by Bardhan and Rudra (1981), Drèze and Mukherjee (1989), Solow (1990), and Osmani (1991). Suppose that daily wages in a labor market start out initially above the market-clearing level for some reason—for example, because the wage was set in the peak season and the economy is now in the slack season. According to the standard account of equilibrating forces in labor markets, when the wage is higher than the market-clearing level, unemployed workers would offer to work for lower wages rather than remain unemployed.

However, in the models of Bardhan and Rudra, Drèze and Mukherjee, Solow, and Osmani, workers' supply side behavior may differ from the standard account, as follows. Suppose that the labor market is a casual one in which hiring takes place afresh each day. If the demand for labor is inelastic, the total wage bill paid to labor over a longer period, such as a month or a year, will be higher the higher is the daily wage. Each of the unemployed knows that he or she will earn more on average over the course of many days if he or she does *not* undercut the established wage and, therefore, will not do so. Wages remain above the market-clearing level as a result.

In this class of models, unlike the models in the earlier subsections, wages are kept above the market-clearing level by the behavior of the *unemployed*. In this way, the wage remains above the market-clearing level, and unemployment persists as a result.

3. The Informal Sector Labor Market

The crucial feature of labor-market dualism just described is that the formal sector offers relatively attractive wages and other terms and conditions of employment whereas the informal sector offers relatively unattractive ones. This leads to the first characterization of the informal economy: workers prefer formal-sector jobs and enter the informal sector only as a last resort. More recently, though, a different view has been put forth: that the informal economy is a desirable sector that workers choose in preference to formal sector work. A third view is that the informal economy has its own internal dualism, combining these two characterizations. A current resource on the informal economy is the ILO's Informal Economy Resource Database, available at http://www.ilo.org/dyn/dwresources/iebrowse. home?p_lang=en.

A. The Informal Economy as a Free-Entry Sector of Last Resort

Most of the poor in the world are working poor. New ILO data show that while open unemployment throughout the world is 6.2 percent of the labor force, another 42.5 percent of those in the labor force are working but earning less than U.S. $2 per day (ILO 2005). It has long been recognized that open unemployment is the tip of the proverbial iceberg: the greater part of the employment problem in developing countries consists of workers who earn so little when they work that they and their families are poor (e.g., Turnham1971, Squire 1981). The working poor are found disproportionately in the informal sector.

Ample empirical research has shown that labor earnings in the informal sector are low, lower even than in the formal sector in a large number of countries. For example, Sudarshan and Unni (2003) see informal work as "a survival activity of the very poor," noting that the dimensions of informal activity are large: 35–85 percent of non-agricultural employment in Asia, 40–97 percent in Africa, and 30–75 percent in the Latin America-Caribbean region.

In the cities of developing countries, we see large numbers of people engaged in work that earns them some cash each day or week. These include hoards of shoe shiners clustered in the town square, lottery ticket vendors seemingly every few feet, would-be construction workers clustered at a particular street corner awaiting the daily round-up, newspaper vendors approaching stopped cars at virtually every traffic light, and (sadly) groups of women, and sometimes men and children, gathered in the red light district. Lewis (1954, 141) referred to "the whole range of casual jobs—the workers on the docks, the young men who rush forward asking to carry your bag as you appear, the jobbing gardener, and the like. *These occupations usually have a multiple of the number they need, each of them earning very small sums from occasional employment; frequently their number could be halved without reducing output in this sector*" (Emphasis added).

Subsequent investigations into these people's lives as well as casual empiricism led analysts to view these types of jobs as having free entry. In a pathbreaking ILO report on Kenya (1972, 6), the criteria defining the informal sector were:

i. Ease of entry.
ii. Reliance on indigenous resources.
iii. Family ownership of enterprises.
iv. Small scale of operation.
v. Labor-intensive and adapted technology.
vi. Skills acquired outside the formal school system.
vii. Unregulated and competitive markets.

The essence of free entry is that all who want a job can get one. ("Job" here is defined to include both self-employment and wage employment.) Barriers to entry into such occupations are small or nonexistent. In some contexts, primarily urban, all that would-be workers need to do is make a minimal investment in the product or service to be sold. In rural contexts, it is obligatory for the family or community to take back into the home those who find such work the best of a bad set of alternatives. One is reminded of Robert Frost's immortal words in his poem "Death of the Hired Man": "Home is the place where, when you have to go there, they have to take you in."

The existence of free-entry employment opportunities in the informal sector helps explain why open unemployment rates in developing countries are comparable to those in developed countries, and often considerably lower (Turnham 1971,

1993; World Bank 1995; ILO 2003). The standard ILO definition of unemployment is a person who did no work for pay in the preceding week, not even for one hour. In poor countries lacking systems of unemployment insurance and cash assistance allowances, the great majority of poor people cannot afford to be without income for as long as a week. So to the extent that the poor can quickly find an opportunity to earn some cash in an informal job, they take it. Open unemployment in their economies is low as a result.

Because of easy entry into economic activities of such kinds, a different wage determination process from the standard marginal productivity rule must be found. Lewis posited income-sharing, a feature taken up by others (e.g., Fei & Ranis 1964, Harberger 1971, Fields 1975). As viewed today, what matters, writes Ranis (2006), is "that the marginal product is low, and sufficiently low to fall below the bargaining wage or income share."

How, then, would we now want to model informal sector wage determination? Essentially, there are four tacks that might be taken, the first two for analytical simplicity and the second two for greater comprehensiveness.

One is to assume that there is a fixed amount of income to be earned in the informal sector, regardless of the number of people working in that sector—that is, the marginal product of labor is literally zero. For example, there may be a fixed number of newspapers to be sold regardless of the number of newspaper vendors. How is the fixed income from newspaper vending to be divided? The easiest simplifying assumption here is full income sharing among the informally employed, so that each earns the average product. The average product is not constant, though—it varies inversely with the number of people in the informal sector. This was the way the urban informal wage was modeled in Fields (1975, 1989).

A second approach is to regard a part of the informal sector as facing, instead of zero marginal product, *constant* marginal product. The dual economy model developed by Harris and Todaro (1970) was formulated to fit the East African case, which they and others regarded as a land surplus economy at the time. Harris and Todaro assumed that anyone who wanted to work in agriculture could find a plot of land, cultivate it, and earn the marginal product from his or her efforts. Agricultural wages were equated to marginal product, not average product, as in Lewis. If the marginal worker and the marginal land are assumed to be as productive as preceding inputs were, a convenient simplifying assumption would be to regard the *marginal* product of labor in agriculture as constant. This assumption was adopted by many in what has come to be called the simplified Harris-Todaro model (Fields 1975, Anand & Joshi 1979, Heady 1981, Stiglitz 1982, Sah & Stiglitz 1985, Bell 1991).

A third approach is intermediate between the first two: a positive but diminishing marginal product. Harberger (1971, 574–575) put it thus:

> [This] variant associates disguised unemployment not just with low wages but
> with situations in which the marginal productivity of labour lies below the
> actual wages earned... There are a variety of activities to which this argument

applies. A classic example is that of fishermen on a lake. The addition of more fishermen increases the total catch, but not proportionately, yet the last fisherman has an equal chance of making a given catch as the first. The expected catch is the same for all, and is equal to their average productivity. But, owing to the fact that the total catch does not increase in proportion to the number of fishermen, the marginal productivity of a fisherman is less than what he earns.

Models with positive but variable marginal product are harder to work with than either of the two preceding ones.

A fourth approach is to model a full demand system for agricultural and non-agricultural products and workers. This was done by Bourguignon (1990). The equations of such systems are so complicated that they are best left to microsimulation and computable general equilibrium exercises.

To conclude, the most common characterization of the informal sector is that it is an easy-entry sector that workers can enter to earn some cash in preference to earning nothing. An alternative view has been gaining popularity in recent years. Let us now turn to it.

B. The Informal Economy as a Desirable Sector

A very different view of the informal sector also appears in the literature. It is the idea that a large number of those working in the informal sector are there *voluntarily*. This view has a long history in the literature (e.g., Hart 1973; Balán, Browning & Jelin 1973). Fields (1990, 66) put it thus:

> Many people are in informal activities by choice. When asked their reasons for doing what they were doing, many informal workers in Costa Rica gave the following answers most frequently: i) They feel they could make more money at the informal sector job they were doing than they could earn in the formal sector, or ii) Even though they made a little less money, they enjoyed their work more, because it allowed them to choose their own hours, to work in the open air, to talk to friends, etc.

The choice approach to the informal sector has been developed more recently in a series of papers by William Maloney. A comprehensive summary of these arguments appears in Maloney (2003).

According to economics textbooks, workers choose among jobs and sectors on the basis of a *package* of characteristics. These include wages, benefits, the work environment, and so on. The variable denoted W on the vertical axis of a standard labor market diagram is ordinarily thought of as a shorthand for this package of benefits, and it is this package of characteristics that Maloney maintains are "roughly comparable" between informal self-employment and formal employment, at least in Mexico. Specifically, Maloney offers a number of reasons why workers might want to be in the informal sector: Some can earn more (or at least hope to earn more) in informal self-employment than they could earn in formal-sector employment; they value the independence of self-employment; they would rather use the money that formal sector protections cost them for investing in their own small informal enterprises; they do not value protections such as health insurance, which formal employment offers to them, in some cases because they already have these protections; and they don't trust the government to deliver on promises such as future pension benefits. For any or all of these reasons, there may be a sizeable numbers of workers who prefer informal self-employment to formal wage employment.

One reason that self-employment is often seen as undesirable is that microenterprises exhibit very high rates of failure. Maloney responds to the precariousness argument thus (2003, 77):

> Small firms will have higher costs, are likely to be informal, and will have very high failure rates. Though this corresponds exactly to the standard picture of the stagnant, precarious, unproductive, unprotected informal worker familiar in the literature, it is, in fact, the opposite. It emerges naturally from the workers trying their luck at entrepreneurship (risk-taking), often failing, and not engaging in the formal institutions until they grow. In sum, there may be nothing pathological about informal self-employment, and to recover the general sense of the word, nothing obviously less decent either.

I agree with Maloney on this point, but I think he goes too far in one respect. He presents an integrated labor-market model (68, 72) in which the total package of benefits is equalized between informal self-employment and formal wage employment. While this model might fit the choice between formal-sector employment and informal self-employment *for those who already have the option of working in the formal sector,* this is a limited group of people. Rather, as argued earlier, throughout the developing world, formal-sector jobs appear to be far fewer in number than the number of people who want them. Thus, in my view, Maloney's characterization applies to a subset of informal-sector workers, but by no means all of them, nor probably even most.

C. The Informal Economy with Its Own Internal Dualism

The preceding subsections put forward two polar views. One is that informal sector employment is *worse* than formal sector employment but superior to unemployment. The other is that employment in the informal economy is *preferred* to formal sector employment.

A way of combining these two polar views would be to regard the informal sector as having *its own internal duality.* On this synthesized approach, some informal activities are preferable to formal-sector jobs and some are not. Such a view is developed at length in Fields (1990), where the two parts of the informal sector are labeled "upper-tier" informal activities and "easy entry" ones. See also House (1984), Tokman (1987), Marcouiller et al. (1997), and Ranis and Stewart (1999).

In fact, dualism within the informal sector is a view that Maloney has come to share. Summarizing the findings of Cunningham and Maloney (2001) for Mexico, Maloney writes (2003, 80): "The single distribution was rejected, supporting a two-tier view, but the share of the population found in the 'lower' tier was only 13 percent of the sample." Perhaps most informal entrepreneurs are in the upper-tier in Mexico, but it remains an open question whether this is the case in India, Bolivia, or Kenya.

Another way of modeling the duality of the informal sector is to specify two informal sectors that are *geographically* distinct. Todaro (1969) had three employment sectors—urban modern employment, urban traditional employment, and agricultural employment—but no unemployment. Harris and Todaro (1970) had urban modern employment, agricultural employment, and unemployment, but no urban informal sector. Fields (1975) had three employment states—urban modern employment, an urban informal sector, and rural agricultural employment—plus unemployment.

If these various sector distinctions are put together, we should have four employment states—employment in the formal sector, employment in the upper-tier informal sector, employment in the easy-entry sector, and employment in rural agriculture—plus unemployment. Adding in rural off-farm employment—what is sometimes called the z-goods sector (Hymer & Resnick 1969; Ranis & Stewart 1993)—would introduce a fifth employment state. To the best of my knowledge, no analytical model has included all five employment states plus unemployment, perhaps because to do so would be too complicated and intractable.

Although six-state models have not been constructed, the literature offers a number of four-state models (consisting of three employment sectors plus unemployment). How the different states link to one another is open to alternative specifications. These are discussed in Section 5.

4. FORMAL-INFORMAL LINKAGES IN THE LABOR MARKET

Based on the models of formal-sector labor markets and informal-sector labor markets reviewed in sections 1 and 2, this section reviews models of linkages between the various sectors. The models reviewed here are: (1) the integrated labor-market model with full market clearing, (2) models with wage dualism but no unemployment, and (3) the Harris-Todaro model, both in its original form and as extended, which features both wage dualism and unemployment.

A. The Integrated Labor Market Model with Wage Equalization and No Unemployment

The integrated labor-market model, also called the unified labor-market model, has as its distinguishing features that (1) each labor market clears, and (2) full

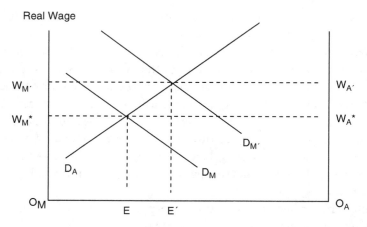

Figure 18.2. The Integrated Labor Market Model: A Higher Demand for Labor in One
Sector Raises Wages in All Sectors

intermarket equilibrium is achieved through actual wage equalization. The model
may be explained with the aid of Figure 18.2.

Suppose, for ease of analysis, that the economy has two sectors, here termed
manufacturing and agriculture. All workers are identical, and so would be willing
to work wherever the wage is higher, be it in manufacturing or in agriculture. The
labor market is assumed to be an integrated one in the sense that the same wage
prevails in both sectors of the economy for a given type of worker—a realistic
enough stylization is some settings, particular for countries in East Asia. For a
model in which workers are not identical, but where the last worker who enters one
sector earns the same amount as he or she would earn in the other, see Roy (1951).

Let us start with a situation in which the demand-for-labor curve in the
manufacturing sector, D_M, is downward-sloping relative to origin O_M, and
likewise, the demand-for-labor curve in the agricultural sector, D_A, is downward-sloping relative to origin O_A. The total labor supply is represented by the
horizontal distance $O_M O_A$. If the standard equilibrating forces in labor markets
are free to operate, as is indeed the case in much of East Asia, wages would
equalize across the two sectors at level W^*. At this wage, $O_M E$ workers would be
demanded in the manufacturing sector, and $O_A E$ workers would be demanded
in the agricultural sector. Furthermore, the total labor demanded in the two
sectors combined would exactly equal the total labor supplied in the economy.
In such an equilibrium, the marginal worker is indifferent between working in
the manufacturing sector or in the agricultural sector, because the two sectors
pay the same wages.

Now suppose that economic growth takes place in the manufacturing sector. Because manufacturing firms need more workers to produce the extra output, the labor-demand-curve in the manufacturing sector shifts rightward to D_M'.

Assuming no change in the agricultural product market, the agricultural employers' demand-for-labor curve would remain stationary at D_A. The labor market is now in disequilibrium, because at the original wage W^*, more labor is demanded than is supplied. To resolve this disequilibrium, some manufacturing employers raise wages in order to retain existing workers and attract new ones, and agricultural employers raise wages to prevent their workers from leaving. The result is that the labor market equilibrates at a new common wage $W' > W^*$. Because of the sector-specific shift in labor demand, more of the country's workers are now in the manufacturing sector than before ($O_M E'$ rather than $O_M E$) and fewer in agriculture ($O_A E'$ rather than $O_A E$).

In the integrated labor-market model, economic growth in *one* sector benefits workers in *all* sectors. Three groups of workers have been identified in this analysis: (i) those who had been working in manufacturing and now earn higher wages than before; (ii) those who are drawn by higher wages into manufacturing from agriculture; and (iii) those who remain in agriculture and earn more than they did previously. In this way, economic growth in a country's export sector reverberates throughout the labor market, benefiting those who produce manufactured goods *and* those who produce agricultural goods.

The extension of the integrated labor-market model from two sectors to N sectors is immediate.

B. Models with Wage Differentials and No Unemployment

In contrast to the integrated labor-market model just discussed, a number of segmented labor-market models are characterized by wage differentials between segments. Models with wage differentials between segmented and no unemployment include the unlimited- supply-of-labor model of Lewis (1954), the intersectoral-shifts model of Kuznets (1955), the crowding model of Bergmann (1971), the minimum-wage model with incomplete coverage of Welch (1974), and the modern-sector-enlargement model of Fields (1979b, 1980).

These models maintain labor market dualism in the sense that real wages are higher in the formal sector than in the informal sector. In this sense, they differ from the integrated labor-market model described in the previous subsection, in which wages are the same in the different sectors. The segmented labor-market models described in this section also maintain a particular kind of supply-side behavior: All workers not employed in the higher-wage formal sector are assumed to take up employment in the lower-wage informal sector. These models, therefore, exhibit no unemployment.

Within this class of models, the most heralded version is the Nobel Prize-winning work of Lewis (1954). As discussed earlier, the distinguishing feature of the Lewis model was that the modern sector faces an unlimited supply of labor at wages only somewhat higher than subsistence levels. It is this that makes the Lewis model "classical," in contrast to a "neoclassical" model in which labor is scarce and has to be bid away from other uses. This feature of the classical model was later elaborated on by Ranis and Fei (1961), Fei and Ranis (1964), and Jorgenson (1967).

The unlimited supply of labor to the modern sector is sometimes called an "infinitely elastic supply curve of labor," but this designation is a misnomer. By definition, a supply curve tells the amount of a good or service that is forthcoming as a function of the relevant price. For it to be a proper function, there can be only one quantity for any price. That is, given the price of labor, the supply function delivers the *unique* quantity of labor available. Thus, in the Lewis model, when the formal sector wage is above the informal sector wage, the potential quantity of labor supplied to the formal sector is *the entire labor force*. However, because formal sector employers do not wish to employ all the workers who would like to work there at that wage, they (the employers) face an effectively unlimited supply of labor. Specifically, this means that no individual employer need raise the wage to attract additional labor, nor must employers as a whole within a substantial range. Indeed, there is a horizontal curve, but that curve is the wage as a function of employment, *not* the amount of labor supplied as a function of the wage.

Over time, the process of savings, investment, capital formation, and economic growth highlighted in many growth models (both classical and neoclassical) shifts the demand-for-labor curve in the formal sector rightward. Workers respond to the increased demand for labor in the formal sector by taking up formal employment to the extent possible. Throughout a long range, the wage in the formal sector remains unchanged, because employers do not need to raise the wage to attract more labor. Ultimately, though, a turning point is reached once the supply of labor to the formal sector is no longer unlimited.

Despite the many insights of the original Lewis model and Fei and Ranis's amplification of it, I find one feature of the model troublesome: the nature of the wage in the informal sector. Lewis used the term "subsistence wage." If the wage is literally a subsistence wage, below which people cannot subsist, then it has a natural floor. But as these models have evolved, the informal sector wage does not take on the character of the minimum needed for survival. It is, rather, more of a basic wage, lower than the real wage received by formal sector workers. The question, then, is whether this wage is a *constant* low wage or whether it *varies* (inversely) with the number of people in the sector.

The great majority of analysts regard production in the informal sector as subject to diminishing returns; see, for example, the earlier Harberger quotation. What diminishing returns in the informal sector implies is that when economic growth takes place and workers are drawn out of the informal sector into the formal sector, those who remain in the informal sector each receive a *higher* income than before; from my reading, this was first pointed out by Sen (1967). The informal sector wage should *not* remain constant. Indeed, the rising wage in the informal sector is a reason for the unlimited supply of labor to the formal sector to run out eventually: because the supply price of labor to the formal sector will have risen due to improved wage opportunities in the *informal* sector.

In the dualistic labor-market model with no unemployment, economic growth reduces poverty in two ways. One is the increase in wages and utility of those who are able to move from the informal to the formal sector. The other is the increase in wages of those who remain informal.

Thus, we see that in these models with wage dualism and no unemployment, as in the other segmented labor-market models, employment and wages in *each* sector of the economy are determined by labor market conditions in *all* sectors of the economy. Partial equilibrium analysis simply cannot explain what we see.

C. Models with Wage Differentials and Unemployment: The Harris-Todaro Model and Extensions of It

In 1970, a major alternative was developed in the context of East Africa. John Harris and Michael Todaro (1970) formulated a model characterized by wage dualism and unemployment. Wage dualism arises in their model because employers in the formal sector are compelled by unions, minimum wage laws, or other institutional forces to pay higher-than-market-clearing wages, while the wage clears the informal-sector labor market. The Harris-Todaro model also featured a spatial distinction: to be hired for a formal-sector job, it was necessary for a worker to be physically present in the urban areas where the formal-sector jobs are assumed to be located.

In the Harris-Todaro model, more workers search for formal-sector jobs than are hired. Employers hire some of the searchers but not all of them. Those not hired end up unemployed ex post. Open unemployment, though a feature of the world, was not a feature of the models reviewed in the previous two subsections.

More specifically, the Harris-Todaro labor market operates as follows. Employers in the formal sector hire workers until the point where the marginal product of labor equals the institutionally determined wage $\overline{W}_F$ On the other hand, in the informal sector, there is assumed to be free entry; thus, all persons who wish to work in the informal sector may do so. Each person employed in the informal sector earns a wage $W_I < \overline{W}_F$.

Workers are assumed to consider the mathematical expected wages from each of two search strategies: (i) Searching for a formal-sector job, which pays a relatively high wage but runs the risk of unemployment, and (ii) Taking an informal-sector job, which offers a low wage with no risk of unemployment. Harris and Todaro's insight was that workers would be expected to allocate themselves between formal-sector and informal- sector search strategies *so that the mathematical expected wages from the two search strategies are equalized:* $E(W_F) = E(W_I)$. Let E_F denote employment in the formal sector and L_F the labor force in the formal sector. In the basic Harris-Todaro model, expected wage equalization leads to the following equilibrium condition:

$$\overline{W}_F \, \frac{E_F}{L_F} = \overline{W}_I.$$

Because $\overline{W}_F > \overline{W}_I$, it follows that $\frac{E_F}{L_F} < 1,$ that is, the formal-sector labor force exceeds formal-sector employment, and, therefore, a Harris-Todaro equilibrium is characterized by open unemployment.

Harris and Todaro's fundamental contribution was to build a model with wage dualism *and* unemployment. The fact that the model remains part of our toolkit more than three decades later is a tribute to its basic insight and analytical power.

At the same time, some of the assumptions of the Harris-Todaro model were judged to be too restrictive, and so the model was generalized in the years that followed to nest their specific formulation within a broader framework. Their model was first extended by Fields (1975), which allowed for on-the-job search from rural agriculture, the existence of an urban informal sector, preferential hiring of the better educated, and employment fixity. The model has subsequently been extended and generalized to allow for duality within the rural sector, mobile capital, endogenous urban wage setting, risk-aversion, a system of demand for goods, and many other factors (Corden & Findlay 1975; Calvo 1978; Moene 1988, 1992; Khan 1989; Fields 1989; Chakravarty & Dutta 1990; Bourguignon 1990; Basu 1997).

5. Contributions of These Models to Understanding and Policy Analysis

Positive economic analysis is about what is and what will be. Normative economic analysis is about what should be. The remainder of this section demonstrates how the segmented labor-market models presented earlier contribute to understanding (the concern of positive economics) and to policy analysis (the concern of normative economics). What all the cases presented here have in common is that it is difficult if not impossible to make sense of them using single-sector models only.

A. Why an Increase in Productivity Might Cause Wages to Fall

The integrated labor-market model maintains that the wage that any worker receives reflects supply and demand for labor in the labor market as a whole. Specifically, the wage is determined by what the last employer is willing to pay in order to attract and employ a worker and by what the last worker requires in order to be attracted and employed.

One common misperception is that the wage "should" vary directly with labor "productivity," commonly measured as value added per worker, in a given firm or sector. According to the integrated labor-market model, nothing could be further from the truth. The following example illustrates why.

Suppose that computers become available, which enable half the formal-sector workers to be replaced at lower cost while keeping total output constant. "Productivity," measured by value added per worker, approximately doubles ("approximately," because productivity would exactly double if the computers cost the same as the dismissed workers, more than double if the computers cost less). However, according to the integrated labor-market model, formal sector wages will *not* double nor necessarily even increase. In fact, to the extent that wages change at all, they are likely to *fall*. Here is why.

The availability of computers that can replace workers induces a substitution effect, which would be expected to result in less labor being demanded to produce a given level of output. For this reason, labor demand would fall approximately in half. Unless the ability to produce at lower cost induces a corresponding increase in the scale of production, the demand for labor in the formal sector will be less after the productivity improvement than it was before.

When the equilibrating forces in labor markets equalize wages across the various sectors, as the integrated labor-market model maintains, a leftward shift of labor demand in one sector of the economy results in lower wages in *all* sectors of the economy. The reason that an increase in "productivity" does not result in higher wages is that employers do not need to pay wages as high as before to attract the desired number of workers. In this way, higher productivity can result in *lower* wages.

The more general point of the integrated labor-market model is that a worker's wage is set not just by that worker's own productivity nor by labor productivity just in that worker's sector. Rather, wages are set by supply and demand for that category of labor in the labor market as a whole.

B. Why Taiwan's Economic Growth Led First to Falling Unemployment at Constant Wages and then to Economy-Wide Wage Increases at Full Employment

The Lewis model's characterization of intersectoral linkages generated two major predictions. The first is that as long as there exists a surplus of labor to the formal sector, economic growth would generate intersectoral shifts of employment but little or no increase in real wages. The second prediction is that once the unlimited supply of labor to the formal sector is exhausted and the turning point is reached, subsequent economic growth is marked by rising real wages economy wide.

The model proved to be remarkably prescient. Take the case of Taiwan, where manufactured exports were the engine of growth. Data on unemployment and real wages (monthly) are displayed in Figure 18.3. At the time Lewis was writing,

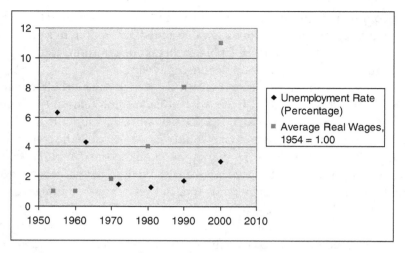

Figure 18.3. Unemployment and Average Real Wages in Taiwan

the open unemployment rate was 6.3 percent, higher than the generally agreed-upon level of full employment. In the next six years of Taiwan's economic growth, unemployment fell to 4.3 percent and real wages in manufacturing rose by only 2 percent (total, not per year), consistent with excess labor continuing to be supplied relative to the amount demanded. But then, in the next decade (the 1960s), unemployment fell to 1.5 percent—a rate indicating severe labor shortages—and real wages shot up by 81 percent. Unemployment remained below 2 percent in the 1970s and 1980s, then rose to 3 percent in the 1990s. At the same time, real wages doubled again in the 1970s and 1980s and rose by another 36 percent in the 1990s, not only in manufacturing but throughout the Taiwanese labor market.

The two phases predicted by Lewis appear clearly in the data for Taiwan: falling unemployment at essentially constant wages, then rapidly rising real wages at full or over-full employment. The dualistic model with intersectoral linkages tells a compelling story, and it did it *before* it happened.

C. Why the Solution to Urban Unemployment in Kenya Was Not Urban Employment Creation but Rural Development

The Harris-Todaro model was formulated in response to the emergence of serious unemployment in urban Kenya. The government of Kenya tried a policy of urban employment creation, which appeared not to have worked. Harris and Todaro's model helped explain why.

The model produced two powerful policy results. The first concerned a policy of formal-sector employment creation to employ the unemployed (who, in the Harris-Todaro model, were all in urban areas, because that is where the formal-sector jobs were assumed to be located). A policy of increasing formal-sector employment by $\Delta E_F = E_F' - E_F$ increases the formal sector labor force by $\Delta E_F \dfrac{\overline{W}_F}{\overline{W}_I}$ and increases open unemployment by $\Delta E_F (\dfrac{\overline{W}_F}{\overline{W}_I} - 1)$. Thus, the solution to urban unemployment is *not* urban employment creation.

The second policy option considered was a policy of rural development. Suppose that such a program could increase the (rural) informal sector wage from $\overline{W}_I$ to $\overline{W}_I'$. From the H-T equilibrium condition, unemployment would then *fall* from $UNEM = E_F(\dfrac{\overline{W}_F}{\overline{W}_I} - 1)$ to $UNEM' = E_F(\dfrac{\overline{W}_F}{\overline{W}_I'} - 1)$. Thus, in the Harris-Todaro model, the solution to urban unemployment is *rural* development.

Soon after the model was published, the government of Kenya followed the Harris-Todaro precepts by putting into place an integrated rural-development program. Indeed, unemployment in Kenya *did* indeed fall. For a more comprehensive welfare economic analysis of various policy options in the Harris-Todaro model, see Fields (2005).

D. Why Poverty Is So Severe in the Urban Informal Sector of Many Developing Countries

Some of the worst poverty in developing countries is found in urban areas (United Nations 2003). The extended Harris-Todaro model helps explain why this is so.

One way in which the Harris-Todaro model has been extended is to have three employment sectors (formal employment, urban informal employment, and agricultural employment) in addition to unemployment. What is important in this particular extension is that the three sectors are located in distinct locations: formal employment and urban informal employment in the urban areas, agricultural employment in the rural areas. In this extension, there are three search strategies: (i) Search for a formal sector job full-time while unemployed. (ii) Give up on the search for a formal sector job and be employed in agriculture. (iii) Search for a formal sector job part-time while informally employed. (Note that search strategies I and ii were those modeled by Harris and Todaro.)

Presumably, those people located nearer to where the formal-sector jobs are stand a better chance of being hired for any given job vacancy. The fact that they do has implications for urban informal wages.

For strictly positive numbers of people to choose each of the three search strategies, the extended Harris-Todaro equilibrium requires that expected wages equalize across the three search strategies. If one group of informal-sector workers has better on-the-job search opportunities than another, the labor-market equilibrium must be one where the group with the better on-the-job search opportunities ends up with a *lower* wage in equilibrium.

Viewed in this way, it is not surprising that some of the worst poverty in the developing world would be found in the *urban* areas: the urban poor consist, at least in part, of those who sought urban formal-sector jobs but who were unlucky enough not to be hired for them. Of course, there is another reason for very low urban informal sector wages—lack of opportunities for wage employment and self-employment in rural areas—which the extended Harris-Todaro explanation complements.

E. Why Expanding Formal-Sector Employment Sometimes Improves Labor Market Conditions and Sometimes Does Not

The same policy can have different effects in the different models. Take the policy of expanding employment in the formal sector.

In all three of the segmented labor-market models, when more formal-sector jobs are created, labor moves from the informal sector to the formal sector to take up the available jobs. Those individuals who are able to make the move are better off in all three models.

The models differ, however, in other respects. In the integrated labor-market model, wages rise by equal amounts in the two sectors. All workers are better off by the same amount.

In the model with wage dualism and no unemployment, the wage level in the formal sector stays the same, but wages rise to some degree in the informal sector. Thus, the remaining informal sector workers benefit from the expansion of employment in the formal sector.

Finally, in the Harris-Todaro model with wage dualism and unemployment, the informal sector wage may or may not rise. What will surely rise, though, is unemployment. In this model, unlike the other ones, formal-sector employment creation produces both winners and losers.

Thus, whether a policy of formal-sector employment creation has favorable labor market effects depends on which labor-market model best fits a particular country's institutional circumstances.

6. A Final Word

I shall now try to summarize the main points of this review and offer some brief concluding thoughts.

First, differences between the various sectors' labor markets appear pervasive. When possible, Occam's razor suggests limiting the analysis to two sectors. But when two sectors are simply not enough, three-sector or *n*-sector models can and have proved insightful.

Second, formal-sector labor markets can be formulated in several alternative ways: in terms of market clearing, in terms of institutional wage setting, in terms of efficiency wages, and in terms of worker-side resistance to wage cuts.

Third, informal-sector labor markets can be modeled as a free-entry sector, as a desirable sector, or as having its own internal duality.

Fourth, the linkages between the different sectors can be modeled in a number of ways: as an integrated labor market, as a model of wage dualism and no unemployment, and as a model of wage dualism with unemployment.

Fifth, a number of external events and policies can be understood only by using segmented labor-market models. In these models, employment and wages in *each* sector of the economy are determined by labor market conditions in *all* sectors of the economy. Single-market analysis simply cannot explain what we see.

The number of possible models combining these various components is enormous. Each of the three components—formal-sector labor market, informal-sector labor market, and intermarket linkages—has three or four alternatives. Even this relatively coarse categorization results in thirty-six different labor-market models.

No analyst would expect that the same model would fit East Africa and East Asia, South Africa and South Korea. Surely, the "correct" model is context specific. Blending empirical observation and analytical modeling has yielded great advances. Coming up with the "correct" model matters for more than understanding; it matters for policy purposes as well. Sound labor market policies require sound labor-market models.

NOTE

1. I am grateful to Mabel Andalón, Gordon Betcherman, Shanta Devarajan, Lisa Dragoset, Louise Fox, Robert Duval Hernández, Maria Laura Sánchez Puerta, and three anonymous referees for helpful comments on an earlier draft.

REFERENCES

Aidt, Toke & Tzannatos, Zafiris. (2002). *Unions and Collective Bargaining: Economic Effects in a Global Environment.* Washington: World Bank.

Akerlof, George & Yellen, Janet, Eds. (1986). *Efficiency Wage Models of the Labor Market.* Cambridge, England: Cambridge University Press.

Anand, Sudhir & Joshi, Vijay. (1979). "Domestic Distortions, Income Distribution and the Theory of Optimum Subsidy." *The Economic Journal* 89: 336–352.

Anand, Sudhir & Kanbur , S.M.R. (1985). "Poverty Under the Kuznets Process." *Economic Journal* 95 (supp.): 42–50.

Anand, Sudhir & Kanbur, S.M.R. (1993). "The Kuznets Process and the Inequality-Development Relationship." *Journal of Development Economics* 40: 25–52.

Ayub, Mahmood (1977). *Income Inequality in a Growth-Theoretic Context: The Case of Pakistan.* Unpublished Ph.D. Dissertation, Yale University.

Balán, J., Browning, H.L. & Jelin, E. (1973). *Men in a Developing Society.* Austin, TX: Institute of Latin American Studies, University of Texas at Austin.

Bardhan, P.K. & Rudra, A. (1981). "Terms and Conditions of Labour Contracts in Agriculture: Results of a Survey in West Bengal 1979." *Oxford Bulletin of Economics and Statistics* 1: 89–111.

Basu, Kaushik (1997). *Analytical Development Economics.* Cambridge, MA: MIT Press.

Becker, Gary S. (1962). "Investment in Human Capital." *Journal of Political Economy* LXX Supplement: 9–49.

Becker, Gary S. (1964). *Human Capital.* New York: Columbia University Press for the National Bureau of Economic Research.

Bell, Clive (1991). "Regional Heterogeneity, Migration, and Shadow Prices." *Journal of Public Economics* 46: 1–27.

Bergmann, Barbara (1971). "The Effect on White Incomes of Discrimination in Employment." *Journal of Political Economy* 79: 294–313.

Besley, Tim & Burgess, Robin. (2004). "Can Labor Regulation Hinder Economic Performance? Evidence from India." *Quarterly Journal of Economics* 19: 91–134.

Blanchard, Olivier & Summers, Lawrence. (1986). "Hysteresis and the European Unemployment Problem." *NBER Macroeconomics Annual:* 15–78.

Bliss, Christopher J. & Stern, Nicholas H. (1978). "Productivity, Wages and Nutrition: 1. The Theory; 2. Some Observations." *Journal of Development Economics* 5: 363–398.

Boudon, Raymond A. (1973). *Mathematical Structures of Social Mobility.* Amsterdam: Elsevier.

Bourguignon, François (1990). "Growth and Inequality in the Dual Model of Development: The Role of Demand Factors." *Review of Economic Studies* 57: 215–228.

Bowles, S. and Heintz, J. (1996). "Wages and Jobs in the South African Economy: An Econometric Investigation." Department of Economics, University of Massachusetts.

Bravo, David (1995). "Cost of Labor Standards in Bolivia." Harvard University.

Burdett, Kenneth & Mortensen, Dale (1998). "Wage Differentials, Employer Size, and Unemployment." *International Economic Review* 39: 257–273.

Cahuc, Pierre & Zylberberg, André. (2004). *Labor Economics.* Cambridge, MA: MIT Press.

Calvo, Guillermo A. (1978). "Urban Unemployment and Wage Determination in LDC's: Trade Unions in the Harris-Todaro Model." *International Economic Review* 19: 65–81.

Chakravarty, Satya R. & Dutta, Bhaskar. (1990). "Migration and Welfare." *European Journal of Political Economy* 6: 119–138.

Chang, C.-H. (1989). "A Study on the Labor Market in Taiwan." In *Institution for Economic Research, Conference on Labor and Economic Development,* Taipei.

Corden, Max & Findlay, Ronald. (1975). "Urban Unemployment, Intersectoral Capital Mobility and Development Policy," *Economica* 42: 59–78.

Cunningham, Wendy V. & Maloney, William F. (2001). "Heterogeneity in the Mexican Micro-Enterprise Sector." *Economic Development and Cultural Change* 50: 131–156.

Dasgupta, Partha & Ray, Debraj. (1986). "Inequality as a Determinant of Malnutrition and Unemployment." *Economic Journal* 96: 1011–1034.

DeSoto, Hernando (1989). *The Other Path*. New York: Harper and Row.

Dixit, Avinash K. (1973). "Models of Dual Economies." In James A. Mirrlees & Nicholas H. Stern, Eds., *Models of Economic Growth: Proceedings of a Conference Held by the International Economic Association at Jerusalem*. New York: International Economic Association.

Doeringer, Peter B. & Piore, Michael J. (1971). *Internal Labor Markets and Manpower Analysis*. Lexington, MA: Heath.

Drèze, Jean & Mukherjee, Anandita. (1989). "Labour Contracts in Rural India: Theories ande Evidence." In S. Chakravarty, Ed., *The Balance Between Industry and Agriculture in Economic Development*. London: Macmillan.

Dunlop, John T. (1944). *Wage Determination Under Trade Unions*. New York: Macmillan.

Eaton, Jonathan & Gersovitz, Mark. (1984). "A Theory of Expropriation and Deviations from Perfect Capital Mobility." *Economic Journal* 94: 16–40.

Ehrenberg, Ronald G. & Smith, Robert S. (2003). *Modern Labor Economics*. Boston: Addison Wesley.

Fallon, Peter & Lucas, Robert. (1991). "The Impact of Changes in Job Security Regulations in India and Zimbabwe." *World Bank Economic Review*, September.

Fallon, Peter & Lucas, Robert. (1993). "Job Security Regulations and the Dynamic Demand for Industrial Labor in India and Zimbabwe." *Journal of Development Economics* 40: 241–275.

Fei, John C.H. & Ranis, Gustav. (1964). *Development of the Labor Surplus Economy*. Homewood, IL: Irwin.

Fei, John C.H., Ranis, Gustav & Kuo, Shirley W.Y. (1978). "Growth and Family Distribution of Income by Factor Components." *Quarterly Journal of Economics* 92: 17–53.

Fei, John C.H., Ranis, Gustav & Kuo, Shirley W.Y. (1979). *Growth with Equity: The Taiwan Case*. Oxford: Oxford University Press.

Fields, Gary S. (1975). "Rural-Urban Migration, Urban Unemployment and Underemployment, and Job Search Activity in LDC's," *Journal of Development Economics* 2: 165–188.

Fields, Gary S. (1979a). "Income Inequality in Urban Colombia: A Decomposition Analysis." *Review of Income and Wealth* 25: 327–341.

Fields, Gary S. (1979b). "A Welfare Economic Approach to Growth and Distribution in the Dual Economy." *Quarterly Journal of Economics* 372: 325–354.

Fields, Gary S. (1980). *Poverty, Inequality, and Development*. New York: Cambridge University Press.

Fields, Gary S. (1984). "Employment, Income Distribution and Economic Growth in Seven Small Open Economies." *The Economic Journal* 94: 74–83.

Fields, Gary S. (1989). "On-the-Job Search in a Labor Market Model: Ex-Ante Choices and Ex-Post Outcomes." *Journal of Development Economics* 30: 159–178.

Fields, Gary S. (1990). "Labour Market Modeling and the Urban Informal Sector: Theory and Evidence." In David Turnham, Bernard Salomé & Antoine Schwarz, Eds., *The Informal Sector Revisited*. Paris: Development Centre of the Organisation for Economic Co-Operation and Development.

Fields, Gary S. (1994). "Changing Labor Market Conditions and Economic Development in Hong Kong, the Republic of Korea, Singapore, and Taiwan, China." *The World Bank Economic Review* 8: 395–414.

Fields, Gary S. (1999). "Employment Generation and Poverty Alleviation in Developing Economies." In Ulrich Hiemenz, Ed., *Growth and Competition in the New Global Economy*. Paris: OECD Development Centre.

Fields, Gary S. (2005). "A Welfare Economic Analysis of Labor Market Policies in the Harris-Todaro Model." *Journal of Development Economics* 76: 127–146.

Fields, Gary S. & Bagg, Walter S. (2003). "Long-Term Mobility and the Private Sector in Developing Countries: New Evidence." In Gary S. Fields & Guy Pfeffermann, Eds., *Pathways Out of Poverty.* Boston: Kluwer Academic Publishers.

Fields, Gary S., Cichello, Paul L., Freije, Samuel, Menéndez, Marta & Newhouse, David. (2003). "Household Income Dynamics: A Four-Country Story." *Journal of Development Studies* 40: 30–54.

Fields, Gary S., Leibbrandt,, Murray & Wakeford, Jeremy. (2000). *Key Labour Market Elasticities.* Report prepared for the Government of South Africa.

Fields, Gary S. & O'Hara Mitchell, Jennifer. (1999). "Changing Income Inequality in Taiwan: A Decomposition Analysis." In Gary Saxonhouse & T.N. Srinivasan, Eds., *Development, Duality, and the International Economic Regime: Essays in Honor of Gustav Ranis.* Ann Arbor, MI: University of Michigan Press.

Fields, Gary S. and Wan, Henry Y. (1989). "Wage-Setting Institutions and Economic Growth." *World Development* 17: 1471–1483.

Ghose, Ajit K. (2003). *Jobs and Incomes in a Globalizing World.* Geneva: International Labour Organization.

Gindling, T.H., Jr. (1991). "An Investigation into Labor Market Segmentation: The Case of San José, Costa Rica." *Economic Development and Cultural Change* 39: 585–605.

Hamermesh, Daniel (1993). *Labor Demand.* Princeton: Princeton University Press.

Harberger, Arnold C. (1971). "On Measuring the Social Opportunity Cost of Labor." *International Labour Review* 103: 559–579.

Harris, John & Todaro, Michael. (1970). "Migration, Unemployment, and Development: A Two Sector Analysis." *American Economic Review* 40: 126–142.

Hart, Keith (1973). "Informal Income Opportunities and Urban Employment in Ghana." *Journal of Modern African Studies* 11: 61–89.

Heady, Christopher J. (1981). "Shadow Wages and Induced Migration." *Oxford Economic Papers* 33: 108–121.

House, William J. (1984). "Nairobi's Informal Sector: Dynamic Entrepreneurs or Surplus Labor?" *Economic Development and Cultural Change* 32: 277–302.

Hymer, Stephen & Resnick, Stephen. (1969). "A Model of an Agrarian Economy with Nonagricultural Activities." *American Economic Review* 59: 493–506.

Inter-American Development Bank (2003). *Good Jobs Wanted.* Washington: Inter-American Development Bank.

International Labour Office. (1972). *Employment, Incomes, and Equality: A Strategy for Increasing Productive Employment in Kenya.* Geneva: Internatuional Labour Organization.

International Labour Office. (1998). *Labour and Social Issues Relating to Export Processing Zones.* Geneva: International Labour Organization.

International Labour Office. (2002). *Women and Men in the Informal Economy: A Statistical Picture.* Geneva: International Labour Organization.

International Labour Office. (2003). *Global Employment Trends 2003.* Geneva: International Labour Organization.

International Labour Office. (2005). *Global Employment Trends 2005.* Geneva: International Labour Organization.

Jhabvala, Renana, Sudarshan, Ratna M. & Unni, Jeemol. (2003). *Informal Economy Centrestage: New Structures of Employment.* New Delhi: Sage Publications.

Jorgenson, Dale W. (1967). "Surplus Agricultural Labour and the Development of a Dual Economy." *Oxford Economic Papers* 19: 288–312.

Khan, M. Ali (1989). "The Harris-Todaro Model." In J. Eatwell et al., *The New Palgrave*. London: MacMillan.

Knight, John B. (1976). "Explaining Income Distribution in Less Developed Countries: A Framework and an Agenda." *Bulletin of the Oxford Institute of Economics and Statistics* 28:208–227.

Kuznets, Simon (1955). "Economic Growth and Income Inequality." *American Economic Review* 45: 1–28.

Lee, Chang-Hee (2002). "The Minimum Wage." *Asian Labour Update* 42.

Leibenstein, Harvey (1957). "Underemployment in Backward Economies." *Journal of Political Economy* 65: 91–103.

Levy, Santiago (2008). "Can Social Programs Reduce Productivity and Growth? A Hypothesis for Mexico." Working Paper, Inter-American Development Bank.

Lewis, W. Arthur (1954). "Economic Development with Unlimited Supplies of Labour." *Manchester School* 22: 139–191.

Lin, C.-C. (1989). "The Basic Labor Standards Law and Operation of Labor Market: Theory and Partial Empirical Results." Academia Sinica.

Lindbeck, Assar & Snower, Dennis. (1988). *Insider-Outsider Theory of Employment and Unemployment*. Cambridge, MA: MIT Press.

Maloney, William F. (2003). "Informal Self-Employment: Poverty Trap or Decent Alternative." In Gary S. Fields & Guy Pfeffermann, Eds., *Pathways Out of Poverty*. Boston: Kluwer.

Marcouiller, Douglas, Ruiz de Castilla, Veronica & Woodruff, Christopher. (1997). "Formal Measures of the Informal Sector Wage Gap in Mexico, El Salvador, and Peru." *Economic Development and Cultural Change* 45: 367–392.

Meade, James A. (1976). *The Just Economy*. London: Allen and Unwin.

Merton, Robert K. (1968). "The Matthew Effect in Science." *Science* 159: 56–63.

Mincer, Jacob (1962). "On-the-Job Training: Costs, Returns, and Some Implications." *Journal of Political Economy* LXX Supplement: 50–79.

Mincer, Jacob (1974). *Schooling, Experience, and Earnings*. New York: Columbia University Press for the National Bureau of Economic Research.

Mirrlees, James A. (1975). "Pure Theory of Underdeveloped Economies." In Lloyd G. Reynolds, Ed., *Agriculture in Development Theory*. New Haven: Yale University Press.

Moene, Karl Ove (1988). "A Reformulation of the Harris-Todaro Mechanism with Endogenous Wages," *Economics Letters* 27: 387–390.

Moene, Karl Ove (1992). "Poverty and Landownership," *American Economic Review* 82:52–64.

Moran, Theodore H. (2002). *Beyond Sweatshops: Foreign Direct Investment and Globalization in Developing Countries*. Washington, DC: Brookings Institution.

Nelson, Richard R. (1966). "A Theory of the Low-Level Equilibrium Trap in Underdeveloped Economies." *American Economic Review* 46: 894–908.

Noe, Raymond A., Hollenbeck, John R., Gerhart, Barry & Wright, Patrick M. (2000). *Human Resource Management*. Boston: Irwin McGraw-Hill.

Osmani, S.R. (1991). "Wage Determination in Rural Labour Markets: The Theory of Implicit Co-Operation." *Journal of Development Economics* 34: 3–23.

Park, Young-Bum (1991). "Union/Non-Union Wage Differentials in the Korean Manufacturing Sector." *International Economic Journal* 5: 79–91.

Raff, Daniel & Summers, Lawrence. (1987). "Did Henry Ford Pay Efficiency Wages?" *Journal of Labor Economics* 5: S57–86.

Ranis, Gustav. (2006). "Is Dualism Worth Revisiting?" In Alain de Janvry & Ravi Kanbur, Eds., *Poverty, Inequality, and Development: Essays in Honor of Erik Thorbecke*. Kluwer.

Ranis, Gustav & Fei, John C. H. (1961). "A Theory of Economic Development." *American Economic Review* 51: 533–565.

Ranis, Gustav & Stewart, Frances. (1993). "Rural Nonagricultural Activities in Development: Theory and Application." *Journal of Development Economics* 40: 75–101.

Ranis, Gustav & Stewart, Frances. (1999). "V-Goods and the Role of the Urban Informal Sector in Development." *Economic Development and Cultural Change* 47: 259–288.

Robinson, Sherman. (1976). "A Note on the U Hypothesis Relating Income Inequality to Economic Development," *American Economic Review* 437–440.

Rosenzweig, Mark. (1988). "Labor Markets in Low Income Countries." In Hollis Chenery & T.N. Srinivasan, eds., *Handbook of Development Economics, Volume 1*. Amsterdam: North Holland.

Roy, A.D. (1951). "Some Thoughts on the Distribution of Earnings," *Oxford Economic Papers* 3: 135–146.

Sah, Raaj Kumar & Stiglitz, Joseph E. (1985). "The Social Cost of Labor and Project Evaluation: A General Approach." *Journal of Public Economics* 28: 135–163.

Schultz, T.W. (1961). "Investment in Human Capital." *American Economic Review* LI: 1–17.

Schultz, T.W. (1962). "Reflections on Investment in Man." *Journal of Political Economy* LXX Supplement: 1–8.

Sen, Amartya K. (1967). "Review of J.C.H. Fei and G. Ranis, *Development of the Labor Surplus Economy: Theory and Policy*." *The Economic Journal* 77: 346–349.

Shapiro, Carl & Stiglitz, Joseph E. (1984). "Equilibrium Unemployment as a Worker Discipline Device." *American Economic Review* 74: 433–444.

Solow, Robert. (1990). *The Labour Market as a Social Institution*. Oxford: Blackwell.

Spinanger, Dean. (1985). "The Labor Market in Panama: An Analysis of the Employment Impact of the Labor Code." Paper presented at the Seminar on Employment Policy in Latin America, Panama.

Squire, Lyn. (1981). *Employment Policy in Developing Countries*. New York: Oxford University Press for the World Bank.

Starr, Gerald (1981). *Minimum Wage Fixing*. Geneva: International Labour Organization.

Stiglitz, Joseph E. (1974). "Alternative Theories of Wage Determination and Unemployment in LDCs: The Labour Turnover Model." *Quarterly Journal of Economics* 88: 194–227.

Stiglitz, Joseph E. (1976). "The Efficiency Wage Hypothesis, Surplus Labor, and the Distribution of Labour in LDCs." *Oxford Economic Papers* 28: 185–207.

Stiglitz, Joseph E. (1982). "The Structure of Labor Markets and Shadow Prices in LDCs." In Richard H. Sabot, ed., *Migration and the Labor Market in Developing Countries*. Boulder, CO: Westview.

Stiglitz, Joseph E. (1985). "Equilibrium Wage Distributions." *The Economic Journal* 95: 595–618.

Tidrick, Gene (1975). "Wage Spillover and Unemployment in a Wage-Gap Economy: The Jamaican Case." *Economic Development and Cultural Change* 23: 306–324.

Todaro, Michael P. (1969). "A Model of Labor Migration and Urban Unemployment in Less Developed Countries." *American Economic Review* 39: 138–148.

Tokman, Victor. (1987). "El Sector Informal: Quince Años Despues," PREALC LIV: 514–529.

Turnham, David. (1971). *The Employment Problem in Less Developed Countries.* Paris: Development Centre of the Organisation for Economic Co-Operation and Development.

Turnham, David. (1993). *Employment and Development: A New Review of Evidence.* Paris: Development Centre of the Organisation for Economic Co-Operation and Development.

Ulrich, Dave. (1997). *Human Resource Champions.* Boston: Harvard Business School Press.

United Nations. (2003). *The Challenge of Slums: Global Report on Human Settlements 2003.* New York: United Nations Human Settlements Programme.

Weiss, Andrew. (1990). *Efficiency Wages.* Princeton: Princeton University Press.

Welch, Finis. (1974). "Minimum Wage Legislation in the United States." *Economic Inquiry* 12: 285–318.

World Bank. (1990). *World Development Report 1990.* Washington: World Bank.

World Bank. (1995). *World Development Report 1995.* Washington: World Bank.

Yoo, Gyeongjoon. (1995). *An Analysis and Decomposition of Changing Labor Income Distribution in Korea.* Unpublished Doctoral Dissertation, Cornell University.

PART IV

WELFARE

CHAPTER 19

WHAT IS WELFARE AND HOW CAN WE MEASURE IT?

KEITH DOWDING

1. INTRODUCTION

Welfare economics is usually considered to be that part of economics concerned with the effects of economic activity on human welfare. Traditionally, it is where economists explicitly keep their normative commitments, thus allowing other parts of their discipline to remain positive or purely explanatory of the processes of economic interaction within institutional contexts. Within welfare economics, topics such as the modeling of individual or household behavior; criteria for judging what is beneficial to society; considerations of how income or wealth distribution affects social welfare; cost-benefit analysis involving externalities, and so on, all have their home. Indeed virtually every other branch of economics is touched upon by welfare economics. Rather than considering the full gamut of issues that are discussed in welfare economics (topics that might be covered in a university course or textbook), this chapter concentrates upon the core issues of normative thinking in welfare economics. These are the questions that concern the very nature of human welfare: what considerations should enter into evaluation of satisfactory human existence, and how might that welfare be measured?

The traditional approach in such treatments of welfare economics begins with the standard economic line on what constitutes human welfare. The standard line is that welfare consists of the satisfaction of human preferences usually understood as what people reveal they want through their choices, though often mediated in normative discussion by what people would choose in ideal informational contexts.[1] At this point, the two fundamental theorems of welfare economics might be mentioned. First, that each Walrasian equilibrium is Pareto efficient, at least if consumers are locally nonsatiated. Second, any Pareto-efficient allocation not on the boundary of the attainable set is a Walrasian equilibrium, provided preferences satisfy appropriate convexity and continuity assumptions.[2] Discussion then proceeds to the problems inherent in the fundamental theorems: the problem of public goods, issues of private information, or the applicability of the continuity and convexity axioms. The theorems might even be questioned in terms of how applicable they are to real public-policy issues such as affordable medical care or decent housing for all. A more philosophical set of criticisms considers the very basis of preference satisfaction: whether this is a vacuous or contentless account of welfare (Sen 1974, 1977, Roemer 1996); and whether it can deal with important political concerns such as rights and freedoms (Sen 1970, Chapter 6*, 1982a). In these discussions the informational basis (Sen 2002, Chapter 11; d'Asprement & Gevers 1977; Fleurbaey 2004) looms large. The consensus is that interpersonally comparable indices of individual well-being are required to avoid Arrow's (1951/1963) conclusion that there is no consistent social welfare function and that different informational bases lead to different policy recommendations. The difficulties of making interpersonal comparisons either with experiential accounts of utility (satisfaction or happiness) and with preference satisfaction accounts (or what I will call choice-based utility) of well-being are well known and widely discussed (see for example Sen 1982b, Mackay 1986, Harsanyi 1987, Elster & Roemer 1991, Hausman 1995; List 2003, Binmore this volume). I will suggest that the two interpretations—which are often confused—create different difficulties. In fact, all approaches to welfare, and not only those using utility as the currency of comparison, face interpersonal comparability problems to which a set of solutions or partial solutions can be addressed (Fleurbaey & Hammond 2004). In Section 4, I will briefly look at social welfare functions without interpersonal comparisons and examine their limitations for all ways of considering human welfare.

In this chapter, I step back from the traditional route of discussing the philosophical issues of welfare economics. The problem with that general approach is that the account and problems inherent in seeing welfare in terms of choice-based utility (whether ordinal or cardinal) or experiential utility are discussed prior to discussing other ways of examining human welfare. Problems with welfarism and utilitarianism, then, lead to the discussion of other approaches as though they avoid such problems when, in reality, their proponents rarely even stand them up to the issues. To be sure, writers often admit (new) difficulties with seeing welfare in terms of rights, responsibilities, or some other concept, but we often lose sight of the fact that they must, as well, grapple with informational or measurement problems that also imply some interpersonal comparisons, or, at the very least, entail judgments about measurement issues. Any welfare economics or political philosophy that does not tell us how to address public policy issues is not worth the name, and that means we must have a way of comparing the welfare of different people in *some* manner in order to make judgments about where to spend public money. All approaches suffer from interpersonal comparability problems—in fact they all face pretty much the same comparability problems, or so I shall argue. I will suggest that these problems are insurmountable for global individual-to-individual comparisons, but are all roughly solvable for what I call global social "type-to-type" (or social-group-to-social-group) comparisons, as long as certain statistical assumptions are satisfied.

I will begin with a very basic question: what is human welfare? And from the answers that historically have been given, I attempt, informally, to discuss the informational problems with which all approaches must grapple, and I suggest the path by which they are practically solved.

2. What Is Human Welfare?

Welfare economics is concerned with the welfare of societies. Welfare in this context can be considered to be the satisfactory functioning of a society. Usually the welfare of societies is thought to depend upon some function of the welfare of their members, and such welfare is considered to be monotonic in that, if the welfare of one person in a society can be increased without thereby decreasing the welfare of anyone else, then the society is also better off; conversely, reducing the welfare of one person without affecting the welfare of anyone else will make society worse off. We could imagine other considerations entering into the calculation, which do not depend on the welfare of people within societies. For example, a longer-lasting society might be thought of as having greater welfare than a shorter-lived one, even if the members of the longer-lasting society had less individual welfare—however that welfare was measured—if stability was something to be valued in itself (see Parfit 1984; Broome 2004 for discussion of welfare issues over generations). However, in keeping with most of welfare economics, I will restrict discussion by assuming throughout that the welfare of a society is exclusively composed of some function of the welfare of its members, though I will argue that we can only judge the relative welfare of society in terms of aggregate measures of which the basic units are types (or groups or classes or sets) of people and cannot take account of individuals as such.[3]

The welfare of individual human beings might be thought of as being composed of their satisfactory state of being. What composes that satisfactory state of being is controversial. It could be composed of something objective—such as how long a biological being survives. Whatever contributes to human survival contributes to their satisfactory state of being. We could then measure the welfare of a society in terms of its mortality rate. One society is judged to have greater welfare than another if its mortality rate is lower. However, most people might consider that there is more to life than simply living. Many would argue that a person in a vegetative state is hardly human, and keeping people alive simply because we are able to do so contributes neither to their individual welfare nor to that of society. Imagine we could keep people alive for long periods even after their bodily organs had shut down. Would doing this for large numbers of people make for a better society? I believe not. However, this belief does not show that mortality rates do not provide some indication of the welfare of a society. It is a mistake to argue that, because we can think of some cases in which a person would sooner be dead, mortality rates do not tell us something about the welfare of a society. Such examples only matter if these cases systematically affect the relevant welfare measure. In other words, comparison of mortality rates across societies can be indicative as long as at least one society does not contain systematic bias—that is, as long as one society does not systematically contain an unusually high proportion of cases in which we judge people would be better off dead. Beyond such systematic bias, any particular cases in which we judge individual welfare not reflected by the mortality rate will be contained in the error terms, when comparing across societies or across groups of people within societies.

Of course, we do not think that survival is the only indication of human welfare. Indicators on morbidity, health, education, as well as the holding of material goods, might all be considered to be objective indicators of the welfare of individuals and the society they inhabit. Again, the fact that we can come up with examples in which we might judge that someone's welfare is not increased by education, health, or material goods should not count against these factors as social indicators, unless we feel the example reveals a bias in the data of some of the societies we are measuring. I come back to these points in Section 6. They raise an important issue that often causes confusion between philosophers and economists. Economists tend to use social indicators to judge relative welfare across countries or social groups within countries. Philosophers come up with examples that show that, even if a given person scored more highly on that indicator, we could not judge that person to have higher welfare. This is then used to critique the social indicator. But such individual examples are not enough on their own. The philosopher needs to demonstrate a bias in the estimates across the societies. The philosopher needs to demonstrate some systematic reason why the indicator is inappropriate.[4]

The definition of human welfare as the satisfactory condition or conditions of being human is as neutral a definition as I can think of. What counts as satisfactory will depend upon what we see as the condition of being human. For example, philosophers working within an Aristotelian tradition see certain needs or functionings as being specifically human. Others, working in a more Kantian tradition, see such lists as too prescriptive, because they are based upon a specific theory of the goal of the good life for humans. Those in the Kantian tradition see freedom as the fundamental criterion of being human and wish to institute that value by assigning rights and privileges (or liberties) to people. A third approach, perhaps more familiar in mainstream economics, is the utilitarian or ordinal form "welfarist" approach. Utilitarianism can be seen either as the maximization of experiential utility or as the maximization of choice-based utility. In the experiential form, human happiness or satisfaction is the satisfactory condition to be maximized; in the second form, the satisfactory condition is whatever people choose for themselves—or at least in politically normative contexts, what people would choose for themselves if ideally placed. The latter form of utilitarianism might fit well with Kantian tradition because what is maximized is what people choose, which seems to imply some kind of freedom, or it might fit well even with an Aristotelian approach—if all people were Aristotelian for example.[5] For that reason, in this chapter, I will distinguish between experiential and choice-based accounts.[6]

We might note here that *welfarism* is defined in terms of a weak ordering, independence, and Pareto indifference, such that only preferences should enter into a social welfare function, and it is the Pareto principle (discussed later) that explicitly brings in individual preferences, and is, thus, part of the very definition of *welfarism*. Often it is then assumed that these preferences must be experiential. However, if any argument can enter into a utility function, then anything that anyone believes is morally relevant can enter into the social-welfare function. Of course, we can still distinguish choice-based welfarism from other approaches, since some theories require elements of welfare (as defined broadly here) to enter for each individual, regardless of whether that individual believes in the relevance or importance of those elements. In that sense, choice-based welfarism is democratic or private in a manner that other approaches may not be. Welfarism, therefore, requires the Pareto principle, even though some theories of human welfare (as that term is understood here) will not.

My justification for what might seem to be a confusing use of the term *welfare*, given the standard meaning of *welfarism* in economic theory, is simply that the usual meaning of *welfare* as used in policy analysis does not imply anything so strict about individual preferences.[7] Most discussions of the needs of the welfare state, for example, are much more catholic in what might be considered morally relevant considerations. For example, it is somewhat tortuous to attempt to discuss welfare rights in terms of individual preferences—especially in terms of experiential utility. Forcing the term *welfare* into the straitjacket of *welfarism* sows more confusion than my usage, or so I believe.

3. Four Approaches to Welfare

Aristotelian Approach

The Aristotelian approach to human welfare suggests that there are particular ways in which humans flourish.[8] These can be seen as needs (Doyal & Gough 1991) though the term *need* often implies instrumental values: we need some *X* in order to provide for some *Y* (White 1975). Rather, here *needs*—or to use the Aristotelian phrase *functionings*—are ends in themselves. They constitute human welfare. Recently, two approaches to functionings—those of Martha Nussbaum and Amartya Sen—have dominated political thought in this area. Sen has maintained a more subjective liberal approach to functionings, whereas Martha Nussbaum (1992, 1995, 2000) has argued that we need to characterize an objective list of functionings:

1. *Life*. Able to live a life of normal length and worth living.
2. *Bodily health*. Adequate nourishment , shelter, and good health
3. *Bodily integrity*. Free from assault, free geographical mobility.
4. *Senses, imagination and thought*. Basic education and freedom of expression.
5. *Emotions*. Able to express emotion and develop attachments.
6. *Practical reason*. Able to for a conception of the good.
7. *Affiliation*. Able to live and interact with others, have self-respect.
8. *Other species*. Able to live and have concern for animals.
9. *Play*. Able to laugh and play.
10. *Environment*. Able to partipate politically and own possessions.

Source: Nussbaum 2000, pp. 78–80

I will not discuss the list in detail. It is sufficient to say that some items appear to be relatively uncontroversial; others, as she admits, are open to debate. Nussbaum is clear that the items are universal and must be promoted in any society, no matter what its culture. Of course, it is precisely because of cultural diversity that some items are controversial. The list was produced following discussion with many people from different walks of life and cultures. The inclusion of being able to live with and show concern for other species has been especially controversial, with those from the developing world showing much less interest than those in the West (Nussbaum 2000, n. 85, 80). Thus, despite their objective nature in the sense that they are supposed to apply across all societies and cultures, the list has been created through discussion and is open to dispute., In addition, while some items are relatively easy to quantify, others seem almost impossible.

Other lists of human needs abound (Chambers 1995; Cummins 1996, 1998; Galtung 1994; Max-Neef 1993; Narayan et al. 2000a, 2000b; Qizilbash 1996; Ramsey 1992; Schwartz 1994; see Alkire 2002, Chapter 2 for a review). Most are specifically directed at examining poverty and hence concerned with raising the living standards of the worst-off in society to some acceptable level. Despite their different heritage, what is interesting about these different lists is how they tend to converge on a central set of needs. The studies of Narayan et al. are, perhaps, the most interesting. In Narayan (2000a) the authors synthesized 81 assessments of poverty conducted by the World Bank in 50 countries. In Narayan (2000b) the authors surveyed poverty-stricken people to see what they considered poverty consisted of. From both these studies Narayan et al. suggest that welfare can be seen in terms of six categories of good:

- Material well-being, including food, assets, and work.
- Bodily well-being: being and appearing healthy and living in a decent physical environment.
- Social well-being: being able to care for and bring up children, having self-respect and dignity and having good relations with one's family and neighbors.
- Security: enjoying civil peace in a safe environment with personal physical security and access to the means of justice, with security in old age and confidence in the future.
- Psychological well-being: having peace of mind, happiness, and harmony.
- Freedom of choice and action.

The list, like Nussbaum's, provides not only for material goods but also for the ability of people to be able to direct their lives. They want freedom as well as material and social goods. Amartya Sen, perhaps the foremost critic of traditional welfare economics, also wants to include freedom and rights within an account of human welfare, which leads him to pursue a version of the Aristotelian approach. For Sen, like Nussbaum, functionings are the ends that provide human flourishing. For both of them, however, social policy should be directed at promoting human capabilities. By *capability,* Nussbaum and Sen mean both the ability and the means by which people can attain their chosen ends. Living and achieving those chosen ends is the functioning in question (see Dowding 2006a for a precise discussion and critique). By developing human capabilities to function, humans can choose which functionings they want to develop for themselves. Capabilities cannot be measured directly, however—and what they constitute often slide into functionings—hence measures across societies rely upon measuring actual functionings across classes of people (see Kuklys 2005). In order to make full comparisons across different societies, a measure or currency is required. This would require us not only to list the important functionings, as Nussbaum and others have done, but also to put a price on the level of each separate functioning. Nussbaum is clear that this is not possible. She states it is "a list of *separate components*" (Nussbaum, 2000, 81, emphasis in original) and means by this that any cost-benefit analysis that weights the elements for trading-off one against the other will have a "tragic aspect." We might specify a minimal level of each functioning, which cannot (except in times of "moral catastrophe"?) be traded. Beyond that level, however, trades are required. At least trades must be made while public policy is publicly financed and funding for one item entails spending less on another. So comparisons and weightings of different functionings are required.

Sen recognizes this problem more specifically. He has two solutions, the first of which is only partial. Although we might not be able to place precise figures on the relative worth of different functionings, we can produce partial comparisons across societies in terms of dominance (Sen 1992). However, this will not take us very far down the path of comparing the welfare of different societies or groups within a society. The second solution he suggests is that we allow different societies to place different weightings upon the desired functionings: so one democratic country might choose to spend more on education at the expense of health, while a second chooses to spend more on health than education. All we can do is compare relative levels of educational attainment and health measures across the two societies. We can gain some partial orderings in this manner. In fact, in practical matters, the World Development Organization provides a Human Development Index (HDI) partially based on these ideas. This index weights a limited set of functionings giving a number between 0 and 1. Where the raw numbers are transformed according to $x\text{–}index = x\text{–}(min_x \,/\, max_x\text{–}min_x)$. The HDI is the average of three indices: life expectancy, education, and GDP.

Life Expectancy (LE) Index = $(LE\text{–}25) \,/\, (85\text{–}25)$

The education index is composed of two other indices:

Adult Literacy Index (ALI) = Adult Literacy Rate/100, and the Gross Enrollment Index (GEI) = Combined Enrollment Ratio/100 to give:
    Education Index = $(2ALI/3) + (GEI/3)$
    GDP Index = $(logGDPpc\text{–}log100) \,/\, (log4000\text{–}log100)$

where *GDPpc* is GDP per capita given in United States dollars.

This measure only provides a partial glimpse at the functionings that might be produced, though more complex formulas might be possible. The index requires, we can see, certain assumptions about the relative worth of each functioning. If a single index is not to be produced, then the only comparisons that can be made about objective functionings measured by such statistics are those at a disaggregated level. Such comparisons across, say, health, education, property rights, nutritional levels, and so on might provide reasonable guides to the relative capability of people in different countries. We might note that these figures on their own do not provide information on distribution within countries.

We can see the problems of the capabilities approach. First the list of relevant functionings must be produced and decisions must be made about whether functionings have intrinsic or only instrumental importance (in order to prevent double counting). Second, for full comparability, an aggregation index must be supplied. Sen's solution is partial comparability using the notion of dominance. But this solution will only allow for an index that can measure comparative deprivation and is unlikely to be able to compare much beyond that. Third, in empirical analysis, whether someone (or some class of people) has chosen to ignore possible functionings or is legally or materially barred from such functionings needs to be decided. For example, if there are few female lawyers in a country is that because of their freely made choices or because it is culturally very difficult for women to become lawyers? After all, they may choose not to become lawyers because they do not want to *because* that is their culture. In other words, translating achieved functionings into inferences about capabilities requires decisions about the true provenance of choices. Where do those choices come from?

Kantian Approaches

For some people, such objective measures of functionings, even in the mild form suggested by Sen, are too paternalistic. What I will call a Kantian approach suggests that we should instead concentrate upon liberty and rights as the satisfactory condition of being human. In the Kantian approaches,[9] freedom constitutes the satisfactory condition of being human. In its most libertarian formulation, freedom is the only thing to be maximized. Various formulations for measuring freedom have been suggested. The pure negative freedom approach suggests that we count, by some means, the number of compossible acts a person is able to do (Steiner 1994, Carter 1999). For two acts to be compossible, they must both be members of a single possible world. In Carter's formulation, the number of compossible acts a that a person i is able to do is given by $\sum_{i=1}^{n} F_{r,i} / (\sum_{i=1}^{n} F_{r,i} + \sum_{i=1}^{n} U_{r,i})$, where F is the number of acts person i is able to do, and U is the number of compossible acts they are unable to do. Each act is measured content independently. That is, each possible act is valued equally with each other possible act. Scratching one's nose is as valuable as praying to one's god, and is as valuable as scratching one's nose while praying to one's god. For this reason some add a component to differentially weight the value of the acts. For example, Kramer's (2003) rival formulation $F^2 / (F + U)$ admits to content evaluation in the measurement. These precise formulas do have an arbitrary character, however (van Hees 2000; Dowding and van Hees 2007). The question of whether to admit evaluation of the compossible acts has best been expressed in Pattanaik and Xu's (1990) "flavour of an impossibility theorem."

They present three axioms:

> *Indifference between no-choice situations: opportunity sets consisting of only one alternative yield the same amount of freedom.* The justification is that an opportunity set of only one item yields no freedom at all.

> *Strict monotonicity: for all distinct alternatives x, y, the opportunity set consisting of both x and y yields strictly more freedom than one consisting of only x.* The justification seems obvious. A set where I can choose from two items yields more freedom than a set with only one of these items.

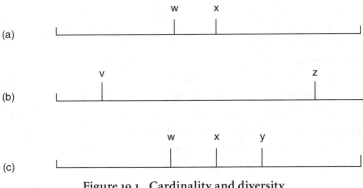

Figure 19.1. Cardinality and diversity

Independence: for all opportunity sets A and B and alternatives x which belong
to neither A nor B, A gives at least as much freedom as B iff the union of
A and {x} gives at least as much freedom as the union of B and {x}. The
idea here is that adding or subtracting the same element from any two
opportunity sets should not affect their relative evaluation.

The three axioms yield a unique cardinality rule that freedom is measured by
the number of alternatives in an opportunity set. However, simple examples seem
to demonstrate the naivety of this cardinality rule. Adding the alternative "blue
car" to the set {red car, train} does not seem to add as much choice as adding it
to the set {bicycle, train}. Intuitively, the simple cardinality rule fails. However,
bringing in content evaluation of alternatives brings its own problems. There have
been several attempts to measure diversity of alternatives within opportunity sets
(Heritier 1996; Bossert et al. 2003), but all fail to overcome the problem (Van Hees
2004). We can see the essential difficulty by means of a simple example. Imagine
measuring diversity along a single dimension. In Figure 19.1 (a), the two items
w and *x*, are closer together than the two items *v* and *z* in Figure 19.1(b). Figure
19.1 (b) seems to provide greater diversity. But now compare Figure 19.1 (b) with
19.1 (c). Here we have three items *w, x,* and *y*. They are still contained within the
broader set (b), but there are now three items. Does (b) or (c) contain the most
freedom? Do we value three options closer together or two alternatives further
apart? Of course, our answer might depend on where we locate our bliss point on
that dimension. But that will mean we define the amount of freedom by our utility,
or our indirect utility. It seems that any measures must either give greater credence
to the number of items, to some form of diversity, or give counter-intuitive results
(Van Hees 2004).

In fact, the problems with the measures of freedom in this literature are
very close to some of the problems noted by critics of the capability/functioning
approach (Cohen 1994, Dowding 2006a). To simply count the alternatives in an
opportunity set seems to miss an important aspect of our evaluation of freedom—

why we value it in the first place. However, bringing in content evaluation seems to reduce the evaluation of freedom to that of utility or at least indirect utility.

One way of trying to grapple with the measurement of freedom, is to shift attention away from freedom and to look more at *rights*. Dowding and Van Hees (2003) distinguish four different ways in which rights exist based on two distinctions. First is the distinction between the formal and material existence of rights. A right exists materially if it is respected, that is, government and the community respect it and rights holders can exercise it. It exists formally if it is specified by some code, such as the list of rights specified by the Universal Declaration of Human Rights. The second dimension pertains to the scope of the right as being a particular ("Person j possesses freedom of speech"), or as a universal ("in this society there is freedom of speech"). The measurement of universal material rights can then be ascertained by the probability that individuals in a society have that right respected or can exercise it. Pogge (2002) and Dowding and Van Hees (2003) argue that a right is violated if the ex ante probability of exercising that right falls below some threshold. Specific ex ante probabilities can be aggregated into the right to perform some action for the act type in question and the act type can be said to materially exist if the probability exceeds a certain threshold. Such calculations might be applied to both negative and positive rights. Alternatively, no threshold need be specified as such; rather, the material rights of different types of people might simply be compared. The approach is very similar to that for calculating capabilities based on actual functionings, and it requires the same sort of statistical assumptions and faces similar problems both over full comparability and whether purported lack of material freedom for a class of acts is, in fact, freely chosen.

Resourcist Approaches

Under this heading, I will discuss a series of mixed views that attempt to capture elements of Kantianism and Aristotelianism in the form of allowing people to choose their conception of the good life while being especially attentive to the distributional considerations of the worst off. These Rawlsian and post-Rawlsian accounts of welfare are diverse, but all recognize that resources of some kind need to be distributed according to some maximizing, maximining, or leximining principles.

Rawls's (1971) principles of social justice are the most discussed and the ones from which many others take their lead. Rawls's (1971, 302) two principles are (1) that each person is to have an equal right to the most extensive total system of equal basic liberties compatible with a similar system of liberty for all, and (2) that social and economic inequalities are to be arranged so that they are both: (a) to the greatest benefit of the least advantaged, consistent with the just savings principle, and (b) attached to offices and positions open to all under the conditions of fair equality of opportunity. The first principle has absolute priority over the second principle, and 2(b) has absolute priority over 2(a). What is to be distributed are primary goods— that is, those things that every rational person is presumed to want—including rights and liberties, wealth and power, because they provide "the clearest basis for interpersonal comparison" (Rawls 1971, 174). However, it is difficult to know how to quantify such primary goods outside of a utility function (which somewhat undermines Rawls's claim), which is why most economists who have attempted to specify welfare functions in terms of the first part of the second principle—the one that does all the work despite being absolutely inferior—typically use utility. Indeed, as an early critique of Rawls pointed out, Rawls's justification for primary goods is otiose since Bentham himself, when proposing codified laws, defined them in terms of rights and liberties, wealth and power, and not utility (Barry 1973, 55). Utility could still be the measure of the relative worth of different rights and liberties, with the priority of given elements instantiated in codified constitutional laws. For Rawls, primary goods are specified simply to justify identifying some elements for special treatment based upon individuals' rational choice of them.

Rawls is a resourcist, since it is clear that what have priority are the social resources such as civil and political liberties, education, health care, and so on, rather than other items that one might choose. That some might lose out because of the natural lottery of genetic or environmental endowment, or simply through poor luck is not of concern beyond what is captured in his two principles. It is not at all clear, however, how these are to be measured even to the extent of being organized to the advantage of the worst off. Hence, most discussions of these principles seem to cash them (so to speak) in terms of money. Dworkin (2000), the resourcist who brought the label to the debate, goes beyond Rawls to include "internal resources" such as absence of physical disabilities and state of health. His idea of a hypothetical insurance market was supposed to distinguish between the bad luck that people have for which they are to blame and that for which they are not. The state is to intervene to remedy only the latter. Roemer's measure (discussed later) is the only empirical offering on the table to capture this (or at least a similar) distinction. In Dworkin's hands, it is difficult to distinguish resourcism from the capabilities approach.

It might be asked what is wrong with operationalizing resources in terms of money. Of course, it can be admitted that simply examining the development of countries in terms of GDP ignores distribution. And, of course, rates of exchange and costs of living need to be controlled for. However, using some relevant equality index, such as the Gini coefficient, and with some relatively simple econometrics, comparisons in terms of income or wealth can be made across countries or across a society. Although it is true that unequally situated people whose income or wealth is identical are unlikely to function identically, it might be argued that equalizing wealth or income (subject to incentive constraints) would be a policy that might promote equality most effectively. Such a measure is relatively easy to calculate, public policy relatively easy to identify, and the process much less subject to rent-seeking activity by those asking for special provisions due to some aspect of their life that entails they can utilize resources less efficiently than others. Concentrating upon money as a resource may not be ideal for promoting equality but it might be the second-best solution.

Utilitarianism

Following Sen (1979, 1999), utilitarianism in welfare economics is usually defined in terms of (i) consequentialism, (ii) welfarism, and (iii) sum ranking. The first is that the rightness of an act should be seen in terms of its consequences alone. Judgment about states must be confined to the utilities in those states. Sum ranking is the thesis that utilities should be aggregated by summing together without paying any attention to the distribution across the utilities of the population. There are many specific approaches that might come under this rubric.

All three aspects of utilitarianism have been criticized. The first is criticized for appearing to invite us to ignore *process*. The same outcome might accrue but through different processes. How the food enters my mouth matters to me. The process criticism misses the mark, however, since the consequence in question is supposed to be a justification of the act in question. If I mind how the food enters my mouth, then the "minding" will enter into the calculation of two different ways of it entering my mouth. A consequence already has the identification of the process contained in its description if there is some difference in the utility of how it might come about. Welfarism is criticized for ignoring relevant nonutility information. If utility is defined experientially then, of course, it leaves out information. If we define *utility* as "happiness," then the utilitarian metric will only count human happiness in its welfare function—a view some espouse (Ng 1997, 1999, 2000). However, a partial defense of choice-based utilitarianism is that any morally important information should enter into the utilities of those concerned about the issue, hence, the consequences of moral judgments must take into account any morally relevant information—at least information judged morally relevant by those whose judgments are considered relevant. Finally, utilitarianism is concerned with maximizing utility and is not concerned with distributional issues, so it might seem inegalitarian. Two defenses for utilitarianism are often offered here. One is that material goods generally have decreasing marginal utility, so utility maximizing will usually not ignore distribution, even as a sideproduct (Carritt 1967). Secondly, some utilitarians suggest that empathy for others is an important aspect of humanity so each will take into account others' utilities within their own utility functions, ensuring that a more egalitarian distribution is attended to (Harsanyi 1953, 1955; see Binmore this volume).

Traditionally, however, development economics did tend to view simple GDP measures as an indicator of the utility of a nation, and so argue that increasing GDP did show an improving situation. But exclusive reliance on GDP does not give any indication of distributional considerations nor does it fit with any extant form of utilitarianism.

Other criticisms of utilitarianism rely upon there being precise measurements of interpersonal utility. It is argued that a utilitarian is committed to giving pleasure wizards—those who gain more utility from resources than others—more resources than ordinary people. And it entails giving less to those who gain less than ordinary people—such as the terminally depressed. As argued later, since such global interpersonal comparability is impossible, we need not be concerned with such fantastic examples. Maximizing utility does seem to suggest that we should spend resources or set up institutions such that, overall, utility is increased the most. This seems to be the conclusion of those happiness approaches that measure experiential utility through surveys.

The idea of maximizing some felt phenomenon as welfare has long been a part of welfare economics, and in a more explicit form it is becoming more popular. Quite how to characterize the felt phenomenon is difficult to specify, with *happiness* and *satisfaction* being the most popular words in the English language used to describe it. The fact that no word in the English language seems quite to cover what is meant suggests that there is no single phenomenon that encompasses it. Nevertheless, people do seem to understand what is being demanded of them when asked in surveys to judge their overall happiness or their satisfaction with different aspects of their lives. Another measure of the welfare of a society can be seen in terms of survey evidence on how happy people feel and what objective conditions contribute to different levels of happiness.

For experiential utility, there is the problem of never being quite sure whether the experiences that one person has are identical to those of another person. We might see two people making identical choices in identical choice situations but cannot tell how happy they are with the choices they make. There are various approaches to measuring experiential utility (see Hammond 1991), though the one that is most extensively used in empirical analyses is happiness surveys. In these surveys samples of populations in different countries have been asked about their life in general and asked if they feel very happy, happy, unhappy or very unhappy or similar terms (Easterlin 1974, 1995, 2000; Simon 1974; Myers 1993; Veenhoven 1999; Clark & Oswald 1994, 1996, 2002; Ng 1996; Frank 1997; Kahneman, Wakker & Sarin 1997; Oswald 1997; Winkelmann & Winkelmann 1998; Di Tella, MacCulloch & Oswald 2001; Van Praag & Ferrer-i-Carbonell 2004; Layard 2005). Comparisons are made across countries or across social groups within countries. Generally, these approaches do not attempt to specify some formal social welfare functional but rather they suggest that maximizing the percentage of people who are happy should be a policy aim. By comparison across social groups, we can also look at the distribution of happiness across types of people, which can inform public policy. Of course the happiness comparisons assume the direct comparability of individual answers to the happiness surveys. Some analyses assume the ordinal scales can also be manipulated as though they were cardinal. Clark and Oswald (2002) propose using such surveys to estimate the monetary value of events which correlate with happiness such as marriage or unemployment using linear equations to estimate a "happiness equation." The coefficient for each life event can be divided by the coefficient for income to estimate the marginal rate of substitution between income and such life events. Since the surveys correlate life events with experiential utility, one might think they avoid the objection that Sen proclaims against

utility approaches of ignoring the provenance of utility. The objective life conditions seem to correlate with overall happiness. However, two sets of evidence show
that individual expectations do affect reported happiness. The happiness literature
shows that terrible events, such as accidents leading to paraplegia, immediately
lower an individual's overall happiness, but that relatively quickly respondents
return to a stated level of happiness not much below what prevailed before the
accident. Similarly, lottery winners at first display high levels of happiness but
soon return to a level not much above that which they enjoyed prior to winning.
Secondly, the related literature examining satisfaction with specific public services
suggests that when objective measures of service quality increase, average levels of
reported satisfaction remain largely constant, suggesting that experienced utility
is related to expectations.

Thus, while public policy might well be informed by such happiness results, we
might think that the welfare of a community is increased if, say, services are better
provided as demonstrated by objective measures (such as how quickly repairs are
provided, how many mistakes are made in calculating benefits, and so on), even if
reported satisfaction remains constant.

Another approach to utilitarianism is to make no assumptions about the
content of utility. Rather, utility is the name given to whatever it is that agents
maximize. While this choice-based approach has many nice features for positive
economics, can it fulfill the role it is assigned in a moral theory? Remembering
from Rawls (1971) that the subject is the structure of society, what people maximize, given the institutions and relationships in which they find themselves, is our
basis for inferences as to what they would maximize under different structures.
And it is those structures that we wish to design. We can imagine that people prefer
to maximize many resources, rights, liberties; and minimize many pains, and so
on. We can note, however, that these maximands and minimands are all external
and, measurement issues aside, comparable. Utilitarianism in this form does not
require any specific assumptions about interpersonal comparisons beyond those
required by other approaches.

All ways of looking at welfare require us to make some interpersonal comparisons. We have seen they all have similar measurement problems. Before looking
again at interpersonal comparisons, I want to examine how far welfare theorists
have taken us without utilizing interpersonal comparisons.

4. INTERPERSONAL NONCOMPARABILITY

A great deal of effort has gone into examining what can be said about the welfare of
a society using only noncomparable ordinal information. Arrow in 1951 sought to
define a social welfare function in terms of individual preference orderings leading

to his famous impossibility theorem that demonstrates that, under his assumptions, there was no nondictatorial social welfare function. In fact, the inputs into such a function do not have to be individual preference profiles; they could be any individual goods such as capabilities or primary goods, as well as preferences understood as experiential or choice-based (Fleurbaey & Hammond 2004). The only requirement is unidimensionality—that is, such a function only discounts views where plural values are thought to be incommensurable. Thus, in an ordinal framework, as long as conditions familiar to Arrow's theorem hold—unrestricted domain, transitivity, completeness, the Pareto principle, anonymity, and independence of irrelevant alternatives—then impossibility results emerge. Only if some dictator assigns the good to each person is the result avoided. Thus, moving outside the preference framework does not avoid Arrow, unless it is accepted that moving out of the framework of preferences and into some substantial theory of the good is moving into a dictatorial social welfare function defined by (the person writing) the theory of the good.

Because of Arrow's result, some have concluded that specifying the welfare of a society requires interpersonal comparisons. However, as is often pointed out, that is not strictly correct, as the result requires all of the conditions of the theorem. Again, a great deal of work has gone into examining possibilities with restrictions on the assumptions. Domain restriction on individual orderings allows the specification of a social welfare function. The most obvious domain restriction in this regard is making all preference orderings single peaked along a single dimension, allowing simple majority rule to define the social preference (Black 1948).

If unrestricted domain is allowed, we might accept majority cycles, though the McKelvey-Schofield results (McKelvey 1976, Schofield 1978) show that in multidimensional settings, a sequence of majority results can lead from one outcome to any other in the policy space. That this does not happen in actual legislative and electoral situations may be due to the empirical fact of people forcing multidimensional issue space into a single ideological dimension or perhaps two dimensions (Schofield 2002, 2006) while, by and large, people have single-peaked preferences. Or it could be due to "structure-induced equilibrium" (Shepsle 1979) and transactional costs where the institutions we use to run our welfare states force results into a restricted set of possible outcomes. Here, history forces outcomes by the structuring of society. While both transaction costs and structure-induced equilibrium might explain stability in actual life, they do not satisfy what the principal subject of political philosophy or welfare economics is supposed to be: the structure of society (Rawls 1971, 1978). Is the equilibrium the just one? Should we allow transactions costs to stop us (trying to) move to the just society?

Apart from natural domain restriction, how else might the impossibility conclusions, drawn from Arrow and related social-choice work, be avoided? One way, which challenges the very heart of the traditional understanding of welfarism, is to examine the Pareto principle, which states that if all individuals strictly prefer x to y then the social preference should be x over y. This axiom is the only one that states that social choice should depend upon individual preferences. In that sense, the Pareto principle is what defines *welfarism* in the traditional sense of depending upon individual utilities alone. We might suggest that such utilities are justified on the grounds of the appeal to nonpaternalism, that is, each person's private views to decide the good for them, and each having an equal input into decisions that affect all.

There might be other grounds for criticizing private preferences as the grounds of social welfare, such as the formation of preferences under limited autonomy, imperfect information, uncertainty, error, and so on. Or, it is argued, that attention to preferences alone ignores other ethical issues that go beyond merely what people prefer. However, all these criticisms might be interpreted as simply suggesting that the utility function needs to be carefully constructed (Broome 1999, Fleurbaey & Hammond 2004). Once a person's utility function has been constructed to represent the person's good (which might be from laundering preferences (Goodin 1986); or constructing them from needs, functionings, primary goods, rights etc.), the Pareto principle does seem reasonable.

Sen (1970, 1982a) suggests that the Pareto principle is not so reasonable where privacy requires stronger grounds on the basis of some sort of rights. His famous impossibility theorem suggests that the Pareto principle and Sen's account of rights—his condition of minimal liberalism (ML)—are incompatible. However, Sen claims ML is a necessary condition of rights, but it conflates Hohfeldian rights and liberties (Dowding 2004) and it is not at all clear that ML is necessary for liberties such as reading or purchasing books.

The most obvious axiom to drop from Arrow's assumptions is independence of irrelevant alternatives, which ensures that a choice between a pair of alternatives depends only on preferences over that pair and not on preferences over any other bundle of goods. Once this axiom is dropped, all sorts of ranking rules can be constructed (though in voting contexts this further opens up the possibilities of manipulation and counter-manipulation). Ranking rules do not bring in cardinality as such, but counting across ranks requires some sort of justification that the difference between each element in a person's ranking can be considered to be of equivalent worth. There are, therefore, numerous possibilities for considering social welfare within an ordinal framework though it would be a mistake to consider them all as utilitarian, if utilitarianism is considered to be some form of experiential utilitarianism. Not only do such ordinal approaches and their problems encompass *utility* as understood in a choice-based framework, but also where *utility* is understood simply as a placeholder name for that which is to be counted in some social ordering framework.

5. INTERPERSONAL COMPARISONS

If we wish to go beyond the limited resources of welfare measurement without interpersonal comparability as seen in the Arrovian framework, then we need to decide what it is we are going to measure interpersonally. We can measure choice-based utility; resources; functionings; or some basket of rights and freedoms. Any public policy that is in any sense redistributive must depend upon some sort of interpersonal comparison. We might try to objectify the comparisons by making them between externally observable objective conditions of people such as needs or functionings, and then making some claims about the relationship of these objective factors and the subjective well-being comparisons that some desire. However, we have also seen that, while reference to needs and functionings might serve well for evaluating the prevalence of poverty, they are less well suited for serving as the basis of comparison going beyond the relative deprivation of the poor (Cohen 1994; Dowding 2006a). But perhaps they can be made to serve this purpose as well as the other possibilities on offer. Let us first consider interpersonal comparisons of utility.

The impossibility of strict global interpersonal comparisons of utility does not mean that we cannot make local interpersonal comparisons—indeed, we make these all the time—nor that we cannot make rough global interpersonal comparisons. I argue that we only need make the latter.

The standard currency in economics for making interpersonal comparisons is von Neumann–Morgernstern utility or some variant that I term "choice-based utility" (Ramsey 1931, Chapter. 7; von Neumann and Morgenstern 1944; Savage 1954, chapters 1–5; Luce and Raiffa 1957, Chapter 2; Jeffrey 1983; Binmore this volume). Here the utility functions are generated, in theory, by individual choices over objectively measured sets of lotteries. Different functions can represent the same behavior up to a positive affine transformation, meaning the same choice behavior can be represented by two utility functions u and v where v can be calculated from u by multiplication by a positive constant k and addition of another constant l. One objection (e.g., Roemer 1996, 16) is that the internal happiness of two people might be represented on an absolute scale underlying the two representative utility functions such that v represents more happiness given the underlying l constant, and each act taken by someone represented by v gives greater increments of utility as represented by the constant k. Hence the external behavior cannot be guaranteed to represent internal feelings and so we are not justified in making choice-based interpersonal comparisons. However, *this* argument relies upon assuming that utility is, at base, experiential and choice-based functions merely represent those experiences.

The assumption of experiential utility can be easily challenged (see Dowding 2006b for more detail on the following argument). Of course people have experiences, and they can roughly suggest how happy they are, or in how much pain they feel if asked to scale those feelings in some manner. But people cannot generally measure the relative experiential utility of some experience against another, say, drinking Sauvignon Blanc rather than Chardonnay. Of course, one may know that on the whole one prefers Sauvignon Blanc to Chardonnay, but the question is, *by how much?* One way is to examine a person's behavior. How often does the individual choose one grape variety over another? How much more is the individual prepared to pay for one than the other? And so on. In that way we can represent relative utility for that person for one grape variety compared to another. In other words there is no internal utility function represented by the choice-based one. There is *only* the utility function based on the externally witnessable behavior.[10]

Consider two individuals who behave in precisely the same way under all choice situations. What warrant would we have for thinking that they experienced different utilities? It might be suggested that they receive different amounts of pleasure even though they live externally identical lives. What evidence could we bring for this inference?[11] If the claim that we would have no warrant for assuming their utilities were identical seems counter-intuitive, this might be because we cannot imagine two humans having such genuinely identical lives. It might be impossible for us to imagine for *people* because it is the uniqueness of expression and demeanor that we recognize agents as people rather than robots. The very variety is what we use to distinguish people, and so imagining two people behaving absolutely identically is not something we can have intuitions about. However, imagine identical behavior in two ants. Given the identity in ant behavior, would anyone wish to argue that they might gain different utilities from what they do? Our intuition that higher animals (e.g., cats, dogs, as well as humans) might get more or less pleasure from life is based on their demeanor even as they live similar lives and make similar choices. And that is the real problem of intercomparability for choice-based utility functions. Life is so complex that we are not comfortable making global comparisons between two people based on their behavior. Taking their lives as wholes, or in part—comparing choices made in a supermarket—does not give us any confidence in personal intercomparability. We do make inexact *local* interpersonal comparisons all the time. We do acknowledge that one person is fussy over the wine they drink, whereas another enjoys any old plonk, and local comparisons are all one requires in ordinary social life.[12] But these local comparisons cannot be aggregated into global ones. The problem of interpersonal comparison as specified here is not that there is some hidden information that is inaccessible through external evaluation but that lives are too complex and the scope for variations among them too subtle to allow interpersonal comparison. Of course, this derivation of the problem of interpersonal comparison of utility makes it no less problematic, but it also makes interpersonal comparison of utility no more problematic than interpersonal comparison of capabilities or resources given the complex and varied lives in different contexts and institutional settings.

I argue below that we can make global type-to-type comparisons for public policy purposes over populations, given certain statistical assumptions. I further argue that this is all we require for public-policy considerations, and hence, although interpersonal comparisons are problematic, the problems are more concerned with practical measurement issues and decisions over reasonable assumptions, than anything deeply philosophical.

6. Welfare Comparisons across Types

We can make comparisons across types of individuals. Such approaches have been made in terms of actual functionings (Kuklys 2005) and in terms of equal opportunities under various headings (such as health and education) by John Roemer (1998; 2002). In Roemer's analysis the distribution of outcomes across different types of people can be compared. He selects types based on a vector of characteristics outside the control of people with each member of a type sharing similar characteristics. The idea is that each type faces similar opportunity sets and how well they do through their choice within each set is a measure of their responsibility. Each type is broken down into centiles against the measure for which they are being compared (health or educational attainment or annual income). So, for example, we could look at the salary at each centile across two types of people (say, men and women) and the differences across the two types at each centile is a measure of the opportunity for each type at that centile for obtaining a higher salary. The difference between the centiles within each type is then assumed to be a measure of responsibility within the type. Each person within a type is responsible for where they end up within that type, but none is responsible for where they are relative to those in a similar position within another type. The approach could be applied to capabilities or material rights. So, for example, health as an example of functioning is measured in some fashion and so the degree of capability of types can be measured relative to the components of a different type. Differences with functionings within each type would then be seen as a measure of the choices people make about how they want to function. That is, variation within a type can be taken to correlate with choices made about lifestyle within a type. Or the approach might be applied to rights, where the degree to which a type can be said to materially have a right is given by the difference at each centile for successfully exercising that right.

Of course, an underlying assumption of such statistical analyses is that the residuals we are trying to capture (and other error terms) are normally distributed across types. That is, any factor that affects the selection of the variable within opportunity sets which is not contained in the data, affects each type in precisely the same manner. For that reason choice of types is important. For example, if we were examining the health of women and men in parts of India, we might find that women's health in many domains is much worse than men's. However, the poor health of some women may stem from choices they make to give up food and health care to conserve resources for their husbands and male offspring (Sen 1999). If that choice is their responsibility, then the differential well-being of men and women with regard to health will not capture their equality of opportunity. Sen uses the example (against welfarism) to suggest that we need to be aware of the provenance of choices. Where women's choice to sacrifice themselves for menfolk is culturally fashioned, that needs to be taken into consideration. As functioning is choice from a capability set, it is no more objective than a choice-based utility function. Either way, measuring achievement in order to calculate opportunities requires the same sorts of assumptions about the provenance of choices made.

Of course, measuring objective characteristics does allows for a straightforward interpersonal comparison. We can judge the health, education, income, wealth, mobility and so on of different types of people. However, unless policy is, for egalitarian reasons, to concentrate upon equalizing outcomes for all in these domains (as suggested by Phillips (1999, 2004)), we must accept some degree of variation. And the liberal line, which Sen takes with regard to public policy, is that variation is best left to individual choices—in Sen's terms to allow variation in functionings with public policy to equalize over capabilities. However, comparisons across types are bound to utilize achieved functionings to measure capabilities.[13] In other words, objectification in terms of functionings only avoids interpersonal comparisons if individual choice over what functionings is ignored, or some metric is devised that allows us to compare differential outcomes across all possible functionings to see how far people equalize across the sets of choices they might make. Of course, choice-based utility is supposed to be the metric by which to make such comparisons, and to the extent that the choice-based utilitarian metric is criticized for failure to handle interpersonal comparison, that criticism will reverberate through any such metric that tries to encapsulate choice together with objective outcome.

All these approaches require us to assume that people are broadly similar, at least across types, and so make reasonably similar decisions when faced with similar choice situations. Variation in their utility functions is derived from the choice they make measured by variation within types. The assumption that people are broadly similar is also standard in traditional utilitarian analyses as it is in the modern equality of opportunity, capabilities, or freedom-of-choice approaches. Harsanyi's (1953, 1955) utilitarian welfare metric assumes everyone's utility function is essentially the same by assuming in one version (as Rawls did subsequently) an original position with a veil of ignorance where variations across people are taken into account as agents do not know what choice they will make. Elsewhere in deriving his aggregation theorem he assumes extended empathy where each takes into account the utility of others when designing institutions that will distribute utility (for criticisms and amendments see Fishburn 1984; Weymark 1991; Hammond 1981, 1983, 1987; Border 1985; Broome 1999, Chapter 6; Roemer 1996, Chapter 4; Binmore 1998, Appendix B; Binmore, this volume). Either way, differences between people are factored into each person's utility function when they choose the basic structure of society (the distributional principles).

We might avoid problems of interpersonal comparisons by simply measuring objective features of society using indicators of health, education, mortality, morbidity, and so on. Public policy, including international aid, might then be determined simply by the objective indicators. Such an approach would take no account of individual responsibility for outcomes, nor individual freedom of choice. Of course, outcomes in these and other domains will correlate to some strong degree with income and wealth, and redistribution across and within types in terms of material wealth would be one process of equalizing across these domains. What effects this would have upon responsible behavior with regard to individual health, education, and so on; and with regard to national wealth acquisition, is one of the major issues debated by egalitarians and their critics and which goes beyond the scope of this chapter.

7. Conclusions

There are limited information welfare measures, including traditionally defined welfarist functions that do not require interpersonal comparisons. However, as has been extensively argued in the literature, these provide little basis on which to build public policy over welfare concerns that embody public discourse about the role of the state in providing for human welfare. Extending the informational base allows for a much broader discussion of those concerns but inevitably raises the problem of interpersonal comparisons. In this chapter, I define social welfare as neutrally as possible as the satisfactory functioning of a society, which itself can be understood as correlating with the satisfactory functioning of members of that society. Within these neutral terms, four broad approaches were discussed. Each may be thought to have its advantages and disadvantages, but rather than concentrating upon the distinctive attributes of each, this chapter has focused on considering the problems that all approaches must address.

All approaches require interpersonal comparisons. I have argued that the problems with this stem from the epistemological problem of complexity and variety of human life. To the extent that we can externally measure the functioning of any individual—in terms of their rights, freedoms, functionings, needs, opportunities, resources, and so on—we can make interpersonal comparisons. There are no particular problems with such comparisons. Problems emerge for comparison because of the complexity and variety of the life choices that people make, even in similar choice situations; the fact that they make choices in very different settings; and the difficulty these two problems engender in creating a metric that can encompass the different possible functionings. Each approach faces the same interpersonal comparison problem, whereas experiential approaches face the additional problem, in theory, of understanding the internal metric that people putatively have. In empirical analysis, this is evaded through survey techniques.

Interpersonal global comparisons are impossible—though we make local interpersonal comparisons every day of our lives. For public policy, however, global comparisons between individuals are not necessary. We can interpersonally compare across types of people based upon the outcomes that accrue to those types, breaking the types down for comparison, not only of the mean each type achieves, but also of the distribution within each type. Comparison at each centile across types allows for distributional comparison. Such analyses require certain statistical assumptions that might not always be justified. Any measure that tries to include the choice that people make given their situations, as well as the actual outcomes they gain, will fail to adequately address that freedom of choice without a theory that specifies what rational choices are. Inevitably such analyses will be both moralized and controversial. The alternative is to accept choices made without criticism.

Public policy can thus be developed at an institutional or structural level (specifying principles of distribution) using rough global comparisons across types of people. And public policy is generally constructed to apply to types. The rough edges of such comparisons can be smoothed with individual local comparisons made by street-level bureaucrats if they are given enough discretion within the legislative framework.

At the end of analysis, with the exception of experiential measures, one might question whether there is anything much to choose between the rival methods of measuring welfare understood as satisfactory functioning. They all require similar means of measuring across types of people; they all face similar problems of interpretation and normative critique; and they may all be tweaked to ensure that the distribution each method adopts might fit with some specific normative intuitions we might have about proper distribution. Experiential measures face additional problems. First, it is unclear whether one is systematically measuring anything at all. Second, even if one is measuring something, it is not clear what this means for economic analysis or distributive justice. That is not to say that happiness surveys cannot contribute to public policy, but they do not provide direct insight into experiences.

Perhaps the only issue that does remain open is how far individual responsibility or choice is allowed to affect the distribution. However, this issue is one that cuts across each approach, rather than one that divides the approaches. Despite all the debate, the issue of individual freedom or responsibility versus needs or equality remains central within each approach as much as across them. The simplest way that public policy might ensure satisfactory human state of being is to provide a basic or citizen's income to each individual sufficient to ensure that satisfactory state of being (Van Parijs 1992, 1995; Dowding et al. 2003; Ackerman et al. 2006). Each individual would receive the same amount in resources with perhaps some recognition of great need in cases of severe disability, together with laws providing for both physical and social access to all positions in society. Differences would then be due to individual choice and the vagaries of luck or network advantage. Even here though, how high that citizen's income is set will depend upon the normative force that choice and responsibility is allowed.

Notes

1. Ken Binmore (this volume) describes this account of utility more precisely.

2. Neither of which requires interpersonal comparisons.

3. In terms of measurement, this sentence is trivial. The point I am making is to emphasize that arguments about the welfare of special cases—individuals for whom the general measure seem inapplicable—are completely beside the point.

4. This may sometimes be provided. A standard example might be that, for example, material goods are less important in a society whose culture is highly ascetic. But even here, the claim that a given social indicator might not be a good indicator across some hypothetical ascetic and materialistic societies is not the same as showing they are not good indicators across any two extant societies. Some *quantitative evidence* is required that the actual societies resemble the hypothetical ones to a high enough degree for the criticism to be sustained.

5. Because choice-based utility might be used in this way, it is sometimes thought to be 'contentless.' That is, other approaches can be colonized by it. Some see this as a distinct problem (Sen 1974, 1979; Roemer 1996), though it might also be seen as a strength.

6. Most people seem to believe that utilitarianism historically should be identified with experiential rather than choice-based utility (Binmore, this volume). I am not convinced, however, that that is what Bentham had in mind: see, for example, Ross 1999.

7. In other words I am *not* using the terms *welfare* and *utility* interchangeably.

8. This is of course a particular interpretation of Aristotle. Some, for example Riley (1988), see Aristotle as a utilitarian. I have no views on the matter and use the term *Aristotelian* simply for convenience.

9. I say approaches as I cover a wide range of ideas here from libertarian to liberal-egalitarian.

10. Note that the happiness surveys themselves do not provide utility functions, and they can only do so if their results are translated into some other currency such as monetary value. Also, we need to think about which measure we trust the most for public policy. If someone says he prefers to read upmarket broadsheet newspapers but buys, at the same price, a downmarket tabloid newspaper, which do we say provides the most welfare? The answer is not always obvious, but in many public-policy arenas the revealed rather than the stated preference evidence is liable to be followed.

11. What if they lived identically but scored their happiness differently on a happiness survey? That would provide one piece of evidence against their having identical utilities. But what could we make of it? Would we think they had different utilities experientially or that there was some cultural difference in how they scored their lives (perhaps by their perception of different reference classes)? They would have to make those inferences from something they were comparing to themselves.

12. Harsanyi's empathetic preferences is one way of formalizing these local comparisons (Binmore, this volume).

13. Quantifying achieved functionings need not be the only device. We can use some measure of constitutional rights to appraise capabilities, but achieved functionings are required to ensure that those constitutional rights are not mere paper rights.

REFERENCES

Ackerman, B., Alstott, A. and van Parijs, P. (2006). *Redesigning Distribution: Basic Income and Stakeholder Grants as Cornerstones for an Egalitarian Capitalism.* London: Verso.

Alkire, S. (2002). *Valuing Freedoms: Sen's Capability Approach and Poverty Reduction.* Oxford: Oxford University Press.

Arrow, K.J. (1951[1963]). *Social Choice and Individual Values.* 2nd ed. New Haven: Yale University Press.

Barry, B. (1973). *The Liberal Theory of Justice.* Oxford: Oxford University Press.

Binmore, K. (1998). *Game Theory and the Social Contract Volume 2: Just Playing.* Cambridge, MA.: MIT Press.

Binmore, K. (this volume). "Interpersonal Comparison of Utility." In H. Kincaid & D. Ross, Eds., *Oxford Handbook of Philosophy of Economic Science.* Oxford: Oxford University Press.

Black, D. (1948). "On the Rationale of Group Decision-making." *Journal of Political Economy* 56: 23–34.

Border, K.C. (1985). "More on Harsanyi's Cardinal Welfare Theorem." *Social Choice and Welfare* 2: 279–281.

Bossert, W., Pattanaik, P.K. & Xu, Y. (2003). "Similarity of Options and the Measurement of Diversity." *Journal of Theoretical Politics* 15 (4): 405–422.

Broome, J. (1999). *Ethics out of Economics.* Cambridge: Cambridge University Press.

Broome, J. (2004). *Weighing Lives.* Oxford: Oxford University Press.

Carritt, E.F. (1967). "Liberty and Equality." In A. Quinton, Ed., *Political Philosophy,* 127–140. Oxford: Oxford University Press.

Carter, I. (1999). *A Measure of Freedom.* Oxford: Oxford University Press.

Chambers, R. (1995). *Poverty and Livelihoods: Whose Reality Counts?* IDS Discussion Paper 347.

Clark, A. and Oswald, A.J. (1994). "Unhappiness and Unemployment." *Economic Journal* 104: 648–659.

Clark, A.E. and Oswald, A.J. (1996). "Satisfaction and Comparison Income." *Journal of Public Economics,* 61: 359–381.

Clark, A. and Oswald, A.J. (2002). "A Simple Statistical Method for Measuring How Life Events Affect Happiness." *International Journal of Epidemiology* 31: 1139–1144.

Cohen, G.A. (1994). "Amartya Sen's Unequal World." *New Left Review* 203: 117–129.

Cummins, R.A. (1996). "The Domains of Life Satisfaction: An Attempt to Order Chaos." *Social Indicators Research* 38 (3): 303–328.

d'Aspremont, C. and Gevers, L. (1977). "Equity and the Informational Basis of Collective Choice." *Review of Economic Studies* 44: 199–209.

Di Tella, R., MacCulloch, R.J. and Oswald, A.J. (2001). "Preferences over Inflation and Unemployment: Evidence from Surveys of Happiness." *American Economic Review* 91: 335–341.

Dowding, K. (2004). "Social Choice and the Grammar of Rights and Freedoms." *Political Studies* 52 (1): 144–161.

Dowding, K. (2006a). "Can Capabilities Reconcile Freedom and Equality?" *Journal of Political Philosophy* 14 (3): 323–336.

Dowding, K. (2006b). "Externalism, Expensive Tastes and Equality." In B. Montero & M.D. White, Eds., *Economics and the Mind.* London: Taylor and Francis.

Dowding, K. and van Hees, M. (2003). "The Construction of Rights." *American Political Science Review* 97 (2): 281–293.

Dowding, K. and van Hees, M. (2007). "Freedom of Choice." In P. Anand, C. Puppe & P. Pattaniak, Eds., *Oxford Handbook of Rational and Social Choice*. Oxford: Oxford University Press.

Dowding, K., De Wispelaere, J. and White, S., Eds. (2003). *The Ethics of Stakeholding* Houndmills, England: Palgrave Macmillan.

Doyal, L. & Gough, I. (1991). *A Theory of Human Need*. Basingstoke, England: Macmillan.

Dworkin, R. (2000). *Sovereign Virtue: The Theory and Practice of Equality*. Cambridge, MA: Harvard University Press.

Easterlin, R.A. (1974). "Does Economic Growth Improve the Human Lot? Some Empirical Evidence." In P.A. David & M.W. Reder, Eds., *Nations and Households in Economic Growth: Essays in Honour of Moses Abramowitz*. New York: Academic Press.

Easterlin, R.A. (1995). "Will Raising the Income of All Increase the Happiness of All?" *Journal of Economic Behavior and Organizations* 27: 35–48.

Easterlin, R.A. (2000). "The Worldwide Standard of Living since 1800." *Journal of Economic Perspectives* 14 (1) :7–26.

Elster, J. and Roemer, J.E., eds. (1991). *Interpersonal Comparisons of Well-Being*. Cambridge, England: Cambridge University Press.

Fishburn, P.C. (1984). "On Harsanyi's Utilitarian Cardinal Welfare Theorem." *Theory and Decision* 17: 21–28.

Fleurbaey, M. (2003). "On the Informational Basis of Social Choice." *Social Choice and Welfare* 21: 347–384.

Fleurbaey, M. and Hammond, P.J. (2004). "Interpersonally Comparable Utility." In S. Barbera, P. J. Hammond & C. Siedl, Eds., *Handbook of Utility Theory, Vol. 2: Extensions*. Dordrecht, The Netherlands: Kluwer.

Frank, R.H. (1997). "The Frame of Reference as a Public Good." *Economic Journal* 107: 1832–1847.

Galtung, J. (1994). *Human Rights in Another Key*. Cambridge, England: Polity Press.

Goodin, R.E. (1986). "Laundering Preferences." In J. Elster & A. Hylland, Eds., *Foundations of Social Choice Theory*. Cambridge, England: Cambridge University Press.

Hammond, P.J. (1981). "Ex-Ante and Ex-Post Welfare Optimality Under Uncertainty." *Economica* 48: 235–250.

Hammond, P.J. (1983). "Ex-Post Optimality as a Dynamically Consistent Objective for Collective Choice Under Uncertainty." In P.K. Pattanaik & M. Salles, Eds., *Social Choice and Welfare*, 175–206. Amsterdam, The Netherlands: North-Holland.

Hammond, P.J. (1987). "On Reconciling Arrow's Theory of Social Choice with Harsanyi's Fundamental Utilitarianism." In G.R. Feiwel, Ed., *Arrow and the Foundations of the Theory of Economic Policy*, 179–192. London: Macmillan.

Hammond, P.J. (1991). "Interpersonal Comparisons of Utility: Why and How they Are and Should be Made." In J. Elster & J. Roemer, Eds., *Interpersonal Comparisons of Well-Being*. Cambridge, England: Cambridge University Press.

Harsanyi, J.C. (1987). "Interpersonal Utility Comparison." In J. Eatwell, M. Milgate & P. Newman, Eds., *The New Palgrave Dictionary of Economics*. London: Macmillan.

Harsanyi, J.C. (1953). "Cardinal Utility in Welfare Economics and the Theory of Risk-Taking." *Journal of Political Economy* 61: 434–435.

Harsanyi, J.C. (1955). "Cardinal Welfare, Individualistic Ethics, and Interpersonal Comparisons of Utility." *Journal of Political Economy* 63: 309–321.

Hausman, D.M. (1995). "The Impossibility of Interpersonal Utility Comparisons." *Mind* 104: 473–490.

Heritier, A. (1996). "The Accommodation of Diversity in European Policy-Making and its Outcome: Regulatory Policy as Patchwork." *Journal of European Public Policy* 3: 149–167.

Jeffrey, R.C. (1983). *The Logic of Decision,* 2nd ed.. Chicago: Chicago University Press.

Kahneman, D., Wakker, P.P. and Sarin, R. (1997). "Back to Bentham? Explorations of Experiential Utility." *Quarterly Journal of Economics* 112: 375–406.

Kramer, M.H. (2003). *The Quality of Freedom.* Oxford: Oxford University Press.

Kuklys, W. (2005). *Amartya Sen's Capability Approach: Theoretical Insights and Empirical Applications.* Berlin, Germany: Springer.

Layard, R. (2005). *Happiness: Lessons from a New Science.* Harmondsworth, England: Penguin.

List, C. (2003). "Are Interpersonal Comparisons of Utility Indeterminate?" *Erkenntnis* 58: 229–260.

Luce, R.D. and Raiffa, H. (1957). *Games and Decisions: Introduction and Critical Survey.* Toronto, Ontario: Dover.

Mackay, A. (1986). "Extended Sympathy and Comparisons of Utility." *Journal of Philosophy* 83: 305–322.

McKelvey, R.D. (1976). "Intransitivities in Multi-dimensional Voting Models and Some Implications for Agenda Control." *Journal of Economic Theory* 12: 472–482.

Max-Neef, M. (1993). *Human Scale Development: Conception, Application and Further Reflections.* London: Apex.

Myers, D.G. (1993). *The Pursuit of Happiness: Who is Happy and Why?* New York: Avon.

Narayan, D., Chambers, R., Shah, M.K. and Petesch, P. (2000a). *Voices of the Poor: Crying Out for Change.* New York: Oxford University Press/World Bank.

Narayan, D., with Patel, R. Schafft, K., Rademacher, A. and Koch-Schutte, S. (2000b). *Voices of the Poor: Can Anyone Hear Us?* New York: Oxford University Press/World Bank.

Ng, Y.-K. (1996). "Happiness Surveys: Some Comparability Issues and an Exploratory Survey Based on Just Perceivable Increments." *Social Indicators Research* 38: 1–27.

Ng, Y.-K. (1997). "A Case for Happiness, Cardinal Utility, and Interpersonal Comparability." *Economic Journal* 197: 1848–1858.

Ng, Y.-K. (1999). "Utility, Informed Preference or Happiness?" *Social Choice and Welfare* 16: 197–216.

Ng, Y. -K. (2000). *Efficiency, Equality and Public Policy: With a Case for Higher Public Spending.* Houndmills, England: Macmillan.

Nussbaum, M. (1992). "Human Functioning and Social Justice: In Defence of Aristotelian Essentialism." *Political Theory* 20: 202–246.

Nussbaum, M. (1995). "Human Capabilities, Female Human Beings." In M. Nussbaum and J. Glover, Eds., *Women Culture and Development: A Study of Human Capabilities.* Oxford: Clarendon Press.

Nussbaum, M. (2000). *Women and Human Development: The Capability Approach.* Cambridge, England: Cambridge University Press.

Oswald, A.J. (1997). "Happiness and Economic Performance." *Economic Journal* 107: 1815–1831.

Parfit, D. (1984). *Reasons and Persons*. Oxford: Oxford University Press.

Pattanaik, P.K., and Xu, Y. (1990). "On Ranking Opportunity Sets in Terms of Freedom of Choice." *Recherches Economiques de Louvain* 56: 383–390.

Pogge, T. (2002). *World Poverty and Human Rights*. Cambridge, England: Polity Press.

Phillips, A. (1999). *Which Equalities Matter?* Cambridge, England: Polity Press.

Phillips, A. (2004). "Defending Equality of Outcome." *Journal of Political Philosophy* 12: 1–19.

Qizilbash, M. (1996). "Capabilities, Well-being and Human Development: A Survey." *Journal of Development Studies* 33 (2): 143–162.

Ramsey, F.P. (1931). *The Foundations of Mathematics and Other Logical Essays*. New York: Harcourt, Brace and Co.

Ramsey, M. (1992). *Human Needs and the Market*. Aldershot, England: Avebury.

Rawls, J. (1971). *A Theory of Justice*. Oxford: Oxford University Press.

Rawls, J. (1978). "The Basic Structure as Subject." In A. Goldman & J. Kim, Eds., *Values and Morals: Essays in Honor of William Frankena, Charles Stevenson and Richard B. Brandt*. Dordrecht, The Netherlands: Reidel.

Riley, J. (1988). *Liberal Utilitarianism: Social Choice Theory and J. S. Mill's Philosophy*. Cambridge, England: Cambridge University Press.

Roemer, J.E. (1996). *Theories of Distributive Justice*. Cambridge, MA.: Harvard University Press.

Roemer, J.E. (1998). *Equality of Opportunity*. Cambridge, MA.: Harvard University Press.

Roemer, J.E. (2002). "Equality of Opportunity: A Progress Report." *Social Choice and Welfare* 19: 455–471.

Ross, D. (1999). *The Concept of Utility from Bentham to Game Theory*. Cape Town: University of Cape Town Press.

Savage, L.J. (1954). *The Foundations of Statistics* London: Chapman and Hall.

Schofield, N. (1978). "Instability of Simple Dynamic Games." *Review of Economic Studies* 45: 575–594.

Schofield, N. (2002). "Representative Democracy as Social Choice." In K. Arrow, A. Sen and K. Suzamura, Eds., *The Handbook of Social Choice and Welfare*. New York: North-Holland.

Schofield, N. (2006). "Social Choice and Elections." In J. Alt, J. Aldrich and A. Lupia, Eds., *A Positive Change in Political Science: The Legacy of Richard McKelvey's Writings*. Ann Arbor: University of Michigan Press.

Schwartz, S.H. (1994). "Are There Universal Aspects in the Structure and Content of Human Values?" *Journal of Social Issues* 50 (4): 19–45.

Sen, A. (1970). *Collective Choice and Social Welfare*. Edinburgh: Oliver and Boyd.

Sen, A. (1974). "Informational Bases of Alternative Welfare Approaches: Aggregation and Income Distribution." *Journal of Public Economics* 3: 387–403.

Sen, A. (1977). "Non-Linear Social Welfare Functions." In R. Butt and J. Hintikka, Eds., *Foundational Problems in the Special Sciences*, 297–302. Boston: Reidel.

Sen, A. (1979). "Utilitarianism and Welfarism." *Journal of Philosophy* 76: 463–489.

Sen, A. (1982a). "The Impossibility of a Paretian Liberal." In A. Sen, *Choice, Welfare and Measurement*. Oxford: Blackwell.

Sen, A. (1982b). "Interpersonal Comparisons of Welfare." In A. Sen, *Choice, Welfare and Measurement*. Oxford: Blackwell.

Sen, A. (1992). *Inequality Reexamined*. Oxford: Oxford University Press.

Sen, A. (1999). *Development as Freedom*. Oxford: Oxford University Press.

Sen, A. (2002). *Rationality and Freedom*. Cambridge, MA: Harvard University Press.

Shepsle, K. (1979). "Institutional Arrangements and Equilibrium in Multidimensional Voting Models." *American Journal of Political Science* 23: 27–59.

Simon, J.A. (1974). "Interpersonal Welfare Comparisons Can bBe Made and Used for Redistribution Decisions." *Kyklos* 27: 63–98.

Steiner, H. (1994). *An Essay on Rights*. Oxford: Blackwell.

Van Hees, M. (2000). *Legal Reductionism and Freedom*. Dordrecht, The Netherlands: Kluwer.

Van Hees, M. (2004). "Freedom of Choice and Diversity of Options: Some Difficulties." *Social Choice and Welfare* 22: 253–266.

Van Parijs, P., Ed. (1992). *Arguing for Basic Income*. London: Verso.

Van Parijs, P. (1995). *Real Freedom for All*. Oxford: Oxford University Press.

Van Praag, B. and Ferrer-i-Carbonell, A. (2004). *Happiness Quantified: A Satisfaction Calculus Approach*. Oxford: Oxford University Press.

Veenhoven, R. (1999). "Freedom and Happiness: A Comparative Study in 44 Nations in the Early 1990s." In E. Dienre and E. Suh, Eds., *Subjective Well-being across Cultures*. Cambridge, MA: MIT Press.

Von Neumann, J. & Morgernstern, O. (1944). *Theory of Games and Economic Behavior*. Princeton: Princeton University Press.

Weymark, J.A. (1991). "A Reconsideration of the Harsanyi–Sen Debate on Utilitarianism." In J. Elster and J. Romer, Eds., *Interpersonal Comparisons of Utility*. Cambridge: Cambridge University Press.

White, A. (1975). *Modal Thinking*. Oxford: Basil Blackwell.

Winkelmann, L. and Winkelmann, R. (1998). "Why Are the Unemployed so Unhappy?" *Economica* 65: 1–15.

CHAPTER 20

INTERPERSONAL COMPARISON OF UTILITY

KEN BINMORE

'Tis vain to talk of adding quantities which after the addition will continue to be as distinct as they were before; one man's happiness will never be another man's happiness: a gain to one man is no gain to another: you might as well pretend to add 20 apples to 20 pears.

Jeremy Bentham

1. INTRODUCTION

There are at least as many views on how the welfare of individuals should be compared as there are authors who write on the subject. An indication of the bewildering range of issues considered relevant in the literature is provided by the book *Interpersonal Comparisons of Well-Being* (Elster & Roemer 1991). However, I plan to interpret the topic narrowly. Although I shall review some traditional approaches along the way, my focus will be on the questions:

What do modern economists mean when they talk about units of utility? How can such utils be compared?

It is widely thought that that the answer to the second question is that utils assigned to different individuals cannot sensibly be compared at all. If this were true, I share the view expressed by Hammond (1976), Harsanyi (1955) and many others that rational ethics would then become a subject with little or no substantive content.

My own answers to the questions offered in this article are mostly a reworking of sections of my book *Natural Justice* (Binmore 2005) and its earlier, two-volume incarnation *Game Theory and the Social Contract* (Binmore 1994, 1996). Many details omitted here are to be found in my *Playing for Real*, forthcoming from Oxford University Press.

2. What Is Utility?

This section offers a brief sketch of the history of utility theory with a view to explaining the origins and tenets of the modern theory.

The word *utility* has always been difficult. Even the arch-utilitarian Jeremy Bentham (1987 [1789]) opens his *Principles of Morals and Legislation* by remarking that his earlier work would have been better understood if he had used *happiness* or *felicity* instead. The emergence of modern utility theory has only served to multiply the philosophical confusion. For example, Amartya Sen (1976) denies that John Harsanyi (1977) can properly be called a utilitarian, because he interprets utility in the modern sense of Von Neumann and Morgenstern rather than in Bentham's original sense.[1]

Bentham's position, later taken up by John Stuart Mill, is that utility should be interpreted as the balance of pleasure and pain experienced by an individual human being. In the fashion of the times, he gave long lists of the phenomena that he felt relevant when estimating a person's utility from the outside.

Victorian economists took up Bentham's idea and incorporated it into their models without paying much attention to its doubtful philosophical and psychological foundations. However, once economists discovered (in the "marginalist revolution" of the early part of the twentieth century) that they did not need to attribute utility functions to economic agents in order to prove most of the propositions that seemed important at the time, all the baggage on utility theory inherited from the Victorian era was swept away. By the late 1930s, it had become fashionable for economists to denounce cardinal utility theory as meaningless nonsense.[2] Even at this late date, Lionel Robbins (1938) is still sometimes quoted to this effect. However, even at the time Robbins was making his name by denouncing classical utility theory, Von Neumann and Morgenstern (1944) were creating the beginnings of the entirely sensible modern theory to which the main part of this paper is devoted.

But Von Neumann and Morgenstern's theory has not satisfied everybody, and now that those who lampooned Bentham's empirical approach are no longer with us, his ideas have been revived as the new field of "happiness studies" (Layard 2005). Amartya Sen offers lists of "capabilities" that might reasonably be expected to promote an agent's well-being. (See Cohen 1989.) There are even neuroscientists who are willing to contemplate the possibility that some kind of metering device might eventually be wired into a brain to measure how much pleasure or pain a person is experiencing. Now that everybody knows of the experiments in which rats press a lever that excites an electrode implanted in a "pleasure center" in their brains to the exclusion of all other options (including food and sex), this idea is perhaps not as wild as it once would have seemed. These and other revivals of Bentham's psychological theory are not necessarily inconsistent with the orthodox approach that I refer to as modern utility theory, but it is important for philosophers to recognize that the modern theory does not depend on any of the psychological or physiological assumptions built into these modern counterparts of the theory of Bentham and Mill.

3. MODERN UTILITY THEORY

Critics of modern utility theory usually imagine that economists still hold fast to the naive beliefs about the way our minds work that are implicit in the work of Bentham and his modern emulators, but orthodox economists gave up trying to be psychologists a long time ago. Far from maintaining that our brains are little machines for generating utility, the modern theory of utility makes a virtue of assuming *nothing whatever* about what causes our behavior.

This doesn't mean that orthodox economists believe that our thought processes have nothing to do with our behavior. We know perfectly well that human beings are motivated by all kinds of considerations. They care about pleasure, and they care about pain. Some are greedy for money.[3] Others just want to stay out of jail. There are even saintly people who would give away the shirt off their back rather than see a baby cry. We accept that people are infinitely various, but we succeed in accommodating their infinite variety within a single theory by denying ourselves the luxury of speculating about what is going on inside their heads. Instead, we pay attention only to what we see them doing.

The modern theory of utility, therefore, abandons any attempt to explain *why* people behave as they do. Instead of an explanatory theory, we have to be content with a descriptive theory, which can do no more than say that a person will be acting inconsistently if that individual did such-and-such in the past, but now plan to do so-and-so in the future.

Such a theory is rooted in observed behavior. It is, therefore, called a theory of "revealed preference," because the data we use in determining what people want is not what they say they want—or what paternalists say they ought to want—but our observations of what they actually choose when given the opportunity.

When using a revealed-preference theory, one must beware of the causal utility fallacy, which says that decision makers choose a over b because the utility of a exceeds that of b. Modern utility theory does not allow such a conclusion. In the psychological theory of Bentham and Mill, one may certainly argue that a person's choice of a over b is *caused* by the utility of a exceeding that of b. But in modern utility theory, the implication goes the other way. It is because the preference $a > b$ has been revealed that we choose a utility function satisfying $u(a) > u(b)$.

For people to behave *as though* their aim were to maximize a utility function, it is only necessary that their choice behavior be consistent. To challenge the theory, one, therefore, needs to argue that people behave inconsistently, rather than that they don't really have utility generators inside their heads.

Rationality as Consistency

Modern utility theory famously began when Oskar Morgenstern turned up at Von Neumann's house in Princeton one day in the early forties complaining that they didn't have a proper basis for the payoffs in the book on game theory they were writing together. So Von Neumann invented a theory on the spot that measures how much a rational person wants something by the size of the risk he is willing to take to get it.

Critics sometimes complain that a person's attitude to taking risks is only relevant when gambling, and so Von Neumann's theory is irrelevant to the kind of moral situations to which utilitarians apply their ideas. However, it is hard to think of a more fundamental moral question than: Who should bear what risk? Utilitarians who want to use the kind of insurance argument employed by Edgeworth (1881) or Harsanyi (1977) in defense of their position certainly have no choice but to accept that attitudes to risk are basic to their approach. Nor is there any lack of support from traditional sources. As it says in the Book of Proverbs: It is the lot that causeth contentions to cease.

The rationality assumptions built into Von Neumann's theory simply require that people make decisions in a consistent way, but his conclusions are surprisingly strong. Anyone who chooses consistently in risky situations will look to an observer as though he or she were trying to maximize the expected value of something. This abstract "something" is what is called utility in the modern theory. To maximize its expected value is simply to take whatever action will make it largest on average.

There are philosophers who follow Kant in claiming that rationality should mean more than mere consistency, so that some utility functions can be dismissed as being less rational than others. However, modern economists follow Hume in treating reason as the "slave of the passions." There can then be nothing irrational about consistently pursuing any end whatever. As Hume extravagantly observed, he might be criticized on many grounds if he were to prefer the destruction of the entire universe to scratching his finger, but his preference could not properly be called *irrational*, because (contra Kant) rationality is about means rather than ends.

Determining a Person's Utility

Von Neumann's theory makes it easy to find a utility function that describes a rational person's behavior if enough data is available on the choices that the individual has made in the past between risky prospects.

Pick two outcomes, W and L, that are, respectively, better and worse than any outcome that we need to discuss. (One can think of W and L as winning or losing everything that there is to be won or lost.) These outcomes will correspond to the boiling and freezing points used to calibrate a thermometer, in that the utility scale to be constructed will assign 0 utils to L, and 100 utils to W.

Suppose we now want to find David Hume's Von Neumann and Morgenstern utility for scratching his finger. For this purpose, consider a bunch of (free) lottery tickets in which the prizes are either W or L. As we offer Hume lottery tickets with higher and higher probabilities of getting W as an alternative to scratching his finger, he will eventually switch from saying no to saying yes. If the probability of W on the lottery ticket that makes him switch is 73 percent, then Von Neumann and Morgenstern's theory says that scratching his thumb should count as being worth 73 utils to Hume. Each extra percentage point added to the indifference probability, therefore, corresponds to one extra util.

As with measuring temperature, it will be obvious that we are free to choose the zero and the unit on the utility scale we construct however we like. We could, for example, have assigned 32 utils to L, and 212 utils to W. One then finds how many utils a scratched finger is worth on this new scale in the same way that one converts degrees Celsius into degrees Fahrenheit. So a scratched thumb worth 73 utils on the old scale is worth 163.4 utils on the new scale.

My guess is that Bentham would have been delighted with the mechanical nature of Von Neumann and Morgenstern's theory, which reduces evaluations of individual welfare to ticking off boxes on a simple Gradgrindian questionnaire, but he would also probably have made the same mistake as many economists in overestimating the extent to which real people make their choices in a consistent manner. Although the utility theory of Von Neumann and Morgenstern performs at least as well as any comparable alternative proposed by the new school of behavioral economists, it is only the rather poor best of a bad lot when it comes to predicting the behavior of laboratory subjects.

Intrapersonal Comparison

Why does a rich man hail a taxicab when it rains while a poor man gets wet? Economists answer this traditional question by making an intrapersonal comparison.

They argue that an extra dollar in Adam's pocket would be worth more to him if he were poor than it would be if he were rich. But how are we to measure such increments in well-being? The unit of measurement certainly cannot be the dollar because, for most of us, an extra dollar becomes less valuable the more of them we have—a phenomenon that economists refer to as the decreasing marginal utility of money.

The answer offered by the Von Neumann and Morgenstern theory is that one can measure the well-being of a person with decreasing (or increasing) marginal utility of money by counting the number of utils by which his total utility is increased when he gains an extra dollar. Because a rational decision maker in the Von Neumann and Morgenstern theory acts as though maximizing expected or average utility, he behaves as though each util is "worth" the same as any other.

Risk Aversion

The Von Neumann and Morgenstern utility function of a person with decreasing marginal utility for money has a concave shape (chords drawn to the curve lie underneath the curve). It follows that such a person is risk averse—that is to say, he prefers to get a sum of money for certain than to participate in a risky enterprise that yields the same amount on average. A risk-loving person (with a convex Von Neumann and Morgenstern utility function) will prefer the risky enterprise. A risk-neutral person will always be indifferent when offered such a choice. In spite of what is commonly said about the beliefs of economists, it is only in the risk-neutral case that they believe in identifying a util with a dollar.

There is sometimes discussion in the philosophical literature about the rationality of "prudent behavior," but the modern theory of utility denies that the extent to which a person is risk averse is a rationality question. As with David Hume's finger, a person's attitudes to taking risks are deemed to be part of his preferences. Epictetus said that one should not say of a man who drinks much wine that he drinks too much, but only that he drinks much wine. We similarly say of a man who risks a lot in gambling dens, not that it is irrational for him to risk so much, but that he behaves as though he has risk-loving preferences.

Gambling and Gut Feelings

In discussing Rawls' (1972) arguments for the use of the maximin criterion in the original position, Kukathas and Pettit (1990, 40) dismiss the maximization of expected Von Neumann and Morgenstern utility as "the gambling strategy." However, numerous economics textbooks to the contrary, a Von Neumann and Morgenstern utility function does not measure how much a person likes or dislikes gambling as an activity. Indeed, as Harsanyi (1992) points out, Von Neumann and Morgenstern's assumptions *do not apply* if a person actually derives pleasure or distress from the process of gambling itself.[4]

Nor is it true that the maximin criterion employed by Rawls (1972), in evaluating the decision problem faced by an individual in the original position, corresponds to the case of infinite risk aversion. The most concave utility function for money would assign zero utils to no dollars and one util to any positive number of dollars—corresponding to the case in which someone cares only about not ending up with nothing at all. But Rawls certainly did not intend that such utility functions should be assigned to the citizens of his ideal society.

Such misunderstandings of the concept of risk aversion derive in part from the entrenched use of the language of the casino and the racetrack in discussing the Von Neumann and Morgenstern theory. However, the rational folk to whom the theory genuinely applies will see no point in taking vacations in Las Vegas. A better exemplar of the theory is a Presbyterian minister considering how to value his house or car. He will not regard the possibility that his house might burn down or his car be stolen as a possible source of excitement. He will make a sober assessment of the probabilities and of the value he places on his property, and then take out insurance to cover himself against the objectively determined risks he faces.

As an example of the power of the theory, imagine that some bullets are loaded into a revolver with six chambers. The cylinder is then spun and the gun pointed at your head. Would you now be prepared to pay more to get one bullet removed when only one bullet was loaded or when four bullets were loaded? Usually, people say they would pay more in the first case because they would then be buying their lives for certain. But the Von Neumann and Morgenstern theory says that you should pay more in the second case, provided only that you prefer life to death and more money to less.[5]

What conclusion should be drawn from such a conflict between one's gut feelings and the recommendations of Von Neumann and Morgenstern's theory? Few people want to admit that their gut feelings are irrational and should, therefore, be amended—which was the reaction of the statistician Savage when trapped by the economist Allais into expressing preferences that were inconsistent with his extension of the Von Neumann and Morgenstern theory. They prefer to deny that the Von Neumann and Morgenstern assumptions characterize rational behavior.

On this subject, it is instructive to consider another informal experiment with which I have teased various experts in economics and finance. Would you prefer (96×69) or (87×78)? Most prefer the former. But $96 \times 69 = 6,624$ and $87 \times 78 = 6,786$. How should we react to this anomaly? Surely not by altering the laws of arithmetic to make $96 \times 69 > 87 \times 78$! So why should we contemplate altering the Von Neumann and Morgenstern assumptions after observing experiments that show they don't match the gut feelings of the man in the street? Our untutored intuitions about statistical matters are no more trustworthy than those that lead a toddler to prefer a candy jar with a big cross-section to a rival with a larger volume. Adults learn to think twice about such matters. If the matter is sufficiently important, we may calculate a little—or perhaps read the label on the packet.

It is such second thoughts about our wants and aspirations that seem to me relevant when ethical issues are at stake. A theory based on gut feelings may perhaps be appropriate in consumer theory when studying impulse buying in supermarkets. But people are likely to be in a much more reflective mood when considering social contract issues. As the old form of English marriage service used to say, this is an occasion for making decisions "advisedly and soberly"—just as a Presbyterian minister contemplates his insurance problem.

Intensity of Preference

In spite of its ancient provenance, the book *Games and Decisions* by Luce and Raiffa (1957) continues to be an excellent reference for one-person decision theory. The fallacies it lists in Chapter 2 remain as relevant now as when the book was written. The third fallacy is of particular importance in discussions of the meaning of utilitarian welfare functions. It says that if the difference in utilities between outcomes a and b exceeds the difference in utilities between outcomes c and d, one is not entitled to deduce that the decision maker would prefer a change from b to a to a change from d to c.

If one wants to make such a claim, it is necessary to add extra assumptions to the standard Von Neumann and Morgenstern theory. In particular, one needs to offer a definition of what it means to say that one preference is held more intensely than another. Von Neumann and Morgenstern themselves (1944, 18) suggest that Adam should be deemed to hold the first preference more intensely than the second if and only if he would always be willing to swap a lottery **L**, in which the prizes a and d each occur with probability 1:2, for a lottery **M**, in which the prizes b and c each occur with probability 1/2. To see why they propose this definition, imagine that Adam is in possession of a lottery ticket **N** that yields the prizes b and d with equal probabilities. Would he now rather exchange b for a in the lottery or d for c? Presumably, Adam will prefer the latter swap if and only if he thinks that b is a greater improvement on a than c is on d. But to say that he prefers the first of the two proposed exchanges to the second is to say that Adam prefers **M** to **L**.

With Von Neumann and Morgenstern's definition, Luce and Raiffa's third fallacy evaporates, but it retains its sting with other definitions of intensity of preference.

4. Interpersonal Comparison of Utility

We have seen that there is a sense in which each util that a rational Adam receives is worth the same to him as all the previous utils he has received. But what of the utils acquired by a rational Eve? In the absence of a Tiresias with experience of both roles, to whom do we appeal when asked to compare the welfare of two such different people as Adam and Eve?

Do We Really Need to Compare Utilities at All?

For example, one might compare Adam's welfare with Eve's by counting their daily consumption of apples. Such a procedure has the advantage of being relatively easy to operationalize, but it is vulnerable to numerous criticisms. Perhaps Eve is rich and Adam is poor, so that she can eat as many apples as she chooses, but his straitened circumstances restrict him to only one apple a day. It would then be surprising if Eve did not derive a great deal less joy from one extra apple per day than Adam.[6]

Even if everybody had equal access to apples, we would still have problems. Suppose that Adam and Eve are both poor, but Adam cares only for fig leaves. Rawls (1982) is only one of many who see no difficulty here, on the grounds that fig leaves can be exchanged for apples in the marketplace. One can, therefore, assess their relative values by quoting their price in dollars. But to grant some a priori legitimacy to the market mechanism begs exactly the sort of question that Rawls is seeking to answer. Even when a market for apples and fig leaves can be taken for granted, the rate at which apples are exchanged for fig leaves in this market tells us little about the relative felicity that Adam and Eve derive from consuming apples and fig leaves. Markets are driven by the relative scarcity of the goods that are traded. If Eve is a pop star, she may be able to trade a nanosecond of her labor for a kidney dialysis machine. But that does not mean that the sacrifice of a nanosecond of her time is worth the same to her as a kidney machine would be to Adam if he were suffering from kidney failure.

One can, of course, invent an index of goods in which the weights attached to fig leaves and apples somehow reflect their use-value rather than their exchange-value. However, objections are not hard to find. For example, it may be that Adam likes martinis mixed only in the proportions of 10 parts of gin to each part of vermouth, whereas the hard-drinking Eve likes them only in the proportions of 1,000 parts of gin to each part of vermouth. It then makes little sense to say that Adam and Eve are equally well off if each are assigned 10 bottles of gin and 1 bottle of vermouth. Adam will now be able to enjoy 11 bottles of martini, whereas Eve will be able to enjoy only 10.01 bottles of martini.[7]

Such examples suggest an idea that it is familiar in the economic theory of the household. Instead of measuring Adam and Eve's welfare in terms of the raw commodities they consume, why not measure their welfare in terms of the characteristic benefits that they get from their consumption? One might ask, for example, how much health, wealth, and wisdom an agent derives from any given bundle of consumption goods. Rawls (1982) proposes just such a list of "primary goods." The primary goods he proposes for aggregation in an index are "the powers and prerogatives of office," "the social basis of self-respect" and "income and wealth."

Economists are not fond of theories that depend on such intangibles. However, even if Rawls' primary goods could be defined in precise terms, one would still be faced with an indexing problem. How do we weigh such primary goods against each other? Rawls seems to think this is a matter on which a broad consensus can be expected.[8] However, I believe that we cannot rely on different individuals valuing some set of primary goods in a similar fashion. Even my own dean is uncharacteristically obtuse when it comes to weighing my self-respect against the prerogatives of her office! Moral philosophy would be a great deal easier if there really were primary goods about which everybody felt pretty much the same, but to make this kind of assumption is to beg a whole set of major questions. Such attempts to evade the problem of interpersonal comparison of utility are admittedly tempting, but they lead only to confusion in the long run.

Interpersonal Comparisons Are Impossible?

As Hammond (1991) documents, establishing a standard for making interpersonal comparisons of utility is widely regarded as impossible or hopelessly intractable. At the time when logical positivism was fashionable, the sound and fury raised against theories of interpersonal comparison reached an almost hysterical pitch. Echoes of the debate still haunt the economics profession today, with the result that expedients like those already reviewed continue to be invented with the aim of somehow allowing interpersonal judgments to be made without utils actually being compared. Meanwhile, a parallel movement within philosophy works hard at making a technical subject out of the notion that ethical values are supposedly incommensurable by their very nature.

I think John Harsanyi's (1977) theory of interpersonal comparisons of utility defuses all these concerns by providing a clear and relatively uncontroversial approach to the subject, but I want first to look at two other approaches—not because I think them satisfactory, but to make it clear that the question isn't really whether interpersonal comparison is possible, but which of all the ways it might be done works best in a given context.[9]

Counting Perception Thresholds

I believe that it was Edgeworth (1881) who first proposed observing how far a parameter controling the environment of a subject needs to be changed before the subject perceives that a change has taken place. If the subject expresses a preference for low-parameter values over high-parameter values, the number of perceptual jumps he experiences as the parameter moves from one end of its range to the other can then be used as a measure of the intensity of his preference between the two extremes. The psychologist Luce (1956) has been a modern exponent of this idea. Rubinstein (1988) has also explored its implications.

If workable, such a procedure would provide an objective method of comparing utils across individuals independently of the social mores of their society of origin. But would such a comparison be meaningful? Even if it were, would it be possible to persuade people to regard it as a relevant input when making fairness judgments?

Like many men, I am not only nearsighted, I am also mildly color-blind. At the Poker table, I have to be quite careful when both blue and green chips are in use. Does it, therefore, follow that I get less pleasure from the use of my eyesight than someone with perfect vision? My hearing is even less reliable than my eyesight. Should those with perfect pitch, therefore, be assumed to take a keener pleasure in music? I have only the haziest idea of how much I am worth, while others keep accounts that are accurate down to the penny. Is this relevant to how much tax we each should pay?

Zero-One Rule

Similar doubts afflict another proposal that gets a better press. Hausman (1994) even argues that, if there is a "correct" way to compare bounded cardinal utilities, then the zero-one rule is it.

The zero-one rule applies when it is uncontroversial that a person's individual preferences are to be measured with a cardinal utility function, usually a Von Neumann and Morgenstern utility function. If Adam and Eve agree that the worst thing that can happen for both of them separately is L and the best is W, then the zero-one rule calls for their utility scales to be recalibrated so that their new Von Neumann and Morgenstern utility functions v_A and v_E satisfy $v_A(L) = v_E(L) = 0$ and $v_A(W) = v_E(W) = 1$. The utility functions obtained after such a recalibration can then be compared without difficulty.

Essentially the same objections to this procedure have been made by Griffin (1986), Hammond (1991), Rawls (1972), and Sen (1970). If Eve is a jaded sophisticate who sees W as only marginally less dull than L, whereas Adam is a bright-eyed youth for whom the difference seems unimaginably great, what sense does it make to adopt a method of utility comparison that treats the two equally? In brief, the objections to the zero-one rule are the same as those that apply to the method of counting perceptual jumps. It certainly provides a way of comparing utils across individuals, but who is to say that the comparisons generated are relevant to anything of interest?

5. Harsanyi and Interpersonal Comparison

Harsanyi (1977) builds on the orthodox Von Neumann and Morgenstern theory of utility. The assumptions of this theory have no bearing on interpersonal comparison, and so he necessarily adds extra assumptions to those of Von Neumann and Morgenstern. It is important to recognize the necessity of making such assumptions, since Von Neumann and Morgenstern's use of "transferable utility" in discussing coalition formation in the second half of their book has left many commentators with the mistaken belief that pure Von Neumann and Morgenstern utility theory allows different individuals, not only to compare their utils, but to pass them from hand to hand if they feel so inclined. My own view is that transferable utility can only make proper sense in the case when the players are all risk neutral, so that their utils can be identified with dollars, but the immediate point is simply that Von Neumann and Morgenstern did not attempt the impossible task of deducing their ideas on transferable utility from the assumptions they wrote into Von Neumann and Morgenstern utility theory.

Harsanyi's (1977) additional assumptions are built on the notion of what I call empathetic preferences. Such preferences were introduced by the philosopher Patrick Suppes (1966), and studied by Sen (1970) and Arrow (1978) under the name of "extended sympathy preferences."

Sympathetic Preferences

In surveying the history of utilitarianism, Russell Hardin (1988) dismisses Hume's emphasis on the importance of sympathetic identification between human beings as idiosyncratic. Although Adam Smith (1975 [1759]) followed his teacher in making human sympathy a major plank in his *Theory of Moral Sentiments,* Hardin is doubtless broadly right in judging that later moral philosophers appeal to human sympathy only when in need of some auxiliary support for a conclusion to which they were led largely by other considerations. Nor is it hard to see why Hume's ideas on human sympathy should have been eclipsed by more peripheral notions. The reasons are much the same as those that led to the eclipse of his even more significant insight into the importance of conventions in human societies. In brief, until game theory came along, no tools were available to operationalize Hume's ideas.

The credit for seeing the relevance of game theory to Hume's idea of a convention probably belongs largely to Thomas Schelling (1960). In the case of Hume's notion of human sympathy, my guess is that it is Harsanyi (1977) who saw the way ahead most clearly. In any case, it is Harsanyi's development of the idea that is followed here.

It is first necessary to recognize that what Hume and Adam Smith called sympathy is nowadays known as *empathy;* psychologists reserve the word *sympathy* for a stronger notion. Adam sympathizes or empathizes with Eve when he imagines himself in her shoes in order to see things from her point of view. When Adam sympathizes with Eve, he identifies with her so strongly that he is unable to separate his interests from hers. For example, before the creation of Eve, Adam perhaps took no interest at all in apples while gathering his daily supply of fig leaves. But, after falling in love with the newly created Eve and observing her fondness for apples, he might then have found himself unable to pass an apple tree without salivating at the thought of how much Eve would enjoy its fruit. In such a case, it would not even be very remarkable if he were to abandon foraging for fig leaves altogether, so as to devote himself entirely to gathering apples for her.

The theory of revealed preference has no difficulty in describing Adam's behavior in such a case of sympathetic identification. If Adam chooses to gather apples rather than fig leaves, he reveals a preference for the consumption of apples by Eve to the consumption of fig leaves by himself. If he is consistent in this behavior, it can be described using a Von Neumann and Morgenstern utility function that depends both on his own consumption and on Eve's consumption. Therefore, no theoretical difficulty exists in incorporating altruistic (or spiteful) preferences into a player's utility function. If Adam really cares for Eve to the extent that he is willing to sacrifice his own physical well-being for hers, then this will be the right and proper way to model the situation.

It is easy to see why the forces of biological evolution might lead to our behaving as though we were equipped with sympathetic preferences. Mothers commonly care for their children more than they do for themselves—just as predicted by the model that sees us merely as machines that our genes use to reproduce themselves. In such basic matters as these, it seems that we differ little from crocodiles or spiders. However, humans do not sympathize only with their children; it is uncontroversial that they also sympathize, to varying degrees, with their husbands and wives, with their extended families, with their friends and neighbors, and with their sect or tribe.

Modern behavioral economists are willing to proceed as though we all sympathize with everybody in much the same way that we sympathize with our near and dear. If this were true, then the Von Neumann and Morgenstern theory would be adequate all by itself to determine a standard of interpersonal comparison, because Adam would only need to consult his own sympathetic utility function to find out how many utils to assign to a change in Eve's situation as compared with some change in his own situation. But Harsanyi's (1977) approach is less naive. He argues that, alongside our personal preferences (which may or may not include sympathetic concerns for others), we also have empathetic preferences that reflect our ethical concerns.

Empathetic Preferences

When Adam *empathizes* with Eve, he does not identify with her so closely that he ceases to separate his own preferences from hers. We weep, for example, with Romeo when he believes Juliet to be dead. We understand why he takes his own life—but we feel no particular inclination to join him in the act. Similarly, a confidence trickster is unlikely to sympathize with his victims, but he will be very much more effective at extracting money from them if he is able to put himself in their shoes with a view to predicting how they will respond to his overtures. I think we unconsciously carry out such feats of empathetic identification on a routine basis when playing the game of life each day with our fellow citizens.

It seems evident to me that empathetic identification is crucial to the survival of human societies. Without it, we would be unable to find our way to equilibria in the games we play except by slow and clumsy trial-and-error methods. However, it is not enough for the viability of a human society that we be able to use empathetic identification to recognize the equilibria of commonly occurring games. The games we play often have large numbers of equilibria. As Hume (1978 [1739]) saw so clearly, society, therefore, needs commonly understood coordinating conventions that select a particular equilibrium when many are available. Sometimes the conventions that have evolved are essentially arbitrary—as in the case of the side of the road on which we drive. However, in circumstances that are more deeply rooted in our social history, we usually overlook the conventional nature of our equilibrium selection criteria. We internalize the criteria so successfully that we fail to notice that selection criteria are in use at all.

We are particularly prone to such sleepwalking when using those conventional rules that we seek to justify by making airy references to "fairness" when asked to explain our behavior. In saying this, I do not have in mind the rhetorical appeals to fairness that typify wage negotiations or debates over taxation. Nor do I have in mind the abstract notions of justice proposed by philosophers like Rawls. I am thinking rather of the give-and-take of ordinary life. Who should wash the dishes tonight? Who ought to buy the next round of drinks? How long is it reasonable to allow a bore to monopolize the conversation over the dinner table? We are largely unconscious of the fairness criteria we use to resolve such questions, but the degree of consensus that we achieve in so doing is really quite remarkable. My guess is that the real reason the idea of Rawls' original position appeals so strongly to our intuition is simply that, in working through its implications, we recognize that it epitomizes the basic principle that underlies the fairness criteria that have evolved to adjudicate our day-to-day interactions with our fellows.

In order to use Rawls' device of the original position successfully as an equilibrium selection criterion, we need to be able to empathize with other people. In particular, we need to recognize that different people have different tastes. The device would obviously be worthless if Eve were to imagine how it would feel to be Adam without substituting his personal preferences for hers. But more than this is necessary. In order to make fairness judgments, Eve must be able to say *how much* better or worse she feels when identifying with Adam than when identifying with herself. Empathetic identification by itself is not sufficient for this purpose. An essential prerequisite for the use of the original position is that we be equipped with empathetic *preferences*.

Adam's *empathetic* preferences need to be carefully distinguished from the *personal* preferences built into his personal utility function. For example, I am expressing an empathetic preference when I say that I would rather be Eve eating an apple than Adam wearing a fig leaf. My own personal preferences are irrelevant to such an empathetic preference. Since I am no beach boy, I would personally much prefer a fig leaf to cover my nakedness than an apple to add to my waistline. However, if I know that apples taste very sweet to Eve and that Adam is totally unself-conscious about his body, I would clearly be failing to empathize success-fully if I were to allow my own impulses toward modesty to influence my judgment about whether Eve is gaining more satisfaction from her apple than Adam is get-ting from his fig leaf.

Harsanyi's Argument

It seems uncontentious that we actually do have empathetic preferences that we reveal when we make "fairness" judgments. Ordinary folk are doubtless less than consistent in the empathetic preferences they reveal, but Harsanyi idealized the situation by taking *homo economicus* as his model of man. In his model, everybody, therefore, has consistent empathetic preferences, which Harsanyi takes to mean that the Von Neumann and Morgenstern rationality requirements are satisfied. Therefore, an empathetic preference can be described using a Von Neumann and Morgenstern utility function.

An orthodox personal utility function of the kind we have considered hitherto simply assigns a utility to each situation that the person in question might encounter. For an empathetic utility function, we have to pair up each such situation with the person whom we are considering in that situation. One such pair might consist of Adam wearing a fig leaf. Another might be Eve eating an apple. An empathetic util-ity function assigns a utility to each such pair. It is, of course, precisely such pairs of possibilities that must be evaluated when people imagine themselves in the original position behind a veil of ignorance that hypothetically conceals their identity.

The next step in Harsanyi's argument is another idealization. He assumes that when someone empathizes with Adam or Eve, he does so entirely successfully. More precisely, if I am totally successful in empathizing with Adam, then the preferences I will express when imagining myself in Adam's position will be identical to Adam's own personal preferences. This is an important point. It escapes Parmenio, for example, in the following exchange quoted from Longinus by Hume (1978 [1739]):

> "Were I Alexander," said Parmenio, "I would accept of these offers made by Darius."
> "So would I too," replied Alexander, "were I Parmenio."

Parmenio makes the mistake of putting himself in Alexander's shoes while retaining his own personal preferences. Alexander corrects him by putting himself in Parmenio's shoes with Parmenio's personal preferences.

The rest of Harsanyi's argument is a straightforward application of the properties of Von Neumann and Morgenstern utility functions. The property that matters here is that any two Von Neumann and Morgenstern utility scales that represent exactly the same preference[10] must be related in the same way as two temperature scales. That is to say, the two scales can differ only in the placing of their zero and their unit. For example, once one knows the number of degrees that the Centigrade and Fahrenheit scales assign to the freezing and boiling points of water, then one knows how to translate any temperature on one scale into the corresponding temperature on the other scale.

The two utility scales to which this fact is now applied are Adam's personal scale and my empathetic scale for Adam. Since Harsanyi's second assumption implies that both scales represent the same preferences, my empathetic scale for Adam is exactly the same as his personal scale, except that the zero and the unit are changed. In particular, a util on my empathetic scale for Adam is obtained by multiplying a util on his personal scale by some constant number a. Similarly, a util on my empathetic scale for Eve is obtained by multiplying a util on her personal scale by some constant number e.

It follows that my empathetic utility function simply expresses the fact that I think that his and her personal utils can be traded off so that e of Adam's personal utils count the same as a of Eve's personal utils. That is to say, Harsanyi's assumptions imply that holding an empathetic preference is exactly the same thing as subscribing to a standard for making interpersonal comparisons between Adam and Eve.

6. Common Interpersonal Comparisons

The interpersonal comparisons described in the preceding section are *idiosyncratic* to the individual making them. If further assumptions are not made, there is nothing to prevent different people comparing utils across individuals in different ways.

Under what circumstances will these different value judgments be the same for everybody in a society? Only then will we have an uncontroversial standard for making interpersonal comparisons available for use in formulating a social contract. Indeed, in the absence of such a *common* standard, many authors would deny that any real basis for interpersonal comparison of utilities exists at all.

Harsanyi (1977, 60) holds that the interpersonal comparisons of utility that we actually make reveal a high degree of agreement across individuals. Rawls (1972) agrees with this assessment. But I am not satisfied simply to note the existence of some measure of consensus in the society in which we live. It seems to me that the standard of interpersonal comparison that a society employs is subject to the same forces of social evolution as its social contract. One cannot, therefore, glibly take a standard for interpersonal comparison as given when discussing social contract issues. One needs to ask how and why such a standard interacts with whatever the current social contract may be—and how it would adapt in response to proposed reforms of the current social contract.

I think that the empathetic preferences we find ourselves holding are a product of *social* evolution. We need such empathetic preferences only because they serve as inputs to the equilibrium selection criteria that lead us to speak of "fairness" when we try to explain to ourselves what we are doing when we use them. However, it is important not to allow oneself to be deceived by this propaganda. Our fairness criteria do not necessarily treat all citizens in an even-handed manner—whatever this might mean. As with all social institutions, the fairness criteria we use will tend to result in certain types of behavior becoming perceived as more successful than others. Those whose behavior is perceived to be successful are more likely to serve as the locus for meme replication than those who are perceived as failures. The point here is that social evolution will tend to favor the survival of whatever empathetic preferences promote the social success of those that hold them at the expense of those that do not. In the medium run, an equilibrium in empathetic preferences will be achieved. In my books, I argue that, in such an *empathetic equilibrium,* everybody will have the same empathetic preferences, and hence we will all share a common standard for making interpersonal comparisons of utility—as Harsanyi and Rawls suggest is actually true for our society. However, this paper is not the place to review my own evolutionary theory.

7. Conclusion

This paper has reviewed only one part of an enormous subject. Its aim has been to clarify how utility is understood by modern economists and to explain why the widespread claims that such a view of utility is incompatible with making interpersonal comparisons is mistaken. It concludes by outlining the theory of interpersonal comparison of John Harsanyi, which I believe is entirely satisfactory for the purpose of making judgments in Rawls' original position.

NOTES

1. I suppose it is idle to suggest that we start using the word *felicity* for Bentham's psychological notion, in order to distinguish it from the very different manner in which modern economists use the word *utility.* Philosophers sometimes speak of "preference satisfaction" when referring to the modern usage, but I suspect they seldom understand how radical the change in attitude has been.

2. A cardinal utility scale operates like a temperature scale, with utils replacing degrees. It is normally contrasted with an ordinal utility scale, in which the amount by which the utility of one outcome exceeds the utility of another outcome is held to be meaningless.

3. Bentham (1789 [1987]) suggests at one point that we should measure felicity in money, as in modern cost-benefit analysis, but who would want to argue that an extra dollar is worth the same to a billionaire as to a beggar?

4. Someone who likes or dislikes the gambling process for its own sake would be unlikely to accept Von Neumann and Morgenstern's assumption that two different lotteries should be regarded as equivalent when they generate the same prizes with the same probabilities. He would prefer whichever lottery squeezed the most drama and suspense from the randomizing process.

5. Suppose that you are just willing to pay X to get one bullet removed from a gun containing one bullet and Y to get one bullet removed from a gun containing four bullets. Let L mean death. Let W mean being alive after paying nothing, C mean being alive after paying X, and D mean being alive after paying Y. Then $u(C) = 1/6\, u(L) + 5/6\, u(W)$ and $\frac{1}{2}\, u(L) + 1/2\, u(D) = 2/3\, u(L) + 1/3\, u(W)$. Simplify by taking $1 = u(L) = 0$ and $w = u(W) = 1$. Then $c = u(C) = 5/6$ and $d = u(D) = 2/3$. Thus $u(D) \pi u(C)$ and so $X < Y$. (This elegant problem is attributed to Zeckhauser by Gibbard (1990) and Kahneman and Tversky (1979). Kahneman and Tversky think the example misleading on the grounds that matters are confused by the question of whether money has value for you after you are dead.)

6. The economists' notion of *consumer surplus* faces precisely this problem—even in the special case of quasilinear utility, for which Varian (1992, 69) describes consumer surplus as being exactly the appropriate welfare measure. An *ordinal* utility function for Adam is quasilinear if it assigns utility $a + U(f)$ to a commodity bundle consisting of a apples and f fig leaves. One can then regard U as defining a *cardinal* utility scale for fig leaves. Adam will always be ready to swap one util's worth of fig leaves for one apple, and so any util on the fig-leaf scale is exactly comparable to any other—if the standard for comparison is the number of apples that Adam will trade for it. But, who is to say that apples (or dollars) are the "appropriate" standard of comparison?

7. Notice that, after Adam and Eve have each been assigned the same bundle of commodities, neither will see any advantage in swapping their bundles. Economists say that an allocation of commodities with this property is *envy-free*. No interpersonal comparisons of utility need be made in identifying such an envy-free allocation. However, I hope the gin and martini example will suffice to indicate why it is wrong to deduce that interpersonal comparisons are therefore irrelevant.

8. Rawls (1972, 94) speaks of the judgment that would be made by a representative agent. He then muddies the waters by saying that only a representative of the least-advantaged social grouping need be considered. But how does one know which group is least advantaged if one has not already decided the scale that determines advantage?

9. My *Game Theory and the Social Contract* contains several other examples. (Binmore 1998)

10. Including preferences over risky alternatives.

REFERENCES

Arrow, K. (1978). "Extended Sympathy and the Problem of Social Choice." *Philosophia* 7: 233–237.

Bentham, J. (1987 [1789]). "An Introduction to the Principles of Morals and Legislation." In *Utilitarianism and Other Essays.* (Introduction by A. Ryan. Essay first published 1789). Harmondsworth, UK: Penguin.

Binmore, K. (1994). *Playing Fair: Game Theory and the Social Contract I*. Cambridge, MA: MIT Press.

Binmore, K. (1998). *Just Playing: Game Theory and the Social Contract II*. Cambridge, MA: MIT Press.

Binmore, K. (2005). *Natural Justice*. New York: Oxford University Press.

Cohen, G. (1989). "Equality of What? On Welfare, Goods and Capabilities." In M. Nussbaum & A. Sen, Eds., *The Quality of Life*. Oxford: Clarendon Press.

Edgeworth, F. (1881). *Mathematical Psychics*. London: Kegan Paul.

Elster, J. & Roemer, J. (1991). *Interpersonal Comparisons of Well-Being*. Cambridge: Cambridge University Press.

Gibbard. A. (1990). *Wise Choices and Apt Feelings: A Theory of Normative Judgment*. Oxford: Clarendon Press.

Griffin, J. (1986). *Well-Being: Its Meaning, Measurement and Moral Importance*. Oxford: Clarendon Press.

Hammond, P. (1976). "Why Ethical Measures of Inequality Need Interpersonal Comparisons." *Theory and Decision* 7: 263–274.

Hammond, P. (1991). "Interpersonal Comparisons of Utility: Why and How They Are and Should Be Made." In J. Elster & J. Roemer, Eds., *Interpersonal Comparisons of Well-Being*. London: Cambridge University Press.

Hardin, R. (1988). *Morality within the Limits of Reason*. Chicago: University of Chicago Press.

Harsanyi, J. (1955). "Cardinal Welfare, Individualistic Ethics, and the Interpersonal Comparison of Utility." *Journal of Political Economy* 63: 309–321.

Harsanyi, J. (1977). *Rational Behavior and Bargaining Equilibrium in Games and Social Situations*. Cambridge: Cambridge University Press.

Harsanyi, J. (1992). "Normative Validity and Meaning of Von Neumann and Morgenstern Utilities." In B. Skyrms, Ed., *Studies in Logic and the Foundations of Game Theory: Proceedings of the Ninth International Congress of Logic, Methodology and the Philosophy of Science*. Dordrecht, The Netherlands: Kluwer.

Hausman, D. (1994). "The Impossibility of Interpersonal Utility Comparisons." Technical Report Working Paper DP1/94, LSE Centre for Philosophy of Natural and Social Sciences.

Hume, D. (1978 [1739]). *A Treatise of Human Nature (Second Edition)*. (L. A. Selby-Bigge, Ed. Revised by P. Nidditch.) Oxford: Clarendon Press.

Kahneman, D. & Tversky, A. (1979). "Prospect Theory: An Analysis of Decision under Risk." *Econometrica* 47: 263–291.

Kukathas, C. & Pettit, P. (1990). *Rawls: A Theory of Justice and its Critics*. Oxford: Polity Press with Blackwell.

Layard, R. (2005). *Happiness: Lessons from a New Science*. London: Allen Lane.

Luce, R. (1956). "Semiorders and a Theory of Utility Discrimination." *Econometrica* 24: 178–191.

Luce, R. & Raiffa, H. (1957). *Games and Decisions*. New York: Wiley.

Rawls, J. (1972). *A Theory of Justice*. Oxford: Oxford University Press.

Rawls, J. (1982). "Social Unity and Primary Goods." In A. Sen & B. Williams, Eds., *Utilitarianism and Beyond*. Cambridge: Cambridge University Press.

Robbins, L. (1938). "Inter-personal Comparisons of Utility." *Economic Journal* 48: 635–641.

Rubinstein, A. (1988). "Similarity and Decision-making under Risk." *Journal of Economic Theory* 46: 145–153.

Schelling, T. (1960). *The Strategy of Conflict.* Cambridge, MA: Harvard University Press.

Sen, A. (1970). *Collective Choice and Social Welfare.* San Francisco: Holden Day.

Sen, A. (1976). "Welfare Inequalities and Rawlsian Axiomatics." *Theory and Decision* 7: 243–262.

Smith, A. (1975 [1759]). *The Theory of Moral Sentiments.* (Edited by D. Raphael & A. Macfie, Eds.). Oxford: Clarendon Press.

Suppes, P. (1966). "Some Formal Models of Grading Principles." *Synthèse* 6: 284–306.

Varian, H. (1992). *Microeconomic Analysis,* 3rd ed. New York: Norton.

Von Neumann, J. & Morgenstern, O. (1944). *The Theory of Games and Economic Behavior.* Princeton: Princeton University Press.

CHAPTER 21

SUBJECTIVE MEASURES OF WELL-BEING: PHILOSOPHICAL PERSPECTIVES

ERIK ANGNER

1. INTRODUCTION

In the last decade, so-called subjective measures of well-being have received increasing amounts of attention. Unlike traditional economic measures, which are typically based on data about income, market transactions, and the like, subjective measures are based on answers to questions such as: "Taking things all together, how would you say things are these days—would you say you're *very happy, pretty happy,* or *not too happy* these days?" (Gurin, Veroff & Feld 1960, 411, italics in original). Proponents of subjective measures (who tend to be psychologists) often present their measures as improvements over traditional economic welfare measures—including measures of income, consumer surplus, and compensating or equivalent variation—for purposes of public policy. Since subjective measures suggest rather different answers to questions about the determinants and distribution of welfare as compared to economic indicators, a shift to subjective measures for public policy purposes could have vast implications.[1]

In response to psychologists' inroads into what is often seen as traditionally economic territory, subjective measures have also been subjected to fierce criticism.[2] Among other things, critics (who tend to be economists) argue that, in general, mental states like happiness cannot be adequately measured, and that, in particular, questionnaire and interview data are inadequate for the purpose. Proponents of subjective measures respond that economic measures are hopelessly indirect, and that they, in any case, have not been properly validated. It is fair to say that the debate between proponents and critics of subjective measures has not so far been very fruitful. It certainly has not generated much convergence in opinion; economists—with a small number of exceptions, like Frey and Stutzer (2002)—still tend to favor economic measures, and psychologists still tend to favor subjective measures.

The goal of this chapter is to explore some fundamental assumptions underlying subjective measures of well-being, as compared to more traditional economic measures. My main thesis is that psychologists and economists have sharply different philosophical commitments, a fact that is seldom made explicit. Although it is perfectly reasonable for social and behavioral scientists to be wary of spending too much time thinking about the philosophical foundations of their enterprise, there are moments when it is eminently useful to do so. In this case, I will maintain, there is good reason to attend to these foundations, since they are directly relevant to the assessment of the various measures.

A better grasp of fundamental commitments, I will argue, goes a long way toward explaining why psychologists' and economists' efforts to measure welfare or well-being are so different, and why there is relatively little fruitful communication and collaboration across fields. Attention to fundamental assumptions also helps identify implicit premises in arguments for and against various approaches, and, therefore, permits a more informed assessment of them. Although my goal here is relatively modest—I do not to presume to determine who is right and who is wrong—I do hope that the discussion will permit deeper and more accurate assessments of the relative advantages and disadvantages of alternative welfare measures as well as their suitability for public policy making.

2. SUBJECTIVE MEASURES OF WELL-BEING

In spite of the fact that subjective measures are often described as a recent phenomenon, their history can be traced back to the early twentieth century. Subjective measures appear to have emerged in studies into marital success and educational psychology in the 1920s and 1930s (Angner undated). As measures of social well-being or welfare, these measures did not gain currency until in the 1960s, when they were rediscovered as a result of developments in gerontology, the epidemiology of mental health, and the social indicator movement. The recent increase in attention coincided with the rise of the so-called positive psychology movement in the 1990s. This movement is motivated by the belief that traditional psychology has spent an inordinate amount of time examining pathology and that positive emotional states are no less worthy of study (Seligman & Csikszentmihalyi 2000; Seligman 2002).[3]

Subjective measures are typically based on data gathered using questionnaires or interviews, though more sophisticated tools like Palm Pilots have been used too.[4] Many researchers use a direct question like that quoted in the introduction to this chapter. Others use small batteries of questions. The widely used Subjective Happiness Scale, due to Sonja Lyubomirsky and Heidi S. Lepper (1999), for instance, has four questions. These questions include the following (Lyubomirsky & Lepper 1999, 151):

1. In general, I consider myself:

    1   2   3   4   5   6   7
    not a very   a very
    happy   happy
    person   person

2. Compared to most of my peers, I consider myself:

    1   2   3   4   5   6   7
    less   more
    happy   happy

After subjects have circled one number for each of the four questions, a total happiness score is computed as the average of the four answers, with one reverse scored (Lyubomirsky & Lepper 1999, 41).

The history of subjective measures offers a fascinating variety of methods used to elicit subjects' happiness (cf. Angner undated). For instance, Goodwin Watson (1930) asks subjects whether they satisfy descriptions like: "Cheerful, gay spirits most of the time. Occasionally bothered by something but can usually laugh it off," "Ups and downs, now happy about things, now depressed. About balanced in the long run," and "Life often seems so worthless that there is little to keep one going. Nothing matters very much, there has been so much of hurt that laughter would be empty mockery" (Watson 1930, 81). Hornell Hart (1940) gives subjects 24 synonyms and 24 antonyms of "happy," and asks them to circle words that apply and cross out words that do not apply to them. Hadley Cantril (1965, 22) relies on a "ladder of life": a ladder-like shape where the rungs have been numbered from 0 to 10. The subject is told: "Here is a picture of a ladder. Suppose we say that the top of the ladder (POINTING) represents the best possible life for you and the bottom (POINTING) represents the worst possible life for you," and asked: "Where on the ladder

(MOVING FINGER RAPIDLY UP AND DOWN THE LADDER) do you feel you personally stand at the *present* time?" (Cantril 1965, 23).[5] In every case, the answers are used to compute a quantitative measure.

A somewhat different approach, called *experience sampling,* has been developed by Daniel Kahneman (1999). Kahneman prompts his subjects every so often—for example, with the use of Palm Pilots—to judge the "quality of their momentary experience" along the "good/bad dimension" (Kahneman 1999, 7). Kahneman adds: "We distinguish two notions of happiness, or well-being (the two terms are used interchangeably in this chapter). *Subjective happiness* is assessed by asking respondents to state how happy they are. *Objective happiness* is derived from a record of instant utility over the relevant period" (Kahneman 1999, 5).[6] More specifically, the objective happiness during some period of time is computed by taking the time integral of the subjective happiness curve. Kahneman and co-authors have since developed other measures, though Kahneman et al. (2004) insist: "Experience sampling is the gold standard" (Kahneman et al. 2004, 1777).

Relying on measures like these, psychologists have inferred the existence of several phenomena. For one thing, psychologists have suggested that there is only a weak relation between income and subjective well-being (SWB). As Ed Diener and Robert Biswas-Diener write, "for middle and upper-income people in economically developed nations, acquiring more income is not likely to strongly enhance SWB. Indeed, some studies find that rising wages predict less well-being" (Diener & Biswas-Diener 2002, 161). Psychologists have also concluded that even rapid economic growth is not associated with measurable increases in subjective well-being (Diener & Biswas-Diener 2002, 139), but that people who live in rich countries are on the average happier than people living in poor countries (Diener & Biswas-Diener 2002, 136). These phenomena—and others like them—are often explained by reference point phenomena (Argyle 1999), the process of adaptation (Frederick & Loewenstein 1999), and misprediction (Loewenstein & Schkade 1999; cf. Loewenstein & Angner 2003). Though still subject to debate, these results indicate that subjective measures may give rather different answers to questions about the determinants and distribution of well-being as compared to economic measures.

An important reason psychologists consider subjective measures of well-being so important is that they believe well-being—as they understand it—has privileged normative status. Some go so far as arguing that public policy should be designed so as to maximize well-being. This is the view of Andrew J. Oswald (1997), who writes: "The relevance of economic performance is that it may be a means to an end. That end is . . . the enrichment of mankind's feeling of well-being. Economic things matter only in so far as they make people happier" (Oswald 1997, 1815). Kahneman adds: "In the present framework . . . it is objective happiness that matters. Policies that improve the frequencies of good experiences and reduce the incidence of bad ones should be pursued" (Kahneman 1999, 15). Finally, Diener and Seligman assert: "Our thesis is that well-being should become a primary focus

of policymakers, and that its rigorous measurement is a primary policy imperative...[We] propose that well-being ought to be the ultimate goal around which
economic, health, and social policies are built" (Diener & Seligman 2004, 1–2).

The enthusiasm for the usefulness of the new measures is unmistakable.
According to Kahneman et al. (2004), subjective measures are

> ...potentially useful to medical researchers for assessing the burden of different
> illnesses (1) and the health consequences of stress (2); to epidemiologists
> interested in social and environmental stressors (3); to economists and policy
> researchers for evaluating policies and for valuing non-market activities (4, 5);
> and to anyone who wishes to measure the well-being of society [6]. (Kahneman
> et al. 2004, 1776)

For the latter purpose, several psychologists have suggested that we establish
"national well-being accounts" (Kahneman et al. 2004) or a "set of national indicators of well-being" (Diener & Seligman 2004, 21) analogous to regular national
accounts. As Diener and Seligman (2004) put it:

> The most important contribution of a national system of well-being indicators
> would be that they could focus the attention of policymakers and the public
> specifically on well-being, and not simply on the production of goods and
> services; one of the main benefits of well-being measures is that they add a
> valuable perspective beyond a cost-benefit market analysis in evaluating societal
> structures and interventions. (Diener & Seligman 2004, 21)

These authors believe that policymakers already care about well-being, but fear
that their attempts to promote it are based on "mere guesses and romantic sentiments" (Diener & Seligman 2004, 21). The hope is, obviously, that national indicators of well-being will allow policymakers to pursue well-being in a scientifically
informed manner.

3. ACCOUNTS OF WELL-BEING

The concept of well-being as I am using it here is nicely captured by Valerie Tiberius
(2006), who writes: "Well-being in the broadest sense is what we have when our
lives are going well for us, when we are living lives that are not necessarily morally
good, but good *for us*" (Tiberius 2006, 493, italics in original). Let us call this the
"core" concept of well-being. Because the concept of well-being is intended to capture what is ultimately (and not just instrumentally) good for the individual, it is
also supposed to capture that which we have reason to promote (as an end and not
just as a means) both in our own lives and in the lives of others (Scanlon 1998, 93).
The core concept of well-being needs to be sharply distinguished from the concept
of financial well-being, or economic welfare, in the sense of access to economic
resources (see Sen 1987, 16). Although it is eminently plausible to assume that some

economic resources are necessary for a life of well-being, as the term is used here, such resources are not constitutive of it. I will assume that both psychologists and economists use the term *well-being* in the core sense. The fact that economists and psychologists argue about which is the best measure of well-being certainly indicates that they take themselves to be measuring the same thing. In addition, the fact that many participants in this debate believe that "well-being ought to be the ultimate goal around which economic, health, and social policies are built" (Diener & Seligman 2004, 1–2) strongly suggests that they use the core concept of well-being.

In accordance with standard practice, I divide accounts of well-being into three main classes: *mental state accounts, preference-satisfaction accounts,* and *objective list accounts.* The tripartite division is sometimes traced to Derek Parfit (1984, 493–502), who writes:

> What would be best for someone, or would be most in this person's interests, or would make this person's life go, for him, as well as possible? Answers to this question I call *theories about self-interest.* There are three kinds of theory. On *Hedonistic Theories,* what would be best for someone is what would make his life happiest. On *Desire-Fulfilment Theories,* what would be best for someone is what, throughout his life, would best fulfil his desires. On *Objective List Theories,* certain things are good or bad for us, whether or not we want to have the good things, or to avoid the bad things. (Parfit 1984, 493, italics in original)

This taxonomy also appears in James Griffin (1986, section 1) and in Daniel M. Hausman and Michael S. McPherson (1996, chapter 6). It is not unproblematic (cf. Scanlon 1993), but will do for present purposes. In what follows, I will discuss the three kinds of account in order.

On the first kind of account, well-being is a mental state or a state of mind. According to these accounts, people are well off to the degree that they are in a particular mental state, be it happiness, satisfaction, elation, or similar. What defines these accounts is that they all see well-being "as having to enter our experience" (Griffin 1986, 13). This requirement is sometimes referred to as the *experience requirement* (Griffin 1986, 13), and accounts that satisfy it as *experiential accounts* (Scanlon 1998, 99). According to such accounts, "something contributes to well-being if, but only if, it affects the quality of one's experience" (Scanlon 1998, 100). There are, of course, many kinds of mental state account, depending on (among other things) what specific mental state is to count.

According to the second kind of account—variously referred to as *state of the world, desire fulfillment,* or *preference satisfaction accounts*—well-being is a matter of preference satisfaction (Griffin 1986, 7). According to these accounts, people are well off to the extent that their preferences are satisfied. These accounts do not satisfy the experience requirement, because people can be made better or worse off by changes in the world that satisfy their preferences, but that do not in any way enter their consciousness (Scanlon 1993, 186). Since people can feel happy (or whatever) even though their preferences are not satisfied, and vice versa, these accounts imply that well-being "can, and it frequently does, come apart from any satisfaction or enjoyment. When you get what you want, you might like it, or you might not. You might not even know you've got it" (Moore & Crisp 1996, 599). Again, there are many kinds of preference-satisfaction account, depending on (among other things) what preferences are to count.

The two kinds of account described so far are collectively referred to as *subjective accounts*, because they describe a person's well-being as (at least partly) a function of his or her feelings, experiences, desires, and so on (Scanlon 1975, 656). By contrast, we can identify what we may call *objective*—or *objective list*—*accounts*, according to which a person's well-being does not depend on such subjective factors. Hence: "Objective accounts of welfare appeal to the thought that there are features of the circumstances, position, or characteristics of persons that enable us to judge how well off they are" (Weale 1998, 704). In this view, then, "certain things are good or bad for beings, independently in at least some cases of whether they are desired or whether they give rise to pleasurable experiences" (Chappell & Crisp 1998, 553). There are many different objective list accounts, depending on (among other things) the exact set of things that are included on the list. Candidates for membership are controversial but include "moral goodness, rational activity, the development of one's abilities, having children and being a good parent, knowledge, and the awareness of true beauty" (Parfit 1984, 499).

Some philosophers believe that it may be possible to form a more plausible account of well-being by combining elements of different accounts (cf. Parfit 1984, 501). Thus, it is possible to maintain that happiness, preference satisfaction, and so on are individually necessary for a life of well-being, although neither one is sufficient by itself (Parfit 1984, 502). On such accounts, which are often referred to as *composite* or *hybrid accounts*, well-being is less like height (which can be accurately captured by a single number) and more like physical fitness (which cannot) (Keller 2004, 35). The appeal of hybrid views is that they appear to combine the most plausible elements of each of the individual accounts just discussed (Parfit 1984, 501). Needless to say, they can also be criticized for including what is least plausible in each individual account.

It should be clear, even from a relatively casual examination, that subjective measures of well-being typically presuppose some mental state account of well-being. We can tell, in part, from the fact that psychologists interested in the measurement of well-being largely appear to adopt the experience requirement. For example, David G. Myers (1992) quotes Madame de la Fayette as saying: "If one thinks that one is happy, that is enough to be happy," and adds that "like Madame de La Fayette, social scientists view well-being as a state of mind. Well-being, sometimes called 'subjective well-being' to emphasize the point, is a pervasive sense that life is good" (Myers 1992, 23; cf. 1992, 27). Similarly, Ed Diener & Eunkook Suh (1997) write: "Subjective well-being research...is concerned with individuals' subjective experiences of their lives. The underlying assumption is that well-being can be defined by people's conscious experiences—in terms of hedonic feelings or cognitive satisfactions" (Diener & Suh 1997, 191). The fact that Diener and Suh argue that well-being is not only *concerned* with individuals' subjective experiences, but is *defined* by them, strongly suggests that Diener and Suh accept the experience requirement.

It is less clear what kind of mental state account is adopted by proponents of subjective measures of well-being. Many psychologists appear to take well-being to be a single homogeneous mental state (Kahneman 1999, 5). Others can be read as treating well-being as a combination of two (Campbell et al. 1976, 8), three (Bradburn & Caplovitz 1965, Section 2.2.5), or more (Diener & Seligman 2004, 1) mental states, each of which is necessary for well-being but neither one of which is (by itself) sufficient. It should also be noted that some proponents of subjective measures of well-being can be understood as defending hybrid views. For example, Kahneman (2000, 691) suggests that subjectively experienced happiness is but one of several constituents of well-being properly understood. What is clear is that there is no such thing as *the* account of well-being adopted by proponents of subjective measures.

By contrast, proponents of economic measures tend to favor preference-satisfaction accounts. In the words of Hausman and McPherson: "Welfare economics identifies welfare with the satisfaction of preferences. This identification is so automatic and ubiquitous that economists seldom realize how controversial it is" (Hausman & McPherson 1997, 17). Notice that the satisfaction of preferences is different from feeling satisfied; economic measures are intended to represent the former rather than the latter. Economists also identify well-being with utility, which is interpreted as an index of preference satisfaction (Mongin & d'Aspremont 1998, 382). This means that economists can legitimately talk about utility—even as identical to well-being—without making any reference to subjective states like happiness, pleasure, and satisfaction. Indeed, economists take a certain amount of pride in eschewing references to such subjective notions (Hausman & McPherson 1997, 17).

Again, it is less clear what kind of preference-satisfaction account is adopted by proponents of traditional economic measures. According to Philippe Mongin and Claude d'Aspremont, economists—whether implicitly or explicitly—rely on a preference-satisfaction account according to which what matters are actual preferences (Mongin & d'Aspremont 1998, 382). The interpretation is supported by the standard technical apparatus, which does not distinguish between actual and ideal preferences. Other economists maintain that what matters are not the preferences that the person actually has, but the preferences he or she would have under some counterfactual conditions. Thus, John C. Harsanyi argues that what matters are a person's *true* preferences, which are "the preferences he *would* have if he had all the relevant factual information, always reasoned with the greatest possible care, and were in a state of mind most conducive to rational choice" (Harsanyi 1982, 55, italics in original).[7]

There is, then, a fundamental difference between the account of well-being adopted by proponents of subjective measures and that adopted by proponents of traditional economic measures. The difference matters because the two accounts diverge, in the sense that it is perfectly possible to be well off according to the one account and not well off according to the other. It is possible to be in the relevant mental state (whether happiness, satisfaction, or whatever) even though our desires are not fulfilled: We could, for instance, be ignorant of the fact that our desires are not fulfilled, or we could be aware of this fact and be happy, satisfied, or whatever anyway. Analogously, it is perfectly possible to not be in the relevant mental state even though our desires are fulfilled: We could, again, be ignorant of the fact that our desires are fulfilled, or we could be aware of this fact but unable to rejoice in it. Since mental state and preference satisfaction accounts diverge, even if we agree that well-being should be measured and promoted, what we measure, and what we promote, will be different depending on what account of well-being we adopt.

In spite of its importance, the fact that economists and psychologists tend to adopt different accounts of well-being is seldom explicitly acknowledged. Consider, for example, some psychologists' criticism of economic measures for being too indirect, in the sense that they do not get directly at what really matters, which is clearly assumed to be some subjectively experienced mental state. In their review "Beyond Money: Toward an economy of well-being," Diener and Seligman (2004) argue:

> Although economics currently plays a central role in policy decisions because it is assumed that money increases well-being, we propose that well-being needs to be assessed more directly, because there are distressingly large, measurable slippages between economic indicators and well-being. (Diener & Seligman 2004, 1)

If the term *well-being* in this passage is interpreted as the psychologists understand it (which is a plausible supposition), the first claim is false: economic measures are used because it is assumed that they reflect preference satisfaction, not positive mental states. However, if the term is used as the economists understand it, Diener and Seligman have no support for the second claim—that there are slippages between economic indicators and well-being—since the evidence they report relates to well-being understood in terms of positive mental states (Diener & Seligman 2004). Either way, the authors fail to properly acknowledge that economists and psychologists operate with different and inconsistent accounts of well-being.

The fact that psychologists and economists tend to be committed to different accounts of well-being helps explain the fact that they go about measuring well-being so differently. First, it explains why psychologists tend to measure well-being by distributing questionnaires asking questions about happiness, satisfaction, and the like, whereas economists tend to compute measures of well-being on the basis of observable choices, market transactions, and such. Second, the difference in accounts of well-being explains why psychologists tend to consider the economic approach to welfare measurement as inadequate, and vice versa. Given that psychologists are ultimately interested in mental states, it strikes them as natural to just ask the person whether (or to what degree) that person is in that state. To them, measures derived from observable choices and market transactions are likely to seem hopelessly indirect. Given that economists are ultimately interested in preference satisfaction, it comes naturally for them to explore whether the person succeeds in securing what that person would choose, on the assumption that choice mirrors preference. To them, measures based on questions about the person's happiness, and so forth, are likely to appear hopelessly irrelevant.

As these remarks suggest, the fact that different measures of well-being presuppose different accounts of well-being is highly relevant to the assessment of those measures. If it turned out that mental state accounts are inadequate, this would constitute prima facie evidence against the subjective measures of well-being (since they were designed to represent mental states). It would not constitute proof, however, since it would remain possible for subjective measures to represent well-being properly understood. Analogously, if it turned out that preference-satisfaction accounts of well-being are inadequate, this would constitute prima facie evidence against the economic measures (as they were designed to represent preference satisfaction). Again, it would not constitute proof, since it would remain possible for economic measures to represent well-being properly understood. Either way, the plausibility of underlying accounts of well-being is eminently relevant to the adequacy of given measures.

4. APPROACHES TO MEASUREMENT

There are (broadly speaking) two different approaches to measurement in the social and behavioral sciences.[8] As David H. Krantz (1991) puts it: "One, which may be termed the *psychometric* approach, introduces latent [unobservable] variables to explain behavioral orderings. The second...treats the numerical representation of behavioral orderings axiomatically" (Krantz 1991, 2, my italics). The second approach is sometimes referred to as the *representational* approach (e.g., in Dawes & Smith 1985, 511). For the reason identified by Dawes and Smith (1985, 512)—the fact that all measurement is at bottom about representation—I will call it the *measurement-theoretic* approach.

The psychometric approach—due in large part to the American Psychological Association's 'Technical Recommendations' (1954) and developed by Lee J. Cronbach and Paul E. Meehl (1955) (cf. John & Benet-Martínez 2000, 351–357)—is largely centered around the concepts of "construct" and "construct validation." A construct is "a variable [that] is abstract and latent rather than concrete and observable" (Nunnally & Bernstein 1994, 85). Construct validation is often described as an instance of ordinary hypothesis testing (Johnson 2001, 11316). On this approach, you start off by simultaneously hypothesizing the existence of a construct and proposing a measure of the construct. On the basis of these assumptions, you derive the prediction that (informally speaking) the measure of the construct will "behave as expected." By exploring differences in the measure of the construct across conditions, and relationships between the measure of the construct and measures of other constructs and overt behavior, you can test whether the prediction is true. If it is, you infer that the construct as well as the proposed measures of it have been validated; if it is not, you infer that either the construct does not exist or the proposed measure is invalid.

The measurement-theoretic approach was first articulated by Dana Scott and Patrick Suppes (1958) but received its canonical statement in Krantz, R. Duncan Luce, Suppes, and Amos Tversky's *Foundations of Measurement* (1971). Instead of latent constructs and construct validation, this approach emphasizes observable orderings and representation theorems (Krantz 1991, 1). On the measurement-theoretic approach, you start off with a set A of objects (e.g., rods, commodity bundles), which can be ordered with respect to some property (e.g., length, preference) by applying a simple observable operation. Then, you prove that if the empirical relation $>$ satisfies certain properties, then there is a function $\phi\,(\cdot)$ from A into some set of numbers such that $\phi\,(\cdot)$ is a *homomorphism*, that is, an assignment of numbers to each member of A such that one object bears relation $>$ to another just in case the former is associated with a greater number than the latter.

There is a great deal of evidence that proponents of subjective measures operate within the psychometric approach. First, there is a purely historical connection in that both subjective measures and psychometrics grew out of personality psychology during the early twentieth century (Angner undated; Winter & Barenbaum 1999, 5). Second, proponents of subjective measures often refer to "psychometric criteria" (Lyubomirsky & Lepper 1999, 140) and "psychometric properties" (Diener et al. 1999, 277). Third, the manner in which subjective measures are defended by their proponents actually conforms to the requirements of the psychometric approach. The psychologists postulate the existence of a construct—happiness, satisfaction, or similar—and propose a measure of it; then, they confirm that the measures "behave as expected" when compared to objective life circumstances, other people's judgment of subjects' happiness, measures of mental health, and so on (cf. Lyubomirsky & Lepper 1999, 145; Diener et al. 1999, 277). In brief, the manner in which the psychologists defend their measures exhibits all the hallmarks of the psychometric approach. Finally, within contemporary psychology, the measurement-theoretic approach is widely regarded as a failure and is not commonly used (John & Benet-Martínez 2000, 341; Cliff 1992).

Meanwhile, there is much evidence that proponents of economic measures operate within the measurement-theoretic approach. First, there is a purely historical connection, because measurement theory was motivated in part by issues relating to utility measurement (Krantz et al. 1971, 9). Second, the manner in which economic measures are defended by their proponents conforms to the demands of the measurement-theoretic approach. The economists begin with the assumption that market choices satisfy certain axioms; on the basis of the axioms, they offer a formal proof that the measure is an index of preference, that is, a utility function (cf. Mas-Colell et al. 1995, 80–82). Because this procedure establishes that the measure is a homomorphism, the actual practice of economists shows the signs of a commitment to the measurement-theoretic approach. Finally, economists do not talk about "constructs," and typically make little effort to validate their measures in the manner favored by the psychometric approach.

Thus, there is a fundamental difference between the approach to measurement adopted by proponents of subjective measures and that adopted by proponents of traditional economic measures. This difference—like that in accounts of well-being—matters, because the different approaches require radically different arguments to validate a given measure. Whereas those operating in accordance with the psychometric approach reason inductively from the claim that a given measure "behaves as expected," those operating in accordance with the measurement-theoretic approach reason deductively from the claim that a given relation satisfies certain axioms. Thus, the two approaches differ both when it comes to the character of the premises and the nature of the inference.

In spite of its importance, the difference between approaches to measurement—like the difference in accounts of well-being—is seldom explicitly acknowledged. For example, economists often reject subjective measures of well-being by saying that mental states like happiness simply cannot be measured: "[the] concept of happiness is one for which there can be no scientific objective measure" (Beckerman 1974, 53). This objection can be understood as presupposing that observable orderings are necessary for measurement, as the measurement-theoretic approach suggests that they are. The criticism does not acknowledge that subjective measures—whatever their flaws—are justified in the manner of the psychometric approach, not the measurement-theoretic one. Similarly, psychologists sometimes criticize economists for failing to properly validate their measures in the manner of the psychometric approach, without mentioning that economists validate their measures in accordance with the measurement-theoretic one.

The fact that psychologists and economists operate within different approaches to measurement helps explain the fact that psychologists and economists go about measuring well-being so differently. First, this difference helps account for the fact that psychologists are comfortable using questionnaire data, whereas welfare economists tend to require observable choices. Second, it helps explain the fact that psychologists validate their measures by establishing construct validity, reliability, and so on, whereas economists tend to establish that a particular function is a utility function. Third, the difference sheds light on the fact that economists' approach to welfare measurement strikes psychologists as terribly inadequate, and the other way around. Given that psychologists operate within the psychometric approach, they are trained to use questionnaires for measurement purposes and to justify their measures by engaging in a process of construct validation. Moreover, they are naturally suspicious of measures that have not been so validated. Given that economists operate within the measurement-theoretic approach, they are trained to use observable orderings for measurement purposes and to justify their measures by offering mathematical proofs. Moreover, they are wary of using measures that are not based on observable orderings and which have not been shown to be homomorphisms.

Finally, the different approaches to measurement help account for the fact that economists adopt preference satisfaction accounts of well-being whereas psychologists adopt mental state accounts. Economists were originally drawn to preference satisfaction accounts after convincing themselves that pleasure and pain could not, whereas preference satisfaction could, be measured scientifically (Mandler 1999, 6; Angner & Loewenstein, in press). Similarly, the recent upswing in interest in happiness appears, at least in part, to be a result of psychologists convincing themselves that happiness and such can, in fact, be scientifically measured. An uncharitable interpretation of these events suggests that economists and psychologists are like the drunken man who looks for his lost key not where he lost it, but where the light is.

A more charitable interpretation, which I favor, is that psychologists and economists assume that accounts of well-being can be judged in part on the grounds of whether they permit the development of adequate measures of well-being. This idea is explicit in several prominent contemporary philosophers. James Griffin argues that we cannot "first fix on the best account of 'well-being' and independently ask about its measurement. One proper ground for choosing between conceptions of well-being would be that one lends itself to the deliberation that we must do and another does not" (Griffin 1986, 1). The idea, presumably, is that the measurement of well-being is necessary for the deliberation that we have to do. Similarly, Christine M. Korsgaard maintains that an account of the quality of life may be assessed "for its utility in determining actual political and economic policy—that is, whether it provides accurate enough measures to assess the effects of policy" (Korsgaard 1993, 54). If Griffin and Korsgaard are correct, the question of what can be adequately measured is highly relevant to the adequacy of accounts of well-being, and to the plausibility of ethical theories in which that concept plays a role.

Anyway, as these reflections indicate, the fact that proponents of subjective and economic measures adopt different approaches to measurement is directly relevant to the assessment of those measures. If it turned out that the psychometric approach is a failure, this would constitute prima facie evidence against subjective measures (since they are justified in the manner of the psychometric approach). It would not constitute proof, however, since it might still be possible to validate subjective measures in some other way. Analogously, if it turned out that the measurement-theoretic approach is a failure, this would constitute prima facie evidence against the economic measures (since they are justified in the manner of the measurement-theoretic approach). Again, it would not constitute proof, since it might still be possible to validate economic measures in some other way. Either way, it should be clear that the adequacy of different approaches to measurement is eminently relevant to the adequacy of measures of well-being.

5. Conclusion

The purpose of this chapter has been to explore some fundamental philosophical commitments underlying subjective measures of well-being, as compared to more traditional economic measures. Though the discussion has been brief, I hope to have established that subjective and economic measures of well-being rest on radically different theoretical foundations. Whereas subjective measures are typically understood as representing some mental state account of well-being, economic measures are typically understood as representing some preference-satisfaction account. Whereas subjective measures are typically justified in accordance with the psychometric approach to measurement, economic measures are typically justified in accordance with the measurement-theoretic approach. These differences are rarely explicit in the writings of either economists or psychologists.

Moreover, I hope to have shown that those commitments have (at least to some extent) helped shape the development of the different measures. Thus, psychologists' long-standing commitment to mental state accounts of well-being appears to have played a role in their adoption of subjective measures, and economists' commitment to preference-satisfaction accounts appears to have figured in their use of, for example, income-based measures. Meanwhile, psychologists' commitment to the psychometric approach to measurement seems to have played a role both in their acceptance of subjective measures and mental state accounts of well-being, and economists' commitment to the measurement-theoretic approach appears to have predisposed them toward choice-based measures and preference-satisfaction accounts of well-being. Radically different philosophical commitments have given psychologists' and economists' efforts to measure well-being or welfare a rather different flavor.

The fact that different theoretical foundations have helped shape measures of well-being suggests that a better understanding of the former permits a better grasp of the latter. And indeed, the discussion of theoretical foundations has helped answer a series of important and connected questions, including: What are these measures intended to represent? That is, what is it that they are measures of? What, in general terms, do psychologists and economists think they have to establish in order to show that something can be measured? What considerations, in particular, make them think that their favored measures of well-being or welfare (as they understand it) meet these demands?

Answers to questions such as these permit a more informed assessment of the relative advantages and disadvantages of alternative welfare measures. As I have suggested, the assessment of a measure of well-being depends to some extent on its philosophical foundations: both on the plausibility of the underlying account of well-being and the adequacy of the relevant approach to measurement. The connection between the measures and their philosophical foundations is of course complicated. Even if it turned out that mental state (preference-satisfaction) accounts of well-being are inadequate, this would not constitute conclusive evidence against subjective (economic) measures of well-being. Even if it turned out that the psychometric (measurement-theoretic) approach to measurement is misguided, this would not constitute conclusive evidence against subjective (economic) measures of well-being. Sorting out these issues would require a much longer study.

Still, the discussion has important implications. One such implication is that some attention to philosophical foundations of measures of well-being is unavoidable. A complete defense of a given measure will have to say something about the nature of well-being and approaches to measurement. Another implication is that there is much to be gained from exploring philosophical foundations. By taking explicit account of philosophical foundations of our efforts to measure well-being, we can hope to gain a better understanding of the nature, strengths, and weaknesses of our measures. Thus, for somebody who wants to understand, attack, or defend a given approach to welfare measurement, attention to fundamental assumptions is well worthwhile. Here, then, is a case in which philosophy of science can make a constructive contribution to a scientific enterprise.

In closing, for the benefit of philosophers who want to know what is in it for them, I want to add that attention to theoretical foundations of welfare measures can have clear benefits from a purely philosophical perspective as well. To begin with, the literature by economists and psychologists raises interesting issues about, and sometimes offers tentative answers to, purely philosophical questions, for example, about the nature of well-being. Having seen this, Sumner (1996) draws heavily on the psychological research in defending an account of well-being as life satisfaction. Also, many philosophical arguments in ethics and political theory rest in part on empirical premises. This, I believe, is what John Rawls was alluding to when he wrote that "the fundamental principles of justice quite properly depend upon the natural facts about men in society" (Rawls 1999, 137). Surely, insofar as the principles of justice depend on empirical facts about the determinants and distribution of well-being, the psychological and economic literature (properly interpreted) is directly relevant to the theory of justice. Similarly, Nicholas Rescher (1972)—relying on the authority of Immanuel Kant—notes: "In social philosophy the actualities of empirical circumstances must ever predominate" (Rescher 1972, ix). The point is that many arguments in moral, social, and political philosophy proceed from, and depend on, empirical facts.

In addition, as we have seen, accounts of well-being can perhaps be judged in part on the grounds of whether they permit the development of adequate measures of well-being. We have seen that this idea is explicit in several contemporary philosophers (Griffin 1986, 1; Korsgaard 1993, 54) and apparently implicit in both the psychological and the economic literature on welfare measurement from the 1930s, or earlier, to the present. If this is correct, then the success (or lack thereof) of attempts to measure, for example, subjective well-being is eminently relevant to the adequacy of the underlying account of well-being. If so, the results of this investigation have implications for the theory of well-being and ethical theories that give the concept some role. Incidentally, Griffin and Korsgaard's position implies that discussing welfare measurement in the absence of a commonly accepted account of well-being does not amount to putting the cart before the horse, as some would have it. The problem has to be attacked, as it were, from both ends.

Finally, the issue of what measure of well-being should be used in the design and evaluation of public policy is of obvious political and practical importance. It is widely (though not universally) agreed that public policy should be designed (at least in part) so as to promote the well-being of the population (see, e.g., Ahlheim 1998, 484). It would not matter which measure we used if they tended to give the same answer to the question about who is well off, and about what conditions tend to make people better off. Judging by available empirical research, however, the measures do not agree in this way. Although it may seem obvious that well-being should be strictly increasing in wealth, for example, this may not be true. Insofar as policy should be designed to promote well-being at all, the choice of measure will have real consequences for the policies that we favor.

Acknowledgments

I am grateful to Harold Kincaid, Don Ross, and the participants in the 2006 Issues in the Philosophy of Economics workshop at the University of Alabama at Birmingham. Errors remain my own.

NOTES

1. As is customary in this literature, I use *welfare* and *well-being* interchangeably. For more about the concept of well-being and efforts to measure it, see Angner (in press, Section 2).

2. I will spell out the criticism in more detail later.

3. For more about positive psychology, see Gillham and Seligman (1999), the special January 2000 issue of *American Psychologist,* and the massive *Handbook of Positive Psychology* (Snyder & Lopez 2002).

4. For useful overviews of subjective measures, see e.g. Diener et al. (1999), Kahneman, Diener, and Schwarz (1999) and Diener, Lucas, and Oishi (2002).

5. The parenthetical notes in small caps are Cantril's instructions to the experimenter (Cantril 1965, 22).

6. The terminology here is unfortunate. Better terms would have been *momentary* (or *instant*) and *overall* well-being, or some such.

7. Interestingly, even though he admits that actual and ideal preferences may fail to coincide, Harsanyi maintains that we should use actual, "manifest," preferences as a basis for welfare measurement (Harsanyi 1982, 55–56).

8. For more on the difference between the two approaches, see Robyn M. Dawes and Tom L. Smith (1985), Joel Michell (1990), David H. Krantz (1991), Charles M. Judd and Gary H. McClelland (1998), and Oliver P. John and Veronica Benet-Martínez (2000).

REFERENCES

Ahlheim, M. (1998). "Measures of Economic Welfare." In S. Barberà, P. J. Hammond, & C. Seidl, Eds., *Handbook of Utility Theory*, Vol. I, 483–568. Dordrecht: Kluwer.

American Psychological Association (1954). "Technical Recommendations for Psychological Tests and Diagnostic Techniques." *Psychological Bulletin* Supplement, 51: 1–38.

Angner, E. (in press). "The Philosophical Foundations of Subjective Measures of Well-Being." In L. Bruni, F. Comim, & M. Pugno, Eds., *Capabilities and Happiness.* Oxford: Oxford University Press.

Angner, E. (undated). "The Evolution of Eupathics: The Historical Roots of Subjective Measures of Well-Being." Unpublished manuscript.

Angner, E., & Loewenstein, G. (in press). "Behavioral Economics." In U. Mäki, Ed., *Handbook of the Philosophy of Science, Vol. 13: Philosophy of Economics.* Amsterdam: Elsevier.

Argyle, M. (1999). "Causes and Correlates of Happiness." In D. Kahneman, E. Diener, & N. Schwarz, Eds., *Well-Being: The Foundations of Hedonic Psychology*, 354–373. New York: Russell Sage.

Beckerman, W. (1974). *Two Cheers for the Affluent Society: A Spirited Defense of Economic Growth.* New York: St. Martin's Press.

Bradburn, N. M., & Caplovitz, D. (1965). *Reports on Happiness: A Pilot Study of Behavior Related to Mental Health.* Chicago: Aldine.

Campbell, A., Converse, P. E., & Rodgers, W. L. (1976). *The Quality of American Life: Perceptions, Evaluations, and Satisfactions.* New York: Russell Sage.

Cantril, H. (1965). *The Pattern of Human Concerns.* New Brunswick: Rutgers University Press.

Chappell, T., & Crisp, R. (1998). "Utilitarianism." In E. Craig, Ed., *The Routledge Encyclopedia of Philosophy*, Vol. 9, 551–557. London: Routledge.

Cliff, N. (1992). "Abstract Measurement Theory and the Revolution that Never Happened." *Psychological Science* 3: 186–190.

Cronbach, L. J., & Meehl, P. E. (1955). "Construct Validity in Psychological Tests." *Psychological Bulletin* 52: 281–302.

Dawes, R., & Smith, T. L. (1985). "Attitude and Opinion Measurement." In G. Lindzey & E. Aronson, Eds., *Handbook of Social Psychology*, 3rd ed., Vol. I, 509–566. New York: Random House.

Diener, E., & Biswas-Diener, R. (2002). "Will Money Increase Subjective Well-Being? A Literature Review and Guide to Needed Research." *Social Indicators Research* 57: 119–169.

Diener, E., Lucas, R. E., & Oishi, S. (2002). "Subjective Well-Being: The Science of Happiness and Life Satisfaction." In C. R. Snyder & S. J. Lopez, Eds., *Handbook of Positive Psychology*, 63–73. Oxford: Oxford University Press.

Diener, E., & Seligman, M. E. P. (2004). "Beyond Money: Toward an Economy of Well-Being." *Psychological Science in the Public Interest* 5: 1–31.

Diener, E., & Suh, E. (1997). "Measuring Quality of Life: Economic, Social, and Subjective Indicators." *Social Indicators Research* 40: 189–216.

Diener, E., Suh, E. M., Lucas, R. E., & Smith, H. L. (1999). "Subjective Well-Being: Three Decades of Progress." *Psychological Bulletin* 125: 276–303.

Frederick, S., & Loewenstein, G. (1999). "Hedonic Adaptation." In D. Kahneman, E. Diener, & N. Schwarz, Eds., *Well-Being: The Foundations of Hedonic Psychology*, 302–329. New York: Russell Sage.

Frey, B. S., & Stutzer, A. (2002). *Happiness and Economics: How the Economy and Institutions Affect Well-Being*. Princeton: Princeton University Press.

Gillham, J. E., & Seligman, M. E. P. (1999). "Footsteps on the Road to a Positive Psychology." *Behaviour and Research Therapy* 37: S163–S173.

Griffin, J. (1986). *Well-Being: Its Meaning, Measurement and Moral Importance*. Oxford: Clarendon.

Gurin, G., Veroff, J., & Feld, S. (1960). *Americans View Their Mental Health: A Nationwide Interview Survey*. New York: Basic Books.

Harsanyi, J. C. (1982). "Morality and the Theory of Rational Behavior." In S. Sen & B. Williams, Eds., *Utilitarianism and Beyond*, 39–62. New York: Oxford University Press.

Hausman, D. M., & McPherson, M. S. (1996). *Economic Analysis and Moral Philosophy*. Cambridge: Cambridge University Press.

Hausman, D. M., & McPherson, M. S. (1997). "Beware of Economists Bearing Advice." *Policy Options* 18: 16–19.

Hart, H. (1940). *Chart for Happiness*. New York: Macmillan.

John, O. P., & Benet-Martínez, V. (2000). "Measurement: Reliability, Construct Validation, and Scale Construction." In H. T. Reiss & C. M. Judd, Eds., *Handbook of Research Methods in Social and Personality Psychology*, 339–369. Cambridge: Cambridge University Press.

Johnson, J. A. (2001). "Personality Psychology: Methods." In N. J. Smelser & P. B. Baltes, Eds., *International Encyclopedia of the Social and Behavioral Sciences*, Vol. 16, 11313–11317. Amsterdam: Elsevier.

Judd, C. M., & McClelland, G. H. (1998). "Measurement." In D. T. Gilbert, S. T. Fiske & G. Lindzey, Eds., *The Handbook of Social Psychology*, 4th ed. 180–232. Boston: McGraw-Hill.

Kahneman, D. (1999). "Objective Happiness." In D. Kahneman, E. Diener, & N. Schwarz, Eds., *Well-Being: The Foundations of Hedonic Psychology*, 3–25. New York: Russell Sage.

Kahneman, D. (2000). "Experienced Utility and Objective Happiness." In D. Kahneman & A. Tversky, Eds., *Choices, Values and Frames*, 673–692. Cambridge: Cambridge University Press.

Kahneman, D., Diener, E., & Schwarz, N., Eds. (1999). *Well-Being: The Foundations of Hedonic Psychology*. New York: Russell Sage.

Kahneman, D., Krueger, A. B., Schkade, D., Schwarz, N., & Stone, A. (2004). "Toward National Well-Being Accounts." *American Economic Review* 94: 429–434.

Kahneman, D., & Tversky, A., Eds., (2000). *Choices, Values and Frames*. Cambridge: Cambridge University Press.

Keller, S. (2004). "Welfare and the Achievement of Goals." *Philosophical Studies* 121: 27–41.

Korsgaard, C. M. (1993). "G. A. Cohen: Equality of What? On Welfare, Goods and Capabilities. Amartya Sen: Capability and Well-Being." In M. Nussbaum & A. Sen, Eds., *The Quality of Life*, 54–61. Oxford: Oxford University Press.

Krantz, D. H. (1991). "From Indices to Mappings: The Representational Approach to Measurement." In D. R. Brown & J. E. K. Smith, Eds., *Frontiers of Mathematical Psychology: Essays in Honor of Clyde Coombs*, 1–52. New York: Springer.

Krantz, D. H., Luce, R. D., Suppes, P., & Tversky, A. (1971). *Foundations of Measurement*, Vol. I. New York: Academic Press.

Loewenstein, G. & Angner, E. (2003). "Predicting and Indulging Changing Preferences." In G. Loewenstein, D. Read & R. Baumeister, Eds., *Time and Decision: Economic and Psychological Perspectives on Intertemporal Choice*, 351–391. New York: Russell Sage.

Loewenstein, G. & Schkade, D. (1999). "Wouldn't It Be Nice? Predicting Future Feelings." In D. Kahneman, E. Diener, & N. Schwarz, Eds., *Well-Being: The Foundations of Hedonic Psychology*, 85–105. New York: Russell Sage.

Lyubomirsky, S. & Lepper, H. S. (1999). "A Measure of Subjective Happiness: Preliminary Reliability and Construct Validation." *Social Indicators Research* 46: 137–155.

Mandler, M. (1999). *Dilemmas in Economic Theory: Persisting Foundational Problems of Microeconomics*. New York: Oxford University Press.

Mas-Colell, A., Whinston, M. D. & Green, J. R. (1995). *Microeconomic Theory*. Oxford: Oxford University Press.

Michell, J. (1990). *An Introduction to the Logic of Psychological Measurement*. Hillsdale: Lawrence Erlbaum Associates.

Mongin, P. & d'Aspremont, C. (1998). "Utility Theory and Ethics." In S. Barberà, P. J. Hammond, & C. Seidl, Eds., *Handbook of Utility Theory*, Vol. I, 371–481. Dordrecht: Kluwer.

Moore, A., & Crisp, R. (1996). "Welfarism in Moral Theory." *Australasian Journal of Philosophy* 74: 598–613.

Myers, D. G. (1992). *The Pursuit of Happiness: Who is Happy and Why?* New York: William Morrow.

Nunnally, J. C. & Bernstein, I. H. (1994). *Psychometric Theory*, 3rd ed. New York: McGraw-Hill.

Oswald, A. J. (1997). "Happiness and Economic Performance." *The Economic Journal* 107: 1815–1831.

Parfit, D. (1984). *Reasons and Persons*. Oxford: Clarendon.

Rawls, J. (1999). *A Theory of Justice*, rev. ed. Cambridge: Belknap.

Rescher, N. (1972). *Welfare: The Social Issues in Philosophical Perspective*. Pittsburgh: University of Pittsburgh Press.

Scanlon, T. M. (1975). "Preference and Urgency." *The Journal of Philosophy* 72: 655–669.

Scanlon, T. M. (1993). "Value, Desire, and Quality of Life." In M. Nussbaum & A. Sen, Eds., *The Quality of Life*, 185–200. Oxford: Oxford University Press.

Scanlon, T. M. (1998). "The Status of Well-Being." In G. B. Peterson, Ed., *The Tanner Lectures on Human Values*, Vol. 19, 91–143. Salt Lake City: The University of Utah Press.

Scott, D. & Suppes, P. (1958). "Foundational Aspects of Theories of Measurement." *The Journal of Symbolic Logic* 23: 113–128.

Seligman, M. E. P. (2002). *Authentic Happiness: Using the New Positive Psychology to Realize Your Potential for Lasting Fulfillment.* New York: Free Press.

Seligman, M. E. P. & Csikszentmihalyi, M. (2000). "Positive Psychology." *American Psychologist* 55: 5–14.

Sen, A. (1987). *Commodities and Capabilities.* New Delhi: Oxford University Press.

Snyder, C. R. & Lopez, S. J. (2002). *Handbook of Positive Psychology.* Oxford: Oxford University Press.

Sumner, L. W. (1996). *Welfare, Happiness, and Ethics.* Oxford: Clarendon.

Tiberius, V. (2006). "Well-Being: Psychological Research for Philosophers." *Philosophy Compass* 1: 493–505.

Watson, G. (1930). "Happiness Among Adult Students of Education." *The Journal of Educational Psychology* 21: 79–109.

Weale, A. (1998). "Welfare." In Edward Craig, Ed., *The Routledge Encyclopedia of Philosophy,* Vol. IX, 702–706. London: Routledge.

Winter, D. G. & Barenbaum, N. B. (1999). "History of Modern Personality Psychology Theory and Research." In Lawrence A. Pervin & Oliver P. John, Eds., *Handbook of Personality: Theory and Research,* 2nd ed. New York: Guilford.

CHAPTER 22

FACTS AND VALUES IN MODERN ECONOMICS

PARTHA DASGUPTA

SOCIAL thinkers frequently remind us that people differ in their views on what constitutes personal well-being, but that even when they don't differ, they disagree over the extent to which one person's well-being can be permitted to be traded off against another's.[1] They point out that some people are concerned mostly about inequalities in income and wealth, while others worry more about inequalities in the access to housing and education (broadly, "life chances"), while still others deplore inequalities in what economists call opportunity sets (e.g., human "capabilities," see Section 2.2). They say that even those who believe income and wealth are the surest determinants of personal well-being disagree over the extent to which inequalities in their distribution among people are defendable. Social thinkers tell us that political differences are to be traced to differences in people's conceptions of personal and social well-being. We are given to understand that people's *ethics* differ.[2]

But if you use this reading of matters to interpret contemporary economic debates, you would face a puzzle: *Professional discussions on some of the most significant issues facing Humanity today are so framed that they provoke debates over facts, not values. More strikingly, economists speak or write as though they agree on values but differ on their reading of facts.* The debates I have in mind are not only about contingent facts, but also about the pathways that characterize social, political, and ecological systems—what one could call deep facts—but they are rarely about values. It is almost as though the protagonists are embarrassed to air their values, because to do so would be to state the obvious and sound grand at the same time. I have yet to read an economic document that doesn't regard as given that involuntary unemployment should be reduced wherever it is extensive, or that destitution should be a thing of the past, or that it would be horrible if the rain forests were to disappear. But there are many disagreements about the most effective ways to reduce involuntary unemployment, destitution, and the extinction rates of rain forests. Disagreements about the magnitude of involuntary unemployment in a country or region, or the extent of destitution in today's world or the rate at which the rain forests are disappearing are also a commonplace. Similarly, the often violent confrontations we see periodically on television over globalization look as though they are prompted by the question whether the process, in the form it has taken shape in recent decades, benefits most people or whether it hurts a substantial number of the poorest of the poor.[3]

It has been shown by philosophers that facts and values are entangled. Even the models we construct to make sense of the world around us reflect prior judgments of what's important and what is not. Such judgments are in part influenced by one's values and personal interests (Putnam 2002). But they are influenced by many other things besides (e.g., the desire to try out an idea or technique just "for size"). Which is why the entanglement can be a source of misunderstanding. Someone who is concerned specifically about the factual aspects of a phenomenon could be thought by others to be making or promoting strong assumptions about value. So, it is possible to overlook that even when values determine—or play a major role in determining—the questions someone is interested in, the answers they arrive at don't necessarily involve value judgments; nor that resolutions of factual questions necessarily settle those normative questions with which they are entangled. Of course, it may be that deep down those economists who, say, worry about the way humanity treats nature and those who regard markets and politics to work well enough to protect and promote nature *do* hold different values, but filter their perceptions of the way the world works through their distinctive ethical receptors—all too often, perhaps, through their private interests. But even if they cloak their ethical differences or private interests by arguing about facts, it is the factual character of the issues they argue about and is the point I am making here.[4]

The near-exclusive engagement over facts on the part of working economists has led public intellectuals to conclude that modern economics must be an ethical desert. A few years ago the late Sir Bernard Williams read a paper at the British Academy in which he attacked economists for inferring human well-being from the choices people actually make. I don't know who had advised Williams on what economists actually write, but he was evidently unaware of a huge empirical literature on valuation (e.g., placing a value on environmental resources) that goes far beyond what he imagined it does.[5]

Such misconceptions have been fuelled by my old friend, Amartya Sen, who, in a pair of books that have been much noted by ethicists, presented what can at best be called a crude caricature of modern economics (Sen,1987, 1999). Among other things, Sen (1987) wrote, "…it is precisely (the) narrowing of the broad (Adam) Smithian view of human beings, in modern economics, that can be seen as one of the major deficiencies of modern economic theory. This impoverishment is closely related to the distancing of economics from ethics." Sen concluded with an observation as general as could be, one nobody could but warm to, that economics and ethics have much to learn from each other. But in the social sciences, general conclusions that appear to be incontrovertible *and* have a warm glow about them are the most suspect. Moreover, Sen didn't point out to the general reader, nor did Williams appear to appreciate, that the shortcuts social scientists resort to are influenced by the scope of the problem they happen to be studying.

Consider the following questions, which are representative of the kinds asked of economists:

(1) The traffic on a highway is heavy, causing delays. There is a proposal to enlarge the road. Should it be accepted, should highway charges be introduced instead, or should the public transport system be extended?

(2) The government in a poor country has, for some decades, been subsidizing the use of the country's natural-resource base. Should it continue to do so? Should the subsidies be enlarged, or should they be reduced?

(3) There are plans among international bodies to help rebuild a poor country, which has been racked by civil strife and corrupt government. What should the mix of government engagement, private enterprise, and civic involvement be?

There is a clear sense in which reasoned responses to the successive questions would be more elaborate, more hesitant, requiring greater sensitivity to life's nuances. For example, it can be argued that people's preferences inferred from choices they make over the use of public and private transport and roads and rail are a reasonable basis for a response to the first question on the list. (How else would we know what the traffic will bear?) Even if it weren't entirely reasonable, I don't believe that Aristotle, whose writings are regarded by moral philosophers as the touchstone of speculations on the ethical life, could help to decide how else one should go about advising what to do. Aristotle (for that matter, Adam Smith, also) does have useful things to say on the third question, but only as a prelude. In sections 4 and 5 I show that as matters stand today, substantive responses to it require a good dose of modern economics, with all its technicalities. I show also that they require, in addition, involvement with anthropology, ecology, demography, epidemiology, psychology, and the nutrition and political sciences. Ethics, on the other hand, would appear to have little to offer at the moment.

There is a reason for this. Modern economics is built on broad ethical foundations, capable of being reduced as special cases to the various ethical theories that are currently on offer (Section 2). Immediately after the publication of Rawls's theory of justice (Rawls 1972), for example, economists derived the theory's implications for the allocation of resources (among contemporaries (Atkinson 1973; Phelps 1973) and across generations (Arrow 1973; Dasgupta 1974; Solow 1974)). They could do it because the foundations of welfare economics were broad enough to permit Rawls's theory to be adopted. But since the basis of welfare economic reasoning was established decades ago, research economists don't find it necessary to rehearse them. The ethical content of modern economics (e.g., that the distribution of individual well-beings matters and that evaluating distributions requires interpersonal comparisons of well-being) is regarded instead as unspoken assumptions in research publications. As the social, political, and ecological pathways of significance for economists, even at their clearest, are at best translucent, contemporary economists spend most of their intellectual energy trying to uncover the trade-offs societies face, rather than the trade-offs that are ethically permissible. To put it another way, economists resist choosing among the various ethical theories currently offered, but work instead from the other, very general, end, often searching for policy mixes that could be shown to enhance human well-being no matter which conception of well-being is adopted and which justification has been offered for adopting it. What is offered in welfare economics is, therefore, frequently a menu of policies, the intellectual battle being conducted over the appropriate reading of the pathways that lead policies to eventualities.

Ethics is missing from the background in none of this. But ethicists, following Sen, would appear to imagine otherwise. (John Rawls was one remarkable exception, and a reason why he has been taken so seriously by economists.) Robbins (1932), for example, continues to be a favorite target for ridicule (Sen 1987; Putnam 2002), for allegedly having steered economists toward a "value-free" enterprise. Here is Putnam (2003, 401) on this:

> "(My) approach demands that we stop attempting to quarantine ethical reflection from economics in the name of "science"...and return to the kind of reasoned and humane evaluation of social wellbeing that Adam Smith saw as an essential part of the task of an economist."

But Robbins wrote over seventy years ago, and the discipline I know to be economics has moved on since then. Putnam (2003, 396) also instructs us that "...the subject of welfare economics... *requires* that we be able to make, and meaningfully discuss, precisely claims about 'the morality' of income distribution, about 'the morality' of using or not using per capita income as our *sole* measure of welfare, about the priorities that *should* be assigned to education, to reducing levels of disease, to reducing the levels of malnutrition...." (Italics in original). And he complains that economists don't do what should be required of them. In a similar vein, the philosopher Martha Nussbaum (2003, 413) speaks of "...the relatively desolate intellectual landscape of economics...," before pausing to confess, "I am not an economist."

As an unreconstructed research economist, I find it hard not to take these charges personally. Here I am, having tried throughout my academic life to uncover and analyze social phenomena and to arrive at policy prescriptions—learning methods and techniques from allied disciplines in order to do so—only to be told that I am no better than an oaf in clodhoppers, rampaging through the human condition. I'm not even sure what to do with the ethicists' charges, other than to note that, over a half-century ago, (Bergson) Burk (1938) and Samuelson (1947) offered a normative framework for policy evaluation, and that the subject "public economics," which in its present guise is now over thirty years old, has routinely engaged in overt ethical reasoning.

But, of course, merely to refer to (Bergson) Burk (1938) and Samuelson (1947) won't do. This paper, therefore, sets itself two related tasks. First, I sketch the ethical reasoning underlying modern economics. This is done in Part I (sections 1 to 3) and the transitional section (Section 4). I want to demonstrate the sense in which contemporary economists regard the *foundations* of welfare economics to be a settled matter. Secondly, in Section 4 and Part II (Section 5), I present a case study, involving five decades of discussion on the problems of economic development in poor countries. The case study is designed to illustrate the thesis of this paper, that professional debates among contemporary economists on even such ethically loaded concerns as poverty and distributive justice have been about facts, not ethical values. To be sure, there is much in the literature on economic development that can be criticised—I offer one particular set of criticisms myself in Section 5.6. But any reasoned critique of the literature would focus on omissions of facts (e.g., the neglect of local ecology in studies of rural poverty), not insensitivity to ethical values. I hope the two parts and the transitional section (Section 4), taken together, go some way toward explaining why ethics has taken a back seat in contemporary economic debates and why economists have been entirely justified to place it there. The real, all-things-considered normative advances that have been made in the subject are due to an improved understanding of social and ecological facts, not to continual reflections on the meaning of poverty or distributive justice, or even of development.[6]

A more detailed plan of the paper is as follows:

Section 1 offers an account of the contemporary economist's model of human agency in a market setting and of the ways in which individual choices are related to collective behavior in the market place. I also sketch the ways in which the model has been adapted to accommodate decision making in non-market environments. sections 2 and 3 build on the model to offer an account of the ethical foundations of modern economics. Although welfare economics is thought to be insensitive to the language of rights, I show that contemporary economists have incorporated rights in their ethics. I describe the way ideas of human rights and human goods— including the recent emphasis placed by a number of ethicists and development activists on "capabilities"—can be and have been subsumed by economists under an overarching notion of human well-being (Section 2).

In Section 3 a distinction is drawn between the "constituents" and "determinants" of well-being. Whereas ethicists are temperamentally drawn to the constituents, economists study the determinants. The nature of the aggregation exercise—from individual to social well-being—is then sketched. In Section 3.1 it is noted that social well-being is a desideratum not only of such teleological theories as classical utilitarianism, but also of a number of intuitionist theories and modern contractual theories of justice. In sections 3.1–3.3 I also show that social well-being can be formalized in three equivalent ways. I show that the third formulation, defined as it is on the determinants of well-being, forms the basis of social cost-benefit analysis. The concept of social well-being is then studied in the context of Kenneth Arrow's famous theorem concerning the general impossibility of constructing democratic voting rules (Section 3.4).

I have had to deploy a certain amount of mathematical formalism in Section 3. This was unavoidable: that there are three equivalent ways of formulating the concept of social well-being is a mathematical fact. I hasten to add though that I don't *do* mathematics in Section 3, but merely use some elementary mathematical notation to illustrate the points that need to be made.

Section 4 is transitional. It responds to a recent complaint of ethicists, that the model of human agency adopted in modern economics is inapplicable to circumstances where people face tragic choices. I study empirical evidence drawn from the world's poorest households concerning allocations of food and health-care among members differing in their gender and age, and on decisions bearing on fertility and reproductive health, to argue that the economist's theory of choice is very much applicable to behavior when people are forced to choose from among terrible courses of action.

Part II (Section 5) contains an account of the evolution of modern development economics. I show that the focus of study of poor economies has changed time and again in response to empirical directives and that debates over policy have typically been generated by disagreements over facts, not values. I first offer reasons that, in the early years of development economics, growth in gross national product (GNP) came to be regarded as the key indicator of economic progress (Section 5.1). This is followed by a discussion of the questions that arose once GNP growth was adopted as a welfare index. They include an exploration of possible tensions between economic growth and egalitarian distributions of income, of the arguments in favor of removing government controls over trade and domestic production, and of uncovering ways of selecting public policies that are consonant with development goals (sections 5.2–5.3). Findings on household food consumption and household behavior (in particular reproductive decisions and the links between female education and fertility behavior) are interpreted next (sections 5.4 and 5.5). I then argue that none of these issues can be addressed satisfactorily unless a study is made of the pathways that connect village poverty in the world's poorest countries to the use of the local natural-resource base there. Both are in turn shown to be related to the prevailing system of property rights to the resource base. This, relatively recent line of inquiry into the persistence of acute poverty in the world's poorest regions, is developed in Section 5.6.

But there is a viewpoint, expressed in advocacy writings by development activists, that sees the lack of economic progress in sub-Saharan Africa and parts of the

Indian subcontinent as being due, in large measure, to a choice of economic policies that don't take people seriously. In Sections 5.7 to 5.9 I argue against this viewpoint, by offering additional evidence to show that differences of opinion among economists over development polices have arisen from differences in the reading of facts, not ethical values, and that people have always been at the centre of attention in the economics of development.

The debates within development economics that are reviewed in the transitional section (Section 4) and Part II don't comprise a full list. The selection of themes here has been much influenced by my own expertise and engagements. But readers wishing to visit most other debates within development economics will find that my thesis holds there too: contemporary economists analyze facts, not values. Part I is intended to explain why.

I. Values

1. Utility Functions and Preference Orderings

Modern economics—by which I mean the style of economics taught and practiced in today's graduate schools—is not much older than the Second World War. In its earliest developments the subject was much influenced by the sharp fact-value distinction prevalent in positivist writings of the 1930s. One task facing economists at the time (at least in the English speaking world) was to elucidate the theory of consumer demand, which studies the dependence of the demand for goods and services in market economies on prices and incomes.

The importance of this task is almost self-evident. If you want to make economic forecasts in a market economy—say, of the effect of government tax policies on the demand for goods and services—you need to discover the functional forms of those demands. Of course, if you want also to identify desirable tax policies, you need to ask more. You need to ask, among other things, why the functional forms are what they are; more generally, you need to ask what motivates people to demand what they do and what constraints they face when they make their choices; and you need to ask at what rates any one person's demands ought to be traded off against those of others. In order to address those questions, you have to dig deeper.

Toward that end, one strand of late-nineteenth and early-twentieth century economics (Edgeworth 1881) was based on the idea that commodity demands are generated by utility maximizing agents, the thought being that the consumption of goods and services yields *utility*—measurable in cardinal units—and that consumers seek to maximize something like the expected value of the utility they would enjoy from consuming goods and services. Interpretations of the concept of utility differed among economists, just as they did among utilitarian philosophers. Some interpreted it as "pleasure," others thought of it as "satisfaction," while yet others regarded it as something like "welfare" or "well-being." Whatever the exact interpretation, the primitive concept in this theory of demand was that of a *utility function*, which is a numerical function defined on commodity bundles.

But there was another strand of thought (Pareto 1909, Slutsky 1915) that regarded someone's utility function to be no more than a numerical representation of an underlying ordering of alternatives, on the basis of which the person does his choosing. The alternatives can be thought of as states of affair, or social states (defined in their generality in Section 2.1). When the theory is applied to demand analysis, however, the alternatives are commodity bundles. The primitive concept in this theory of demand is that of an *ordering* of commodity bundles (sometimes called a "preference ordering" of commodity bundles): Utility is a derived notion.[7] Although the theory is frequently associated with Hicks and Allen (1934) and is regarded as modern economics' first showpiece, their work was a rediscovery of Pareto (1909) and Slutsky (1915) in the English speaking world.

The theory of commodity demand was designed originally to study the consumer who appears today in elementary economics textbooks. About the only thing this person is reported to be doing is buying and selling goods in markets where the prices are given. To this consumer, a feasible social state is a commodity bundle he can afford. The theory focuses on a particular type of personal freedom, where the constraints someone faces are shaped only by market prices and the earned and unearned incomes he is able to command. Today we all know him as *Economic Man*.

Intellectuals find Economic Man impossible to take. Since they also like to think that economics continues to do little more than offer accounts of Economic Man, they find modern economics impossible to take as well. They accuse Economic Man of being deracinated, alienated, and atomized, and liken him to a "balloon tethered to nothing." They charge economists with imagining that the motivations of Economic Man reflect his "rational self-interest," and insist that they can't reflect his rational self-interest, because there is no adequate self for such a person to be. Where are his emotions, they ask; where are the tragic choices he faces from time to time; where is his sense of fellowship with others; his commitment to causes and to his own self; and what about all those activities he engages in outside the market?[8]

The creators of the theory of consumer choice had expressly set themselves a very limited goal. They took Economic Man's political, social, and family engagements as given. For example, they recognized that in every economy there are a number of *public* goods (of varying quality), such as security, the legal framework, cultural treasures, places of tranquillity, public health systems, and knowledge. They assumed that decisions on the supply of public goods are reached through the political process.[9] In fact, even before the advent of modern consumer-choice theory, economists had noted that transactions can give rise to *externalities*, and that a central task of government is to curb or encourage externalities by means of taxes and subsidies (Pigou 1920) and by establishing markets for externalities (Lindahl 1958 [1928]).

The concept of externalities generalizes the notion of public goods (Arrow 1971). By an "externality," economists mean the effects that transactions have on people who have not been a party to the negotiations that led to the transactions. This linking of externalities to the legal system (in particular, to the structure of property rights) was the central insight of Coase (1960). In a pure market economy, primary education and public health measures, to take only two examples, involve externalities. If I become literate, I benefit, but so do others, because they can now communicate with me via nonoral means. Similarly, if I am immunized against an infectious disease, I benefit, but so do others, because they are no longer in danger from me. That is why there can be an under-supply of goods and services conferring positive externalities. By the same token, there can be an oversupply of goods and services inflicting negative externalities (e.g., pollution). A commodity is *private* if transactions in it involve no externalities.

One of the commodities Economic Man purchases in the market is leisure. Consumer-choice theorists imagined that Economic Man spends his leisure time not only chatting, gardening, and reading books, but also engaging in those political and social activities that help to determine the extent of taxation for financing the supply of public goods, for curbing negative externalities and encouraging positive externalities, and for redistributing income and wealth. However, in the immediate post-War years, economists didn't study those other activities. No doubt markets and politics are intertwined, but as there was then no adequate "political economy" to offer guidance on what those links could be, expenditures on the production of public goods and externalities were taken to be incurred by a government bent on maximizing social well-being (sections 3.1 to 3.3). Government decisions on taxation, redistribution, and the supply of public goods were taken to be a given backdrop against which individual choices in the market for private goods and externalities are made. As we confirm later, the assumptions concerning Economic Man's motivations and activities reflect sociology, not psychology.[10] There was a large ceteris paribus clause in the study of Economic Man.

However, contemporary economists entertain wide-ranging interpretations of utility. A person's ordering of alternatives could reflect a lot more than just the chooser's personal preferences. It could reflect an amalgam of his preferences and purposes, his personal and social values, his beliefs about what others are like, what actions they and nature are likely to take, and so forth. Individuals are taken to be pluralists in their intellectual and emotional makeup.

The shift in the notion of utility from a primitive concept to a derived notion has been complete and permanent. Moreover, a high or low value of utility, per se, has no meaning in the economist's account. What has meaning are utility *comparisons*—across social states and across people. Of course, if the underlying ordering possesses sufficient structure, the corresponding utility would possess a cardinal representation, and comparisons among social states could yield utility differences that are large, or small, or medium relative to one another.[11] The theory even allows for "tragic choices" (Section 4). I think economists have been ill-advised to call numerical representations of orderings utility functions: it has misled many anti-utilitarian ethicists into thinking that modern welfare economics is beyond the pale. But a research enterprise should be judged by what it accomplishes, not by its ill-chosen nomenclature.[12]

2. Institutions and Human Flourishing

An alternative to the program that starts with individuals' orderings of states of affair is to ask what bodies of laws, institutions, and public policies are most likely to enable people to flourish. The tactic is to study the effect of the character of the public sphere on personal decisions—and back again—in an iterative way. I am thinking here of the kind of enquiry that was undertaken by Rawls (1972). But it didn't start with Rawls. It has been a recurring theme in modern economics.

To begin with, advances in modeling strategic behavior made it possible for economists to admit a richer set of alternatives than the one faced by Economic Man. So, the alternatives (we will call them "social states") are taken now to be more than just bundles of market commodities. They are mixtures of marketed goods, public goods, goods produced within the household, and time and resources spent on education, politics, networking, even gossiping. A social state includes the allocation of resources (who gets what, when, where, and why) and anything else deemed relevant for personal or social choice (see later).[13] Moreover, a key notion in the social sciences—*commitment*—is no longer a primitive in economics. Commitment to an undertaking can be seen as being strategic, as a way of tying one's hands, as it were, so that the undertaking is credible, not only to others, but to one's own self too.

The ordering of alternatives revealed from the choices an agent makes depends on economic institutions. For example, that the concern someone has toward the poor in the minimal state should be expected to be different from the concern the same person would have in a welfare state; the reason being that, in the welfare state the person faces additional taxation to finance redistribution, whereas, in the minimal state, redistribution can only be achieved by means of voluntary transfers. In principle, the person shouldn't have to worry about the poor in the welfare state (it's the government's task to enforce redistributive measures). In contrast, she will be active on their behalf in the minimal state. Since the choices the person faces in the two societies differ greatly, the individual chooses differently.

2.1 Well-Being: Goods and Rights

The primary concept in the research program that asks what bodies of laws, institutions, and public policies are most likely to enable people to flourish is an individual's *well-being,* which is to be distinguished from his utility. Unlike utility, well-being isn't necessarily related to the ordering on the basis of which the person chooses. The centrality in the realization of well-being of social institutions and the latter's role as a basis for resource allocation is clear enough: social life is an expression of a person's sense of social unity, and commodities and an absence of coercion are the means by which people can pursue their own conception of the good.

The objects of choice in ethical theories are social states. Formally, a *social state* is a complete history of the world, extending from the known past to the indefinite future—as complete, that is, as current powers of discrimination will allow. *All* ethical theories evaluate social states; the theories differ in what is ethically significant in social states. One broad class of theories begins by identifying *individual well-beings* as the ethically significant features of social states and proceeds to aggregate them into a measure of *social well-being* (Section 3). In what follows, I report on that strand of welfare economics that has been built on those theories, although environmental economists frequently include additional features of social states in their evaluative exercises.

As the conceptual move from individual to social well-being involves an aggregation exercise, welfare economics is viewed by moral philosophers as being "goal-based." Rights-based theories are frequently offered in contrast. "The distinction between rights-based and goal-based theories," writes Waldron (1984, 13), "[lies in the idea] that a requirement is rights-based if it is generated by a concern for some individual interest, goal-based if it is generated by concern for something taken to be an interest of society as a whole." Rights-based theories according to this reckoning reject aggregation, because it is held that in such an exercise the interests of the individual can get swamped by claims made on behalf of a multitude of others. "A goal," writes Dworkin (1978, 91), "is a non-individuated political aim." Goal-based theories are thought to be collectivist. Worse, they are dismissed as being technocratic, formulaic, and ultimately, "algorithmic" (O'Neill 1986).

I have never felt I understood the distinction drawn by these authors. In the theories they commend, rights don't go against interest; they reinforce some interests against the claims of other, less urgent or vital, interests. Moreover, rights need to be justified; they can't be plucked from air. Even those rights that are regarded as fundamental have as their basis the thought that they are necessary for human flourishing. They are seen as protecting and promoting a certain class of human interests, such as agency, independence, choice, and self-determination.[14] The starting point in this line of thought is the unarguable fact that different people know different things, possess different skills and talents, and not all people can learn or observe the same things. These features of life offer a powerful justification for the right to individual discretion in thinking, choosing, and acting (Section 2.2). Freedom of expression, including a nondocile press ("the public have a right to know"), are examples. (They enable people to create and innovate.) The private right to certain kinds of property is another. (It can be justified on the grounds that it creates incentives to accumulate and innovate, enabling economies, and thus people, to prosper.) Democracy is still another. (There is some evidence that in poor countries democracy has helped to spur economic development; Section 5.7.) So also is it more generally with institutions, such as the household: it has instrumental value for the individual. (The cost per person in a household declines initially with numbers in the household.) The search for the instrumental worth of institutions, activities, and goods has been a recurring feature of modern economics.

Meanwhile, problems of interpretation have been compounded by the claim that fundamental rights are inviolable: "Individuals have rights, and there are things no person or group may do to them [without violating their rights]" (Nozick 1974, ix). Such rights impose rigid constraints on what people may or may not do. Social states in which Nozickian rights are violated to the slightest extent are rejected in Nozick's scheme of things. Trade-offs are not permitted. In an otherwise very different theory of justice, Rawls (1972) arrived at a lexicographically ordered hierarchy of rights.

Moral philosophers often say that theories that regard social well-being as the ethically significant feature of social states permit trade-offs between different people's interests, whereas rights-based theories prohibit trade-offs between urgent (or vital) interests and mere desires. But there are always degrees to which interests are frustrated and the corresponding rights (if there are corresponding rights) aren't met. Moreover, as inviolability means a zero rate of trade-off, we wouldn't depart from the practical spirit of inviolability (assuming that rights are inviolable), if we allowed trade-offs between rights, and between rights and other goods, such as utility, provided that the trade-off rate is very small in appropriate regions of the space of states of affair.

Nevertheless, the language that contemporary economists use to discuss public policy could appear to be at variance with the generality I am claiming here for the ethical foundations of modern economics. There is a familiar caricature of welfare economics, that it reduces dilemmas in social ethics to the formula: "Choose x so as to maximize $W(x)$, subject to the constraint $F(x) \geq 0$." If this isn't the most narrow-minded, goal-based, algorithmic social ethics, one may ask, what is?

In fact the formula is consistent with any number of ethical theories. The formula doesn't specify the domain and form of the function $W(x)$. (In sections 3.1 and 3.2 we confirm that modern economics isn't restricted to any particular domain or form of W.) Nor is the formula dependent on any particular *justification* for the domain and form of $W(x)$ that has been adopted, which means that it can accommodate a wide variety of ethical theories (Section 3.1). The stricture, "Max W," isn't a monopoly of classical utilitarianism; we see below that there are prominent contractual and intuitionist theories that also give rise to it.

2.2 *"Capabilities" as Well-Being*

To illustrate, human rights are frequently interpreted today by ethicists and development activists in terms of the extent to which human *capabilities* are protected and promoted. Formally, capabilities are taken to be "the alternative combinations of functionings that are feasible for [a person] to achieve" (Sen 1999, 75). A seeming advantage of working with capabilities is that they appear to be clear and objective, whereas the notion of well-being is vague and, possibly, subjective. The problem is that it hasn't been uncommon of authors to champion capabilities as an alternative to the welfare economist's mode of discourse even while displaying an unwillingness to offer any hint about how various capabilities are to be compared with one another.

Capabilities are a special version of what economists call *opportunity sets*. The earliest attempts (e.g., Suppes 1987) to rank opportunity sets without first offering an account of ways to value and rank the objects in those sets showed that the enterprise wasn't going to work. Since then, however, we have been offered capability theories built on air. Martha Nussbaum (reported approvingly in Putnam 2003) has produced a list of nine "central human capabilities," *every one of which*, she insists, is "...non-negotiable up to some threshold level (which, typically, will be specified over time by judicial and legislative action)."[15] The problem is that it is all too easy to regard "central human capabilities" as being non-negotiable when one is under no obligation to estimate the costs required to protect and promote them. What would Nussbaum's prescription be if a country is so poor that it simply can't afford every one of the nine central human capabilities for all members of society? When the protection and promotion of rights demand resources, there is no getting away from admitting trade-offs and from having to value those trade-offs.[16]

Many would regard it absurd that an ethical theory could value the capacity to form life plans but remain indifferent to its realization and the experiential states that go with its realization. (Rawls 1972, in an extended discussion [424–433], called the connection between well-being and the exercise of our capacities the Aristotelian Principle.) The acquisition of skills involves resources, meaning that there are trade-offs among them. But not all skills have equal weight. Numeracy and literacy are *basic* skills; they prove useful to people no matter what they wish to be and do. Health is also a vital aspect of well-being. Good health is not only desired and desirable in itself, it is also necessary for one's projects and purposes regardless of what they happen to be. In a similar vein, it wouldn't be odd if someone were to insist on her freedom to speak even if she had no immediate intention of speaking. We value freedom of speech because it would be vital to our well-being under many, possibly unforeseen, circumstances. In contrast, there are skills and privileges that are so specialized that only those with very specific aptitudes and desires would rationally wish to acquire them.

Arrow (1995) has built on these considerations to show why the freedom to be and do should be valued (Arrow calls that freedom, *flexibility*) and why capability sets that include health and basic skills are more valuable than those that don't. He has also shown that the ethical worth of capability sets rests on the prior notion of well-being. To follow Arrow's argument, consider an individual deliberating over alternative life plans. We index possible capability sets by the number n, and we let F_n be the capability set n. Let us denote an element of F_n by x_n. We think of x_n as a life plan, which can be interpreted as a combination of functionings that are feasible for the person to achieve. Imagine now that, in the first instance, the individual chooses a capability set from a collection of capability sets and that subsequently the individual selects a life plan from that chosen set.[17]

That future contingencies are uncertain means that the worth of any life plan to the individual is uncertain. So we let the random variable $\tilde{\varepsilon}$ reflect that uncertainty and imagine that the person has to choose a capability set *before* observing the realization of $\tilde{\varepsilon}$. For simplicity of exposition we assume that *after* she chooses a capability set, the uncertainty resolves itself (i.e., the true value of $\tilde{\varepsilon}$ is revealed) and that the individual then proceeds to select a life plan from the capability set that was chosen. Let $V(x_n, \varepsilon)$ be the person's well-being if the person were to choose x_n from F_n when ε is the realization of $\tilde{\varepsilon}$. We now let $\bar{x}_n(\varepsilon)$ be the person's best life plan in F_n, should ε be realized.[18] As the person chooses a capability set before $\tilde{\varepsilon}$ reveals itself, the person values each capability set, n, in terms of that person's uncertain well-being under the optimum policy $\bar{x}_n(\varepsilon)$. For concreteness, let us imagine that choice under uncertainty involves maximizing expected well-being. (It may be that the probabilities in the exercise are entirely subjective.) In that case, the value the individual would attach to F_n is $E[V(\bar{x}_n(\varepsilon), \varepsilon)]$, where E is the expectation operator. Write $V(n) = E[V(\bar{x}_n(\varepsilon), \varepsilon)]$. It follows that $V(n)$ is the value she would attach to capability set n. Notice that all capability sets can be ranked by the individual in question.

Consider two capability sets n and n^*. n is worth more than n^* to the person iff $V(n) > V(n^*)$. Arrow's analysis shows that capability theory reduces to an ethics that is grounded on individual and social well-being.[19]

3. Individual and Social Well-Being

In measuring well-being, be that of a person or of a collectivity of persons, one may study either well-being's constituents or its determinants. In practice, a mixture of constituents and determinants are used, as for example, in the United Nations Development Programme's composite Human Development Index (HDI).[20] But it pays to study them separately, which is what we do in the following section.

3.1 *Direct Measures, 1: Constituents*

A person's well-being is composed of a variety of objects (health and satisfaction at work are but two). They are the *constituents* of well-being. As well-being itself is an aggregate, measuring someone's well-being involves an aggregation exercise; which means acknowledging trade-offs among the constituents, implying in turn that weights are awarded to the constituents.

Say a person values health, but also values a creative life that (in this individual's case) involves a certain neglect of health. Improvements in the individual's health and enrichment of a creative life involve a trade-off. In order to evaluate the individual's personal good she could use health as the benchmark and reflect on what weight she should rationally place on the creative life. Alternatively, the individual could use creative life as the benchmark and reflect on what weight she should rationally award to health. Unless the person suffers from reasoning defects, it should not matter which way she evaluates the alternatives: the individual will reach the same conclusion.[21] It should not be supposed, however, that the weights she rationally places on these two constituents are fixed. If her health were bad, she would place a higher weight—at the margin—on her health relative to her creative life, than if her health were good, other things being equal.

Consider an N-person society. People are denoted variously by i, j, and k (i, j, $k = 1, 2, \ldots, N$). They are not necessarily to be thought of as contemporaries, as the set $\{1, 2, \ldots, N\}$ could include future people. Let x be a social state and $V_i(x)$ individual i's well-being in x. $V_i(x)$ is a scalar function. As it is an aggregate of the constituents of i's well-being, the units in which $V_i(x)$ is measured could be any one of the constituents of well-being. For example, it could be health (measured in terms of, say, i's nutritional status).

Those personal characteristics that are ethically relevant are embodied in the V_i functions. Other things being equal, the well-being function of an infant differs from that of an adult male, that of an adult male differs from that of a lactating female, and so on. The point is that, if nothing else, their nutritional, health-care, and emotional needs differ. The subscript under person i's well-being function captures such differences. When nutritionists and applied econometricians refer to "adult-equivalent" scales for food or income needs in a household, it is to this they allude. For empirical purposes, they use deflators and magnifiers to construct the well-being functions of various categories of people from a representative adult's well-being function.[22]

Policy evaluation involves well-being comparisons. Imagine that person k is the evaluator. So k could be a citizen (thinking about things before casting his vote on political candidates; see Section 3.4), or k could be an ethicist hired to offer guidance to the government, or k could be a government decision maker, and so on. Now k's evaluation of person i's well-being is unlikely to be the same as someone else's evaluation of i's well-being. This isn't to claim that well-being is an entirely subjective matter (although aspects of it surely are). But if nothing else, there are always differences in the way any two people measure the same object. Let $V_{ki}(x)$ denote k's evaluation of i's well-being in social state x. Suppose now that, in k's evaluation, individual i's well-being is predicted to be higher if policy A, rather than policy B, were chosen, but that the reverse is predicted for individual j. How should k rank the policies?

It may be assumed that k has a theory of how policies lead to outcomes. Here we are to interpret outcomes (or consequences) as social states. So, if k believes that A will result in social state x and B in social state y, his role as a policy evaluator would be to compare x and y.

Social well-being is an aggregate of individual well-beings. Imagine that certain types of interpersonal comparisons of individual well-beings are possible (e.g., that person i is healthier than person j). Like individual well-being functions, social well-being is a scalar. The units in which social well-being is measured could be someone's well-being, which, as we observed earlier, would be measured in terms of one of the constituents of that person's well-being. To give an example, it could be that social well-being is measured in terms of an index of person 1's health (e.g., nutritional status).

Let us write k's evaluation of social well-being in x as $W_k(x)$, where

$$W_k(x) = W_k(V_{k1}(x), V_{k2}(x), \ldots, V_{kN}(x)). \tag{22.1}$$

k would judge x to be socially more desirable than y if and only if $W_k(x) > W_k(y)$. W_k is k's *social well-being function*. It embodies ethical values, not only through each of the V_{ki} functions, but also through W_k's functional form.

Suppose $W_k(x) > W_k(y)$. Since k believes that policy A leads to x and policy B leads to y, he would recommend A over B. This mode of reasoning is called *social cost-benefit analysis*.

A relatively weak ethical principle, much used in modern economics, is that W_k satisfies the criterion of *efficiency*: if x and y are identical in all respects other than that at least one of the constituents of someone's well-being is greater in x than in y, then $W_k(x) > W_k(y)$.[23]

Sen, like Isaiah Berlin before him, has argued in favor of ethical theories that admit a plurality of human values, and has remarked: "To insist that there should be only one homogeneous magnitude that we value is to reduce drastically the range of our evaluative reasoning." (Sen 1987, 77). Note, though, that the ethical reasoning k deploys to arrive at the V_{ki}s in expression (1) insists on no such thing. In fact, it involves the reverse of what Sen seems to be accusing modern economists of doing. Contemporary economists don't claim that people value some homogeneous magnitude. Instead, they see k as arriving at the homogeneous magnitude V_{ki} *from* the plurality of values i holds. The constituents of well-being themselves reflect the plurality of values.

Economists have explored alternative structures of W when the Vs are cardinally measurable. Of particular interest is the case where W is additive in the Vs (it is enormously useful in both theoretical and empirical applications). In that case social well-being in x is

$$W_k(x) = V_{k1}(x) + V_{k2}(x) + \ldots + V_{kN}(x). \tag{22.1a}$$

Formula (22.1a) satisfies the criterion for efficiency. It is also harbored by a variety of ethical theories. For example, if the V_{ki}s are taken to be "happiness" or "satisfaction" and the views of an "ideally rational and impartial spectator" (Rawls 1972, 184) are sought, (22.1a) would represent classical utilitarianism. However, the additive form in (22.1a) isn't restricted to teleological theories, it can also be arrived at from intuitionist, even contractual considerations. Koopmans (1972) and Maskin (1978) identified intuitively appealing ethical axioms, which, when imposed on $W_k(x)$, require that $W_k(x)$ is the additive form (22.1a). In an earlier work, Harsanyi (1955) had arrived at (22.1a) from an exercise that Rawls subsequently called a hypothetical choice behind the "veil of ignorance." In contrast to Rawls, Harsanyi had postulated that, when evaluating a social state, the chooser would assign an equal probability of being in any person's situation.

Experience shows that there are enormous computational advantages in adopting (22.1a); the fundamental papers by Ramsey (1928) and Koopmans (1965) on optimum saving and Mirrlees (1971) on optimum income taxation are among the most prominent examples.

A much used alternative to (1a) is the Rawlsian form:

$$W_k(x) = \text{(lexicographic)-min} \{V_{k1}(x), V_{k2}(x), \ldots, V_{kN}(x)\}. \tag{22.1b}$$

Note that (22.1b) also satisfies the criterion for efficiency.

Hammond (1976) and d'Aspremont and Gevers (1977) provided axiomatic foundations for formula (22.1b).[24] Atkinson (1973) used (22.1b) to estimate optimum income taxation in a simple version of a model pioneered by Mirrlees (1971), where private incentives play a role in wealth creation. By making a not-implausible set of assumptions regarding individual motivation, Atkinson showed that taxation would not be significantly more progressive if (22.1b) were adopted than if (22.1a) were adopted. This is an unexpected result, which means that it is informative. (I shall offer an explanation for the finding in Section 5.3.) It also has a wider message: given the way the world probably is, it can be that even apparently radically different ethical theories arrive at similar policy conclusions.

3.2 Direct Measures, 2: Utility and Other Goods

In fact, economists haven't usually adopted expression (22.1) to formulate the concept of social well-being. They have devised a different, but equivalent, method. (Later we will see why they have done so.)

Imagine that evaluator k knows the ordering on the basis of which i would choose. Let $U_{ki}(x)$ be the numerical function k constructs from i's ordering: it is k's construction of i's utility function. Theoretical economists typically define social well-being on individual utilities, not on individual well-beings (Samuelson 1947; Graaff 1962). In a classic treatise on public finance, however, Musgrave (1959) argued that basing social well-being exclusively on individual utilities is an improper restriction because of the presence of what he called *merit goods*. Such goods are worth more than what they contribute to utility. As we noted in Section 2, individual and group "rights" also constitute a class of merit goods. Many regard the distribution of wealth to be a merit good. Musgrave argued that when we evaluate social states, the supply of merit goods ought to be valued over and beyond the contribution they make to individual utilities. This reasoning has been pervasive in applied welfare and development economics.

Well-being isn't the same as utility. The two are different because people not infrequently choose for reasons that have little to do with their own well-being. As we noted earlier, the context can matter. It could be that a person is socially obliged to choose in certain ways, or it could be that the person is led to value things not in that person's own interest. More generally, many choices are made within the context of the household. Such choices can be a reflection of the household's internal dynamics (for example, the balance of power and responsibility among its members). In a series of books and articles that are dismissive of much modern economics, Amartya Sen has argued that individual utilities cannot be accepted as the only basis for social evaluation, because, among other things, "...deprived people tend to come to terms with their deprivation" (Sen 1999, 63). But in reiterating this over the years, he has been pushing against an open door. I know of no economist who has argued, for example, that there is little need to invest in women's reproductive health programs in the poorest countries because poor women there are resigned to their fate and don't appear much to insist on them; or that governments in poor countries ought not to invest in primary education in rural areas because parents there don't care for education, and the children, being unaware of education, don't care either. Nor do I know of any modern economist who has sought justification for democracy and civil liberties solely from the intensity of the desires that citizens have for democracy and civil liberties. Economists have certainly asked whether poor countries can *afford* democracy and civil liberties, as have political leaders (Section 5.7),. However, that question has to do with the possibility that democracy and civil liberties hinder growth in incomes in poor countries, something that citizens there would be expected to care about, and would be justified in doing so.

Following the leads of (Bergson) Burk (1938) and Musgrave (1959), economists regard social well-being to be a function not only of individual utilities, but also explicitly of those characteristics of social states that possess ethical relevance over and above their relevance as determinants of utilities (e.g., democracy and civil liberties). Formally, this amounts to evaluator k defining social well-being as a function H_k having the property that, for all social states, x,

$$H_k(x) = H_k(U_{k1}(x), U_{k2}(x), \ldots, U_{kN}(x), G_{k1}(x), G_{k2}(x), \ldots, G_{kN}(x)) \qquad (22.2)$$
$$= \quad W_k(V_{k1}(x), V_{k2}(x), \ldots, V_{kN}(x)),$$

where $\{G_{k1}(x), G_{k2}(x), \ldots, G_{kN}(x)\}$ are N functions of x, reflecting the non-utility *merits* of x.

Notice that H_k is a function of x not only through the U_{ki}s, but also through the G_{ki}s. Notice too that there is no unique H_k satisfying equation (22.2), which is another reason why k and j may arrive at different social well-being functions. As H_k is anchored to W_k in equation (22.2), the G_{ki}s are defined in such a way that H_k satisfies the criterion of *efficiency*: If x and y are identical in all respects other than that one or more of the arguments of H_k is greater in x than in y, then $H_k(x) > H_k(y)$.

We turn now to the familiar, but more restricted, concept of *Pareto efficiency*. We say that a feasible social state y is *Pareto inefficient* if there is a feasible social state x such that $U_{ki}(x) \geq U_{ki}(y)$ for all i and $U_{ki}(x) > U_{ki}(y)$ for at least one i. And we say that a feasible social state, say z, is *Pareto efficient* if it is *not* Pareto inefficient. Finally, we say that H_k is *Paretian* if, for any feasible set of social states, the one it commends most is Pareto efficient. Notice now that, unless each G_{ki} ($i = 1, 2, \ldots, N$) is an increasing function of each of U_{ki} ($i = 1, 2, \ldots, N$), H_k would *not* be Paretian, even though, by construction, it satisfies the criterion of efficiency.[25]

One advantage of working with H_k, rather than W_k, is that H_k is in part based on observable behavior (U_{ki}, remember, is the numerical function evaluator k uses to represent the ordering on the basis of which i would choose) and in part on nonutility merits of social states (reflected in $G_{ki}(x)$, $i = 1, 2, \ldots, N$)—for example, the extent to which democracy, privacy, and civil liberties are honoured. One can think of the latter as the adjustments k ought to make to her evaluation, once the utility contributions to social well-being have been estimated by her. Of course, to say that the latter move consists of "adjustments" is to say neither that it is an afterthought, nor that the adjustments would necessarily be small.

Another reason economists work with H_k, rather than W_k, is that it forces them to think hard as to why they should go beyond the U_{ki}s when evaluating policies. Enthusiasm for "nonutility" features of social states can, after all, be a code for paternalism, even authoritarianism.[26] And finally, there are huge practical advantages in working with H_k, rather than W_k. Pinning down the U_{ki}s enables k to estimate the way people would respond to public policies, such as taxes and subsidies and the supply of basic needs. Suppose instead that k were to work with W_k. Then k would certainly know how to think ethically about social states directly in terms of individual well-being functions; but k wouldn't know which public policies to support, because k wouldn't be able to tell how people would respond to the policies. (V_{ki}, remember, doesn't necessarily conform to the ordering on the basis of which person i would choose.)[27]

3.3 *Indirect Measures: Determinants*

There is yet another way to measure well-being. It is to value well-being's *determinants*, which are the commodity inputs that produce well-being. The determinants consist of such goods as food and nutrition, medical care, clothing, potable water, shelter, access to knowledge and information, resources devoted to national security, and aggregate goods like income and wealth. In the previous two sub-sections we noted that it is possible to evaluate policies by comparing the constituents of social well-being, as in k's judgment, "Choose policy A, not policy B, because A will lead to x and B to y, and I estimate $H_k(x) > H_k(y)$." But policies can also be evaluated in terms of their effect on the determinants of social well-being. If undertaken with sufficient precision and care, either procedure would do the job. This is to say that policies can be evaluated on the basis of a suitable measure of either the constituents or the determinants of social well-being.[28]

3.3.1 Social Cost-Benefit Analysis

To illustrate, consider an investment project, which is a flow of the services of commodity inputs and outputs. The project, therefore, is a flow of the determinants of well-being. The social worth of an input or output is the contribution it makes to social well-being. That contribution is called the commodity's *shadow price,* or alternatively, its "social scarcity price" (or alternatively still, its "accounting price"). A commodity's shadow price isn't necessarily the same as its market price. To take an example, the price received by sufferers from urban pollution in, say, Dhaka is zero, but the shadow price isn't zero, because Dhaka residents suffer from bronchial disorders due to the pollution. To take another example, in an evaluative framework where poverty in terms of income and wealth is a concern, the shadow price attributable to a project's benefit flowing to the needy would be higher than to a commensurate benefit flowing to the rich. And so on. However, shadow prices depend not only on ethical values, technology, and available resources, but also on the institutions that influence the allocation of resources. Shadow prices do a huge amount of work for us: they summarize both facts and values. Project evaluation involves valuing the project inputs and outputs in terms of their shadow prices and then aggregating them in a suitable way. The way the aggregation is done is this.

The difference between the sum of the shadow values of a project's outputs in a given period and the sum of the shadow values of the inputs in that same period is called the project's *shadow profit* for that period. The project's shadow profit is estimated for each year of it life. What remains to be estimated is a set of social discount rates—one for each pair of adjacent periods—that would enable the evaluator to aggregate the project's flow of shadow profits. (Social discount rates are themselves intertemporal shadow prices.) It can be shown that, in evaluating a project, the sum of the present discounted flow of the project's shadow profits is the appropriate aggregate index: if the present discounted sum is positive, the project should be accepted; if it is negative, the project should be rejected.

To see why this is the correct criterion for project evaluation, let social states now be denoted as vectors. The idea is to regard a social state as a complete allocation of goods and services, covering who gets what and receives what. Let x be a social state. A project is a perturbation to x. Call the perturbation Δx. Suppose person k is the project evaluator. Her social well-being function is $W_k(V_{k1}(x), V_{k2}(x), \ldots, V_{kN}(x))$, as in equation (22.1). If the project were undertaken, social well-being would change by the amount,

$$\Sigma_i \, (\partial W_k / \partial V_{ki})(\partial V_{ki} / \partial x).(\Delta x). \tag{22.3}$$

The expression represents the sum of all the small changes (Δx) that are brought about by the project, valued at shadow prices $\Sigma_i(\partial W_k/\partial V_{ki}).\,(\partial V_{ki}/\partial x)$. So, expression (22.3) is the social profitability of the project, evaluated by k at shadow prices. Since time is implicit in expression (22.1), expression (22.3) denotes the present discounted sum of the flow of the project's shadow profits.[29]

There is a beautiful relationship between the present discounted sum of the flow of a project's shadow profits and the (true) wealth of a nation. We are to identify a capital asset not only in terms of its characteristics, but also its location, date, uncertain contingency, and the identity of the person or group who owns it. By *inclusive wealth* we mean the shadow value (or social worth) of *all* capital assets, including not only manufactured assets, but also knowledge and skills, and natural capital (e.g., ecosystems). Since W_k is a function of the entire distribution of goods and services, the shadow value of a unit of a particular type of capital asset owned by someone who is poor would be greater than the shadow value of a unit of that same type of capital asset owned by someone who is rich, other things being equal. So inclusive wealth is not simply the sum of individual wealths, but is a weighted sum of individual wealths. It can be shown that the sum of the present discounted flow of a project's shadow profits is its contribution to the economy's inclusive wealth, meaning that wealth, when inclusively measured, is an aggregate index of social well-being. As a nation's wealth is the social worth of its capital assets, it is a measure of the nation's opulence. That isn't to say that inclusive wealth *is* social well-being, it is to say only that a policy reform (e.g., an investment project) increases social well-being when, and only when, it raises inclusive wealth.

3.3.2 Inclusive Wealth and Sustainable Development: Theory

Interestingly, social well-being and inclusive wealth move together *over time* as well. It can be shown that, under a well-defined set of circumstances, the necessary and sufficient condition for social well-being to be a nondeclining function of time is that inclusive wealth per head is a nondeclining function of time. The theorem has been proved and put to work in an increasingly general context by Dasgupta and Mäler (2000) and Arrow et al. (2003a, 2003b). The theorem gives operational meaning to the intuitive notion of *sustainable development*, made popular by the famous Brundtland Commission Report (WCED, 1987), which defined it "...as development that meets the needs of the present without compromising the ability of future generations to meet their own needs."

The Brundtland Commission's definition of sustainable development focuses on the maintenance of the overall productive base of an economy. But as the Commission Report left it, that base is an unspecified aggregate of the determinants of social well-being. The theorem that connects movements over time of social well-being and inclusive wealth per head tells us *how* to measure the overall productive base. Since it links a precise aggregate of the determinants of social well-being to social well-being itself, the theorem also tells us why we should be interested in the productive base. In Section 5.5 I report on an application of the theorem to the world's poorest regions, so as to explore whether economic development over the past three decades there has been sustainable.

3.3.3 Why Determinants?

Following Sen (1987) and Dreze and Sen (1990), Anand and Ravallion (1993) and UNDP (1994, 14–15) have criticized those who regard gross national product (GNP) to be an index of social well-being, on the grounds that it is, instead, a measure of a country's opulence. The criticism is faulty in two ways. First, opulence is a stock concept, and GNP is not a return on any index of opulence that I am aware of.[30] Secondly, and more importantly, the connection that was drawn in Section 3.3.1 between the constituents and determinants of well-being tells us that it isn't a mistake to seek to measure social well-being in terms of an index of opulence. The point isn't that opulence misleads, but rather that we should search for the *right* measure of opulence. And the right measure of opulence is (inclusive) wealth.

Roughly speaking, the constituents and determinants of well-being can be thought of as "ends" and "means," respectively. Ethicists regard the constituents as the obvious objects of study, in contrast to economists and statisticians, who gravitate toward the determinants. There is a cultural divide here, and they often clash. Consider, however, education and skills. Are they constituents or determinants? They are in fact both. The acquisition of education is partly an end in itself and partly a means to increasing future opportunities (or capabilities), by improving skills. Aristotelian ethics emphasizes the former, while the economics of human capital stresses the latter. That education has both flavors doesn't pose problems, so long as we are able to track the two. Double-counting is a virtue when a commodity offers joint benefits. Education ought to be counted twice. (It is the same with health.) Schultz (1961, 1974) and Becker (1964, 1983), who pioneered the economics of human capital, contributed greatly to our understanding of the process of economic development, by drawing attention away from Aristotelian virtues. If governments in today's poor countries were persuaded that education doesn't foster growth in national wealth, but is solely an end in itself, they would have an excuse to neglect it even more than they currently do. Governments could argue that poor countries can't afford such luxuries as education.

Why bother about the determinants of well-being, when the natural thing would be to measure the real thing, namely, the constituents?

There are several reasons. First, without an understanding of the ways in which the constituents are "produced" by their determinants, we would not know which institutions best promote human interests and which ones are likely to prove disastrous. Should markets be relied upon to produce and allocate food, clothing, shelter, and information? Should the State be involved in the supply of education, public-health care, roads and ports? Should local communities be engaged in the management of spatially confined natural resources? What kinds of institutions should people depend on for insurance and credit? And so on. Second, policy alternatives, such as investment projects, are easiest to frame in terms of the commodity determinants of well-being. It is not an accident that projects are formulated in terms of commodity flows. (At their rawest, commodity flows are what investment projects involve.) And third, shadow profits are a linear index of a project's inputs and outputs. Linearity greatly eases estimation.

3.4 Social Well-Being Functions and Arrow's Voting Rules

Where does Kenneth Arrow's celebrated Impossibility Theorem fit into this? There have been a number of readings of Arrow's monograph (Arrow 1963 [1951]). Several don't fit well with the axioms Arrow imposed on the mechanisms for social choice he wished to study. My own reading is this:

The title of Arrow's monograph is *Social Choice and Individual Values*. Arrow's concern was to discover *democratic voting rules*, in a world where voter k ranks social states in accordance with W_k (equivalently, H_k).[31] Arrow's presumption was that people cast their votes on the basis of their ethical evaluation of social states. In the theory I have just sketched, W_k in expression (22.1) reflects k's values. To say that people differ in their values is to say that the W_ks differ. Arrow assumed that the only information voter k is allowed to provide on her ballot paper is the ordering of social states induced by W_k and that the only pieces of information the voting rule is permitted to entertain *are* the individual orderings. A voting rule aggregates the N orderings induced by the W_ks into a final ordering. Social choice is made on the basis of that final ordering. Arrow's voters fill their ballot papers on the basis of ethical considerations (W_k); they do not vote on the basis of their personal interest (V_k), nor on the basis of what they would personally have chosen (U_k). Arrow's Impossibility Theorem states that if the number of social states exceeds two, it isn't possible to devise a voting rule satisfying a set of simple ethical principles (e.g., that it should be democratic, that it should yield an efficient outcome) if the set of possible W_k functions is unrestricted. But the theorem prevents no one from reasoning ethically.[32]

Typically though, people don't vote directly on social states. Depending on the context, the alternatives on which people vote are policies, or laws, or rules, or candidates; but ultimately it is social states on which people vote. To take an example, even when people cast their votes for political candidates, they, in effect, vote for social states, because candidates represent policies, and different policies lead to different social states. Once again however, disagreements over facts rear their head. Thus, imagine that there are several policies (candidates) to choose from. Even if all voters have the same ethical ordering of social states (i.e., W_k and the V_{ki}s in expression (22.1) are independent of k), they would rank policies differently if they were to read the pathways that lead policies to eventualities differently. Arrow's Impossibility Theorem states that if the number of policies exceeds two, it is not possible to devise a voting rule satisfying a set of simple ethical principles (e.g., that it should be democratic, that it should yield an efficient outcome) if voters' beliefs about the character of the pathways that lead from policies to eventualities are drawn from an unrestricted set of belief systems. But the theorem doesn't prevent people from reasoning ethically. In other words, even if people held the same ethical values, the Impossibility Theorem would rear its head if people believed in diverse theories concerning the ways in which various agencies in society would be expected to respond to policies and the ways in which Nature would react to the treatment meted out to it. In Section 5 we shall see how disagreements over such facts have dominated 50 years of development economics.

It is a deep insight of modern economics that we should not worry about others when going about our daily business in the market place for private goods. The market system helps to save enormously on information costs: when shopping, we don't have to look constantly into other people's affairs so as to determine who needs what and why. But markets are an effective institution only for transactions in private goods. The public sphere includes the supply of public goods and merit goods (more generally, externalities), one class of such goods being the (public) institutions that are required to ensure that markets work well. Modern economics urges people to worry about others in the public sphere and vote on the basis of the public interest, which in the notation here, are the H_ks (or the W_ks). Civic awareness, or so modern economists have shown, is to recognise and embrace this dichotomy between the public and private spheres of our lives (Arrow 1974).

TRANSITION

4. Tragic Choices, Gender-Based Allocations, and Partial Orderings

There are contemporary ethicists who question the basis on which modern economics is constructed, by claiming that not all social states are rankable. Some maintain that to imagine that choices are made on the basis of an underlying ordering is to misconceive personhood (Sen 1987, Putnam 2002). Ethical reasoning, they say, can at best yield *partial* orderings of alternatives, not orderings.[33] In the language of Section 2, this means that if k were ethically sensitive, k would be unable to construct not only W_k (or H_k), but the individual V_{ki}s (or the U_{ki}s and the G_{ki}s) as well, each of which, remember, was taken to be a numerical representation of an ordering of alternatives. There is even the suggestion by ethicists that when the alternatives are "tragic," to claim to be able to rank them all is to reveal oneself as being shallow, lacking in the higher sensibility.

4.1 Personal Choice

In the context of personal choice, the origins of Agamemnon's marital difficulties have been cited as illustration (Sen 1987). Aeschylus reported that the goddess

Artemis had sent adverse weather to Aulis. As leader of the Greeks, Agamemnon was faced with a cruel choice: sacrifice his daughter, Iphigenia, so as to permit the Greek fleet to sail to Troy, or spare her, in which case the ships would be unable to sail and the Greeks would suffer humiliation, possibly, too, an eventual attack from their enemies. Agamemnon was faced with a tragic choice and decided it was necessary to sacrifice Iphigenia. Sen speculates instead that although Agamemnon chose as he did, he would not have chosen it on the grounds that it was the less bad option, because *both options were so horrible as to be unrankable.*

But we are not offered reasons why one cannot rank tragic choices.[34] Even while acknowledging that either choice would destroy his integrity, Agamemnon could have insisted—and in at least one reading of Aeschylus' play (Williams 1993), *did* insist— that he chose the lesser of two evils, even that it was *necessary* he chose the way he did. While the ancients, as far as I know, did not have the term "evil" in their lexicon, no disservice is done by my use of it here, because Agamemnon's dilemma has been used by Nussbaum (2000a) to illustrate tragic choices in contemporary poor societies. Nussbaum (2003, 415–416) has gone further to recommend the classics to economists and policy makers on the remarkable ground that, by reading about tragic choices they would better appreciate the tragedies befalling members of the world's poorest households; which, if you think about it, is pretty insulting to the many social scientists who have discovered such choices in the Indian subcontinent and sub-Saharan Africa and have explored the circumstances under which they are made.

In a revelatory, but now sadly under-acknowledged work, the demographer Pravin Visaria observed that the female-male ratio in India had shown a decline since the Indian Census of 1901 and was, worse, considerably less than one (Visaria 1967). In order to answer a question the epidemiologist Lincoln Chen posed in response to Visaria's finding, namely, "Where have the women gone?," D'Souza and Chen (1980), Chen et al. (1981), and Chen (1982) uncovered male bias in household allocations of food and health care in parts of the Indian subcontinent.[35] The authors arrived at their finding by studying mortality and anthropometric statistics and inferring household commodity allocations from the statistics. A number of development economists subsequently explored the idea that in a social environment where female children are costlier to the household than male children (girls depart on marriage, and dowries can be crippling), such forms of discrimination as Visaria had observed in the census data were the response of poor households to a constantly stressful economic situation.[36]

It had not gone unnoticed by economists that a household is not a person. A household's choices reflect its internal dynamics; for example, the balance of power among its members that is likely to be founded on economic dependence, the social status of women vis-a-vis men, and so on. If we imagine that mothers are likely to have greater empathy with daughters than fathers have, we should expect discrimination against female children to be less in households where women are educated, or have access to paid employment, or control the household budget, other things being equal. Extending this thought, we would expect nourishment to be better and discrimination against women to be less in households where women are educated, or have access to paid employment, or control the household budget, other things being equal. There is evidence of this.[37]

There is evidence, too, that gender discrimination in the Indian subcontinent differs across ecological zones and rules of property inheritance; and that the character of gender discrimination in sub-Saharan Africa differs from that in the Indian subcontinent. In a wide ranging book, Boserup (1970) observed that women have a prominent role in agriculture involving hoe farming (such as in sub-Saharan Africa), in contrast to regions (such as the Indian subcontinent) where plough farming is predominant. Boserup drew a connection between hoe cultivation, polygamy, and the position of women.

Substantiating that connection *within* Africa has proved to be difficult. In a fundamental body of work, the anthropologist Jack Goody has stressed that someone's economic importance in a system cannot be inferred only from her involvement in agriculture, it depends also on her engagement in such complementary activities as drawing water and collecting wood fuel on a daily basis. He has used the role of women in economic activity in its widest sense to provide an explanation not only for the practice of polygamy in sub-Saharan Africa, but also for why cultivable land is awarded to married women by their spouse's clan and why men are obliged to offer bridewealth at marriage.[38]

Boserup's thesis regarding the connection between women's position in society and their role in agriculture has been applied by Bardhan (1974) and Sopher (1980) to the Indian subcontinent. They noted a North-South divide in women's life chances there, being a lot dimmer in the wheat growing North than in the rice growing South (the East falls somewhere in between). The authors observed, too, that the now-famous state, Kerala, is an outlier even in the South. That a prominent caste in Kerala, in contrast to those in the North, are matrilineal and that the fact that among them it is customary for female residence to be matrilocal may, also, have had something to do with the emergence of the divide. Evidence, such as we have, that norms of behavior in part emerge from local influences, such as the influence of one's neighbors and peer group, is consistent with this thought.[39]

My point here is not to argue in favor of, or against, the discussed behaviors or indeed any of a number of other explanations that have been offered for gender discrimination in the Indian subcontinent and sub-Saharan Africa. Instead, the question I want to touch upon here is whether it makes sense to interpret gender discrimination within a household in terms of the relative voices of members, each of whom is able to rank household allocations in a complete manner, or whether, because the choices are frequently tragic, it is more appropriate to imagine that they are *unable* to rank them completely.

Putnam (2002), like Sen (1987), would seem to believe that the matter can be settled by reflection. It seems to me though that the question is an empirical one. By this I don't mean determining whether undergraduates are able to rank alternatives presented to them via a computer programme in a university laboratory, but whether people living in raw economic circumstances can explain why they view matters the way they do. The problem with concluding that choice mechanisms within poor households are based on partial orderings of food and health-care allocations is that we would not be able to explain *systematic* gender discrimination in many parts of the Indian subcontinent and sub-Saharan Africa. If tragic choices were nonrankable, some households would choose one way, others in other ways. But what we observe from the data are, after controlling for other factors, systematic biases in food and health-care allocations within the household. Until better reasons are offered than the ones put forward by contemporary ethicists, economists have little reason to reject the hypothesis they have worked with over the years.

4.2 *Social Choice*

That *social* choice is frequently arrived at from partial orderings of alternatives has, however, been the working hypothesis in modern economics. In Section 2 we noted that the W_ks differ from one another. Even if someone evaluating a project (say, person k) were convinced that a project is socially desirable, insofar as expression (22.3) is positive, person k would balk, because there are others involved in reaching a decision, and he should expect their social well-being functions to differ from his. A good project evaluator, therefore, conducts a sensitivity analysis of the project, by identifying ranges of values for the most contentious parameters under which the project is acceptable and ranges for which it is not acceptable. The choice mechanism would be expected to differ from place to place and from time to time. Political pressures often intrude on decision making. When it doesn't intrude, sensitivity analysis helps those involved to deliberate, discuss, and select projects in a manner that makes their choices consistent with one another over time. In fact sensitivity analysis is routinely practiced in social cost-benefit analysis.[40]

II. Facts

The framework presented in sections 2 and 3 is useful for classifying debates on economic policy. Imagine there are two policy options, A and B. Individuals j and k could disagree about their merits for three reasons:

(α) j and k differ in the way they measure individual well-beings. ("In assessing a person's well-being, you place far too much weight on personal income relative to education," says k to j.) In the notation of expression (22.1), j and k construct V_{ji} and V_{ki} differently.

(β) j and k differ in the way they conceive social well-being. ("You don't place sufficient weight on equality of well-beings," says j to k.) In the notation of expression (22.1), j and k construct W_j and W_k differently.

(γ) *j* and *k* have different theories regarding the likely effects of the policy options. (*k* says to *j*: "You think *A* would result in greater impoverishment of the poor than *B*. I disagree.")

[Corresponding disagreements could arise if *j* and *k* were to deliberate matters in terms of H_j and H_k (the left-hand side of equation (22.2)).]

Policy discussions among professional economists usually take the form γ. In the following section, I illustrate this by tracing aspects of the development of development economics. My idea isn't to offer a historical survey. Rather, I sketch a number of debates that have taken place over the decades. Not unnaturally, the selection reflects my own expertise and involvement.

5. The Development Debate

The economics of development is an inquiry into the poverty of nations and is concerned to discover ways out for them. (In order to discuss economic policy, the objects of study in development economics used to be called *underdeveloped countries*, a term that has undergone several transformations over the past five decades: *less developed countries, developing countries*, the *Third World*, the *South*, and so on. Some economists, including myself, merely refer to them as *poor*.) The subject has a wide engagement. Not only do academic economists and anthropologists study it, but government departments, non-governmental organizations (NGOs), and international agencies contribute thinking to it, too. Although much has been written—and continues to be written—on the meaning of poverty, there is an intuitive sense in which people can be judged to be poor: *people are poor if they have very limited access to the resources they need to be able to function.*

5.1 *Development as Economic Growth*

This may seem overly rough and ready and aggregative. After all, there are many kinds of resources, and one can be well-off in some (food), but poor in others (health care). Moreover, *needs* requires elucidation. (That too has elicited book-length inquiries.) And what, after all, should one mean by something being "very limited" and by someone's "ability to function"? All these are valid concerns. But at a very early stage in the development of the economics of development, *income* came to be seen as the appropriate index of the resources a person needs to be able to function. Whatever else people may need, it was argued, they need income to be able to purchase goods and services. There is no evidence in the development literature, however, that income was ever regarded as an end in itself. Investigations into the incidence and magnitude of poverty has been a recurrent activity in development economics. The World Bank's oft-cited estimate, that some 1.2 billion people live under $1 a day, is the kind of fact that offers a glimpse of the magnitude of poverty (Section 5.4).[41]

In moving from "personal" to "national," the obvious generalization of income is gross national product (GNP). GNP is an index of the goods provided in an economy. (For simplicity, we regard national income and GNP to be the same object here.) As an index of economic development, this may seem a limitation, but even when you go beyond GNP, you find yourself returning to it. For example, if various public goods are to be supplied by government (local or national), the government would require resources. If those resources are to be obtained from taxes, there has to be sufficient income in the economy *to* tax, which brings us back to GNP. In consequence of its widespread use in policy discussions, GNP has now become so ingrained in our collective subconscious that, even as you ask someone, "Growth in what?," you know the answer to be "Growth in GNP."

The use of GNP as a development index has been routinely criticized as well, not just by ethicists (Bauer 1971; see also Section 5.7). This being so, its staying power may seem surprising. The simple reason behind it is that the belief among development economists has been that improvements in the material conditions of life are necessary before all else. It is because this belief could only be substantiated or refuted by an appeal to facts, not values, that the long-running controversy about whether income is a suitable index of development has been over facts.

To trace the origins of the dominance of GNP in development thinking, it helps to recall a passage in an article that gave rise to the modern literature on economic development:

> The central problem in the theory of economic development is to understand the process by which a community which was previously saving and investing 4 or 5 per cent of its national income or less, converts itself into an economy where voluntary saving is running at about 12 to 15 per cent of national income or more. This is the central problem because the central fact of economic development is rapid capital accumulation (including knowledge and skills with capital).

Now, this passage was not written by a Stalinist, nor by a descendant of some nineteenth-century English entrepreneur obsessed with capital accumulation. It was written by the late W. Arthur Lewis (Lewis 1954), as humane an economist as you could find. And his reasoning went something like this:

Imagine that a dollar's worth of investment converts itself into a perpetual flow of an additional 10 cents of income each year, which is to say that the real rate of return on investment is 10% per year. This means that the capital sum required to generate a dollar of income annually is $10. So, if 5 percent of GNP were invested each year, GNP would grow at an annual rate of 0.5 percent (0.05/10), whereas, if 15 percent of GNP were invested each year, GNP would grow at an annual rate of 1.5 percent (0.15/10). Suppose population is expected to grow at 1 percent annually. Then, at a 5 percent investment rate GNP per capita would *decline* at 0.5 percent a year, whereas at a 15 percent investment rate GNP per capita would *increase* at 0.5 percent a year. One path would represent decay, the other path, development.[42]

5.2 The Quality of Economic Growth: Investment in What?

A research agenda's fecundity can be measured by the number of answerable questions it gives rise to. By this count, the agenda proposed in Lewis' paper was enormously fecund. First, it's all very well to raise the rate of investment, but how would anyone know what the country should be investing in? Heavy industries (e.g., steel)? Light industries (e.g., garments)? Agriculture? Roads, ports, and electricity? Public health? Primary education? Reproductive health programs?) Secondly, who should do the investing: the government or private sector or local communities? Third, and relatedly, should the government have a strategy for economic development (e.g., creating heavy industries)? Fourth, should we expect growth in GNP to lead to a reduction in absolute poverty within society even without the active agency of government? And so on.

The fourth question gave rise to the famous "trickle down" view of economic growth, the thought being that, if the economy were to take off, no one would be left behind: Formal employment would be created and wages would rise. Most development economists will give you a straight answer if you ask them whether economic growth can be relied upon to trickle down reasonably fast. It won't be the same answer though. However, no economist will ask you why you want to know, which goes to show that there is a common ethical basis on which the development debate has been conducted. Even though the motivation behind the question is prompted by ethical concerns, the question itself concerns the factual. The problem economists face is that the statistics are confounding. So the debate has been and continues to be, over facts.[43]

The controversy over trade liberalization, and more recently, "globalization" through free international capital movements, is in part a response to the third of the foregoing questions, which has to do with choice of appropriate economic policies. An earlier intuition, that economic growth is facilitated by protection of domestic industries against foreign imports has been argued by a number of trade and development economists as being dubious (Bhagwati & Desai, 1970, Bhagwati & Srinivasan 1975). Protectionist policies not only distort domestic prices in such a way as to waste resources, they also help to create a social environment where corruption is able to thrive, meaning that even more resources are wasted (Krueger 1978, Bhagwati 1982). Moreover, theoretically at least, learning through work in advanced export sectors would be expected to enhance human productivity, thereby economic performance (Lucas 1993). The phrase "export led growth" is an expression of this thought.

The debate continues. Some economists have observed that the governments of recent development successes, particularly Taiwan and South Korea, protected selected industries from foreign competition and advanced the cause of a selected group of export industries by offering what in effect were subsidies (Amsden 1989, Wade 1990). However, those favoring less government intervention ask in return whether those economies would have performed even better had their governments not tried to pick future industrial winners. Being counterfactuals, these questions are very hard to answer. But they involve analyses of facts, not values.

Of the four, it is the second question that has proved to be the most contentious among public intellectuals. Until recently, even the left-right distinction was frequently drawn in terms of an answer to it. But the question is bogus. You cannot judge who should do the investing (public, private, or communitarian) without an understanding of the strengths and weaknesses of the various institutions in the economy. As we noted in Section 2, modern economics tells us that there are activities that ought almost invariably to be left to the private realm, certain others to the realm of markets, some to communities, others still to the public arena. But there is a wide range whose placement can be determined only by comparing the efficiency with which institutions operate with the other public policies and norms of behavior that are in place. It is all well and good to imagine, as I did in my illustration of Lewis' reasoning, that the rate of return on investment is 10 percent a year. But if there is widespread corruption in the public sector or property rights to capital assets are insecure (see later) or the government is predatory, the rate of return could be woefully low, perhaps even negative. Growing recognition of this has meant that although development economists discussed *policy* in earlier years, they now study the character of *institutions*. The two are interrelated: Good policies can't be plucked from air; the efficacy of economic policies depends on the character of institutions.[44]

The development of the theory of social cost-benefit analysis for poor countries was a response to the first question. We observed in Section 3.3 that the theory was built on wide ethical foundations. In the event, though, not much use has been made of social cost-benefit analysis in the choice of investment projects in poor countries: the techniques were felt to be overly complicated. (Little & Mirrlees 1991, offer an interesting assessment.) I don't know if this has mattered hugely, because until the late 1970s the productive gains enjoyed by an economy from having a healthy and educated population were generally not appreciated. Not only were political leaders in most poor countries uninterested in primary health care and basic education, but the techniques of social cost-benefit analysis were designed mainly for industrial and agricultural projects. However, growing empirical evidence of the validity of a theory of economic development in which human capital plays a central role (Leibenstein 1957, on health; Schultz 1961, 1974; and Becker 1981, 1983, on education), meant that the long-held belief that steel mills in the world's poorest countries yield higher social profits than schools and public health programs was false. One implication of the theory of human capital is that improvements in education and health are appreciated, not only to be consonant with growth in GNP, but also to be sources of economic growth. Obvious though this implication may sound today, the idea that education is an engine of macroeconomic growth was formulated in a testable model only recently, by Lucas (1988). The widespread acceptance of human capital theory (World Bank 1993, 1998) is an instance of how the discovery of facts is absorbed in the social sciences, but its general absorption took time.

5.3 Growth vs Distribution

GNP is an aggregate measure, estimated on the basis of market prices. If the individual human being is to be the focus of attention, development economics had to care about the distribution of income, especially the incidence of poverty. A country's GNP can be large even while its distribution is highly unequal and even while some live in abject poverty. A nation can enjoy huge private incomes but suffer from public squalor. More subtly, there can be a conflict between the prospects of large GNP in the future and equality in the distribution of contemporary income. The latter observation is the source of the long-standing debate on growth versus distribution.

The conflict can be fuelled by two forces. First, if the rich in fact invest more than the poor (because, say, they can afford to!), a redistribution in favor of the poor would reduce the rate of investment and thereby economic growth, other things being equal. Second, redistribution may blunt incentives to work, to take risks, to invest, more generally, to undertake productive activities. It is remarkable that the latter possibility was formulated in a meaningful way only recently, in a bold and original paper by Mirrlees (1971). Mirrlees's article showed clearly that whether the incentive effects are significant can only be discovered empirically, by studying the demand for leisure (and risk-avoidance), and by uncovering the productivity of work (and risk). An early theoretical exercise by Atkinson (1973) on a version of Mirrlees's model suggested that the incentive effects can in principle be so powerful, that even as egalitarian an ethic as that of Rawls (equation (22.1b)) could recommend low marginal tax rates on high incomes. The implication was that, although governments ought to be engaged in income transfers, they ought not to be as vigorous as egalitarians might instinctively want them to be.

Set against the foregoing two reasons behind a conflict between growth and redistribution (more generally, between efficiency and equity) are drivers that go the other way. If small agricultural farms are more productive than large ones (say because it is easier for the land owner in small farms to monitor farm laborers' work effort; Eswaran & Kotwal 1985), a redistribution of land in favour of the landless could enhance economic growth. Adelman and Morris (1973) had earlier uncovered empirical evidence that land redistribution in South Korea and Taiwan had been an engine of economic growth there. Empirical work at the World Bank (Chenery et al. 1974; Ahluwalia 1976a,b), showing that poor countries in the contemporary world could enjoy economic growth with some redistribution, was consistent with those findings.

A second driver was identified with health, which is an aspect of human capital. Using results obtained by nutritionists and epidemiologists, it has been argued that investment in nutrition and health care for the poor could increase their productivity to an extent that economy-wide labor productivity would increase. It has been argued also that markets alone shouldn't be expected to eliminate hunger and malnutrition speedily. Perhaps economic growth trickles down, but it doesn't cascade down.

The reasoning is this:

Stunting is a reflection of long-term undernourishment, while wasting is a manifestation of short-term undernourishment. Each significantly limits the capacity for physical work, where strength and endurance are needed. Moreover, the energy required for maintaining human life is substantial, in that 60 to 75 percent of the energy intake of someone in daily nutrition balance goes toward maintenance, the remaining 40 to 25 percent is spent on discretionary activities (work and leisure). Maintenance requirements are, therefore, like fixed costs, meaning that the metabolic processes converting nutrition intake into nutritional status are nonlinear. Which is to say that the effects on the nutritional status of a marginally undernourished person of small alterations in their mean nutrition intake are amplified, they aren't proportional to the alterations. Dasgupta and Ray (1986, 1987) showed that because of such nonlinearities, markets can't eliminate undernutrition easily. The point is that the undernourished are at a severe disadvantage in their ability to obtain food. Because their capacity to work is impaired, the undernourished are unable to offer the quality of work needed to obtain the food they require if they are to improve their nutritional status. It was shown as well that, over time, undernourishment can be both a cause and consequence of someone falling into a *poverty trap*. Because undernourishment displays hysteresis (there are further positive feedbacks between nutrition and infection), poverty can even be dynastic. Once a household falls into a poverty trap, it can prove especially hard for descendants to emerge out of it.[45] Similarly, enhancements of family environments improve the early development of cognitive as well as socioemotional competencies among children (personality factors, confidence, motivation). The development of such competencies is impeded in adolescence if they are not acquired in early childhood (Heckman 2000, 2008).

The pathways triggered by these two drivers (land ownership and health and education) suggest that it is possible, not only to recommend economic growth *with* redistribution, but that one can even advocate patterns of redistribution *before* economic growth takes place (Adelman 1979, Deininger & Squire 1998). Notice once again that the confounding problems in all this have involved facts, broadly construed—not values.[46]

5.4 *Estimating Poverty*

Poverty is self-evidently multidimensional. This makes estimating the magnitude and extent of poverty in today's world most problematic. In fact the problems remain huge even if one adopts a narrow view of poverty. Let us see why.

It could be thought that, because food is a key determinant of well-being, poverty should be identified with low nutrition intake. Problems of measurement abound even so, because one has to ask whether a person's diet is deficient in macronutrients (protein, carbohydrates) or micronutrients (iron, iodine, phosphorus) or in both. In those societies where diets aren't built round root vegetables (cassava, yam) someone whose energy intake is adequate can be assumed to enjoy an adequate intake of protein. So, a seemingly uncomplicated way to estimate poverty is to identify a level of energy intake (e.g., 2,000 kilocalories per day) such that a person is deemed to be poor if his daily intake is below it. The idea then would be to measure intakes in population samples.

Clearly though, intakes should be matched with energy requirements (a sedentary person's daily requirements would be lower than the requirements of someone involved in strenuous work, other things being equal). Moreover, even though the poorest people everywhere spend most of their income on food (the proportion has been found to be as high as 80%), they buy other things too (clothes, bedding, the occasional finery). A nutrition-based notion of poverty would seem to be overly limiting. So poverty is often defined today in terms of a minimum income or expenditure level, in that a person is judged to be poor if his income or expenditure is below that level.

Once the poverty line has been agreed upon, the simplest way to measure its extent is to estimate the proportion of people who are below the line. This yields the "headcount ratio" of the poor. Because the cost of living differs across countries, new empirical problems arise when we seek global figures for poverty. Economic statisticians have, therefore, estimated international differences in the cost of living. Instead of using official exchange rates among national currencies, they use purchasing power parity (PPP) exchange rates, so as to make national poverty lines comparable to one another.

In some countries (many in Latin America), poverty is defined in terms of low income, while in others (e.g., India) low expenditure is the criterion. This adds to the difficulties in making international comparisons of poverty. Problems are compounded by the fact that neither reported income nor reported expenditure is likely to reflect the worth of resources rural people may have obtained from their local commons (Section 5.6.1). It has transpired also that the length of the recall period in sample surveys influences poverty estimates. In the mid-1990s, the National Sample Survey in India conducted experiments in which households were randomly assigned one of two questionnaires with different reporting periods. In one questionnaire, people were asked to recall their expenditure on items of high frequency (food, tobacco) over the previous 7 days, on items of low frequency (clothing, footwear) over the previous 365 days, and on all other items over the previous 30 days. In the other questionnaire, people were asked to recall their expenditure on all items over a uniform period of the previous 30 days. Interestingly, the headcount ratio obtained from answers to the former questionnaire was *half* that obtained from the latter.[47]

Despite the empirical difficulties, a picture is emerging about absolute poverty in the contemporary world. Although the number of people living under the World Bank's criterion of $1 a day has increased in Africa and some countries in Latin America during the past fifteen years or so, the total number in the world who are below that poverty line has declined. High rates of growth in income per head in China and India have pulled up sufficiently large numbers of people from below the poverty line to have made this possible. Interestingly, though, the total number of people in the world living below $2 a day has risen. China's and India's high growth rates haven't lifted sufficiently large numbers above the higher poverty line. These findings offer a glimpse of the relationship between economic growth and poverty alleviation experienced in recent years.

5.5 Female Education and Fertility

In the contemporary world, the world's poorest regions have experienced the fastest rate of population growth. Sub-Saharan Africa and the Indian subcontinent—the world's poorest regions—have experienced unprecedented population increase over the past four decades, averaging well over 2 percent a year. Declines in child mortality rates there were not matched by declines in fertility rates, at least, not until recently in some parts of India and Bangladesh. Is there a connection between poverty and fertility? What accounts for the persistence of high fertility rates in the poor world?[48]

Caldwell (1980) documented a number of historical cases and suggested that mass education can be expected to reduce high fertility rates. Subsequent writings on population growth in poor countries have stressed that there is a negative link between education (especially female education) and fertility. So it is now a commonplace that an absence of female education is a prime cause of pro-natalism (Sen 1994, 1999; Dreze and Sen, 1995).

But there are two problems with the latter viewpoint. First, the extent to which fertility decline "responds" to increases in female education in both time series and cross- section data not only differ substantially across space and time, there are also places in Africa where the response has been found to have the "wrong" sign; that is, increases in primary education for women have been associated with *increases* in total fertility rate (TFR) (Jolly & Gribble 1993). Secondly, fertility rates in the world's poorest regions remained much the same until recently, even while infant mortality rates declined, which means that there must have been other significant reasons for the pro-natalism; an absence of female education could hardly prescribe an invariant fertility rate. In any event, Susan Cochrane, to whom we owe the first, clear studies showing the links between female education and fertility reduction, was herself reluctant to attribute causality to her findings (Cochrane 1979, 1983)—as have scholars studying more recent data (Cohen 1993, Jolly & Gribble 1993)—because it is extremely difficult to establish causality. Women's education may well reduce fertility; on the other hand, the initiation of childbearing may itself be a factor in the termination of education. Moreover, even when education is made available by the state, households may choose not to take up the opportunity: the ability (or willingness) of governments in poor countries to enforce school attendance is often greatly limited. The private costs and benefits of education and the mores of the community to which people belong influence their decisions. It could be that the very characteristics of a community that are reflected in low education attainment for women are also those encouraging high fertility;

for example, absence of associational activities among women, or lack of communication with the outside world, or inheritance rules that place women at a disadvantage. (We discussed some of these issues in Section 4.1.) Demographic theories striving for generality would regard both women's education and fertility to be "endogenous" variables. The negative relationship between education and fertility in such theories would be an association, not a causal relationship. The two variables would be interpreted as "moving together" in samples, nothing more.

The Green Revolution of the early 1970s enabled world food production to keep pace with world population growth. I believe this fact led social scientists to conclude during the 1980s that, even in the world's poorest regions, population is not a problem.[49] But cereal yields have stagnated in recent years, even while population has continued to grow at high rates. Moreover, there is not much area left on the globe that is agriculturally promising. These twin facts may be a reason why economic demographers appear now to have shifted to the view that high population growth has hampered economic development in the world's poorest regions (Birdsall et al. 2001). But this revised viewpoint suffers from the same weakness as the one that says that high population growth has posed no problems for economic development there: both regard population change to be an exogenous factor. Excepting for societies where fertility has been restricted by government fiat (as in China), population change shouldn't be taken to be exogenously given. Below I explore a recent point of view that is based on institutional and ecological fundamentals, not female education, nor fertility behavior. In order to elaborate on the viewpoint, I discuss the role the local natural-resource base plays in rural life among the world's poorest. I argue that to ignore that base leads generally to wrong policy prescriptions.[50]

5.6 The Role of Natural Capital in Rural Lives

The issue in fact is broader than the neglect of the local natural-resource base in *development* economics. Twentieth century economics, more generally, has in large measure been detached from the environmental sciences. Judging by the profession's writings, we economists see nature at best as a backdrop from which resources can be considered in isolation. We also assume that the processes characterizing the Earth system are linear. Moreover, macroeconomic forecasts routinely exclude environmental resources. Accounting for nature, if it comes into the calculus at all, is an afterthought to the real business of doing economics.

One can argue that this practice has given rise to a puzzling cultural phenomenon: One group of scientists (usually earth scientists) see in humanity's current use of Nature's services symptoms of a deep malaise (e.g., Ehrlich & Ehrlich 2004, Steffen et al. 2004), even while another group of scientists (usually economists) document the fact that people today are on average better off in many ways than they had ever been and wonder why the gloom (e.g., Simon 1990, Johnson 2001). In ignoring the role of natural capital in economic activities, development economists have merely followed their professional colleagues. However, while policies and institutions matter, ecology matters too. The neglect of nature has been not only unfortunate, but ironic too. One has only to think of agricultural land, threshing grounds, grazing fields, village tanks and ponds, woodlands and forests, streams and water holes in inland villages, and of woodlands and forests, coastal fisheries, mangroves and coral reefs in coastal villages in order to recognize the importance of spatially localized natural resources in the lives of the rural poor. Recall also that some 60 to 70 percent of people in the world's poorest regions live in rural areas. Nevertheless, barring agricultural land, natural capital has been absent from most of the models on the basis of which development economists have drawn policy recommendations. Leading books on the economics of development ignore the local natural-resource base and the wide variety of institutions that have evolved for managing them.[51]

5.6.1 Property Rights and the Local Commons

Talk of capital assets makes one think of their ownership and to the *rights* to those assets. Who owns the assets that characterize the local natural-resource base? Anthropologists and economists working at the fringes of official development economics have discovered that, barring agricultural land, they are mostly neither private nor the property of the state, but are communally owned. They are the *local commons*. As a proportion of total assets, the local commons range widely across ecological zones. In India they are most prominent in arid regions, mountain regions, and unirrigated areas; they are least prominent in humid regions and river valleys. (There is a rationale behind this, based on the need to pool risks.)

Are they important? In a pioneering study, Jodha (1986) reported evidence from over 80 villages in 21 dry districts in India, that among poor families the proportion of income based directly on their local commons is in the range 15 to 25 percent. In a study of 29 villages in south-eastern Zimbabwe, Cavendish (2000) arrived at even larger estimates: the proportion of income based directly on the local commons is 35 percent, with the figure for the poorest quintile reaching 40 percent.

Are the local commons managed communally? Not invariably, but in many cases they are or have been in the past. Where they are managed, the commons aren't open to outsiders, but only to those having historical rights through kinship ties and community membership. Communal management of local resources makes connection with "social capital," viewed as a complex of interpersonal networks, and hints at the basis upon which cooperation has traditionally been built. As the local commons have been seats of nonmarket relationships, transactions involving them are often not mediated by market prices. So their fate is frequently unreported in national economic accounts. However, a large empirical literature has confirmed that resource users in many cases cooperate, on occasion through democratic means. Case studies have shown, too, that cooperation can forestall rural and coastal communities from experiencing the "tragedy of the commons." The empirical literature on the local commons is valuable because it has unearthed how institutions that are neither part of the market system nor of the state develop organically to cope with resource allocation problems.[52]

Thus far, the good news about communitarian institutions. There are, however, two pieces of bad news. First, a general finding from studies on the management of local commons is that entitlements to their products is frequently based on private holdings: richer households enjoy a greater proportion of the benefits from the commons. Beteille (1983), for example, drew on examples from India to show that access to the commons is often restricted to the elite (e.g., caste Hindus). Cavendish (2000) has reported that, in absolute terms, richer households in his sample took more from the commons than poor households. That women are sometimes excluded has also been recorded—for example, from communal forestry (Agarwal 2001).[53]

The second piece of bad news is that local commons have degraded in recent years in many parts of the poor world. Why should this happen now in those places where they had been managed in a sustainable manner previously?

One reason is deteriorating external circumstances, which lower both the private and communal profitability of investment in the resource base. There are many ways in which circumstances can deteriorate. Increased uncertainty in property rights are a prime example. You and your community may think that you together own the forest your forefathers passed on to you, but if you don't possess a deed to the forest, your communal rights are insecure. In a dysfunctional state of affairs the government may confiscate the property. Political instability (in the extreme, civil war) is another source of uncertainty: your communal property could be taken away from you by force. Political instability is also a direct cause of environmental degradation: civil disturbance all too frequently expresses itself through the destruction of physical capital.

When people are uncertain of their rights to a piece of property, they are reluctant to make the investments necessary to protect and improve it. If the security of a communal property is uncertain (owing to whichever of the aforementioned reasons), the private returns expected from collective work on it are low. The influence would be expected to run the other way, too, with growing resource scarcity contributing to political instability, as rival groups battle over resources. The feedback could be positive, exacerbating the problem for a time, reducing private returns on investment further. Groups fighting over spatially localized resources are a frequent occurrence today (Homer-Dixon 1994). Over time, the communitarian institutions themselves disintegrate.[54]

The second reason is rapid population growth, which can trigger resource depletion if institutional practices are unable to adapt to the increased pressure on resources. In Côte d'Ivoire, for example, growth in rural population has been accompanied by increased deforestation and reduced fallows. Biomass production has declined, as has agricultural productivity (Lopez 1998). However, rapid population growth in the world's poorest regions in recent decades itself requires explanation. Increased economic insecurity, due to deteriorating institutions, is one identifiable cause: children yield a higher return in such circumstances than other forms of capital assets (Bledsoe 1994; Guyer 1994; Heyser 1996). This means that even if rapid population growth is a proximate cause of environmental destruction, the underlying cause would be expected to lie elsewhere. Thus, when positive links are observed in the data between population growth, environmental degradation, and poverty, they should not be read to mean that one of them is the prior cause of the others. Over time, each could in turn be the cause of the others.[55]

The third reason is that management practices at the local level are on occasion overturned by central fiat. A number of states in the Sahel imposed rules that in effect destroyed communal management practices in the forests. Villages ceased to have the authority to enforce sanctions on those who violated locally instituted rules. There are now a number of enumerations of the ways in which state authority can damage local institutions and turn the local commons into open-access resources (Thomson *et al* 1986; Somanathan,1991; Baland & Platteau 1996).

And the fourth reason is that the management of local commons often relies on social norms of behavior that are founded on reciprocity. But institutions based on reciprocity are fragile. They are especially fragile in the face of growing opportunities for private investment in substitute resources (Dasgupta 1993, 2007; Campbell et al. 2001). This is a case where an institution deteriorates even when there is no deterioration in external circumstances or in population pressure. However, when traditional systems of management collapse and aren't replaced by institutions that can act as substitutes, the use of the local commons becomes unrestrained. The commons then deteriorate, leading to the proverbial tragedy of the commons. In a recent study, Balasubramanian and Selvaraj (2003) have found that one of the oldest sources of irrigation—village tanks—have deteriorated over the years in a sample of villages in southern India because of a gradual decline in collective investment in their maintenance. The decline has come about as richer households have invested increasingly in private wells. Because poor households depend not only on tank water, but also on the fuelwood and fodder that grow round the tanks, the move to private wells by richer households has accentuated the economic stress experienced by the poor.

History tells us that the local commons can be expected to decline in importance in tandem with economic development (North & Thomas 1973). Ensminger's (1992) study of the privatization of common grazing lands among the Orma in northeastern Kenya established that the transformation took place with the consent of the elders of the tribe. She attributed this to cheaper transportation and widening markets, making private ownership of land more profitable. The elders were from the stronger families, and Ensminger didn't fail to notice that privatization accentuated inequality within the tribe.

The point isn't to lament the decline of the commons; it is to identify those who are likely to get hurt by the transformation of economic regimes. That there are winners in the process of economic development is a truism. Much the harder task is to identify the likely losers and have policies in place that act as safety nets for them. This involves the analysis of facts, broadly construed, not values.

5.6.2 Inclusive Wealth and Sustainable Development: Application

The weakening of institutions that once managed the local commons is symptomatic of a wider social problem. Property rights to environmental resources are frequently unspecified or are unenforced even if they are specified, meaning that their market prices are all too often zero. People, therefore, have little incentive to economize on their use. But as environmental resources *in situ* are socially valuable, their shadow prices are positive (Section 3.3). Earlier we noted that one way to measure social well-being is to estimate inclusive wealth, where wealth includes the social value not only of manufactured capital assets and knowledge and skills, but also environmental assets. We noted also that under certain circumstances social well-being is sustainable when, and only when, inclusive wealth per head does not decline over time. GNP is an inadequate measure of economic development because, among other things, it doesn't recognize the degradation of capital assets. Huge quantities of economic transactions are thereby absent from the measure. As it happens, the United Nations Development Programme's Human Development Index (HDI) is also impervious to the degradation of capital assets. In this sense, HDI is no better than GNP per head as a measure of social well-being. There are many circumstances where a nation's GNP per head would increase over a period of time and its HDI improve, even while inclusive wealth per head declines. In broad terms, the circumstances involve growing markets in certain classes of goods and services (e.g., petroleum products, transportation) and an absence of markets and collective policies for environmental goods and services (e.g., ecosystem services). This is why blanket proposals for free trade reflect faulty economics: the market mechanism can't be expected to function efficiently when markets for many environmental resources are simply missing.

Of course, a situation in which GNP per head increases and HDI improves while inclusive wealth per head declines can't go on forever. An economy that eats into its productive base in order to raise current production cannot do so indefinitely. Eventually GNP per head and HDI would have to decline too, unless policies were to so change that inclusive wealth per head begins to accumulate. Using data published by the World Bank (Hamilton & Clemens 1999), Dasgupta (2004 [2001], 2007) and Arrow et a.l (2004) have shown that even while GNP per head and HDI have both increased in the Indian subcontinent over the past three decades, inclusive wealth per head has declined somewhat. The decline has occurred because, relative to population growth, investments in manufactured capital, knowledge and skills, and improvements in institutions have not compensated for the degradation of natural capital. In sub-Saharan Africa, both GNP per head and wealth per head have declined, even while HDI has shown an improvement. The evidence also suggests that among the world's poorest regions, those that have experienced higher rates of population growth have faired worse in terms of accumulation of inclusive wealth per head.

The findings are, however, very tentative, not only because the World Bank's estimates of shadow prices are most crude, but also because the circumstances in which inclusive wealth per head is an appropriate index of social well-being are restrictive (they are at best a first approximation to the world as we now know it). There is much that remains to be done to improve the way we go about identifying sustainable development. Nevertheless, they explain the puzzling cultural phenomenon noted earlier. A current manifestation of the phenomenon is that, when development activists insist that development must be sustainable if it is to be viewed *as* development (e.g., recent issues of the United Nations' annual *Human Development Report*), they frequently advertise ethical criteria (e.g., HDI) that have no bearing on the sustainability of development. It is a curious state of affairs.

5.7 Freedom and Development

In a classic essay on social and political history, the late T.H. Marshall (1964) codified the modern concept of citizenship by identifying three social revolutions that took place sequentially in Western Europe: those of civil liberties in the eighteenth century, political liberties in the nineteenth, and socioeconomic liberties in the twentieth. Each type of liberty is valuable, but are they compatible, or are we faced with trade-offs among them?

Lipset (1959) famously observed that growth in GNP per head helps to promote democratic practice. The converse, that democratic practice and civil liberties promote material prosperity, has also been suggested by social scientists. Democracy and civil liberties, including the existence of a free press, have been seen not only as ends in themselves, some have seen them also as the means to economic progress. Understandably, rulers in the world's poorest countries have thought otherwise. That political and civil liberties on the one hand, and economic progress on the other, involve trade-offs when countries are poor has been the stated conviction of people in power in most of today's poorest countries. However, in their pioneering empirical work on what they termed *social capability*, Adelman and Morris (1965, 1967) saw societal openness to discussions and ideas as a driver of economic progress. Their work had little impact on development economics. In view of the indifference development activists showed until recently to the lack of political and civil liberties in large parts of the poor world (most especially sub-Saharan Africa), one can but conclude that the presence of substantial trade-offs among the various categories of freedom was the unstated conviction among them. "Food before freedom" was a slogan in frequent use among development activists until the demise of the Soviet Union.

In a crude statistical analysis of what in 1970 were 51 countries with the lowest GNP per head, Dasgupta (1990) found that, during the period 1970–1980, those nations whose citizens had enjoyed greater political and civil liberties had also on average performed better in terms of growth in GNP per head and improvements in life expectancy at birth. The correlation wasn't strong, but it was positive and significant. Of course, correlation isn't causation, but the finding did imply that political and civil liberties are not luxuries in poor countries; they don't necessarily hinder economic progress. Subsequently, several more elaborate investigations were published. They included not only poor nations but rich nations too. The most elaborate among them was Barro (1996), who found that among those nations where freedom was highly restricted, there was a positive correlation between political and civil liberties, on the one hand, and growth in GNP per head, on the other, but that among those where freedom was considerable, there was a negative correlation.[56] During the decade of the 1970s, the bulk of the worst offenders of restrictions in citizens' freedom were governments in the world's poorest countries, most of them in sub-Saharan Africa. Barro's findings were, therefore, consistent with those reported by Dasgupta.

That said, Barro's and Dasgupta's are only two empirical studies.[57] More importantly, neither author investigated whether, among poor countries, there was a positive link between political and civil liberties and increases in *inclusive wealth* per head, meaning that, as matters stand, we don't know the links between democracy and sustainable development in the contemporary world.[58] It is, therefore, as well to be circumspect about Sen's (1999) insistence that we regard development *as* freedom The redeployment of terms doesn't illuminate what development really amounts to. Freedom isn't a unitary good; rather, there are trade-offs among its various components. As the components are many, Sen's appeal to the notion of a person's capabilities (Section 2.2) as a way of repackaging freedom is, also, of no help.[59] Democracy, for example, means many things at once: regular and fair elections, government transparency, political pluralism, a free press, freedom of association, freedom to complain about degradation of the natural environment, and so on. We still have little empirical understanding of which aspects are most potent in bringing about sustainable development. That being so, a commitment to democracy today can't be based on grounds that it promotes sustainable development. We should favor democracy because (i) it is innately a good thing and (ii) it isn't known to hinder economic progress and may possibly even help to bring it about.

So we return to matters of fact, broadly construed. Empirical investigations into the possible links between crude measures of democracy and economic development would require that the criterion taken to be the indicator of democratic practice should be explicit and independent of the chosen measure of economic development (say, GNP per head). The cross-country indexes of civil and political liberties used by Dasgupta (1990) and Barro (1996), would appear to satisfy the requirement, because the way they were constructed bore little-to-no relation to economic activity.

However, so far as I know, at levels of aggregation below that of the nation, there are no consistent sets of indexes of democracy and civil liberties that are independent of material well-being. And yet, democratic practice and civic engagement could differ widely among regions within a country. Suppose we wish to inquire whether differences in the economic performance of the states or provinces in, say, India or China can be explained, at least in part, in terms of differences in the practice of local democracy. What should we look for? Problems are compounded because most of us *want* to believe that democracy is allied to the other things that make life good. Empirical investigations are thus vulnerable to what econometricians call the "warm glow effect," meaning that we are tempted to read signs of democratic practice in precisely those societies that have prospered in other ways.[60]

For these reasons, scholars today find it difficult to resist claiming more than is uncovered when they study the links between democracy, civil liberties, and economic progress. In a breathless passage on Sen (1999) on human capabilities, Kuper (2000, 663) refers to the instrumental value of democracy by saying that it has been "...demonstrated repeatedly that nondemocratic regimes are in fact unfailingly detrimental to human rights and well-being."

If only the demonstration were in hand. Alas, it isn't. The evidence is fragmentary and often qualitative. Below the level of nations, the evidence mostly amounts to citing instances, occasionally dressed up in the form of case studies, that are especially vulnerable to the warm-glow effect. Counter-citings aren't hard to find. At the level of nations, India and China have been used repeatedly to settle one intellectual score or another.

5.8 Ethical Complaints and Empirical Problems

But recent criticisms of GNP by development activists have been built on the language of morality.[61] Reports on poverty frequently proclaim that contemporary economists have adopted the wrong ethical standards, that if they would only frame the prevailing state of affairs the right way, we would know what should be done to alleviate poverty. We are often encouraged to think that to rename poverty, or development is to explain why and how it occurs. I believe this is what attracts us to the voluminous debate on quality-of-life indexes in academic publications and international development reports. The problem is that to describe is not the same as to explain. Moreover, as the subject of poverty raises passions, writers all too often end up assuming the moral high ground. Alternatives to GNP are proposed, preceded by such captions as "development with a human face," or "putting people first," or "humanizing economics," or prefaced by such solemn pronouncements as that "the poor should be regarded as agents, not patients," or that "freedom should be seen as a social commitment"—the suggestion being that those who don't preach morality when trying to uncover the social, political, and ecological processes that harbor poverty and destitution, overlook the human race or regard economic activity as having priority over human interests.

Not surprisingly then, academic expressions of moral superiority haven't been substitutes for anything other than academic expressions of moral superiority. Moreover, the urge to moralize has led to a proliferation of "rights" (Nussbaum 2003; Putnam 2003). The problem is that when aspects of the human good are transformed, willy nilly, into rights, the very notion of rights is debased, its force weakened. The moral rhetoric can also backfire. Making good points with bad arguments can disguise the fact that there are good arguments that would have served the purpose.

The following is an example of the kind of mistake one makes when attempting overkill: In giving expression to their moral outrage over the enormous inequality in today's world, the authors of UNDP (1998, 30) wrote: "New estimates show that the world's 225 richest people have a combined wealth of over $1 trillion U.S., equal to the annual income of the poorest 47 percent of the world's people (2.5 billion)."

But wealth is a stock, whereas income is a flow. As they differ in dimension, they can't be compared. The stock has to be converted into an equivalent flow (or vice versa) before comparisons can be made. (The authors of UNDP, 1999, repeated the mistake.) If we were to pursue UNDP's reasoning, we could follow the standard practice of converting wealth into a figure for permanent income by using a 5 percent annual interest rate, that is, divide wealth by 20. When this conversion is made on the data, my calculations, albeit they are very crude, tell me that the world's richest 225 people, having a combined annual income of over $50 billion U.S., earn more than the combined annual incomes of people in the world's twelve poorest countries, or about 7 percent of the world's population (385 million). This is still a sobering statistic.

5.9 Differences Over Facts, not Values

It isn't faulty ethics that has prevented contemporary economists from identifying sure-fire exits from poverty. After all, it is a concern with ethics that has prompted many of us to study the phenomenon in the first place. Alternative descriptions of poverty are easy enough to document, that the poor often don't enjoy food security, go hungry, don't own assets, are stunted and wasted, don't live long, can't read or write, are not empowered, can't ensure themselves against crop failure or household calamity, don't have control over their own lives, live in unhealthy surroundings, and so forth. There is no surprise there: modern economic theory explains why they would all be expected to go together.[62] What has proved to be really hard is uncovering the pathways that make people poor and keep them in poverty. In Section 5.4 I offered an account of how very perplexing the problems associated with gathering and analyzing survey data are. One class of debates is over which variables are best predictors of the value of some other variable (e.g., children's educational attainment). Such debates are partly factual and partly methodological (what are the best procedures for *uncovering* a fact?), but even the latter are over procedures for identification, estimation, and model control. A recent discussion among development economists in South Africa has been over what are the the the most important determinants of black children's educational attainment (Case & Deaton 1999, Bhorat et al 2001). The pupil-teacher ratio, food-energy intake per household member, and parents' educational attainments could be expected to be among those determinants. All investigators would appear to take it for granted that an improvement in children's education performance *is a good thing.* As that is a shared value, the investigators don't make a point of it.

At a deep level, then, disagreements over the right means to further given ends arise far more frequently in development economics than disputes over the nature of appropriate ends. To see explorations in ethical values as the corrective for the deficiencies of contemporary development economics is at best self-indulgence masquerading as moral sensitivity; at worst it is a distraction. We would, for example, have been far ahead in our understanding of the recent economic history of the world's poorest countries if development economists had taken nature seriously.

It is hard to overstate the significance of the latter. Like human metabolic pathways (Section 5.3), ecological processes are overwhelmingly nonlinear (see e.g., Steffen et al. 2004). Nevertheless, our intuition about development prospects have been formed mostly by linear analogies. Thus, when *The Independent* (1999, 4 December) says in its editorial that "... economic growth is good for the environment, because countries need to put poverty behind them in order to care," or when *The Economist* (1999, 4 December, 17) writes that "... trade improves the environment, because it raises incomes, and the richer people are, the more willing they are to devote resources to cleaning up their living space," they express the belief that environmental damages can always be undone if and when it is so desired. However, as we noted in our discussion of poverty traps (Section 5.3), pathways driven by nonlinear processes are often irreversible. Unless note is taken of that fact, policies adopted in the name of development may well be that very development's undoing.[63]

Earlier we noted that discussions on economic development based on the United Nations' Human Development Index (HDI) can mislead because the index lacks ethical foundation. We noted, too, that discussions founded on "capabilities" end nowhere because the capability theory doesn't offer ways to value the inevitable trade-offs among capability sets. But the working economist's loudest complaint against HDI- and capabilities-style reasoning is practical, not first-order normative. To instruct those in charge of implementing policy that their task is to raise HDI or improve capabilities isn't helpful because the instruction is altogether too flabby. It encourages coordination failure among those implementing policy: almost every policy should be expected to promote some element or other of someone's favourite goal included in HDI or capabilities. Adopting either would make it most difficult to hold public officials responsible (Seabright 2001). To insist that if the inclusive wealths (or as a first approximation, the *net* incomes) of the intended beneficiaries of a policy aren't rising one shouldn't be allowed to claim that they are benefiting, is not only an ethically justifiable directive (sections 3.3.1 to 3.3.2 and 5.6.2), it makes practical sense, also.

All this isn't to say that disputes over ends can't or don't occur, it is only to say that even if differences in ends are the sources of the disputes, people soon enough bypass those sources and argue instead about history (for example, about which person or group committed which atrocity, when) and about the ways in which social, political, and ecological processes work.

In their influential World Bank monograph on the incidence of undernourishment in poor countries, Reutlinger and Pellekaan (1986, 6) wrote:

> long run economic growth is often slowed by widespread chronic food insecurity. People who lack energy are ill-equipped to take advantage of opportunities for increasing their productivity and output. That is why policymakers in some countries may want to consider interventions that speed up food security for the groups worst affected without waiting for the general effect of long-run growth.

Then there are economists who advocate policies based on an opposite causal mechanism, such as the one in World Bank (1986, 7):

> The best policies for alleviating malnutrition and poverty are those which increase growth and the competitiveness of the economy, for a growing and competitive economy facilitates a more even distribution of human capital and other assets and ensures higher incomes for the poor. Progress in the battle against malnutrition and poverty can be sustained if, and only if, there is satisfactory economic growth.

There doesn't appear to me to be a conflict in values in the quotations here. Rather, it reads as though there is disagreement over the most effective means for eliminating destitution. That the publications are from the same institution and from the same year should not cause surprise: we are all still woefully ignorant of the ways in which human societies and nature respond to policies.

NOTES

1. An earlier version was published in *Economics and Philosophy*, 2005, 2 (2): 221–278, under the title, "What Do Economists Analyze and Why: Values or Facts?." I am grateful to Harold Kincaid and Donald Ross for encouraging me to prepare a revised and extended version of that paper for this volume. They also offered me suggestions on what to revise. Shamik Dasgupta clarified a number of philosophical points. For their comments on the previous article, I am particularly grateful to Kenneth Arrow and Geoffrey Brennan.

2. Within economics, among the most prominent expositions of this view include Robbins (1932), Samuelson (1947), Graaff (1962), and Joan Robinson (1964). Within political theory, see Barry (1965).

3. For contrasting opinions on the question, see Stiglitz (2002) and pretty nearly any recent issue of the weekly magazine, *The Economist*.

4. Ehrlich and Ehrlich (1996) offer an illuminating account of how expert scientific findings are willfully ignored, even distorted, when they prove awkard to private interests. The authors cite contemporary debates on global warming (in particular, its anthropogenic causes) and the depletion of biological diversity as examples.

5. See, for example, Freeman (1993). I personally found the accusation ironic, because I had published a treatise only a few years earlier on destitution and

well-being, where well-being was given a wider interpretation than one based exclusively on "revealed preference," which is what Williams was attacking. See Dasgupta (1993). I go into these matters in greater detail in sections 2 and 3.

6. My choice of subject for the case study has been prompted by Hilary Putnam's and Martha Nussbaum's criticisms, quoted earlier. Both sets of criticism were based on a belief that there is an absence of ethical concern among professional economists studying economic development.

7. For convenience, I define the technical terms just used in the text: Let X be a set of alternatives (e.g., states of affair, or (more narrowly) commodity bundles). By a *partial ordering* of X we mean a binary relation R (e.g., "at least as good as") among members of X, satisfying (i) "reflexivity": for all x in X, xRx; and (ii) "transitivity": for all x, y, z in X, xRy and yRz implies xRz. A partial ordering R is an *ordering* if it satisfies (iii) "completeness": for all x, y in X, either xRy or yRx. (Note that R is a partial ordering of X if there is at least one pair of members of X that are not related to each other via R.) From R we may induce the "strict" binary relation, P (e.g., "better than"), which is defined as follows: for all x, y in X, xPy if an only if xRy and *not* yRx.

By a *numerical representation* of an ordering R we mean a real-valued function U defined on X, such that for all x, y in X, xRy if and only if $U(x) \geq U(y)$. It follows that xPy if and only if $U(x) > U(y)$.

It is obvious that if X is a finite set, every ordering defined on it has a numerical representation. In fact, any order preserving transformation of a numerical representation of a given ordering is itself a numerical representation of that same ordering. This is what economists mean when they say that U is *ordinal*. If, on the other hand, X is an infinite set, some structure (viz. "continuity") has to be imposed on an ordering if it is to possess a numerical representation. (Example: the lexicographic ordering of points on the unit square does not possess a numerical representation.)

8. In one form or other these charges appear in Sen (1987, 1999), Nussbaum (2000a,b, 2003), and Putnam (2002, 2003).

9. Public goods are commodities that are (i) jointly consumable and (ii) nonexcludable. Fresh air used to be a prototypical public good. In a classic paper Samuelson (1954) showed that the supply of public goods involves the now-familiar Prisoners' Dilemma and concluded that the dilemma would be resolved effectively, not by markets, but by politics.

10. I owe this way of putting the matter to Robert Solow.

11. Among the most general formulations are to be found in Gorman (1968) and Koopmans (1972).

12. Pareto (1909) had used the term *ophelimity* in lieu of utility, but it has not been adopted by economists.

13. See, for example, Samuelson (1954), Schelling (1960, 1978), Arrow (1971, 1974), Becker (1981, 1983), Dasgupta (1993, 2004 [2001]), and Persson and Tabellini (2000) for a coverage of this range of objects.

14. The literature on this is huge. Scanlon (1978) contains a brief but lucid statement.

15. Nussbaum (2003, 416). Her list, as catalogued by Putnam (2003), consists of (1) Life (including freedom from premature mortality), (2) Bodily Health (including reproductive health, adequate nourishment, and shelter), (3) Bodily Integrity (e.g., security against violent assault, having opportunities for sexual satisfaction and for choice in matters of reproduction) (4) Senses, Imagination, and Thought (e.g., being

able to have pleasurable experiences and avoid nonbeneficial pain), (5) Emotional Development (not having it blighted by fear and anxiety), (6) Practical Reason (being able to form a conception of the good life), (7) Affiliation (e.g., freedom of assembly), (8) Other species (being able to live with concern for and in relation to the world of nature), and (9) Control over one's material and political environment.

16. To confirm why trade-offs can't be avoided, see UNDP (2003), which attempts to cost the Millennium Development Goals for the world's poorest countries. The goals include not only aggregate poverty reduction and the availability of potable water, but also reductions in the incidence of malaria, tuberculosis, and HIV-AIDS.

It is an attractive feature of Nozick's and Rawls' theories of rights that they are within the financial reach of any society. Even the poorest society should be able to ensure that people enjoy democracy and civil liberties; and even the poorest society can in addition follow Rawls, if it desires, and choose the social state where the poorest is better off than the poorest in every other social state. (Rawls, 1972, however, notably restricted applications of his theory of justice to countries that are not overly poor.)

17. Readers will recognize that this very stylized version can be extended in any number of ways: Capabilities evolve over time (later additions being constrained by earlier choices); at the earliest stages of one's life, the choices are made by others (hopefully on one's behalf!); and so on.

18. Formally, $\bar{x}_n(\varepsilon)$ is any element in F_n that maximizes $V(x_n,\varepsilon)$. In many contexts $\bar{x}_n(\varepsilon)$ would be unique.

19. Theories of justice accommodated within the broad perspective of modern economics are often contrasted with those deontological theories that are founded upon ideas of *procedural fairness* (Hayek 1960, Rawls 1972, Nozick 1974). The contrast, it is commonly said, lies in the fact that the criteria by which fairness of a procedure is judged are independent of any prior assessment of the possible outcomes in applying the procedure.

In such theories, problems lie with the prior notion of fairness. Examples are often taken from gambling. For instance, if there are two people on a lifeboat and food enough for only one, a procedure frequently advocated in those theories is to allocate the food on the basis of the toss of an unbiased coin. The rogue word here is *unbiased*. Although it means equal chance of either outcome, its ethical force occurs from the idea of empirical probabilities, that if such a coin were tossed over and over again, each outcome would occur approximately 50 percent of the time. Never mind that the procedure itself relies on a single toss. Were we to know nothing about empirical probabilities, we wouldn't even begin to have an intuitive sense of what an unbiased coin is. The fairness of the procedure rests squarely on our previous evaluation of probable consequences.

20. HDI is a suitably normalised linear combination of gross national product per head, life expectancy at birth, and literacy. See Section 5.

21. Tversky and Kahneman (1986) found experimental evidence that the way a decision problem is framed can matter to the decision maker even when the alternative ways of framing the problem are logically equivalent. It should not be overly difficult to offer an explanation for framing effects in terms of selection advantages: words can be, and often are, used as purely signalling devices. However, if the person in the example I am considering in the text suffered from such framing defects, she could enhance her well-being indefinitely by merely switching her benchmark back and forth even while remaining at the same social state. Psychologists would be justified in calling her deluded.

22. Equivalently, they could conduct the exercise by using an "infant-equivalent scale"; and so on, for any other category of persons.

23. Efficiency, as defined earlier, is to be contrasted from the well-known concept of *Pareto efficiency*. The latter is efficiency on the subspace of utilities. See Section 3.2.

24. A revealing difference between the axioms postulated by Koopmans and Maskin, on the one hand, and those postulated by Hammond and d'Aspremont-Gevers, on the other, is in their specifications of the extent to which, for each k, the V_{ki}s ($i = 1, 2, \ldots, N$) are measurable and comparable among the is.

25. To confirm this, consider a feasible set of social states. Pick an efficient social state from that set ("efficiency" defined earlier). Ignore the uninteresting case where each G_{ki} is an increasing function of each of the U_{ki}s. Consider now the projection of the chosen point on the N-dimensional subspace of individual utilities. Clearly, it is not an efficient point on the projection of the feasible set of social states on that subspace; which is another way of saying that it is not Pareto-efficient. Sen's (1970) "liberal paradox" is an instance of this observation.

26. Berlin (1959) is a classic on this (often hidden) code. He noted that Marx's notion of "false consciousness" has been used by tyrannies to justify their actions.

27. In theoretical welfare economics, when the model being subjected to analysis is of an aggregate form, say, involving (aggregate) consumption, investment, and leisure, such constituents as health and education are often assumed to be subsumed under the former two, and social well-being is regarded to be based solely on individual utilities. The point in such exercises frequently is to study the way various forms of the function H_k reflect concerns about equality among people.

28. Rawls' two principles of justice (Rawls 1972, 302–303) are directed in part at the production and distribution of certain constituents (political and civil liberties) and in part at the production and distribution of certain determinants (income and wealth): Rawls offered a mix of constituents and determinants. In the text I am claiming that it is in theory possible to evaluate exclusively in terms of one or the other.

29. Discussions on even the choice of appropriate discount rates in public projects (i.e., social discount rates) have typically been about facts, not values: should the rates chosen correspond the market rate of interest and, if so, which one? On this see Arrow et al (1996). Differences of views on social discount rates are usually handled by sensitivity analysis. See Section 4.2.

The briefest account I know of project evaluation is in Daily et al (1999). For fuller discussions, including practical methods for estimating shadow prices and the associated social discount rates, see Arrow and Kurz (1970), Little and Mirrlees (1968, 1974), Dasgupta et al. (1972), and Dasgupta (2004 [2001]).

30. One can even argue that, because it doesn't take note of capital depreciation, GNP cannot be a measure of opulence. See Section 5.6.

31. Majority rule is an example of a voting rule. What I am calling a "voting rule" was named a "social welfare function" by Arrow (1963 [1951]). There is, unfortunately, a profusion of technical terms in modern economics. But as long as we use them consistently, we won't run into problems.

32. The restriction that individual orderings and *only* individual orderings are permitted to be introduced in the aggregation exercise has been much criticized in the social choice literature. But no one has provided evidence of what additional information could be made permissible at a polling station without jeopardising the electoral process. Intensity of feeling? That would be subject to serious distortions owing to exaggerated

claims. Special needs of the voter? That would violate a central principle of democracy, namely, equal citizenship (anonymity of the voter). Interpersonal comparisons of well-being? But who is to conduct the comparisons, something that are expected to have already been undertaken by the civic minded voters when they cast their votes? And so forth.

Voting rules in many national elections (e.g., presidential elections in the United States, parliamentary elections in the United Kingdom) require voters to disclose even less information than Arrow made a requirement in his theory. Election rules there insist that voter k names only the candidate who is highest on the ordering induced by W_k. The restriction is not only unnecessary, but overly limiting too: it can distort election outcomes when the number of candidates exceeds two. On this see Dasgupta and Maskin (2004).

33. "Orderings" and "partial orderings" were defined in note 7.

34. The protagonist in William Styron's *Sophie's Choice* faced an even crueler dilemma when forced to choose one of her two children for certain death in the gas chamber. (Failure to comply would have led to the certain death of both children in the gas chamber.) Having been forced to choose thus destroyed her, but her humanity shone through when, in the closing passages of the book, she also disclosed the reason for the choice she had made.

35. The literature emanating from them is huge. See, for example, Sen and Sengupta (1983) and Behrman (1988a,b).

36. See especially Rosenzweig and Schultz (1982). In support of this interpretation, a sample from northern India revealed that higher birth-order girls are discriminated against even more strongly than lower birth-order girls. See M. Das Gupta (1987).

37. See Cochrane (1979), Behrman and Wolfe (1984), Kennedy (1989), and Sen (1990), among others. To the best of my knowledge, McElroy and Horney (1981) is the earliest study to use bargaining theory (specifically, the well-known Nash bargaining solution) to explain household commodity demands. Earlier, Kalai and Smorodinsky (1975) had developed a model of bargaining that would appear to be better suited for studying household choices (Sen 1990; Dasgupta 1993).

38. See Goody (1973), Goody and Tambiah (1973), Goody (1976), Williamson (1976), and Goody et al. (1981).

39. See Blume and Durlauf (2001) for a general analysis of the effect of what economists call "social preferences" on collective behavior; and Dasgupta (1993, 2002, 2003) for a model of fertility behavior based on such preferences.

40. See, for example, the case studies in Dasgupta et al. (1972). Nussbaum (2000b) imagines that project evaluators produce a single number (the present discounted value of the flow of social profits) and consider their job done. Of the many project evaluation reports I have read over the years, this was rarely the practice.

41. The first of what has become an annual *World Development Report* of the World Bank, was centred on poverty in sub-Saharan Africa and the Indian subcontinent (World Bank 1978). The *Report*'s fourth chapter bore the title "Prospects for Growth and Alleviation of Poverty." The annual *Report*'s immediate focus returns periodically to poverty (World Bank 1990, 2000). Much earlier, the Perspective Planning Division of the Government of India produced a blueprint for guaranteeing a basic minimum income for all (Pant et al. 1962). Nothing came of it though.

42. It is worth noting in passing that investment rates in East Asian countries (e.g., South Korea, Taiwan) during the 1980s frequently exceeded 40 percent of GNP.

43. A recent statistical analysis issued from the World Bank, by Dollar and Kraay (2000), had the revealing title "Growth *Is* Good for the Poor."

44. The World Bank's annual *World Development Report* is a good indicator of the evolution of thinking on economic development. World Bank (1997, 2002) were devoted to the role of the State and to the building of productive institutions.

45. I have discussed these pathways in greater detail elsewhere (Dasgupta 1993, 1997). For a historical account of the way improvements in nutrition intake and economic development reinforced each other during the economic rise of the West, see Fogel et al. (1983) and Fogel (1994, 2004). Identifying poverty traps at the household level from economic data is fraught with difficulties, because one has to locate once-similar households whose economic conditions have diverged over time. Jalan and Ravallion (2002) have found evidence of poverty traps in contemporary rural China.

46. A frequent illustration is the contrast offered by South Korea and Ghana. GNP per head was roughly the same in the two countries in 1960. But South Korea enjoyed one towering advantage over Ghana: the government in South Korea had effected land reform and introduced universal primary education. That early advantage shows today, in that when GNP is measured in United States dollars, the ratio of South Korea's and Ghana's GNP per head is of the order of 20:1.

47. For a discussion of the finding, see Deaton and Dreze (2002).

48. *Total fertility rate* (TFR) is the number of children who would be born to a woman if she were to live to the end of her childbearing years and bear children in accordance with current age-specific fertility rates. It is the best single index of natalism. In the late 1970s, TFR in sub-Saharan Africa was 6.6, that in the Indian subcontinent, 5.3. In the mid 1990s, the corresponding figures were 5.6 and 3.4, respectively. As a matter of comparison, we note that the corresponding figures for the world as a whole were 3.7 and 2.8.

49. See, for example, Kelley (1988). Sen (1994) was even contemptuous of those ecologists who expressed concern about Earth's capacity to sustain 8–10 billion people at a reasonable standard of living.

50. The thesis has been developed more fully in Dasgupta (1982, 1993, 2003, 2004, 2004 [2001]) and Dasgupta and Mäler (1991).

51. As examples, see Dreze and Sen (1990) and Ray (1998). I have grumbled about the absence of natural capital from official development economics many times before. (See, for example, Dasgupta 1982, 1993, 2004, 2004 [2001]; Dasgupta & Mäler 1991). Since 1996, Professor Charles Perrings, Editor of the journal *Environment and Development Economics* (Cambridge University Press), has been active in promoting the inclusion of natural capital in development economics.

52. See Chopra *et al* (1989), Feeny *et al* (1990), Ostrom (1990), Bromley *et al* (1992), Baland and Platteau (1996), Ghate *et al* (2007) and the references there. The economic theory of the local commons was developed in Dasgupta and Heal (1979, ch. 3).

53. McKean (1992) stressed that benefits from the commons are frequently captured by the elite. Agarwal and Narain (1996) exposed the same phenomenon in their study of water management practices in a semi-arid village in the Gangetic plain.

54. Recently de Soto (2000) has argued that the absence of well-defined property rights and their protection is the central fact of underdevelopment. Rightly, he stressed the inability of poor people to obtain credit because of a lack of collateral. In the text I am offering a multicausal explanation for poverty.

55. For the theory, see Dasgupta (1993, 2003); for a recent empirical study on South Africa that tests the theory, see Aggarwal *et al* (2001)

56. Political and civil liberties, even though they are distinct goods, are highly correlated in the contemporary world. See Taylor and Jodice (1983).

57. Sen (1999) has notably observed that famines haven't occurred in democracies. In the text I am focussing not on extreme events, but on the prospects of escape from persistent ills like malnutrition. Although famines receive more attention in the press, malnutrition and disease are quantitatively of greater significance, because they are persistent and they involve far larger numbers of people.

58. The sole (but very partial) exception is the valuable paper by Barrett and Graddy (2000), who in a cross country study, have shown that, controlling for income differences, urban air-borne pollutants and several of water-borne pollutants are negatively and significantly correlated with the extent to which citizens enjoy political and civil liberties. People have greater voice in more open societies and that greater voice is able to translate itself into more effective political action.

59. In his review of Sen (1999), Seabright (2001) enlarges on the question of when repackaging a concept makes that concept less problematic.

60. Roemer (1999) makes a similar point about the temptations the political "left" yielded to in the 1960s and 1970s, to define "socialism" as the confluence of all good things.

61. Since 1990 the shrillest have been the authors of the annual *Human Development Report* of the United Nations Development Programme.

62. See Dasgupta (1993). For confirmation that there are no surprises there, see the summary and discussion of the findings of a large-scale survey undertaken by the World Bank, in Narayan (2000). I need hardly add at this point in the article that there is no acknowledgement in the publication that the findings confirmed what contemporary economists had predicted. This isn't to play down the usefulness of repeated confirmations of theoretical predictions. I merely protest against the way empirical findings confirming predictions of modern economic theory are thrown back at the theorists as showing evidence that they are ethically insensitive.

63. For explorations into the implications of ecological non-linearities for economic policy, see Dasgupta (1982, 2004 [2001]) and Dasgupta and Mäler (2004).

REFERENCES

Adelman, I. (1979). *Redistribution Before Growth*. Leiden: University of Leiden.

Adelman, I. & Morris, C.T. (1965). "A Factor Analysis of the Interrelationship between Social and Political Variables and per Capita Gross National Product." *Quarterly Journal of Economics* 79 (3): 555–578.

Adelman, I. & Morris, C.T. (1967). *Society, Politics and Economic Development*. Baltimore, MD: Johns Hopkins University Press.

Adelman, I. & Morris, C.T. (1973). *Economic Growth and Social Equity in Developing Countries*. Stanford, CA: Stanford University Press.

Agarwal, A. & Narain, S. (1996). *Dying Wisdom: Rise, Fall and Potential of India's Traditional Water Harvesting Systems.* New Delhi: Centre for Science and Development.

Agarwal, B. (2001). "Participatory Exclusions, Community Forestry, and Gender: An Analysis for South Asia and a Conceptual Framework." *World Development* 29 (10): 1623–1648.

Aggarwal, R., Netanyahu, S. & Romano, C. (2001). "Access to Natural Resources and the Fertility Decision of Women: The Case of South Africa." *Environment and Development Economics* 6 (2): 209–236.

Ahluwalia, M.S. (1976a). "Inequality, Poverty and Development." *Journal of Development Economics* 3 (4): 307–342.

Ahluwalia, M.S. (1976b). "Income Distribution and Development: Some Stylized Facts." *American Economic Review* (Papers & Proceedings) 66 (2): 128–135.

Amsden, A. (1989). *Asia's Next Giant: South Korea and Late Industrialization.* New York: Oxford University Press.

Anand, S. & Ravallion, M. (1993). "Human Development in Poor Countries: On the Role of Private Incomes and Public Services." *Journal of Economic Perspectives* 7 (1): 133–150.

Arrow, K.J. (1963 [1951]). *Social Choice and Individual Values,* 2nd ed.. New York: John Wiley.

Arrow, K.J. (1971). "Political and Economic Evaluation of Social Effects of Externalities." In M. Intriligator, Ed., *Frontiers of Quantitative Economics, Vol. I.* Amsterdam: North Holland.

Arrow, K.J. (1973). "Rawls' Principle of Just Savings." *Swedish Journal of Economics* 75 (3): 323–335.

Arrow, K.J. (1974). *The Limits of Organization.* New York: W.W. Norton.

Arrow, K.J. (1995). "A Note On Flexibility and Freedom." In K. Basu, P. Pattanaik & K. Suzumura, Eds., *Choice, Welfare, and Development.* Oxford: Clarendon Press.

Arrow, K.J., Dasgupta, P., Goulder, L., Daily, G., Ehrlich, P., Heal, G., Levin, S., Mäler, K.-G., Schneider, S., Starrett, D. & Walker, B. (2004). "Are We Consuming Too Much?" *Journal of Economic Perspectives* 18 (3): 147–172.

Arrow, K.J., Dasgupta, P. & Mäler, K.-G. (2003a). "The Genuine Saving Criterion and the Value of Population." *Economic Theory* 21 (1): 217–225.

Arrow, K.J., Dasgupta, P. & Mäler, K.-G. (2003b). "Evaluating Projects and Assessing Sustainable Development in Imperfect Economies." *Environmental and Resource Economics* (Symposium on the Economics of Non-Convex Environments) 26 (4): 647–685.

Arrow, K.J. & Kurz, M. (1970). *Public Investment, the Rate of Return and Optimal Fiscal Policy.* Baltimore: Johns Hopkins University Press.

Atkinson, A.B. (1973). "How Progressive Should Income Tax Be?" In M. Parkin & R. Nobay, Eds., *Essays in Modern Economics.* London: Longman.

Baland, J.-M. & Platteau, J.-P. (1996). *Halting Degradation of Natural Resources: Is There a Role for Rural Communities?* Oxford: Clarendon Press.

Balasubramanian, R. & Selvaraj, K.N. (2003). "Poverty, Private Property and Common Pool Management: The Case of Irrigation Tanks in South India." Working Paper No. 2–03. South Asian Network for Development and Environmental Economics, Kathmandu.

Bardhan, P.K. (1974). "On Life and Death Questions." *Economic and Political Weekly* 9 (32–34, Special Number): 1293–1305.

Barrett, S. & Graddy, K. (2000). "Freedom, Growth and the Environment." *Environment and Development Economics* 5 (4): 433–456.

Barro, R.J. (1996). "Democracy and Growth." *Journal of Economic Growth* 1(1): 1–27.

Barry, B. (1965). *Political Argument*. London: Routledge & Kegan Paul.

Bauer, P.T. (1971). *Dissent on Development*. London: Weidenfeld & Nicolson.

Becker, G. (1964). *Human Capital*. New York: Columbia University Press.

Becker, G. (1981). *A Treatise on the Family*. Cambridge, MA: Harvard University Press.

Becker, G. (1983). *Human Capital: A Theoretical and Empirical Analysis, with Special Reference to Education*. Chicago: University of Chicago Press.

Behrman, J.R. (1988a). "Nutrition, Health, Birth Order and Seasonality: Intrahousehold Allocation Among Children in Rural India." *Journal of Development Economics* 28 (1): 43–62.

Behrman, J.R. (1988b). "Intrahousehold Allocation of Nutrients in Rural India: Are Boys Favoured? Do Parents Exhibit Inequality Aversion?" *Oxford Economic Papers* 40 (1): 32–54.

Behrman, J. & Wolfe, B.L. (1984). "More Evidence on Nutrition Demand: Income Seems Overrated and Women's Schooling Underemphasized." *Journal of Development Economics* 14(1–2): 105–128.

(Bergson, A.) Burk, A. (1938). "A Reformulation of Certain Aspects of Welfare Economics." *Quarterly Journal of Economics* 52 (3): 310–334.

Berlin, I. (1959). "Two Concepts of Liberty." In *Four Essays on Liberty*. Oxford: Oxford University Press.

Beteille, A., Ed. (1983). *Equality and Inequality: Theory and Practice*. Delhi: Oxford University Press.

Bhagwati, J. (1982). "Directly Unproductive, Profit Seeking (DUP) Activities." *Journal of Political Economy* 90 (5): 988–1002.

Bhagwati, J. & Desai, P. (1970). *India: Planning for Industrialization*. Oxford: Oxford University Press.

Bhagwati, J. & Srinivasan, T.N. (1975). *Foreign Trade Regimes and Economic Development: India*. New York: Columbia University Press.

Bhorat, H., Leibbrandt, M., Mazia, M., van der Berg, S. & Woolard, I. (2001). *Fighting Poverty* Cape Town: University of Cape Town Press.

Birdsall, N., Kelley, A.C. & and Sinding, S.W., Eds. (2001). *Population Matters: Demographic Change, Economic Growth, and Poverty in the Developing World*. Oxford: Oxford University Press.

Bledsoe, C. (1994). " 'Children are Like Young Bamboo Trees': Potentiality and Reproduction in sub-Saharan Africa." In K. Lindahl-Kiessling and H. Landberg, Eds., *Population, Economic Development and the Environment*. Oxford: Oxford University Press.

Blume, L. & Durlauf, S.N. (2001). "The Interactions-Based Approach to Socioeconomic Behavior." In S.N. Durlauf & H. Peyton Young, Eds., *Social Dynamics*. Cambridge, MA: MIT Press.

Boserup, E. (1970). *Women's Role in Economic Development*. New York: St. Martin's Press.

Bromley, D.W. et al., Eds. (1992). *Making the Commons Work: Theory, Practice and Policy*. San Francisco: ICS Press.

Caldwell, J.C. (1980). "Mass Education as a Determinant of the Timing of Fertility Decline." *Population and Development Review* 6 (2): 225–256.

Campbell, B., Manando, A., Nemarundwe, N., Sithole, B., De Jong, W., Luckert, M. & Matose, F. (2001). "Challenges to Proponents of Common Property Resource Systems: Despairing Voices from the Social Forests of Zimbabwe." *World Development* 29 (4): 589–600.

Case, A. & Deaton, A. (1999). "School Inputs and Educational Outcomes in South Africa." *Quarterly Journal of Economics* 114 (3): 1047–1084.

Cavendish, W. (2000). "Empirical Regularities in the Poverty-Environment Relationships of Rural Households: Evidence from Zimbabwe." *World Development* 28 (11): 1979–2003.

Chen, L.C., Huq, E. & D'Souza, S. (1981). "Sex Bias in the Family Allocation of Food and Health Care in Bangladesh." *Population and Development Review* 7 (1): 55–70.

Chen, L.C. (1982). "Where Have the Women Gone? Insights from Bangladesh on the Low Sex Ratio of India's Population." *Economic and Political Weekly* 17 (10): 365–372.

Chenery, H. et al. (1975). *Redistribution with Growth*. New York: Oxford University Press.

Chopra, K., Kadekodi, G.K. & Murty, M.N. (1989). *Participatory Development: People and Common Property Resources*. New Delhi: Sage Publications.

Coase, R. (1960). "The Problem of Social Cost." *Journal of Law and Economics* 3 (1): 1–44.

Cochrane, S. (1979). *Fertility and Education: What Do We Really Know?* Baltimore, MD: Johns Hopkins University Press.

Cochrane, S. (1983). "Effects of Education and Urbanization on Fertility." In R. Bulatao & R. Lee, Eds., *Determinants of Fertility in Developing Countries*, Vol II. New York: Academic Press.

Cohen, B. (1993). "Fertility Levels, Differentials and Trends." In K.A. Foote, K.H. Hill & L.G. Martin, Eds., *Demographic Change in Sub-Saharan Africa*. Washington, DC: National Academy Press.

Daily, G., Dasgupta, P., Soderqvist, T., Aniyar, S., Arrow, K.J., Ehrlich, P., Jansson, A.M., Jansson, B.O., Kautsky, N., Levin, S., Lubchenco, J., Mäler, K.-G., Simpson, D., Starrett, D., Tilman, D. & and Walker, B. (1999). "The Nature of Value and the Value of Nature." *Science* 289 (21 July): 395–396.

Das Gupta, M. (1987). "Selective Discrimination Against Female Children in India." *Population and Development Review* 13 (1): 77–100.

Dasgupta, P. (1974). "On Some Alternative Criteria for Justice Between Generations." *Journal of Public Economics* 3 (4): 405–423.

Dasgupta, P. (1982). *The Control of Resources*. Cambridge, MA: Harvard University Press.

Dasgupta, P. (1990). "Well-Being and the Extent of Its Realization in Poor Countries." *Economic Journal* 100 (Supplement): 1–32.

Dasgupta, P. (1993). *An Inquiry into Well-Being and Destitution*. Oxford: Clarendon Press.

Dasgupta, P. (1997). "Nutritional Status, the Capacity for Work and Poverty Traps." *Journal of Econometrics* 77 (1): 5–38.

Dasgupta, P. (2003). "Population, Poverty, and the Natural Environment." In K.-G. Mäler & J. Vincent, Eds, *Handbook of Environmental and Resource Economics*. Amsterdam: North Holland.

Dasgupta, P. (2004). "World Poverty: Causes and Pathways." In F. Bourguignon & B. Pleskovic, Eds., *Annual World Bank Conference on Development Economics 2003: Accelerating Development*, 159–196. New York: World Bank and Oxford University Press.

Dasgupta, P. (2004 [2001]). *Human Well-Being and the Natural Environment*, 2nd ed. Oxford: Oxford University Press.

Dasgupta, P. (2007). *Economics: A Very Short Introduction*. Oxford: Oxford University Press.

Dasgupta P. & Heal, G.M. (1979). *Economic Theory and Exhaustible Resources*. Cambridge, England: Cambridge University Press.

Dasgupta, P. & Mäler, K.-G. (1991). "The Environment and Emerging Development Issues." *Proceedings of the Annual World Bank Conference on Development Economics 1990*, 101–132. Washington, DC: World Bank.

Dasgupta, P. & Mäler, K.-G. (2000). "Net National Product, Wealth, and Social Well-Being." *Environment and Development Economics* 5 (1): 69–93.

Dasgupta, P. & Mäler, K.-G., Eds. (2004). *The Economics of Non-Convex Ecosystems*. Dordrecht, The Netherlands: Kluwer.

Dasgupta, P., Marglin, S. & Sen, A. (1972). *Guidelines for Project Evaluation*. New York: United Nations.

Dasgupta, P. & Maskin, E. (2004)."The Fairest Vote of All." *Scientific American* 290 (3): 92–97.

Dasgupta, P. & Ray, D. (1986). "Inequality as a Determinant of Malnutrition and Unemployment, 1: Theory." *Economic Journal* 96 (4): 1011–1034.

Dasgupta, P. & Ray, D. (1987). "Inequality as a Determinant of Malnutrition and Unemployment, 2: Policy." *Economic Journal* 97 (1): 177–188.

d'Aspremont, C. & Gevers, L. (1977). "Equity and the Informational Basis of Collective Choice." *Review of Economic Studies* 44 (2): 199–209.

Deaton, A. & Dreze, J. (2002). "Poverty and Inequality in India, a Reexamination." *Economic and Political Weekly*, September 7: 3729–3748.

Deininger, K. & Squire, L. (1998). "New Ways of Looking at Old Issues: Inequality and Growth." *Journal of Development Economics* 57 (2): 259–287.

de Soto, H. (2000). *The Mystery of Capital*. New York: Basic Books.

Dollar, D. & Kraay, A. (2000). "Growth *Is* Good for the Poor." Discussion Paper, World Bank, Washington, DC.

Dreze, J. & Sen, A. (1990). *Hunger and Public Action*. Oxford: Clarendon Press.

Dreze, J. & Sen, A. (1995). *India: Economic Development and Social Opportunities*. Oxford : Oxford University Press.

D'Souza, S. & Chen, L.C. (1980). "Sex Differentials in Mortality in Rural Bangladesh." *Population and Development Review* 6 (2): 257–270.

Dworkin, R. (1978). *Taking Rights Seriously*. London: Duckworth.

Edgeworth, F.Y. (1881). *Mathematical Psychics*. London: K. Kegan Paul.

Ehrlich, P.R. & Ehrlich, A.H. (1996). *Betrayal of Science and Reason: How Anti-Environmentalism Threatens Our Future*. Washington, DC: Island Press.

Ehrlich, P.R. & Ehrlich, A.H. (2004). *One With Nineveh: Politics, Consumption and the Human Future*. Washington, DC: Island Press.

Ensminger, J. (1992). *Making a Market: The Institutional Transformation of an African Society*. New York: Cambridge University Press.

Eswaran, M. & Kotwal, A. (1985). "A Theory of Contractual Structure in Agriculture." *American Economic Review* 75 (3): 352–368.

Feeny, D., Berkes, F., McCay, B.J. & Acheson, J.M. (1990). "The Tragedy of the Commons: Twenty-two Years Later." *Human Ecology* 18 (1): 1–19.

Fogel, R.W. (1994). "Economic Growth, Population Theory, and Physiology: The Bearing of Long-Term Processes on the Making of Economic Policy." *American Economic Review* 84 (2): 369–395.

Fogel, R.W. (2004). *The Escape from Hunger and Premature Death, 1700–2100: Europe, America, and the Third World*. Cambridge, England: Cambridge University Press.

Fogel, R.W., Engerman, S.L., Margo, R., Sokoloff, K., Steckel, R., Trussell, T.J., Villaflor, G. & Wachter, K.W. (1983). "Secular Changes in American and British Stature and Nutrition." *Journal of Interdisciplinary History* 14(4): 445–481.

Freeman III, A.M. (1993). *The Measurement of Environmental and Resource Values: Theory and Methods*. Washington, D.C.: Resources for the Future.

Ghate, R., Jodha, N.S., & Mukhopadhyay, P. (2008). *Promise, Trust and Evolution: Managing the Commons of South Asia*. Oxford: Oxford University Press.

Goody, J. (1973). "Polygyny, Economy, and the Role of Women." In J. Goody, Ed., *The Character of Kinship*. Cambridge, England: Cambridge University Press.

Goody, J. (1976). *Production and Reproduction: A Comparative Study of the Domestic Terrain*. Cambridge, England: Cambridge University Press.

Goody, J., Duly, C., Beeson, I. & Harrison, G. (1981). "Implicit Sex Preference: A Comparative Study." *Journal of Biosocial Sciences* 13(4): 455–466.

Goody, J. & Tambiah, S.J. (1973). *Bridewealth and Dowry*. Cambridge, England: Cambridge University Press.

Gorman, W.M. (1968). "The Structure of Utility Functions." *Review of Economic Studies* 35 (4): 367–390.

Graaff, J. de V. (1962). *Theoretical Welfare Economics*. Cambridge, England: Cambridge University Press.

Guyer, J.L. (1994). "Lineal Identities and Lateral Networks: The Logic of Polyandrous Motherhood." In C. Bledsoe & G. Pison, Eds., *Nupitality in Sub-Saharan Africa: Contemporary Anthropological and Demographic Perspectives*. Oxford: Clarendon Press.

Hamilton, K. & Clemens, M. (1999). "Genuine Savings Rates in Developing Countries." *World Bank Economic Review* 13 (2): 333–356.

Hammond, P. (1976)."Equity, Arrow's Conditions and Rawls' Difference Principle." *Econometrica* 44 (5): 793–804.

Harsanyi, J.C. (1955). "Cardinal Welfare, Individualistic Ethics and Interpersonal Comparisons of Utility." *Journal of Political Economy* 63 (3): 309–321.

Hayek, F. (1960). *The Constitution of Liberty*. London: Routledge & Kegan Paul.

Heckman, J.J. (2000). "Policies to Foster Human Capital." *Research in Economics* 54 (1): 3–56.

Heyser, N. (1996). *Gender, Population and Environment in the Context of Deforestation: A Malaysian Case Study*. Geneva: United Nations Research Institute for Social Development.

Hicks, J.R. & Allen, R.G.D. (1934). "A Reconsideration of the Theory of Value, Parts 1 & 2." *Economica* NS, 1(1&2): 52–76 & 196–219.

Homer-Dixon, T.F. (1994). "Environmental Scarcities and Violent Conflict: Evidence from Cases." *International Security* 19 (1): 5–40.

Jalan, J. & Ravallion, M. (2002). "Geographic Poverty Traps? A Micro Model of Consumption Growth in Rural China." *Journal of Econometrics* 17 (4): 329–346.

Jodha, N.S. (1986). "Common Property Resources and the Rural Poor." *Economic and Political Weekly* 21: 1169–1181.

Johnson, D. Gale (2001). "On Population and Resources: A Comment." *Population and Development Review* 27 (4): 739–747.

Jolly, C.L. & Gribble, J.N. (1993). "The Proximate Determinants of Fertility." In K.A. Foote, K.H. Hill & L.G. Martin, Eds., *Demographic Change in Sub-Saharan Africa*. Washington, DC: National Academy Press.

Kalai, E. & Smorodinsky, M. (1975). "Other Solutions to Nash's Bargaining Problem." *Econometrica* 43 (3): 513–518.

Kelley, A. C. (1988). "Economic Consequences of Population Change in the Third World." *Journal of Economic Literature* 26 (4): 1685–1728.

Kennedy, E. (1989). *The Effects of Sugarcane Production on Food Security, Health, and Nutrition in Kenya: A Longitudinal Analysis*, Research Report No. 78. Washington, D.C.: International Food Policy Research Institute.

Koopmans, T.C. (1965). "On the Concept of Optimal Economic Growth." *Pontificiae Academiae Scientiarum Scripta Varia*, 28. Reprinted, 1966, in *The Econometric Approach to Development Planning*. Amsterdam: North Holland.

Koopmans, T.C. (1972). "Representation of Preference Orderings over Time." In C.B. McGuire & R. Radner, Eds., *Decision and Organization*. Amsterdam: North Holland.

Krueger, A.O. (1978). *Liberalization Attempts and Consequences*. New York: National Bureau of Economic Research.

Kuper, A. (2000). "Rawlsian Global Justice: Beyond *The Law of Peoples*." *Political Theory* 28: 640–674.

Leibenstein, H. (1957). *Economic Backwrdness and Economic Growth*. New York: John Wiley.

Lewis, W.A. (1954). "Economic Development with Unlimited Supplies of Labour." *Manchester School of Economic and Social Studies* 22 (2): 139–191.

Lindahl, E.R. (1958 [1928]). "Some Controversial Questions in the Theory of Taxation." In R.A. Musgrave & A.T. Peacock, Eds., *Classics in the Theory of Public Finance*. London: MacMillan. (Originally published in Swedish in 1928.)

Lipset, S.M. (1959). "Some Social Requisites of Democracy: Economic Development and Political Legitimacy." *American Political Science Review* 53 (1): 69–105.

Little, I.M.D. & Mirrlees, J.A. (1968). *Manual of Industrial Project Analysis in Developing Countries: Social Cost Benefit Analysis*. Paris: OECD.

Little, I.M.D. & Mirrlees, J.A. (1974). *Project Appraisal and Planning for Developing Countries*. London: Heinemann.

Little, I.M.D. & Mirrlees, J.A. (1991). "Project Appraisal and Planning Twenty Years On." *Proceedings of the Annual Conference on Development Economics 1990*. Washington, DC: World Bank.

Lopez, R. (1998). "The Tragedy of the Commons in Cote d'Ivoire Agriculture: Empirical Evidence and Implications for Evaluating Trade Policies." *World Bank Economic Review* 12 (1): 105–132.

Lucas, R. (1988). "On the Mechanics of Economic Development." *Journal of Monetary Economics* 22 (1): 3–42.

Lucas, R. (1993). "Making a Miracle." *Econometrica* 61 (2): 251–272.

Marshall, T.H. (1964). *Class, Citizenship and Social Development*. Garden City, NY: Doubleday & Co.

Maskin, E. (1978). "A Theorem on Utilitarianism." *Review of Economic Studies* 45 (1): 94–96.

McElroy, M.B. & Horney, M.J. (1981). "Nash Bargained Household Decisions: Toward a Generalization of the Theory of Demand." *International Economic Review* 22 (2): 333–349.

McKean, M. (1992). "Success on the Commons: A Comparative Examination of Institutions for Common Property Resource Management." *Journal of Theoretical Politics* 4 (2): 256–268.

Mirrlees, J.A. (1971). "An Exploration in the Theory of Optimum Income Taxation." *Review of Economic Studies* 38 (1): 175–208.

Musgrave, R. (1959). *Theory of Public Finance*. New York: McGraw Hill.

Narayan, D., with Patel, R., Schafft, K., Rademacher, A. & Koch-Schulte, S. (2000). *Voices of the Poor: Can Anyone Hear Us?* Oxford: Oxford University Press.

North, D. & Thomas, R.P. (1973). *The Rise of the Western World: A New Economic History*. Cambridge, England: Cambridge University Press.

Nozick, R. (1974). *Anarchy, State and Utopia*. New York: Basic Books.

Nussbaum, M (2000a). *Women and Human Development*. Cambridge, England: Cambridge University Press.

Nussbaum, M. (2000b). "The Costs of Tragedy: Some Moral Limits of Cost-Benefit Analysis." *Journal of Legal Studies* 29 (6): 1005–1036.

Nussbaum, M. (2003). "Tragedy and Human Capabilities: A Response to Vivian Walsh." *Review of Political Economy* 15 (3): 413–418.

O'Neill, O. (1986). *Faces of Hunger: An Essay on Poverty, Justice and Development*. London: Allen and Unwin.

Ostrom, E. (1990). *Governing the Commons: The Evolution of Institutions for Collective Action*. Cambridge, England: Cambridge University Press.

Pant, P. et al (1962). *Perspectives of Development: 1961–1976, Implications of Planning for a Minimum Standard of Living*. New Delhi: Planning Commission of India.

Pareto, V. (1909). *Manuel d'economie Politique*. Paris: Giard et Briere.

Persson, T. & Tabellini. G. (2000). *Political Economics: Explaining Economic Policy*. Cambridge, MA: MIT Press.

Phelps, E.S. (1973). "Taxation of Wage Income for Economic Justice." *Quarterly Journal of Economics* 87 (3): 331–354.

Pigou, A.C. (1920). *The Economics of Welfare*. London: Macmillan.

Putnam, H. (2002). *The Collapse of the Fact/Value Distinction*. Cambridge, MA: Harvard University Press.

Putnam, H. (2003). "For Ethics and Economics without the Dichotomies." *Review of Political Economy* 15 (3): 395–412.

Ramsey, F.P. (1928). "A Mathematical Theory of Saving." *Economic Journal* 38 (4): 543–549.

Rawls, J. (1972). *A Theory of Justice*. Oxford: Oxford University Press.

Ray D. (1998). *Development Economics*. Princeton: Princeton University Press.

Reutlinger, S. & Pellekaan, H. (1986). *Poverty and Hunger: Issues and Options for Food Security in Developing Countries*. Washington, DC: World Bank Publication.

Robbins, L. (1932). *An Essay on the Nature and Significance of Economic Science*. London: MacMillan.

Robinson, Joan (1964). *Economic Philosophy*. Harmondsworth, England: Penguin Books.

Roemer, J. (1999). "Does Democracy Engender Justice?" In I. Shapiro & C. Hacker-Cordon, Eds., *Democracy's Value*. Cambridge, England: Cambridge University Press.

Rosenzweig, M.R. & Schultz. T.P. (1982). "Market Opportunities, Genetic Endowments and the Intrafamily Allocation of Resources: Child Survival in Rural India." *American Economic Review* 72 (4): 803–815.

Samuelson, P.A. (1947). *Foundations of Economic Analysis*. Cambridge, MA: Harvard University Press.

Samuelson, P.A. (1954). "The Pure Theory of Public Expenditure." *Review of Economics and Statistics* 36 (4): 387–389.

Scanlon, T.M. (1978). "Rights, Goals and Fairness." In S. Hampshire, Ed., *Public and Private Morality*. Cambridge, England: Cambridge University Press.

Schelling, T. (1960). *The Strategy of Conflict*. Cambridge, MA: Harvard University Press.

Schultz, T.W. (1961). "Investment in Human Capital." *American Economic Review* 51 (1): 1–17.

Schultz, T.W. (1974). *The Economics of the Family: Marriage, Children and Human Capital*. Chicago: University of Chicago Press.

Seabright, P. (2001). "The Road Upward." *New York Review of Books*, March 29: 41–43.

Sen, A. (1970). *Collective Choice and Social Welfare*. San Francisco: Holden Day.

Sen, A. (1987). *On Ethics and Economics*. Oxford: Basil Blackwell.

Sen, A. (1990). "Gender and Cooperative Conflict." In I. Tinker, Ed., *Persistent Inequalities: Women and Economic Development*. Oxford: Oxford University Press.

Sen, A. (1994). "Population: Delusion and Reality." *New York Review of Books* (September 22): 62–71.

Sen, A. (1999). *Development as Freedom*. Oxford: Oxford University Press.

Sen, A. & Sengupta, S. (1983). "Malnutrition of Rural Children and the Sex Bias." *Economic and Political Weekly* 18 (19–21, Annual Number): 855–864.

Simon, J.L. (1990). *Population Matters: People, Resources, Environment, Immigration*. New Brunswick, NJ: Transaction Press.

Slutsky, E. (1915). "Sulla Teoria del Bilancio del Consumatore." *Giornale degli Economisti e Rivista di Statistica*, 51 (July), 1–26. Translated as "On the Theory of the Budget of the Consumer." In K.E. Boulding & G.J. Stigler, Eds., 1963, *Readings in Price Theory*. London: Allen & Unwin.

Solow, R.M. (1974). "Intergenerational Equity and Exhaustible Resources." *Review of Economic Studies* 41 (Symposium Issue): 29–45.

Sopher, D.E., Ed. (1980). *An Exploration of India: Geographical Perspectives on Society and Culture*. Ithaca, NY: Cornell University Press.

Steffen, W., Sanderson, A., Tyson, P.D., Jäger, J., Matson, P.A., Moore III, B., Oldfield, F., Richardson. K., Schellnhuber, H.J., Turner II, B.L. & Wasson, R.J. (2004). *Global Change and the Earth System*. Berlin: Springer.

Stiglitz, J.E. (2002). *Globalization and Its Discontents*. New York: W.W. Norton.

Suppes, P. (1987). "Maximizing Freedom of Decision: An Axiomatic Analysis." In G. Feiwel, Ed., *Arrow and the Foundation of the Theory of Economic Policy*. London: McMillan.

Taylor, C.L. & Jodice, D.A. (1983). *World Handbook of Political and Social Indicators, 1*. New Haven, Connecticut: Yale University Press.

Tversky, A. & Kahneman, D. (1986). "Rational Choice and the Framing of Decisions." *Journal of Business* 59 (S): 251–278.

UNDP (1994, 1998, 1999, 2003). *Human Development Report*. New York: Oxford University Press.

Visaria, P.M. (1967). "The Sex Ratio of the Population of India and Pakistan and Regional Variations During 1901–61." In A. Bose, Ed., *Patterns of Population Change in India*. Bombay: Allied Publishers.

Wade, R. (1990). *Governing the Market: Economic Theory and the Role of Government in East Asian Industrialization*. Princeton, NJ: Princeton University Press.

Waldron, J. (1984). "Introduction." In J. Waldron, Ed., *Theories of Rights*. Oxford: Oxford University Press.

Williams, B. (1993). *Shame and Necessity*. Berkeley, CA: University of California Press.

Williamson, N.E. (1976). *Sons or Daughters? A Cross Cultural Survey of Parental Preferences*. Beverley Hills, CA: Sage Publications.

World Bank (1978, 1986, 1990, 1993, 1997, 1998, 2000, 2002). *World Development Report*. New York: Oxford University Press.

WCED—World Commission on Environment and Development.— (1987). *Our Common Future*. New York: Oxford University Press.

Author Index

Subject Index

CPSIA information can be obtained
at www.ICGtesting.com
Printed in the USA
BVHW010321041019
560188BV00003B/3/P